CAPTAIN AMERICA

WINTER SOLDIER

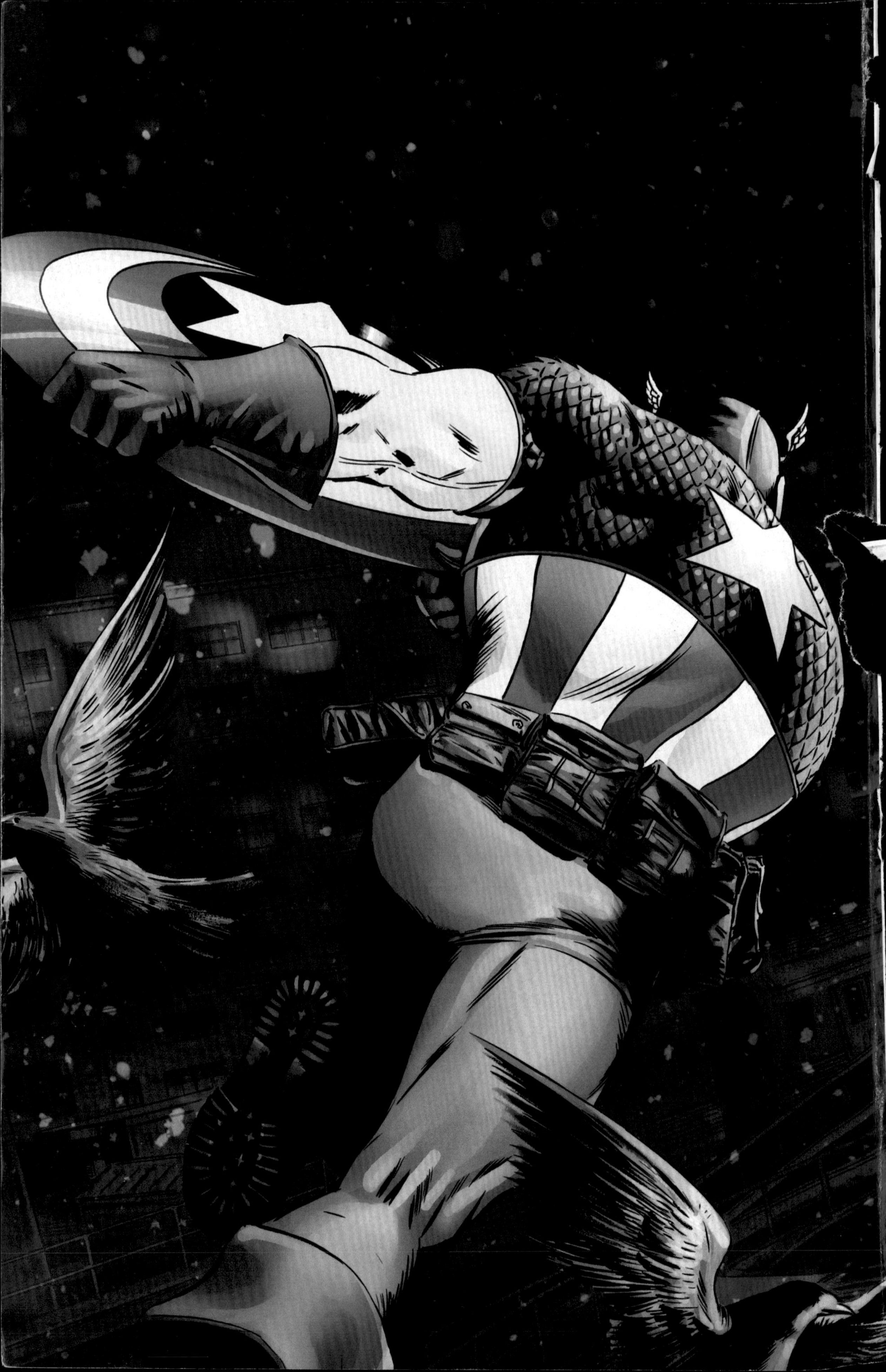

CAPTAIN AMERICA

WINTER SOLDIER

WRITER: Ed Brubaker

"OUT OF TIME"
ARTIST: Steve Epting
FLASHBACK ART: Michael Lark

"THE LONESOME DEATH OF JACK MONROE"
ARTISTS: John Paul Leon & Tom Palmer

"WINTER SOLDIER"
ARTIST: Steve Epting with Mike Perkins
FLASHBACK ART & #9: Michael Lark

COLORIST: Frank D'Armata
LETTERERS: VC's Randy Gentile, Chris Eliopoulos & Joe Caramagna
ASSISTANT EDITORS: Nicole Wiley, Molly Lazer,
Andy Schmidt & Aubrey Sitterson
EDITOR: Tom Brevoort

Captain America created by Joe Simon & Jack Kirby

COLLECTION EDITOR: Jennifer Grünwald • ASSOCIATE EDITOR: Caitlin O'Connell
ASSOCIATE MANAGING EDITOR: Kateri Woody • EDITOR, SPECIAL PROJECTS: Mark D. Beazley
VP PRODUCTION & SPECIAL PROJECTS: Jeff Youngquist • SVP PRINT, SALES & MARKETING: David Gabriel

EDITOR IN CHIEF: C.B. Cebulski • CHIEF CREATIVE OFFICER: Joe Quesada
PRESIDENT: Dan Buckley • EXECUTIVE PRODUCER: Alan Fine

CAPTAIN AMERICA: WINTER SOLDIER ULTIMATE COLLECTION. Contains material originally published in magazine form as CAPTAIN AMERICA #1-9 and #11-14. Eighth printing 2018. ISBN 978-0-7851-4341-3. Published by MARVEL WORLDWIDE, INC., a subsidiary of MARVEL ENTERTAINMENT, LLC. OFFICE OF PUBLICATION: 135 West 50th Street, New York, NY 10020. Copyright © 2010 MARVEL No similarity between any of the names, characters, persons, and/or institutions in this magazine with those of any living or dead person or institution is intended, and any such similarity which may exist is purely coincidental. Printed in Canada. DAN BUCKLEY, President, Marvel Entertainment; JOHN NEE, Publisher; JOE QUESADA, Chief Creative Officer; TOM BREVOORT, SVP of Publishing; DAVID BOGART, SVP of Business Affairs & Operations, Publishing & Partnership; DAVID GABRIEL, SVP of Sales & Marketing, Publishing; JEFF YOUNGQUIST, VP of Production & Special Projects; DAN CARR, Executive Director of Publishing Technology; ALEX MORALES, Director of Publishing Operations; DAN EDINGTON, Managing Editor; SUSAN CRESPI, Production Manager; STAN LEE, Chairman Emeritus. For information regarding advertising in Marvel Comics or on Marvel.com, please contact Vit DeBellis, Custom Solutions & Integrated Advertising Manager, at vdebellis@marvel.com. For Marvel subscription inquiries, please call 888-511-5480. Manufactured between 5/9/2018 and 5/29/2018 by SOLISCO PRINTERS, SCOTT, QC, CANADA.

1098

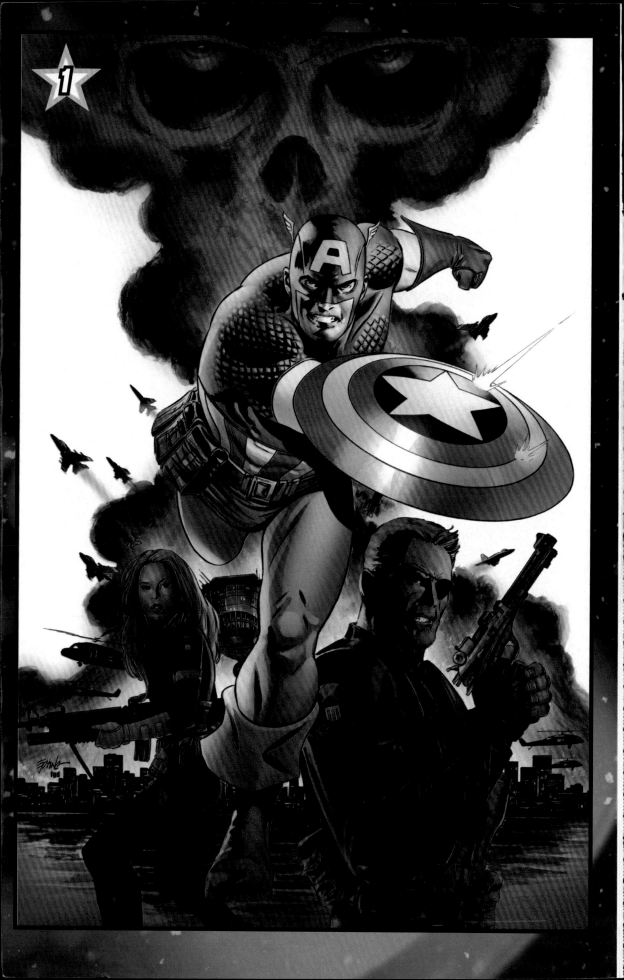

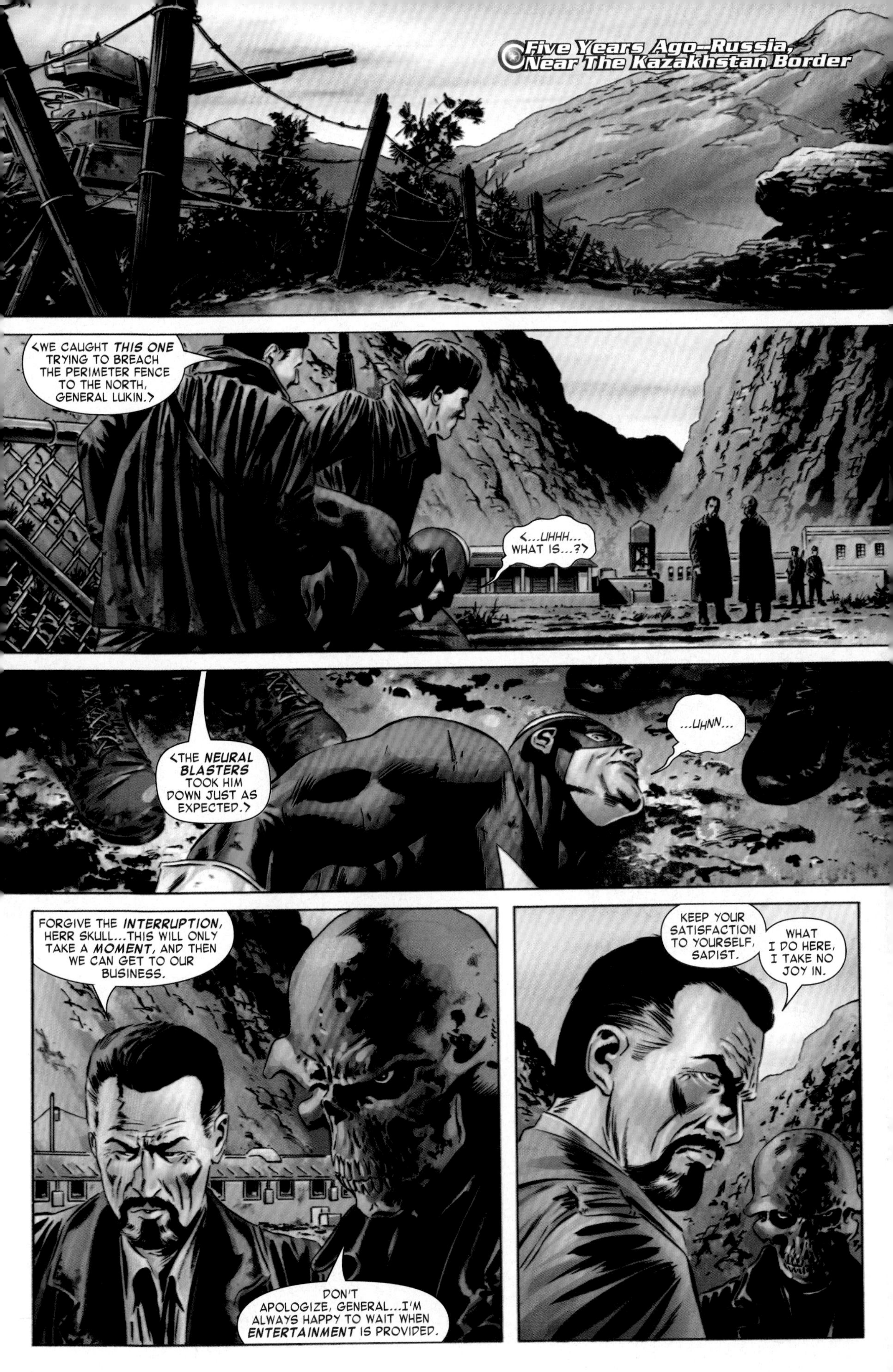
Five Years Ago--Russia, Near The Kazakhstan Border
<WE CAUGHT THIS ONE TRYING TO BREACH THE PERIMETER FENCE TO THE NORTH, GENERAL LUKIN.>
<...UHHH... WHAT IS...?>
<THE NEURAL BLASTERS TOOK HIM DOWN JUST AS EXPECTED.>
...UHNN...
FORGIVE THE INTERRUPTION, HERR SKULL...THIS WILL ONLY TAKE A MOMENT, AND THEN WE CAN GET TO OUR BUSINESS.
DON'T APOLOGIZE, GENERAL...I'M ALWAYS HAPPY TO WAIT WHEN ENTERTAINMENT IS PROVIDED.
KEEP YOUR SATISFACTION TO YOURSELF, SADIST.
WHAT I DO HERE, I TAKE NO JOY IN.

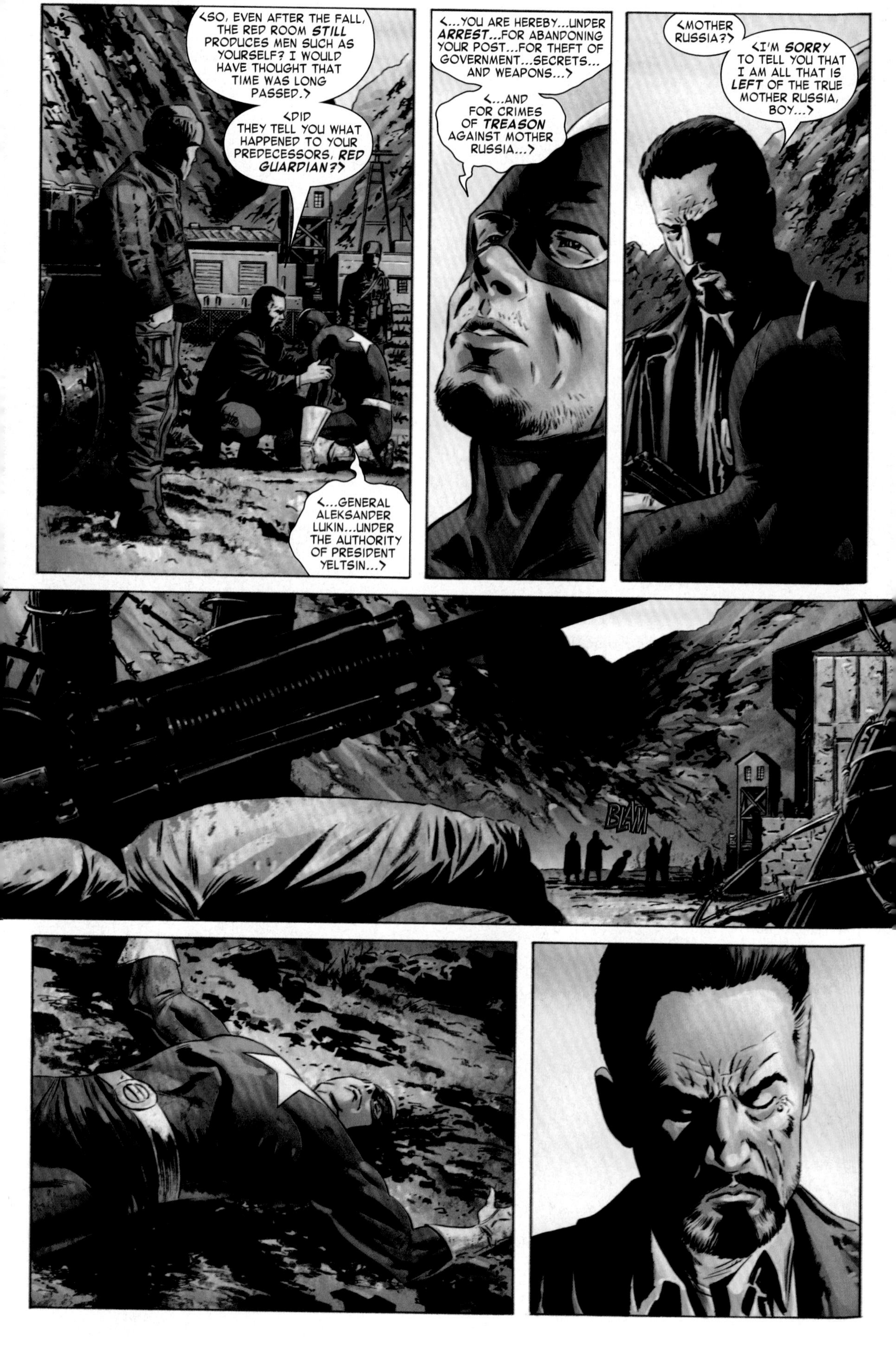
<SO, EVEN AFTER THE FALL, THE RED ROOM STILL PRODUCES MEN SUCH AS YOURSELF? I WOULD HAVE THOUGHT THAT TIME WAS LONG PASSED.>
<DID THEY TELL YOU WHAT HAPPENED TO YOUR PREDECESSORS, RED GUARDIAN?>
<...GENERAL ALEKSANDER LUKIN...UNDER THE AUTHORITY OF PRESIDENT YELTSIN...>
<...YOU ARE HEREBY...UNDER ARREST...FOR ABANDONING YOUR POST...FOR THEFT OF GOVERNMENT...SECRETS... AND WEAPONS...>
<...AND FOR CRIMES OF TREASON AGAINST MOTHER RUSSIA...>
<MOTHER RUSSIA?>
<I'M SORRY TO TELL YOU THAT I AM ALL THAT IS LEFT OF THE TRUE MOTHER RUSSIA, BOY...>
BLAM

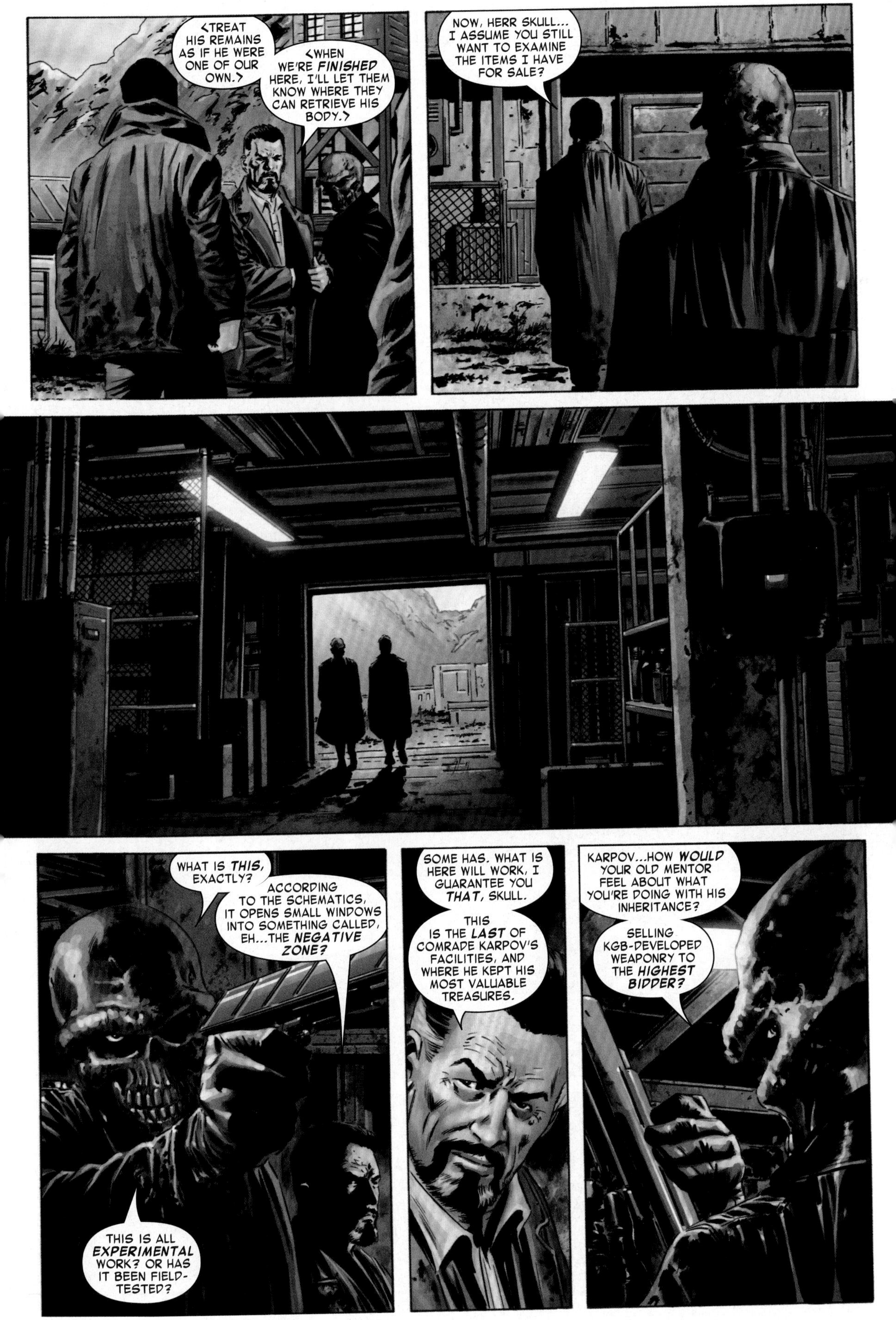
<TREAT HIS REMAINS AS IF HE WERE ONE OF OUR OWN.>
<WHEN WE'RE *FINISHED* HERE, I'LL LET THEM KNOW WHERE THEY CAN RETRIEVE HIS BODY.>
NOW, HERR SKULL... I ASSUME YOU STILL WANT TO EXAMINE THE ITEMS I HAVE FOR SALE?
WHAT IS *THIS,* EXACTLY?
ACCORDING TO THE SCHEMATICS, IT OPENS SMALL WINDOWS INTO SOMETHING CALLED, EH...THE *NEGATIVE ZONE?*
THIS IS ALL *EXPERIMENTAL* WORK? OR HAS IT BEEN FIELD-TESTED?
SOME HAS. WHAT IS HERE WILL WORK, I GUARANTEE YOU *THAT,* SKULL.
THIS IS THE *LAST* OF COMRADE KARPOV'S FACILITIES, AND WHERE HE KEPT HIS MOST VALUABLE TREASURES.
KARPOV...HOW *WOULD* YOUR OLD MENTOR FEEL ABOUT WHAT YOU'RE DOING WITH HIS INHERITANCE?
SELLING KGB-DEVELOPED WEAPONRY TO THE *HIGHEST BIDDER?*

WHY DO YOU THINK HE LEFT THIS IN *MY* HANDS AND NOT HIS *SUPERIORS'*?

HE KNEW IF THE SOVIET UNION WERE TO COLLAPSE, THERE MUST STILL BE MEN WILLING TO DO THE RIGHT THING FOR THE CAUSE.

AND I AM NOT SELLING *EVERYTHING* YOU SEE HERE. MOST OF IT IS LEAVING THIS SAD COUNTRY, ALONG WITH MYSELF AND MY MEN.

I SEE. THEN I--

--MEIN *GOTT!*

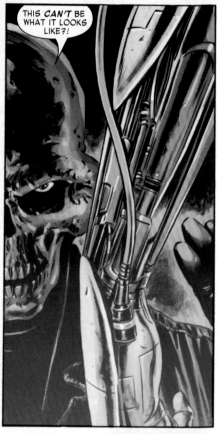

THIS *CAN'T* BE WHAT IT LOOKS LIKE?!

AH, YES. I'VE BEEN GOING OVER THE PAPERWORK COMRADE KARPOV LEFT ON THIS ONE.

HE WAS APPARENTLY *VERY USEFUL* IN THE COLD WAR. A SECRET WEAPON, OF A SORT, AGAINST THE UNITED STATES.

HOW MUCH DO YOU *WANT* FOR IT?

I THINK *NOT*, HERR SKULL. I HAVE MY *OWN* PLANS FOR THAT ITEM. UNLESS, OF COURSE, YOU WOULD BE WILLING TO EXCHANGE IT FOR THE *COSMIC CUBE*, AS IT IS KNOWN?

THE *CUBE?* WHAT DO *YOU* KNOW ABOUT *THAT?*

WE KNOW OF MANY THINGS YOU HOLD CLOSE, SKULL.

AND I WOULD VALUE THIS COSMIC CUBE *QUITE HIGHLY* IF IT IS WHAT I HAVE HEARD.

OH, IT IS, *BELIEVE ME.* BUT IT'S *NOT* IN MY POSSESSION.

EVEN IF IT *WAS,* YOU CAN'T THINK YOU'D HAVE *ANYTHING* THAT WOULD MAKE ME GIVE IT UP.

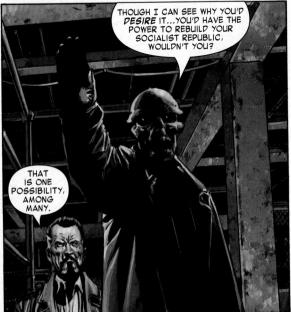

THOUGH I CAN SEE WHY YOU'D *DESIRE* IT...YOU'D HAVE THE POWER TO REBUILD YOUR SOCIALIST REPUBLIC, WOULDN'T YOU?

THAT IS ONE POSSIBILITY, AMONG MANY.

WELL, YOU CAN KEEP *DREAMING*... MY SPIES ARE COMBING THE WORLD FOR SIGNS OF IT EVEN AS WE SPEAK.

THE CUBE WILL BE *MINE,* AND NO ONE ELSE'S.

AND WHEN THAT DAY COMES, THIS WHOLE WORLD WILL KNOW *FEAR,* GENERAL... LIKE YOU'VE *NEVER* SEEN.

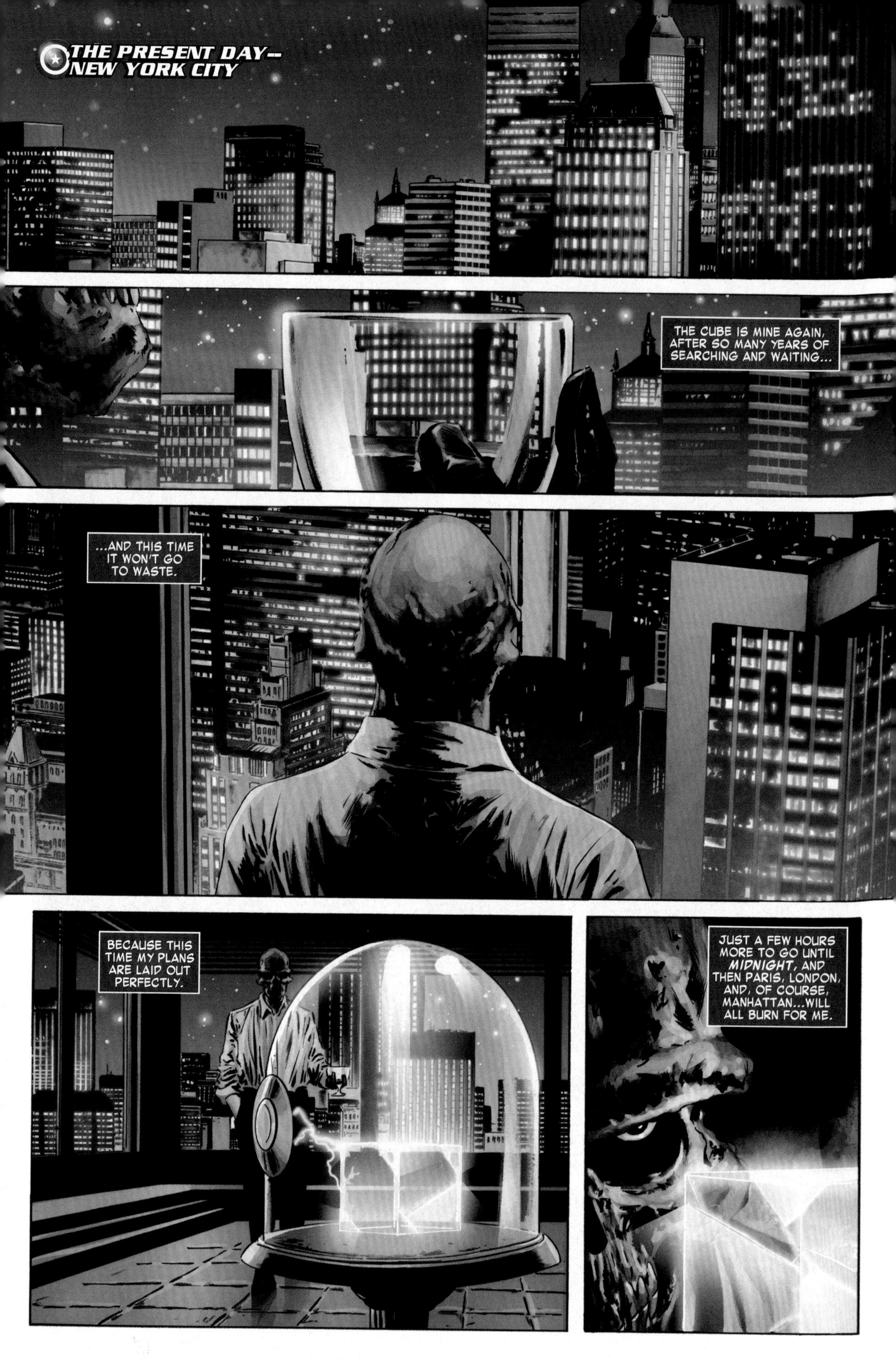
THE PRESENT DAY--
NEW YORK CITY
THE CUBE IS MINE AGAIN, AFTER SO MANY YEARS OF SEARCHING AND WAITING...
...AND THIS TIME IT WON'T GO TO WASTE.
BECAUSE THIS TIME MY PLANS ARE LAID OUT PERFECTLY.
JUST A FEW HOURS MORE TO GO UNTIL *MIDNIGHT,* AND THEN PARIS, LONDON, AND, OF COURSE, MANHATTAN...WILL ALL BURN FOR ME.

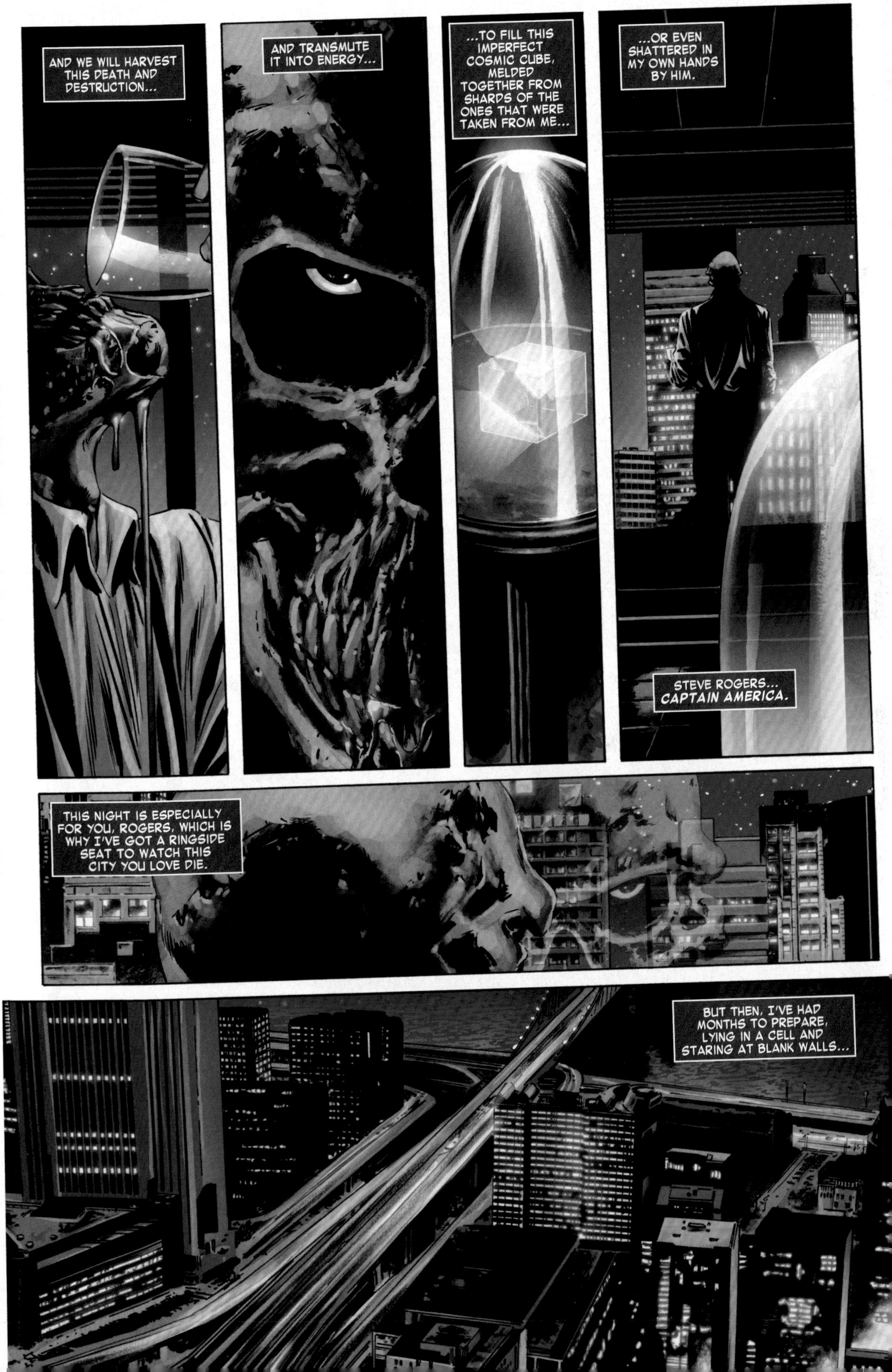
AND WE WILL HARVEST THIS DEATH AND DESTRUCTION...
AND TRANSMUTE IT INTO ENERGY...
...TO FILL THIS IMPERFECT COSMIC CUBE, MELDED TOGETHER FROM SHARDS OF THE ONES THAT WERE TAKEN FROM ME...
...OR EVEN SHATTERED IN MY OWN HANDS BY HIM.
STEVE ROGERS... CAPTAIN AMERICA.
THIS NIGHT IS ESPECIALLY FOR YOU, ROGERS, WHICH IS WHY I'VE GOT A RINGSIDE SEAT TO WATCH THIS CITY YOU LOVE DIE.
BUT THEN, I'VE HAD MONTHS TO PREPARE, LYING IN A CELL AND STARING AT BLANK WALLS...

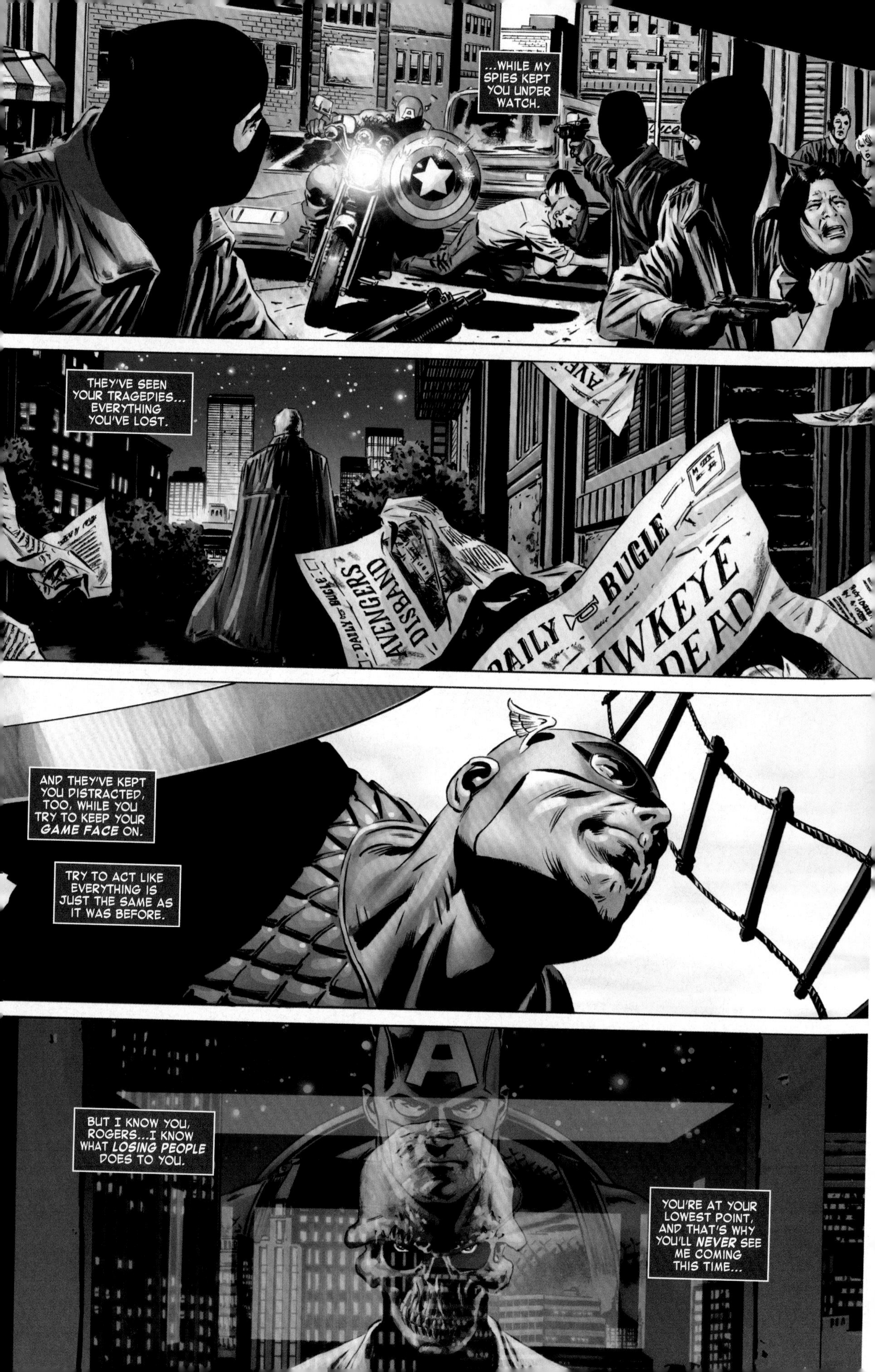

...WHILE MY SPIES KEPT YOU UNDER WATCH.
THEY'VE SEEN YOUR TRAGEDIES... EVERYTHING YOU'VE LOST.
DAILY BUGLE
AVENGERS DISBAND
DAILY BUGLE
AND THEY'VE KEPT YOU DISTRACTED, TOO, WHILE YOU TRY TO KEEP YOUR GAME FACE ON.
TRY TO ACT LIKE EVERYTHING IS JUST THE SAME AS IT WAS BEFORE.
BUT I KNOW YOU, ROGERS...I KNOW WHAT LOSING PEOPLE DOES TO YOU.
YOU'RE AT YOUR LOWEST POINT, AND THAT'S WHY YOU'LL NEVER SEE ME COMING THIS TIME...

"HOW *ARE* YOU, STEVE, REALLY?"

"I'M SORRY, WHAT WAS THE *QUESTION?*"

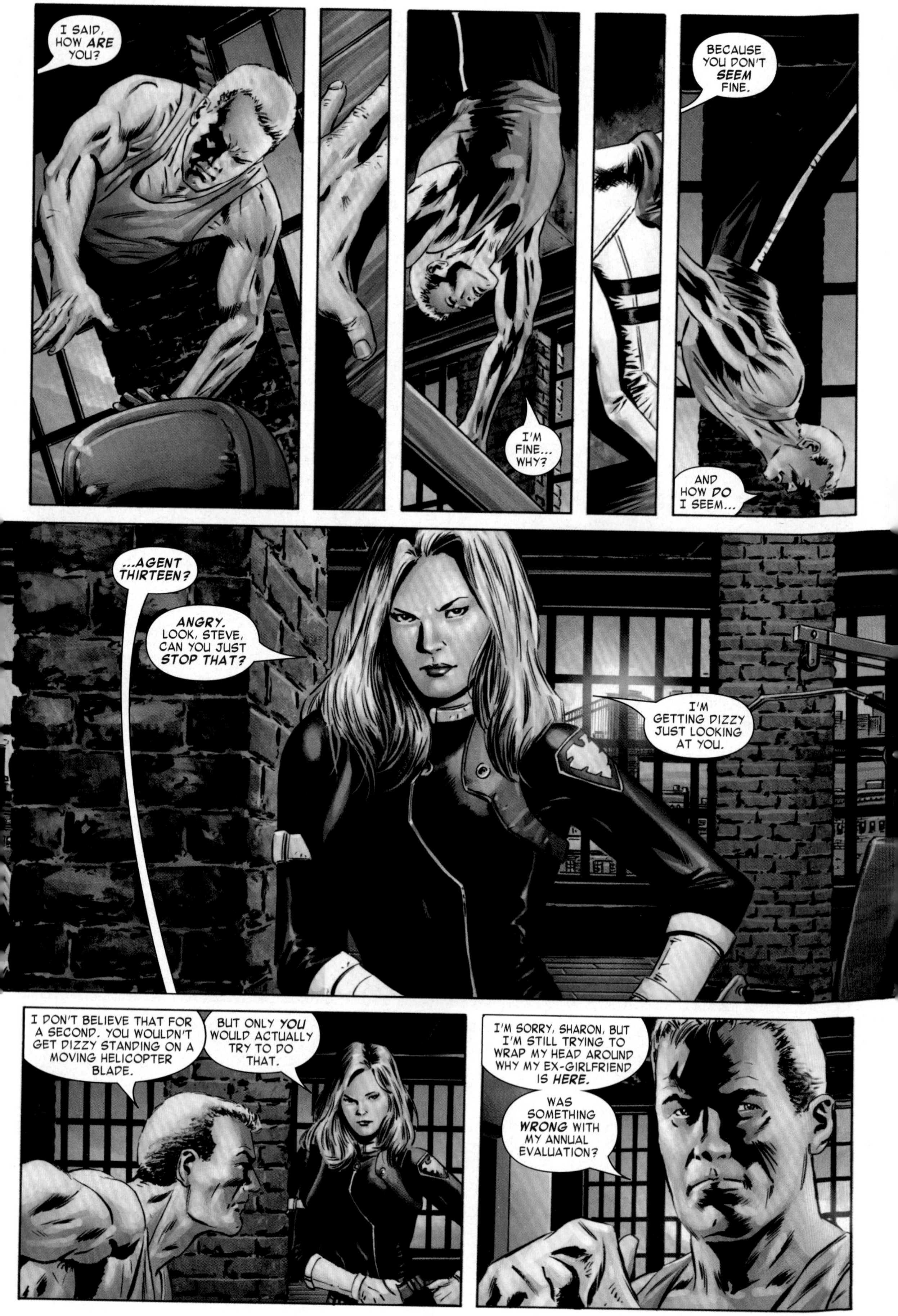
I SAID, HOW ARE YOU?
I'M FINE... WHY?
BECAUSE YOU DON'T SEEM FINE.
AND HOW DO I SEEM...
...AGENT THIRTEEN?
ANGRY. LOOK, STEVE, CAN YOU JUST STOP THAT?
I'M GETTING DIZZY JUST LOOKING AT YOU.
I DON'T BELIEVE THAT FOR A SECOND. YOU WOULDN'T GET DIZZY STANDING ON A MOVING HELICOPTER BLADE.
BUT ONLY YOU WOULD ACTUALLY TRY TO DO THAT.
I'M SORRY, SHARON, BUT I'M STILL TRYING TO WRAP MY HEAD AROUND WHY MY EX-GIRLFRIEND IS HERE.
WAS SOMETHING WRONG WITH MY ANNUAL EVALUATION?

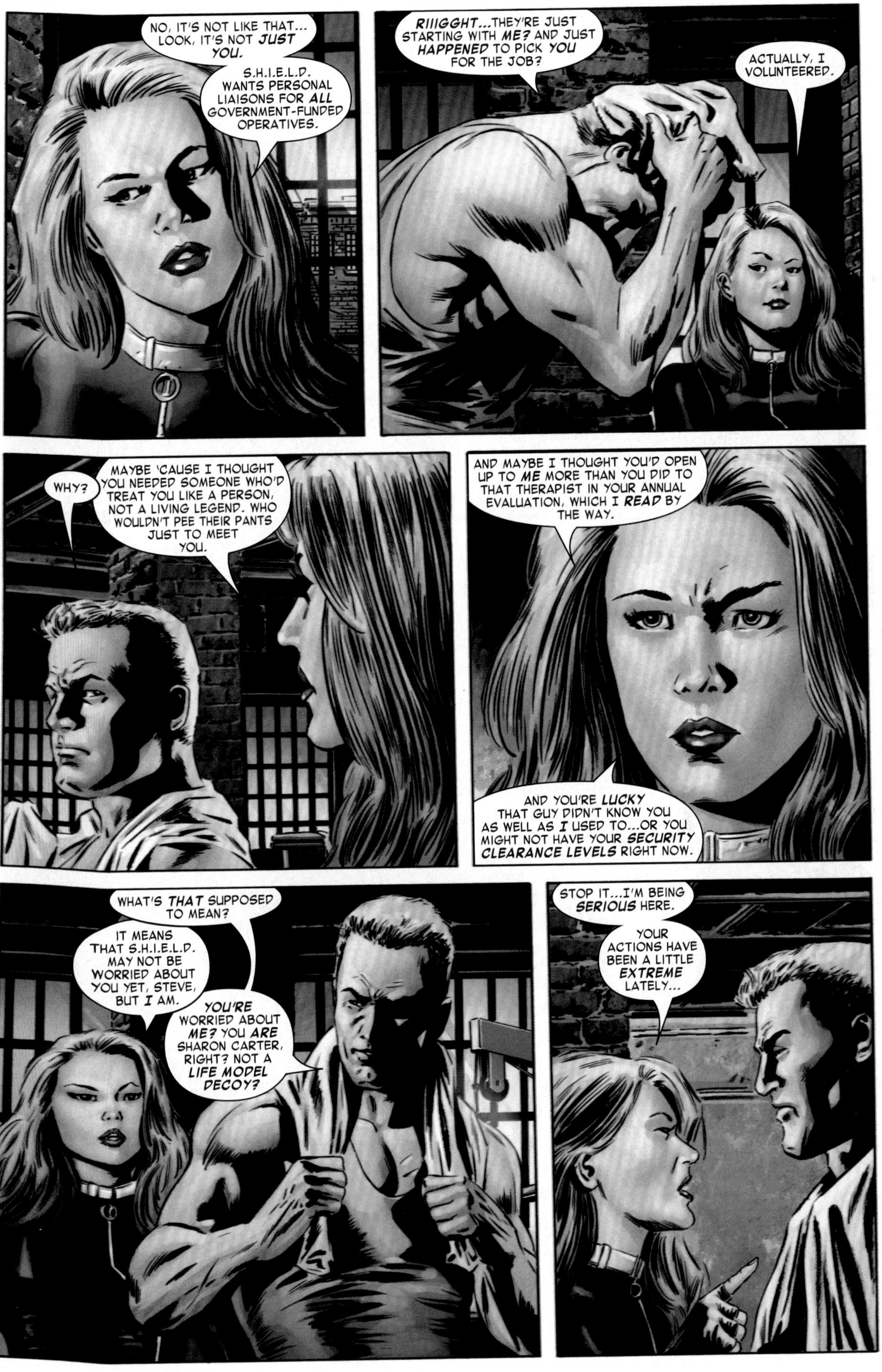
NO, IT'S NOT LIKE THAT... LOOK, IT'S NOT JUST YOU.
S.H.I.E.L.D. WANTS PERSONAL LIAISONS FOR ALL GOVERNMENT-FUNDED OPERATIVES.
RIIIGGHT... THEY'RE JUST STARTING WITH ME? AND JUST HAPPENED TO PICK YOU FOR THE JOB?
ACTUALLY, I VOLUNTEERED.
WHY?
MAYBE 'CAUSE I THOUGHT YOU NEEDED SOMEONE WHO'D TREAT YOU LIKE A PERSON, NOT A LIVING LEGEND. WHO WOULDN'T PEE THEIR PANTS JUST TO MEET YOU.
AND MAYBE I THOUGHT YOU'D OPEN UP TO ME MORE THAN YOU DID TO THAT THERAPIST IN YOUR ANNUAL EVALUATION, WHICH I READ BY THE WAY.
AND YOU'RE LUCKY THAT GUY DIDN'T KNOW YOU AS WELL AS I USED TO...OR YOU MIGHT NOT HAVE YOUR SECURITY CLEARANCE LEVELS RIGHT NOW.
WHAT'S THAT SUPPOSED TO MEAN?
IT MEANS THAT S.H.I.E.L.D. MAY NOT BE WORRIED ABOUT YOU YET, STEVE, BUT I AM.
YOU'RE WORRIED ABOUT ME? YOU ARE SHARON CARTER, RIGHT? NOT A LIFE MODEL DECOY?
STOP IT...I'M BEING SERIOUS HERE.
YOUR ACTIONS HAVE BEEN A LITTLE EXTREME LATELY...

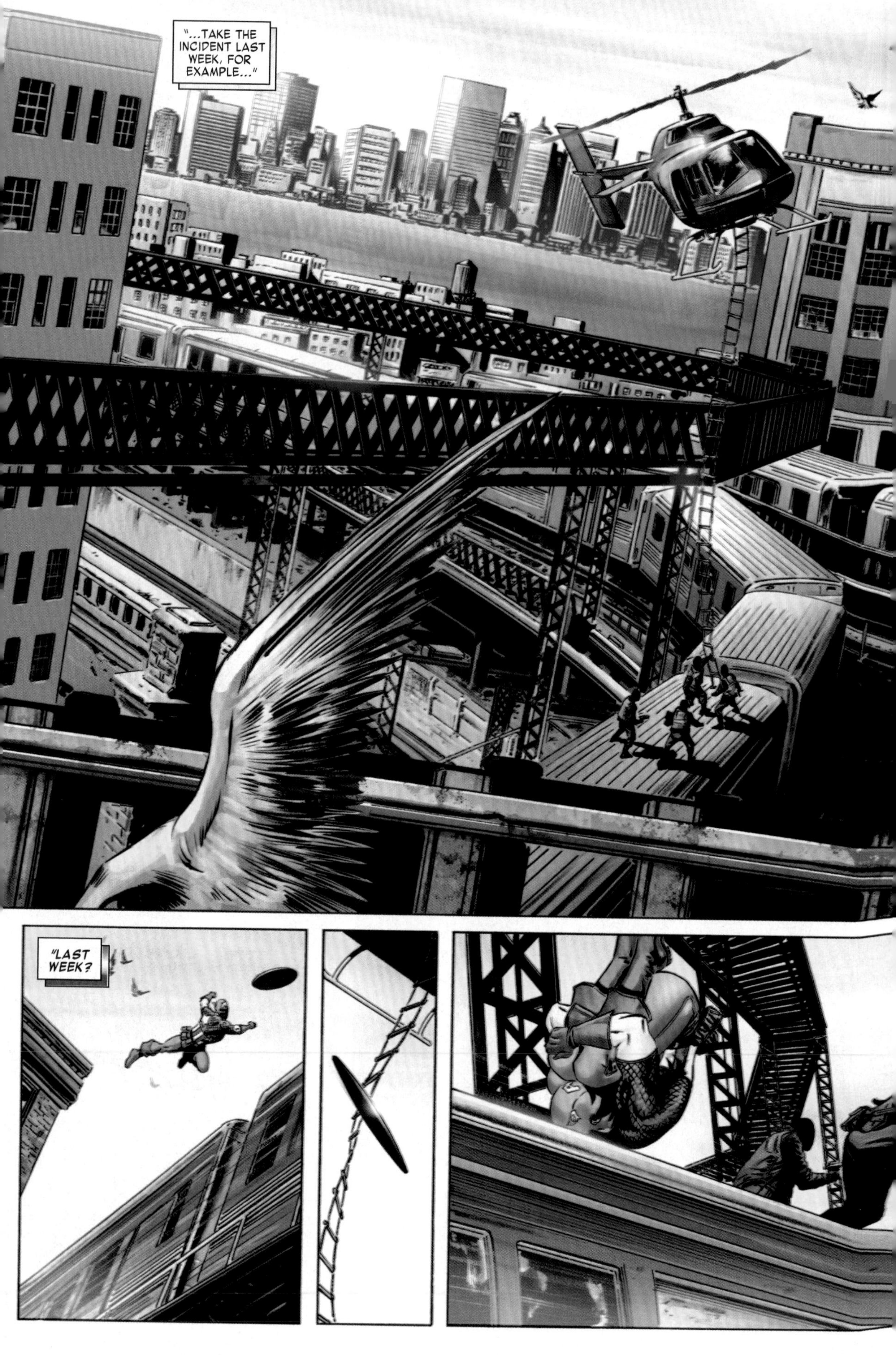
"...TAKE THE INCIDENT LAST WEEK, FOR EXAMPLE..."
"LAST WEEK?

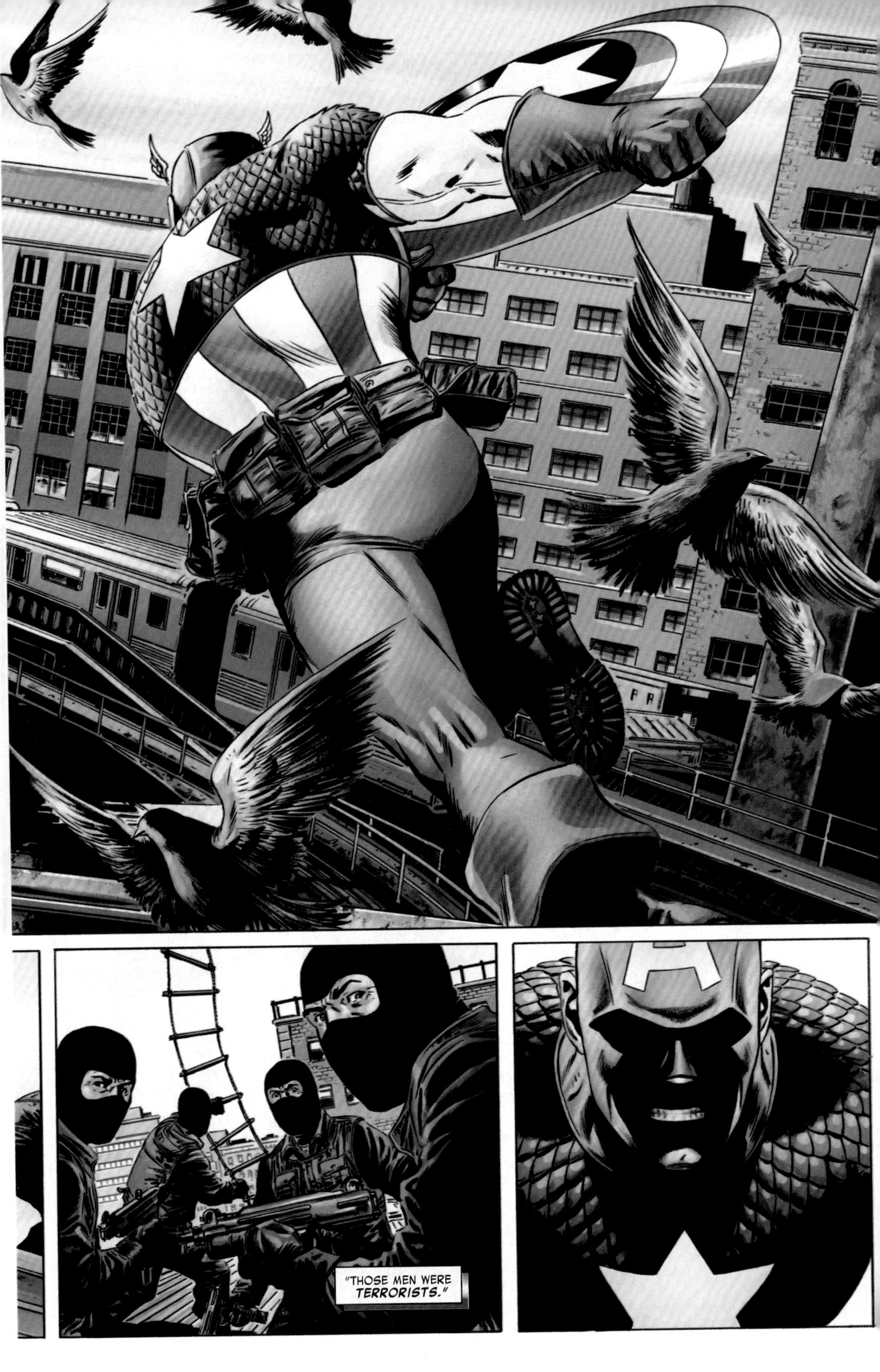
"THOSE MEN WERE TERRORISTS."

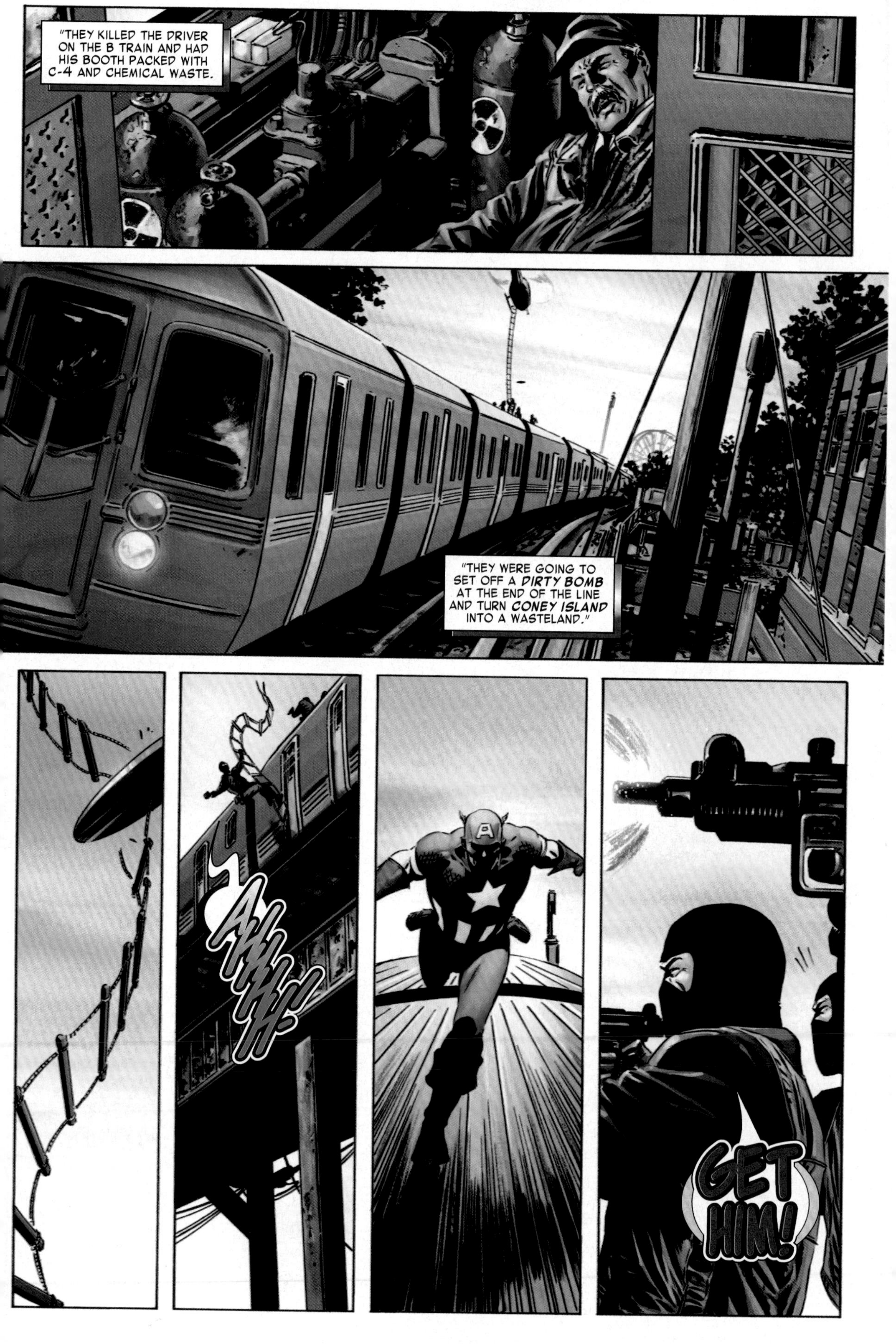
"THEY KILLED THE DRIVER ON THE B TRAIN AND HAD HIS BOOTH PACKED WITH C-4 AND CHEMICAL WASTE.
"THEY WERE GOING TO SET OFF A DIRTY BOMB AT THE END OF THE LINE AND TURN CONEY ISLAND INTO A WASTELAND."
AHHHH!
GET HIM!

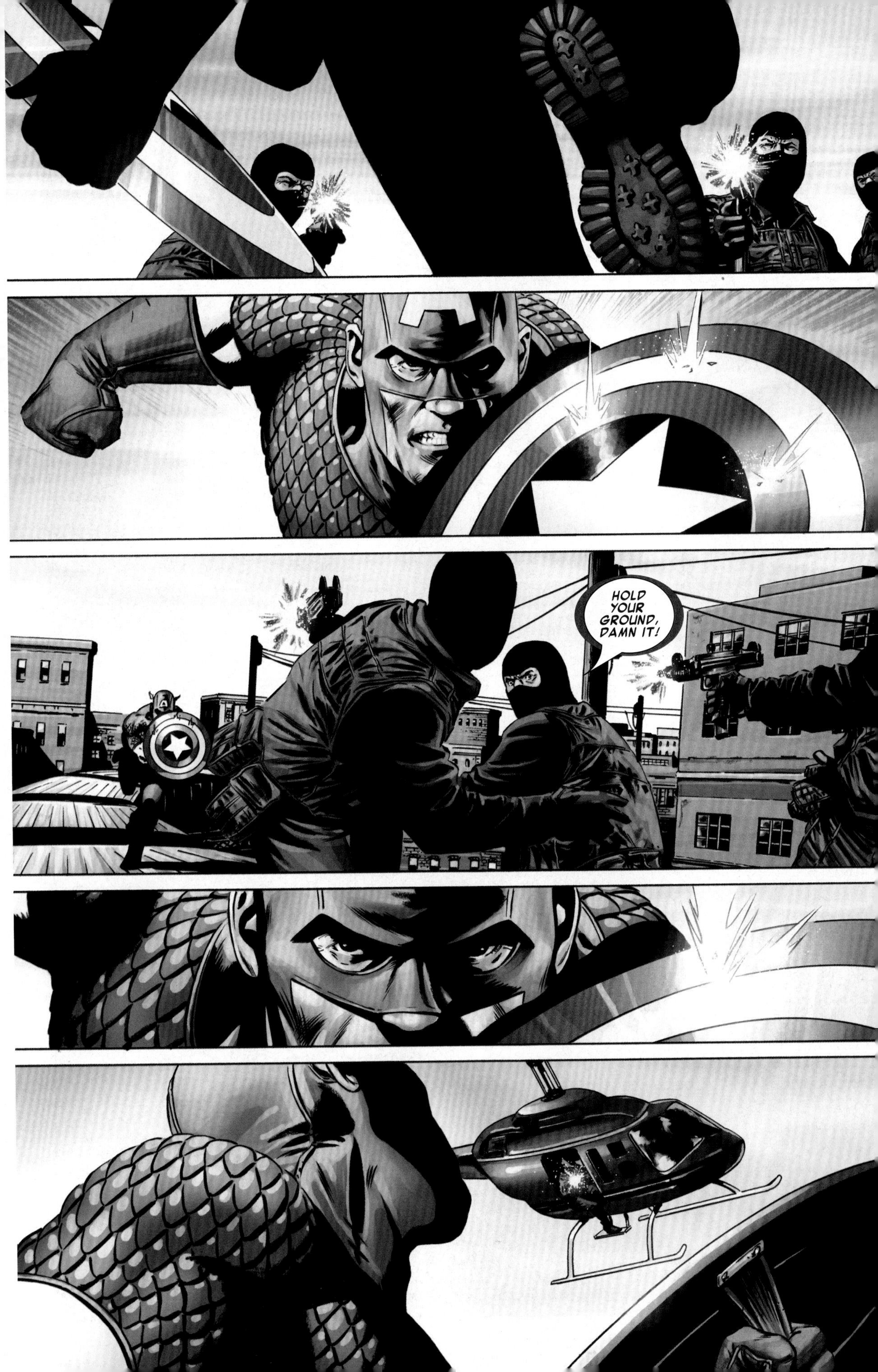
HOLD YOUR GROUND, DAMN IT!

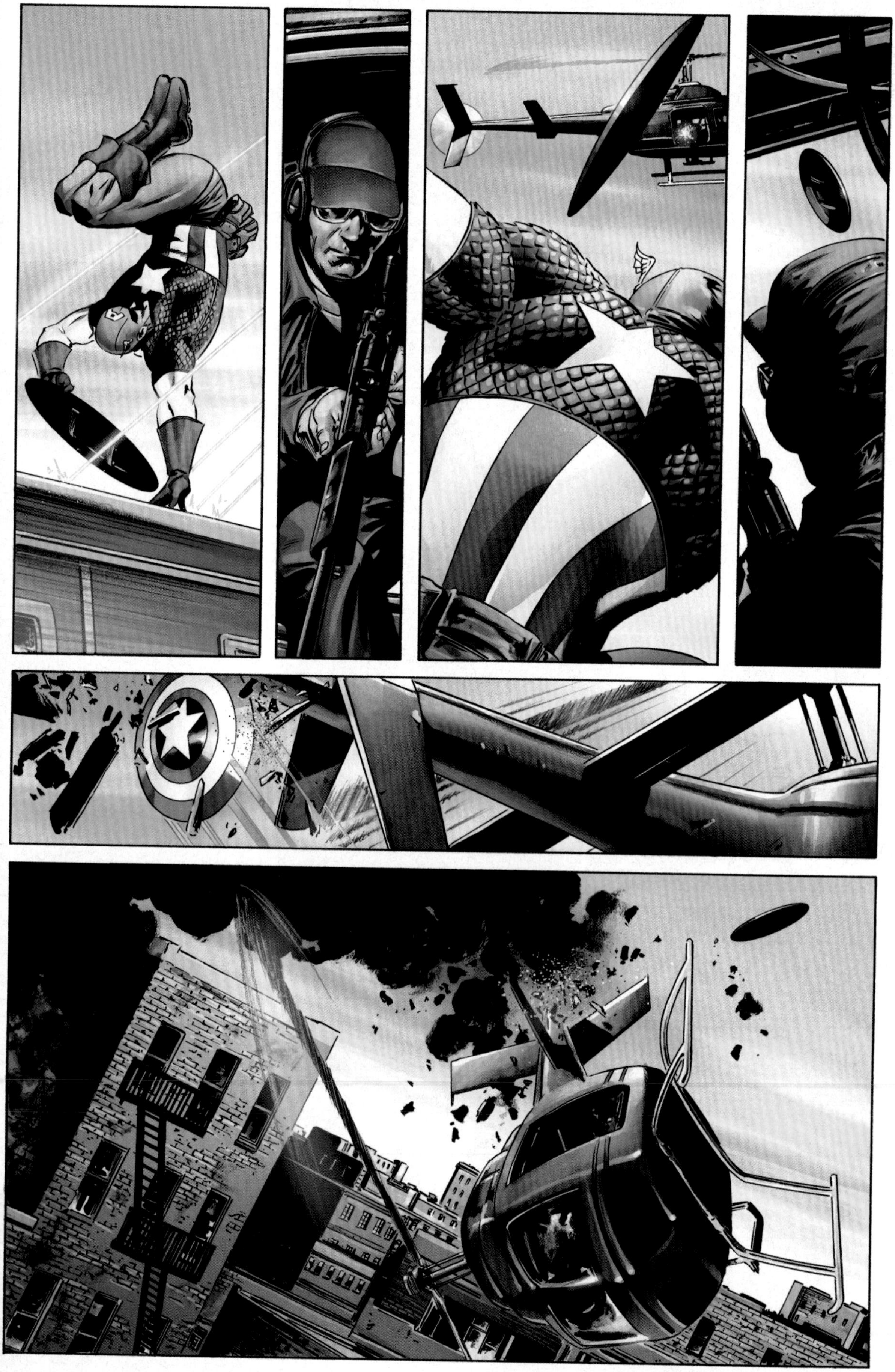

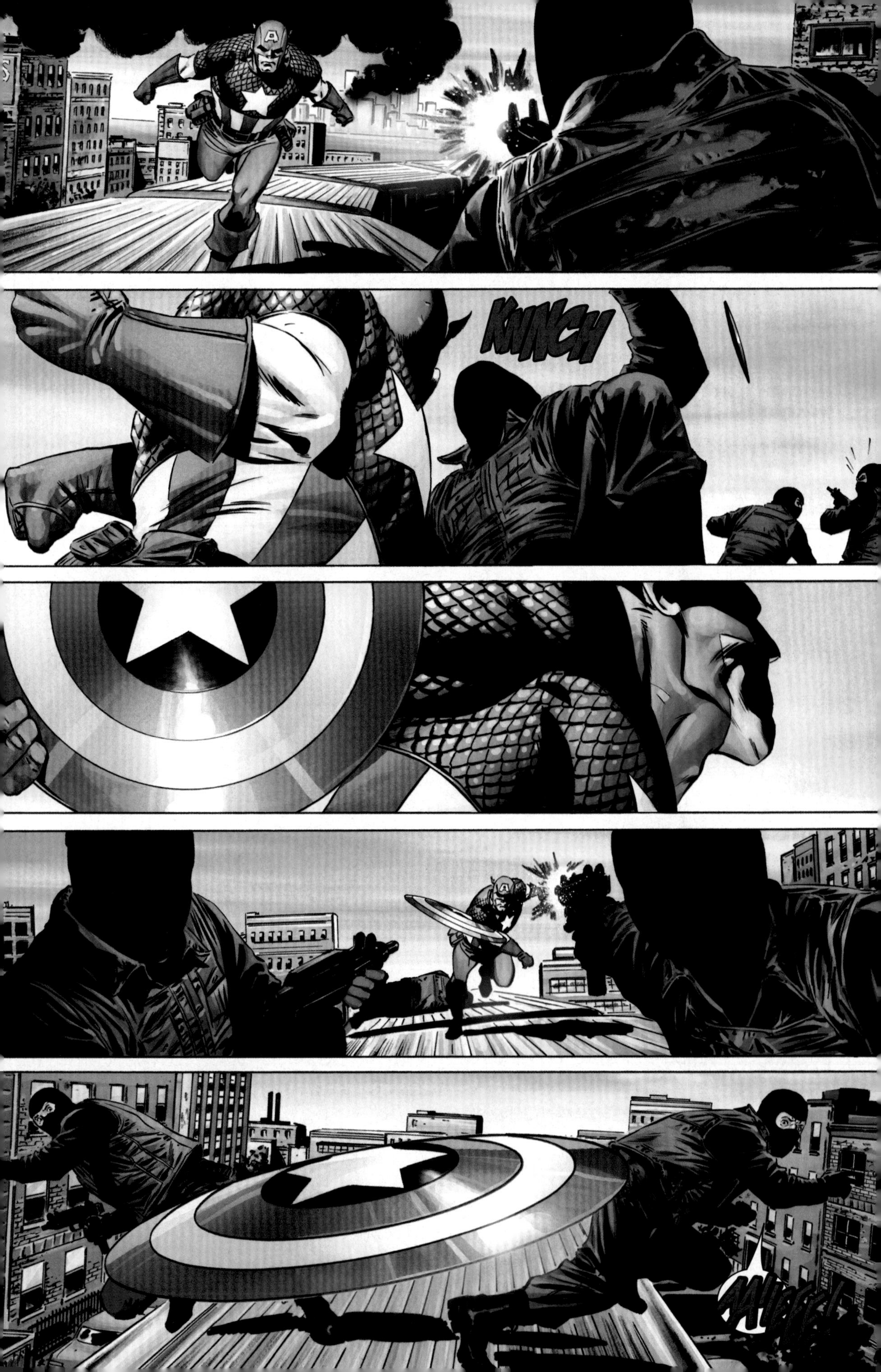
KVNCH

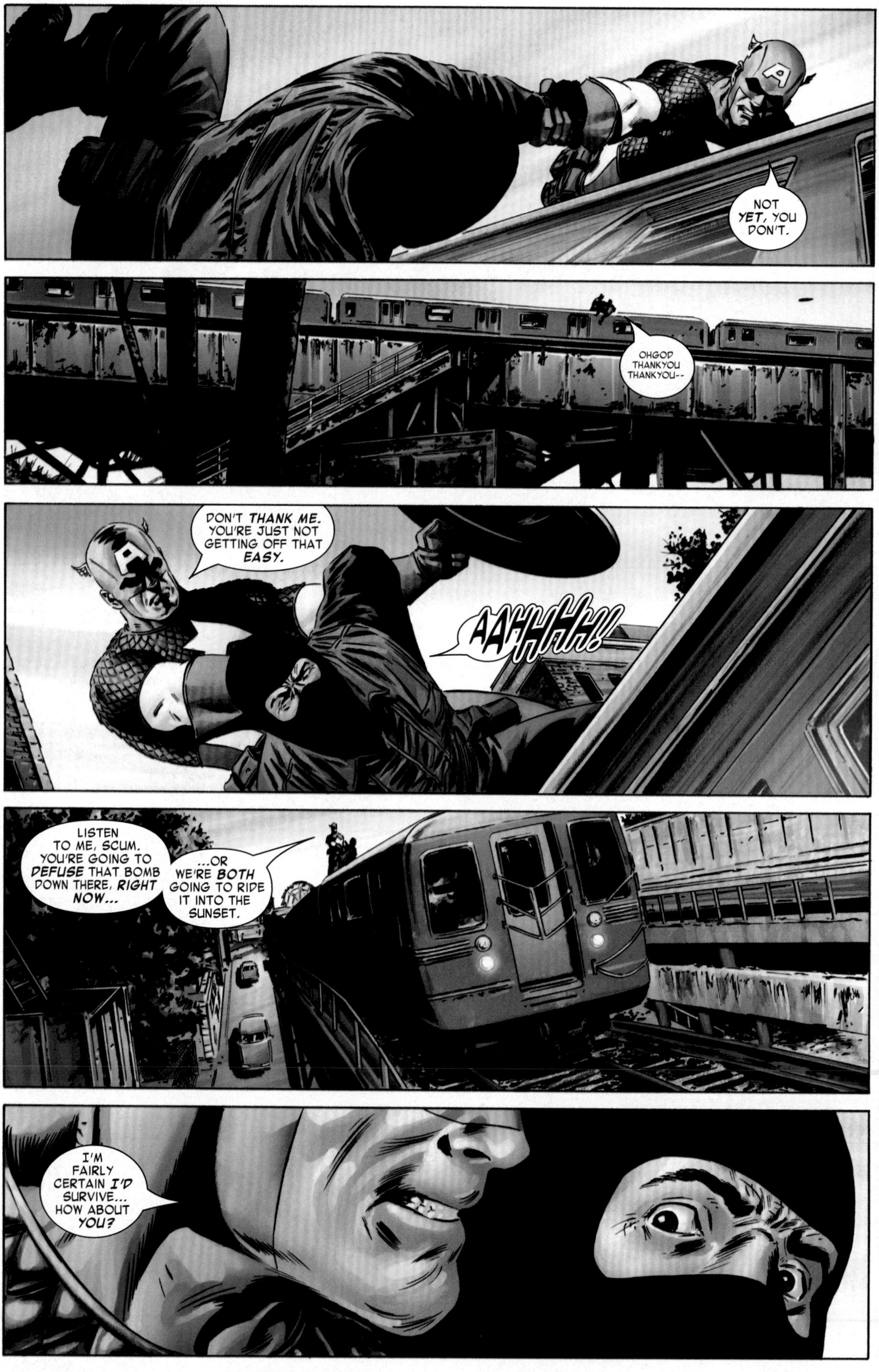
NOT *YET*, YOU DON'T.
OHGOD THANKYOU THANKYOU--
DON'T *THANK ME*. YOU'RE JUST NOT GETTING OFF THAT *EASY*.
AAHHHHH!
LISTEN TO ME, SCUM. YOU'RE GOING TO *DEFUSE* THAT BOMB DOWN THERE, *RIGHT NOW...*
...OR WE'RE *BOTH* GOING TO RIDE IT INTO THE SUNSET.
I'M FAIRLY CERTAIN *I'D* SURVIVE... HOW ABOUT *YOU?*

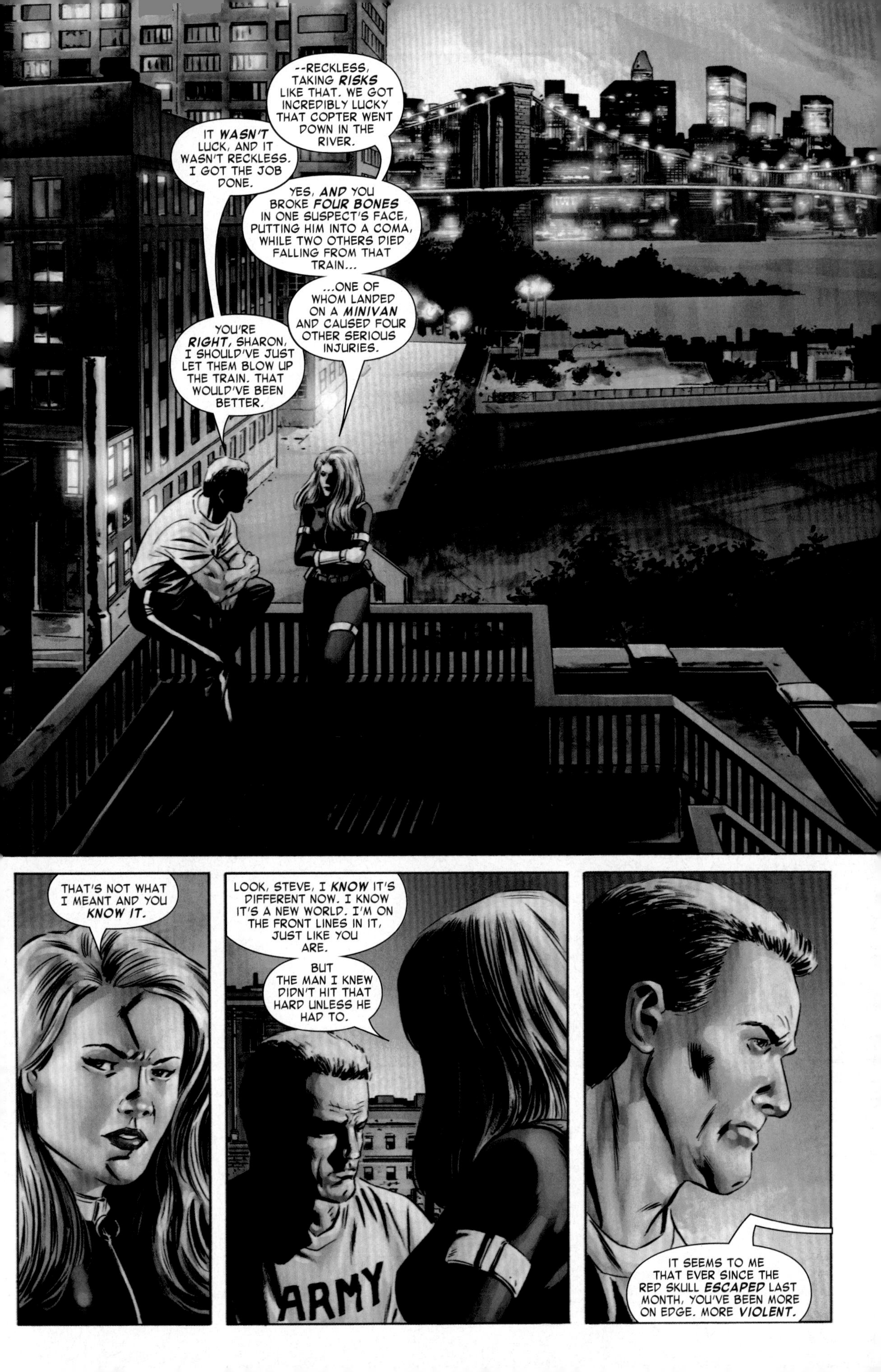
--RECKLESS, TAKING *RISKS* LIKE THAT. WE GOT INCREDIBLY LUCKY THAT COPTER WENT DOWN IN THE RIVER.
IT *WASN'T* LUCK, AND IT WASN'T RECKLESS. I GOT THE JOB DONE.
YES, *AND* YOU BROKE *FOUR BONES* IN ONE SUSPECT'S FACE, PUTTING HIM INTO A COMA, WHILE TWO OTHERS DIED FALLING FROM THAT TRAIN...
...ONE OF WHOM LANDED ON A *MINIVAN* AND CAUSED FOUR OTHER SERIOUS INJURIES.
YOU'RE *RIGHT,* SHARON, I SHOULD'VE JUST LET THEM BLOW UP THE TRAIN. THAT WOULD'VE BEEN BETTER.
THAT'S NOT WHAT I MEANT AND YOU *KNOW IT.*
LOOK, STEVE, I *KNOW* IT'S DIFFERENT NOW. I KNOW IT'S A NEW WORLD. I'M ON THE FRONT LINES IN IT, JUST LIKE YOU ARE.
BUT THE MAN I KNEW DIDN'T HIT THAT HARD UNLESS HE HAD TO.
ARMY
IT SEEMS TO ME THAT EVER SINCE THE RED SKULL *ESCAPED* LAST MONTH, YOU'VE BEEN MORE ON EDGE. MORE *VIOLENT.*

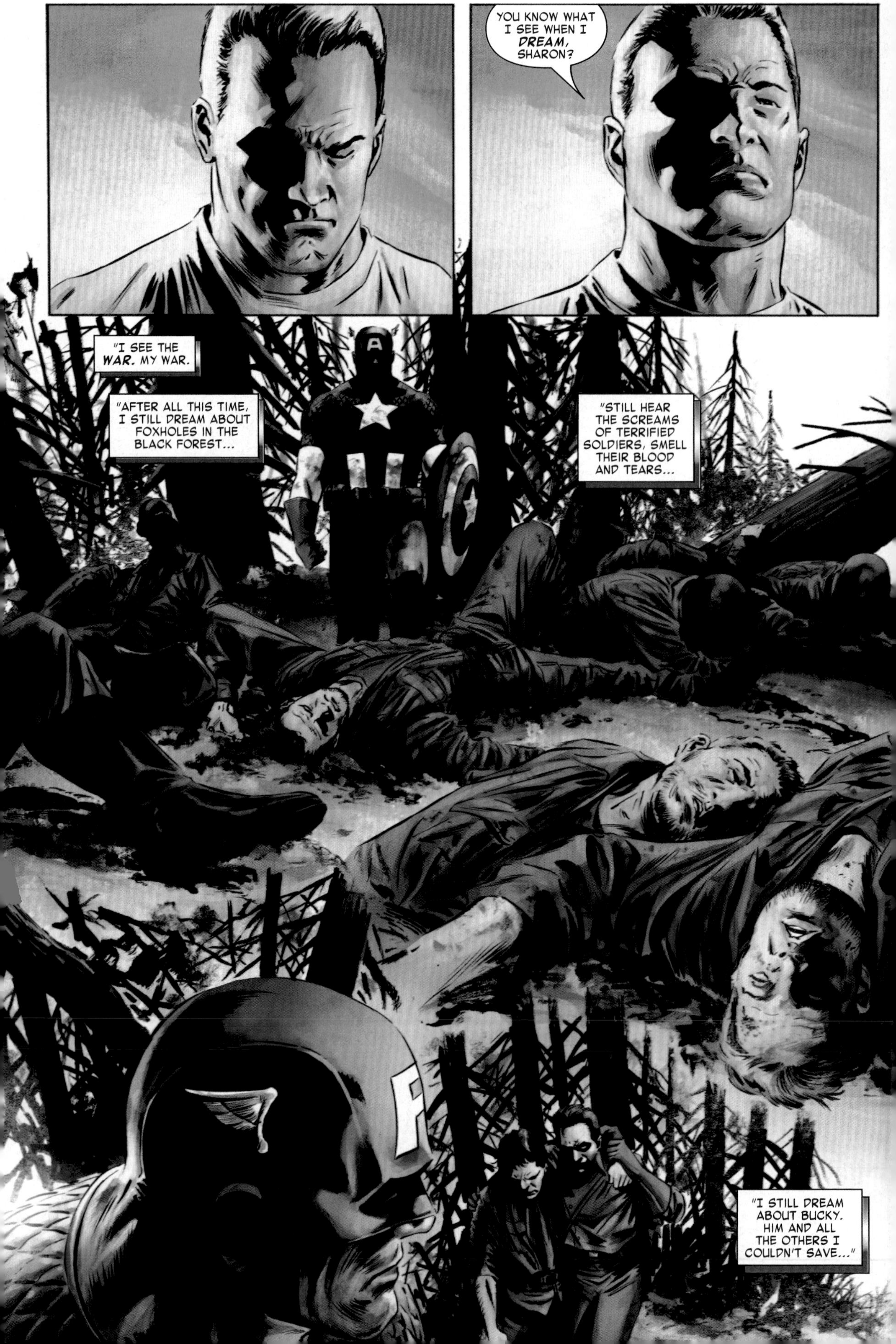
YOU KNOW WHAT I SEE WHEN I *DREAM*, SHARON?
"I SEE THE *WAR.* MY WAR.
"AFTER ALL THIS TIME, I STILL DREAM ABOUT FOXHOLES IN THE BLACK FOREST...
"STILL HEAR THE SCREAMS OF TERRIFIED SOLDIERS, SMELL THEIR BLOOD AND TEARS...
"I STILL DREAM ABOUT BUCKY. HIM AND ALL THE OTHERS I COULDN'T SAVE..."

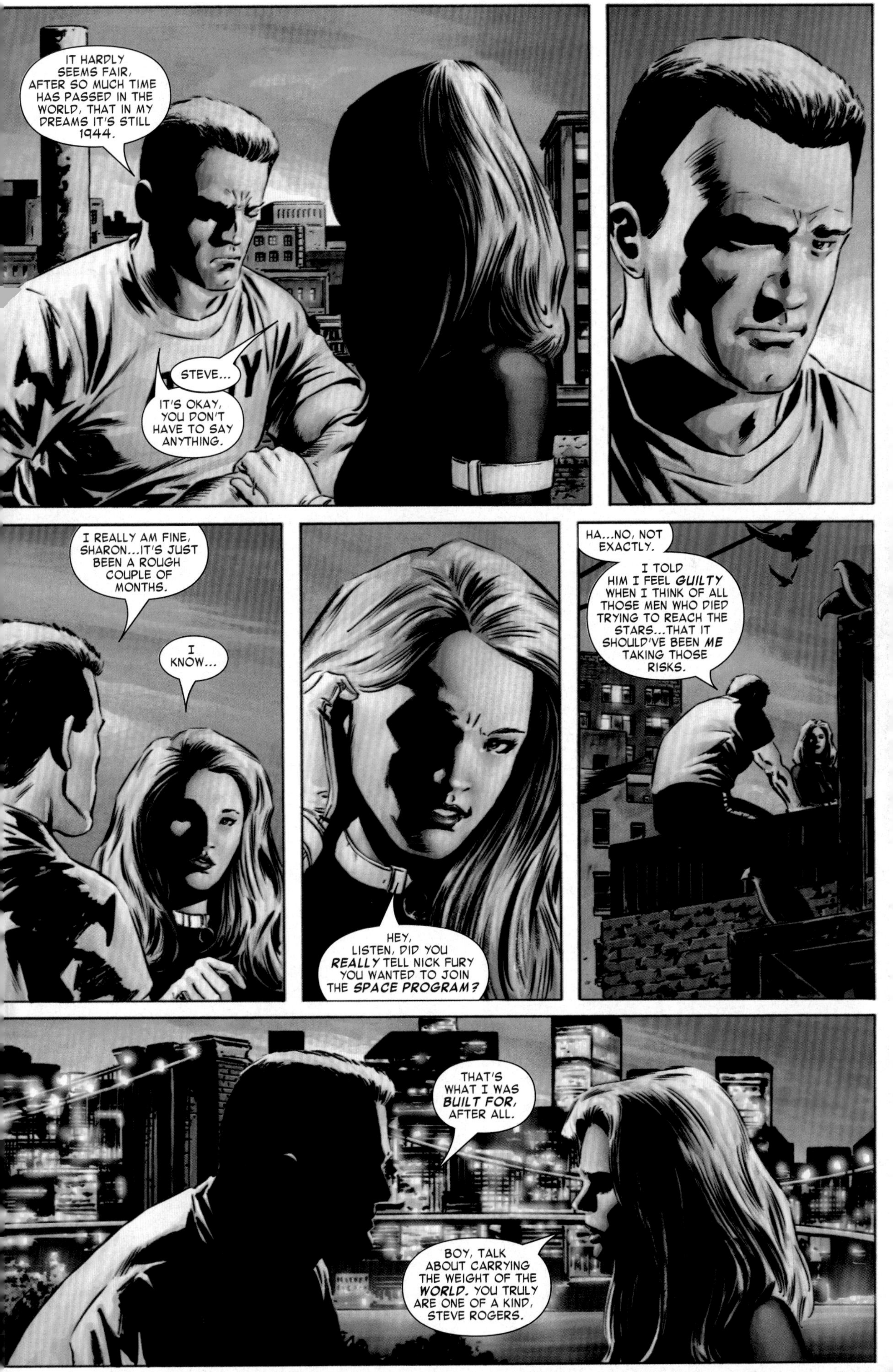
IT HARDLY SEEMS FAIR, AFTER SO MUCH TIME HAS PASSED IN THE WORLD, THAT IN MY DREAMS IT'S STILL 1944.
STEVE...
IT'S OKAY, YOU DON'T HAVE TO SAY ANYTHING.
I REALLY AM FINE, SHARON...IT'S JUST BEEN A ROUGH COUPLE OF MONTHS.
I KNOW...
HEY, LISTEN, DID YOU REALLY TELL NICK FURY YOU WANTED TO JOIN THE SPACE PROGRAM?
HA...NO, NOT EXACTLY.
I TOLD HIM I FEEL GUILTY WHEN I THINK OF ALL THOSE MEN WHO DIED TRYING TO REACH THE STARS...THAT IT SHOULD'VE BEEN ME TAKING THOSE RISKS.
THAT'S WHAT I WAS BUILT FOR, AFTER ALL.
BOY, TALK ABOUT CARRYING THE WEIGHT OF THE WORLD. YOU TRULY ARE ONE OF A KIND, STEVE ROGERS.

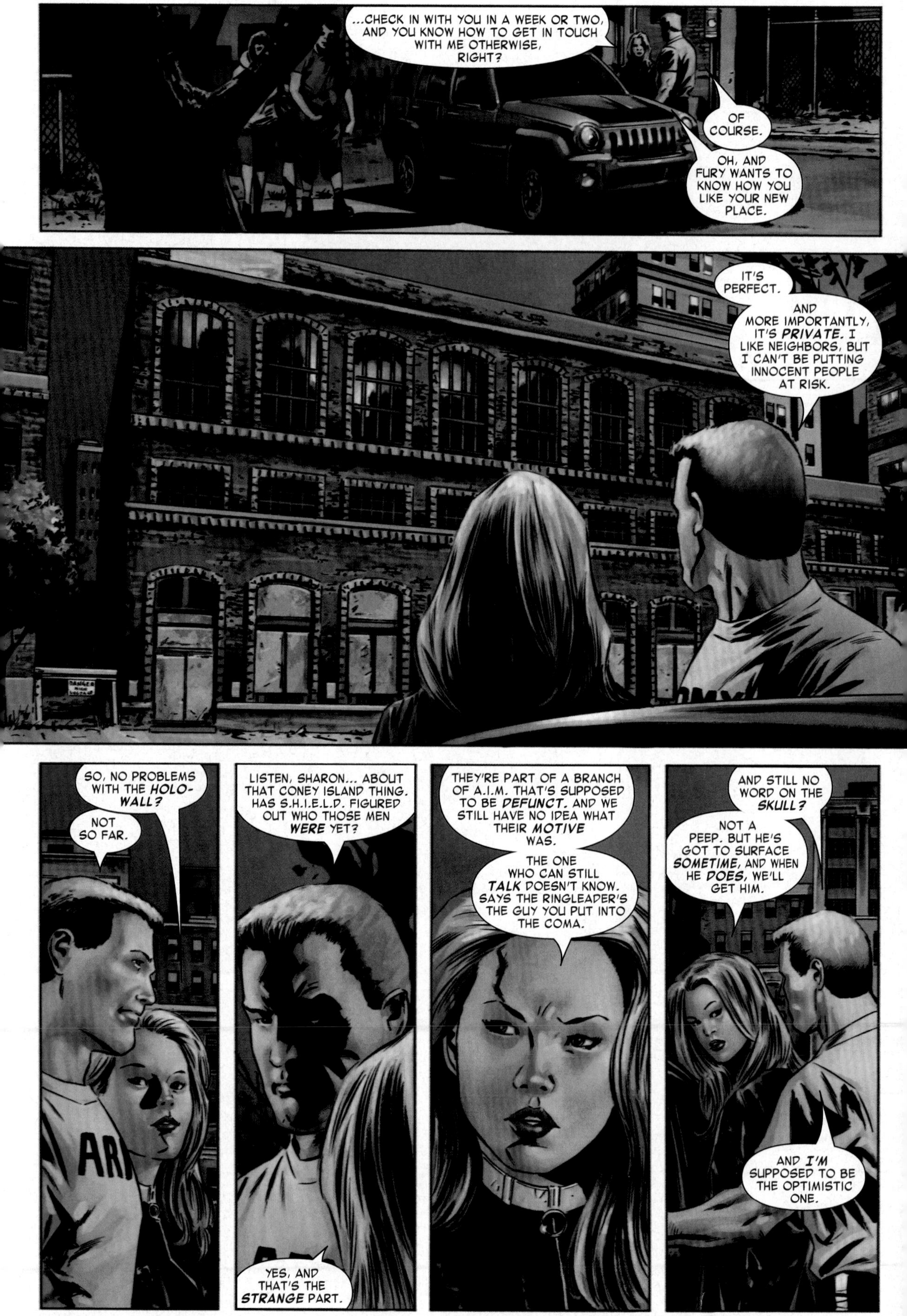
...CHECK IN WITH YOU IN A WEEK OR TWO, AND YOU KNOW HOW TO GET IN TOUCH WITH ME OTHERWISE, RIGHT?
OF COURSE.
OH, AND FURY WANTS TO KNOW HOW YOU LIKE YOUR NEW PLACE.
IT'S PERFECT.
AND MORE IMPORTANTLY, IT'S PRIVATE. I LIKE NEIGHBORS, BUT I CAN'T BE PUTTING INNOCENT PEOPLE AT RISK.
SO, NO PROBLEMS WITH THE HOLO-WALL?
NOT SO FAR.
LISTEN, SHARON... ABOUT THAT CONEY ISLAND THING. HAS S.H.I.E.L.D. FIGURED OUT WHO THOSE MEN WERE YET?
YES, AND THAT'S THE STRANGE PART.
THEY'RE PART OF A BRANCH OF A.I.M. THAT'S SUPPOSED TO BE DEFUNCT. AND WE STILL HAVE NO IDEA WHAT THEIR MOTIVE WAS.
THE ONE WHO CAN STILL TALK DOESN'T KNOW. SAYS THE RINGLEADER'S THE GUY YOU PUT INTO THE COMA.
AND STILL NO WORD ON THE SKULL?
NOT A PEEP. BUT HE'S GOT TO SURFACE SOMETIME, AND WHEN HE DOES, WE'LL GET HIM.
AND I'M SUPPOSED TO BE THE OPTIMISTIC ONE.

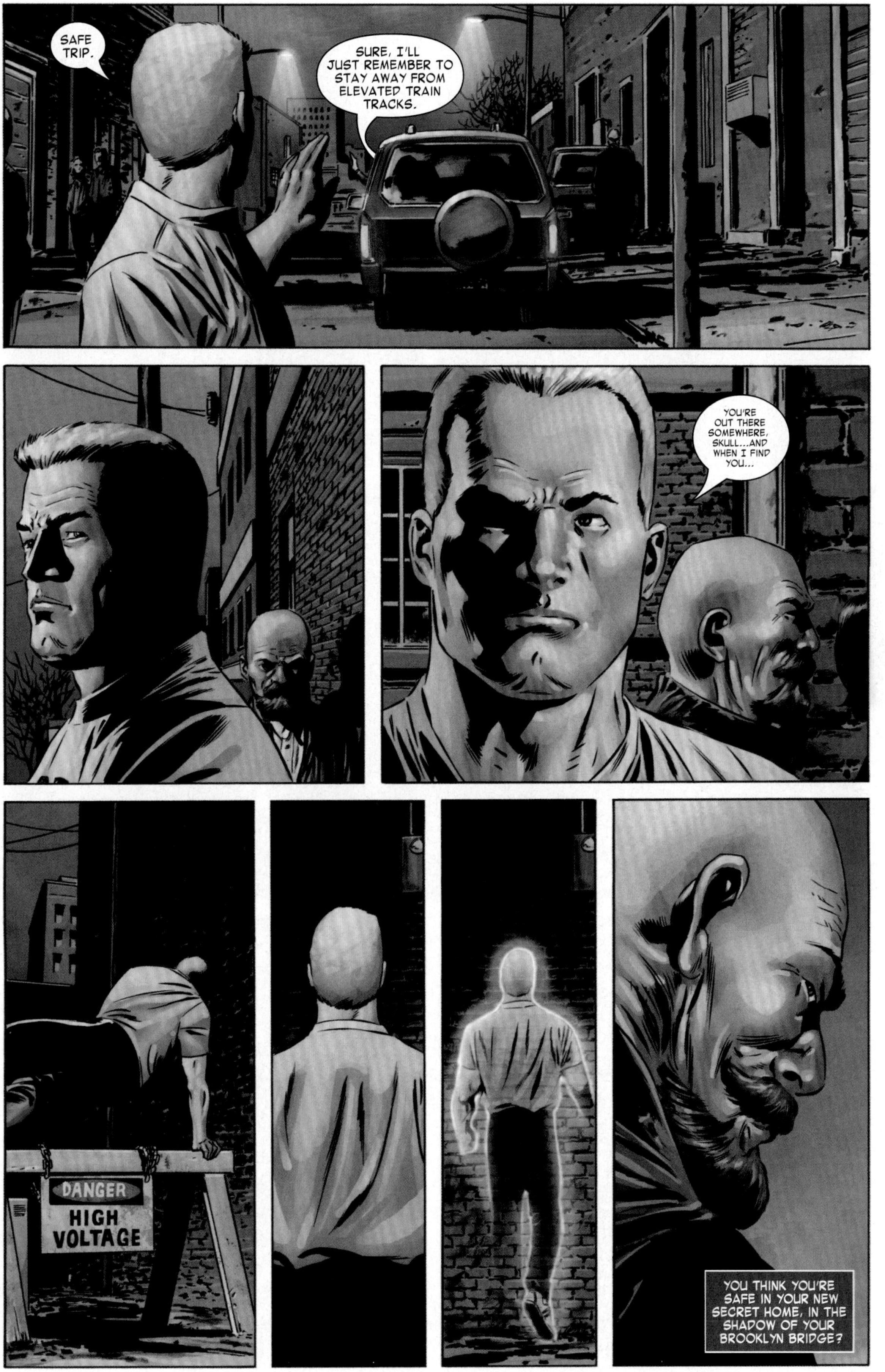
SAFE TRIP.
SURE, I'LL JUST REMEMBER TO STAY AWAY FROM ELEVATED TRAIN TRACKS.
YOU'RE OUT THERE SOMEWHERE, SKULL...AND WHEN I FIND YOU...
DANGER
HIGH VOLTAGE
YOU THINK YOU'RE SAFE IN YOUR NEW SECRET HOME, IN THE SHADOW OF YOUR BROOKLYN BRIDGE?

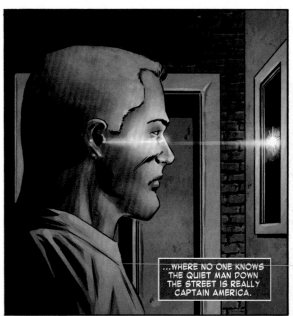

...WHERE NO ONE KNOWS THE QUIET MAN DOWN THE STREET IS REALLY CAPTAIN AMERICA.

BUT I'LL ALWAYS BE ABLE TO FIND YOU, ROGERS.

I COULD PUT A BULLET BETWEEN YOUR EYES ANYTIME I WANT, AND YOU'D NEVER SEE IT COMING.

BUT THAT WOULD BE TOO EASY. I NEED TO MAKE YOU SUFFER.

BECAUSE YOU DO IT SO WELL, ROGERS... SUFFERING, I MEAN.

AND THAT'S OUR DESTINY, AFTER ALL, ISN'T IT...?

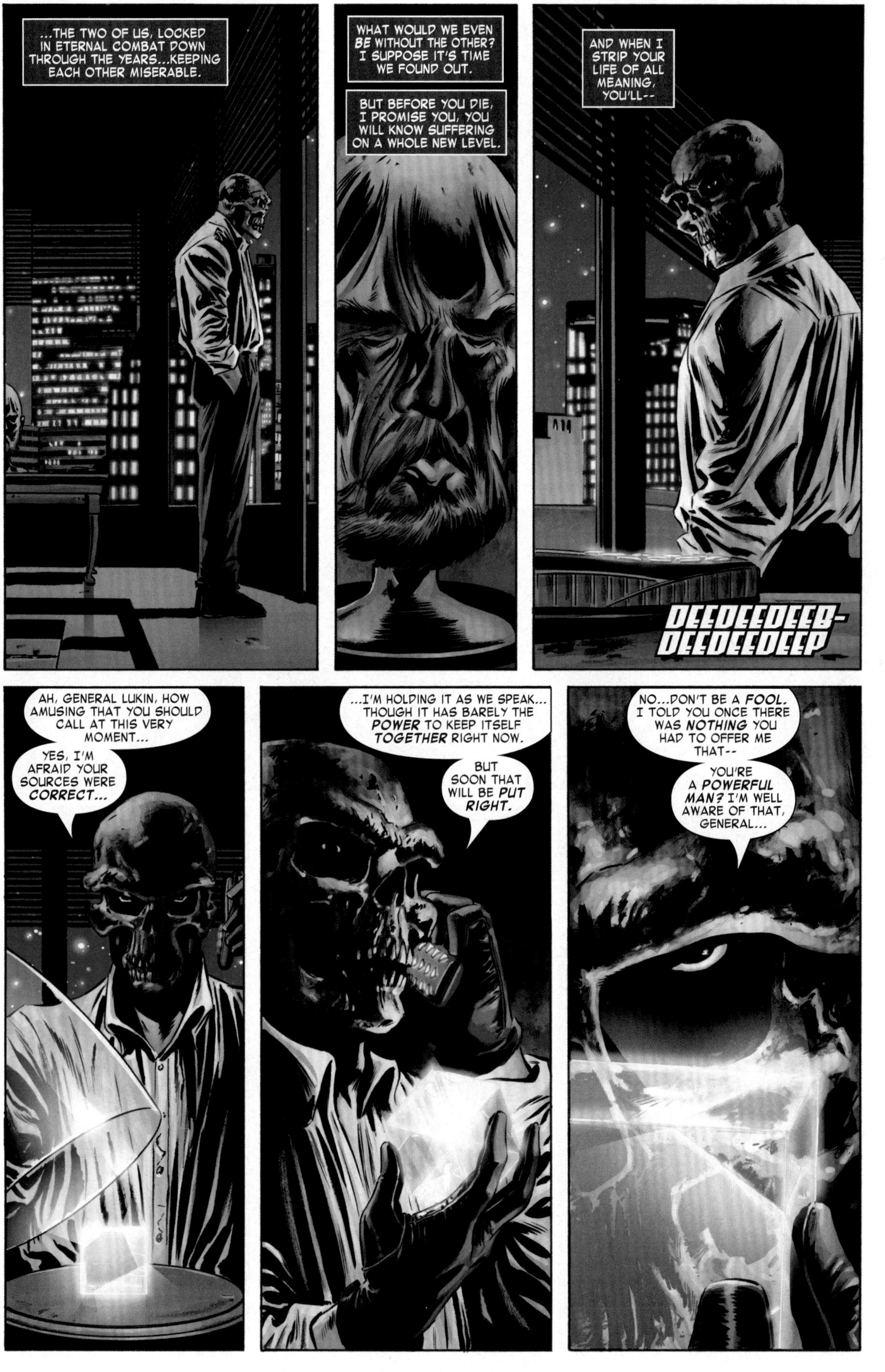
...THE TWO OF US, LOCKED IN ETERNAL COMBAT DOWN THROUGH THE YEARS...KEEPING EACH OTHER MISERABLE.
WHAT WOULD WE EVEN BE WITHOUT THE OTHER? I SUPPOSE IT'S TIME WE FOUND OUT.
BUT BEFORE YOU DIE, I PROMISE YOU, YOU WILL KNOW SUFFERING ON A WHOLE NEW LEVEL.
AND WHEN I STRIP YOUR LIFE OF ALL MEANING, YOU'LL--
DEEDEEDEEB-DEEDEEDEEP
AH, GENERAL LUKIN, HOW AMUSING THAT YOU SHOULD CALL AT THIS VERY MOMENT...
YES, I'M AFRAID YOUR SOURCES WERE CORRECT...
...I'M HOLDING IT AS WE SPEAK... THOUGH IT HAS BARELY THE POWER TO KEEP ITSELF TOGETHER RIGHT NOW.
BUT SOON THAT WILL BE PUT RIGHT.
NO...DON'T BE A FOOL. I TOLD YOU ONCE THERE WAS NOTHING YOU HAD TO OFFER ME THAT--
YOU'RE A POWERFUL MAN? I'M WELL AWARE OF THAT, GENERAL...

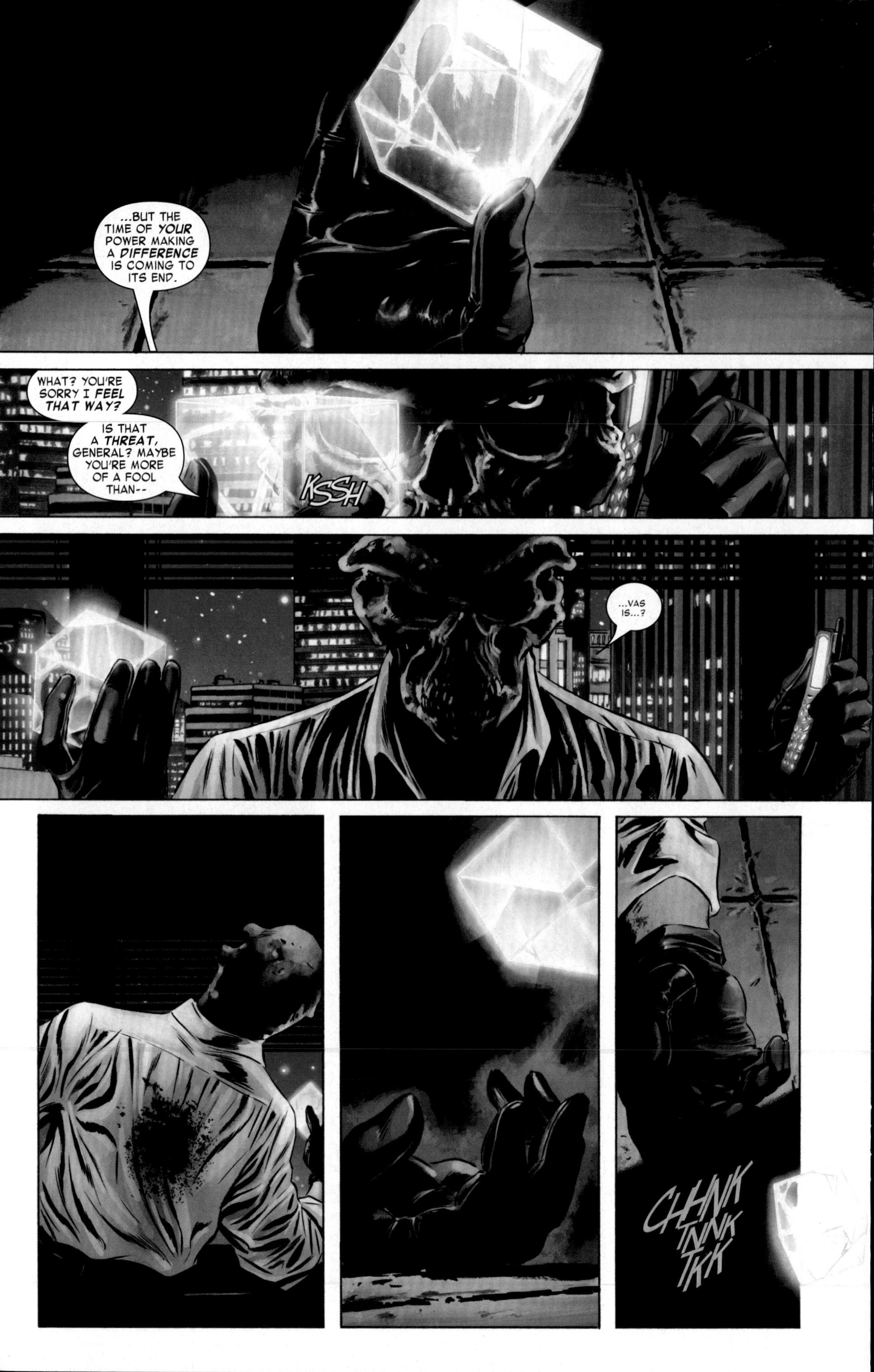
...BUT THE TIME OF YOUR POWER MAKING A DIFFERENCE IS COMING TO ITS END.
WHAT? YOU'RE SORRY I FEEL THAT WAY?
IS THAT A THREAT, GENERAL? MAYBE YOU'RE MORE OF A FOOL THAN--
KSSH
...VAS IS...?
CLINK
TINK
TKK

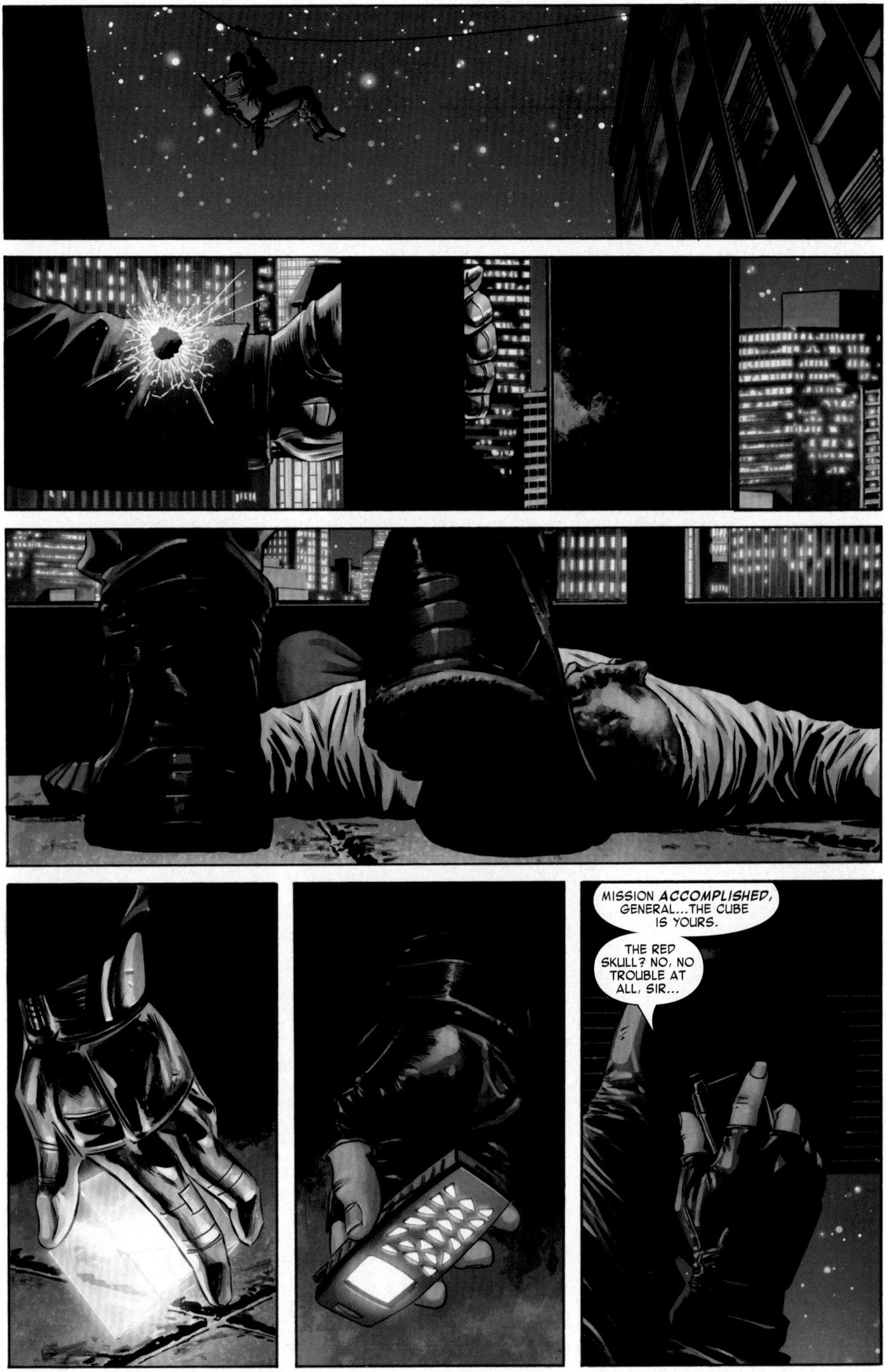
MISSION ACCOMPLISHED, GENERAL...THE CUBE IS YOURS.
THE RED SKULL? NO, NO TROUBLE AT ALL, SIR...

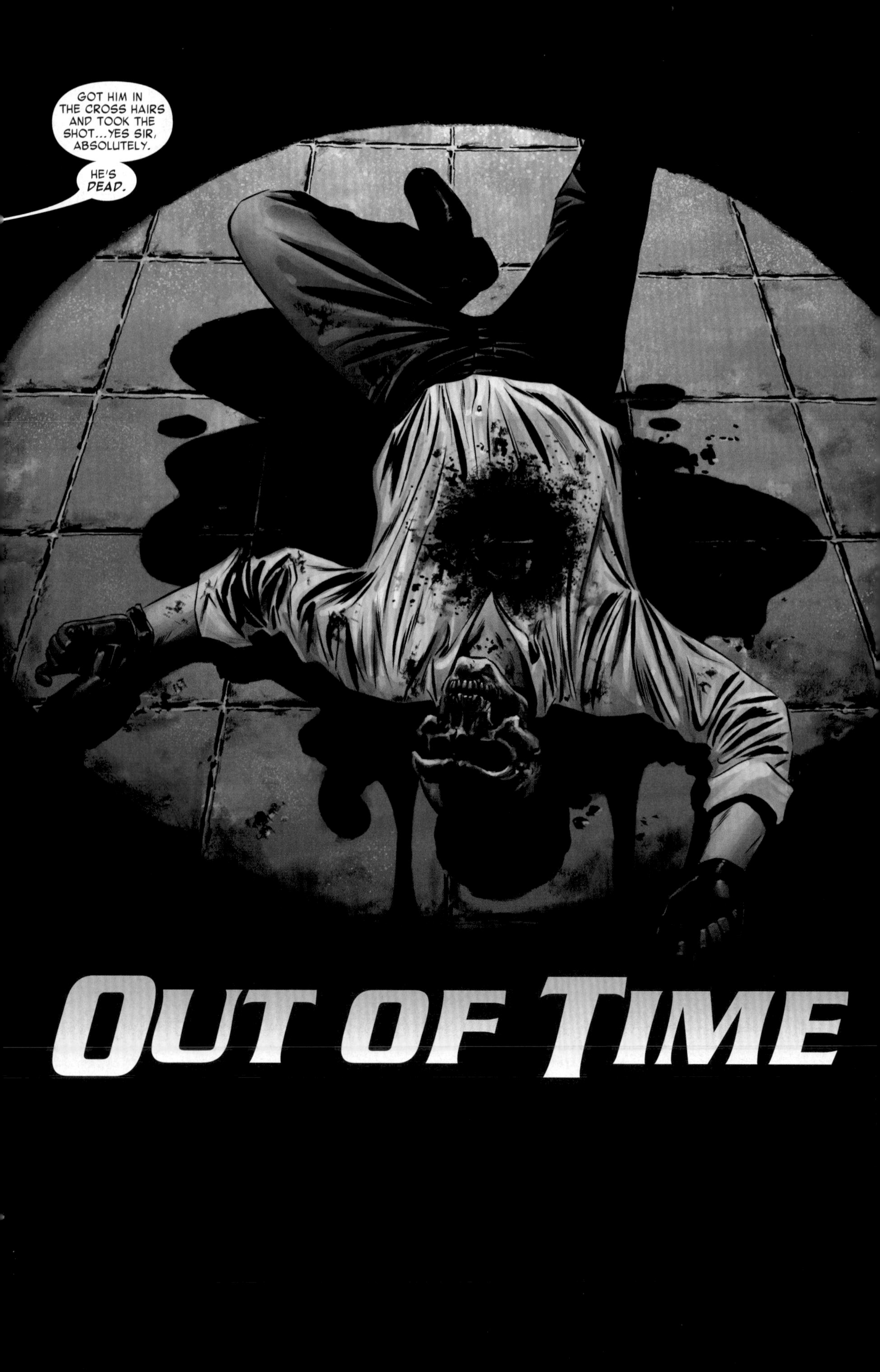
GOT HIM IN THE CROSS HAIRS AND TOOK THE SHOT...YES SIR, ABSOLUTELY.
HE'S DEAD.
OUT OF TIME

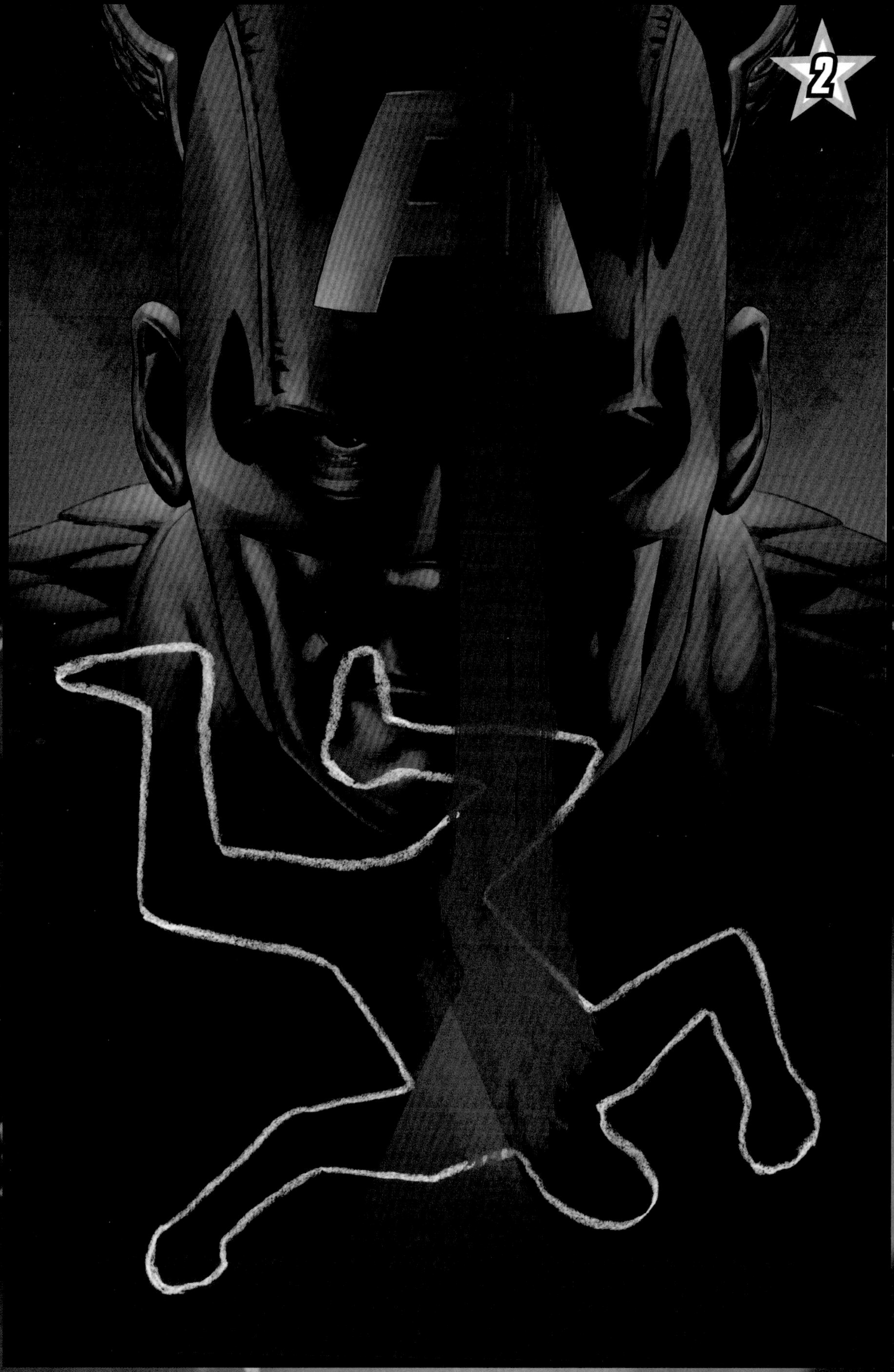
2

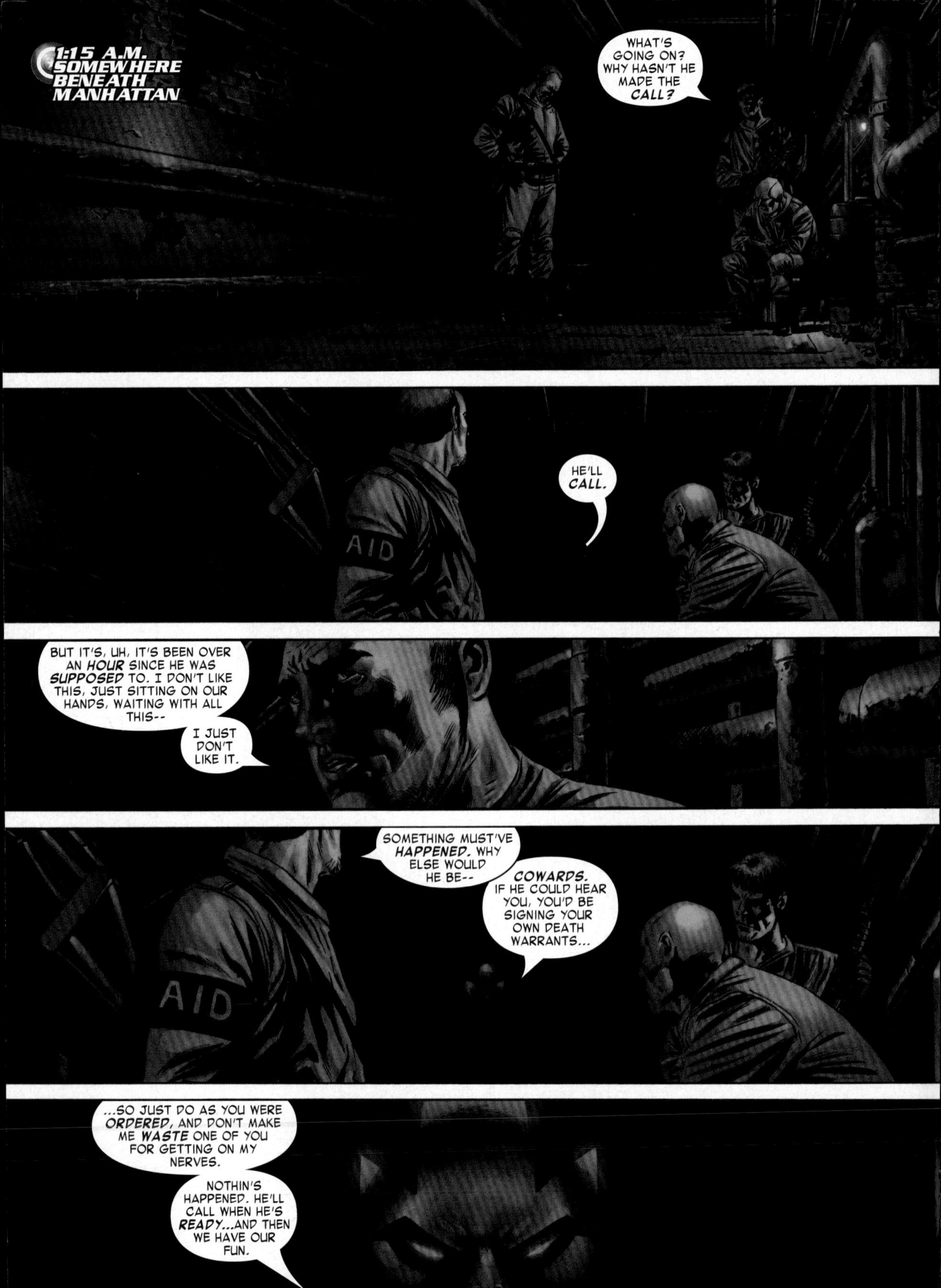

1:15 A.M. SOMEWHERE BENEATH MANHATTAN
WHAT'S GOING ON? WHY HASN'T HE MADE THE CALL?
HE'LL CALL.
AID
BUT IT'S, UH, IT'S BEEN OVER AN HOUR SINCE HE WAS SUPPOSED TO. I DON'T LIKE THIS, JUST SITTING ON OUR HANDS, WAITING WITH ALL THIS--
I JUST DON'T LIKE IT.
SOMETHING MUST'VE HAPPENED. WHY ELSE WOULD HE BE--
COWARDS. IF HE COULD HEAR YOU, YOU'D BE SIGNING YOUR OWN DEATH WARRANTS...
AID
...SO JUST DO AS YOU WERE ORDERED, AND DON'T MAKE ME WASTE ONE OF YOU FOR GETTING ON MY NERVES.
NOTHIN'S HAPPENED. HE'LL CALL WHEN HE'S READY...AND THEN WE HAVE OUR FUN.

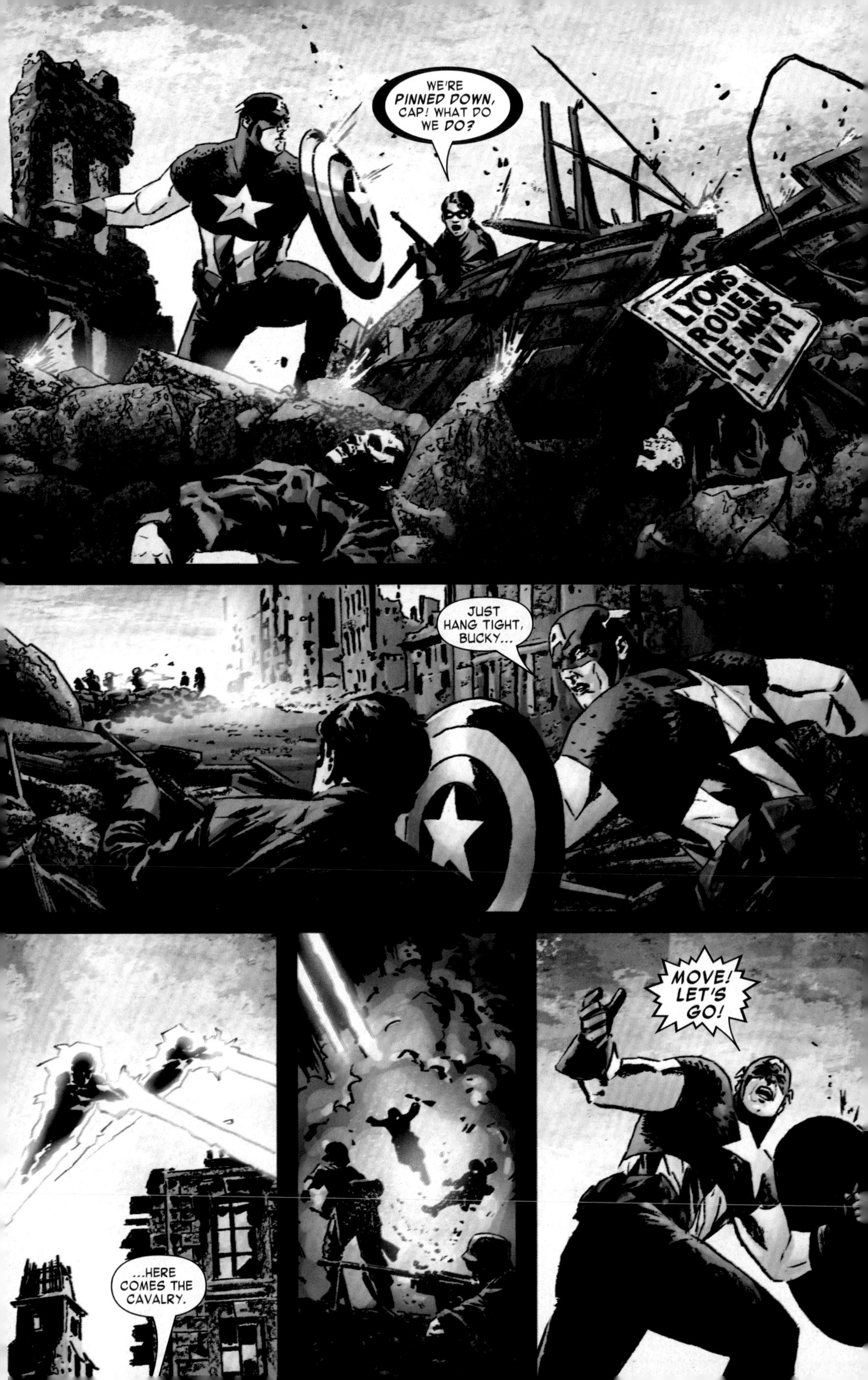
WE'RE PINNED DOWN, CAP! WHAT DO WE DO?
LYONS ROUEN LE MANS LAVAL
JUST HANG TIGHT, BUCKY...
...HERE COMES THE CAVALRY.
MOVE! LET'S GO!

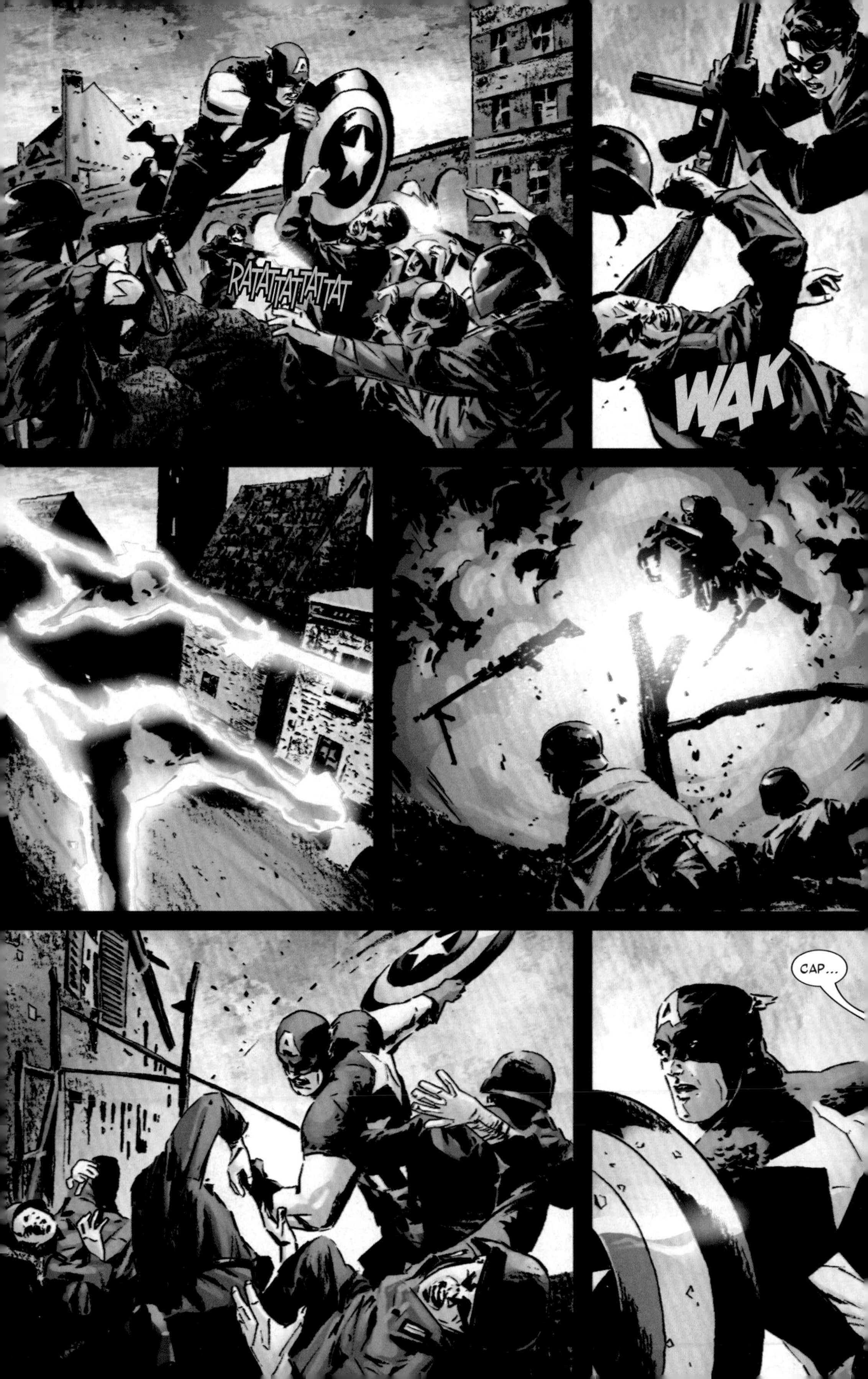
RATATATTATTATTAT
WAK
CAP...

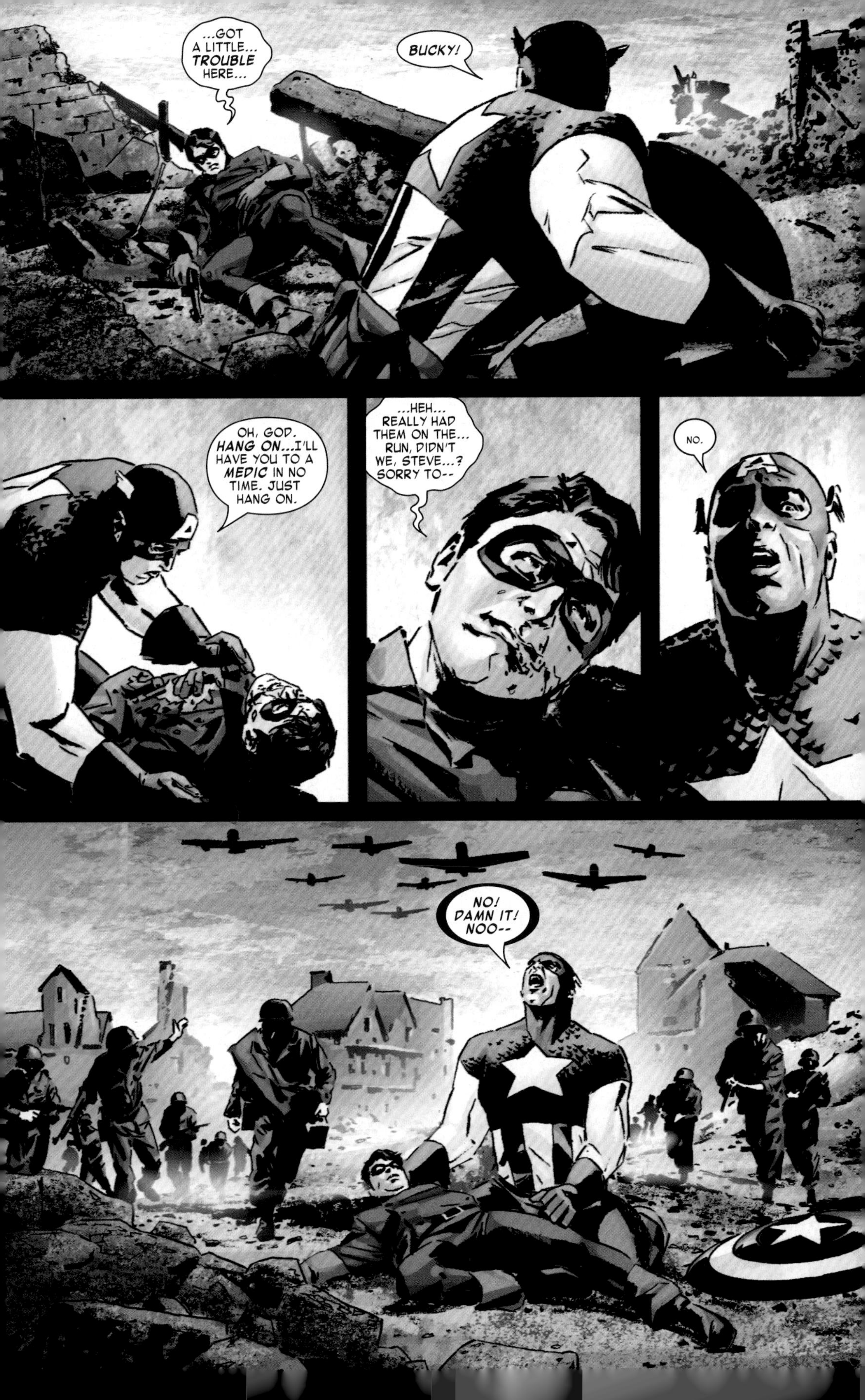
...GOT A LITTLE... TROUBLE HERE...
BUCKY!
OH, GOD. HANG ON...I'LL HAVE YOU TO A MEDIC IN NO TIME. JUST HANG ON.
...HEH... REALLY HAD THEM ON THE... RUN, DIDN'T WE, STEVE...? SORRY TO--
NO.
NO! DAMN IT! NOO--

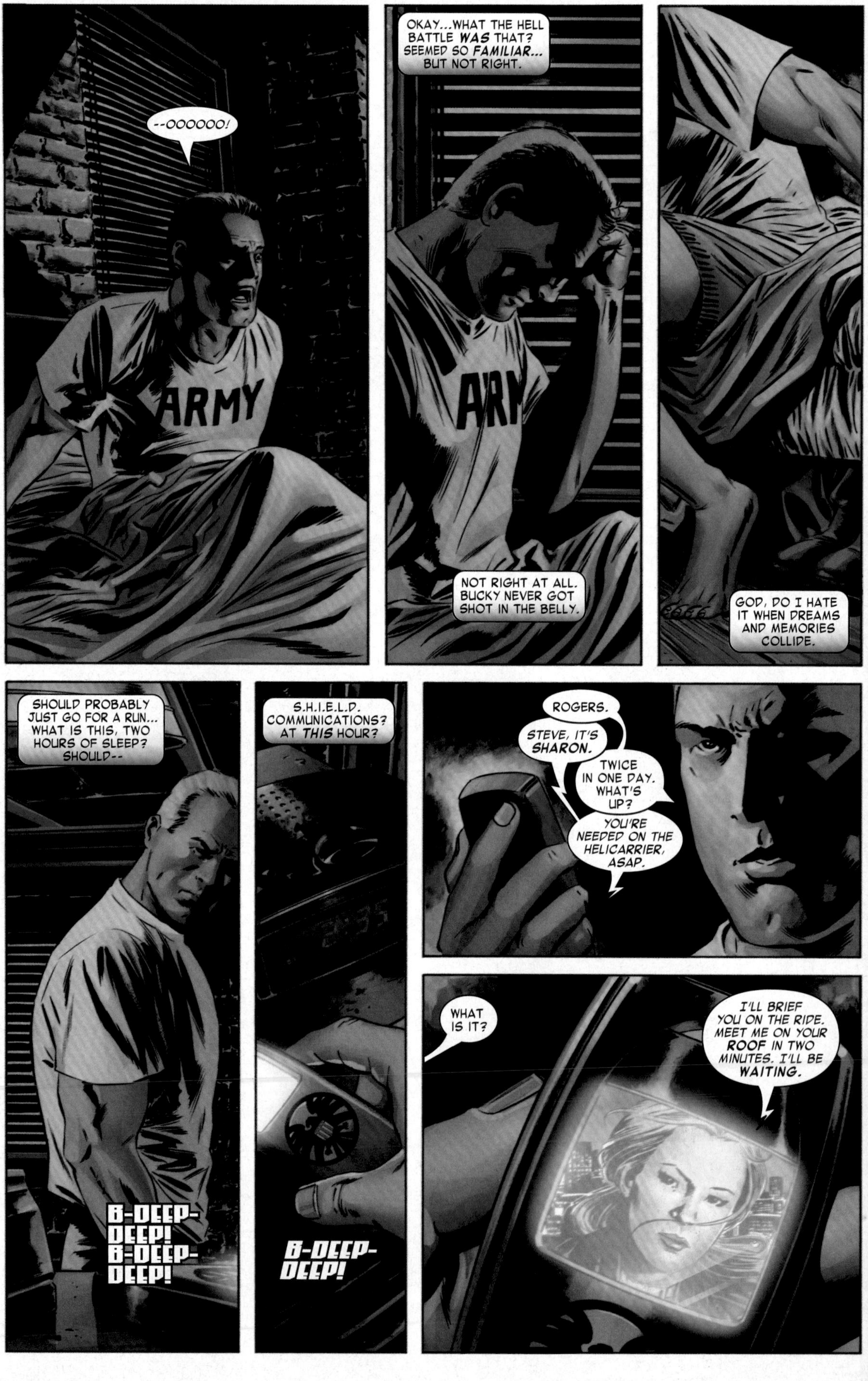
--OOOOOO!
OKAY...WHAT THE HELL BATTLE WAS THAT? SEEMED SO FAMILIAR... BUT NOT RIGHT.
NOT RIGHT AT ALL. BUCKY NEVER GOT SHOT IN THE BELLY.
GOD, DO I HATE IT WHEN DREAMS AND MEMORIES COLLIDE.
SHOULD PROBABLY JUST GO FOR A RUN... WHAT IS THIS, TWO HOURS OF SLEEP? SHOULD--
B-DEEP-DEEP! B-DEEP-DEEP!
S.H.I.E.L.D. COMMUNICATIONS? AT THIS HOUR?
B-DEEP-DEEP!
ROGERS.
STEVE, IT'S SHARON.
TWICE IN ONE DAY. WHAT'S UP?
YOU'RE NEEDED ON THE HELICARRIER, ASAP.
WHAT IS IT?
I'LL BRIEF YOU ON THE RIDE. MEET ME ON YOUR ROOF IN TWO MINUTES. I'LL BE WAITING.

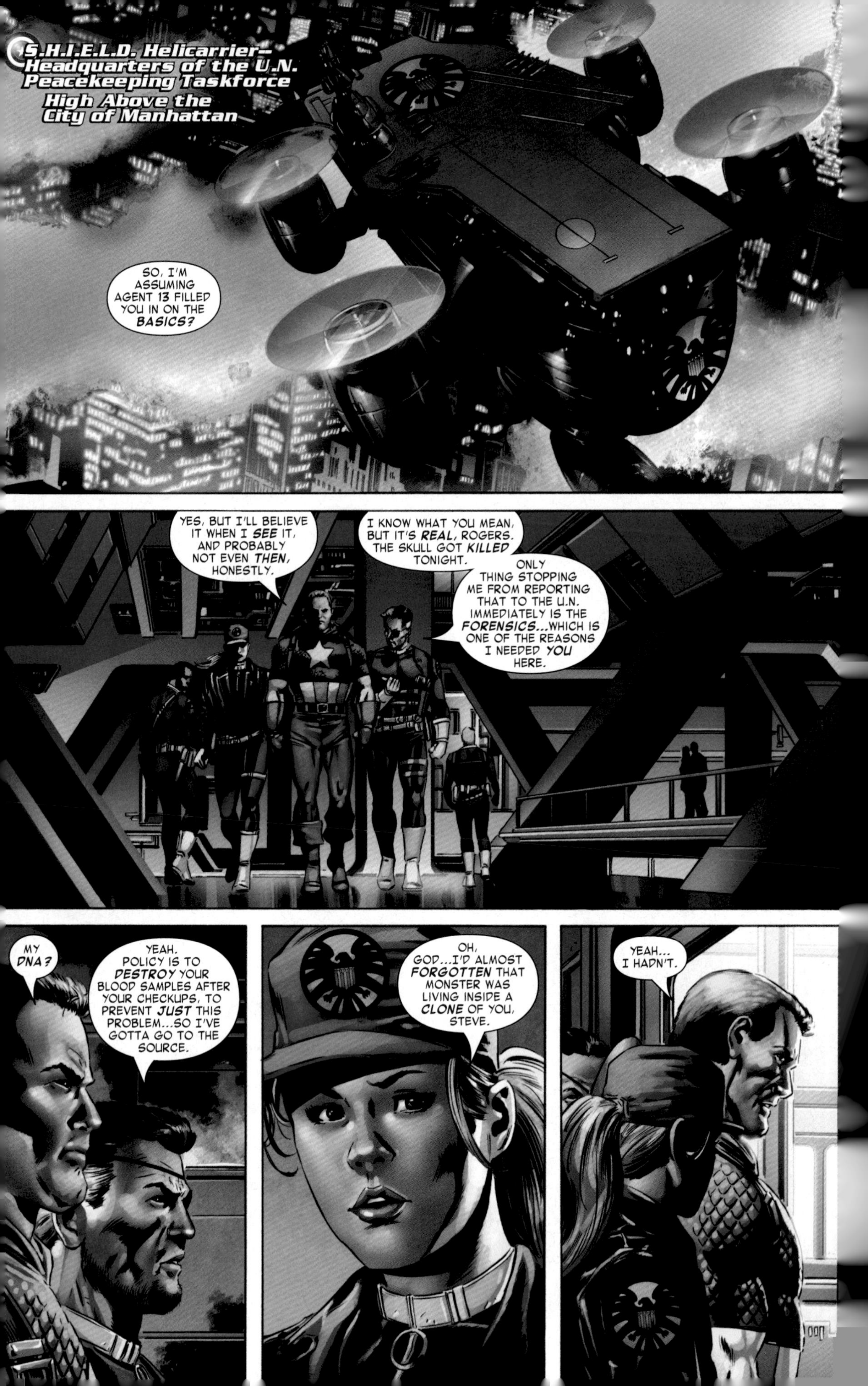
S.H.I.E.L.D. Helicarrier-- Headquarters of the U.N. Peacekeeping Taskforce
High Above the City of Manhattan
SO, I'M ASSUMING AGENT 13 FILLED YOU IN ON THE BASICS?
YES, BUT I'LL BELIEVE IT WHEN I SEE IT, AND PROBABLY NOT EVEN THEN, HONESTLY.
I KNOW WHAT YOU MEAN, BUT IT'S REAL, ROGERS. THE SKULL GOT KILLED TONIGHT.
ONLY THING STOPPING ME FROM REPORTING THAT TO THE U.N. IMMEDIATELY IS THE FORENSICS...WHICH IS ONE OF THE REASONS I NEEDED YOU HERE.
MY DNA?
YEAH. POLICY IS TO DESTROY YOUR BLOOD SAMPLES AFTER YOUR CHECKUPS, TO PREVENT JUST THIS PROBLEM...SO I'VE GOTTA GO TO THE SOURCE.
OH, GOD...I'D ALMOST FORGOTTEN THAT MONSTER WAS LIVING INSIDE A CLONE OF YOU, STEVE.
YEAH... I HADN'T.

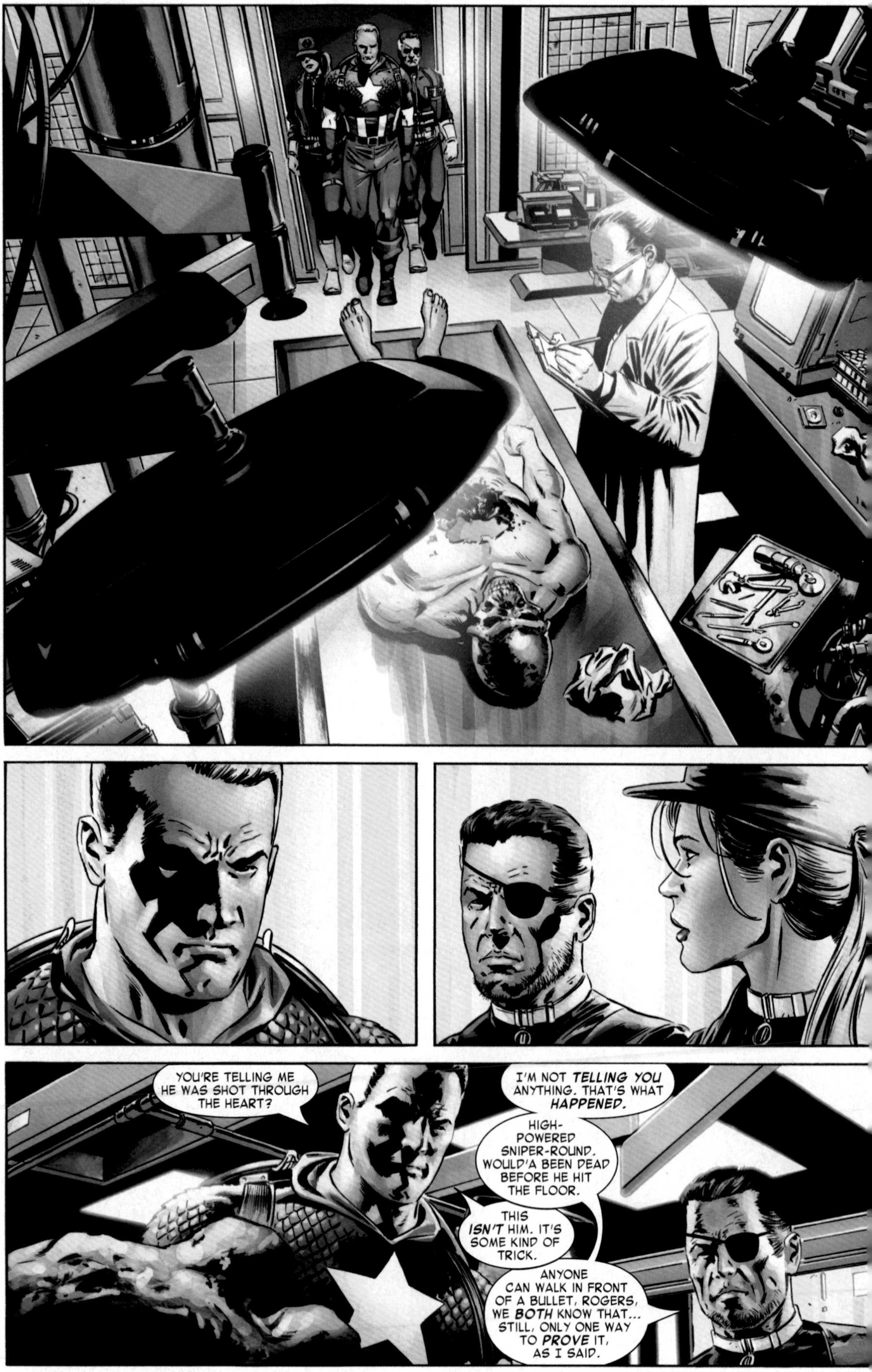
YOU'RE TELLING ME HE WAS SHOT THROUGH THE HEART?
I'M NOT TELLING YOU ANYTHING. THAT'S WHAT HAPPENED.
HIGH-POWERED SNIPER-ROUND. WOULD'A BEEN DEAD BEFORE HE HIT THE FLOOR.
THIS ISN'T HIM. IT'S SOME KIND OF TRICK.
ANYONE CAN WALK IN FRONT OF A BULLET, ROGERS, WE BOTH KNOW THAT... STILL, ONLY ONE WAY TO PROVE IT, AS I SAID.

DOCTOR? WOULD YOU TAKE A DNA SAMPLE FROM THE CAPTAIN HERE?

OH, UH... OF *COURSE*, COLONEL FURY. I MEAN, IF THAT'S... UH...OKAY WITH--

DO IT.

IF THAT REALLY IS HIM, WHAT WAS HE *DOING* IN NEW YORK? THE SKULL IS NEVER ANY PLACE WITHOUT A *REASON*.

WE DON'T KNOW THAT YET. HE WAS *FOUND* IN A PENTHOUSE ON THE UPPER WEST SIDE. IT WAS MOSTLY UNFURNISHED, RENTED UNDER A FAKE NAME.

YOU JUST *HAPPENED* TO FIND HIM?

NO, SOMEONE CALLED IN A TIP TO THE COPS. WE SCRAMBLED THEIR LINE AND GOT THERE FIRST, TO KEEP A *LID* ON IT.

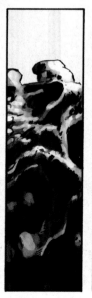

I WANT TO SEE THAT *CRIME SCENE*. NOW.

OF COURSE YOU DO.

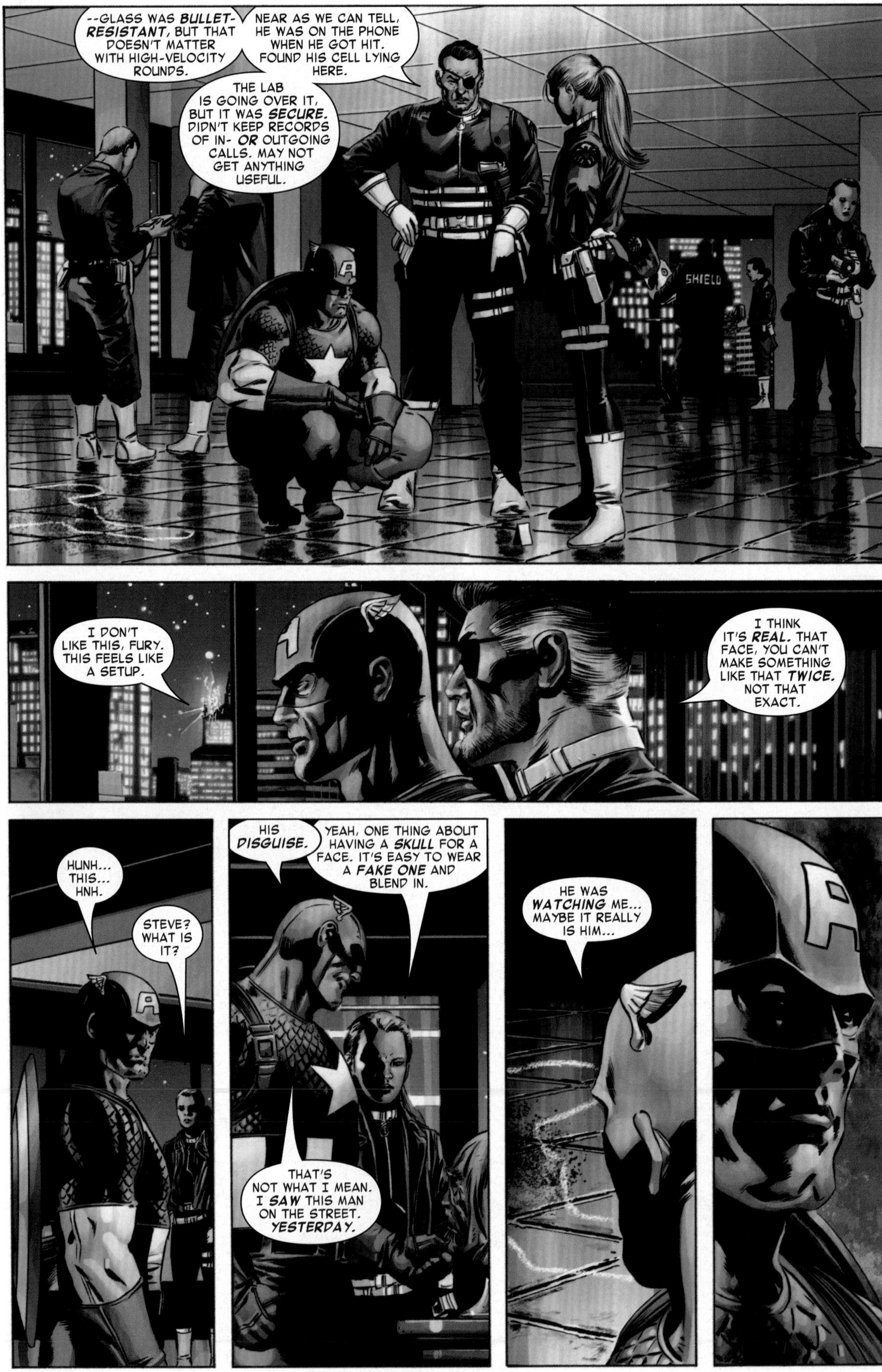
--GLASS WAS BULLET-RESISTANT, BUT THAT DOESN'T MATTER WITH HIGH-VELOCITY ROUNDS.
NEAR AS WE CAN TELL, HE WAS ON THE PHONE WHEN HE GOT HIT. FOUND HIS CELL LYING HERE.
THE LAB IS GOING OVER IT, BUT IT WAS SECURE. DIDN'T KEEP RECORDS OF IN- OR OUTGOING CALLS. MAY NOT GET ANYTHING USEFUL.
SHIELD
I DON'T LIKE THIS, FURY. THIS FEELS LIKE A SETUP.
I THINK IT'S REAL. THAT FACE, YOU CAN'T MAKE SOMETHING LIKE THAT TWICE. NOT THAT EXACT.
HUNH... THIS... HNH.
STEVE? WHAT IS IT?
HIS DISGUISE.
YEAH, ONE THING ABOUT HAVING A SKULL FOR A FACE. IT'S EASY TO WEAR A FAKE ONE AND BLEND IN.
THAT'S NOT WHAT I MEAN. I SAW THIS MAN ON THE STREET. YESTERDAY.
HE WAS WATCHING ME... MAYBE IT REALLY IS HIM...

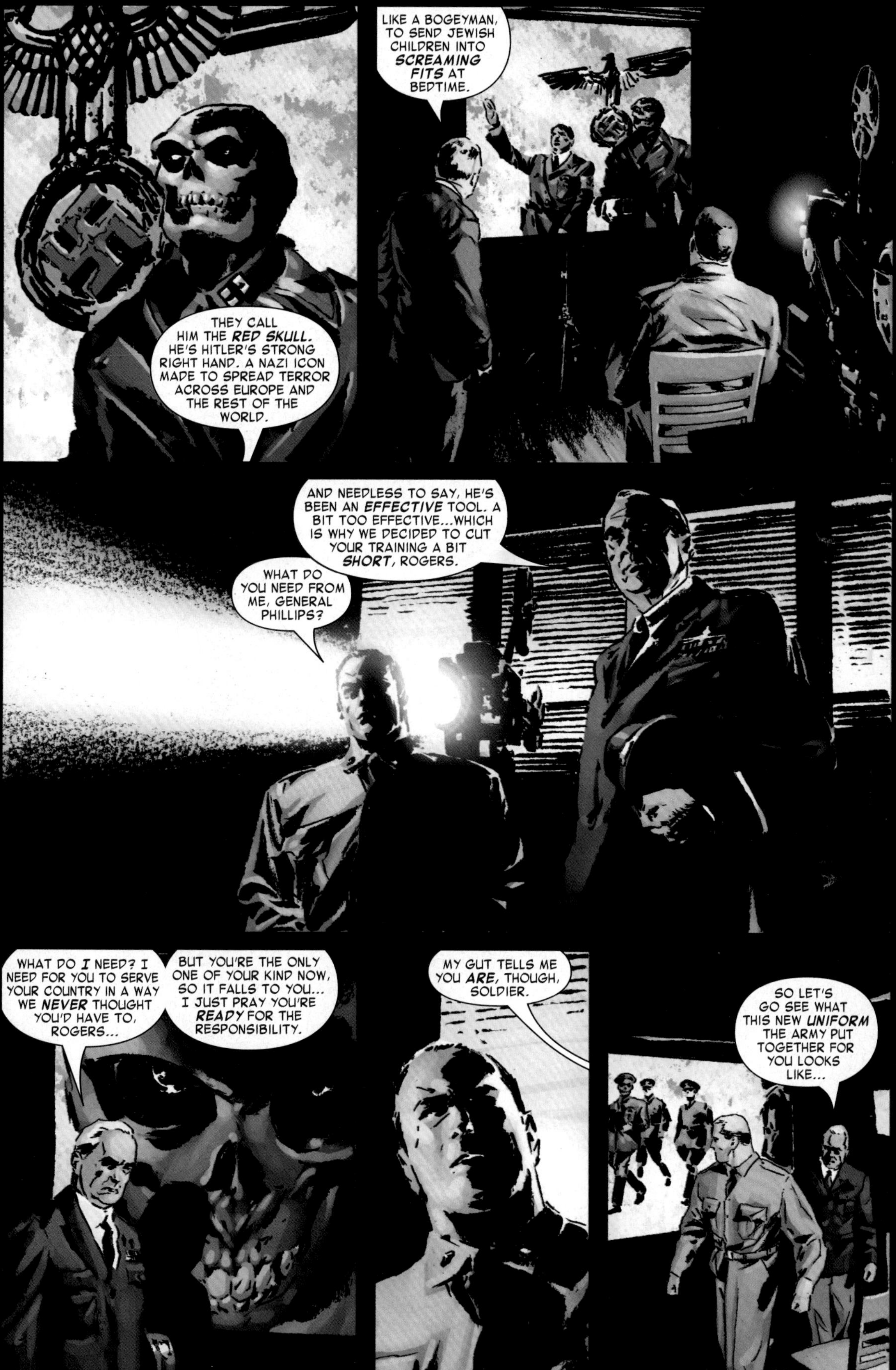
THEY CALL HIM THE RED SKULL. HE'S HITLER'S STRONG RIGHT HAND. A NAZI ICON MADE TO SPREAD TERROR ACROSS EUROPE AND THE REST OF THE WORLD.
LIKE A BOGEYMAN, TO SEND JEWISH CHILDREN INTO SCREAMING FITS AT BEDTIME.
AND NEEDLESS TO SAY, HE'S BEEN AN EFFECTIVE TOOL. A BIT TOO EFFECTIVE...WHICH IS WHY WE DECIDED TO CUT YOUR TRAINING A BIT SHORT, ROGERS.
WHAT DO YOU NEED FROM ME, GENERAL PHILLIPS?
WHAT DO I NEED? I NEED FOR YOU TO SERVE YOUR COUNTRY IN A WAY WE NEVER THOUGHT YOU'D HAVE TO, ROGERS...
BUT YOU'RE THE ONLY ONE OF YOUR KIND NOW, SO IT FALLS TO YOU... I JUST PRAY YOU'RE READY FOR THE RESPONSIBILITY.
MY GUT TELLS ME YOU ARE, THOUGH, SOLDIER.
SO LET'S GO SEE WHAT THIS NEW UNIFORM THE ARMY PUT TOGETHER FOR YOU LOOKS LIKE...

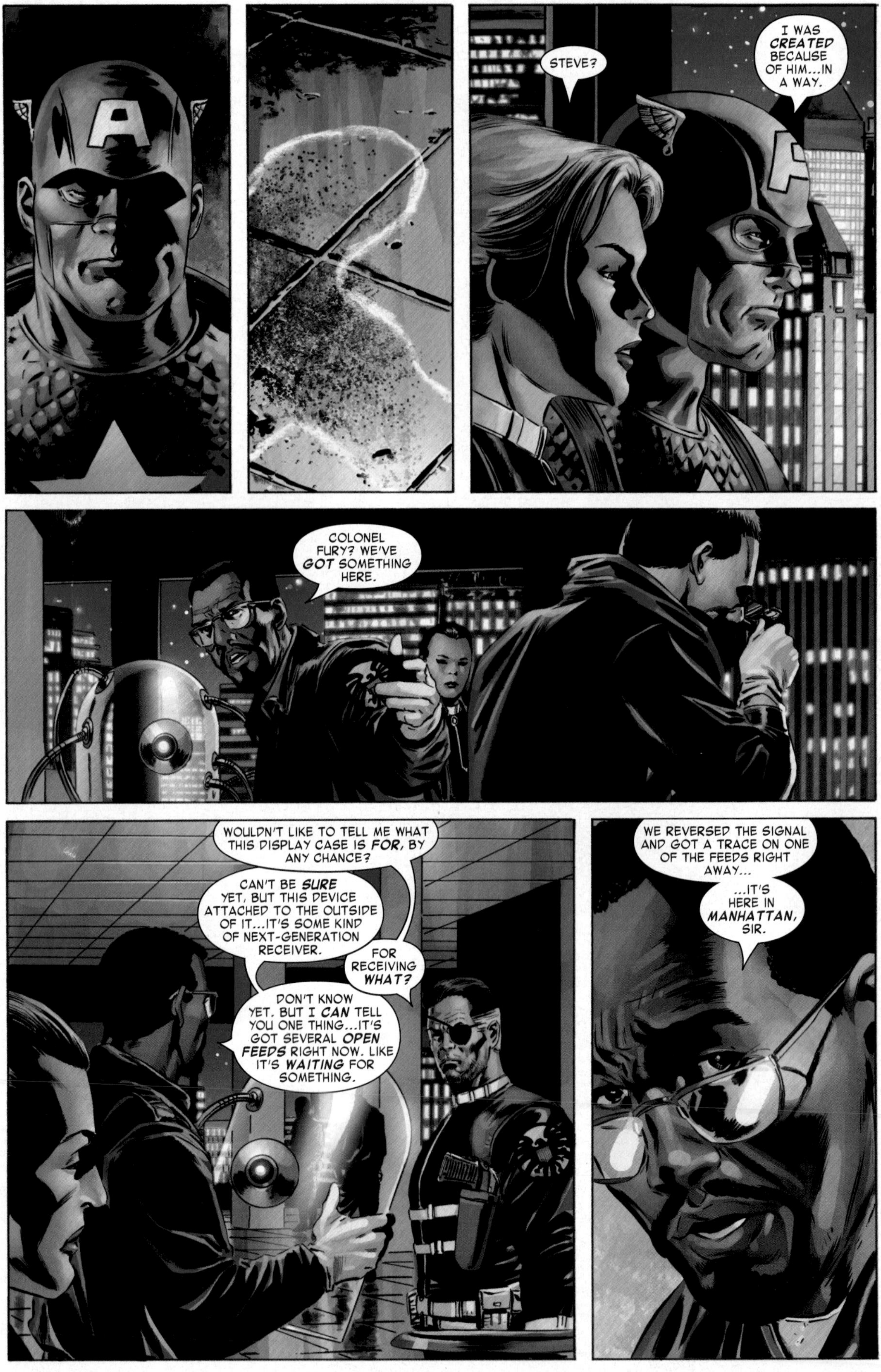
STEVE?
I WAS CREATED BECAUSE OF HIM...IN A WAY.
COLONEL FURY? WE'VE GOT SOMETHING HERE.
WOULDN'T LIKE TO TELL ME WHAT THIS DISPLAY CASE IS FOR, BY ANY CHANCE?
CAN'T BE SURE YET, BUT THIS DEVICE ATTACHED TO THE OUTSIDE OF IT...IT'S SOME KIND OF NEXT-GENERATION RECEIVER.
FOR RECEIVING WHAT?
DON'T KNOW YET. BUT I CAN TELL YOU ONE THING...IT'S GOT SEVERAL OPEN FEEDS RIGHT NOW. LIKE IT'S WAITING FOR SOMETHING.
WE REVERSED THE SIGNAL AND GOT A TRACE ON ONE OF THE FEEDS RIGHT AWAY...
...IT'S HERE IN MANHATTAN, SIR.

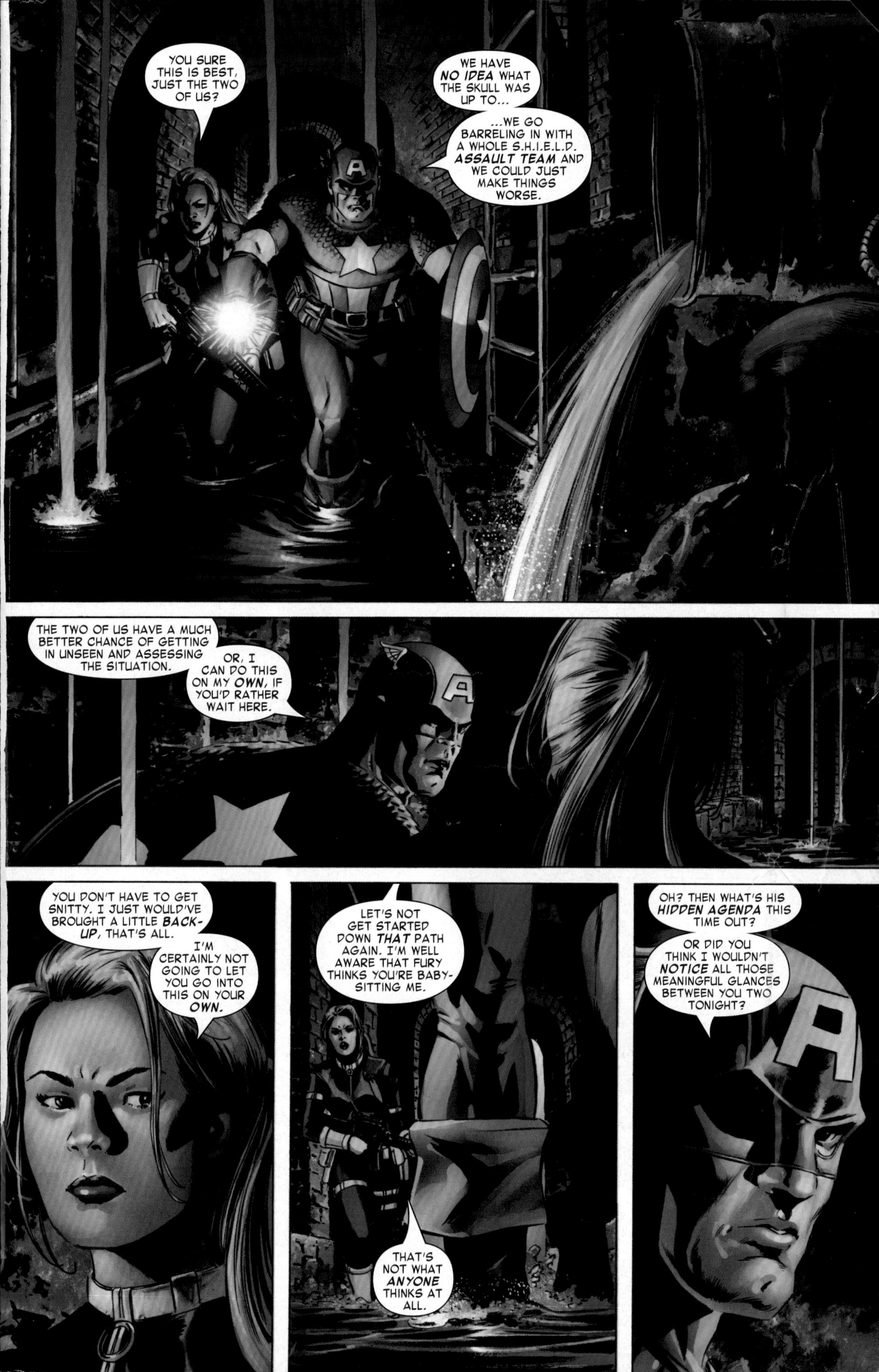
YOU SURE THIS IS BEST, JUST THE TWO OF US?
WE HAVE NO IDEA WHAT THE SKULL WAS UP TO...
...WE GO BARRELING IN WITH A WHOLE S.H.I.E.L.D. ASSAULT TEAM AND WE COULD JUST MAKE THINGS WORSE.
THE TWO OF US HAVE A MUCH BETTER CHANCE OF GETTING IN UNSEEN AND ASSESSING THE SITUATION.
OR, I CAN DO THIS ON MY OWN, IF YOU'D RATHER WAIT HERE.
YOU DON'T HAVE TO GET SNITTY. I JUST WOULD'VE BROUGHT A LITTLE BACK-UP, THAT'S ALL.
I'M CERTAINLY NOT GOING TO LET YOU GO INTO THIS ON YOUR OWN.
LET'S NOT GET STARTED DOWN THAT PATH AGAIN. I'M WELL AWARE THAT FURY THINKS YOU'RE BABY-SITTING ME.
THAT'S NOT WHAT ANYONE THINKS AT ALL.
OH? THEN WHAT'S HIS HIDDEN AGENDA THIS TIME OUT?
OR DID YOU THINK I WOULDN'T NOTICE ALL THOSE MEANINGFUL GLANCES BETWEEN YOU TWO TONIGHT?

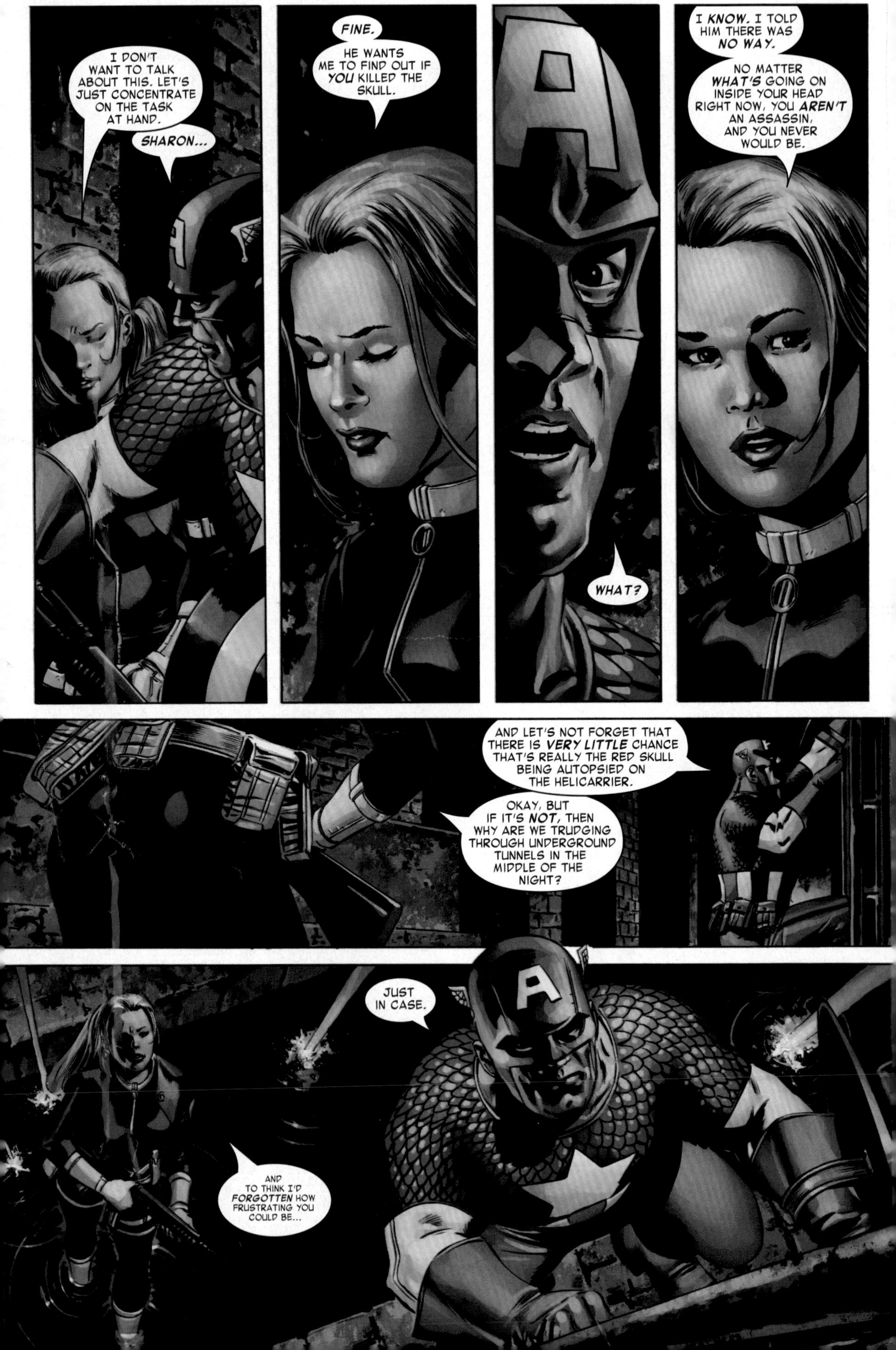
I DON'T WANT TO TALK ABOUT THIS. LET'S JUST CONCENTRATE ON THE TASK AT HAND.
SHARON...
FINE.
HE WANTS ME TO FIND OUT IF YOU KILLED THE SKULL.
WHAT?
I KNOW. I TOLD HIM THERE WAS NO WAY.
NO MATTER WHAT'S GOING ON INSIDE YOUR HEAD RIGHT NOW, YOU AREN'T AN ASSASSIN, AND YOU NEVER WOULD BE.
AND LET'S NOT FORGET THAT THERE IS VERY LITTLE CHANCE THAT'S REALLY THE RED SKULL BEING AUTOPSIED ON THE HELICARRIER.
OKAY, BUT IF IT'S NOT, THEN WHY ARE WE TRUDGING THROUGH UNDERGROUND TUNNELS IN THE MIDDLE OF THE NIGHT?
JUST IN CASE.
AND TO THINK I'D FORGOTTEN HOW FRUSTRATING YOU COULD BE...

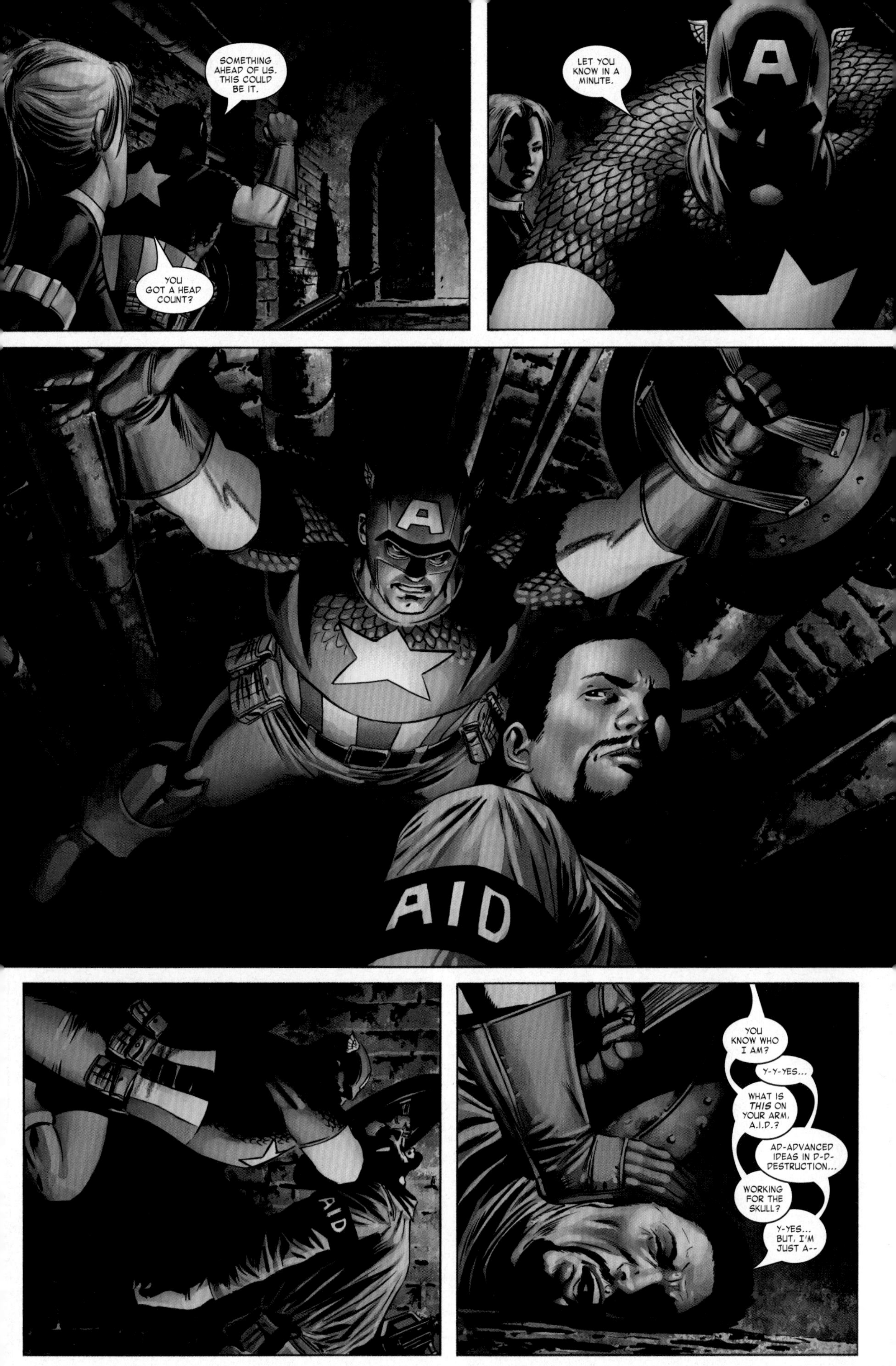

SOMETHING AHEAD OF US. THIS COULD BE IT.
YOU GOT A HEAD COUNT?
LET YOU KNOW IN A MINUTE.
AID
AID
YOU KNOW WHO I AM?
Y-Y-YES...
WHAT IS *THIS* ON YOUR ARM, A.I.D.?
AD-ADVANCED IDEAS IN D-D-DESTRUCTION...
WORKING FOR THE SKULL?
Y-YES... BUT, I'M JUST A--

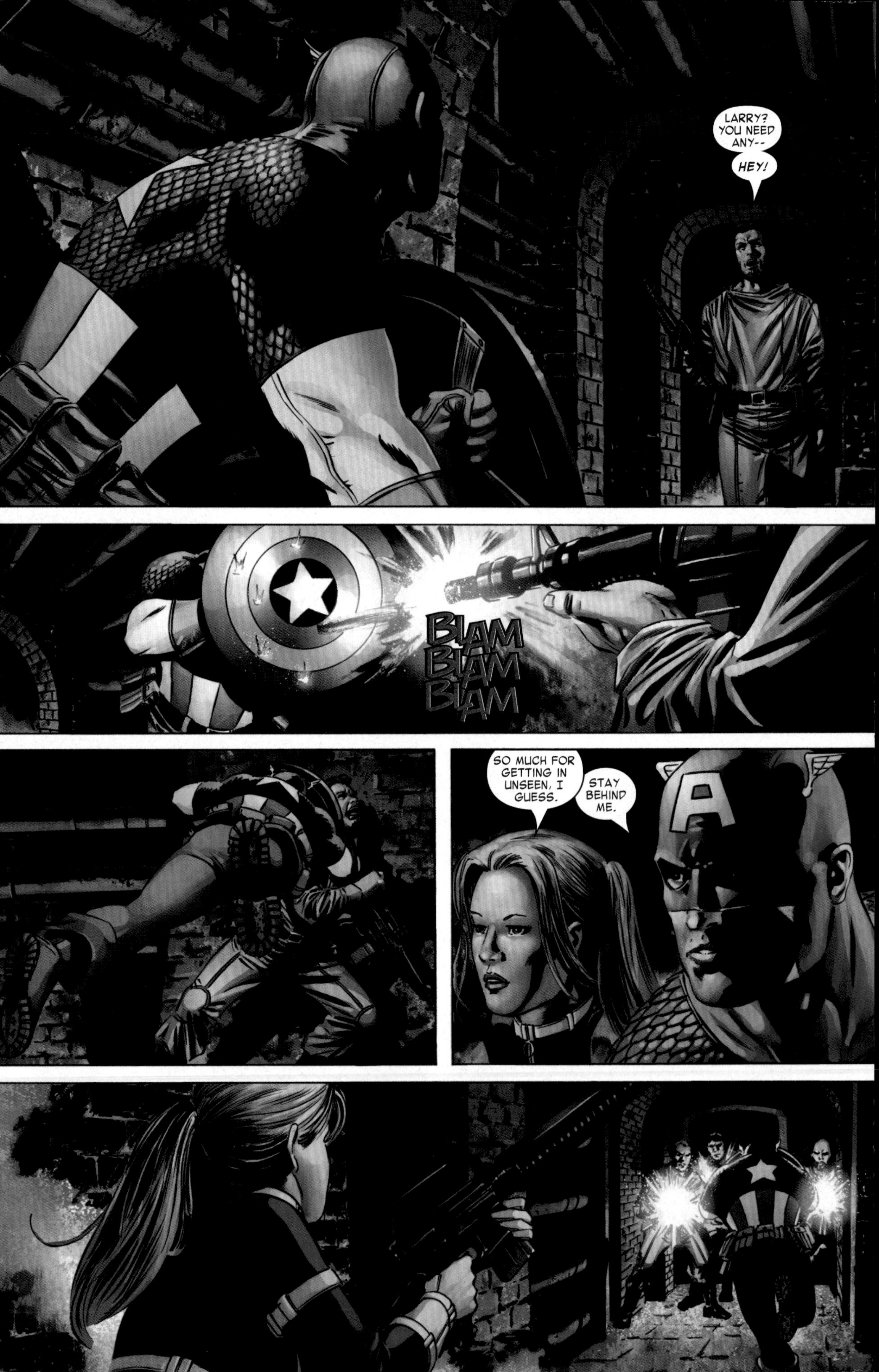
LARRY? YOU NEED ANY--
HEY!
BLAM BLAM BLAM
SO MUCH FOR GETTING IN UNSEEN, I GUESS.
STAY BEHIND ME.

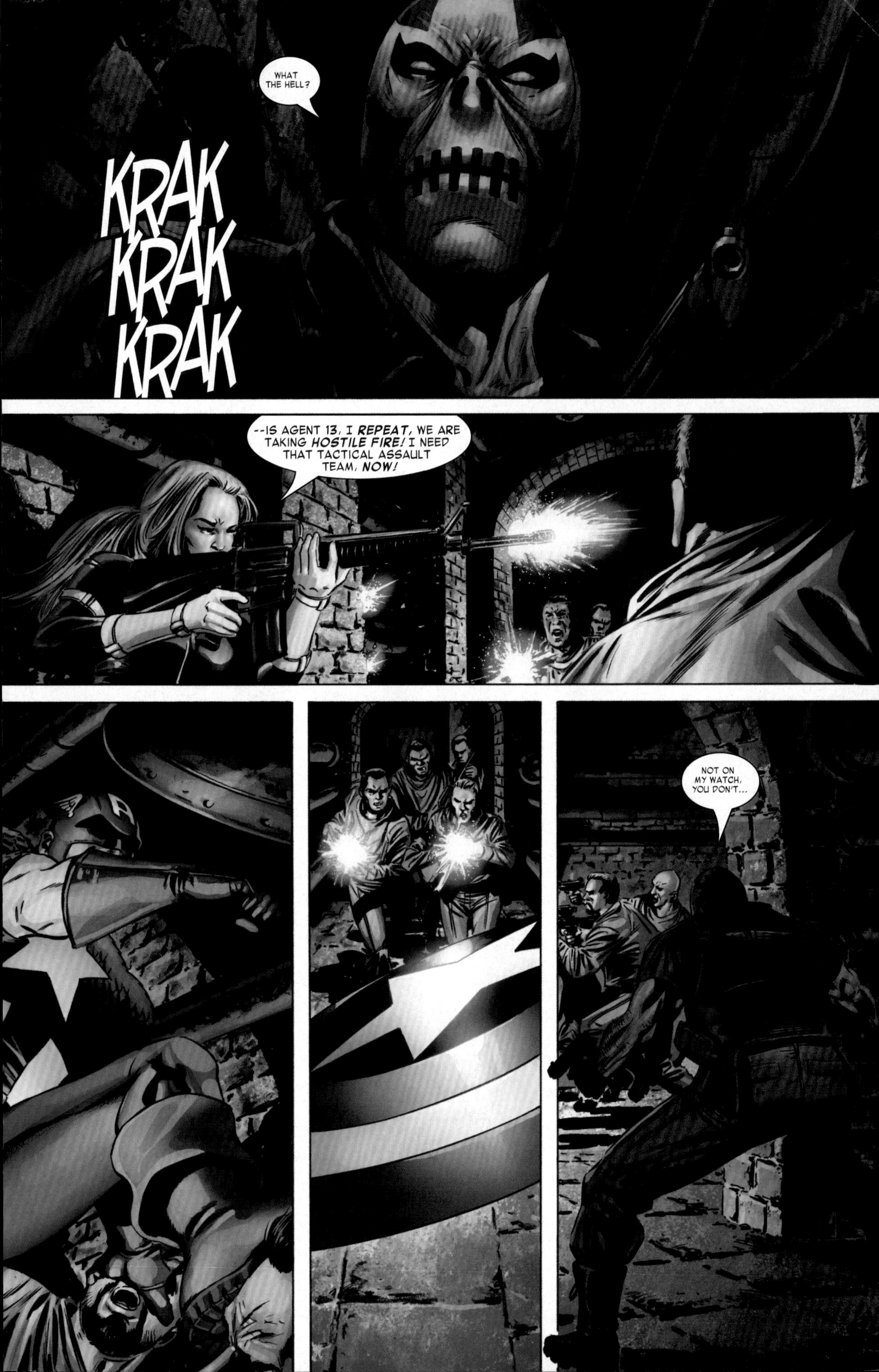
WHAT THE HELL?
KRAK KRAK KRAK
--IS AGENT 13, I REPEAT, WE ARE TAKING HOSTILE FIRE! I NEED THAT TACTICAL ASSAULT TEAM, NOW!
NOT ON MY WATCH, YOU DON'T...

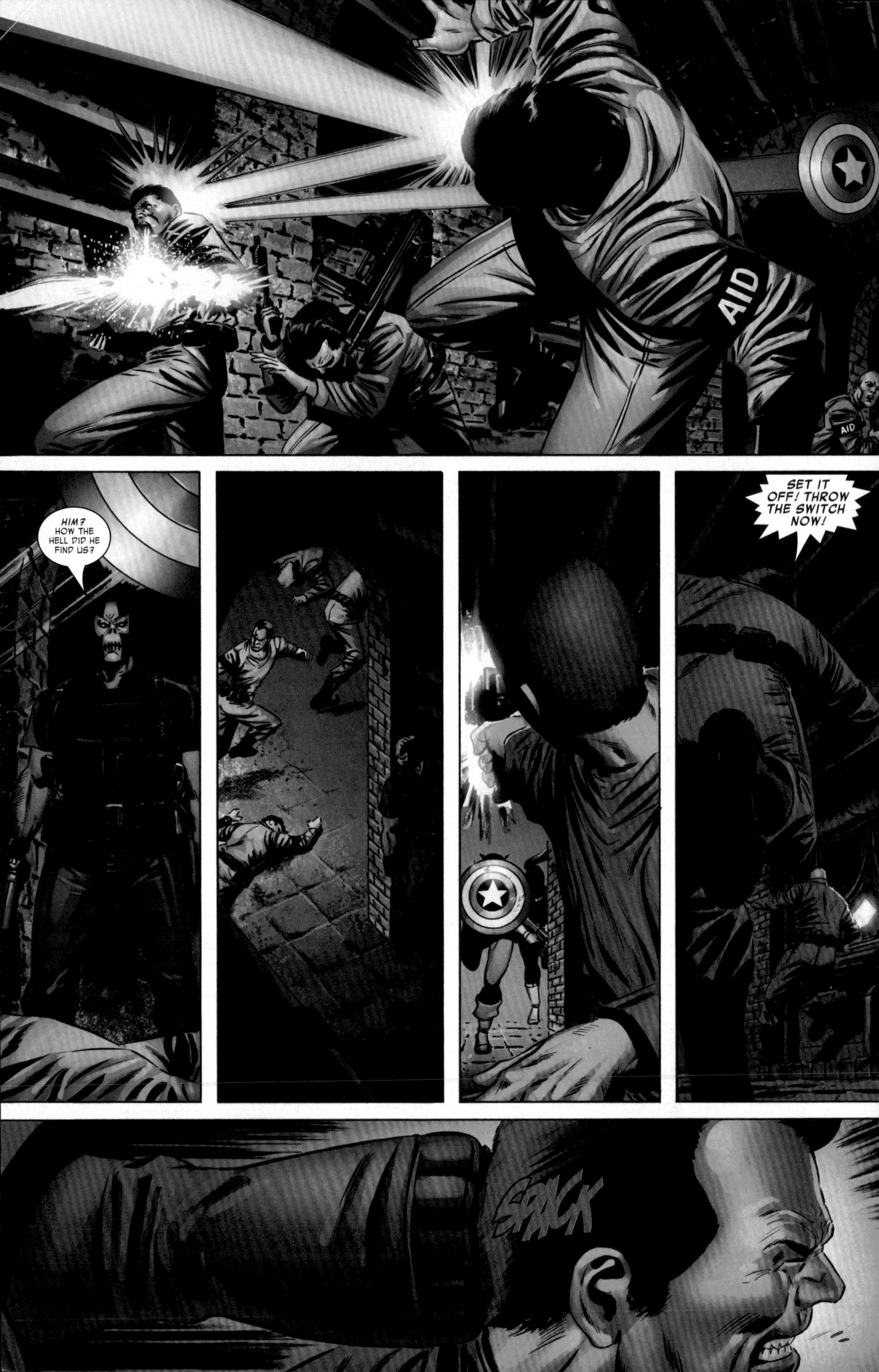
AID
AID
HIM? HOW THE HELL DID HE FIND US?
SET IT OFF! THROW THE SWITCH NOW!
SPACK

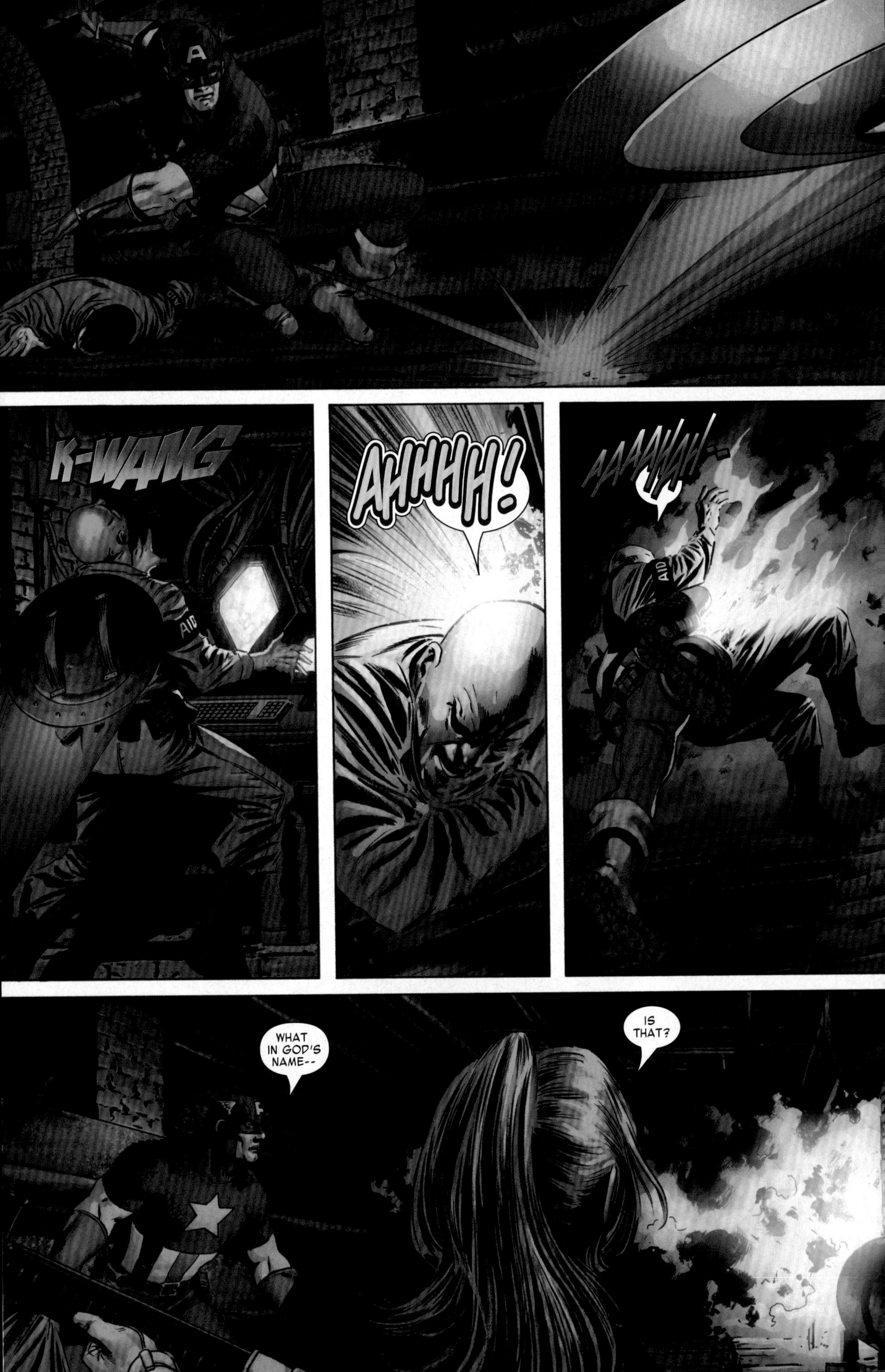
K-WAMG
AHHHH!
AAAAAHAH--
WHAT IN GOD'S NAME--
IS THAT?

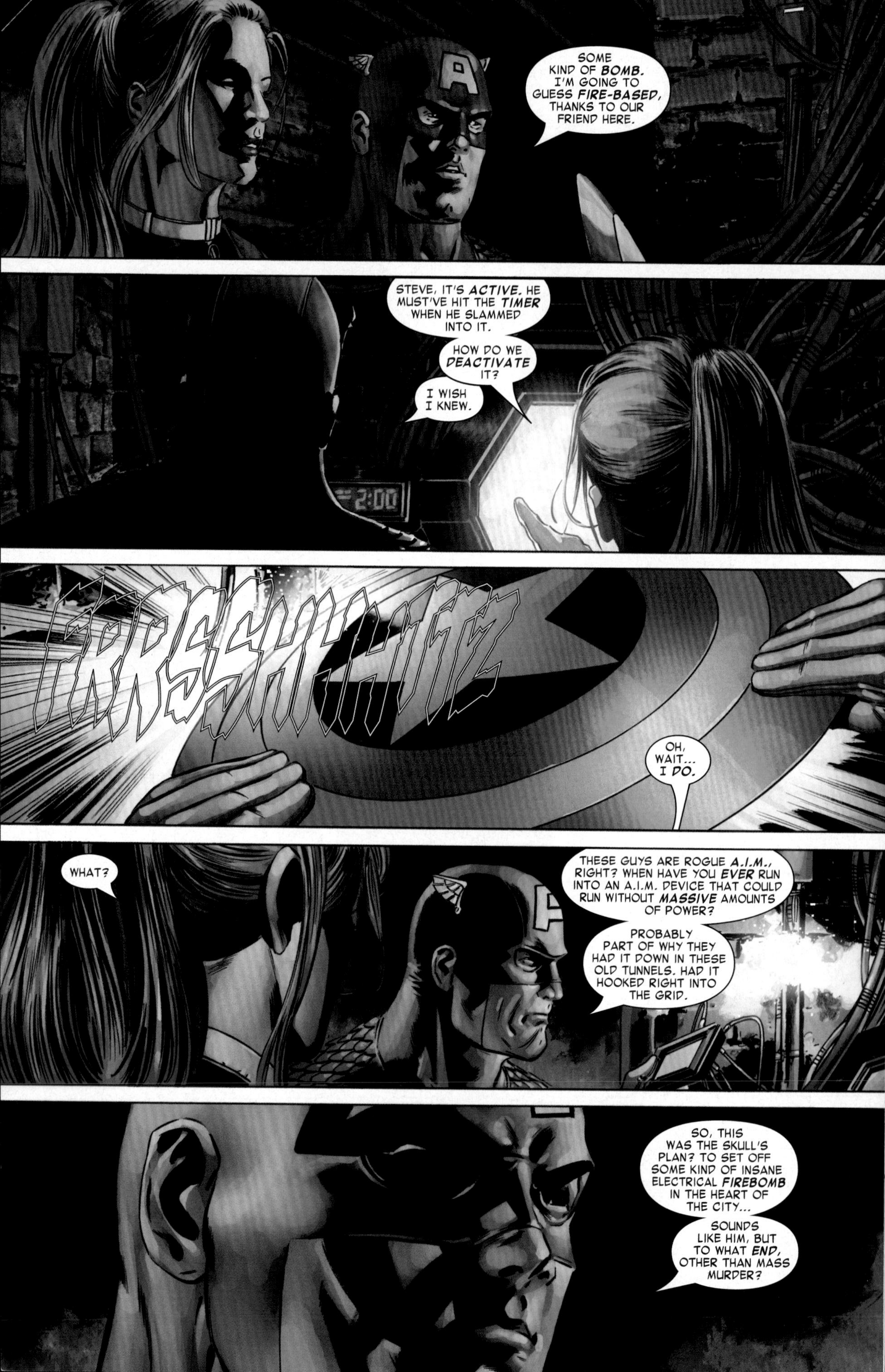
SOME KIND OF BOMB. I'M GOING TO GUESS FIRE-BASED, THANKS TO OUR FRIEND HERE.
STEVE, IT'S ACTIVE. HE MUST'VE HIT THE TIMER WHEN HE SLAMMED INTO IT.
HOW DO WE DEACTIVATE IT?
I WISH I KNEW.
2:00
FRRSSHHHHZZ
OH, WAIT... I DO.
WHAT?
THESE GUYS ARE ROGUE A.I.M., RIGHT? WHEN HAVE YOU EVER RUN INTO AN A.I.M. DEVICE THAT COULD RUN WITHOUT MASSIVE AMOUNTS OF POWER?
PROBABLY PART OF WHY THEY HAD IT DOWN IN THESE OLD TUNNELS. HAD IT HOOKED RIGHT INTO THE GRID.
SO, THIS WAS THE SKULL'S PLAN? TO SET OFF SOME KIND OF INSANE ELECTRICAL FIREBOMB IN THE HEART OF THE CITY...
SOUNDS LIKE HIM, BUT TO WHAT END, OTHER THAN MASS MURDER?

THAT'S NOT *ENOUGH?*

NOT FOR THE SKULL. NOT USUALLY.

AGENT 13 TO COLONEL FURY. WE NEED A SCIENCE TEAM DOWN HERE *NOW.* FOUND A MEAN-LOOKING W.M.D. OF *SOME* KIND.

IT'S NEUTRALIZED FOR NOW, BUT--

WE'VE GOT BIGGER PROBLEMS THAN *THAT,* AGENT.

GOT A WEIRD ENERGY SIGNATURE OFF THAT GLASS CASE, SO WE RAN A *THERMAL SCAN...*AND NOW WE *KNOW* WHAT WAS INSIDE OF IT.

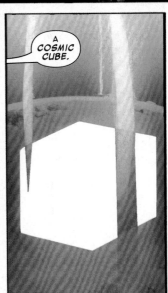

A *COSMIC CUBE.*

WHICH MEANS WHOEVER *KILLED* THE RED SKULL TONIGHT HAS *GOT* IT...

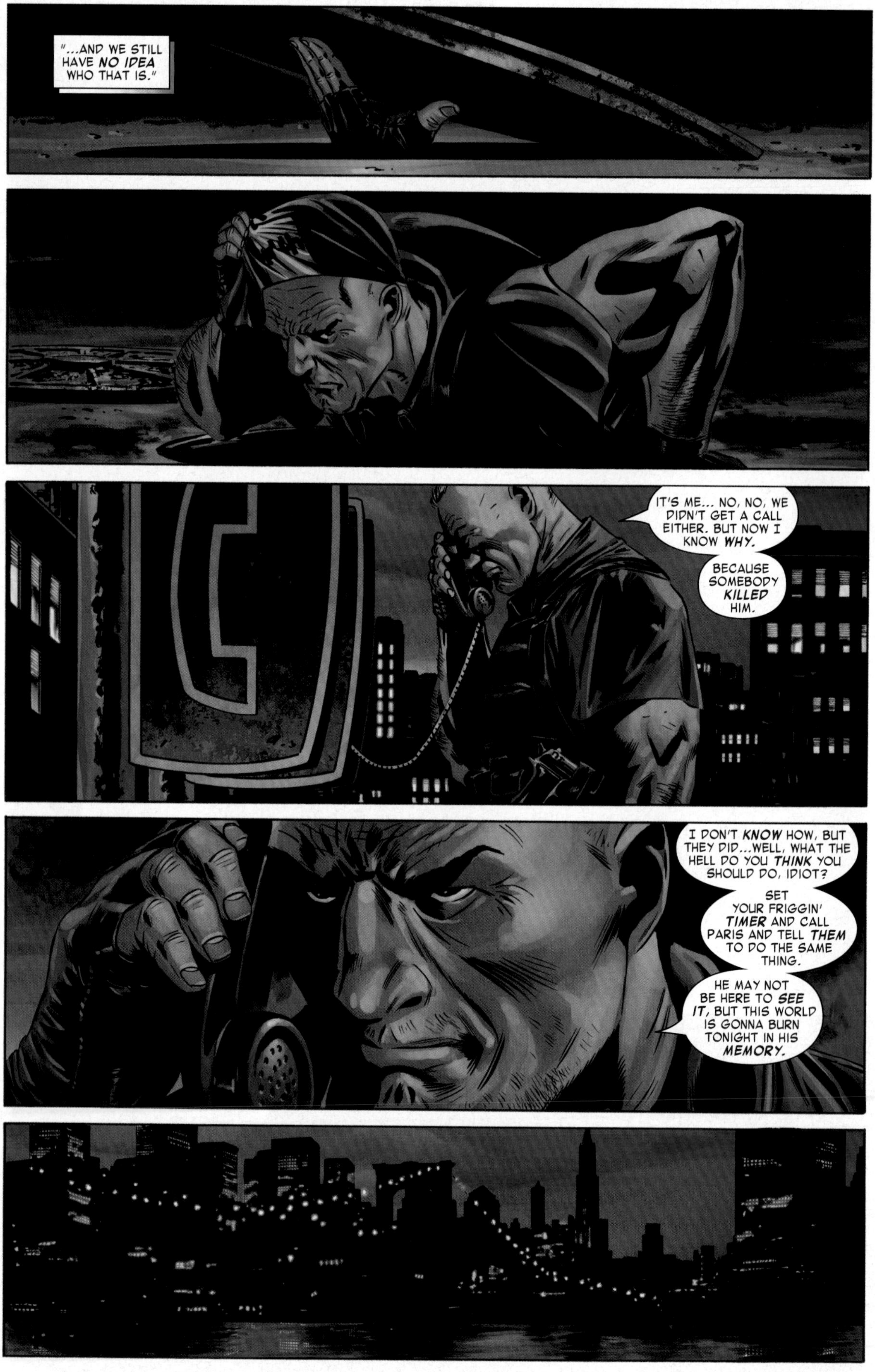
"...AND WE STILL HAVE NO IDEA WHO THAT IS."
IT'S ME... NO, NO, WE DIDN'T GET A CALL EITHER. BUT NOW I KNOW WHY.
BECAUSE SOMEBODY KILLED HIM.
I DON'T KNOW HOW, BUT THEY DID...WELL, WHAT THE HELL DO YOU THINK YOU SHOULD DO, IDIOT?
SET YOUR FRIGGIN' TIMER AND CALL PARIS AND TELL THEM TO DO THE SAME THING.
HE MAY NOT BE HERE TO SEE IT, BUT THIS WORLD IS GONNA BURN TONIGHT IN HIS MEMORY.

3

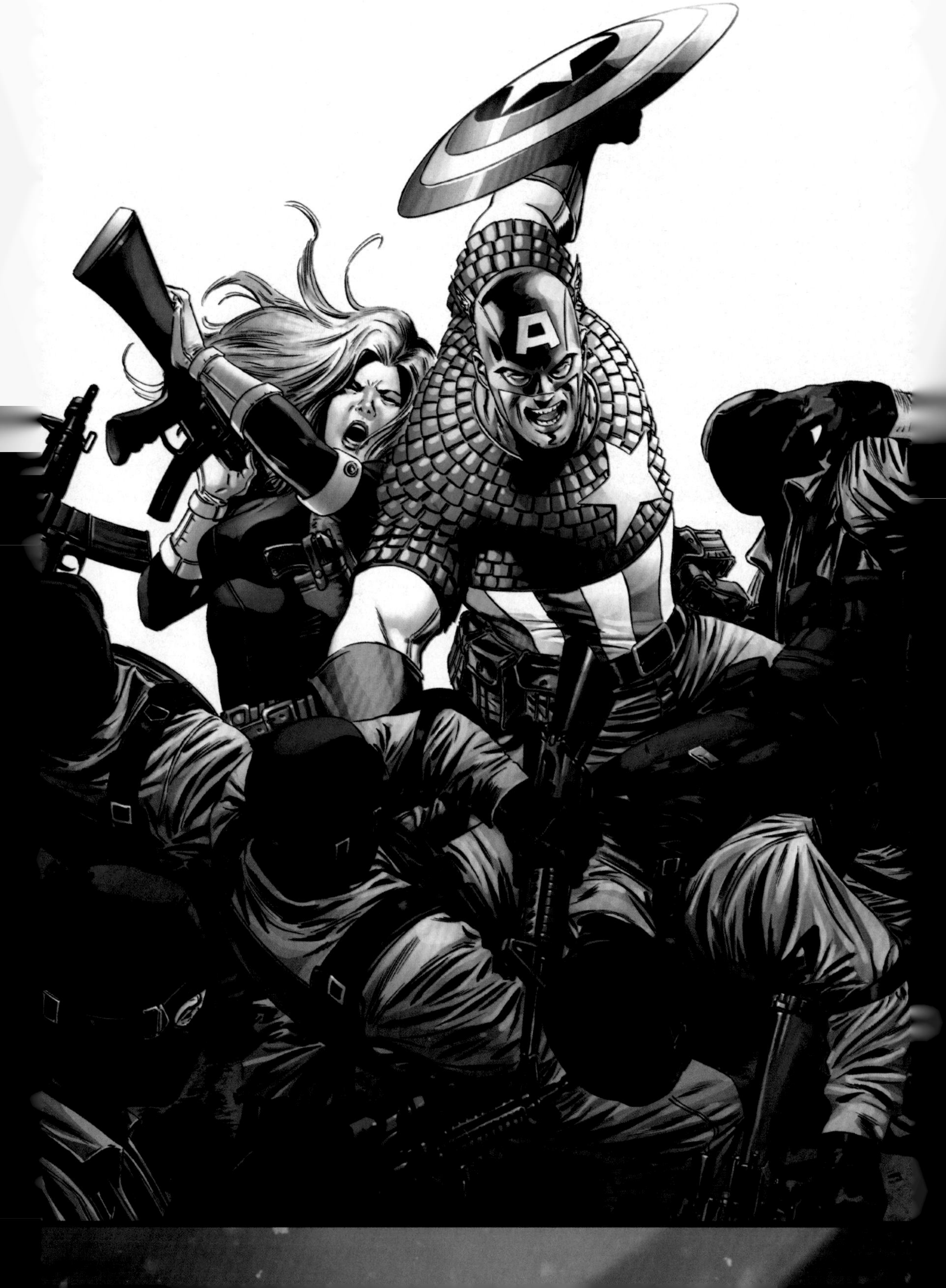

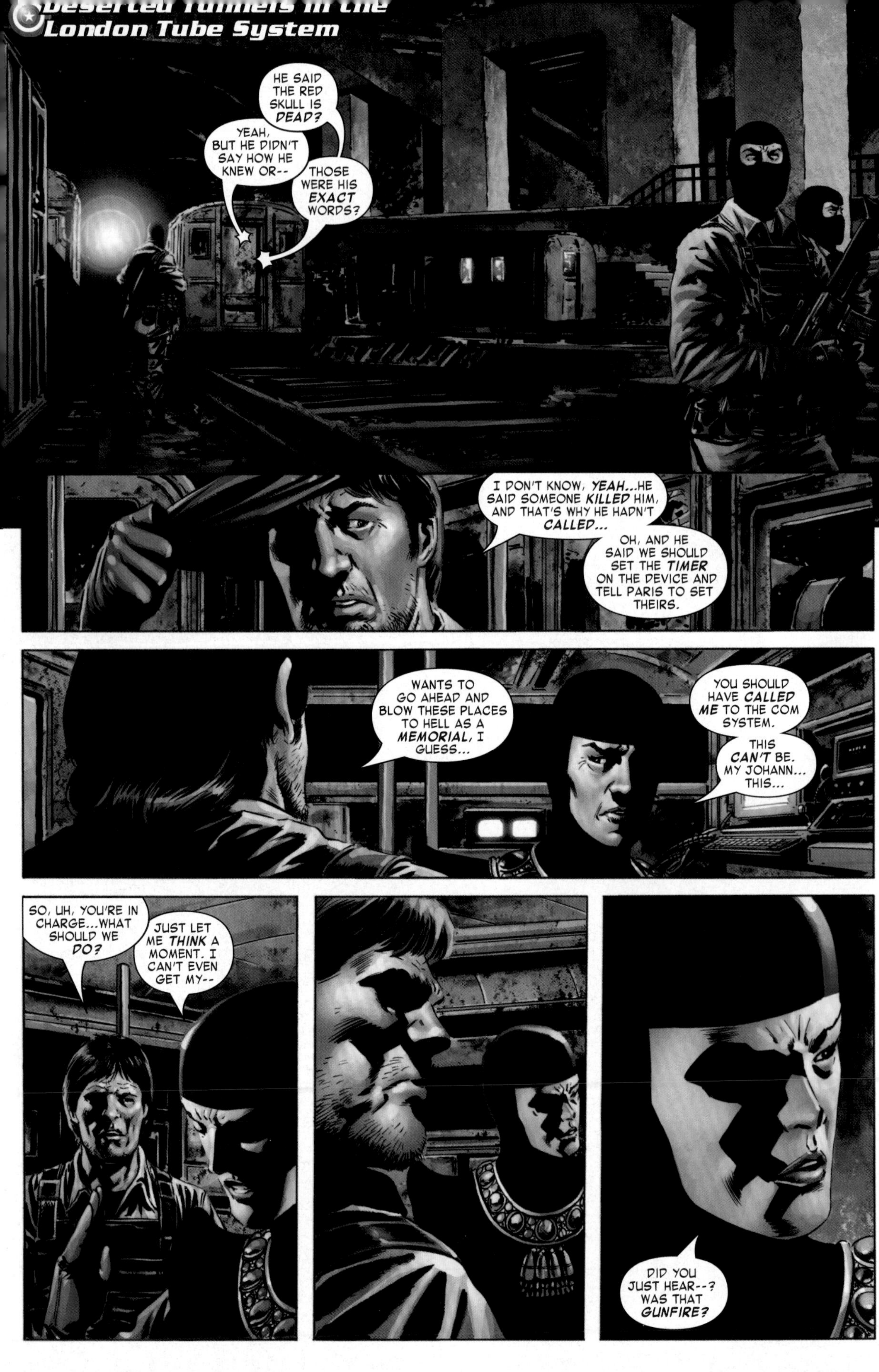
London Tube System
HE SAID THE RED SKULL IS DEAD?
YEAH, BUT HE DIDN'T SAY HOW HE KNEW OR--
THOSE WERE HIS EXACT WORDS?
I DON'T KNOW, YEAH...HE SAID SOMEONE KILLED HIM, AND THAT'S WHY HE HADN'T CALLED...
OH, AND HE SAID WE SHOULD SET THE TIMER ON THE DEVICE AND TELL PARIS TO SET THEIRS.
WANTS TO GO AHEAD AND BLOW THESE PLACES TO HELL AS A MEMORIAL, I GUESS...
YOU SHOULD HAVE CALLED ME TO THE COM SYSTEM.
THIS CAN'T BE. MY JOHANN... THIS...
SO, UH, YOU'RE IN CHARGE...WHAT SHOULD WE DO?
JUST LET ME THINK A MOMENT. I CAN'T EVEN GET MY--
DID YOU JUST HEAR--? WAS THAT GUNFIRE?

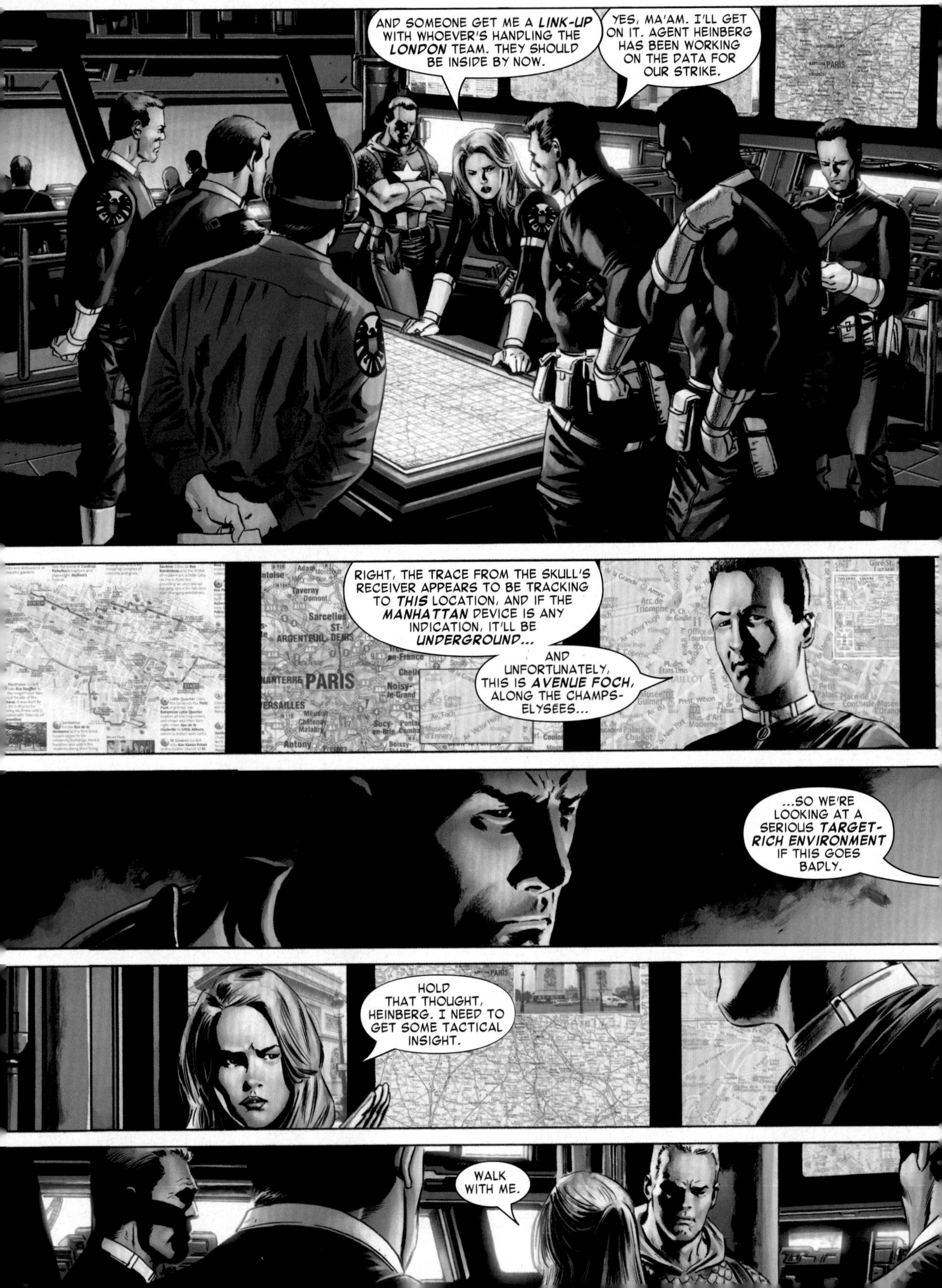
AND SOMEONE GET ME A LINK-UP WITH WHOEVER'S HANDLING THE LONDON TEAM. THEY SHOULD BE INSIDE BY NOW.
YES, MA'AM. I'LL GET ON IT. AGENT HEINBERG HAS BEEN WORKING ON THE DATA FOR OUR STRIKE.
RIGHT, THE TRACE FROM THE SKULL'S RECEIVER APPEARS TO BE TRACKING TO THIS LOCATION, AND IF THE MANHATTAN DEVICE IS ANY INDICATION, IT'LL BE UNDERGROUND...
AND UNFORTUNATELY, THIS IS AVENUE FOCH, ALONG THE CHAMPS-ELYSEES...
...SO WE'RE LOOKING AT A SERIOUS TARGET-RICH ENVIRONMENT IF THIS GOES BADLY.
HOLD THAT THOUGHT, HEINBERG. I NEED TO GET SOME TACTICAL INSIGHT.
WALK WITH ME.

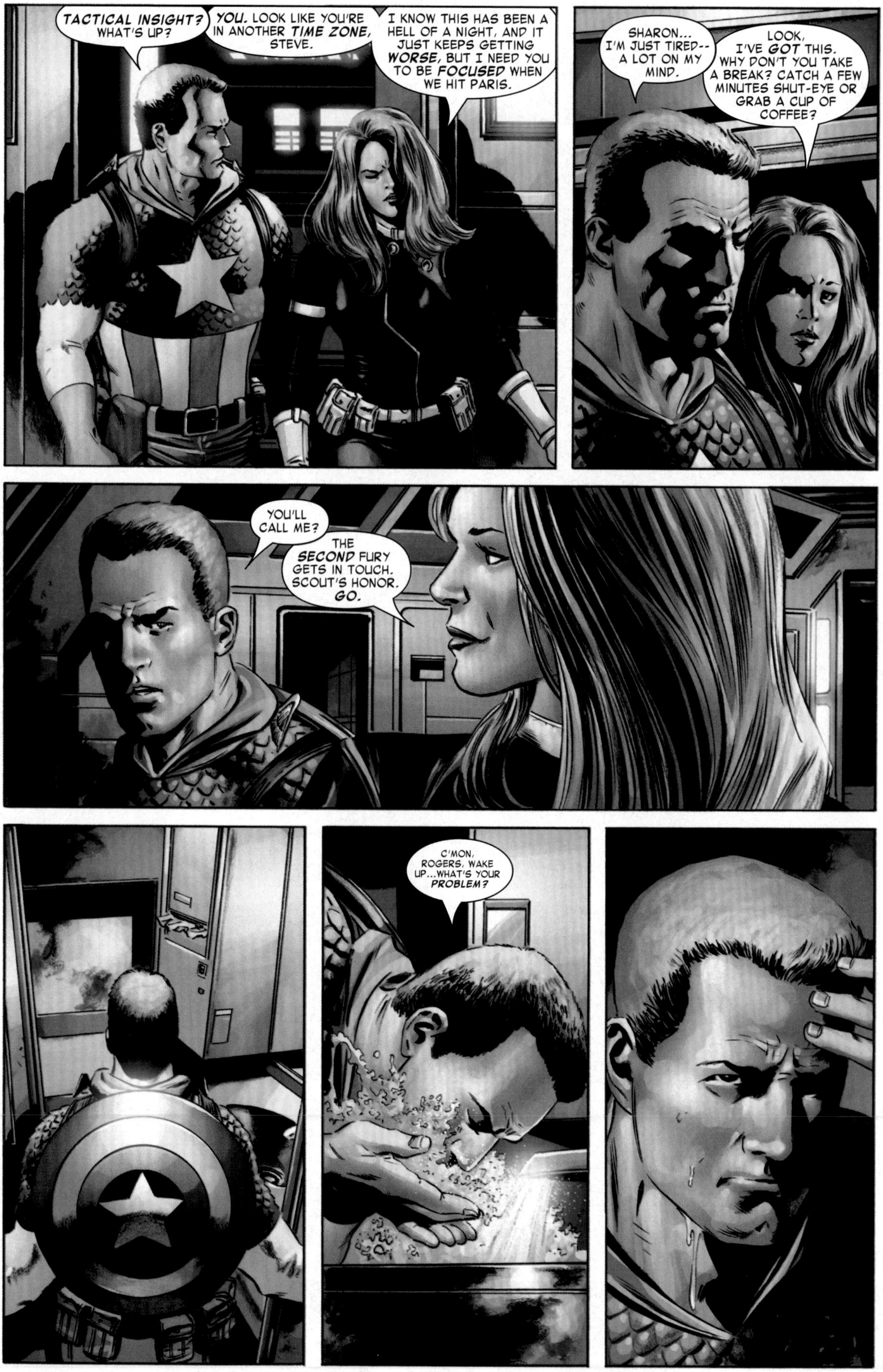
TACTICAL INSIGHT? WHAT'S UP?
YOU. LOOK LIKE YOU'RE IN ANOTHER TIME ZONE, STEVE.
I KNOW THIS HAS BEEN A HELL OF A NIGHT, AND IT JUST KEEPS GETTING WORSE, BUT I NEED YOU TO BE FOCUSED WHEN WE HIT PARIS.
SHARON... I'M JUST TIRED-- A LOT ON MY MIND.
LOOK, I'VE GOT THIS. WHY DON'T YOU TAKE A BREAK? CATCH A FEW MINUTES SHUT-EYE OR GRAB A CUP OF COFFEE?
YOU'LL CALL ME?
THE SECOND FURY GETS IN TOUCH. SCOUT'S HONOR. GO.
C'MON, ROGERS, WAKE UP...WHAT'S YOUR PROBLEM?

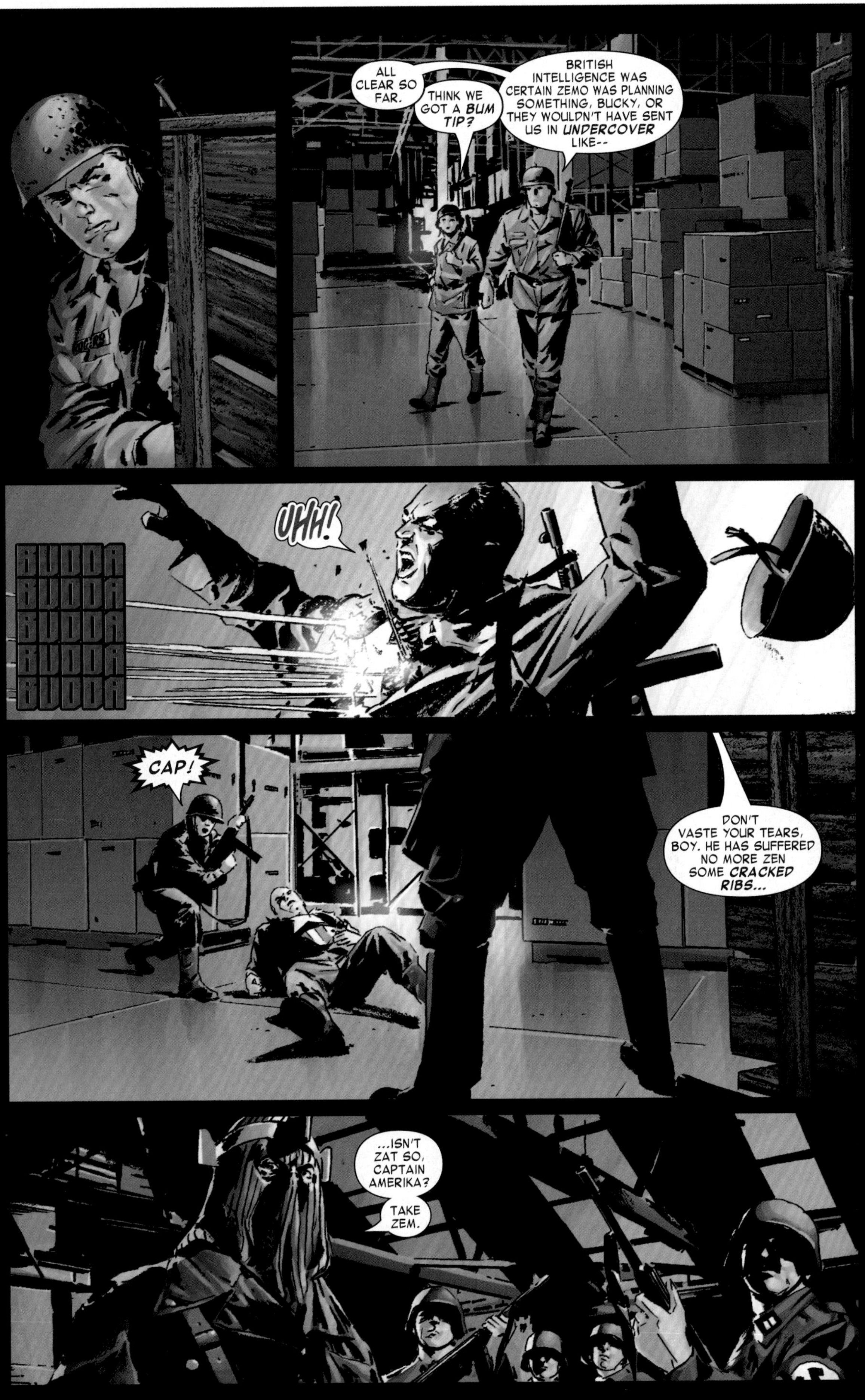
ALL CLEAR SO FAR.
THINK WE GOT A BUM TIP?
BRITISH INTELLIGENCE WAS CERTAIN ZEMO WAS PLANNING SOMETHING, BUCKY, OR THEY WOULDN'T HAVE SENT US IN UNDERCOVER LIKE--
BUDDA BUDDA BUDDA BUDDA BUDDA
UHH!
CAP!
DON'T VASTE YOUR TEARS, BOY. HE HAS SUFFERED NO MORE ZEN SOME CRACKED RIBS...
...ISN'T ZAT SO, CAPTAIN AMERIKA?
TAKE ZEM.

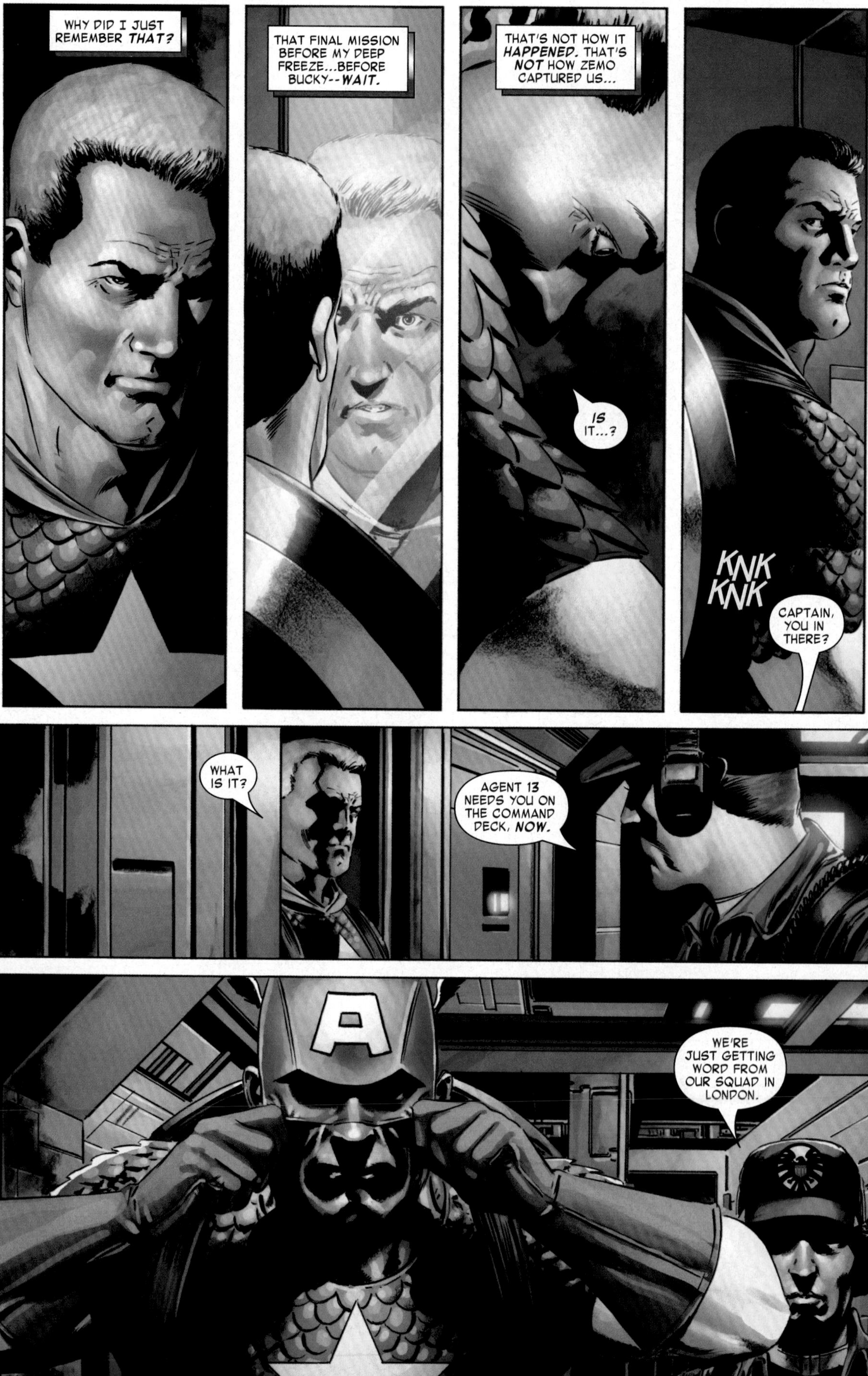
WHY DID I JUST REMEMBER *THAT?*
THAT FINAL MISSION BEFORE MY DEEP FREEZE...BEFORE BUCKY--*WAIT.*
THAT'S NOT HOW IT *HAPPENED.* THAT'S *NOT* HOW ZEMO CAPTURED US...
IS IT...?
KNK KNK
CAPTAIN, YOU IN THERE?
WHAT IS IT?
AGENT 13 NEEDS YOU ON THE COMMAND DECK, *NOW.*
WE'RE JUST GETTING WORD FROM OUR SQUAD IN LONDON.

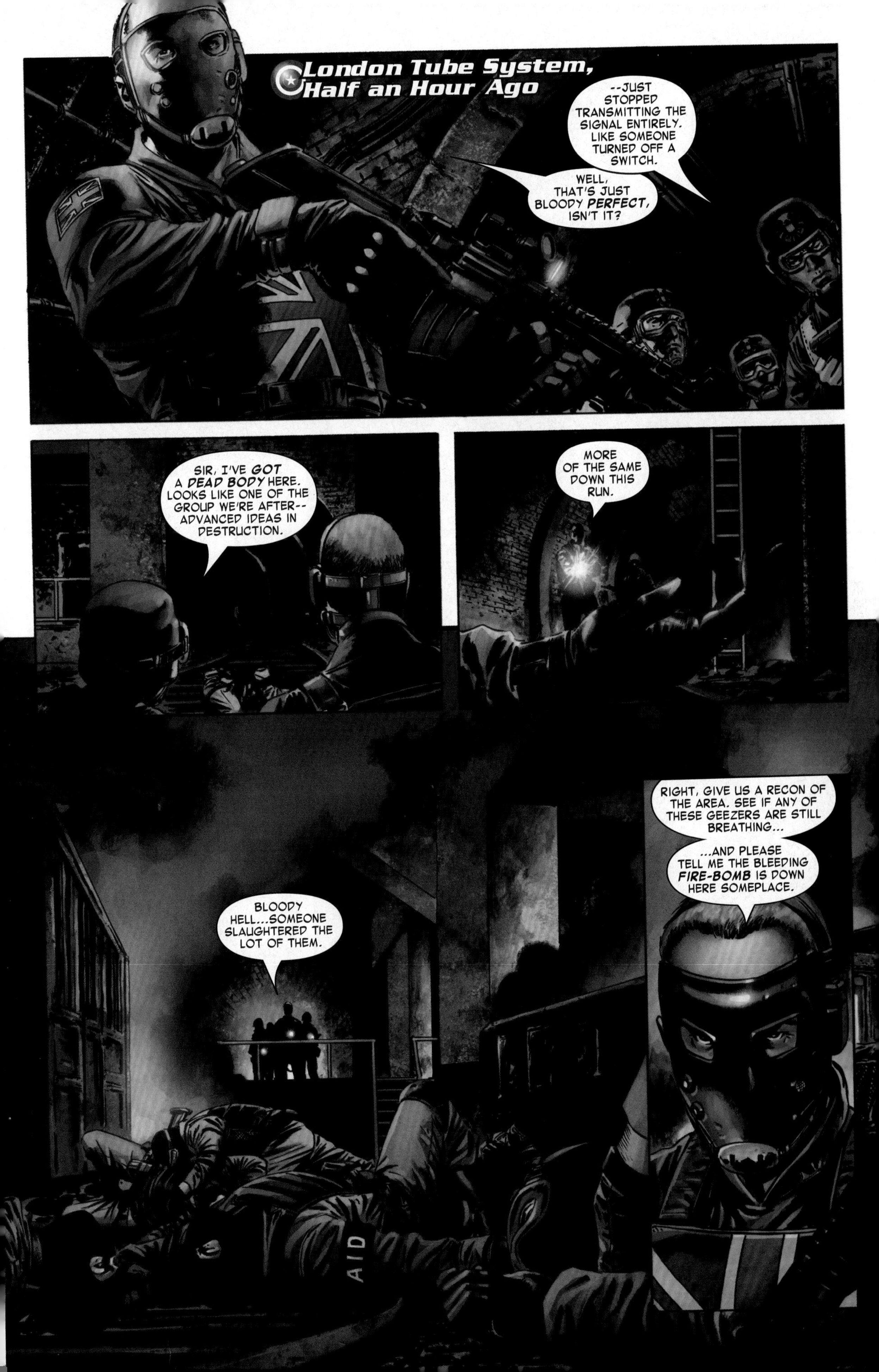
London Tube System, Half an Hour Ago
--JUST STOPPED TRANSMITTING THE SIGNAL ENTIRELY. LIKE SOMEONE TURNED OFF A SWITCH.
WELL, THAT'S JUST BLOODY PERFECT, ISN'T IT?
SIR, I'VE GOT A DEAD BODY HERE. LOOKS LIKE ONE OF THE GROUP WE'RE AFTER-- ADVANCED IDEAS IN DESTRUCTION.
MORE OF THE SAME DOWN THIS RUN.
RIGHT, GIVE US A RECON OF THE AREA. SEE IF ANY OF THESE GEEZERS ARE STILL BREATHING...
...AND PLEASE TELL ME THE BLEEDING FIRE-BOMB IS DOWN HERE SOMEPLACE.
BLOODY HELL...SOMEONE SLAUGHTERED THE LOT OF THEM.
AID

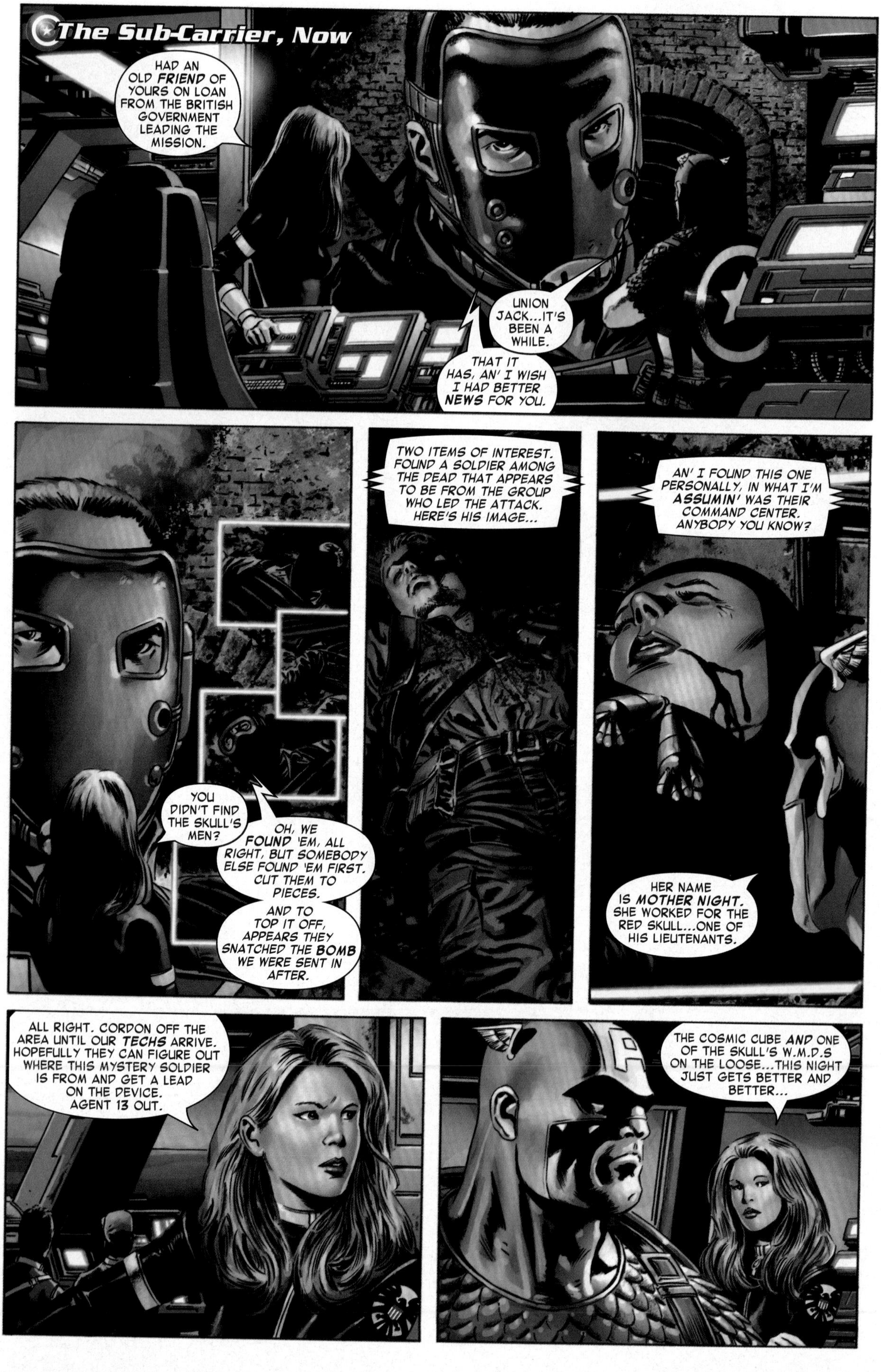

The Sub-Carrier, Now
HAD AN OLD FRIEND OF YOURS ON LOAN FROM THE BRITISH GOVERNMENT LEADING THE MISSION.
UNION JACK...IT'S BEEN A WHILE.
THAT IT HAS, AN' I WISH I HAD BETTER NEWS FOR YOU.
YOU DIDN'T FIND THE SKULL'S MEN?
OH, WE FOUND 'EM, ALL RIGHT, BUT SOMEBODY ELSE FOUND 'EM FIRST. CUT THEM TO PIECES.
AND TO TOP IT OFF, APPEARS THEY SNATCHED THE BOMB WE WERE SENT IN AFTER.
TWO ITEMS OF INTEREST. FOUND A SOLDIER AMONG THE DEAD THAT APPEARS TO BE FROM THE GROUP WHO LED THE ATTACK. HERE'S HIS IMAGE...
AN' I FOUND THIS ONE PERSONALLY, IN WHAT I'M ASSUMIN' WAS THEIR COMMAND CENTER. ANYBODY YOU KNOW?
HER NAME IS MOTHER NIGHT. SHE WORKED FOR THE RED SKULL...ONE OF HIS LIEUTENANTS.
ALL RIGHT. CORDON OFF THE AREA UNTIL OUR TECHS ARRIVE. HOPEFULLY THEY CAN FIGURE OUT WHERE THIS MYSTERY SOLDIER IS FROM AND GET A LEAD ON THE DEVICE. AGENT 13 OUT.
THE COSMIC CUBE AND ONE OF THE SKULL'S W.M.D.S ON THE LOOSE...THIS NIGHT JUST GETS BETTER AND BETTER...

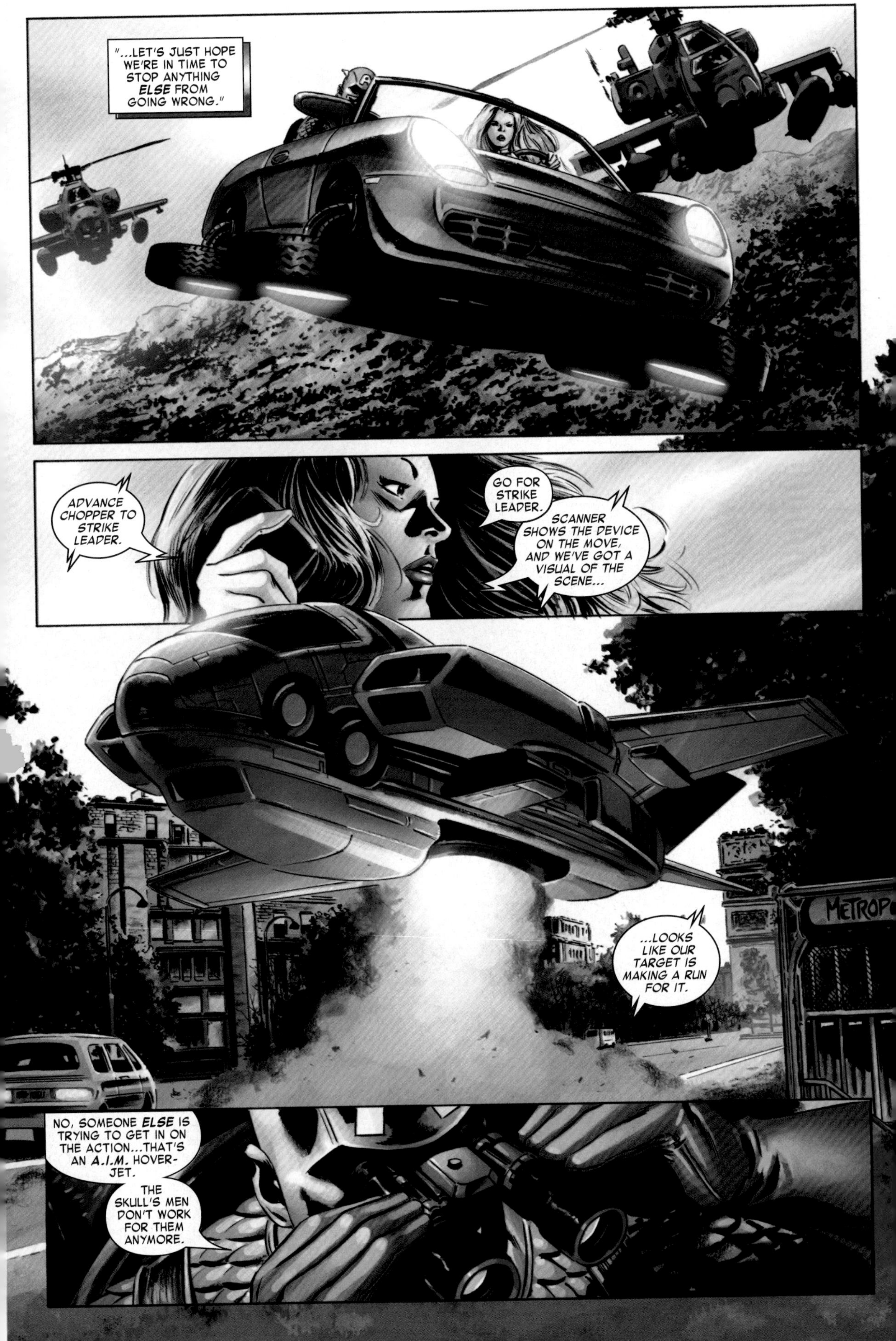
"...LET'S JUST HOPE WE'RE IN TIME TO STOP ANYTHING ELSE FROM GOING WRONG."
ADVANCE CHOPPER TO STRIKE LEADER.
GO FOR STRIKE LEADER.
SCANNER SHOWS THE DEVICE ON THE MOVE, AND WE'VE GOT A VISUAL OF THE SCENE...
METROP
...LOOKS LIKE OUR TARGET IS MAKING A RUN FOR IT.
NO, SOMEONE ELSE IS TRYING TO GET IN ON THE ACTION...THAT'S AN A.I.M. HOVER-JET.
THE SKULL'S MEN DON'T WORK FOR THEM ANYMORE.

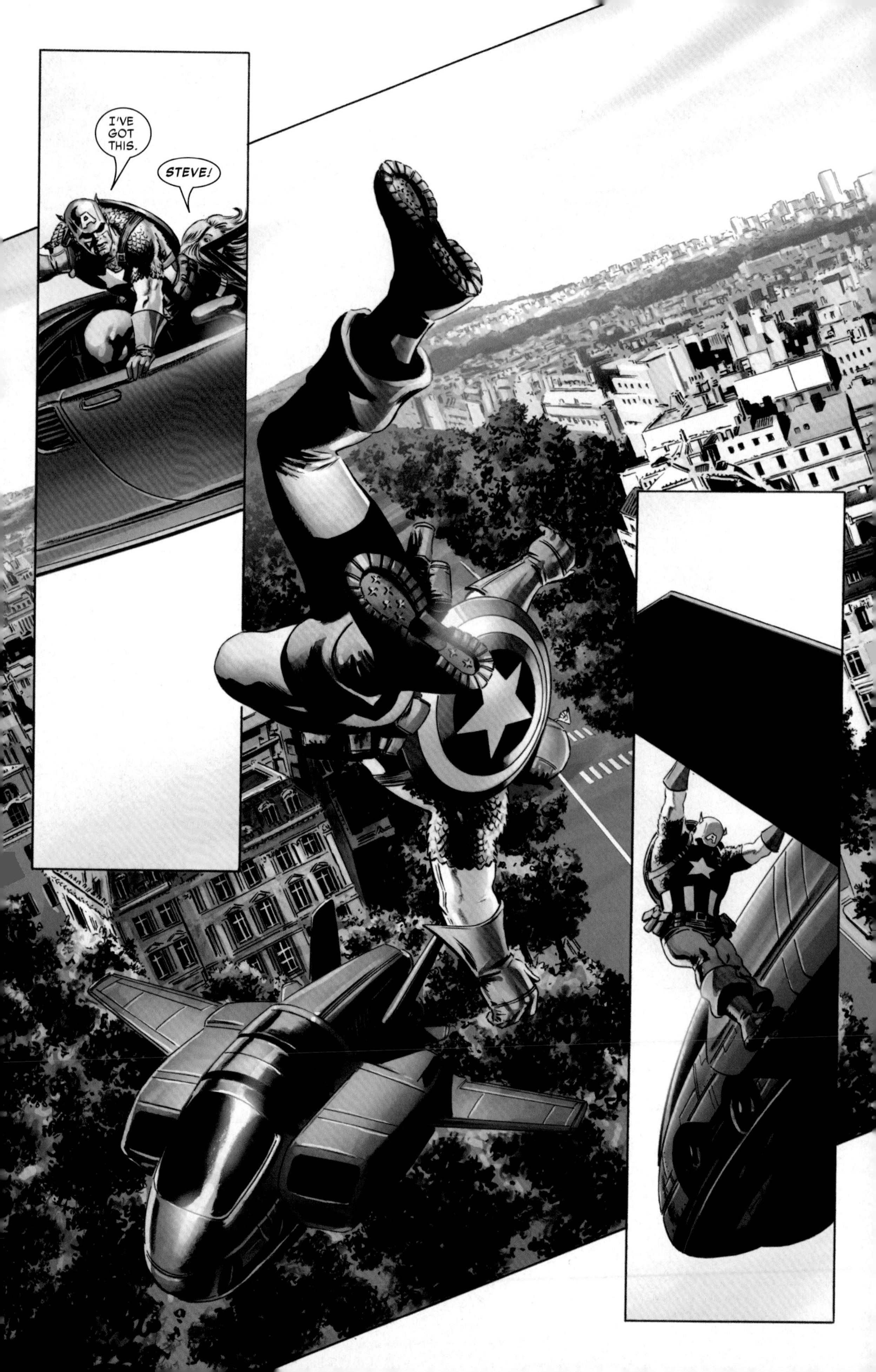
I'VE GOT THIS.
STEVE!

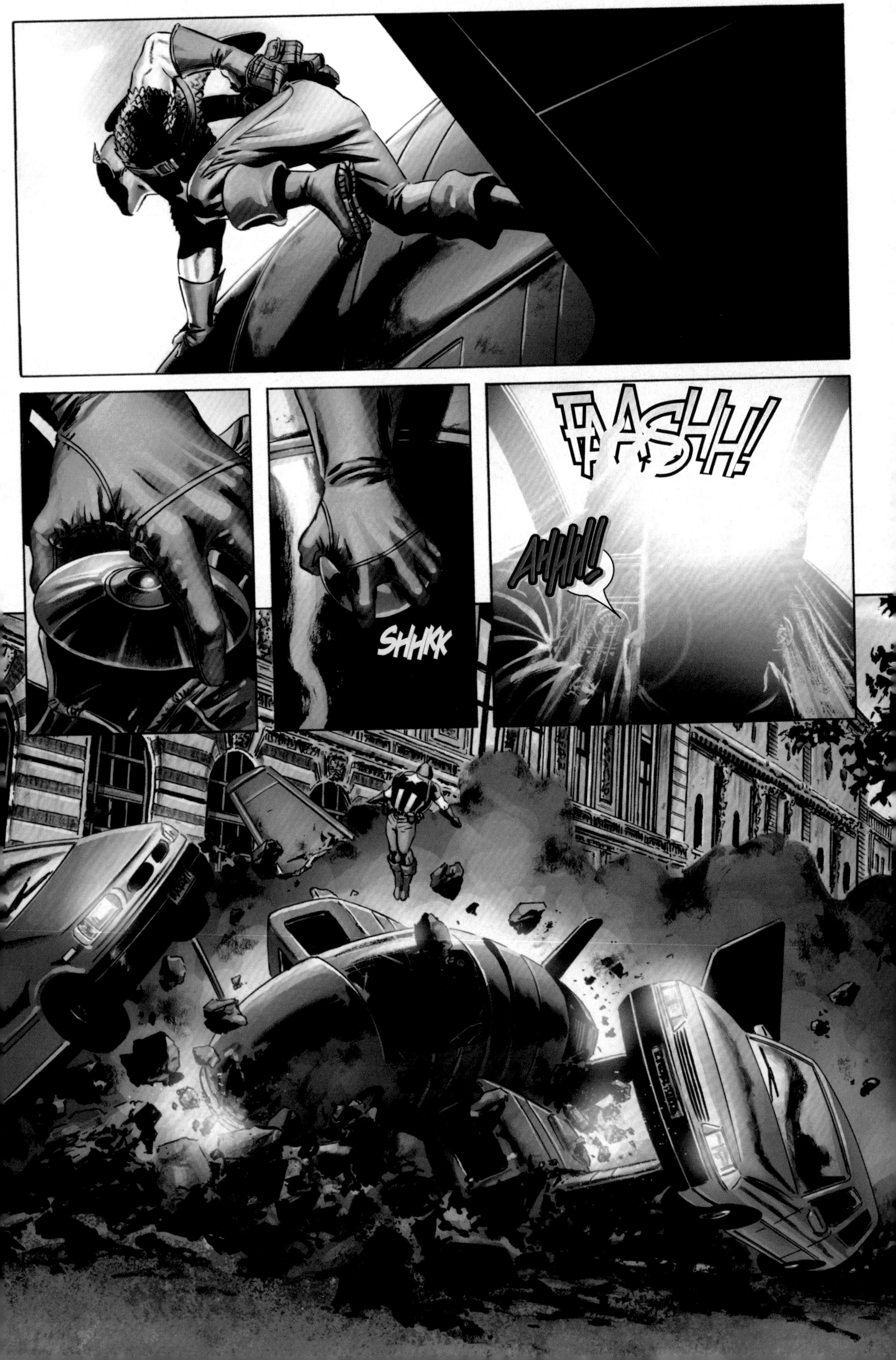

SHHKK
FAASHH!
AHHH!!

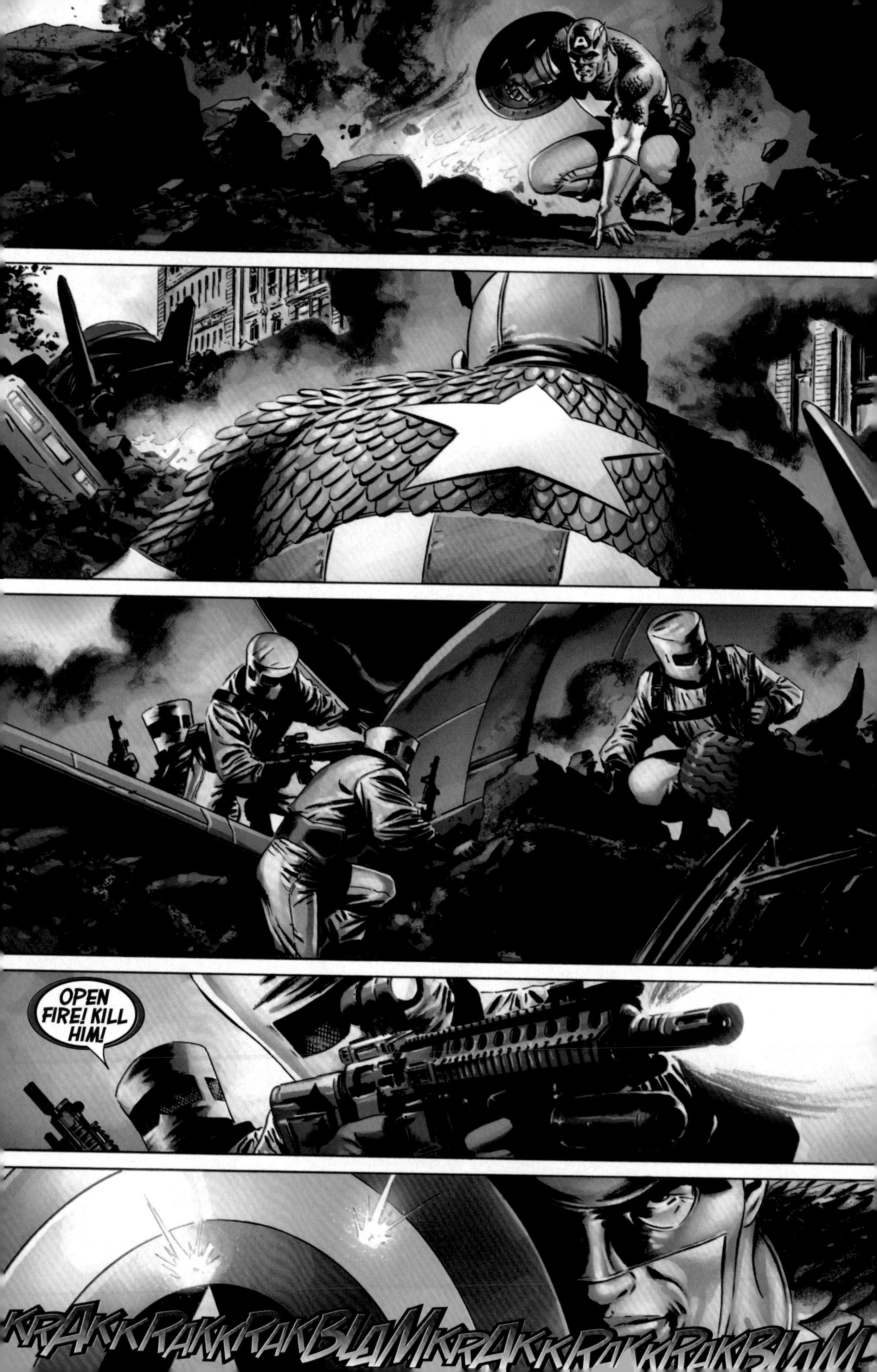
OPEN FIRE! KILL HIM!
KRAKKRAKKRAKKRAKBLAMKRAKKRAKKRAKKRAKBLAM

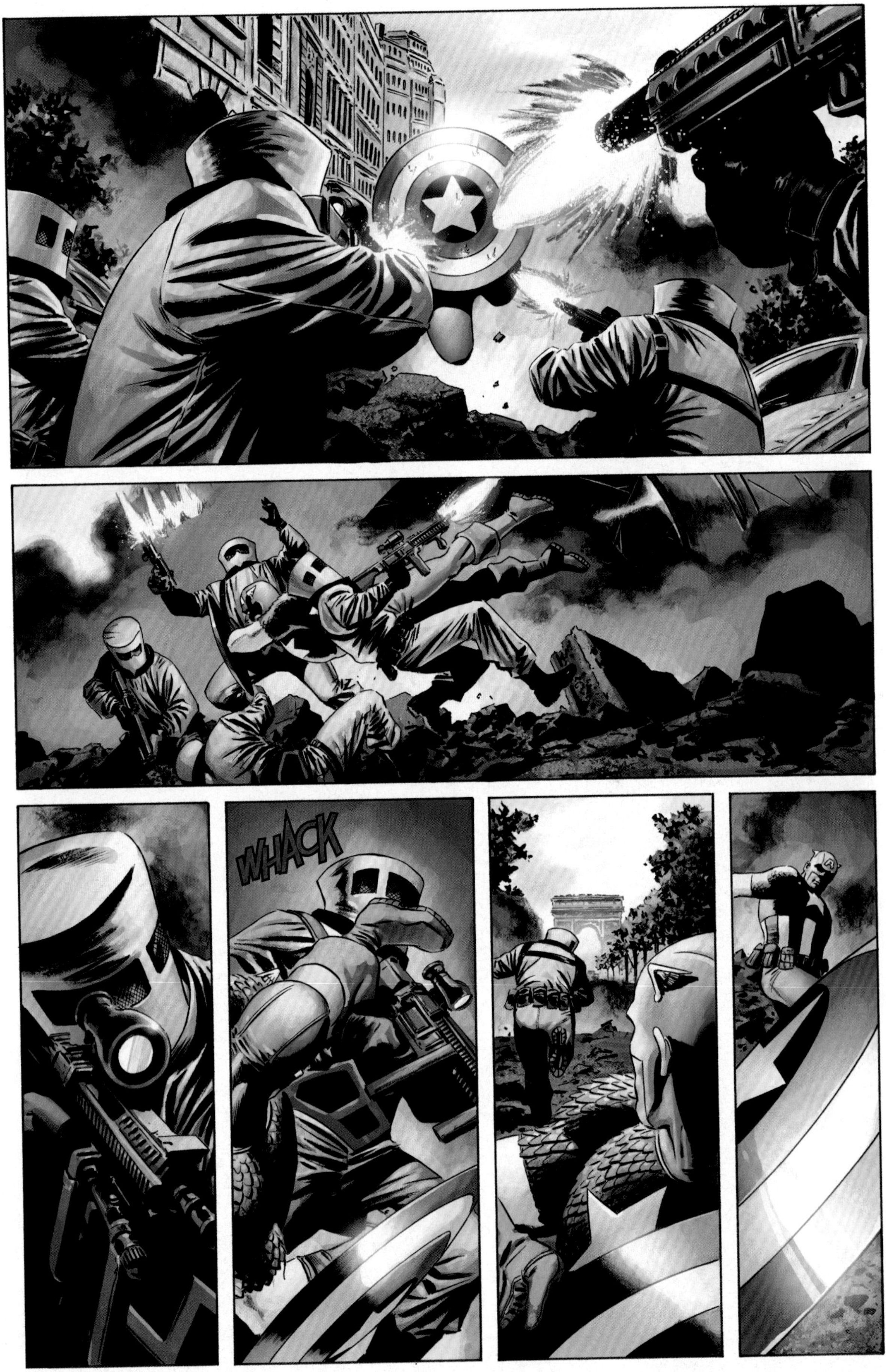
WHACK

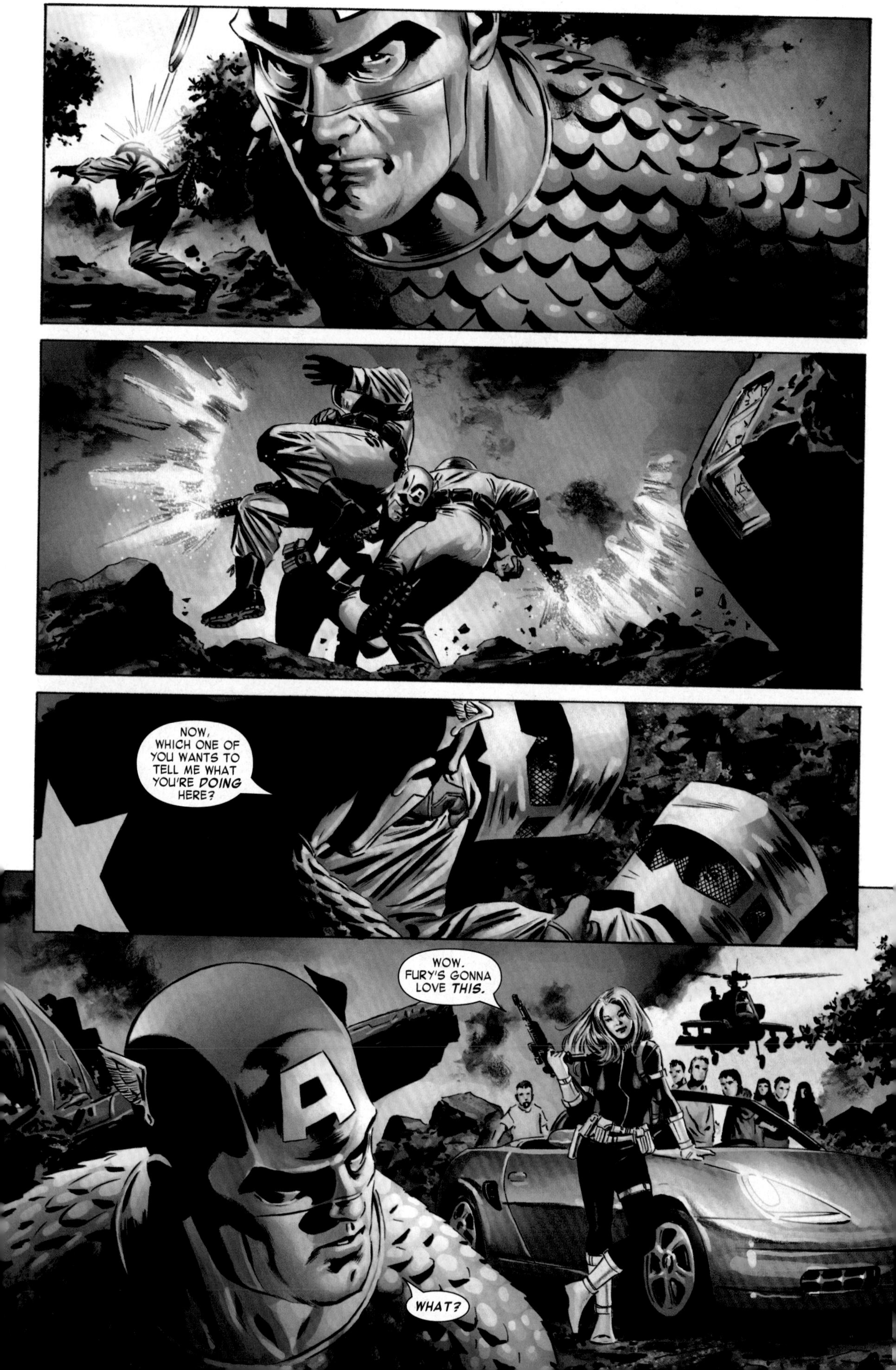
NOW, WHICH ONE OF YOU WANTS TO TELL ME WHAT YOU'RE *DOING* HERE?
WOW. FURY'S GONNA LOVE *THIS.*
WHAT?

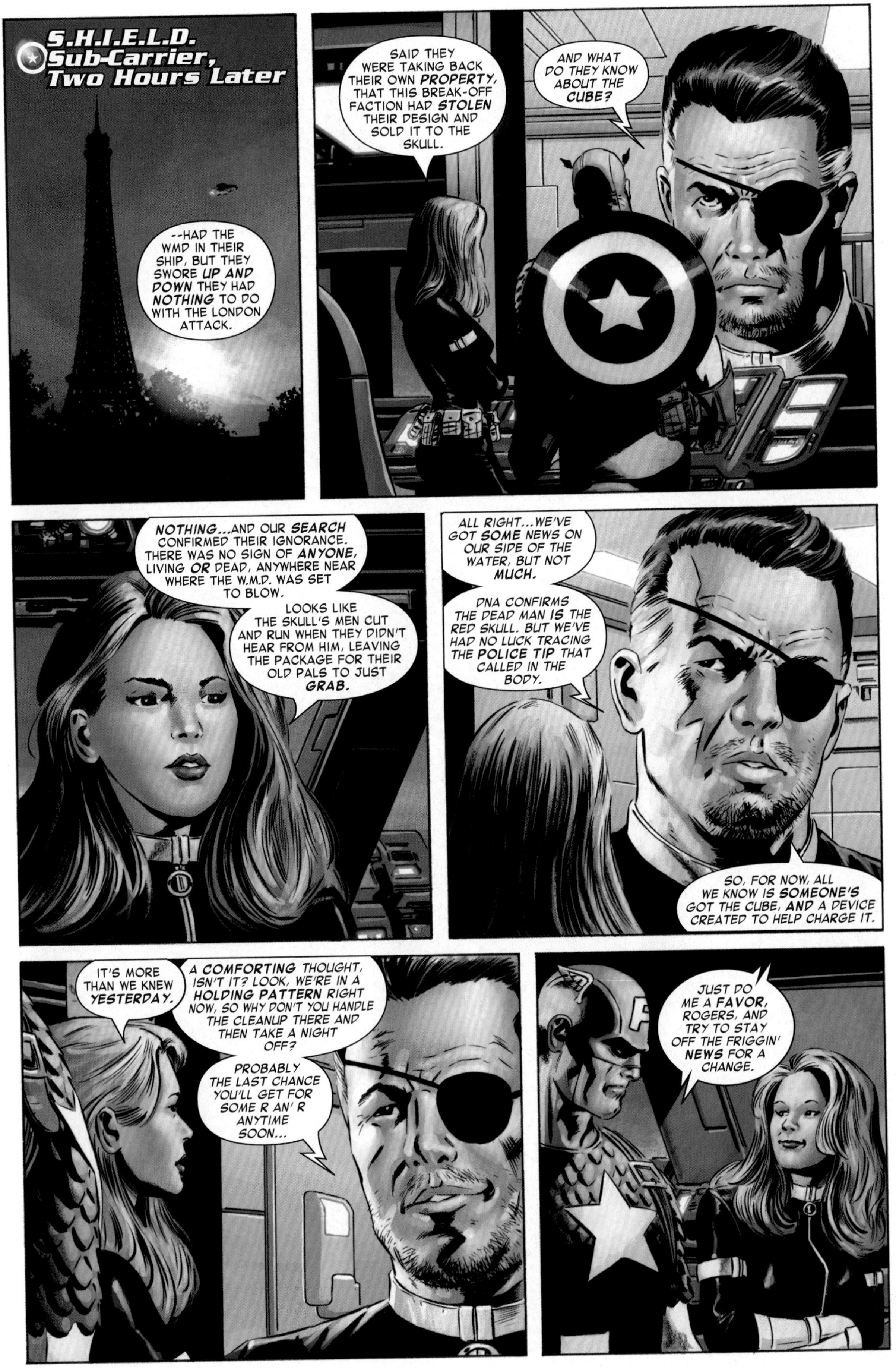
S.H.I.E.L.D. Sub-Carrier, Two Hours Later
--HAD THE WMD IN THEIR SHIP, BUT THEY SWORE UP AND DOWN THEY HAD NOTHING TO DO WITH THE LONDON ATTACK.
SAID THEY WERE TAKING BACK THEIR OWN PROPERTY, THAT THIS BREAK-OFF FACTION HAD STOLEN THEIR DESIGN AND SOLD IT TO THE SKULL.
AND WHAT DO THEY KNOW ABOUT THE CUBE?
NOTHING...AND OUR SEARCH CONFIRMED THEIR IGNORANCE. THERE WAS NO SIGN OF ANYONE, LIVING OR DEAD, ANYWHERE NEAR WHERE THE W.M.D. WAS SET TO BLOW.
LOOKS LIKE THE SKULL'S MEN CUT AND RUN WHEN THEY DIDN'T HEAR FROM HIM, LEAVING THE PACKAGE FOR THEIR OLD PALS TO JUST GRAB.
ALL RIGHT...WE'VE GOT SOME NEWS ON OUR SIDE OF THE WATER, BUT NOT MUCH.
DNA CONFIRMS THE DEAD MAN IS THE RED SKULL. BUT WE'VE HAD NO LUCK TRACING THE POLICE TIP THAT CALLED IN THE BODY.
SO, FOR NOW, ALL WE KNOW IS SOMEONE'S GOT THE CUBE, AND A DEVICE CREATED TO HELP CHARGE IT.
IT'S MORE THAN WE KNEW YESTERDAY.
A COMFORTING THOUGHT, ISN'T IT? LOOK, WE'RE IN A HOLDING PATTERN RIGHT NOW, SO WHY DON'T YOU HANDLE THE CLEANUP THERE AND THEN TAKE A NIGHT OFF?
PROBABLY THE LAST CHANCE YOU'LL GET FOR SOME R AN' R ANYTIME SOON...
JUST DO ME A FAVOR, ROGERS, AND TRY TO STAY OFF THE FRIGGIN' NEWS FOR A CHANGE.

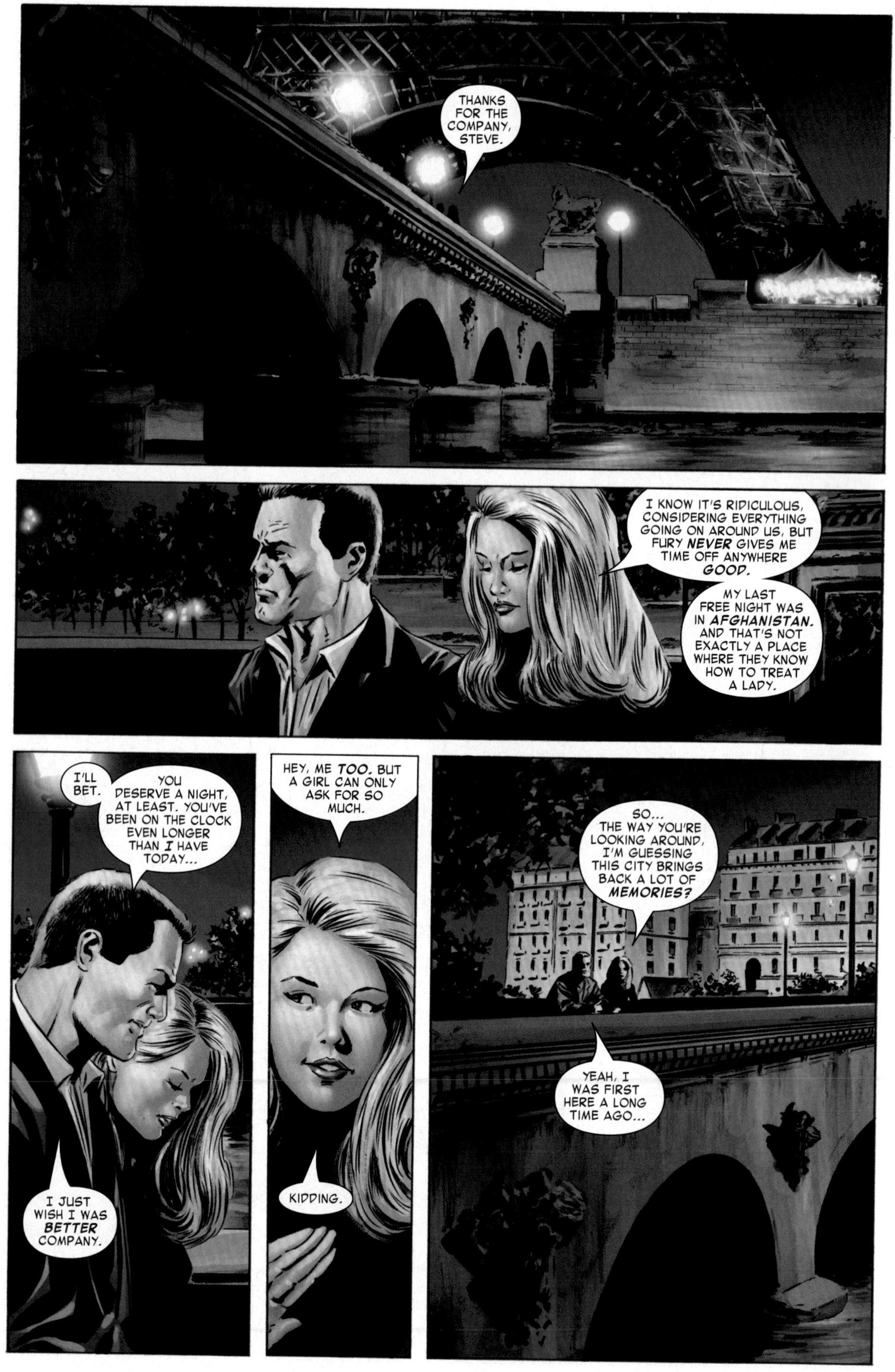

THANKS FOR THE COMPANY, STEVE.
I KNOW IT'S RIDICULOUS, CONSIDERING EVERYTHING GOING ON AROUND US, BUT FURY **NEVER** GIVES ME TIME OFF ANYWHERE **GOOD.**
MY LAST FREE NIGHT WAS IN **AFGHANISTAN.** AND THAT'S NOT EXACTLY A PLACE WHERE THEY KNOW HOW TO TREAT A LADY.
I'LL BET.
YOU DESERVE A NIGHT, AT LEAST. YOU'VE BEEN ON THE CLOCK EVEN LONGER THAN ***I*** HAVE TODAY...
I JUST WISH I WAS **BETTER** COMPANY.
HEY, ME **TOO.** BUT A GIRL CAN ONLY ASK FOR SO MUCH.
KIDDING.
SO... THE WAY YOU'RE LOOKING AROUND, I'M GUESSING THIS CITY BRINGS BACK A LOT OF **MEMORIES?**
YEAH, I WAS FIRST HERE A LONG TIME AGO...

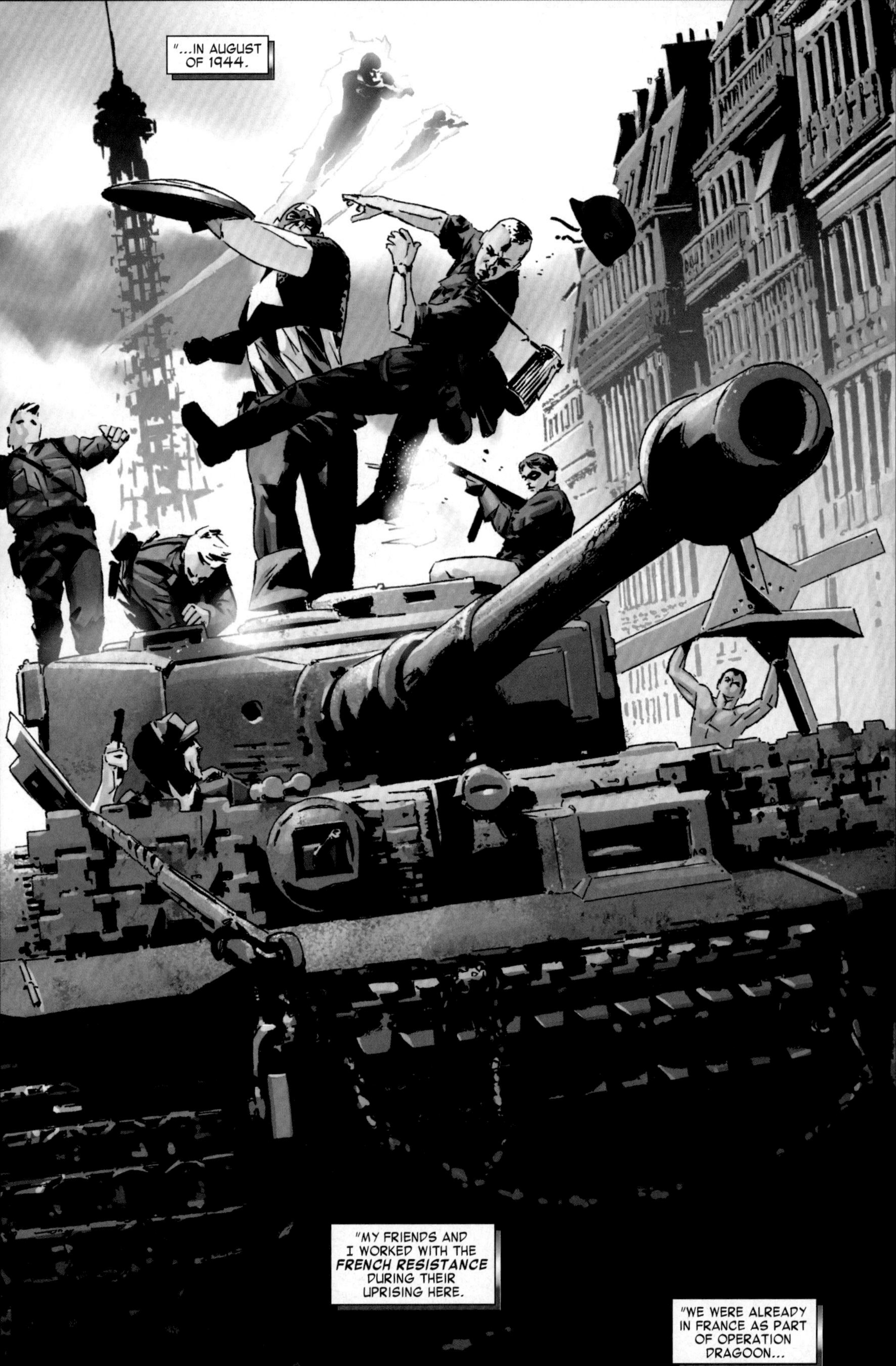
"...IN AUGUST OF 1944.
"MY FRIENDS AND I WORKED WITH THE *FRENCH RESISTANCE* DURING THEIR UPRISING HERE.
"WE WERE ALREADY IN FRANCE AS PART OF OPERATION DRAGOON...

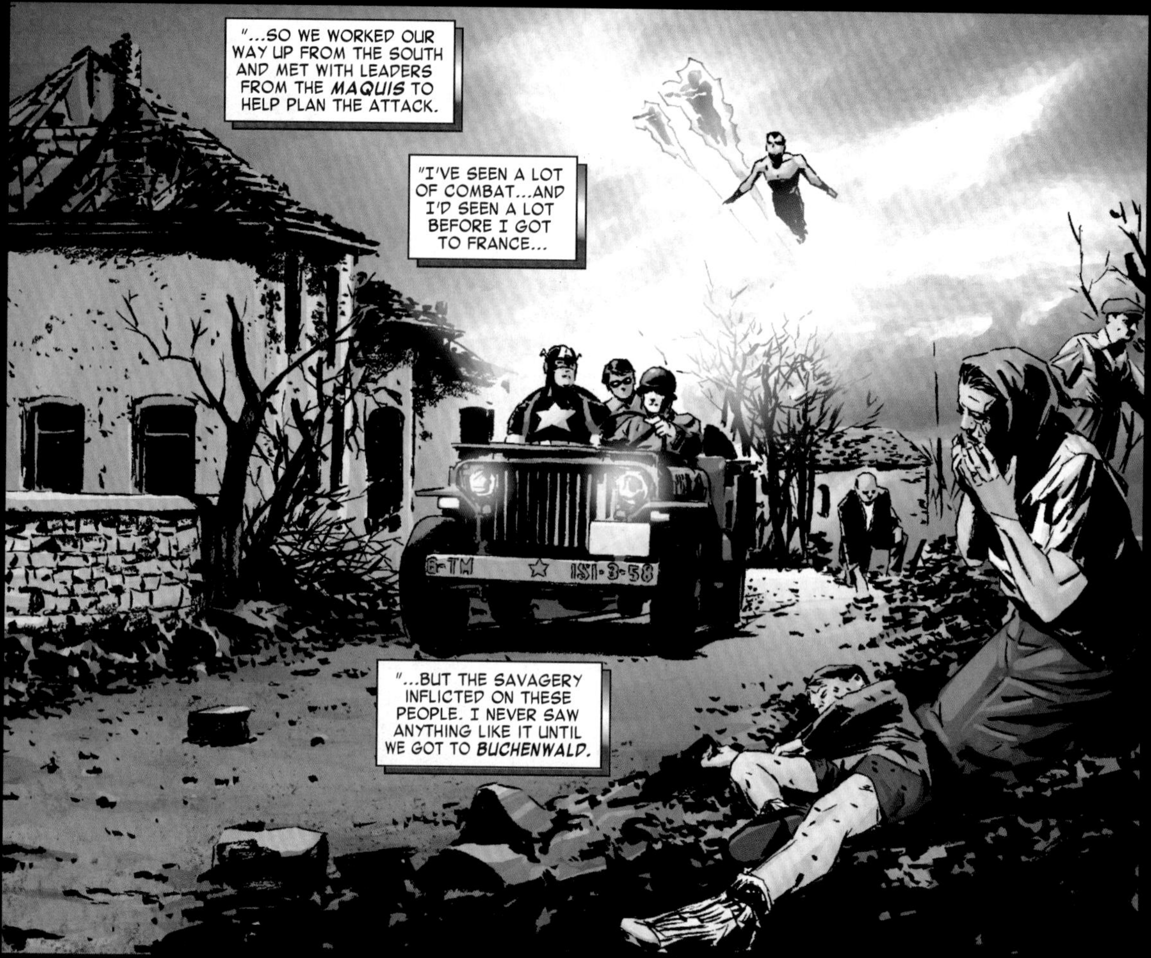
"...SO WE WORKED OUR WAY UP FROM THE SOUTH AND MET WITH LEADERS FROM THE *MAQUIS* TO HELP PLAN THE ATTACK.
"I'VE SEEN A LOT OF COMBAT...AND I'D SEEN A LOT BEFORE I GOT TO FRANCE...
"...BUT THE SAVAGERY INFLICTED ON THESE PEOPLE. I NEVER SAW ANYTHING LIKE IT UNTIL WE GOT TO *BUCHENWALD*.

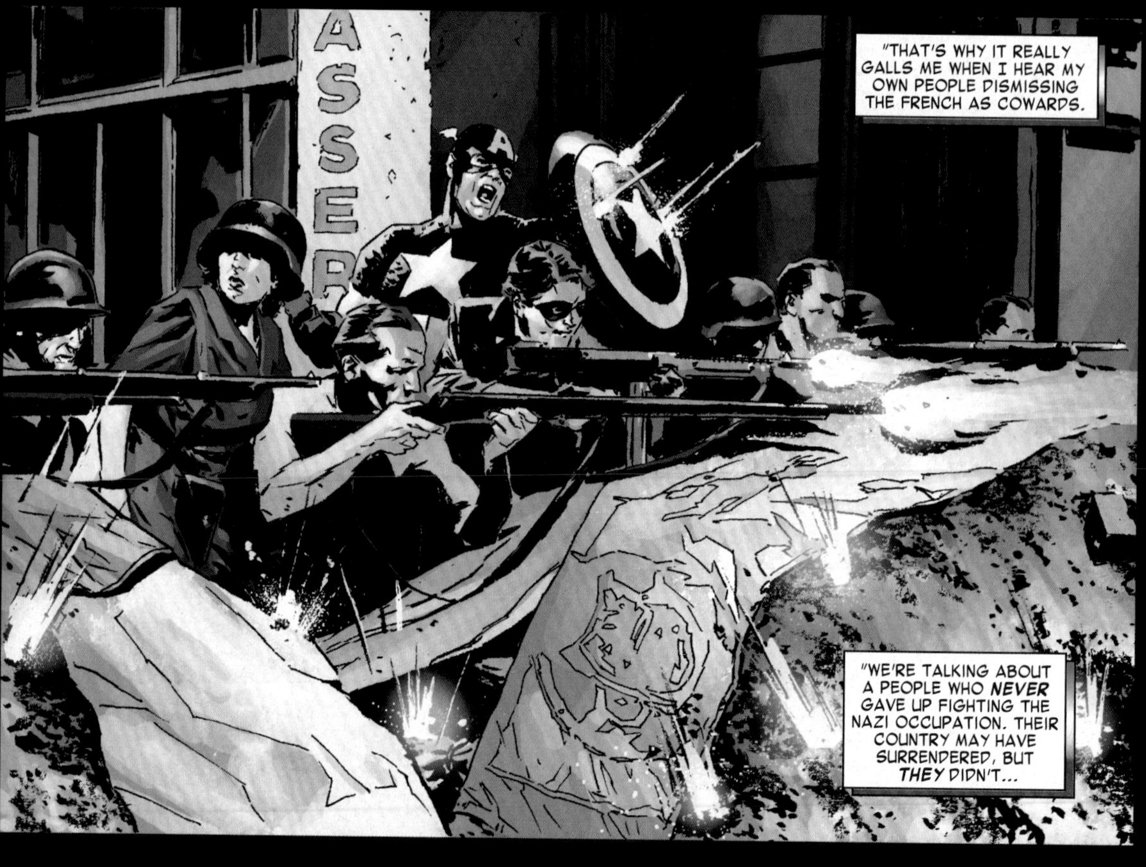
"THAT'S WHY IT REALLY GALLS ME WHEN I HEAR MY OWN PEOPLE DISMISSING THE FRENCH AS COWARDS.
"WE'RE TALKING ABOUT A PEOPLE WHO *NEVER* GAVE UP FIGHTING THE NAZI OCCUPATION. THEIR COUNTRY MAY HAVE SURRENDERED, BUT *THEY* DIDN'T...

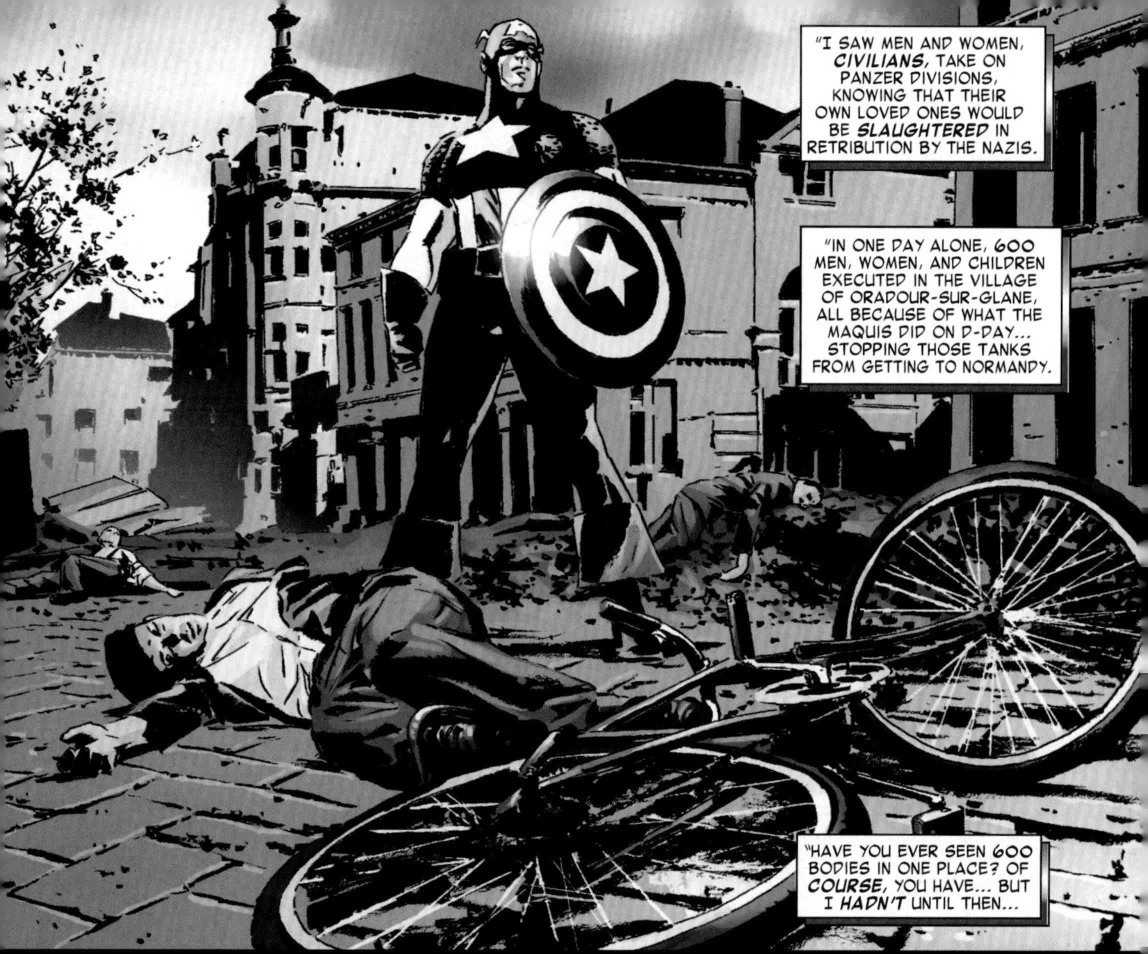
"I SAW MEN AND WOMEN, CIVILIANS, TAKE ON PANZER DIVISIONS, KNOWING THAT THEIR OWN LOVED ONES WOULD BE SLAUGHTERED IN RETRIBUTION BY THE NAZIS.
"IN ONE DAY ALONE, 600 MEN, WOMEN, AND CHILDREN EXECUTED IN THE VILLAGE OF ORADOUR-SUR-GLANE, ALL BECAUSE OF WHAT THE MAQUIS DID ON D-DAY... STOPPING THOSE TANKS FROM GETTING TO NORMANDY.
"HAVE YOU EVER SEEN 600 BODIES IN ONE PLACE? OF COURSE, YOU HAVE... BUT I HADN'T UNTIL THEN...

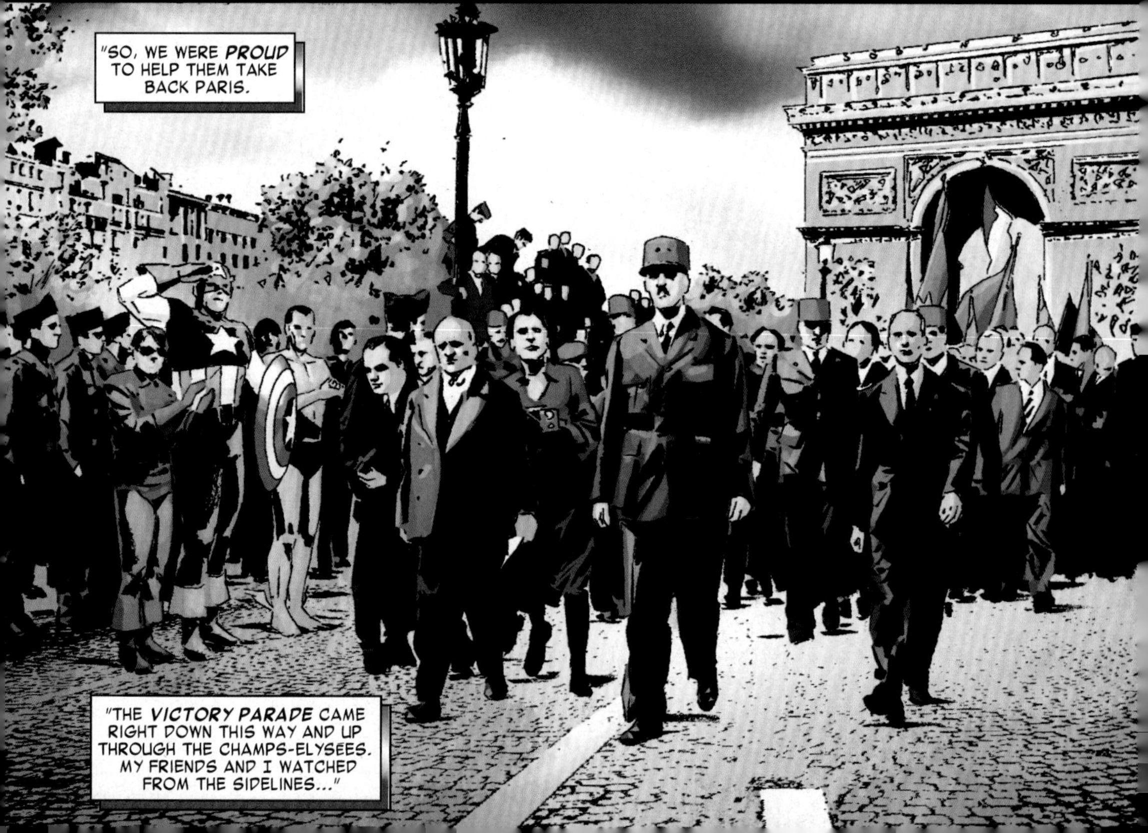
"SO, WE WERE PROUD TO HELP THEM TAKE BACK PARIS.
"THE VICTORY PARADE CAME RIGHT DOWN THIS WAY AND UP THROUGH THE CHAMPS-ELYSEES. MY FRIENDS AND I WATCHED FROM THE SIDELINES..."

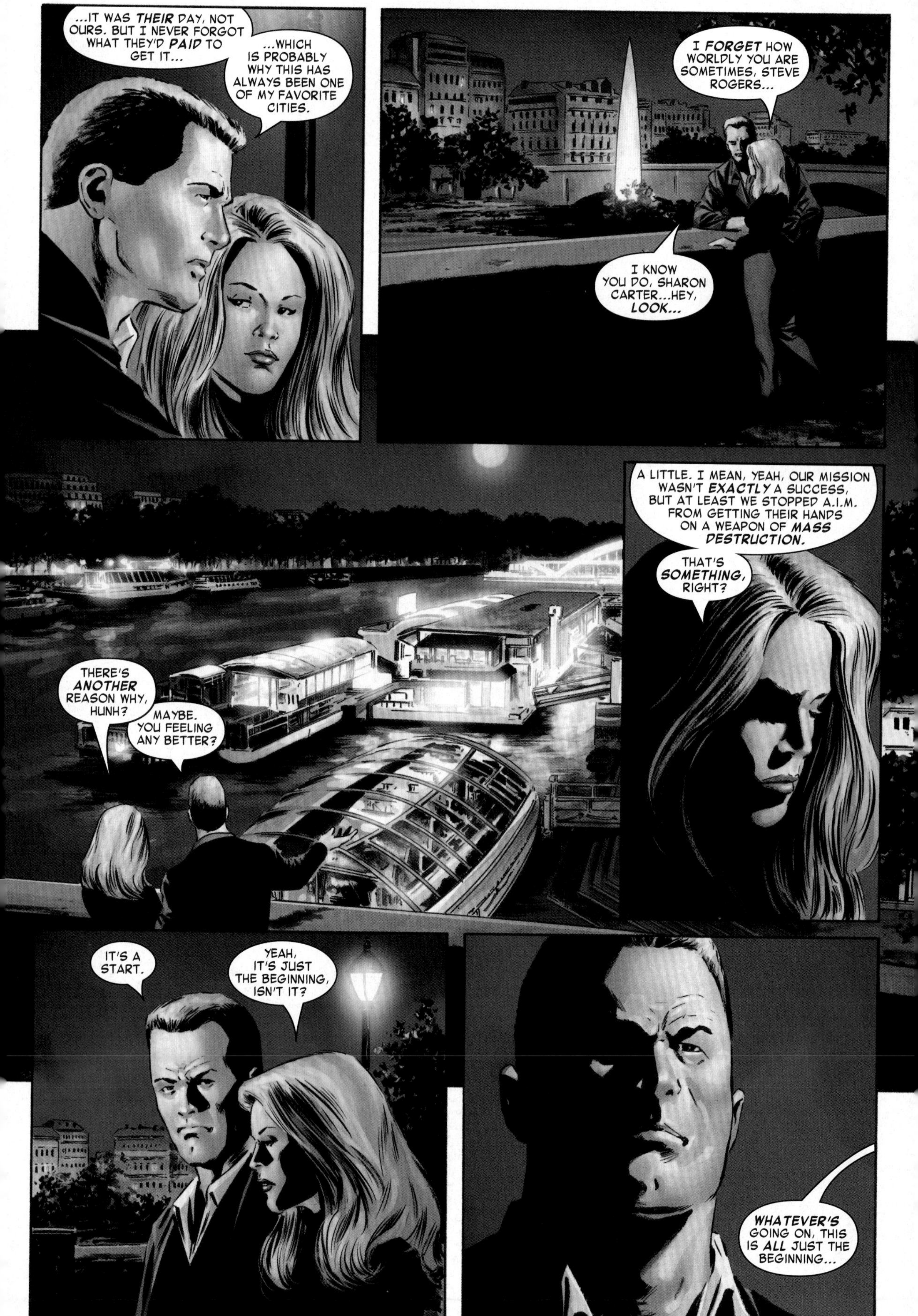
...IT WAS THEIR DAY, NOT OURS. BUT I NEVER FORGOT WHAT THEY'D PAID TO GET IT...
...WHICH IS PROBABLY WHY THIS HAS ALWAYS BEEN ONE OF MY FAVORITE CITIES.
I FORGET HOW WORLDLY YOU ARE SOMETIMES, STEVE ROGERS...
I KNOW YOU DO, SHARON CARTER...HEY, LOOK...
THERE'S ANOTHER REASON WHY, HUNH?
MAYBE. YOU FEELING ANY BETTER?
A LITTLE. I MEAN, YEAH, OUR MISSION WASN'T EXACTLY A SUCCESS, BUT AT LEAST WE STOPPED A.I.M. FROM GETTING THEIR HANDS ON A WEAPON OF MASS DESTRUCTION.
THAT'S SOMETHING, RIGHT?
IT'S A START.
YEAH, IT'S JUST THE BEGINNING, ISN'T IT?
WHATEVER'S GOING ON, THIS IS ALL JUST THE BEGINNING...

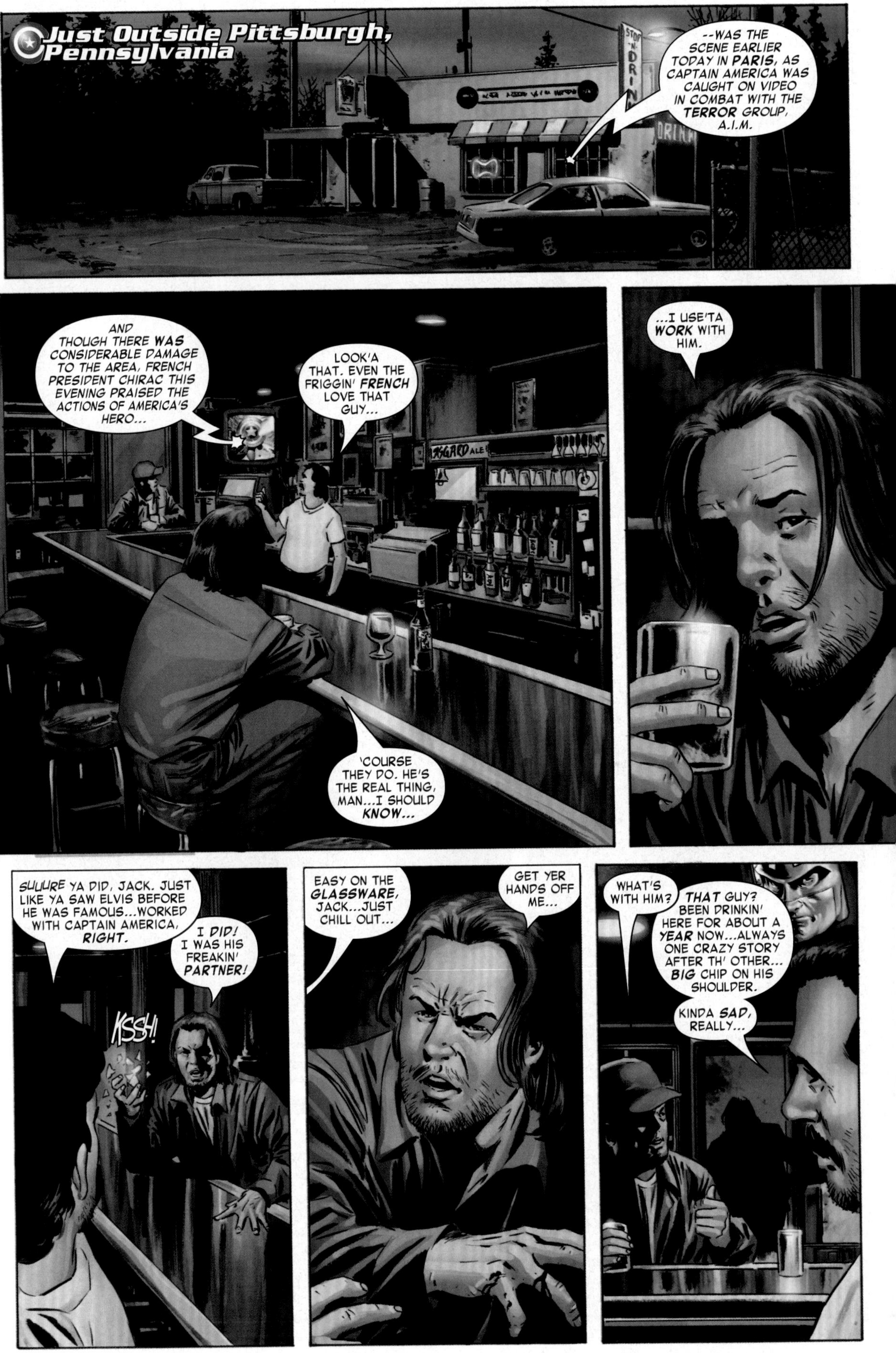

Just Outside Pittsburgh, Pennsylvania
--WAS THE SCENE EARLIER TODAY IN PARIS, AS CAPTAIN AMERICA WAS CAUGHT ON VIDEO IN COMBAT WITH THE TERROR GROUP, A.I.M.
AND THOUGH THERE WAS CONSIDERABLE DAMAGE TO THE AREA, FRENCH PRESIDENT CHIRAC THIS EVENING PRAISED THE ACTIONS OF AMERICA'S HERO...
LOOK'A THAT. EVEN THE FRIGGIN' FRENCH LOVE THAT GUY...
'COURSE THEY DO. HE'S THE REAL THING, MAN...I SHOULD KNOW...
...I USE'TA WORK WITH HIM.
SUUURE YA DID, JACK. JUST LIKE YA SAW ELVIS BEFORE HE WAS FAMOUS...WORKED WITH CAPTAIN AMERICA, RIGHT.
I DID! I WAS HIS FREAKIN' PARTNER!
KSSH!
EASY ON THE GLASSWARE, JACK...JUST CHILL OUT...
GET YER HANDS OFF ME...
WHAT'S WITH HIM?
THAT GUY? BEEN DRINKIN' HERE FOR ABOUT A YEAR NOW...ALWAYS ONE CRAZY STORY AFTER TH' OTHER... BIG CHIP ON HIS SHOULDER.
KINDA SAD, REALLY...

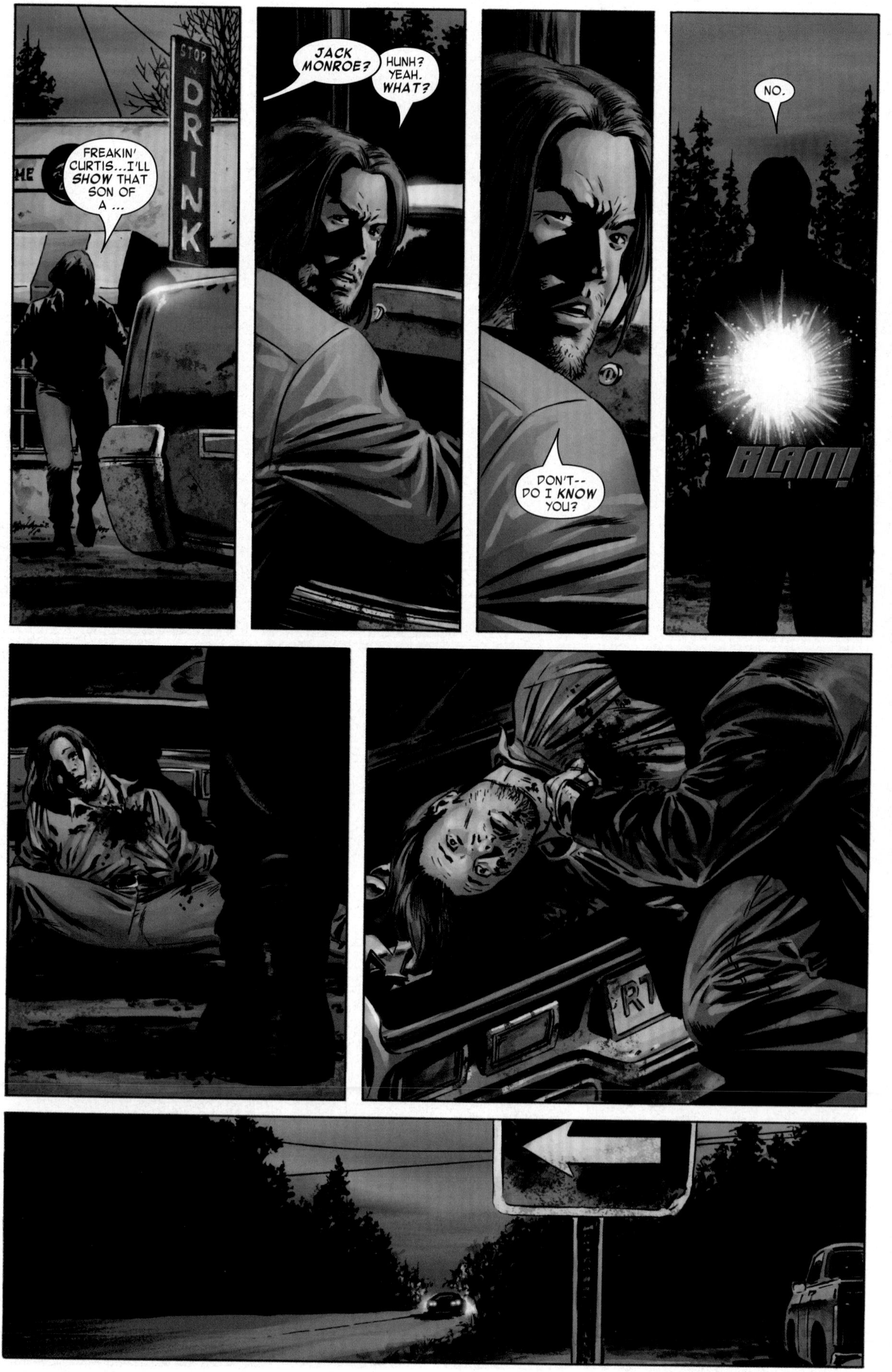
STOP
DRINK
FREAKIN' CURTIS...I'LL SHOW THAT SON OF A ...
JACK MONROE?
HUNH? YEAH. WHAT?
DON'T-- DO I KNOW YOU?
NO.
BLAM!

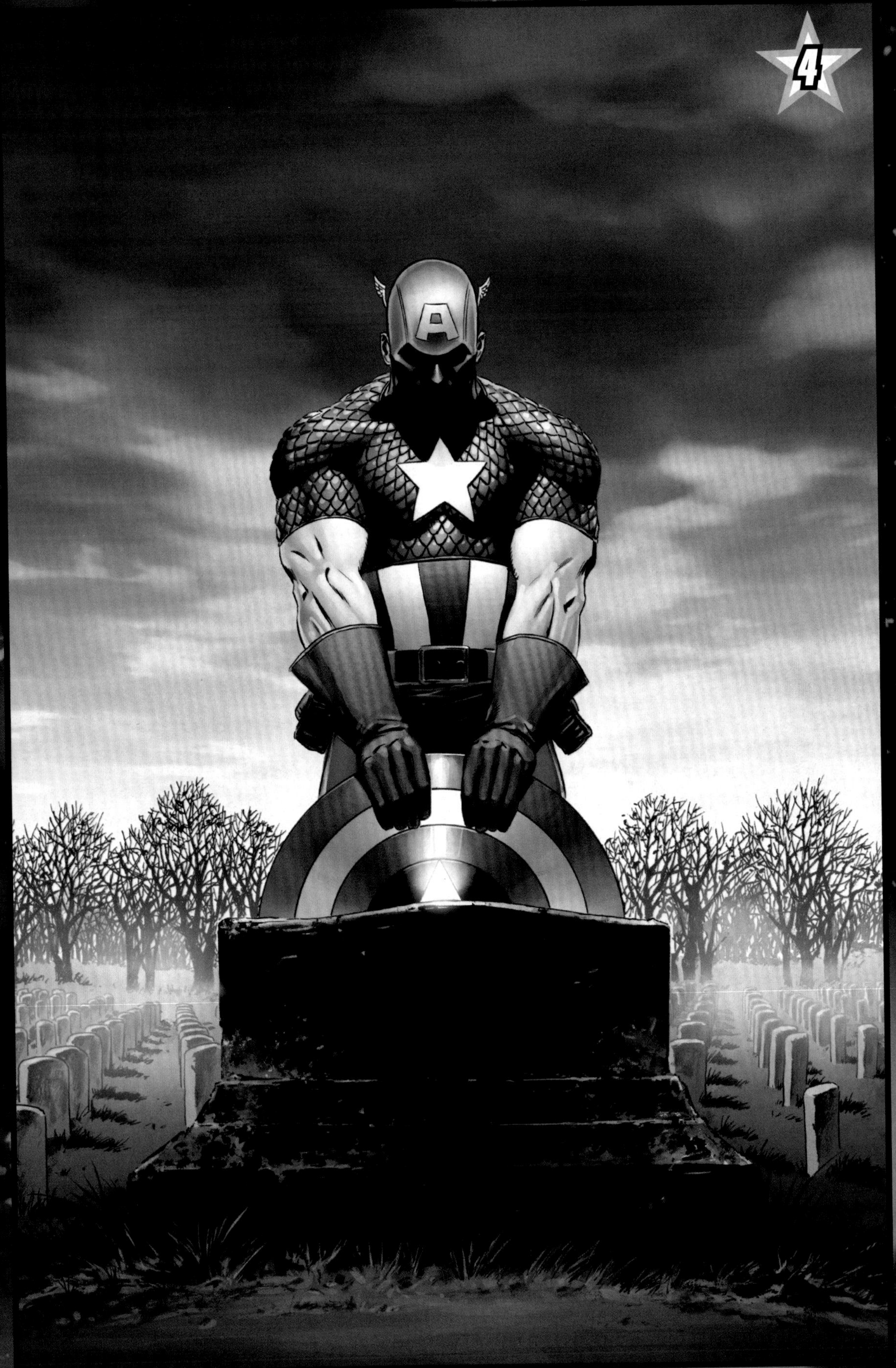
4

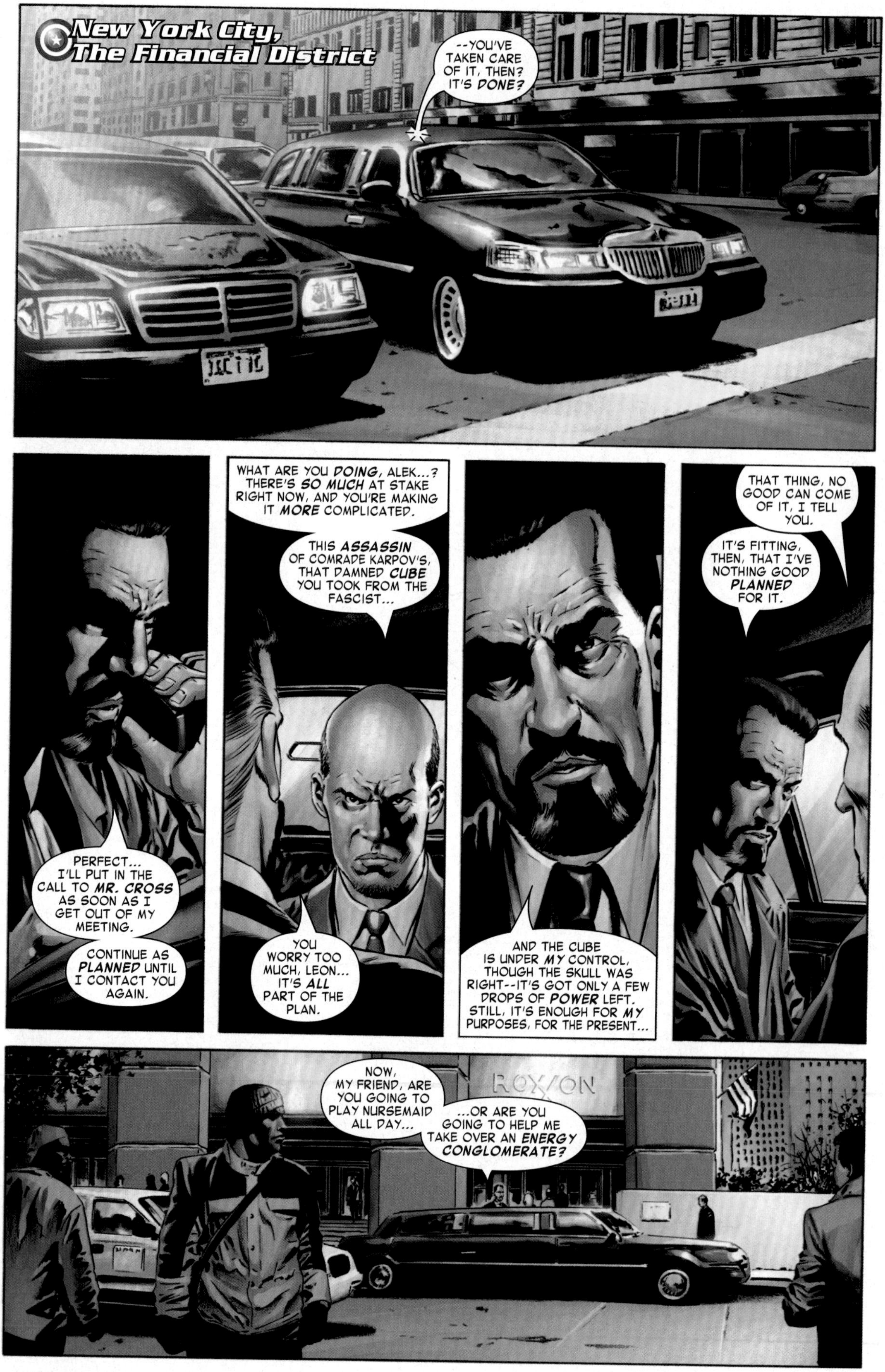

New York City, The Financial District
--YOU'VE TAKEN CARE OF IT, THEN? IT'S DONE?
PERFECT... I'LL PUT IN THE CALL TO MR. CROSS AS SOON AS I GET OUT OF MY MEETING.
CONTINUE AS PLANNED UNTIL I CONTACT YOU AGAIN.
WHAT ARE YOU DOING, ALEK...? THERE'S SO MUCH AT STAKE RIGHT NOW, AND YOU'RE MAKING IT MORE COMPLICATED.
THIS ASSASSIN OF COMRADE KARPOV'S, THAT DAMNED CUBE YOU TOOK FROM THE FASCIST...
YOU WORRY TOO MUCH, LEON... IT'S ALL PART OF THE PLAN.
AND THE CUBE IS UNDER MY CONTROL, THOUGH THE SKULL WAS RIGHT--IT'S GOT ONLY A FEW DROPS OF POWER LEFT. STILL, IT'S ENOUGH FOR MY PURPOSES, FOR THE PRESENT...
THAT THING, NO GOOD CAN COME OF IT, I TELL YOU.
IT'S FITTING, THEN, THAT I'VE NOTHING GOOD PLANNED FOR IT.
ROXXON
NOW, MY FRIEND, ARE YOU GOING TO PLAY NURSEMAID ALL DAY...
...OR ARE YOU GOING TO HELP ME TAKE OVER AN ENERGY CONGLOMERATE?

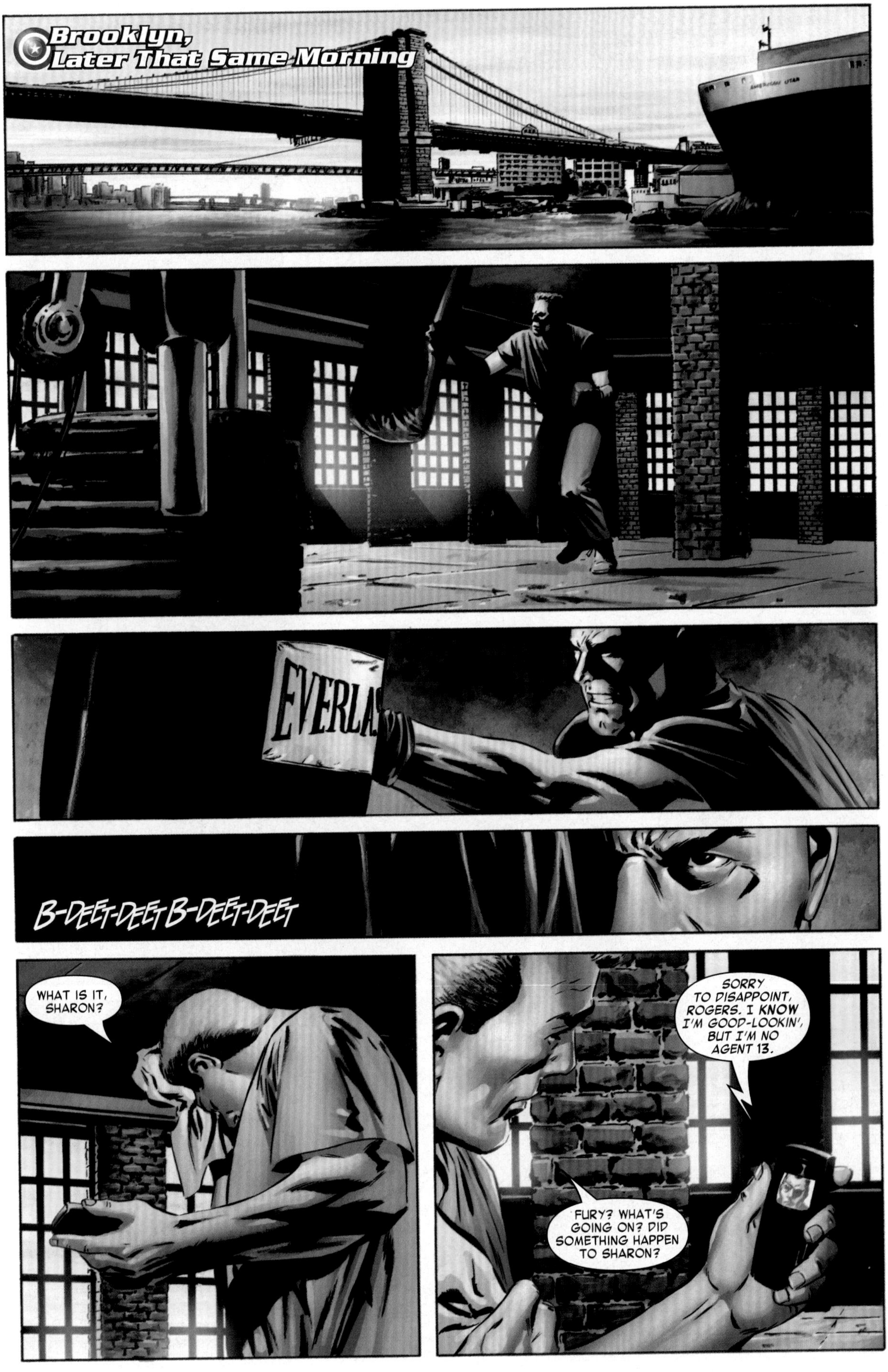
Brooklyn, Later That Same Morning
EVERLAS
B-DEET-DEET B-DEET-DEET
WHAT IS IT, SHARON?
SORRY TO DISAPPOINT, ROGERS. I KNOW I'M GOOD-LOOKIN', BUT I'M NO AGENT 13.
FURY? WHAT'S GOING ON? DID SOMETHING HAPPEN TO SHARON?

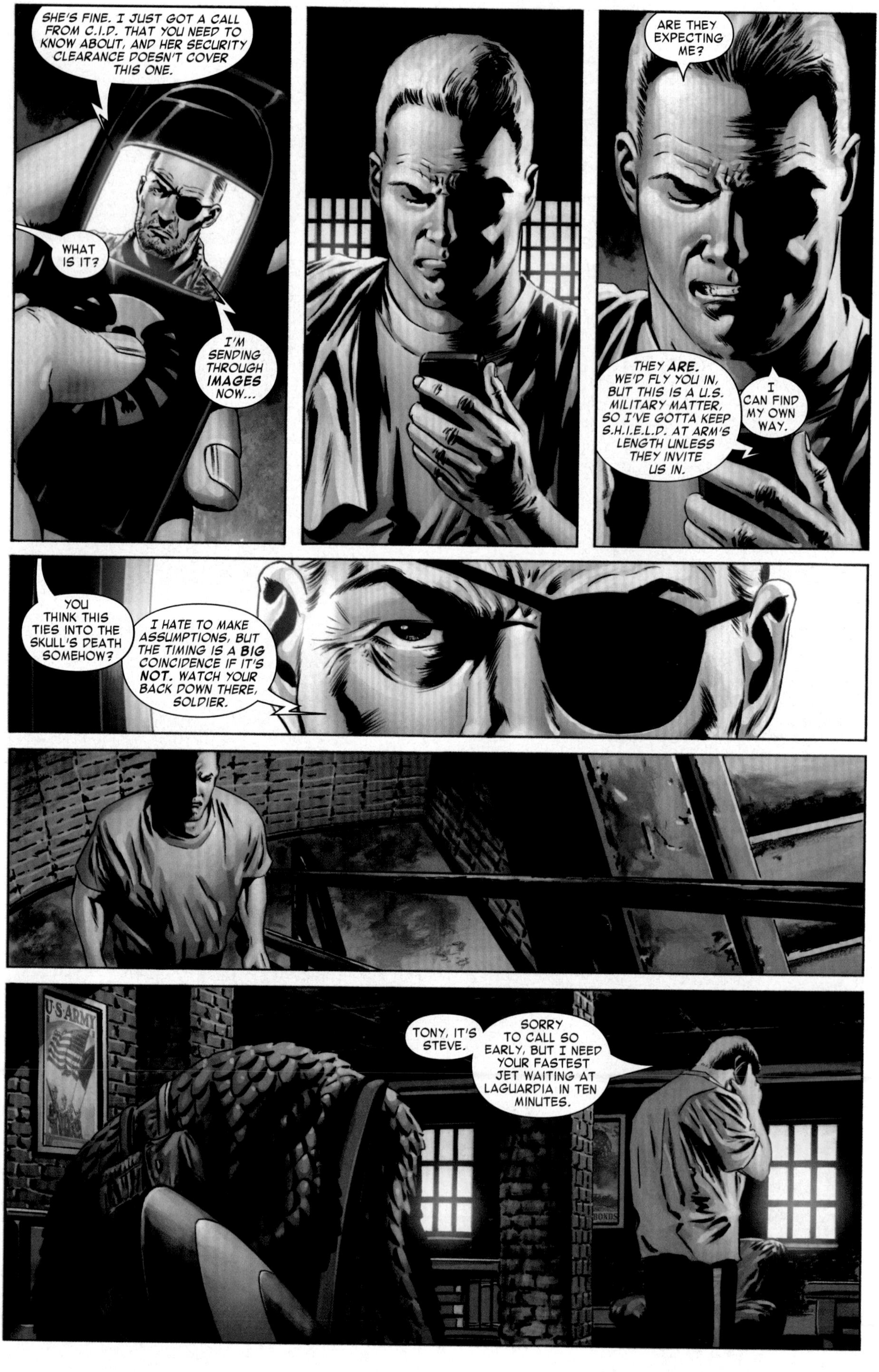

SHE'S FINE. I JUST GOT A CALL FROM C.I.D. THAT YOU NEED TO KNOW ABOUT, AND HER SECURITY CLEARANCE DOESN'T COVER THIS ONE.
WHAT IS IT?
I'M SENDING THROUGH IMAGES NOW...
ARE THEY EXPECTING ME?
THEY ARE. WE'D FLY YOU IN, BUT THIS IS A U.S. MILITARY MATTER, SO I'VE GOTTA KEEP S.H.I.E.L.D. AT ARM'S LENGTH UNLESS THEY INVITE US IN.
I CAN FIND MY OWN WAY.
YOU THINK THIS TIES INTO THE SKULL'S DEATH SOMEHOW?
I HATE TO MAKE ASSUMPTIONS, BUT THE TIMING IS A BIG COINCIDENCE IF IT'S NOT. WATCH YOUR BACK DOWN THERE, SOLDIER.
U.S. ARMY
TONY, IT'S STEVE.
SORRY TO CALL SO EARLY, BUT I NEED YOUR FASTEST JET WAITING AT LAGUARDIA IN TEN MINUTES.

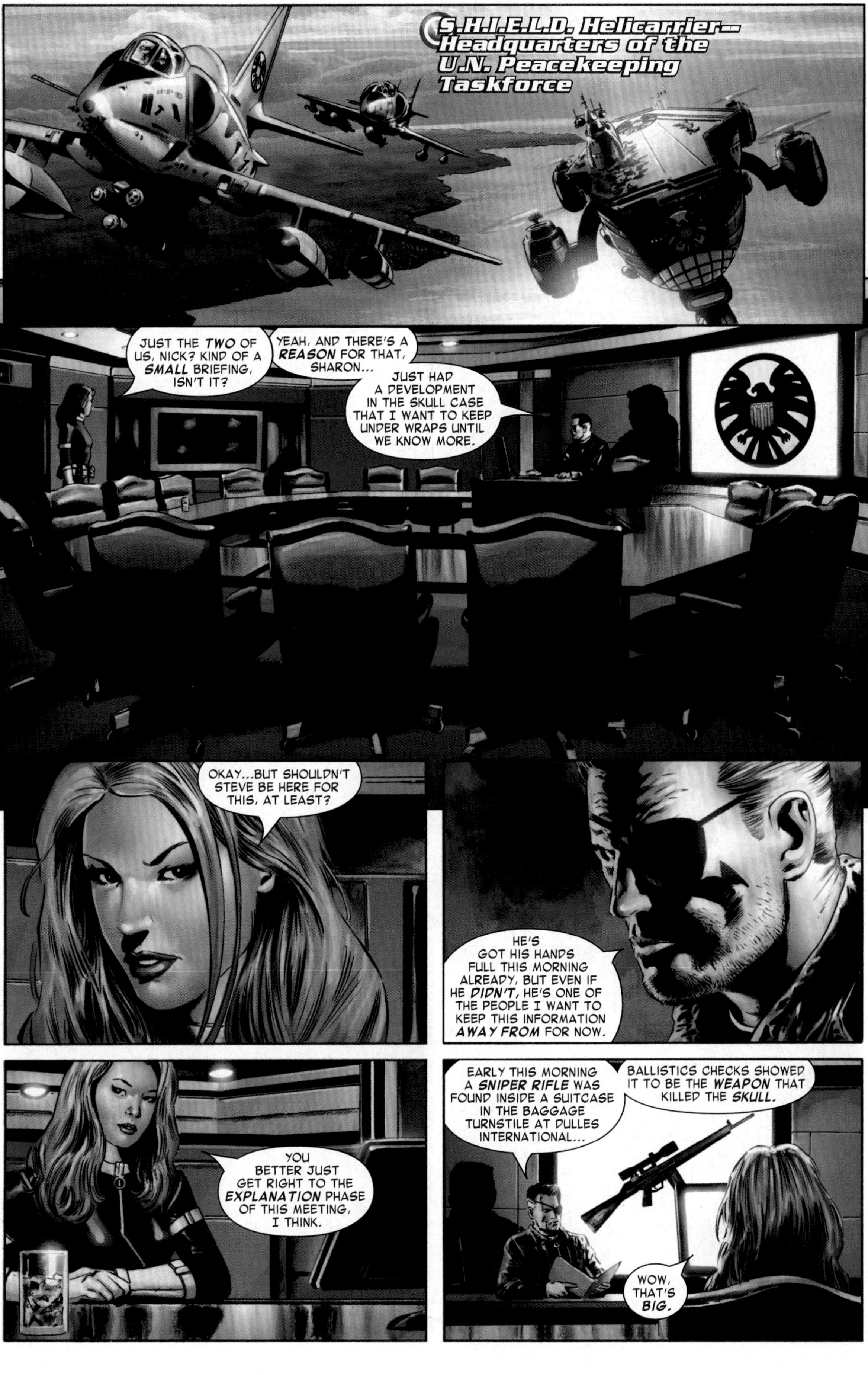
S.H.I.E.L.D. Helicarrier-- Headquarters of the U.N. Peacekeeping Taskforce
JUST THE TWO OF US, NICK? KIND OF A SMALL BRIEFING, ISN'T IT?
YEAH, AND THERE'S A REASON FOR THAT, SHARON...
JUST HAD A DEVELOPMENT IN THE SKULL CASE THAT I WANT TO KEEP UNDER WRAPS UNTIL WE KNOW MORE.
OKAY...BUT SHOULDN'T STEVE BE HERE FOR THIS, AT LEAST?
HE'S GOT HIS HANDS FULL THIS MORNING ALREADY, BUT EVEN IF HE DIDN'T, HE'S ONE OF THE PEOPLE I WANT TO KEEP THIS INFORMATION AWAY FROM FOR NOW.
YOU BETTER JUST GET RIGHT TO THE EXPLANATION PHASE OF THIS MEETING, I THINK.
EARLY THIS MORNING A SNIPER RIFLE WAS FOUND INSIDE A SUITCASE IN THE BAGGAGE TURNSTILE AT DULLES INTERNATIONAL...
BALLISTICS CHECKS SHOWED IT TO BE THE WEAPON THAT KILLED THE SKULL.
WOW, THAT'S BIG.

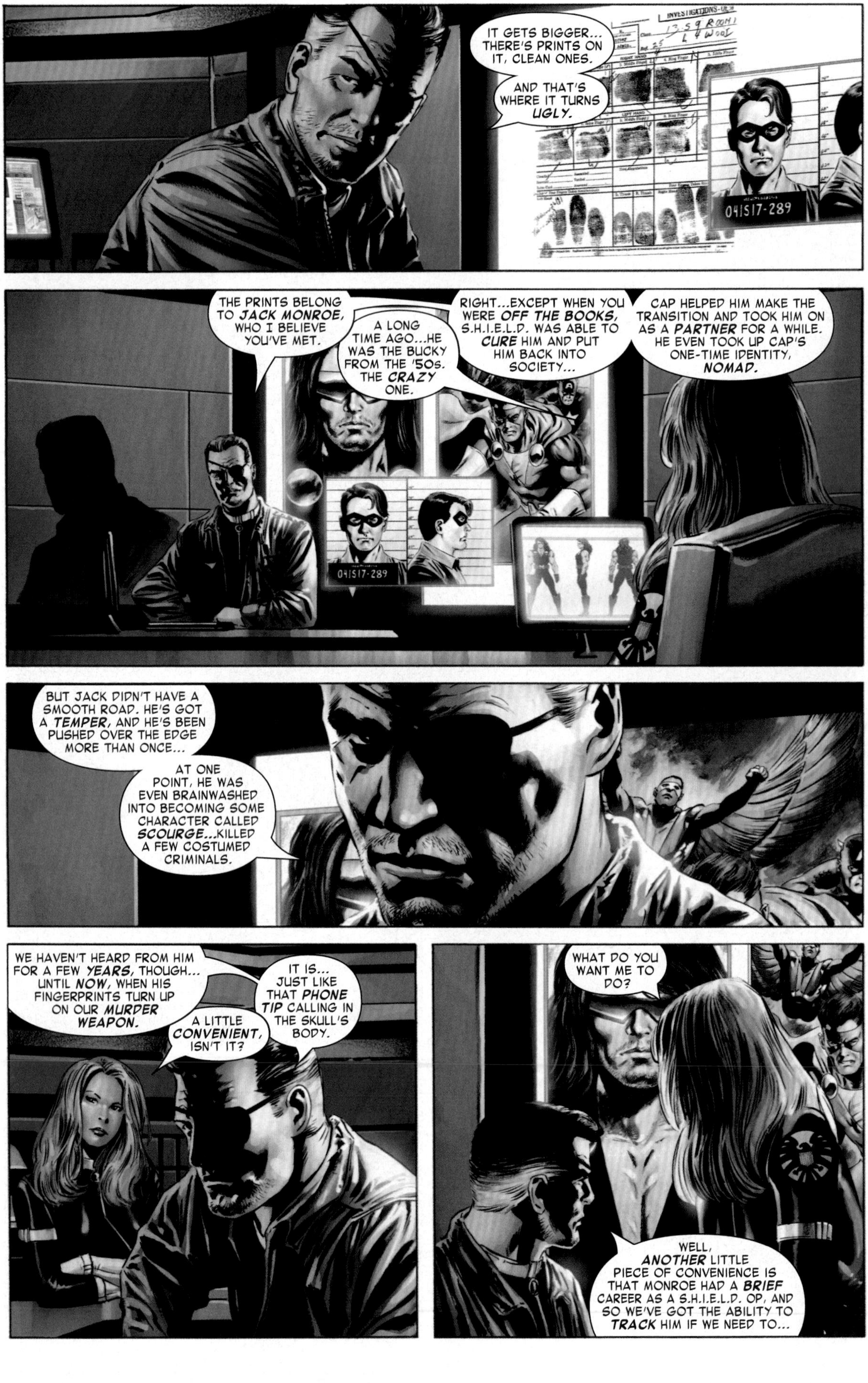
IT GETS BIGGER... THERE'S PRINTS ON IT, CLEAN ONES.
AND THAT'S WHERE IT TURNS UGLY.
041S17-289
THE PRINTS BELONG TO JACK MONROE, WHO I BELIEVE YOU'VE MET.
A LONG TIME AGO...HE WAS THE BUCKY FROM THE '50s. THE CRAZY ONE.
RIGHT...EXCEPT WHEN YOU WERE OFF THE BOOKS, S.H.I.E.L.D. WAS ABLE TO CURE HIM AND PUT HIM BACK INTO SOCIETY...
CAP HELPED HIM MAKE THE TRANSITION AND TOOK HIM ON AS A PARTNER FOR A WHILE. HE EVEN TOOK UP CAP'S ONE-TIME IDENTITY, NOMAD.
041S17-289
BUT JACK DIDN'T HAVE A SMOOTH ROAD. HE'S GOT A TEMPER, AND HE'S BEEN PUSHED OVER THE EDGE MORE THAN ONCE...
AT ONE POINT, HE WAS EVEN BRAINWASHED INTO BECOMING SOME CHARACTER CALLED SCOURGE...KILLED A FEW COSTUMED CRIMINALS.
WE HAVEN'T HEARD FROM HIM FOR A FEW YEARS, THOUGH... UNTIL NOW, WHEN HIS FINGERPRINTS TURN UP ON OUR MURDER WEAPON.
IT IS... JUST LIKE THAT PHONE TIP CALLING IN THE SKULL'S BODY.
A LITTLE CONVENIENT, ISN'T IT?
WHAT DO YOU WANT ME TO DO?
WELL, ANOTHER LITTLE PIECE OF CONVENIENCE IS THAT MONROE HAD A BRIEF CAREER AS A S.H.I.E.L.D. OP, AND SO WE'VE GOT THE ABILITY TO TRACK HIM IF WE NEED TO...

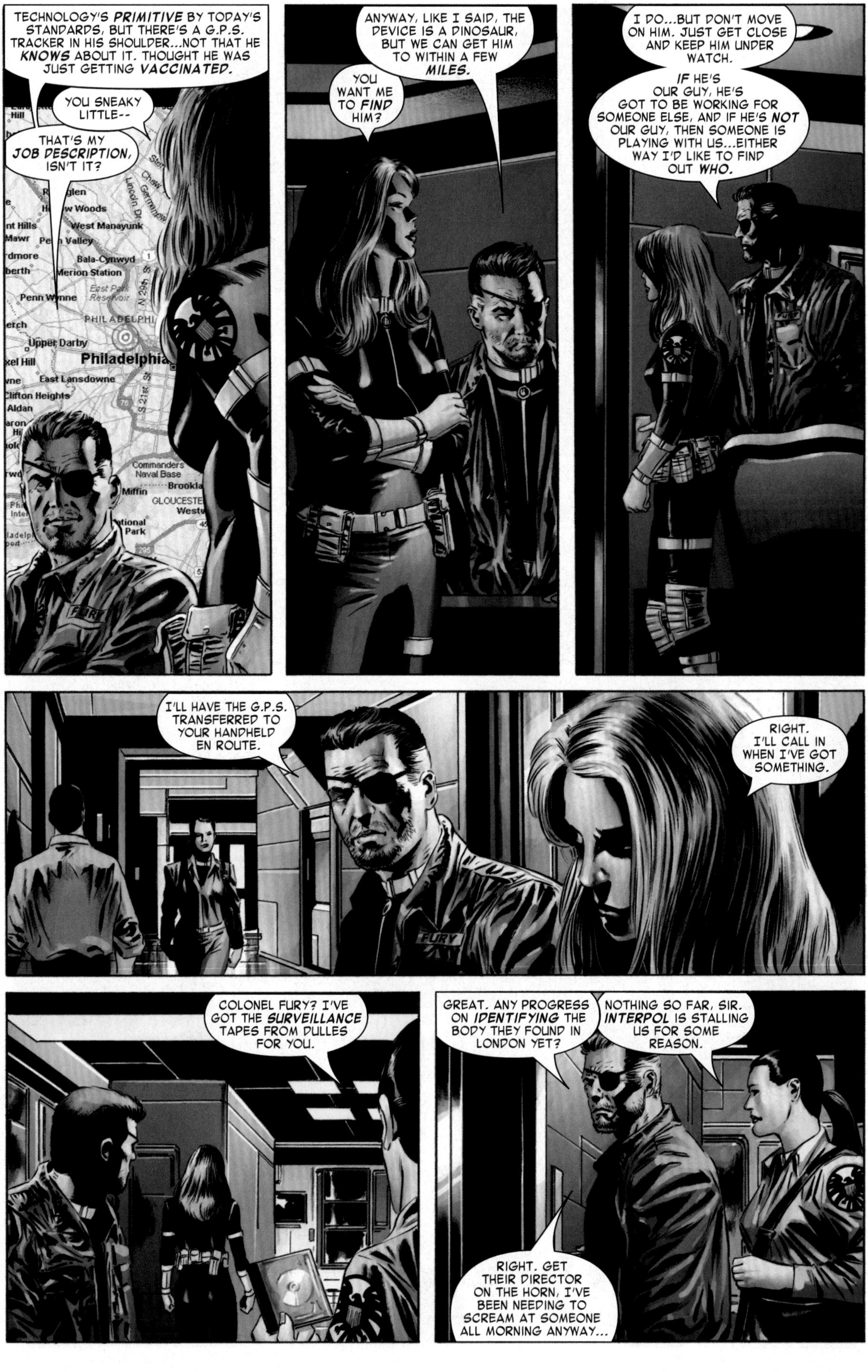
TECHNOLOGY'S *PRIMITIVE* BY TODAY'S STANDARDS, BUT THERE'S A G.P.S. TRACKER IN HIS SHOULDER...NOT THAT HE *KNOWS* ABOUT IT. THOUGHT HE WAS JUST GETTING *VACCINATED.*
YOU SNEAKY LITTLE--
THAT'S MY *JOB DESCRIPTION,* ISN'T IT?
West Manayunk
Bala-Cynwyd
Merion Station
Penn Wynne
Upper Darby
Philadelphia
East Lansdowne
Clifton Heights
Aldan
Commanders Naval Base
Miffin
GLOUCESTER
FURY
ANYWAY, LIKE I SAID, THE DEVICE IS A DINOSAUR, BUT WE CAN GET HIM TO WITHIN A FEW *MILES.*
YOU WANT ME TO *FIND* HIM?
I DO...BUT DON'T MOVE ON HIM. JUST GET CLOSE AND KEEP HIM UNDER WATCH.
IF HE'S OUR GUY, HE'S GOT TO BE WORKING FOR SOMEONE ELSE, AND IF HE'S *NOT* OUR GUY, THEN SOMEONE IS PLAYING WITH US...EITHER WAY I'D LIKE TO FIND OUT *WHO.*
FURY
I'LL HAVE THE G.P.S. TRANSFERRED TO YOUR HANDHELD EN ROUTE.
RIGHT. I'LL CALL IN WHEN I'VE GOT SOMETHING.
FURY
COLONEL FURY? I'VE GOT THE *SURVEILLANCE* TAPES FROM DULLES FOR YOU.
GREAT. ANY PROGRESS ON *IDENTIFYING* THE BODY THEY FOUND IN LONDON YET?
NOTHING SO FAR, SIR. *INTERPOL* IS STALLING US FOR SOME REASON.
RIGHT. GET THEIR DIRECTOR ON THE HORN, I'VE BEEN NEEDING TO SCREAM AT SOMEONE ALL MORNING ANYWAY...

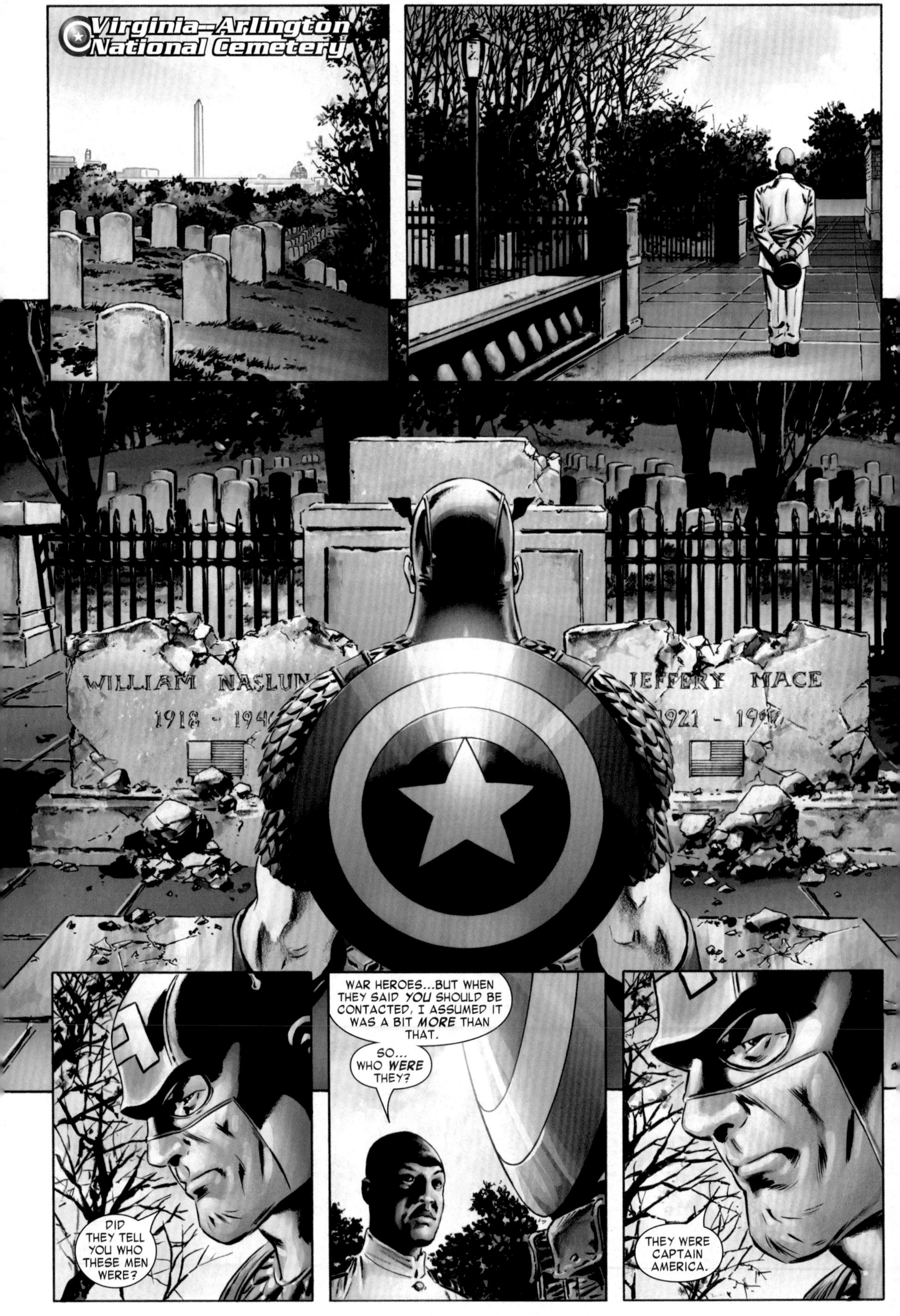
Virginia—Arlington National Cemetery
WILLIAM NASLUN
1918 - 194
JEFFERY MACE
1921 - 19
DID THEY TELL YOU WHO THESE MEN WERE?
WAR HEROES...BUT WHEN THEY SAID YOU SHOULD BE CONTACTED, I ASSUMED IT WAS A BIT MORE THAN THAT.
SO... WHO WERE THEY?
THEY WERE CAPTAIN AMERICA.

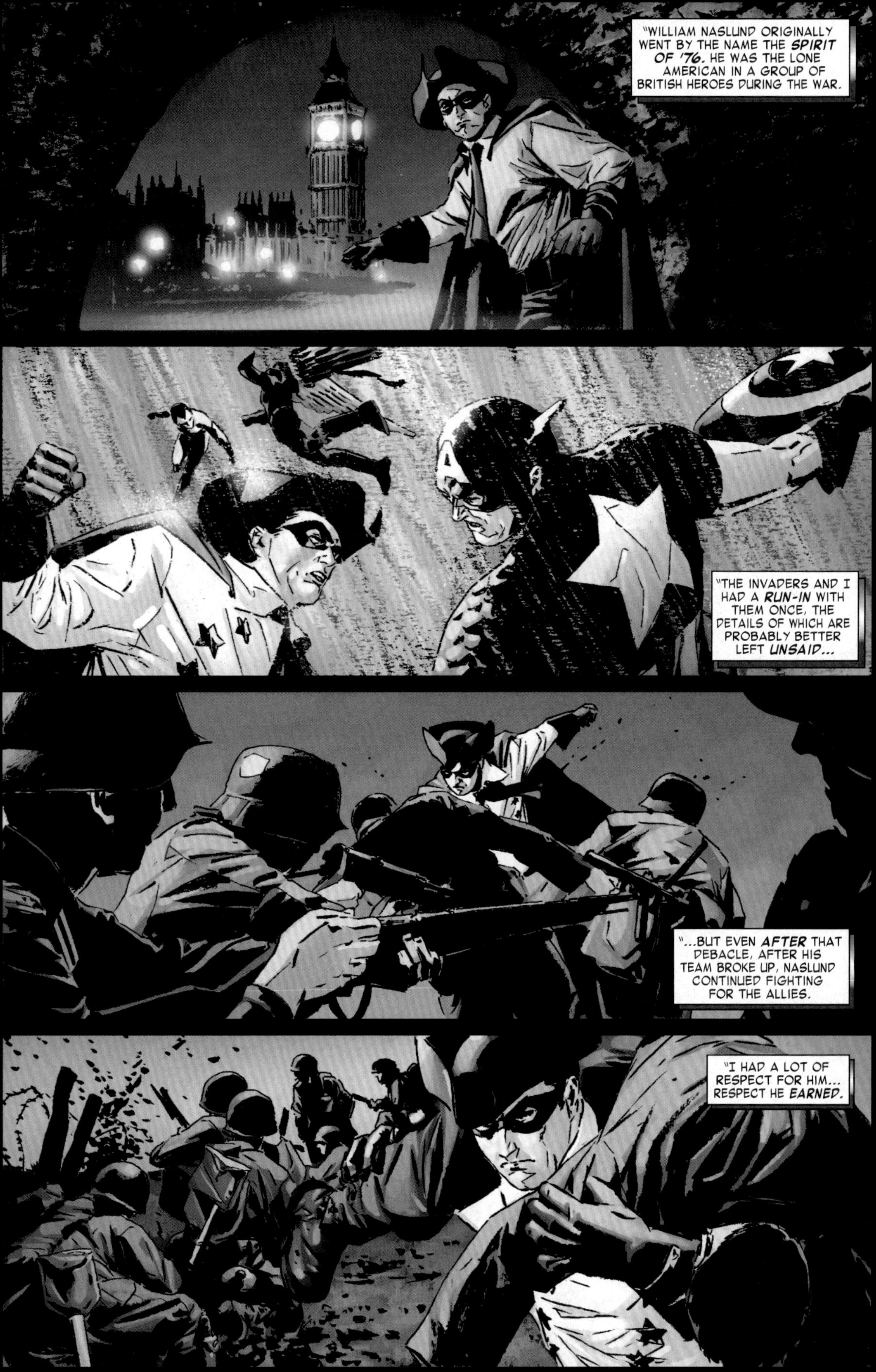
"WILLIAM NASLUND ORIGINALLY WENT BY THE NAME THE SPIRIT OF '76. HE WAS THE LONE AMERICAN IN A GROUP OF BRITISH HEROES DURING THE WAR.
"THE INVADERS AND I HAD A RUN-IN WITH THEM ONCE, THE DETAILS OF WHICH ARE PROBABLY BETTER LEFT UNSAID...
"...BUT EVEN AFTER THAT DEBACLE, AFTER HIS TEAM BROKE UP, NASLUND CONTINUED FIGHTING FOR THE ALLIES.
"I HAD A LOT OF RESPECT FOR HIM... RESPECT HE EARNED.

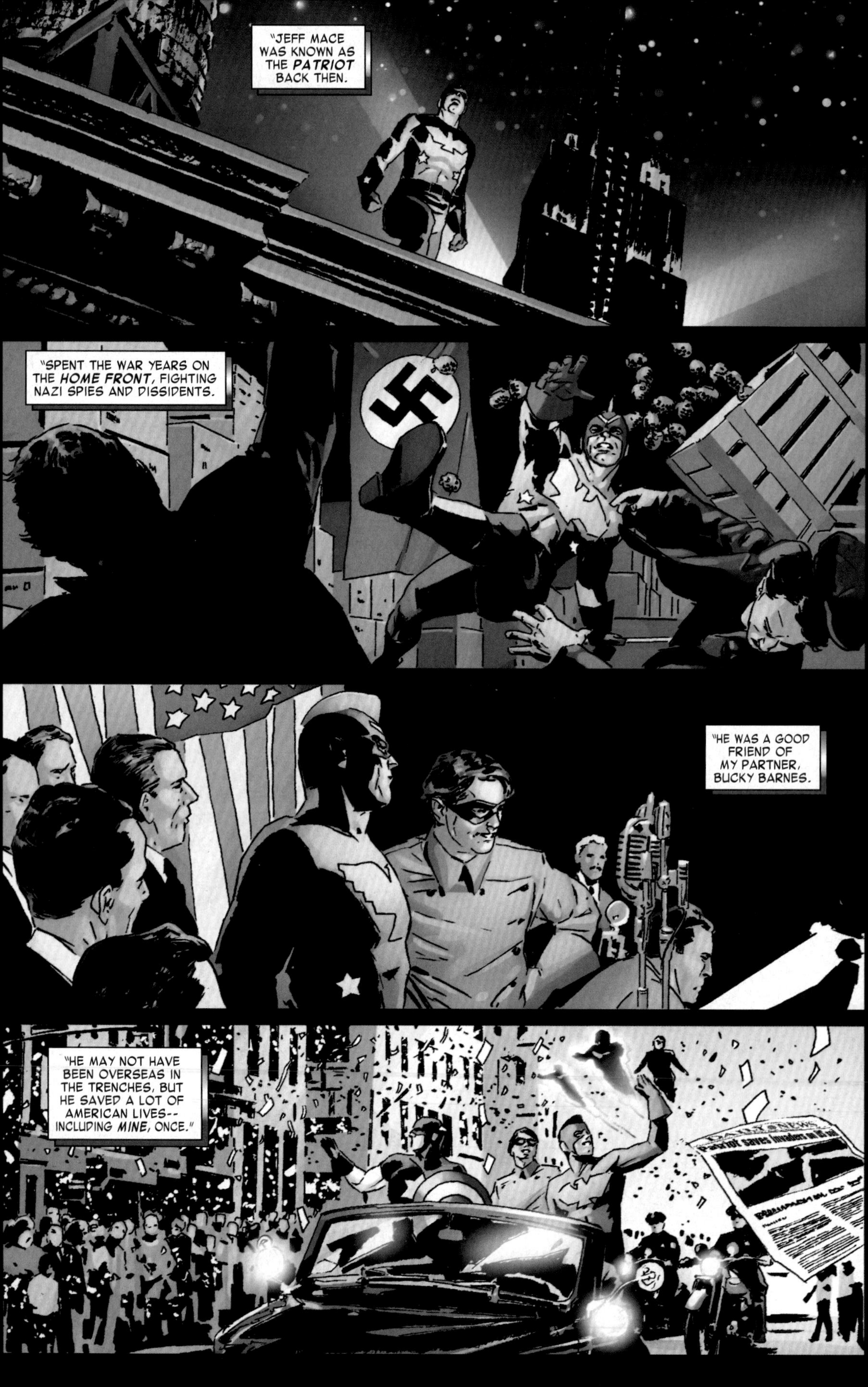
"JEFF MACE WAS KNOWN AS THE *PATRIOT* BACK THEN.
"SPENT THE WAR YEARS ON THE *HOME FRONT,* FIGHTING NAZI SPIES AND DISSIDENTS.
"HE WAS A GOOD FRIEND OF MY PARTNER, BUCKY BARNES.
"HE MAY NOT HAVE BEEN OVERSEAS IN THE TRENCHES, BUT HE SAVED A LOT OF AMERICAN LIVES--INCLUDING *MINE,* ONCE."

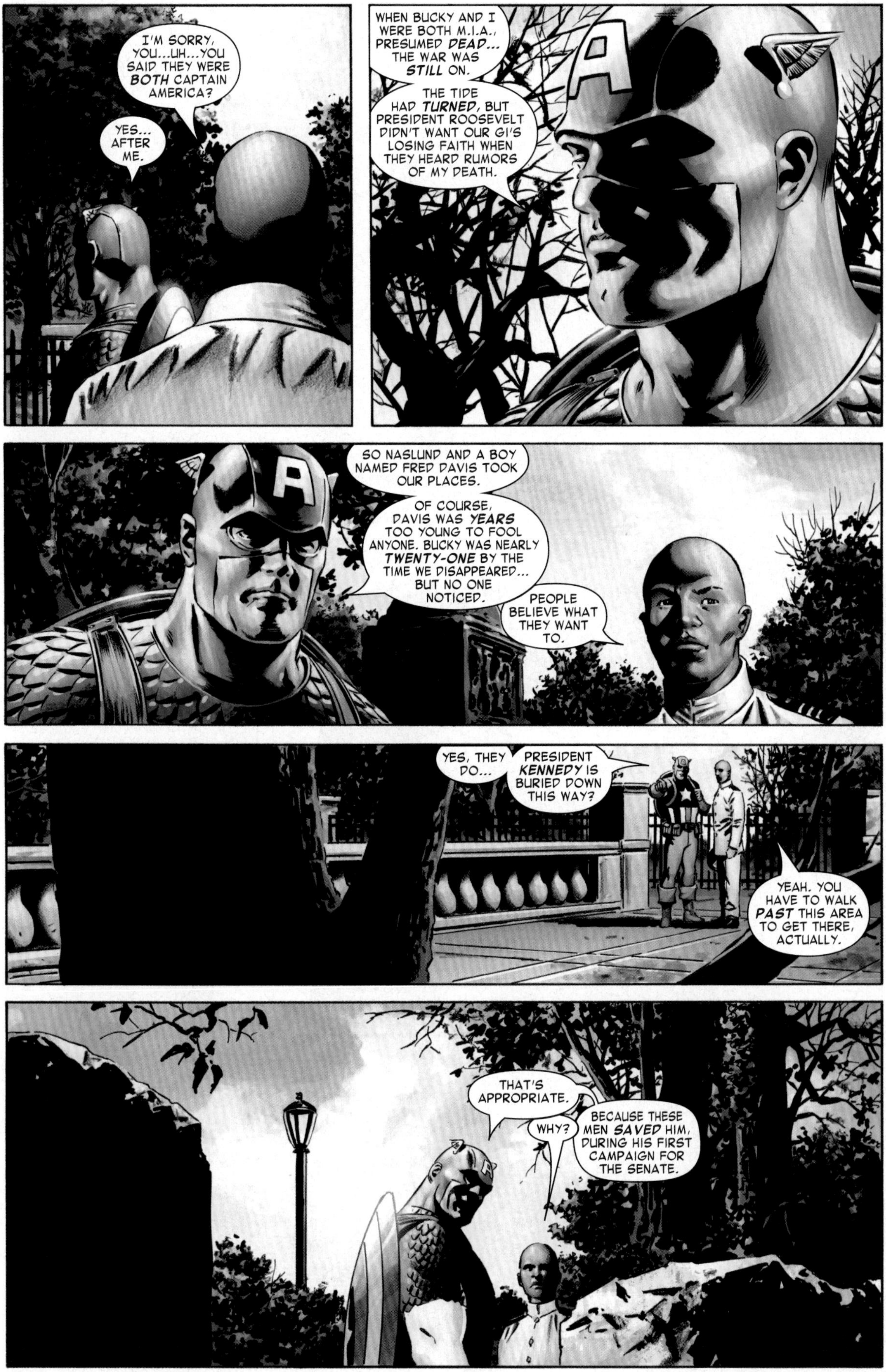
I'M SORRY, YOU...UH...YOU SAID THEY WERE *BOTH* CAPTAIN AMERICA?
YES... AFTER ME.
WHEN BUCKY AND I WERE BOTH M.I.A., PRESUMED *DEAD*... THE WAR WAS *STILL* ON.
THE TIDE HAD *TURNED*, BUT PRESIDENT ROOSEVELT DIDN'T WANT OUR GI'S LOSING FAITH WHEN THEY HEARD RUMORS OF MY DEATH.
SO NASLUND AND A BOY NAMED FRED DAVIS TOOK OUR PLACES.
OF COURSE, DAVIS WAS *YEARS* TOO YOUNG TO FOOL ANYONE. BUCKY WAS NEARLY *TWENTY-ONE* BY THE TIME WE DISAPPEARED... BUT NO ONE NOTICED.
PEOPLE BELIEVE WHAT THEY WANT TO.
YES, THEY DO...
PRESIDENT *KENNEDY* IS BURIED DOWN THIS WAY?
YEAH. YOU HAVE TO WALK *PAST* THIS AREA TO GET THERE, ACTUALLY.
THAT'S APPROPRIATE.
WHY?
BECAUSE THESE MEN *SAVED* HIM, DURING HIS FIRST CAMPAIGN FOR THE SENATE.

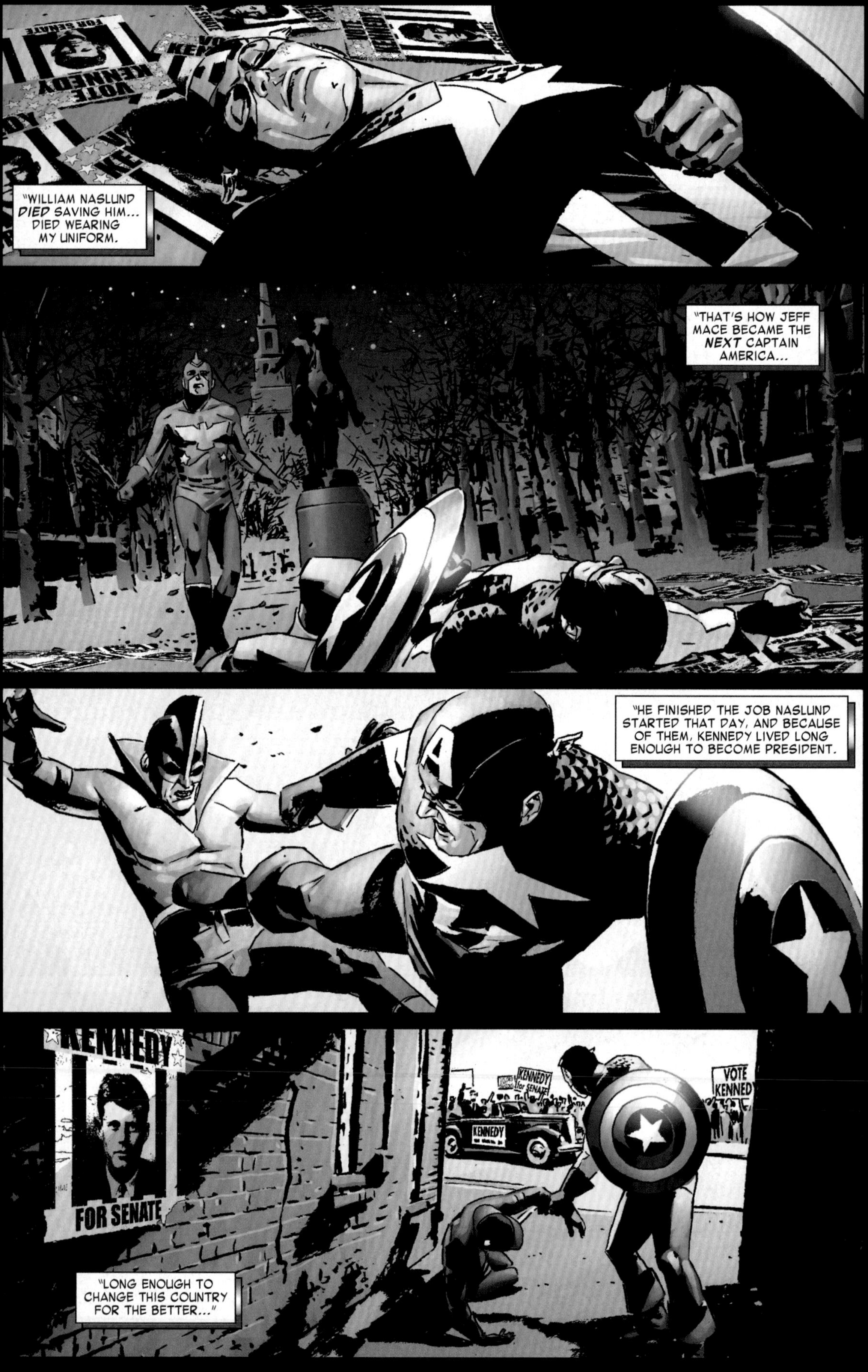
"WILLIAM NASLUND *DIED* SAVING HIM... DIED WEARING MY UNIFORM.
"THAT'S HOW JEFF MACE BECAME THE *NEXT* CAPTAIN AMERICA...
"HE FINISHED THE JOB NASLUND STARTED THAT DAY, AND BECAUSE OF THEM, KENNEDY LIVED LONG ENOUGH TO BECOME PRESIDENT.
KENNEDY
FOR SENATE
KENNEDY for SENATE
KENNEDY
VOTE KENNEDY
"LONG ENOUGH TO CHANGE THIS COUNTRY FOR THE BETTER..."

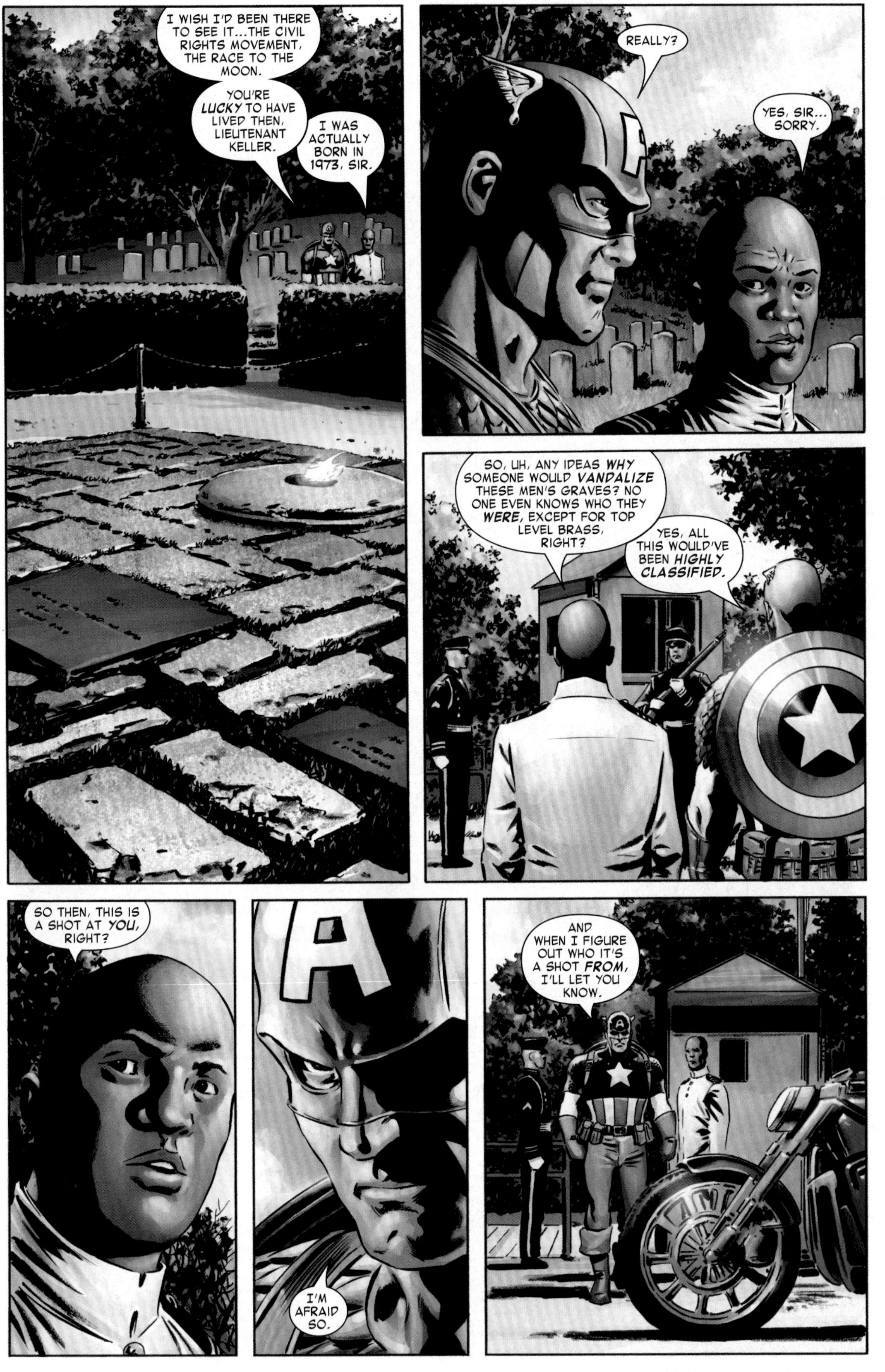
I WISH I'D BEEN THERE TO SEE IT...THE CIVIL RIGHTS MOVEMENT, THE RACE TO THE MOON.
YOU'RE LUCKY TO HAVE LIVED THEN, LIEUTENANT KELLER.
I WAS ACTUALLY BORN IN 1973, SIR.
REALLY?
YES, SIR... SORRY.
SO, UH, ANY IDEAS WHY SOMEONE WOULD VANDALIZE THESE MEN'S GRAVES? NO ONE EVEN KNOWS WHO THEY WERE, EXCEPT FOR TOP LEVEL BRASS, RIGHT?
YES, ALL THIS WOULD'VE BEEN HIGHLY CLASSIFIED.
SO THEN, THIS IS A SHOT AT YOU, RIGHT?
I'M AFRAID SO.
AND WHEN I FIGURE OUT WHO IT'S A SHOT FROM, I'LL LET YOU KNOW.

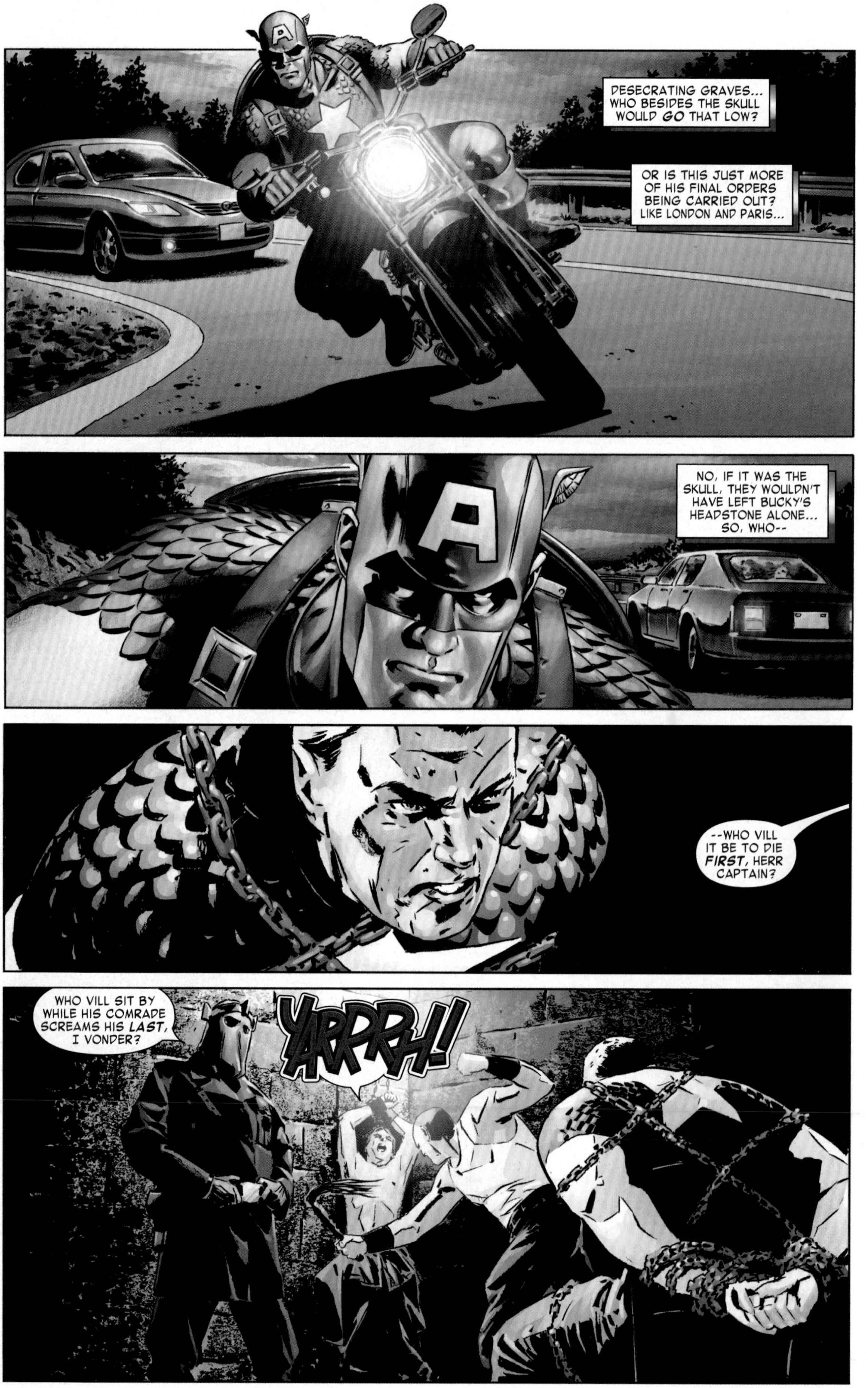
DESECRATING GRAVES... WHO BESIDES THE SKULL WOULD *GO* THAT LOW?
OR IS THIS JUST MORE OF HIS FINAL ORDERS BEING CARRIED OUT? LIKE LONDON AND PARIS...
NO, IF IT WAS THE SKULL, THEY WOULDN'T HAVE LEFT BUCKY'S HEADSTONE ALONE... SO, WHO--
--WHO VILL IT BE TO DIE *FIRST*, HERR CAPTAIN?
WHO VILL SIT BY WHILE HIS COMRADE SCREAMS HIS *LAST*, I VONDER?
YARRRH!

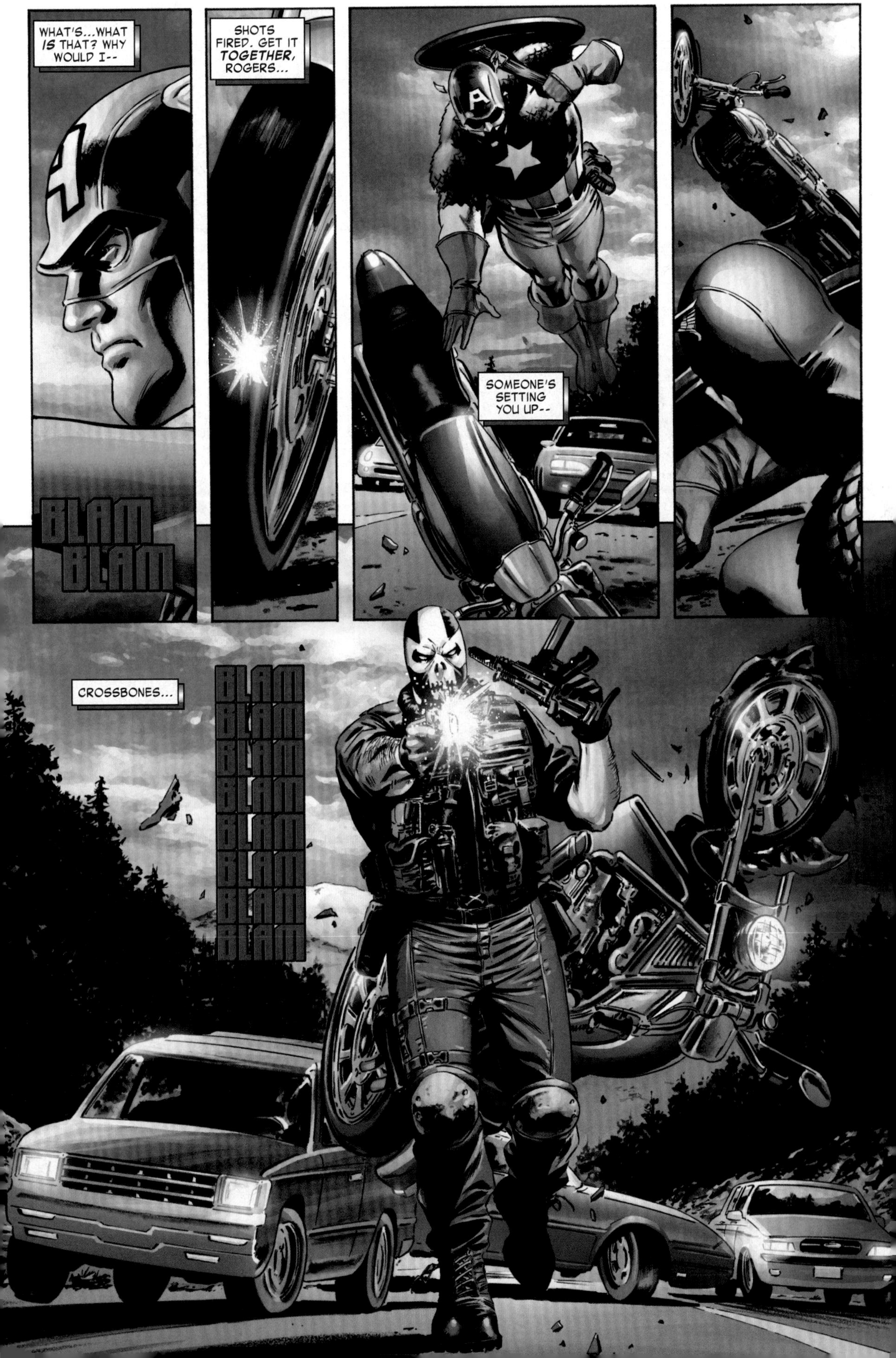
WHAT'S...WHAT IS THAT? WHY WOULD I--
BLAM BLAM
SHOTS FIRED. GET IT TOGETHER, ROGERS...
SOMEONE'S SETTING YOU UP--
CROSSBONES...
BLAM BLAM BLAM BLAM BLAM BLAM BLAM BLAM

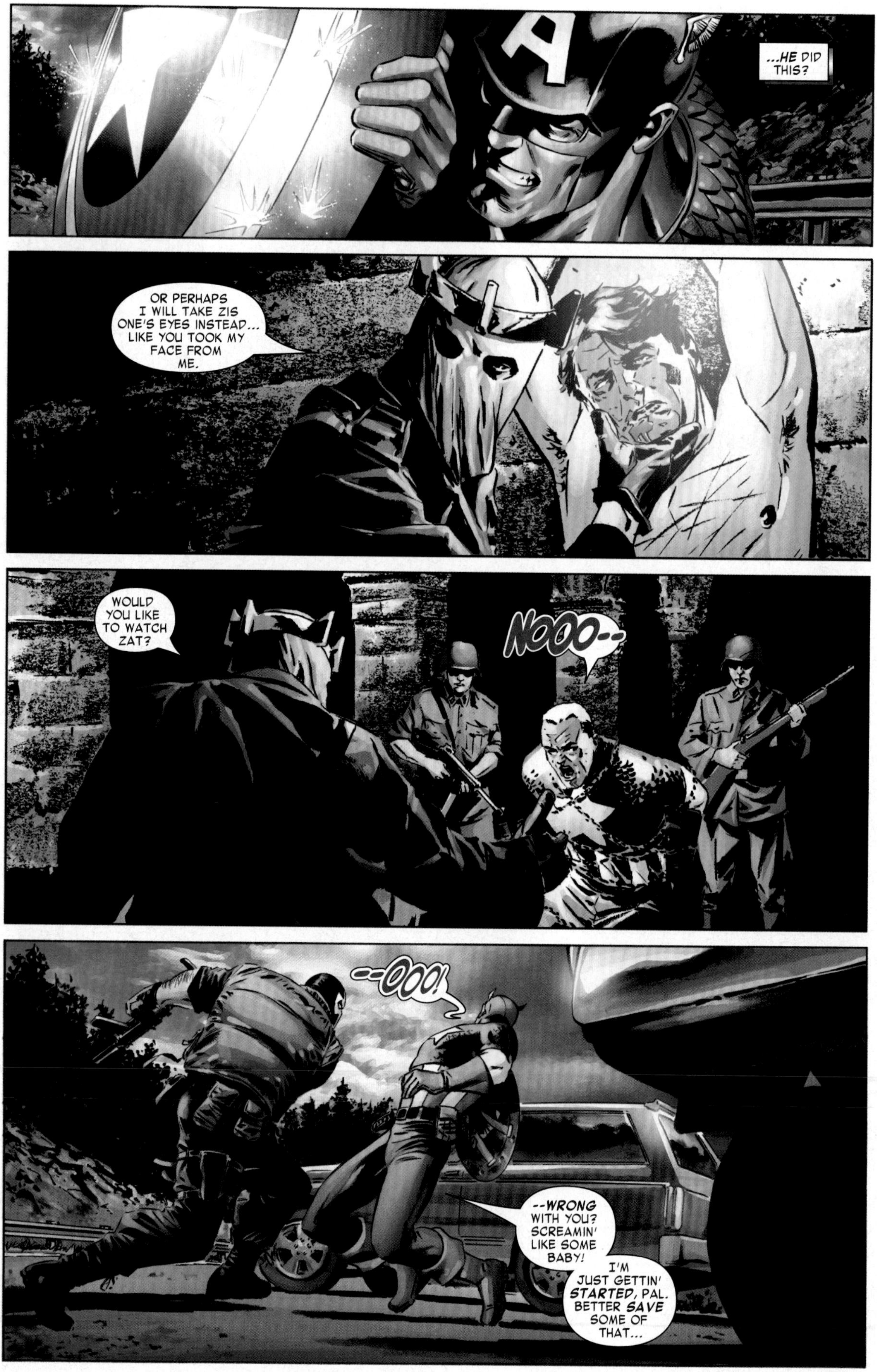
...HE DID THIS?
OR PERHAPS I WILL TAKE ZIS ONE'S EYES INSTEAD... LIKE YOU TOOK MY FACE FROM ME.
WOULD YOU LIKE TO WATCH ZAT?
NOOO--
--OOO!
--WRONG WITH YOU? SCREAMIN' LIKE SOME BABY!
I'M JUST GETTIN' STARTED, PAL. BETTER SAVE SOME OF THAT...

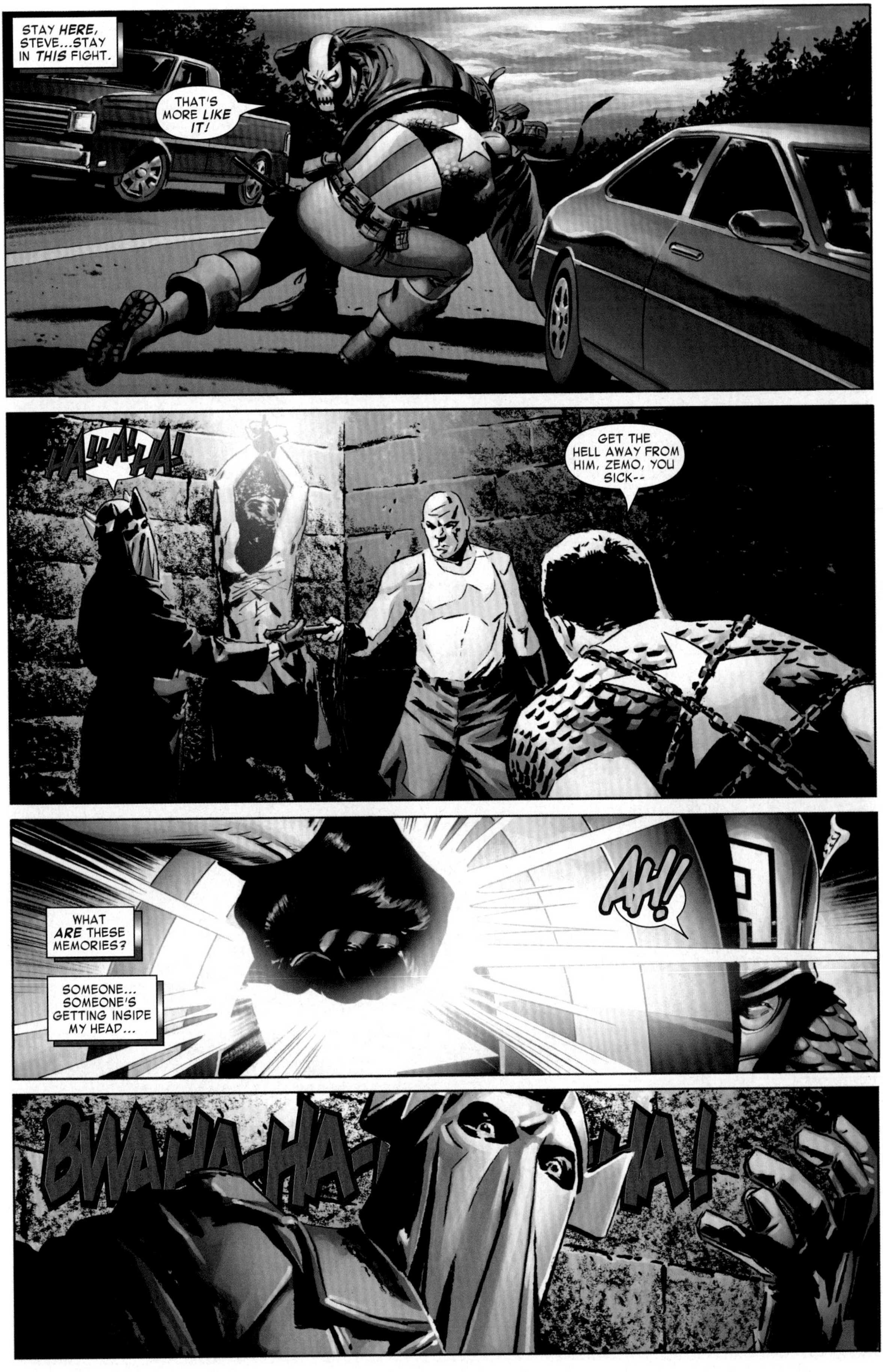
STAY HERE, STEVE...STAY IN THIS FIGHT.
THAT'S MORE LIKE IT!
HA-HA-HA!
GET THE HELL AWAY FROM HIM, ZEMO, YOU SICK--
WHAT ARE THESE MEMORIES?
SOMEONE... SOMEONE'S GETTING INSIDE MY HEAD...
AH!
BWAHA-HA-HA-HA!

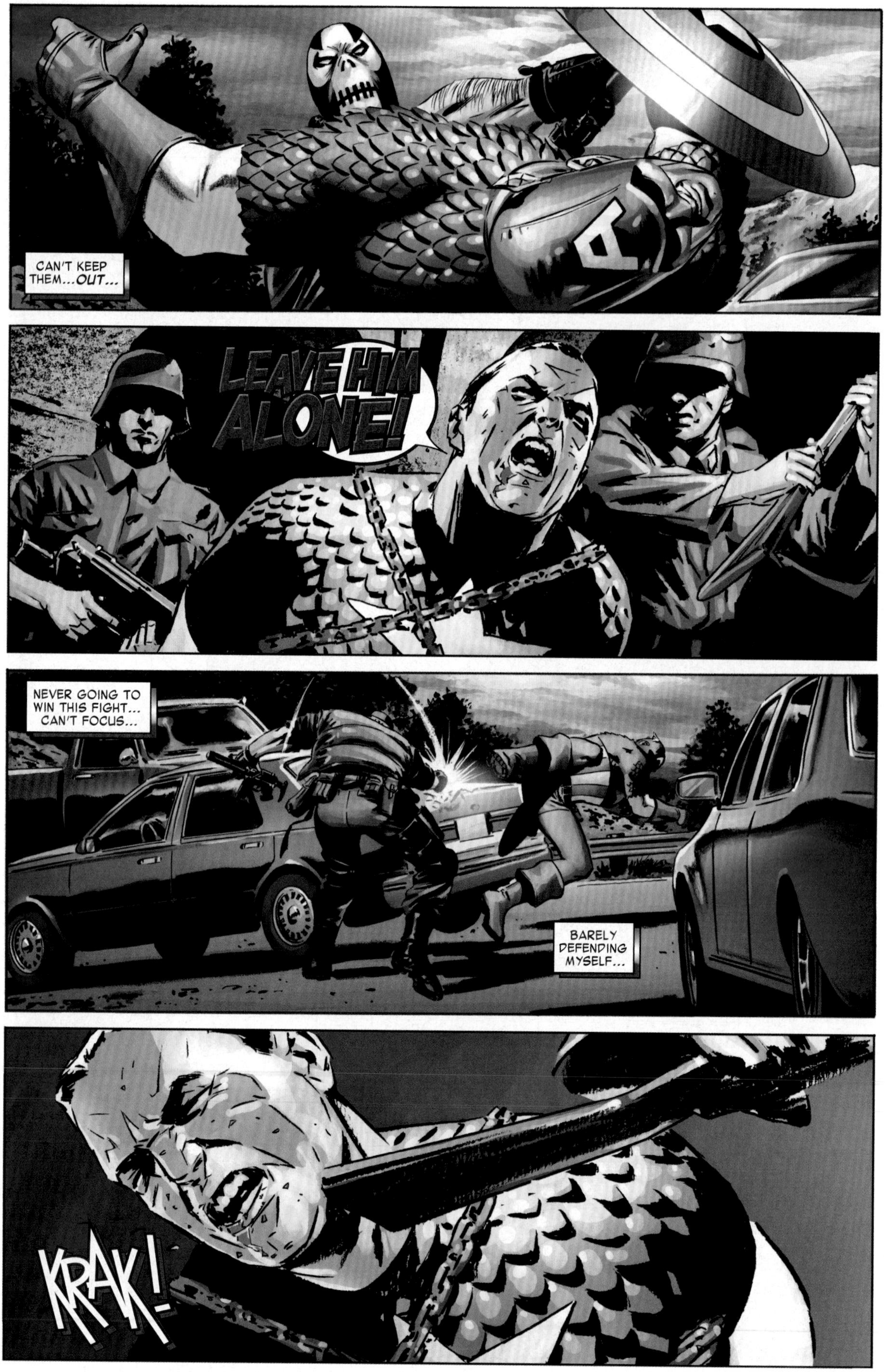
CAN'T KEEP THEM...OUT...
LEAVE HIM ALONE!
NEVER GOING TO WIN THIS FIGHT... CAN'T FOCUS...
BARELY DEFENDING MYSELF...
KRAK!

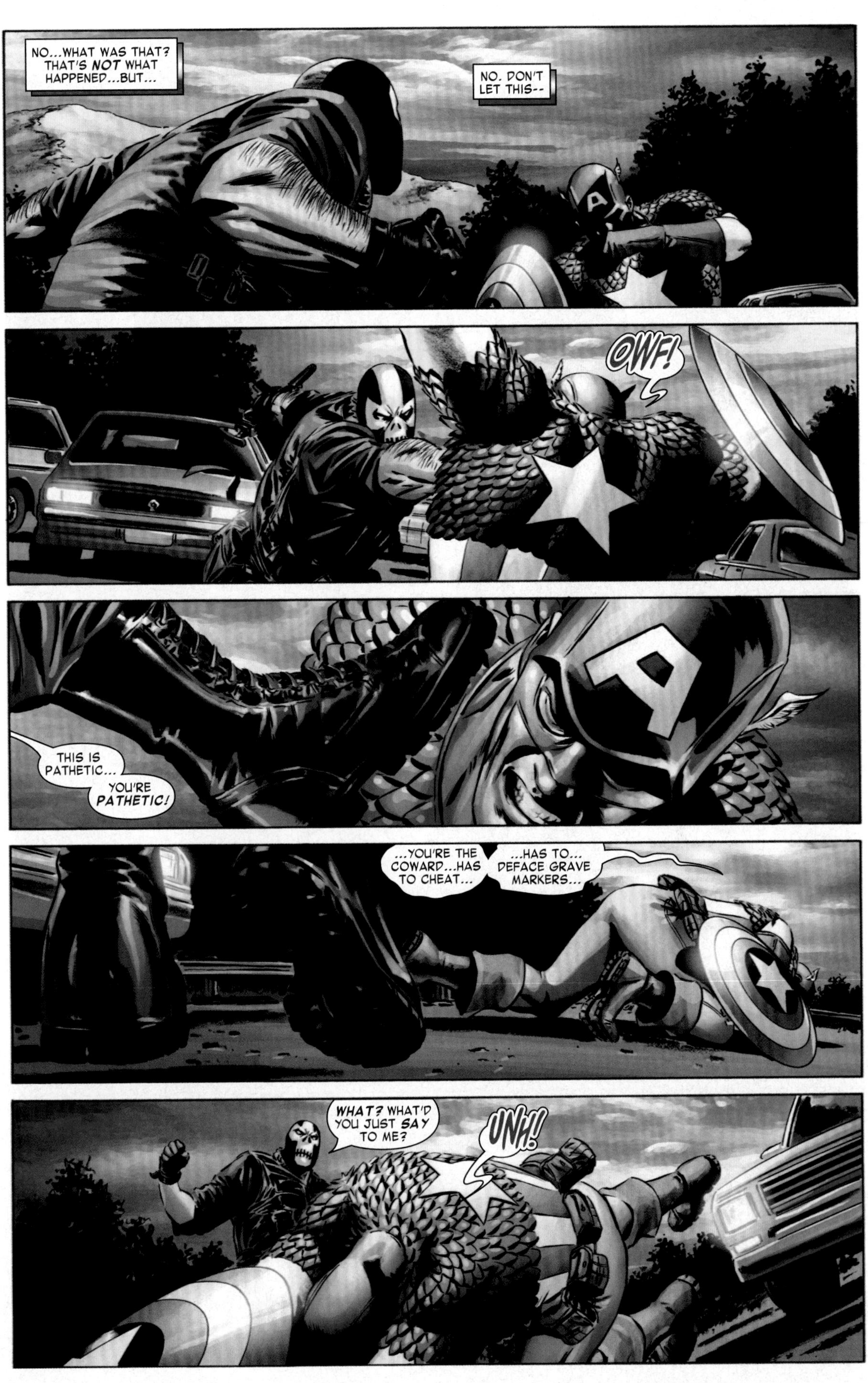

NO...WHAT WAS THAT? THAT'S NOT WHAT HAPPENED...BUT...
NO. DON'T LET THIS--
OWF!
THIS IS PATHETIC...
YOU'RE PATHETIC!
...YOU'RE THE COWARD...HAS TO CHEAT...
...HAS TO... DEFACE GRAVE MARKERS...
WHAT? WHAT'D YOU JUST SAY TO ME?
UNH!

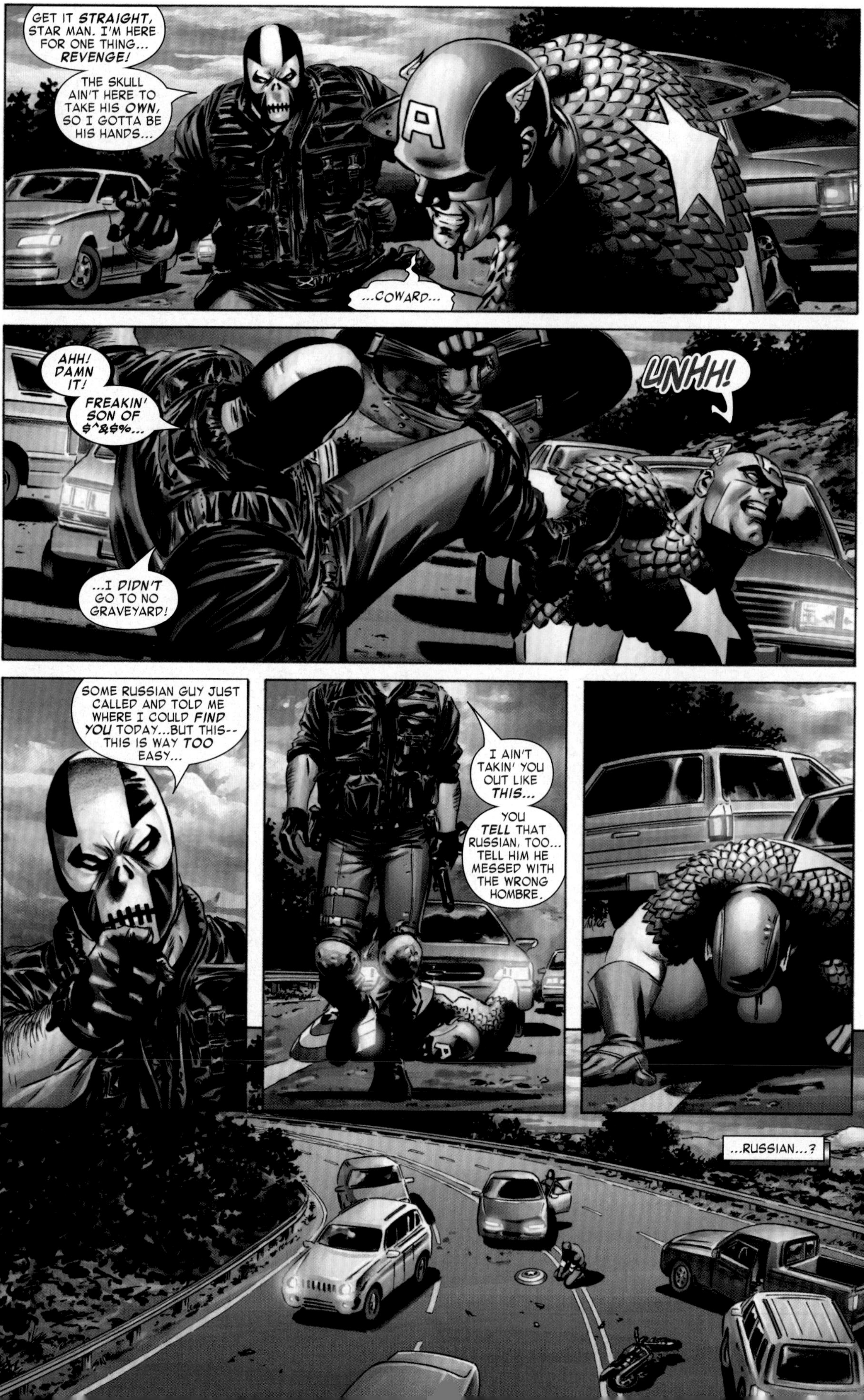
GET IT STRAIGHT, STAR MAN. I'M HERE FOR ONE THING... REVENGE!
THE SKULL AIN'T HERE TO TAKE HIS OWN, SO I GOTTA BE HIS HANDS...
...COWARD...
AHH! DAMN IT!
FREAKIN' SON OF $^&$%...
UNHH!
...I DIDN'T GO TO NO GRAVEYARD!
SOME RUSSIAN GUY JUST CALLED AND TOLD ME WHERE I COULD FIND YOU TODAY...BUT THIS-- THIS IS WAY TOO EASY...
I AIN'T TAKIN' YOU OUT LIKE THIS...
YOU TELL THAT RUSSIAN, TOO... TELL HIM HE MESSED WITH THE WRONG HOMBRE.
...RUSSIAN...?

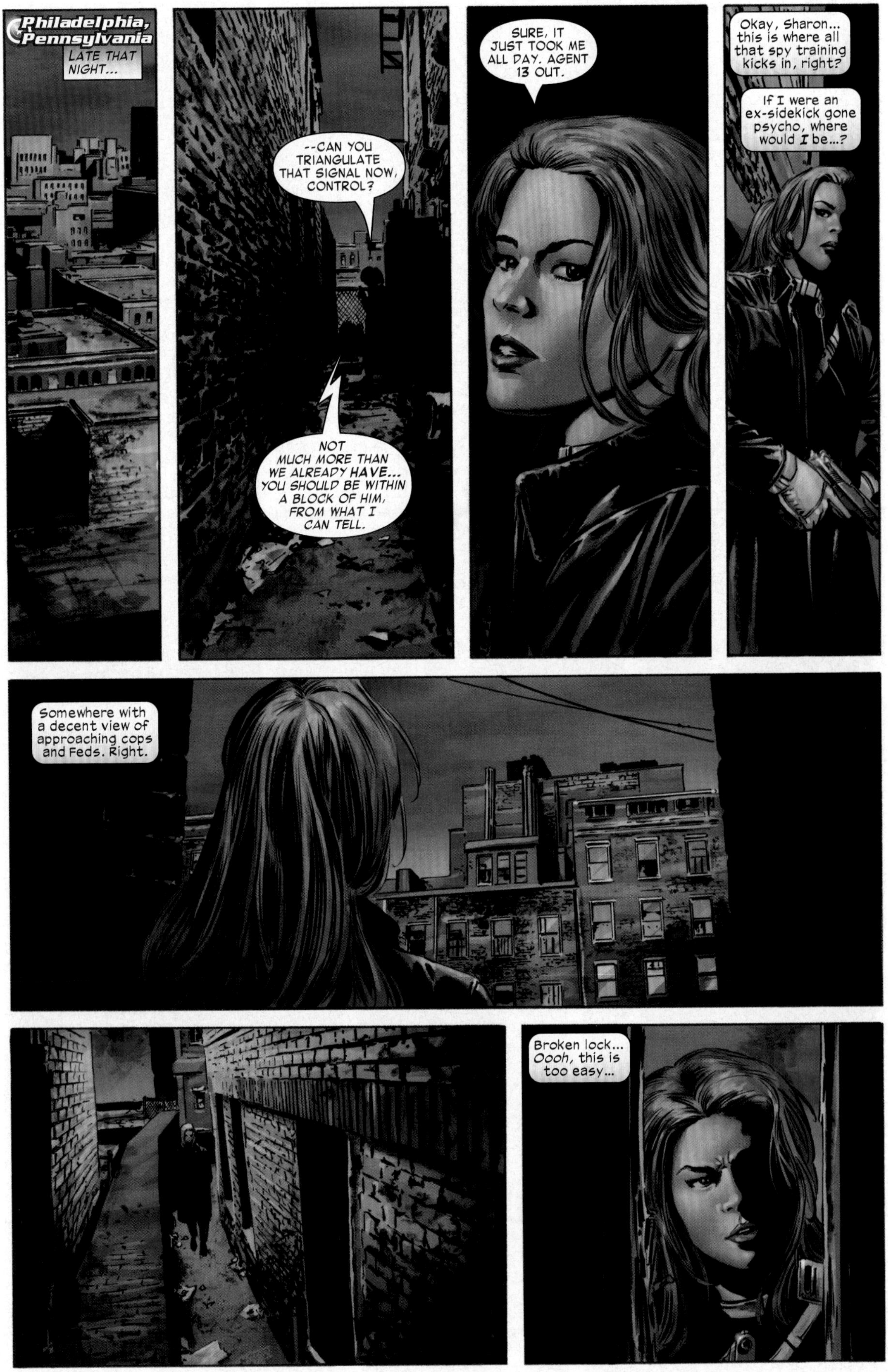
Philadelphia, Pennsylvania
LATE THAT NIGHT...
--CAN YOU TRIANGULATE THAT SIGNAL NOW, CONTROL?
NOT MUCH MORE THAN WE ALREADY HAVE... YOU SHOULD BE WITHIN A BLOCK OF HIM, FROM WHAT I CAN TELL.
SURE, IT JUST TOOK ME ALL DAY. AGENT 13 OUT.
Okay, Sharon... this is where all that spy training kicks in, right?
If I were an ex-sidekick gone psycho, where would I be...?
Somewhere with a decent view of approaching cops and Feds. Right.
Broken lock... Oooh, this is too easy...

Easy, girl... remember, Fury said just get an eyeball and then back off.

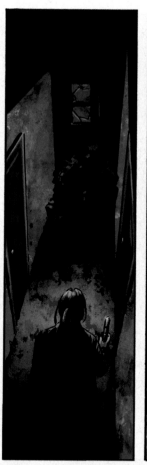

AHHH!

WRONG DOOR.

WHU--?

CRACK

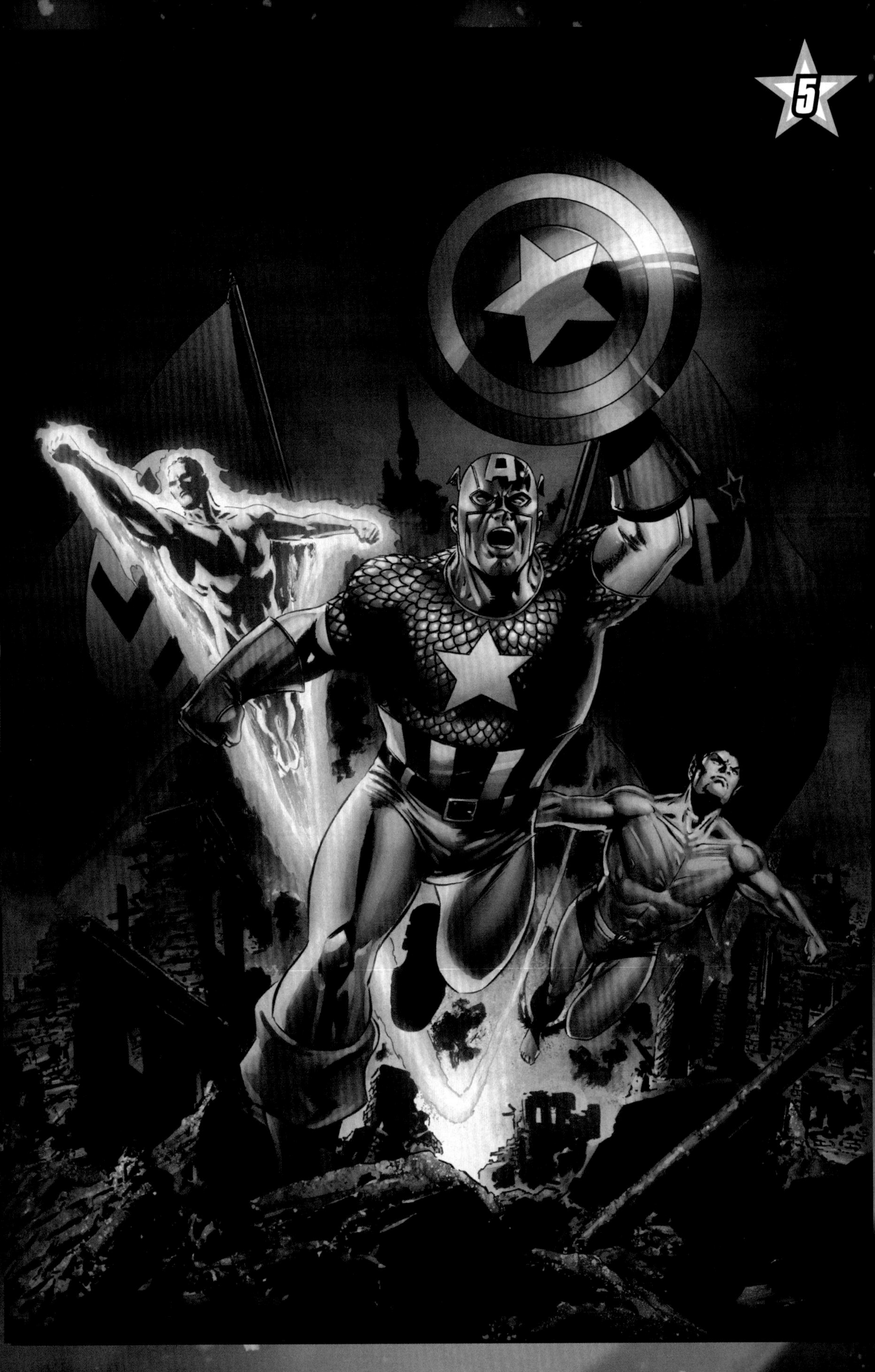
5

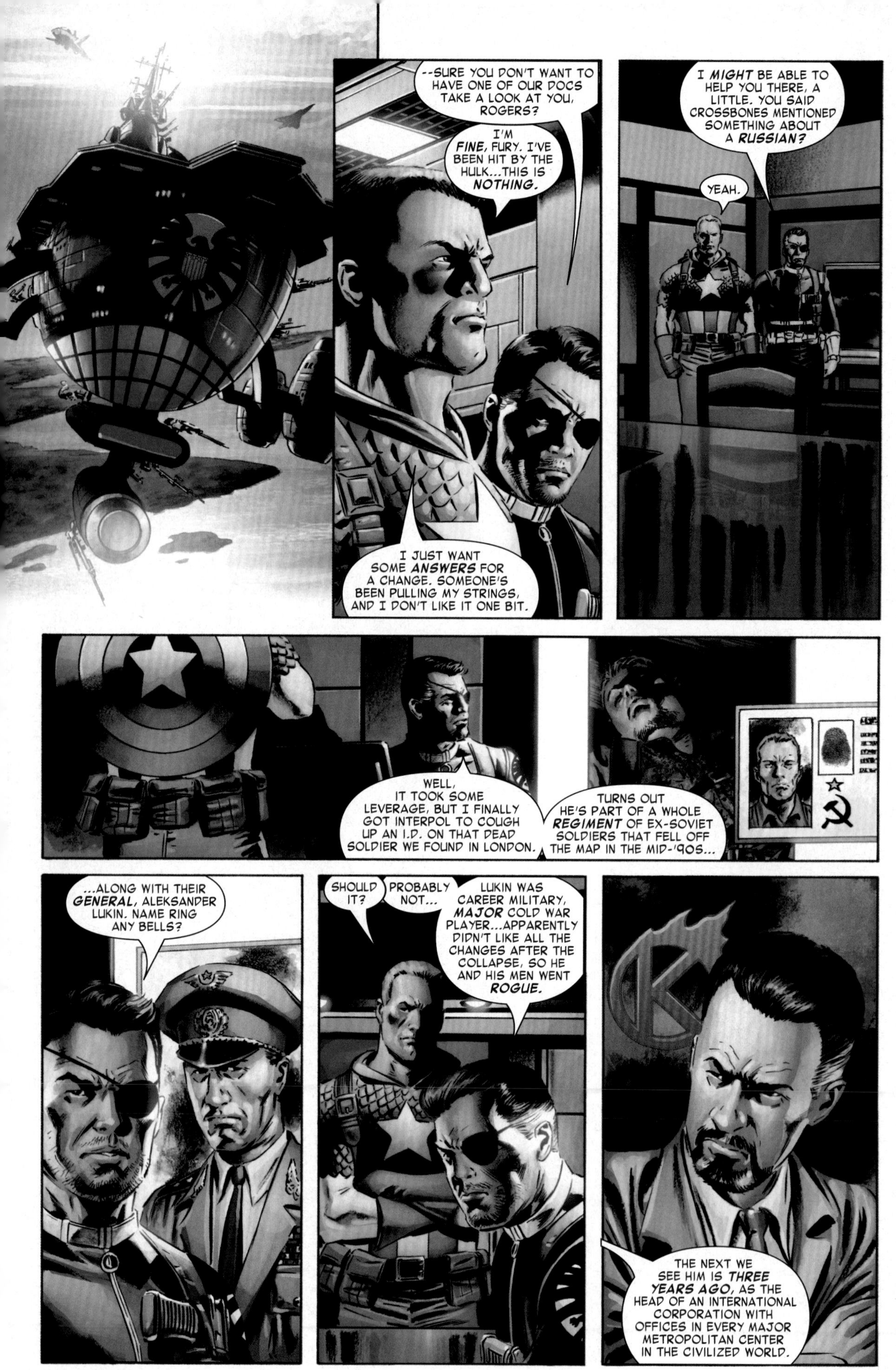
--SURE YOU DON'T WANT TO HAVE ONE OF OUR DOCS TAKE A LOOK AT YOU, ROGERS?
I'M FINE, FURY. I'VE BEEN HIT BY THE HULK...THIS IS NOTHING.
I JUST WANT SOME ANSWERS FOR A CHANGE. SOMEONE'S BEEN PULLING MY STRINGS, AND I DON'T LIKE IT ONE BIT.
I MIGHT BE ABLE TO HELP YOU THERE, A LITTLE. YOU SAID CROSSBONES MENTIONED SOMETHING ABOUT A RUSSIAN?
YEAH.
WELL, IT TOOK SOME LEVERAGE, BUT I FINALLY GOT INTERPOL TO COUGH UP AN I.D. ON THAT DEAD SOLDIER WE FOUND IN LONDON.
TURNS OUT HE'S PART OF A WHOLE REGIMENT OF EX-SOVIET SOLDIERS THAT FELL OFF THE MAP IN THE MID-'90S...
...ALONG WITH THEIR GENERAL, ALEKSANDER LUKIN. NAME RING ANY BELLS?
SHOULD IT?
PROBABLY NOT...
LUKIN WAS CAREER MILITARY, MAJOR COLD WAR PLAYER...APPARENTLY DIDN'T LIKE ALL THE CHANGES AFTER THE COLLAPSE, SO HE AND HIS MEN WENT ROGUE.
THE NEXT WE SEE HIM IS THREE YEARS AGO, AS THE HEAD OF AN INTERNATIONAL CORPORATION WITH OFFICES IN EVERY MAJOR METROPOLITAN CENTER IN THE CIVILIZED WORLD.

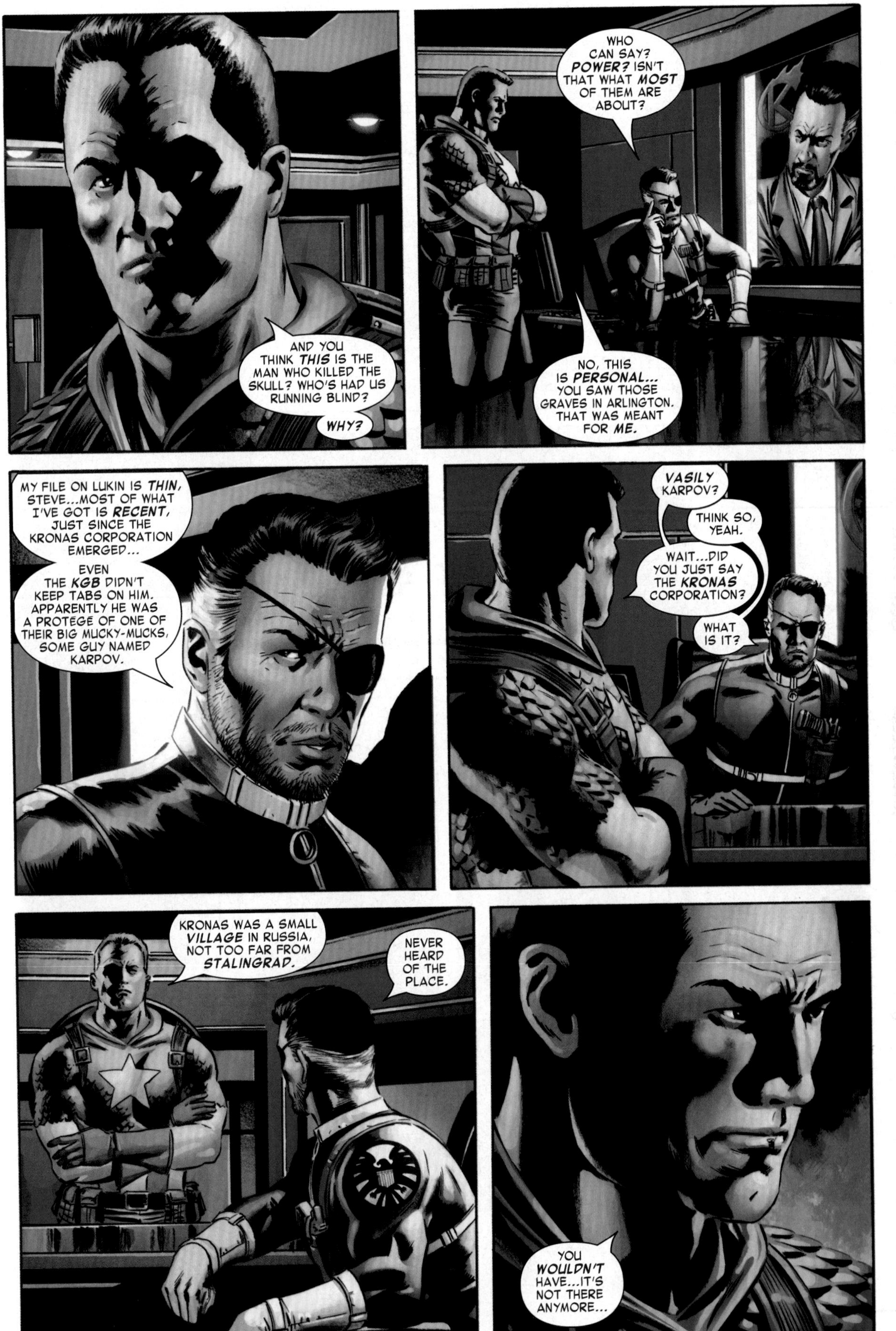
AND YOU THINK THIS IS THE MAN WHO KILLED THE SKULL? WHO'S HAD US RUNNING BLIND?
WHY?
WHO CAN SAY? POWER? ISN'T THAT WHAT MOST OF THEM ARE ABOUT?
NO, THIS IS PERSONAL... YOU SAW THOSE GRAVES IN ARLINGTON. THAT WAS MEANT FOR ME.
MY FILE ON LUKIN IS THIN, STEVE...MOST OF WHAT I'VE GOT IS RECENT, JUST SINCE THE KRONAS CORPORATION EMERGED...
EVEN THE KGB DIDN'T KEEP TABS ON HIM. APPARENTLY HE WAS A PROTEGÉ OF ONE OF THEIR BIG MUCKY-MUCKS, SOME GUY NAMED KARPOV.
VASILY KARPOV?
THINK SO, YEAH.
WAIT...DID YOU JUST SAY THE KRONAS CORPORATION?
WHAT IS IT?
KRONAS WAS A SMALL VILLAGE IN RUSSIA, NOT TOO FAR FROM STALINGRAD.
NEVER HEARD OF THE PLACE.
YOU WOULDN'T HAVE...IT'S NOT THERE ANYMORE...

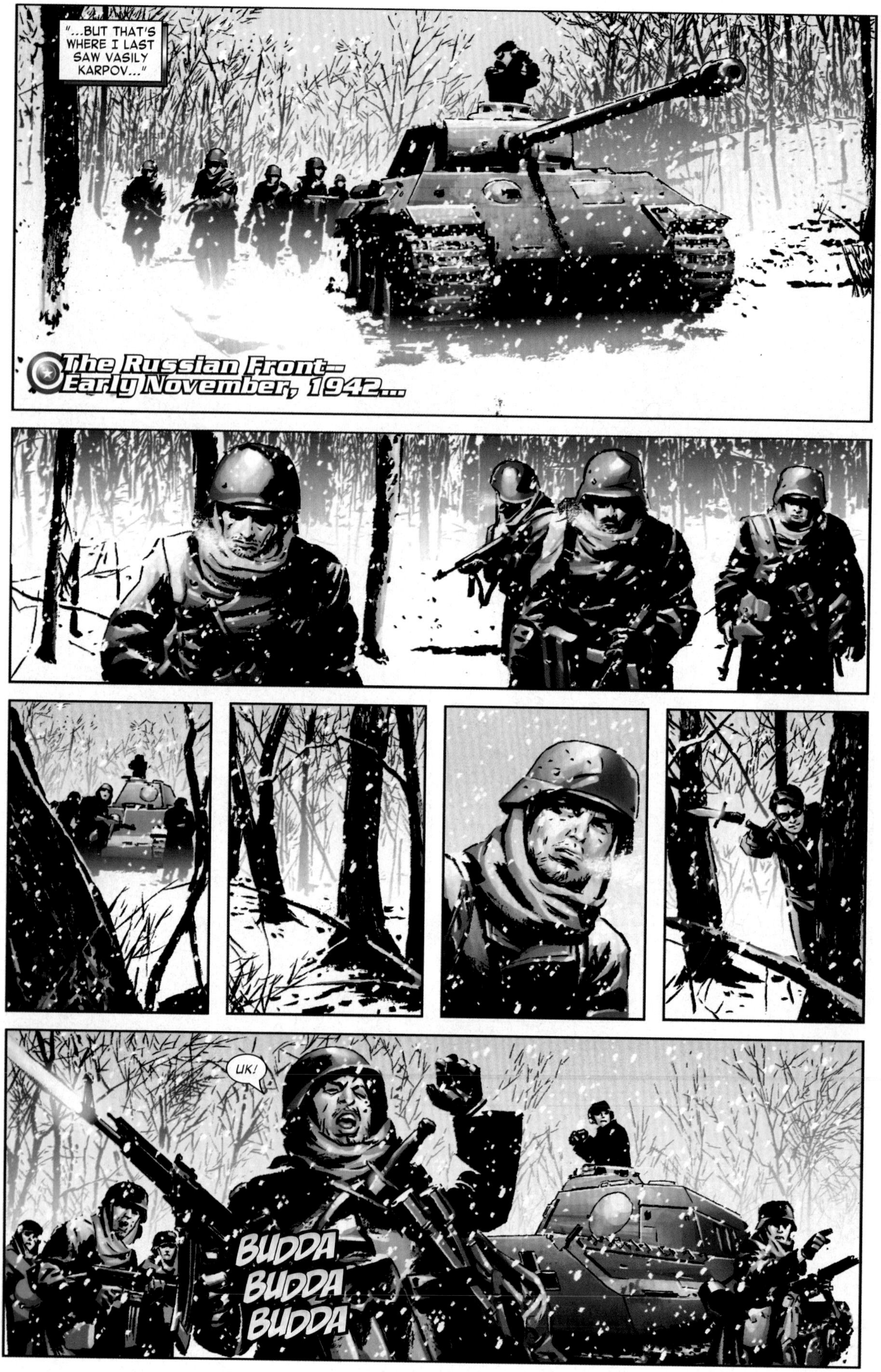
"...BUT THAT'S WHERE I LAST SAW VASILY KARPOV..."
The Russian Front-- Early November, 1942...
UK!
BUDDA BUDDA BUDDA

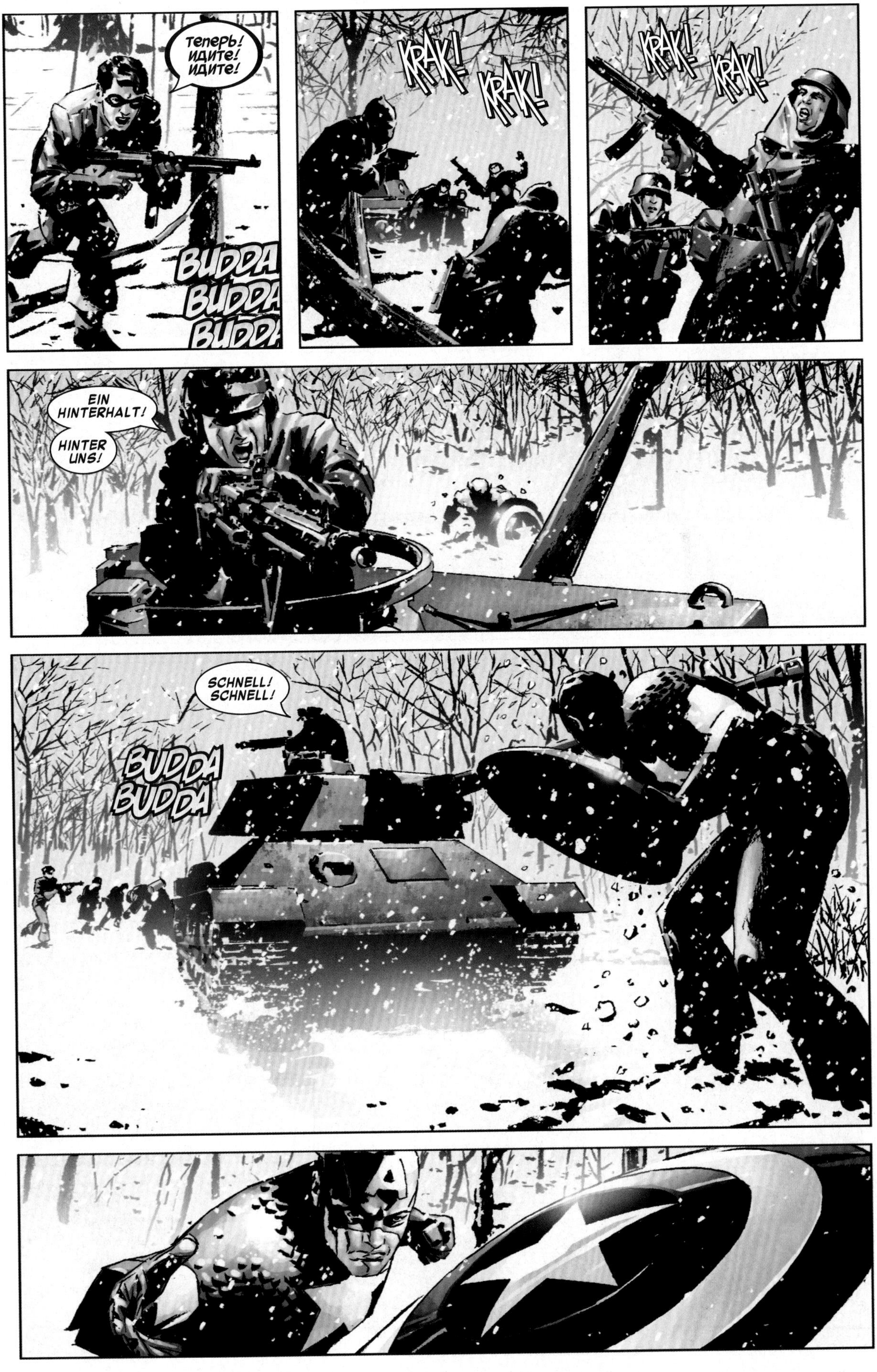
теперь! идите! идите!
BUDDA BUDDA BUDDA
KRAK! KRAK!
KRAK! KRAK!
EIN HINTERHALT!
HINTER UNS!
SCHNELL! SCHNELL!
BUDDA BUDDA

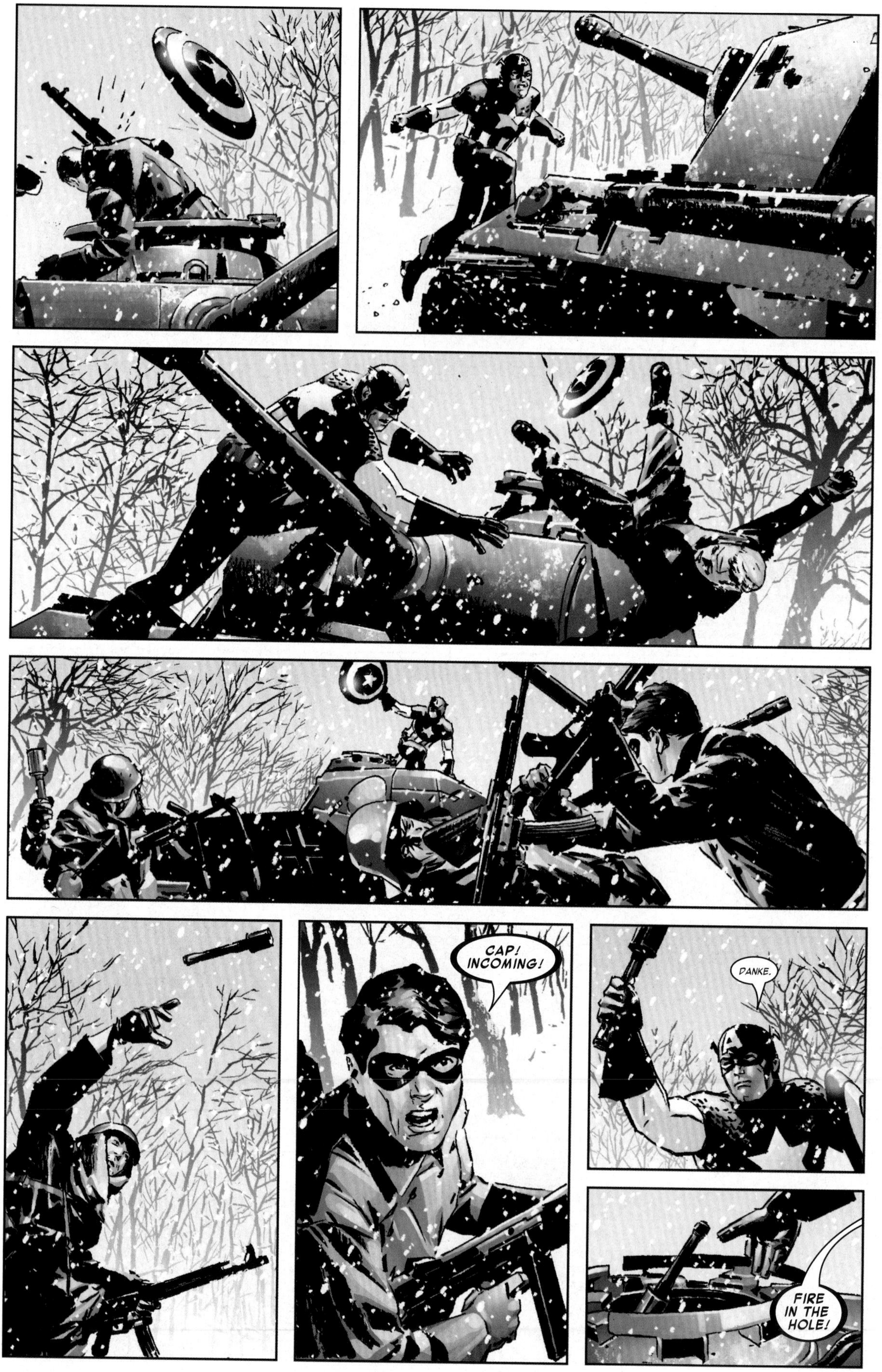
CAP! INCOMING!
DANKE.
FIRE IN THE HOLE!

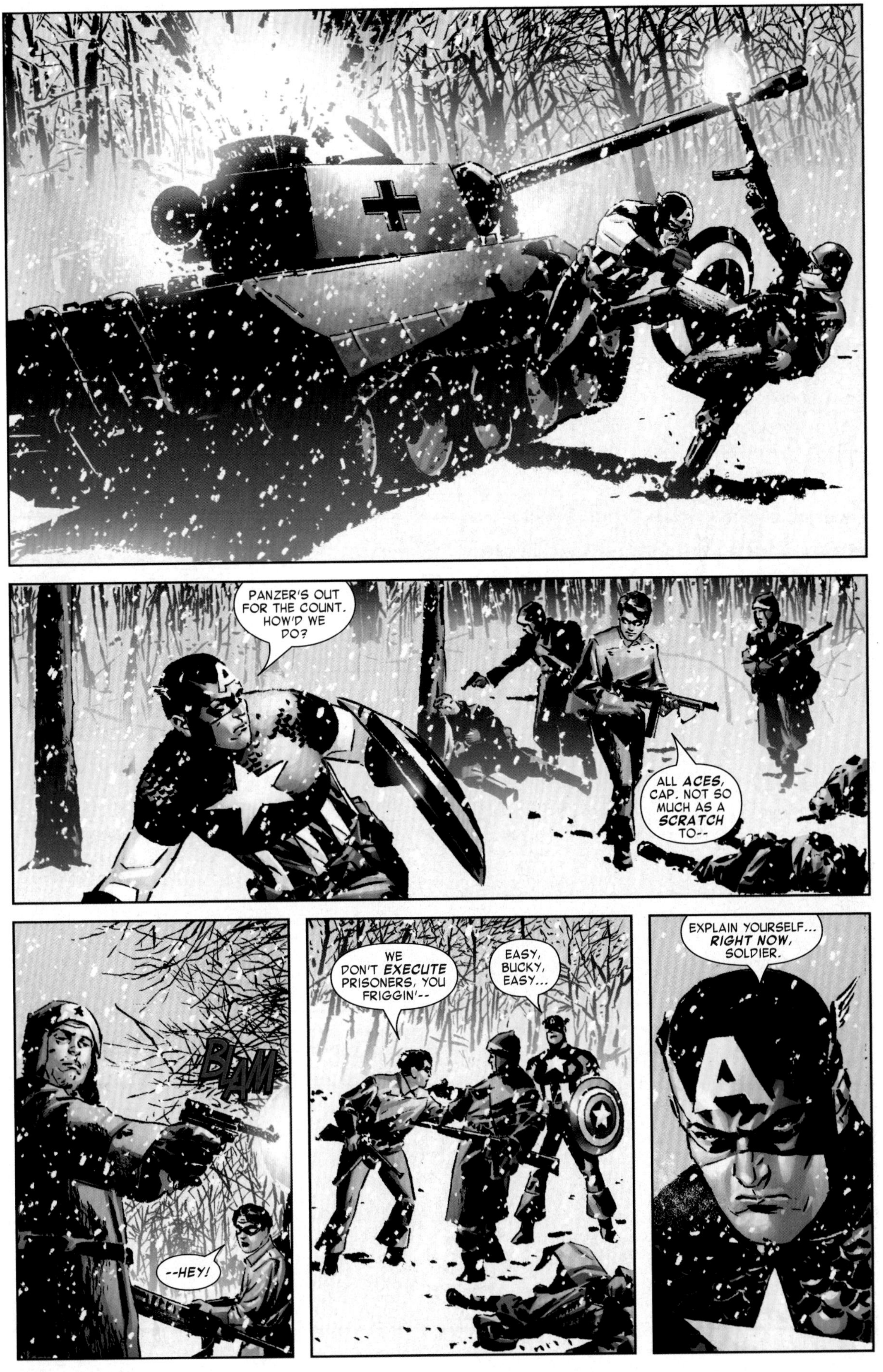
PANZER'S OUT FOR THE COUNT. HOW'D WE DO?
ALL ACES, CAP. NOT SO MUCH AS A SCRATCH TO--
BLAM
--HEY!
WE DON'T EXECUTE PRISONERS, YOU FRIGGIN'--
EASY, BUCKY, EASY...
EXPLAIN YOURSELF... RIGHT NOW, SOLDIER.

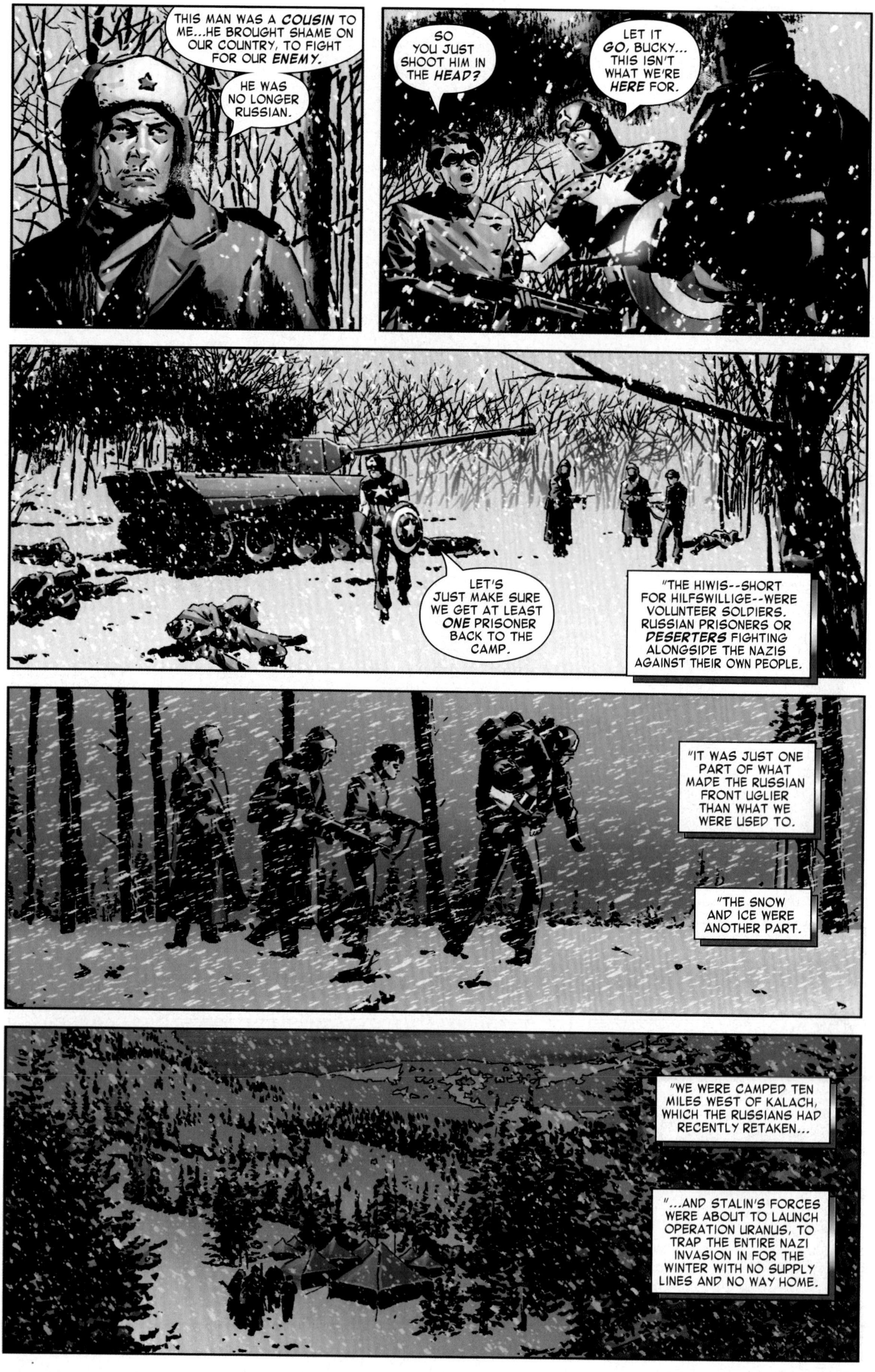
THIS MAN WAS A COUSIN TO ME...HE BROUGHT SHAME ON OUR COUNTRY, TO FIGHT FOR OUR ENEMY.
HE WAS NO LONGER RUSSIAN.
SO YOU JUST SHOOT HIM IN THE HEAD?
LET IT GO, BUCKY... THIS ISN'T WHAT WE'RE HERE FOR.
LET'S JUST MAKE SURE WE GET AT LEAST ONE PRISONER BACK TO THE CAMP.
"THE HIWIS--SHORT FOR HILFSWILLIGE--WERE VOLUNTEER SOLDIERS. RUSSIAN PRISONERS OR DESERTERS FIGHTING ALONGSIDE THE NAZIS AGAINST THEIR OWN PEOPLE.
"IT WAS JUST ONE PART OF WHAT MADE THE RUSSIAN FRONT UGLIER THAN WHAT WE WERE USED TO.
"THE SNOW AND ICE WERE ANOTHER PART.
"WE WERE CAMPED TEN MILES WEST OF KALACH, WHICH THE RUSSIANS HAD RECENTLY RETAKEN...
"...AND STALIN'S FORCES WERE ABOUT TO LAUNCH OPERATION URANUS, TO TRAP THE ENTIRE NAZI INVASION IN FOR THE WINTER WITH NO SUPPLY LINES AND NO WAY HOME.

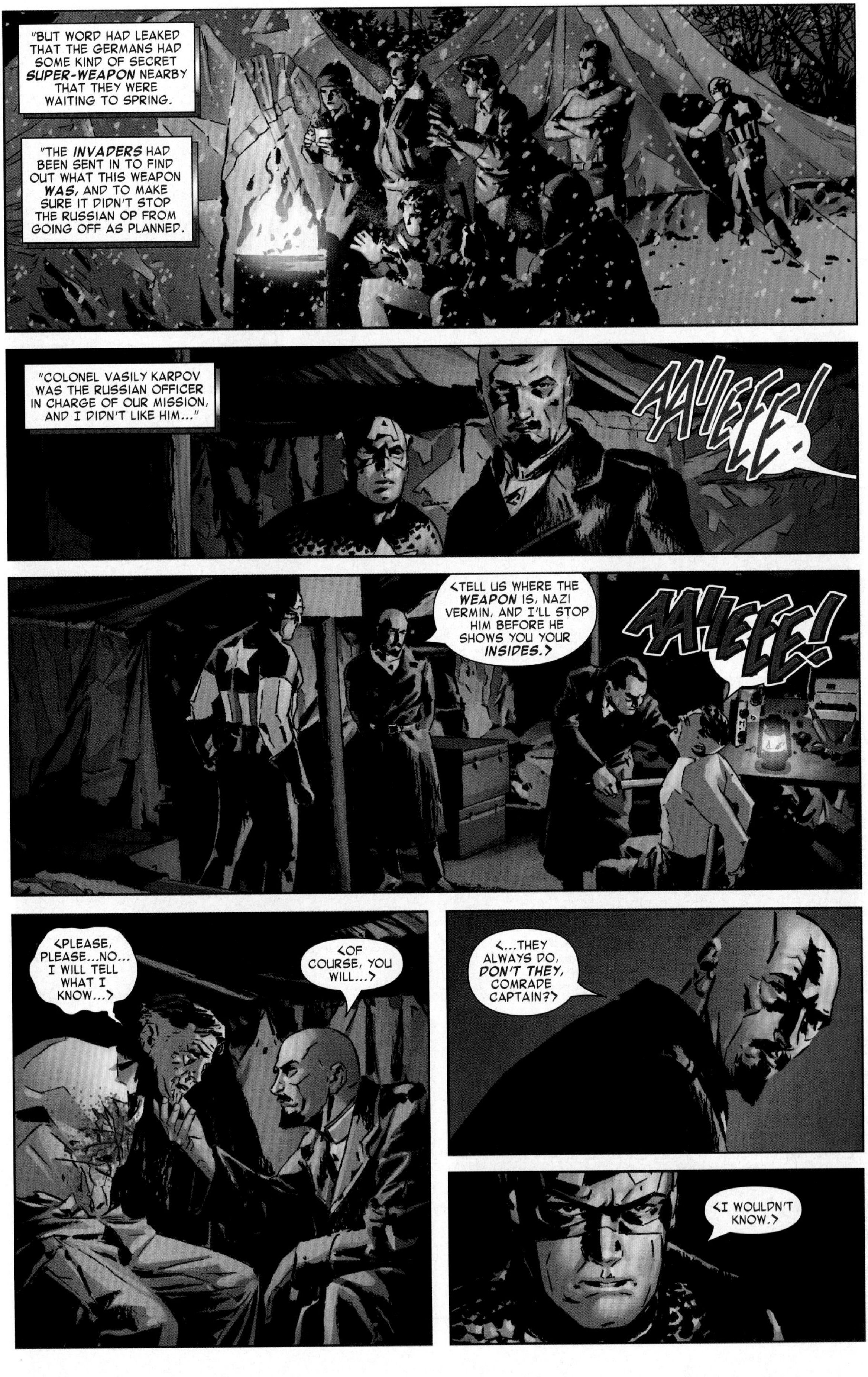
"BUT WORD HAD LEAKED THAT THE GERMANS HAD SOME KIND OF SECRET SUPER-WEAPON NEARBY THAT THEY WERE WAITING TO SPRING.
"THE INVADERS HAD BEEN SENT IN TO FIND OUT WHAT THIS WEAPON WAS, AND TO MAKE SURE IT DIDN'T STOP THE RUSSIAN OP FROM GOING OFF AS PLANNED.
"COLONEL VASILY KARPOV WAS THE RUSSIAN OFFICER IN CHARGE OF OUR MISSION, AND I DIDN'T LIKE HIM..."
AAAIIEEEE!
<TELL US WHERE THE WEAPON IS, NAZI VERMIN, AND I'LL STOP HIM BEFORE HE SHOWS YOU YOUR INSIDES.>
AAAIIEEEE!
<PLEASE, PLEASE...NO... I WILL TELL WHAT I KNOW...>
<OF COURSE, YOU WILL...>
<...THEY ALWAYS DO, DON'T THEY, COMRADE CAPTAIN?>
<I WOULDN'T KNOW.>

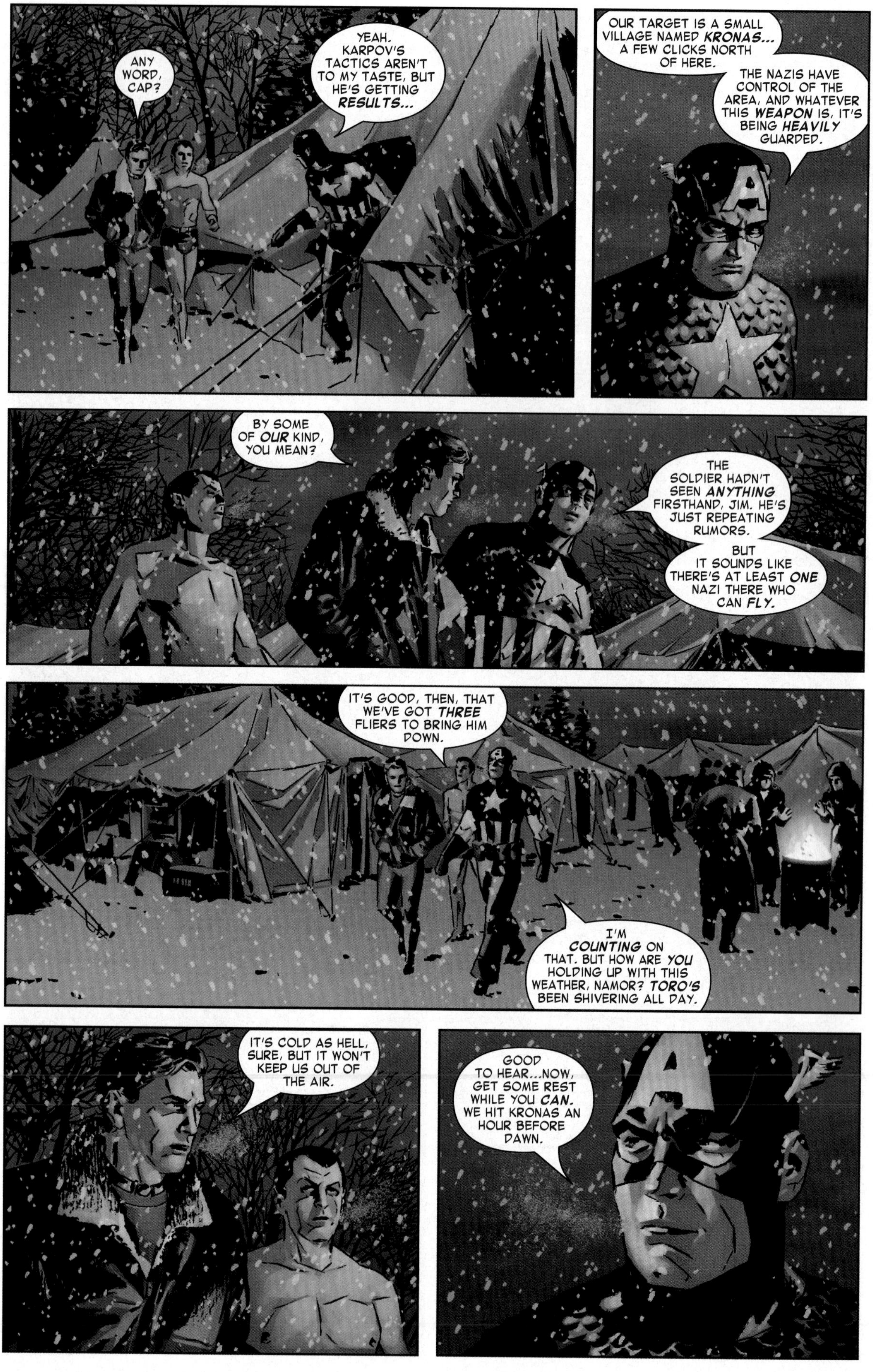
ANY WORD, CAP?
YEAH. KARPOV'S TACTICS AREN'T TO MY TASTE, BUT HE'S GETTING RESULTS...
OUR TARGET IS A SMALL VILLAGE NAMED KRONAS... A FEW CLICKS NORTH OF HERE.
THE NAZIS HAVE CONTROL OF THE AREA, AND WHATEVER THIS WEAPON IS, IT'S BEING HEAVILY GUARDED.
BY SOME OF OUR KIND, YOU MEAN?
THE SOLDIER HADN'T SEEN ANYTHING FIRSTHAND, JIM. HE'S JUST REPEATING RUMORS.
BUT IT SOUNDS LIKE THERE'S AT LEAST ONE NAZI THERE WHO CAN FLY.
IT'S GOOD, THEN, THAT WE'VE GOT THREE FLIERS TO BRING HIM DOWN.
I'M COUNTING ON THAT. BUT HOW ARE YOU HOLDING UP WITH THIS WEATHER, NAMOR? TORO'S BEEN SHIVERING ALL DAY.
IT'S COLD AS HELL, SURE, BUT IT WON'T KEEP US OUT OF THE AIR.
GOOD TO HEAR...NOW, GET SOME REST WHILE YOU CAN. WE HIT KRONAS AN HOUR BEFORE DAWN.

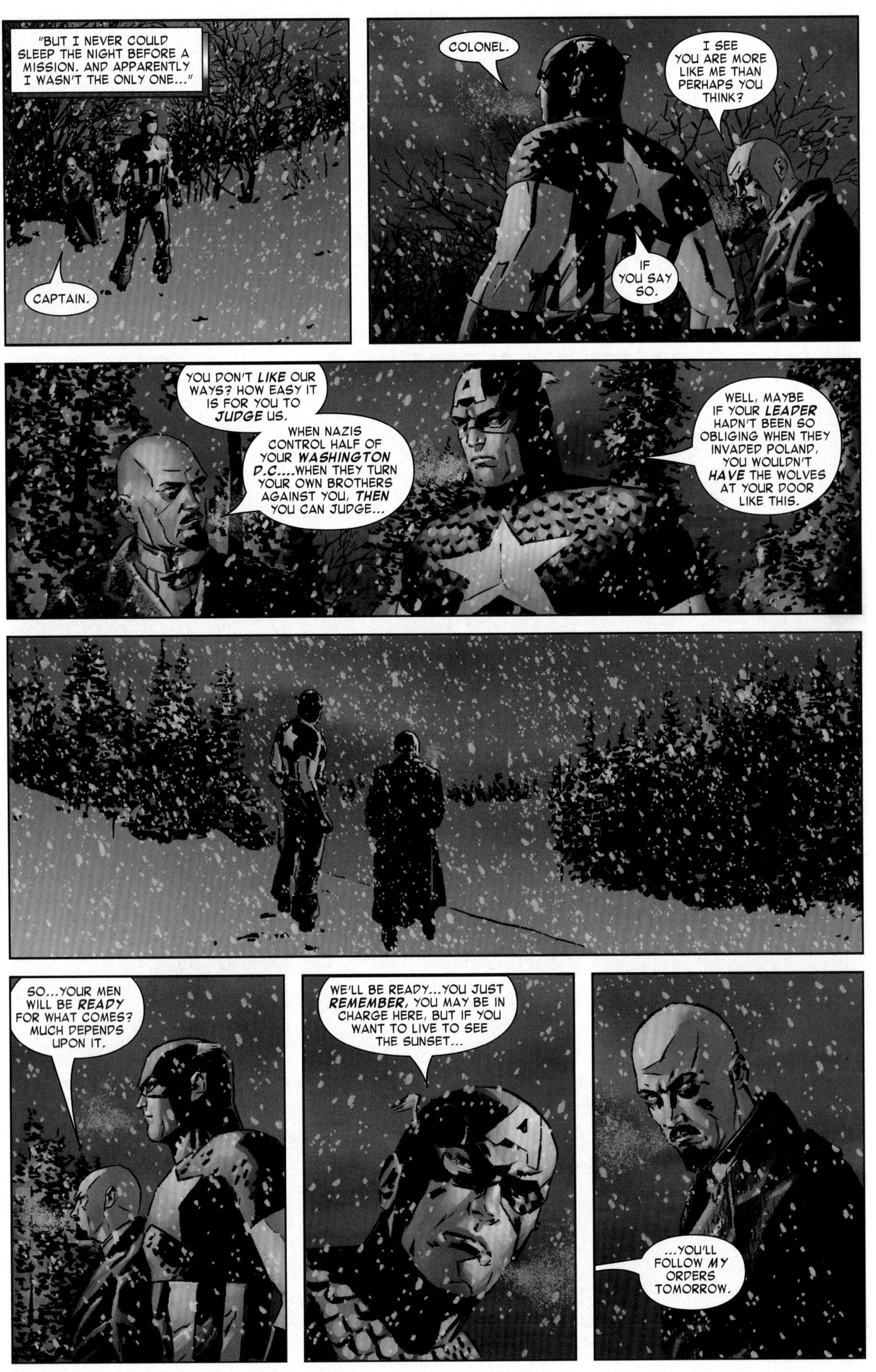

"BUT I NEVER COULD SLEEP THE NIGHT BEFORE A MISSION. AND APPARENTLY I WASN'T THE ONLY ONE..."
CAPTAIN.
COLONEL.
I SEE YOU ARE MORE LIKE ME THAN PERHAPS YOU THINK?
IF YOU SAY SO.
YOU DON'T LIKE OUR WAYS? HOW EASY IT IS FOR YOU TO JUDGE US.
WHEN NAZIS CONTROL HALF OF YOUR WASHINGTON D.C.... WHEN THEY TURN YOUR OWN BROTHERS AGAINST YOU, THEN YOU CAN JUDGE...
WELL, MAYBE IF YOUR LEADER HADN'T BEEN SO OBLIGING WHEN THEY INVADED POLAND, YOU WOULDN'T HAVE THE WOLVES AT YOUR DOOR LIKE THIS.
SO... YOUR MEN WILL BE READY FOR WHAT COMES? MUCH DEPENDS UPON IT.
WE'LL BE READY... YOU JUST REMEMBER, YOU MAY BE IN CHARGE HERE, BUT IF YOU WANT TO LIVE TO SEE THE SUNSET...
...YOU'LL FOLLOW MY ORDERS TOMORROW.

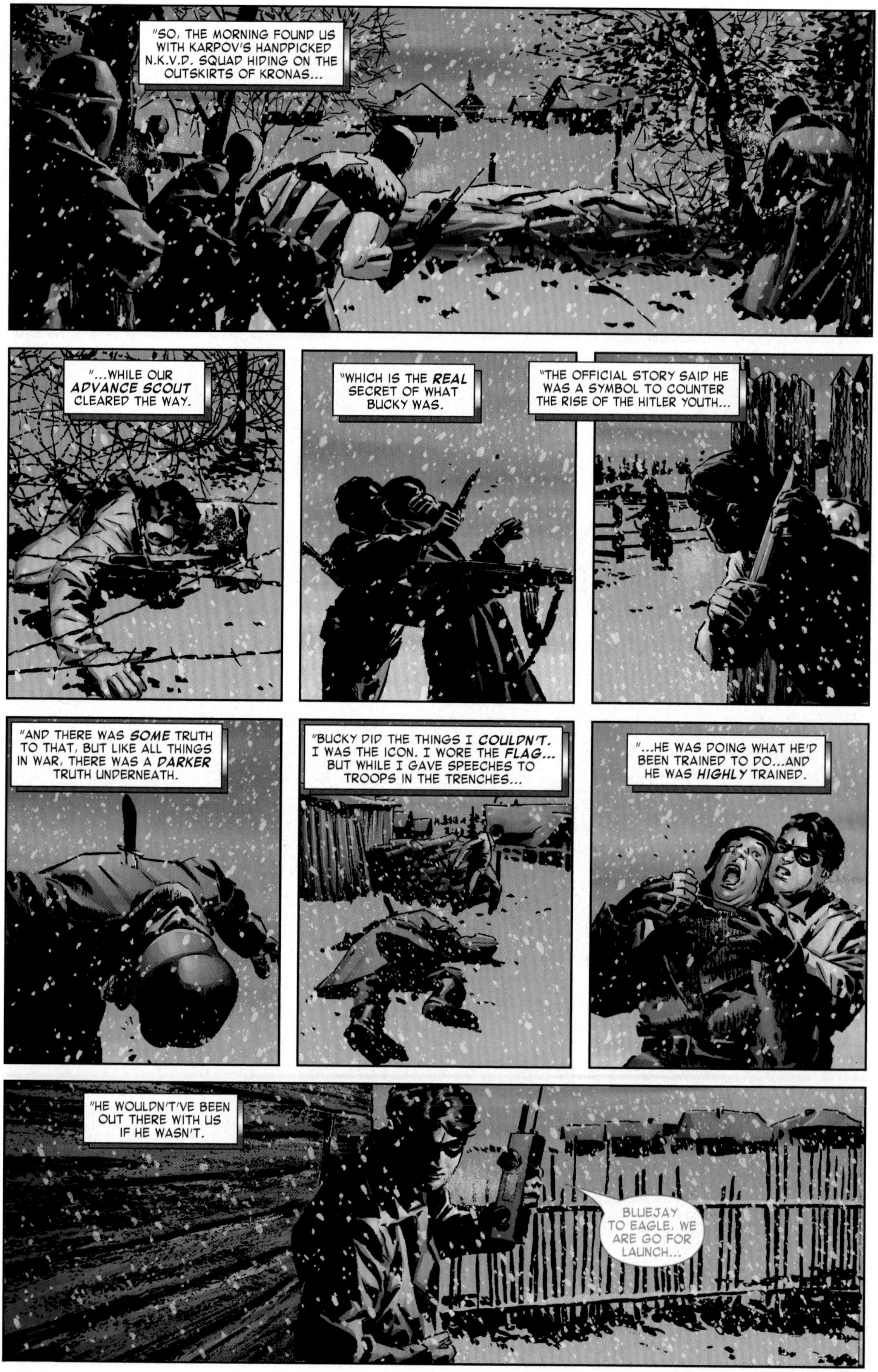
"SO, THE MORNING FOUND US WITH KARPOV'S HANDPICKED N.K.V.D. SQUAD HIDING ON THE OUTSKIRTS OF KRONAS...
"...WHILE OUR ADVANCE SCOUT CLEARED THE WAY.
"WHICH IS THE REAL SECRET OF WHAT BUCKY WAS.
"THE OFFICIAL STORY SAID HE WAS A SYMBOL TO COUNTER THE RISE OF THE HITLER YOUTH...
"AND THERE WAS SOME TRUTH TO THAT, BUT LIKE ALL THINGS IN WAR, THERE WAS A DARKER TRUTH UNDERNEATH.
"BUCKY DID THE THINGS I COULDN'T. I WAS THE ICON. I WORE THE FLAG... BUT WHILE I GAVE SPEECHES TO TROOPS IN THE TRENCHES...
"...HE WAS DOING WHAT HE'D BEEN TRAINED TO DO...AND HE WAS HIGHLY TRAINED.
"HE WOULDN'T'VE BEEN OUT THERE WITH US IF HE WASN'T.
BLUEJAY TO EAGLE, WE ARE GO FOR LAUNCH...

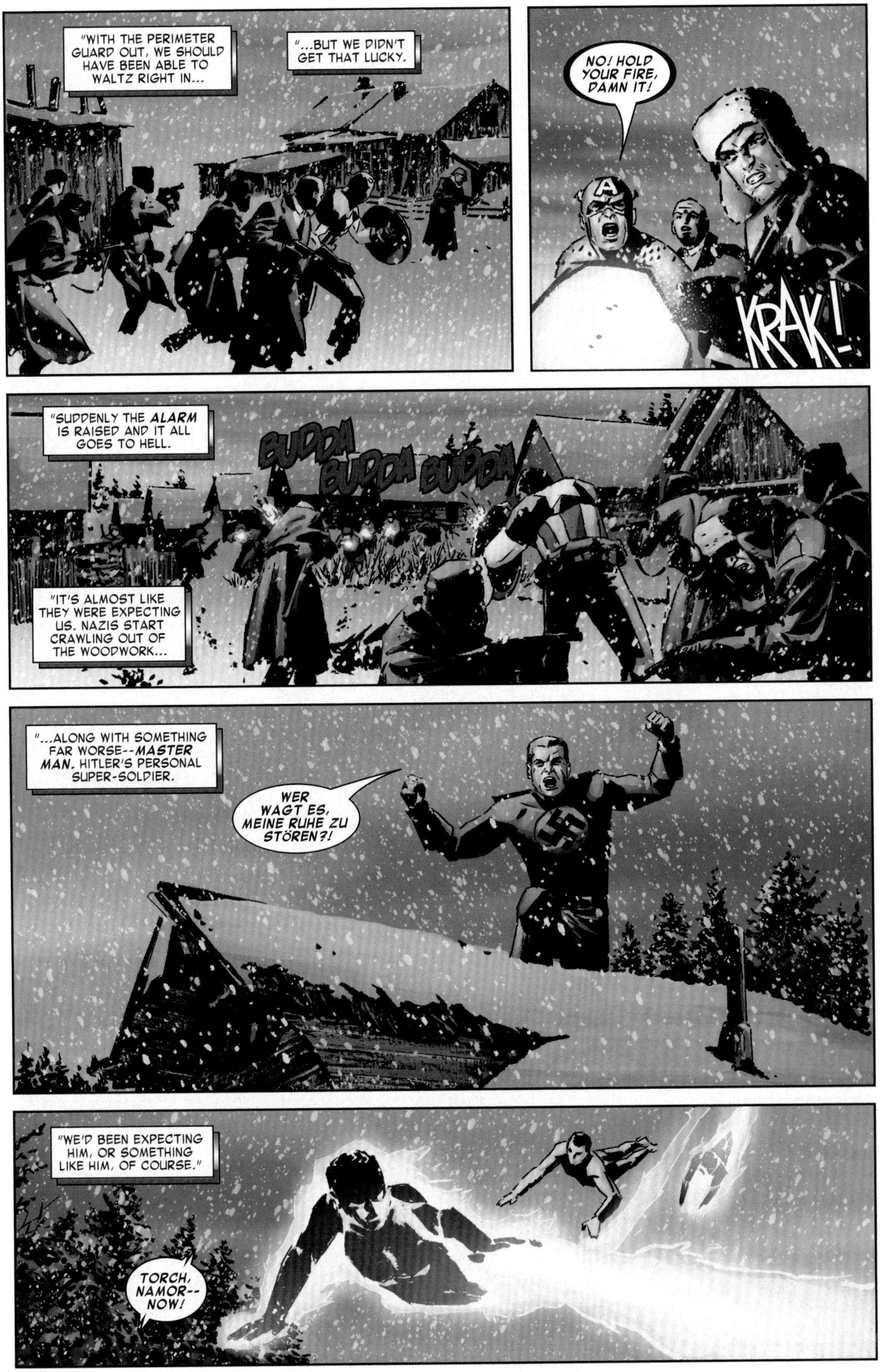
"WITH THE PERIMETER GUARD OUT, WE SHOULD HAVE BEEN ABLE TO WALTZ RIGHT IN...
"...BUT WE DIDN'T GET THAT LUCKY.
NO! HOLD YOUR FIRE, DAMN IT!
KRAK!
"SUDDENLY THE ALARM IS RAISED AND IT ALL GOES TO HELL.
BUDDA BUDDA BUDDA
"IT'S ALMOST LIKE THEY WERE EXPECTING US. NAZIS START CRAWLING OUT OF THE WOODWORK...
"...ALONG WITH SOMETHING FAR WORSE--MASTER MAN. HITLER'S PERSONAL SUPER-SOLDIER.
WER WAGT ES, MEINE RUHE ZU STÖREN?!
"WE'D BEEN EXPECTING HIM, OR SOMETHING LIKE HIM, OF COURSE."
TORCH, NAMOR-- NOW!

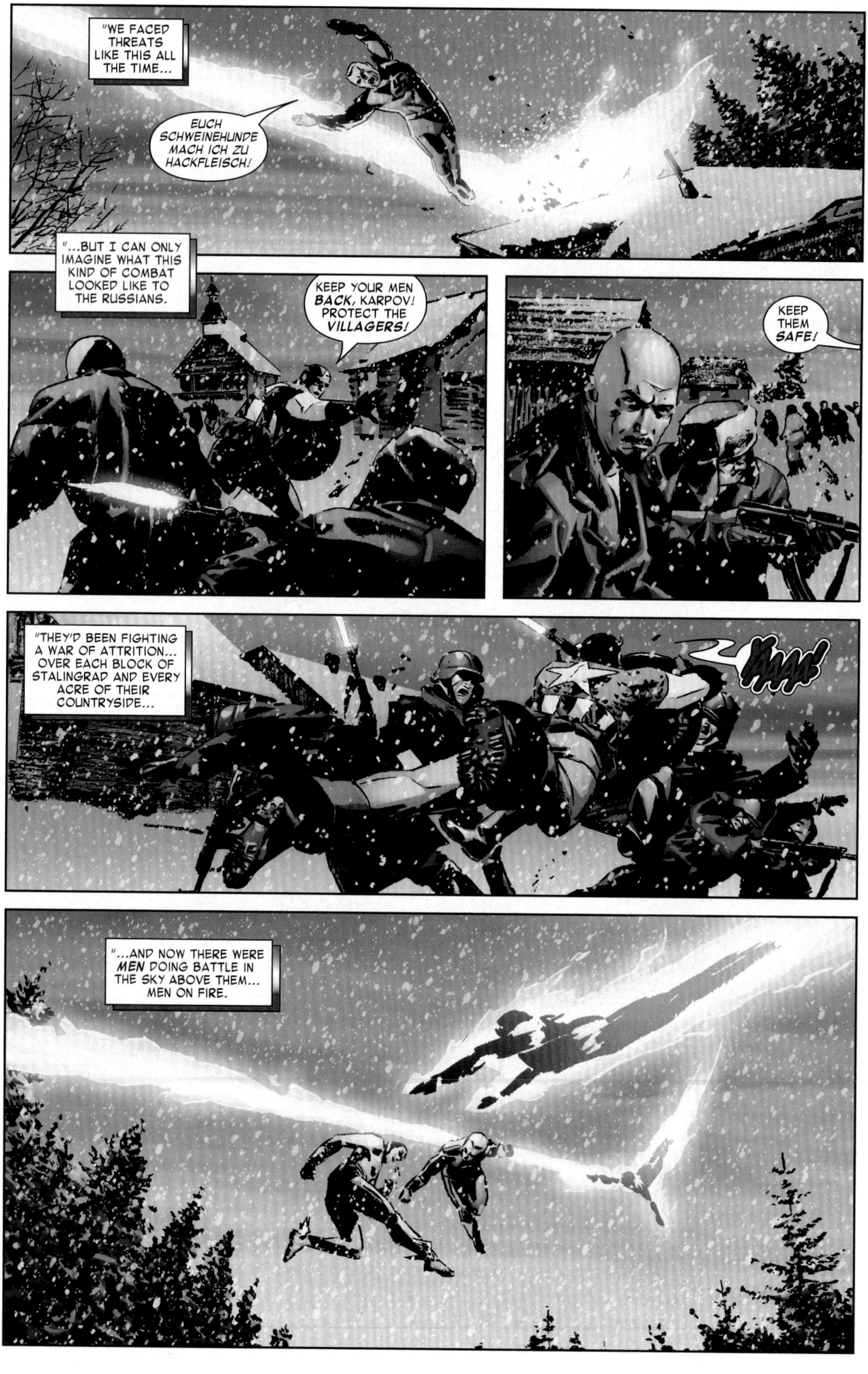
"WE FACED THREATS LIKE THIS ALL THE TIME...
EUCH SCHWEINEHUNDE MACH ICH ZU HACKFLEISCH!
"...BUT I CAN ONLY IMAGINE WHAT THIS KIND OF COMBAT LOOKED LIKE TO THE RUSSIANS.
KEEP YOUR MEN BACK, KARPOV! PROTECT THE VILLAGERS!
KEEP THEM SAFE!
"THEY'D BEEN FIGHTING A WAR OF ATTRITION... OVER EACH BLOCK OF STALINGRAD AND EVERY ACRE OF THEIR COUNTRYSIDE...
YAAAA!
"...AND NOW THERE WERE MEN DOING BATTLE IN THE SKY ABOVE THEM... MEN ON FIRE.

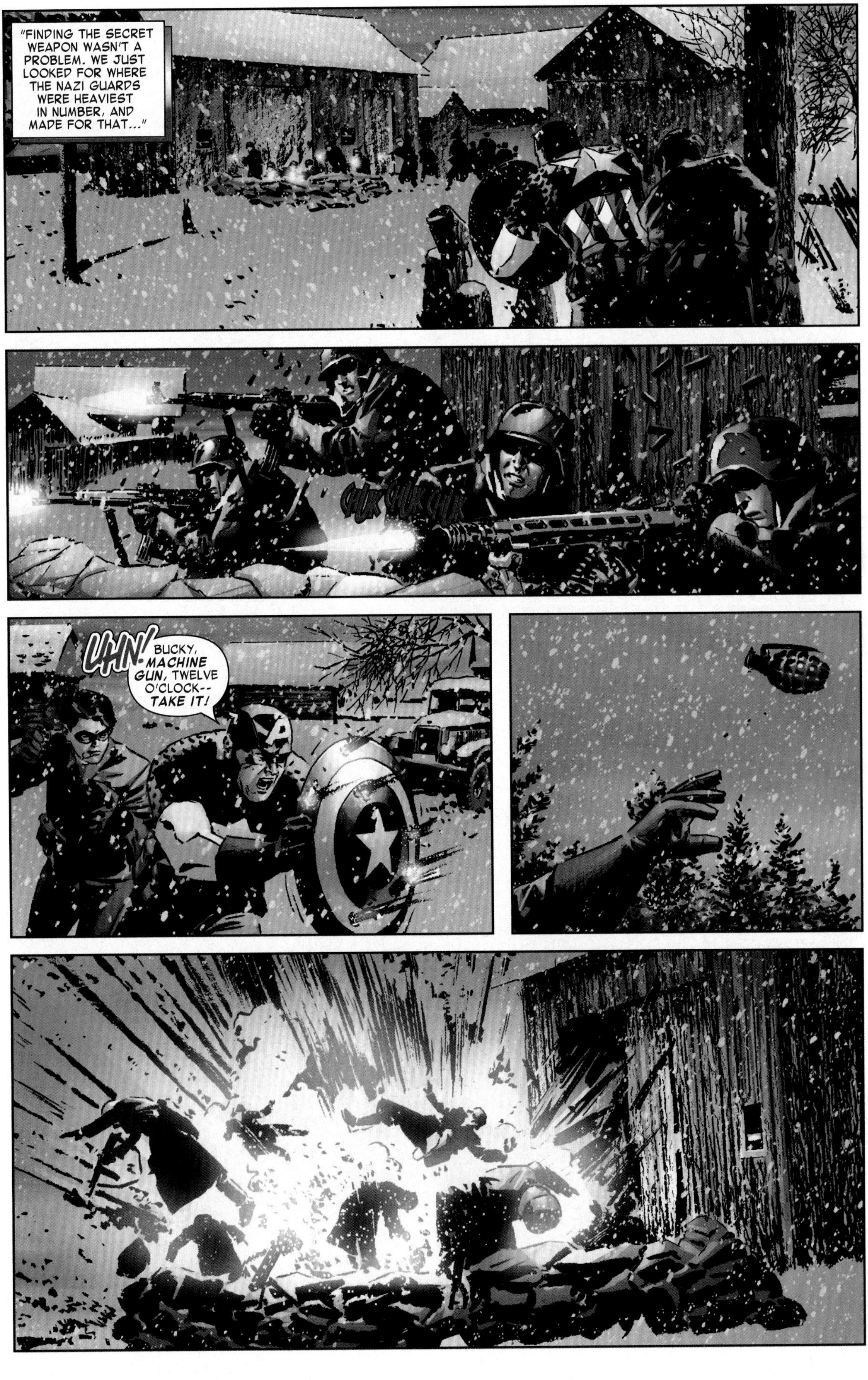
"FINDING THE SECRET WEAPON WASN'T A PROBLEM. WE JUST LOOKED FOR WHERE THE NAZI GUARDS WERE HEAVIEST IN NUMBER, AND MADE FOR THAT..."
CHUK CHUK CHUK
UHN!
BUCKY, MACHINE GUN, TWELVE O'CLOCK-- TAKE IT!

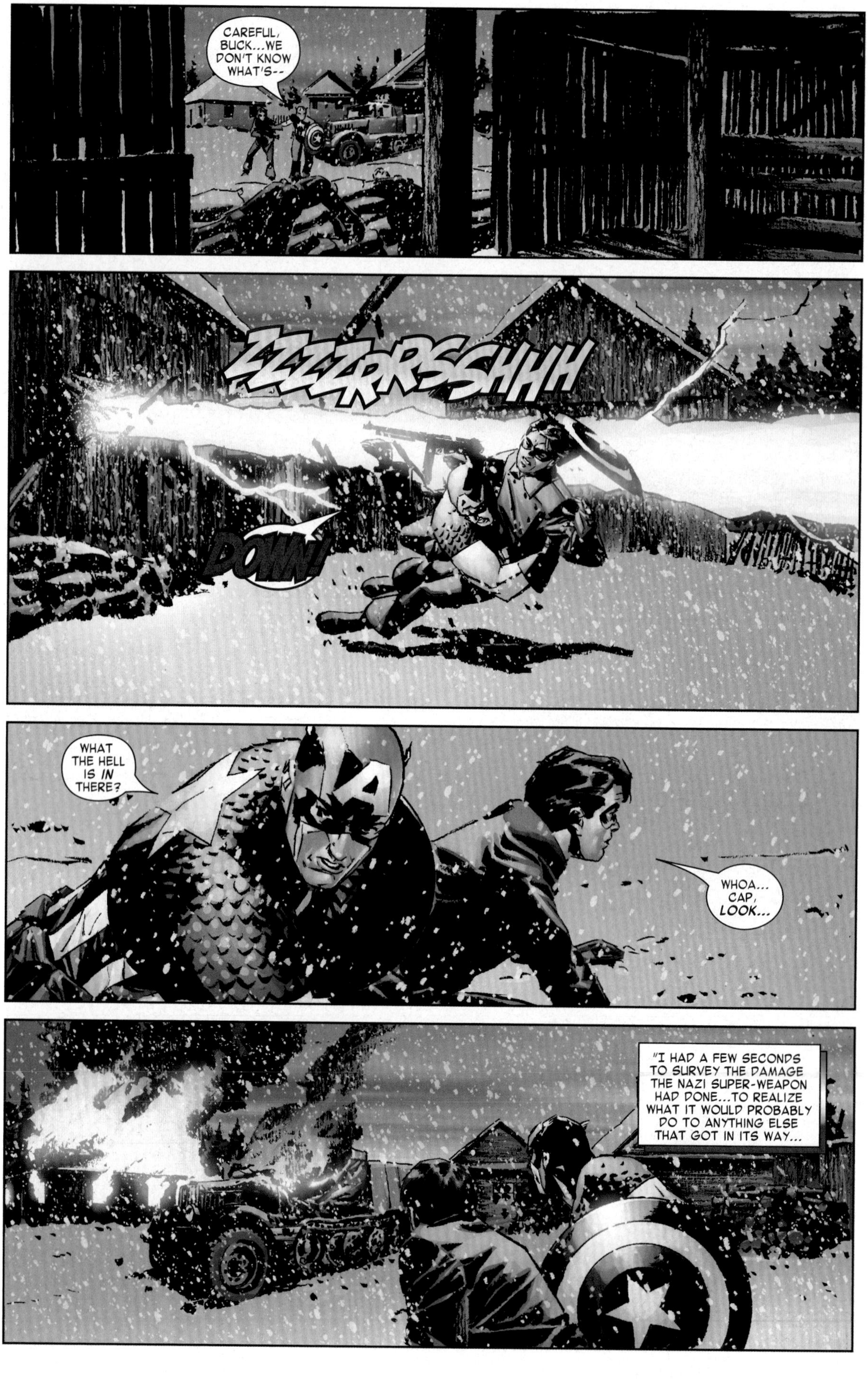
CAREFUL, BUCK...WE DON'T KNOW WHAT'S--
ZZZZRRSSHHH
DOWN!
WHAT THE HELL IS *IN* THERE?
WHOA... CAP, *LOOK*...
"I HAD A FEW SECONDS TO SURVEY THE DAMAGE THE NAZI SUPER-WEAPON HAD DONE...TO REALIZE WHAT IT WOULD PROBABLY DO TO ANYTHING ELSE THAT GOT IN ITS WAY...

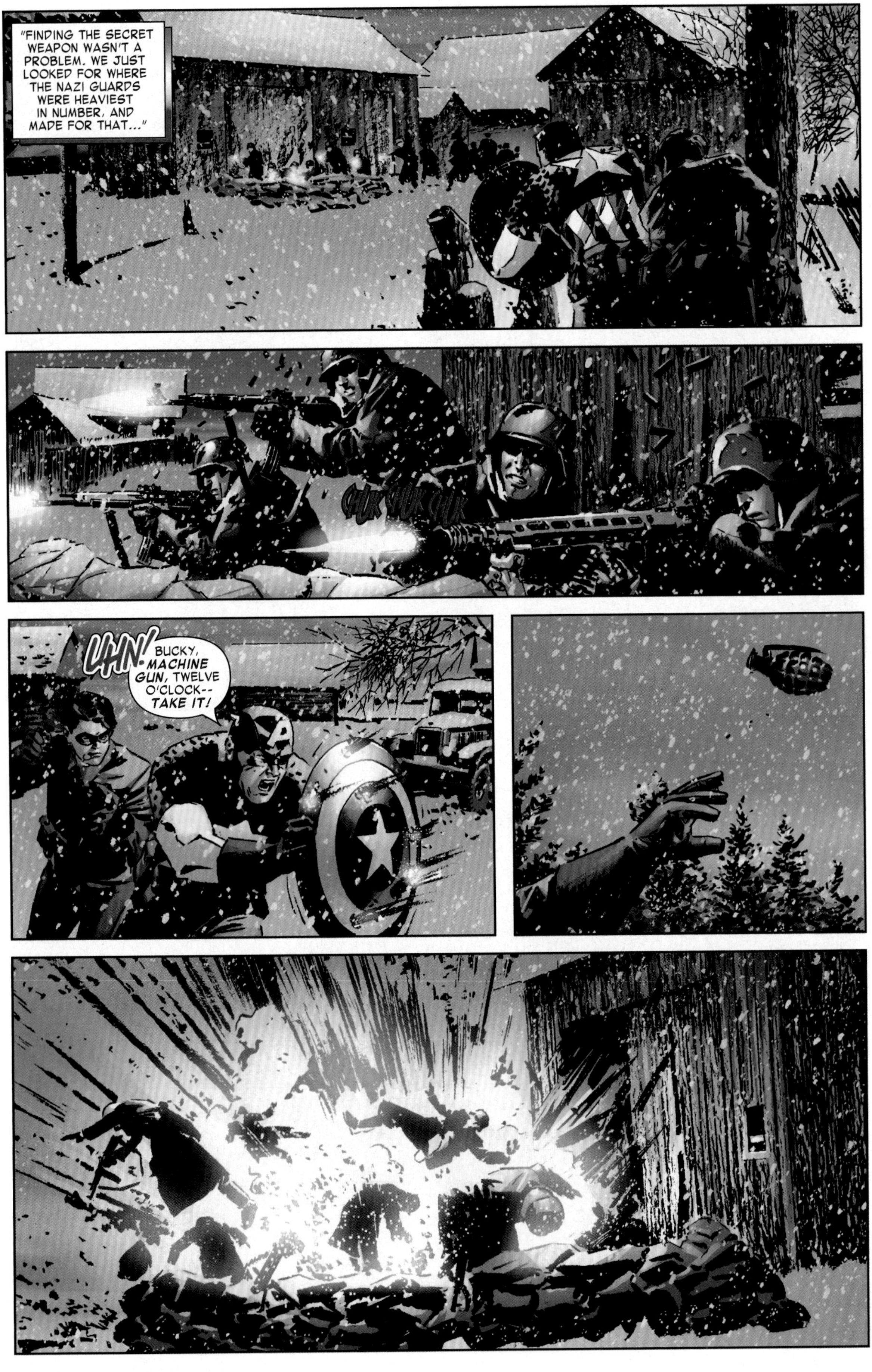
"FINDING THE SECRET WEAPON WASN'T A PROBLEM. WE JUST LOOKED FOR WHERE THE NAZI GUARDS WERE HEAVIEST IN NUMBER, AND MADE FOR THAT..."
CHUK CHUK CHUK
UHN!
BUCKY, MACHINE GUN, TWELVE O'CLOCK-- TAKE IT!

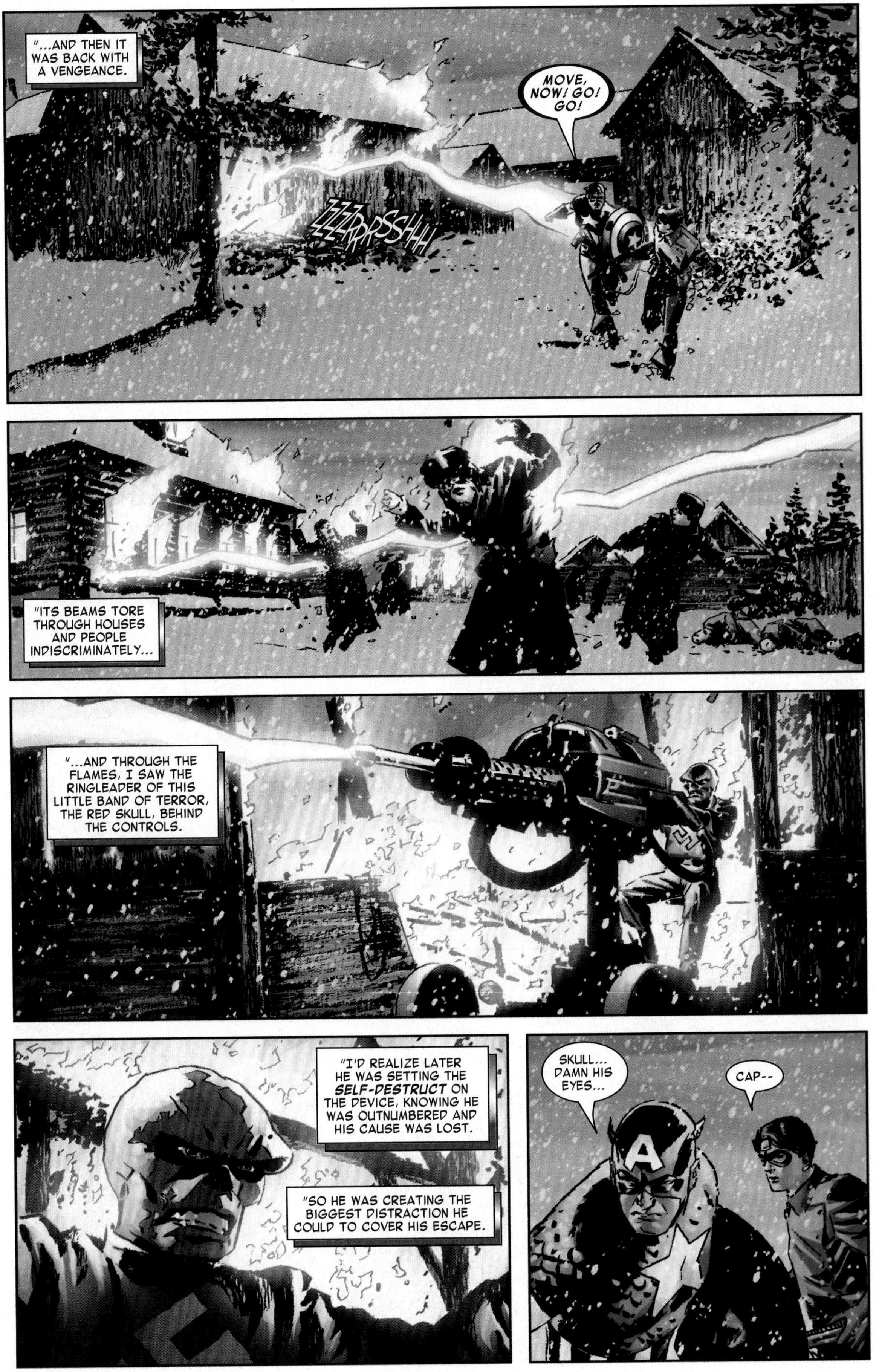
"...AND THEN IT WAS BACK WITH A VENGEANCE.
MOVE, NOW! GO! GO!
ZZZZRRRSSHHH
"ITS BEAMS TORE THROUGH HOUSES AND PEOPLE INDISCRIMINATELY...
"...AND THROUGH THE FLAMES, I SAW THE RINGLEADER OF THIS LITTLE BAND OF TERROR, THE RED SKULL, BEHIND THE CONTROLS.
"I'D REALIZE LATER HE WAS SETTING THE SELF-DESTRUCT ON THE DEVICE, KNOWING HE WAS OUTNUMBERED AND HIS CAUSE WAS LOST.
"SO HE WAS CREATING THE BIGGEST DISTRACTION HE COULD TO COVER HIS ESCAPE.
SKULL... DAMN HIS EYES...
CAP--

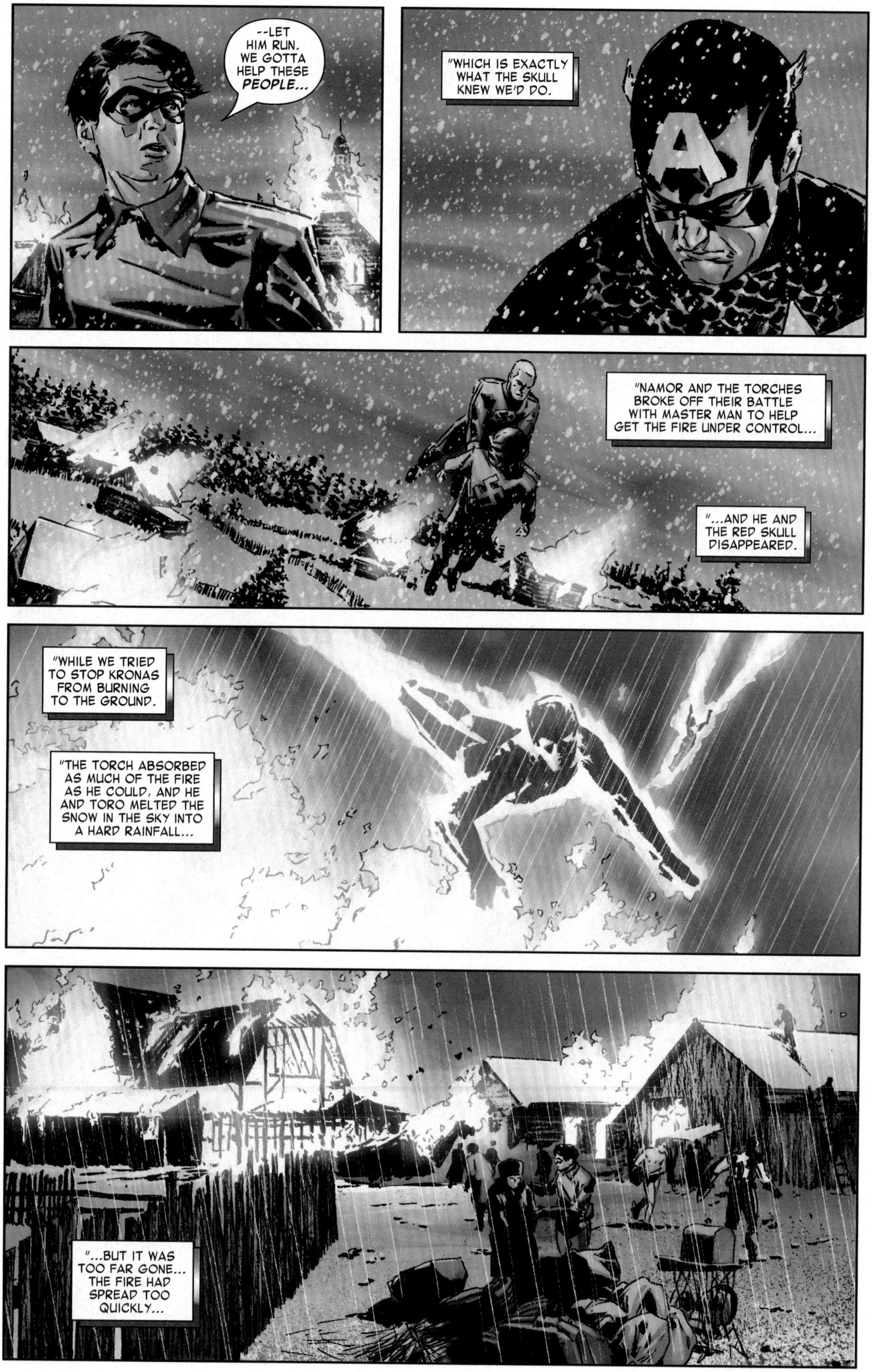
--LET HIM RUN. WE GOTTA HELP THESE PEOPLE...
"WHICH IS EXACTLY WHAT THE SKULL KNEW WE'D DO.
"NAMOR AND THE TORCHES BROKE OFF THEIR BATTLE WITH MASTER MAN TO HELP GET THE FIRE UNDER CONTROL...
"...AND HE AND THE RED SKULL DISAPPEARED.
"WHILE WE TRIED TO STOP KRONAS FROM BURNING TO THE GROUND.
"THE TORCH ABSORBED AS MUCH OF THE FIRE AS HE COULD, AND HE AND TORO MELTED THE SNOW IN THE SKY INTO A HARD RAINFALL...
"...BUT IT WAS TOO FAR GONE... THE FIRE HAD SPREAD TOO QUICKLY...

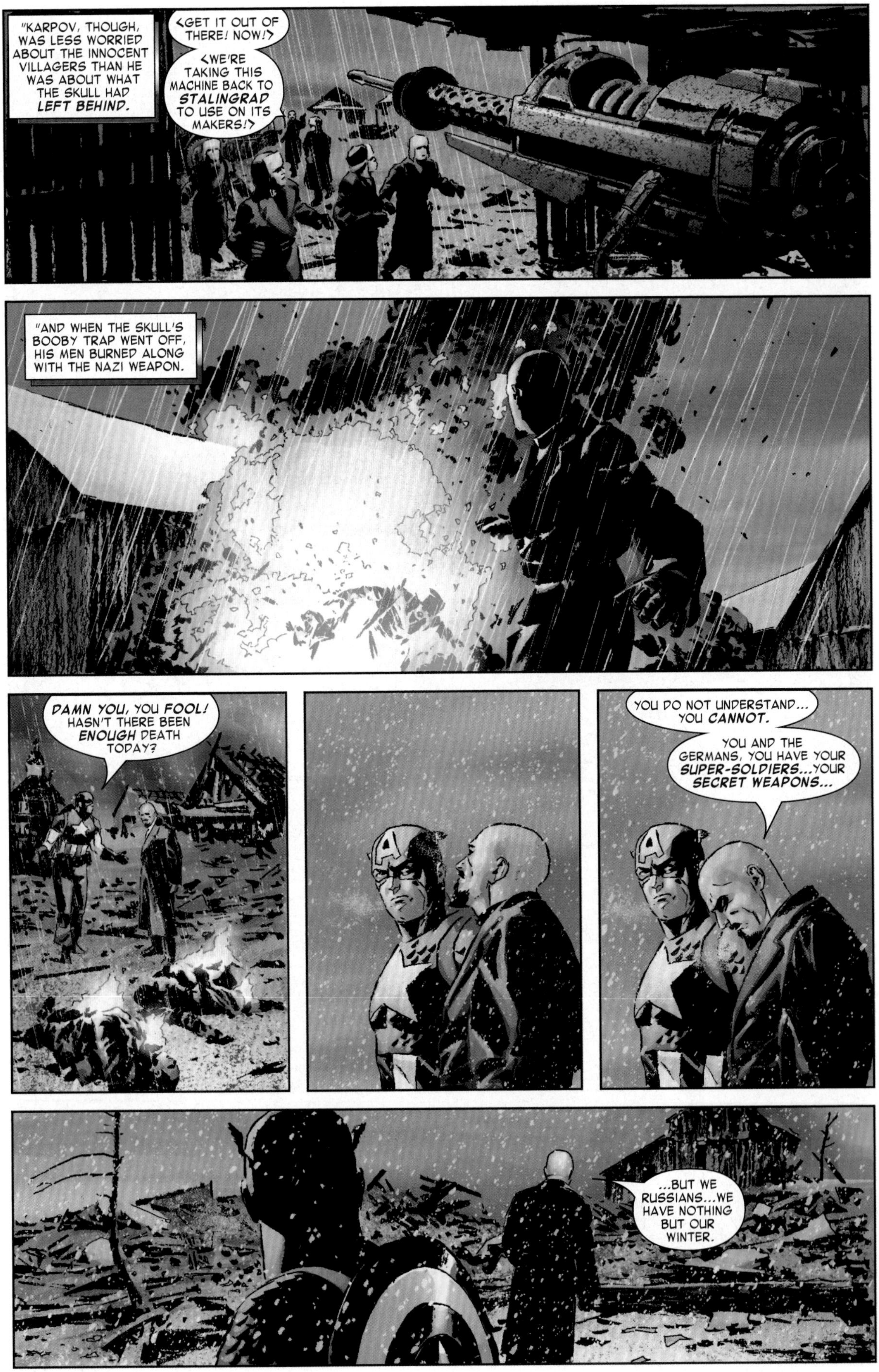
"KARPOV, THOUGH, WAS LESS WORRIED ABOUT THE INNOCENT VILLAGERS THAN HE WAS ABOUT WHAT THE SKULL HAD LEFT BEHIND.
<GET IT OUT OF THERE! NOW!>
<WE'RE TAKING THIS MACHINE BACK TO STALINGRAD TO USE ON ITS MAKERS!>
"AND WHEN THE SKULL'S BOOBY TRAP WENT OFF, HIS MEN BURNED ALONG WITH THE NAZI WEAPON.
DAMN YOU, YOU FOOL! HASN'T THERE BEEN ENOUGH DEATH TODAY?
YOU DO NOT UNDERSTAND... YOU CANNOT.
YOU AND THE GERMANS, YOU HAVE YOUR SUPER-SOLDIERS...YOUR SECRET WEAPONS...
...BUT WE RUSSIANS...WE HAVE NOTHING BUT OUR WINTER.

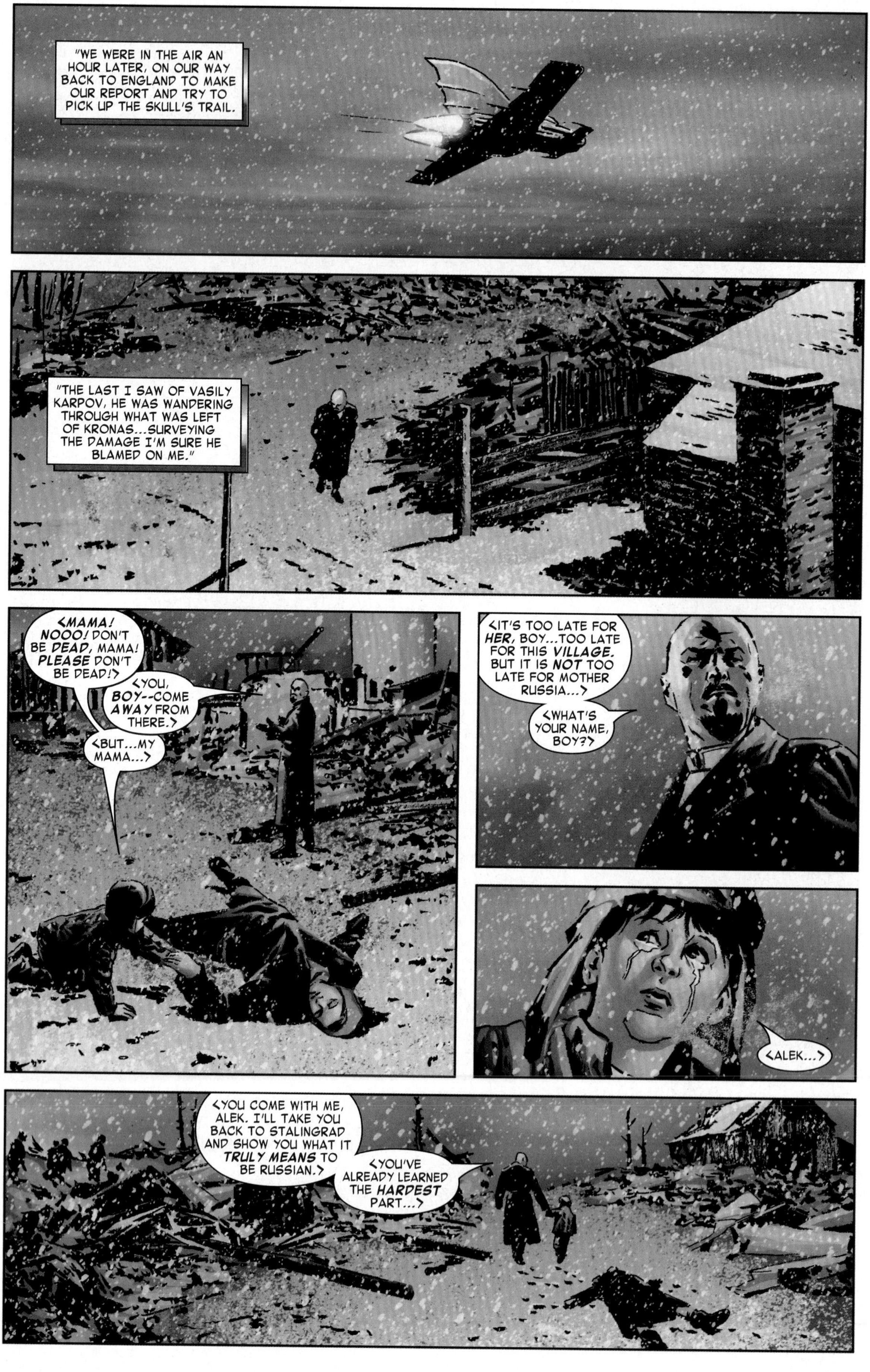
"WE WERE IN THE AIR AN HOUR LATER, ON OUR WAY BACK TO ENGLAND TO MAKE OUR REPORT AND TRY TO PICK UP THE SKULL'S TRAIL.
"THE LAST I SAW OF VASILY KARPOV, HE WAS WANDERING THROUGH WHAT WAS LEFT OF KRONAS...SURVEYING THE DAMAGE I'M SURE HE BLAMED ON ME."
<MAMA! NOOO! DON'T BE DEAD, MAMA! PLEASE DON'T BE DEAD!>
<YOU, BOY--COME AWAY FROM THERE.>
<BUT...MY MAMA...>
<IT'S TOO LATE FOR HER, BOY...TOO LATE FOR THIS VILLAGE. BUT IT IS NOT TOO LATE FOR MOTHER RUSSIA...>
<WHAT'S YOUR NAME, BOY?>
<ALEK...>
<YOU COME WITH ME, ALEK. I'LL TAKE YOU BACK TO STALINGRAD AND SHOW YOU WHAT IT TRULY MEANS TO BE RUSSIAN.>
<YOU'VE ALREADY LEARNED THE HARDEST PART...>

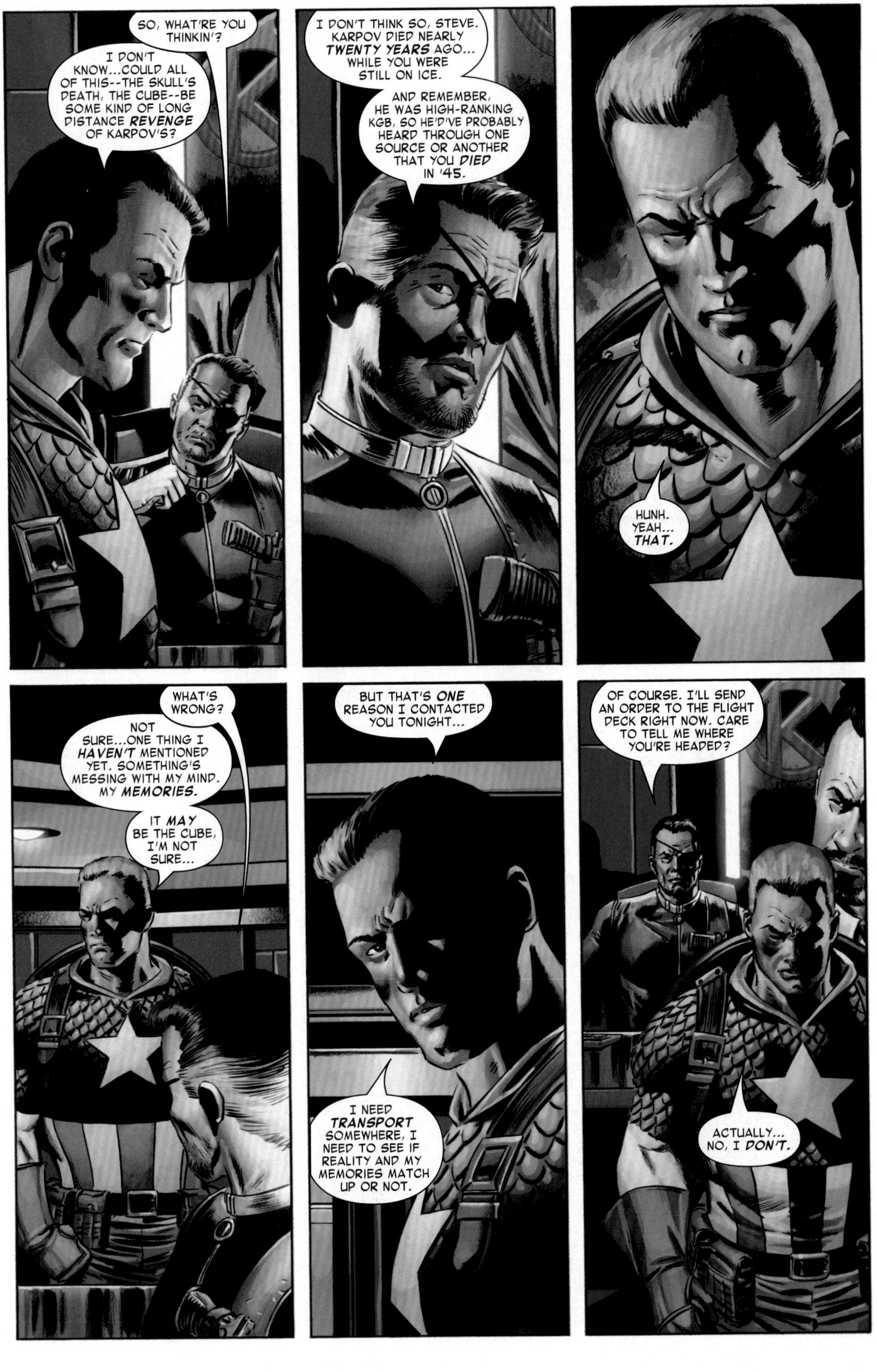
SO, WHAT'RE YOU THINKIN'?
I DON'T KNOW...COULD ALL OF THIS--THE SKULL'S DEATH, THE CUBE--BE SOME KIND OF LONG DISTANCE REVENGE OF KARPOV'S?
I DON'T THINK SO, STEVE. KARPOV DIED NEARLY TWENTY YEARS AGO... WHILE YOU WERE STILL ON ICE.
AND REMEMBER, HE WAS HIGH-RANKING KGB, SO HE'D'VE PROBABLY HEARD THROUGH ONE SOURCE OR ANOTHER THAT YOU DIED IN '45.
HUNH. YEAH... THAT.
WHAT'S WRONG?
NOT SURE...ONE THING I HAVEN'T MENTIONED YET. SOMETHING'S MESSING WITH MY MIND. MY MEMORIES.
IT MAY BE THE CUBE, I'M NOT SURE...
BUT THAT'S ONE REASON I CONTACTED YOU TONIGHT...
I NEED TRANSPORT SOMEWHERE, I NEED TO SEE IF REALITY AND MY MEMORIES MATCH UP OR NOT.
OF COURSE. I'LL SEND AN ORDER TO THE FLIGHT DECK RIGHT NOW. CARE TO TELL ME WHERE YOU'RE HEADED?
ACTUALLY... NO, I DON'T.

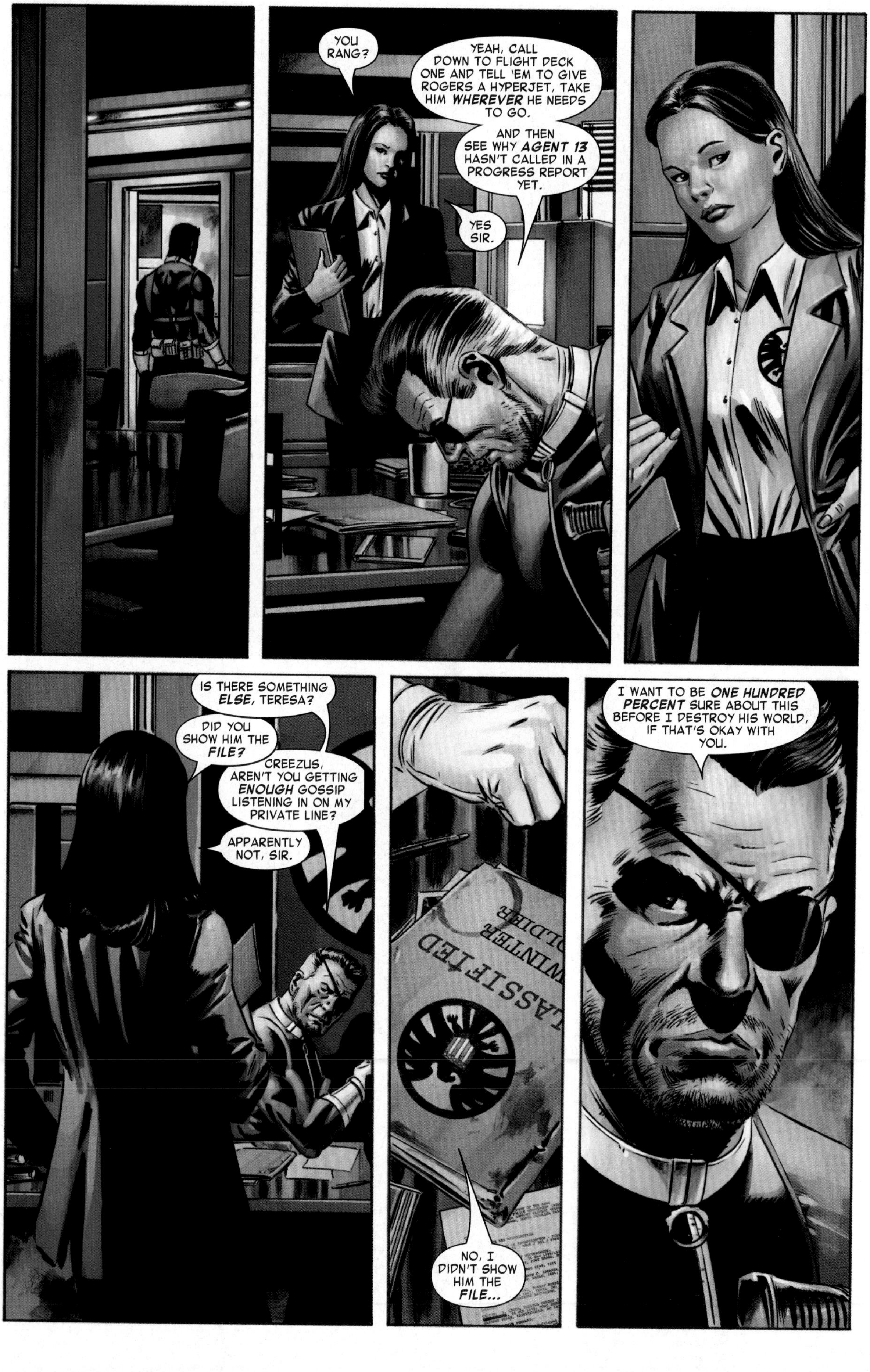
YOU RANG?
YEAH, CALL DOWN TO FLIGHT DECK ONE AND TELL 'EM TO GIVE ROGERS A HYPERJET, TAKE HIM WHEREVER HE NEEDS TO GO.
AND THEN SEE WHY AGENT 13 HASN'T CALLED IN A PROGRESS REPORT YET.
YES SIR.
IS THERE SOMETHING ELSE, TERESA?
DID YOU SHOW HIM THE FILE?
CREEZUS, AREN'T YOU GETTING ENOUGH GOSSIP LISTENING IN ON MY PRIVATE LINE?
APPARENTLY NOT, SIR.
CLASSIFIED
WINTER SOLDIER
NO, I DIDN'T SHOW HIM THE FILE...
I WANT TO BE ONE HUNDRED PERCENT SURE ABOUT THIS BEFORE I DESTROY HIS WORLD, IF THAT'S OKAY WITH YOU.

6

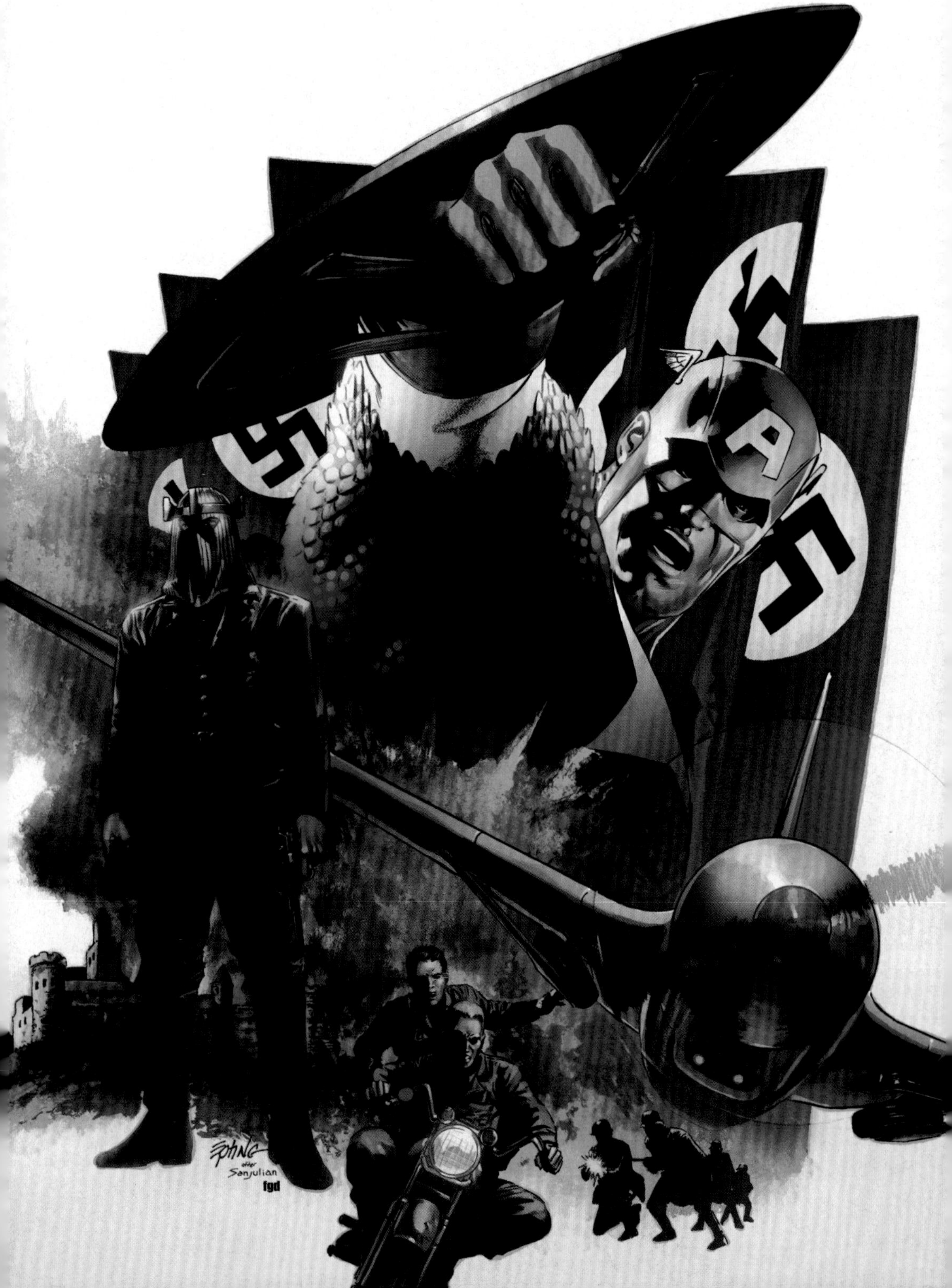
Epting
after
Sanjulian
fgd

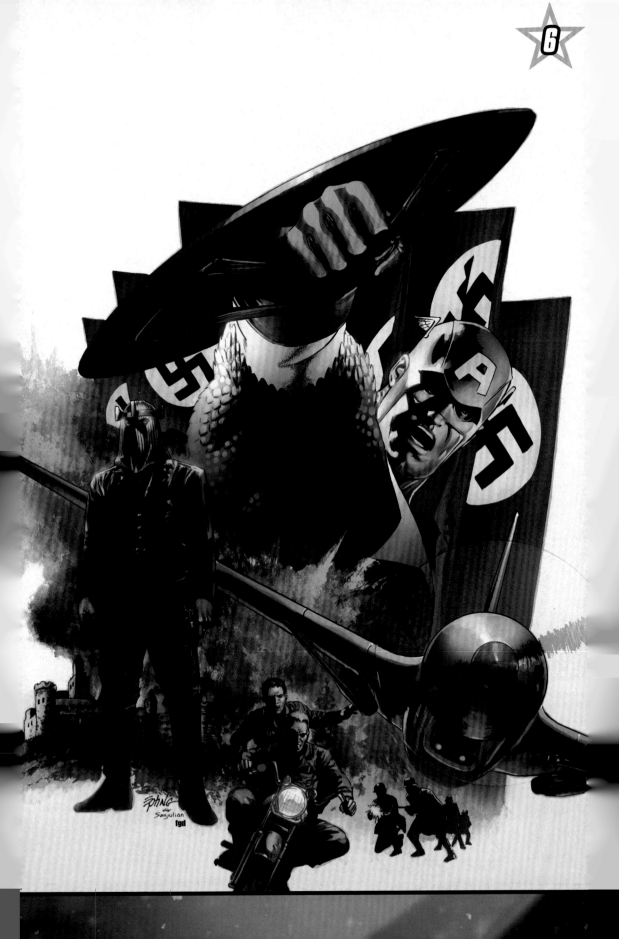

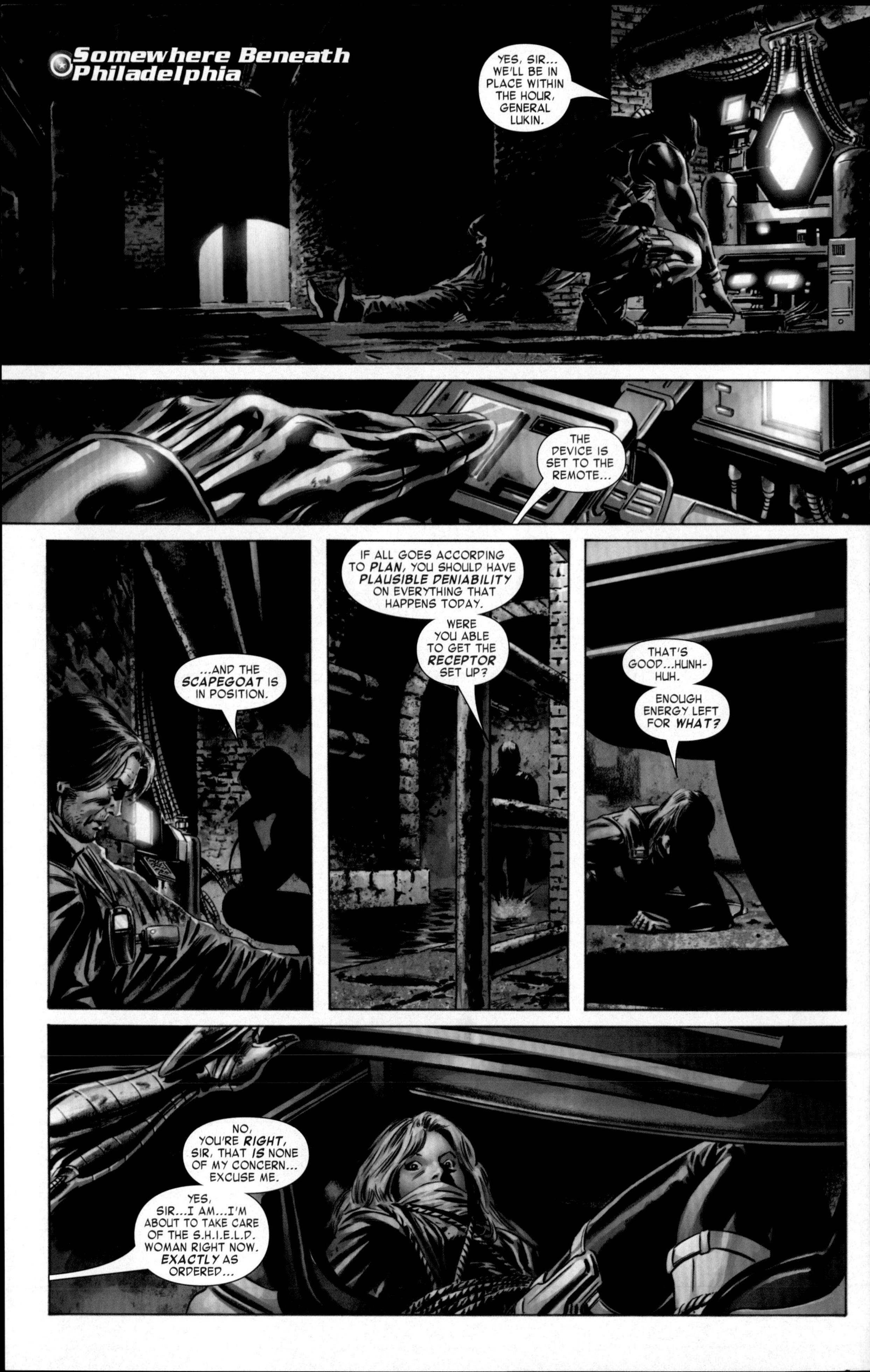
Somewhere Beneath Philadelphia
YES, SIR... WE'LL BE IN PLACE WITHIN THE HOUR, GENERAL LUKIN.
THE DEVICE IS SET TO THE REMOTE...
...AND THE SCAPEGOAT IS IN POSITION.
IF ALL GOES ACCORDING TO PLAN, YOU SHOULD HAVE PLAUSIBLE DENIABILITY ON EVERYTHING THAT HAPPENS TODAY.
WERE YOU ABLE TO GET THE RECEPTOR SET UP?
THAT'S GOOD...HUNH-HUH.
ENOUGH ENERGY LEFT FOR WHAT?
NO, YOU'RE RIGHT, SIR, THAT IS NONE OF MY CONCERN... EXCUSE ME.
YES, SIR...I AM...I'M ABOUT TO TAKE CARE OF THE S.H.I.E.L.D. WOMAN RIGHT NOW. EXACTLY AS ORDERED...

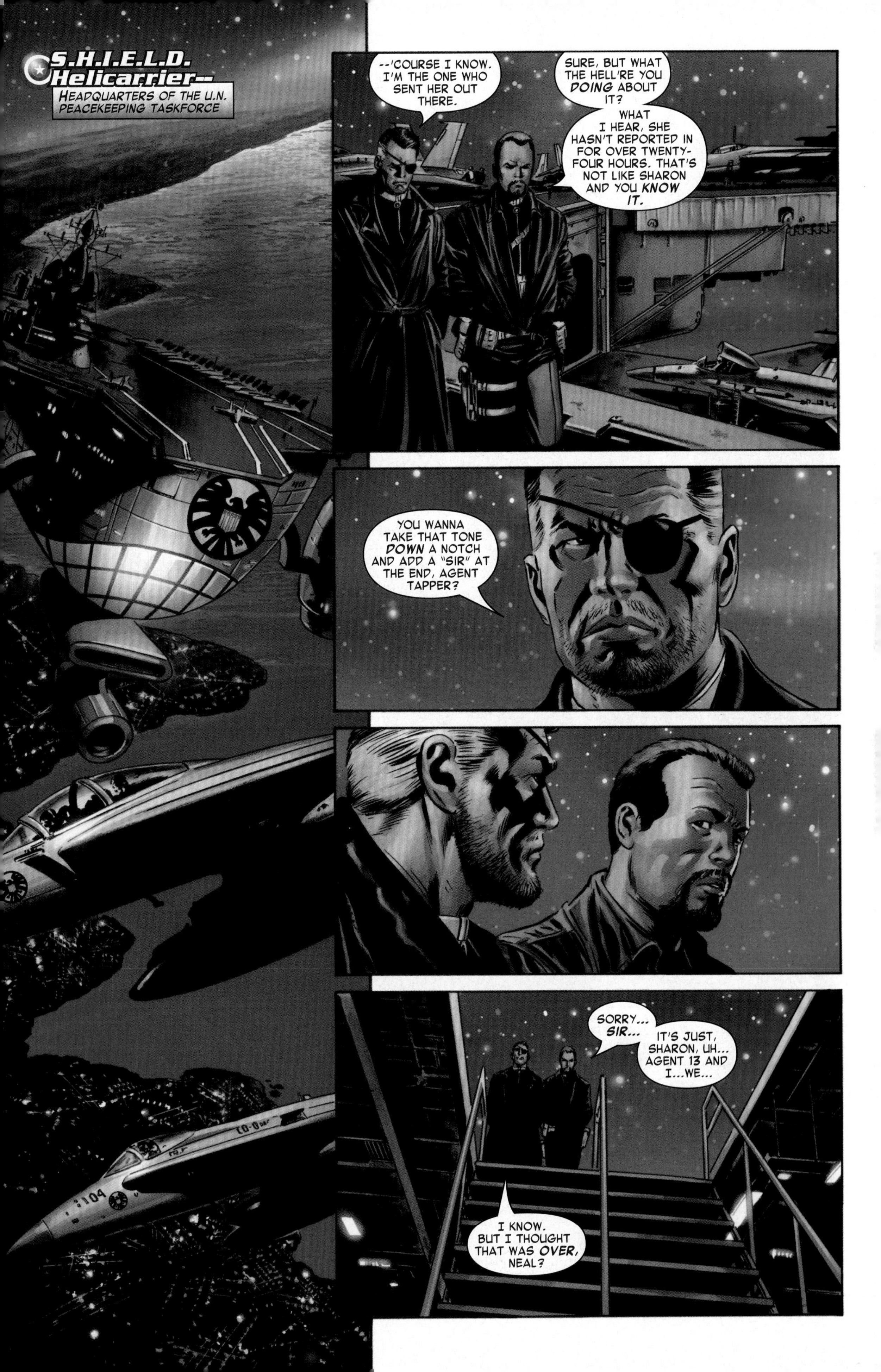
S.H.I.E.L.D. Helicarrier--
HEADQUARTERS OF THE U.N. PEACEKEEPING TASKFORCE
--'COURSE I KNOW. I'M THE ONE WHO SENT HER OUT THERE.
SURE, BUT WHAT THE HELL'RE YOU DOING ABOUT IT?
WHAT I HEAR, SHE HASN'T REPORTED IN FOR OVER TWENTY-FOUR HOURS. THAT'S NOT LIKE SHARON AND YOU KNOW IT.
YOU WANNA TAKE THAT TONE DOWN A NOTCH AND ADD A "SIR" AT THE END, AGENT TAPPER?
SORRY... SIR...
IT'S JUST, SHARON, UH... AGENT 13 AND I...WE...
I KNOW. BUT I THOUGHT THAT WAS OVER, NEAL?

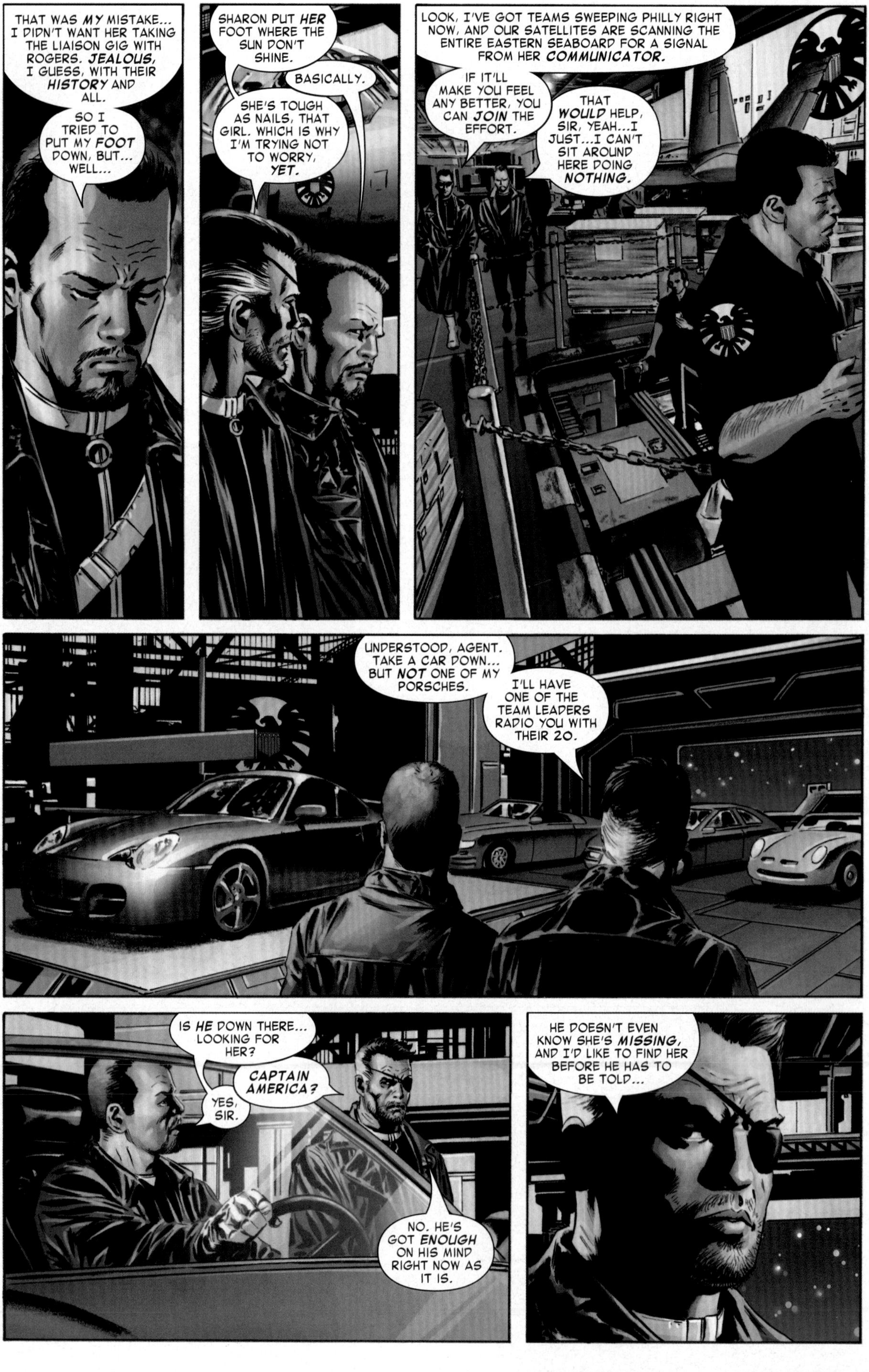
THAT WAS MY MISTAKE... I DIDN'T WANT HER TAKING THE LIAISON GIG WITH ROGERS. JEALOUS, I GUESS, WITH THEIR HISTORY AND ALL.
SO I TRIED TO PUT MY FOOT DOWN, BUT... WELL...
SHARON PUT HER FOOT WHERE THE SUN DON'T SHINE.
BASICALLY.
SHE'S TOUGH AS NAILS, THAT GIRL. WHICH IS WHY I'M TRYING NOT TO WORRY, YET.
LOOK, I'VE GOT TEAMS SWEEPING PHILLY RIGHT NOW, AND OUR SATELLITES ARE SCANNING THE ENTIRE EASTERN SEABOARD FOR A SIGNAL FROM HER COMMUNICATOR.
IF IT'LL MAKE YOU FEEL ANY BETTER, YOU CAN JOIN THE EFFORT.
THAT WOULD HELP, SIR, YEAH...I JUST...I CAN'T SIT AROUND HERE DOING NOTHING.
UNDERSTOOD, AGENT. TAKE A CAR DOWN... BUT NOT ONE OF MY PORSCHES.
I'LL HAVE ONE OF THE TEAM LEADERS RADIO YOU WITH THEIR 20.
IS HE DOWN THERE... LOOKING FOR HER?
CAPTAIN AMERICA?
YES, SIR.
NO. HE'S GOT ENOUGH ON HIS MIND RIGHT NOW AS IT IS.
HE DOESN'T EVEN KNOW SHE'S MISSING, AND I'D LIKE TO FIND HER BEFORE HE HAS TO BE TOLD...

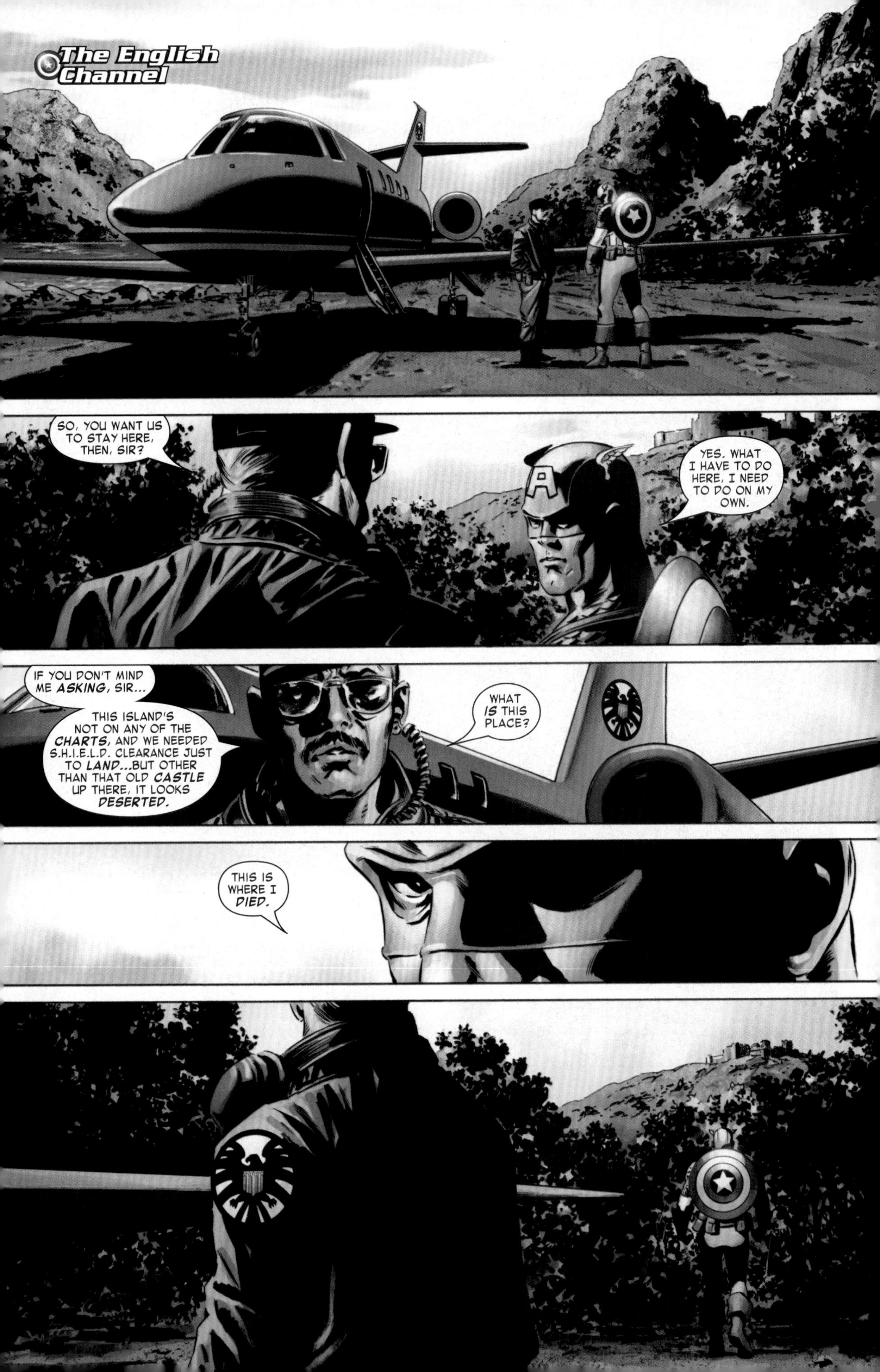
The English Channel
SO, YOU WANT US TO STAY HERE, THEN, SIR?
YES. WHAT I HAVE TO DO HERE, I NEED TO DO ON MY OWN.
IF YOU DON'T MIND ME ASKING, SIR...
THIS ISLAND'S NOT ON ANY OF THE CHARTS, AND WE NEEDED S.H.I.E.L.D. CLEARANCE JUST TO LAND...BUT OTHER THAN THAT OLD CASTLE UP THERE, IT LOOKS DESERTED.
WHAT IS THIS PLACE?
THIS IS WHERE I DIED.

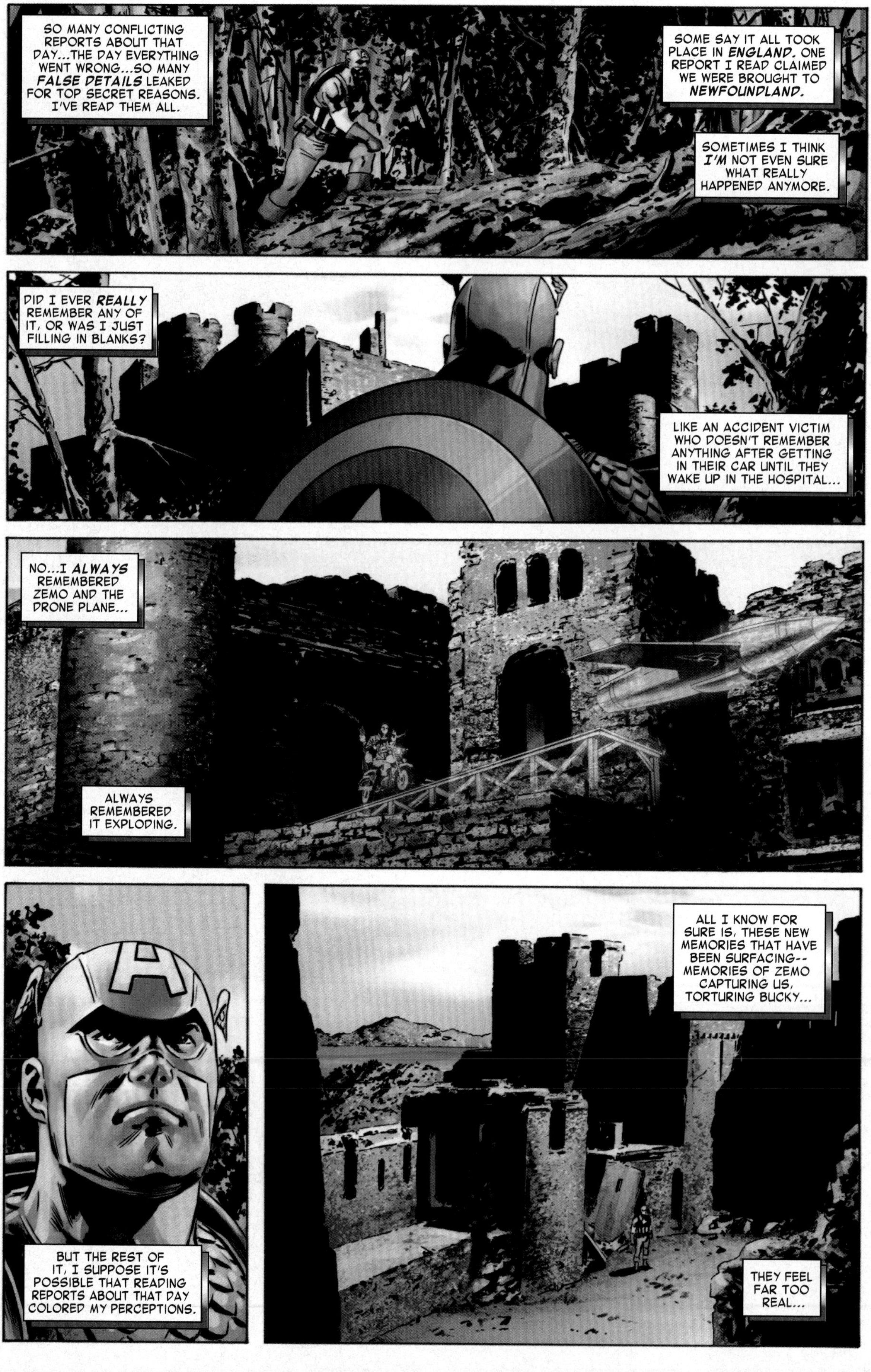
SO MANY CONFLICTING REPORTS ABOUT THAT DAY...THE DAY EVERYTHING WENT WRONG...SO MANY FALSE DETAILS LEAKED FOR TOP SECRET REASONS. I'VE READ THEM ALL.
SOME SAY IT ALL TOOK PLACE IN ENGLAND. ONE REPORT I READ CLAIMED WE WERE BROUGHT TO NEWFOUNDLAND.
SOMETIMES I THINK I'M NOT EVEN SURE WHAT REALLY HAPPENED ANYMORE.
DID I EVER REALLY REMEMBER ANY OF IT, OR WAS I JUST FILLING IN BLANKS?
LIKE AN ACCIDENT VICTIM WHO DOESN'T REMEMBER ANYTHING AFTER GETTING IN THEIR CAR UNTIL THEY WAKE UP IN THE HOSPITAL...
NO...I ALWAYS REMEMBERED ZEMO AND THE DRONE PLANE...
ALWAYS REMEMBERED IT EXPLODING.
BUT THE REST OF IT, I SUPPOSE IT'S POSSIBLE THAT READING REPORTS ABOUT THAT DAY COLORED MY PERCEPTIONS.
ALL I KNOW FOR SURE IS, THESE NEW MEMORIES THAT HAVE BEEN SURFACING-- MEMORIES OF ZEMO CAPTURING US, TORTURING BUCKY...
THEY FEEL FAR TOO REAL...

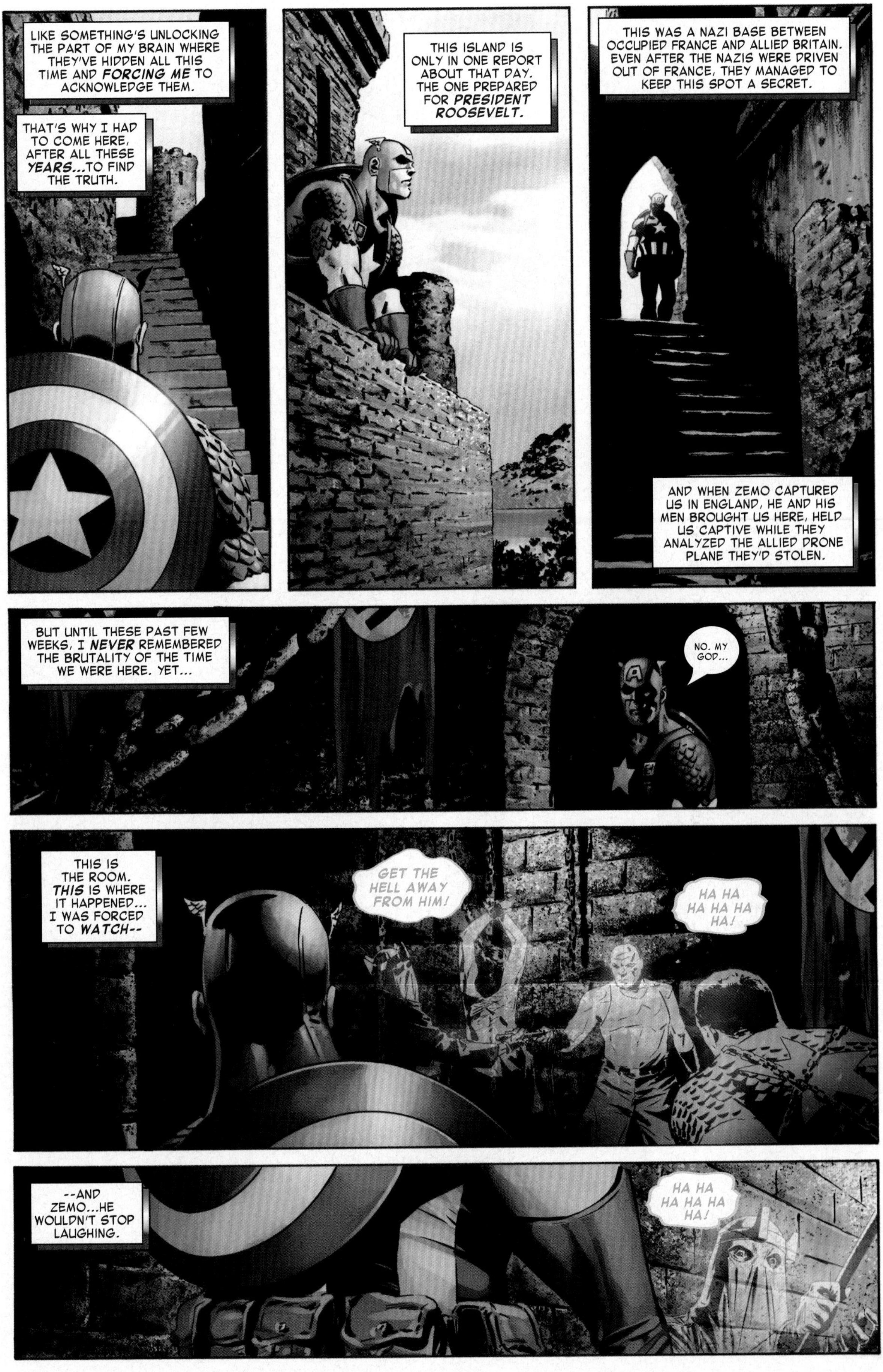
LIKE SOMETHING'S UNLOCKING THE PART OF MY BRAIN WHERE THEY'VE HIDDEN ALL THIS TIME AND FORCING ME TO ACKNOWLEDGE THEM.
THAT'S WHY I HAD TO COME HERE, AFTER ALL THESE YEARS...TO FIND THE TRUTH.
THIS ISLAND IS ONLY IN ONE REPORT ABOUT THAT DAY. THE ONE PREPARED FOR PRESIDENT ROOSEVELT.
THIS WAS A NAZI BASE BETWEEN OCCUPIED FRANCE AND ALLIED BRITAIN. EVEN AFTER THE NAZIS WERE DRIVEN OUT OF FRANCE, THEY MANAGED TO KEEP THIS SPOT A SECRET.
AND WHEN ZEMO CAPTURED US IN ENGLAND, HE AND HIS MEN BROUGHT US HERE, HELD US CAPTIVE WHILE THEY ANALYZED THE ALLIED DRONE PLANE THEY'D STOLEN.
BUT UNTIL THESE PAST FEW WEEKS, I NEVER REMEMBERED THE BRUTALITY OF THE TIME WE WERE HERE. YET...
NO. MY GOD...
THIS IS THE ROOM. THIS IS WHERE IT HAPPENED... I WAS FORCED TO WATCH--
GET THE HELL AWAY FROM HIM!
HA HA HA HA HA HA!
--AND ZEMO...HE WOULDN'T STOP LAUGHING.
HA HA HA HA HA HA!

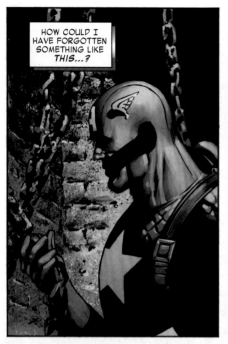
HOW COULD I HAVE FORGOTTEN SOMETHING LIKE *THIS...?*

MAYBE A BETTER QUESTION IS...WHY AM I REMEMBERING IT ALL *NOW?*

--AMERIKANER!

--AMERIKANER!

BUDDABUDDABUDD--

WHAT--? NAZI SOLDIERS?

ZEMO? NO, WHAT IS--THIS ISN'T REAL... IT *CAN'T* BE.

KAPITAN AMERIKANER! GET HIM! KILL HIM!

BULLETS ARE REAL ENOUGH.

WHATEVER'S GOING ON HERE, ONE THING'S CLEAR...

...I'VE GOTTA GET OUT--*NOW!*

KRAK!

KRAK!

KRAK!

BUDDABUDDABUDDABUDDABUDDABUDDABUDDABUDDA

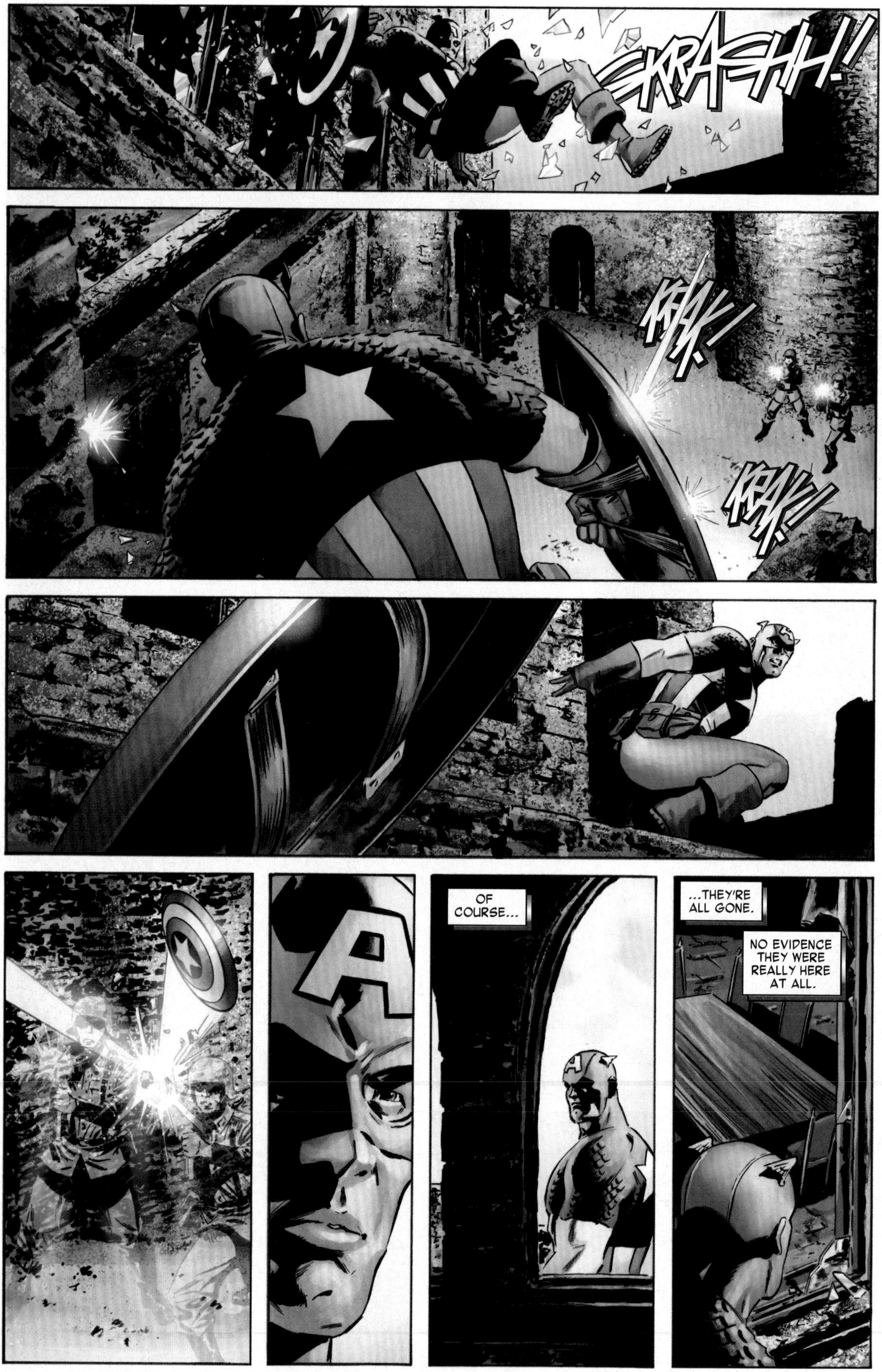
SKRASHH!!
KRAK!
KRAK!!
OF COURSE...
...THEY'RE ALL GONE.
NO EVIDENCE THEY WERE REALLY HERE AT ALL.

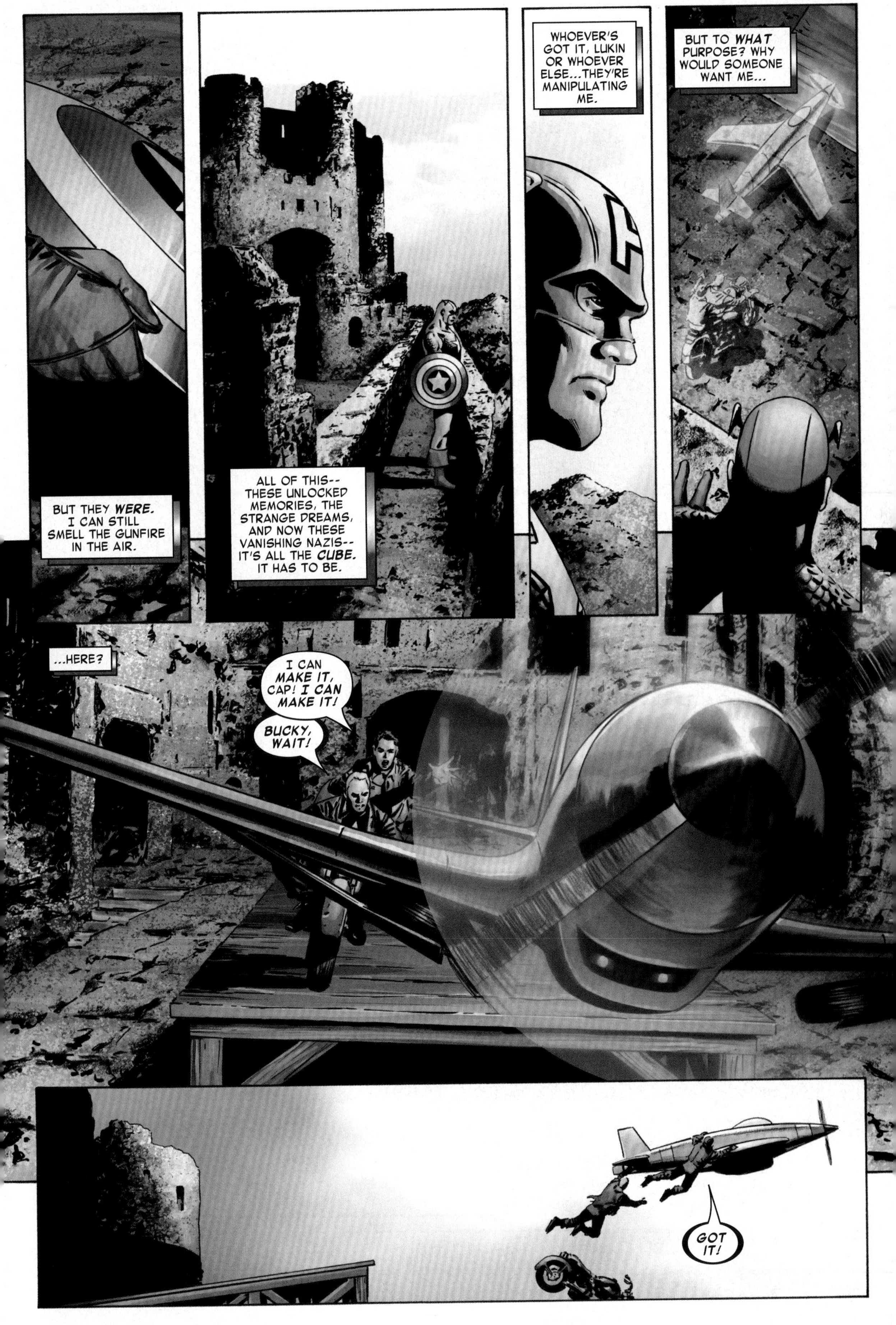
BUT THEY *WERE.* I CAN STILL SMELL THE GUNFIRE IN THE AIR.
ALL OF THIS-- THESE UNLOCKED MEMORIES, THE STRANGE DREAMS, AND NOW THESE VANISHING NAZIS-- IT'S ALL THE *CUBE.* IT HAS TO BE.
WHOEVER'S GOT IT, LUKIN OR WHOEVER ELSE...THEY'RE MANIPULATING ME.
BUT TO *WHAT* PURPOSE? WHY WOULD SOMEONE WANT ME...
...HERE?
I CAN *MAKE IT,* CAP! *I CAN MAKE IT!*
BUCKY, WAIT!
GOT IT!

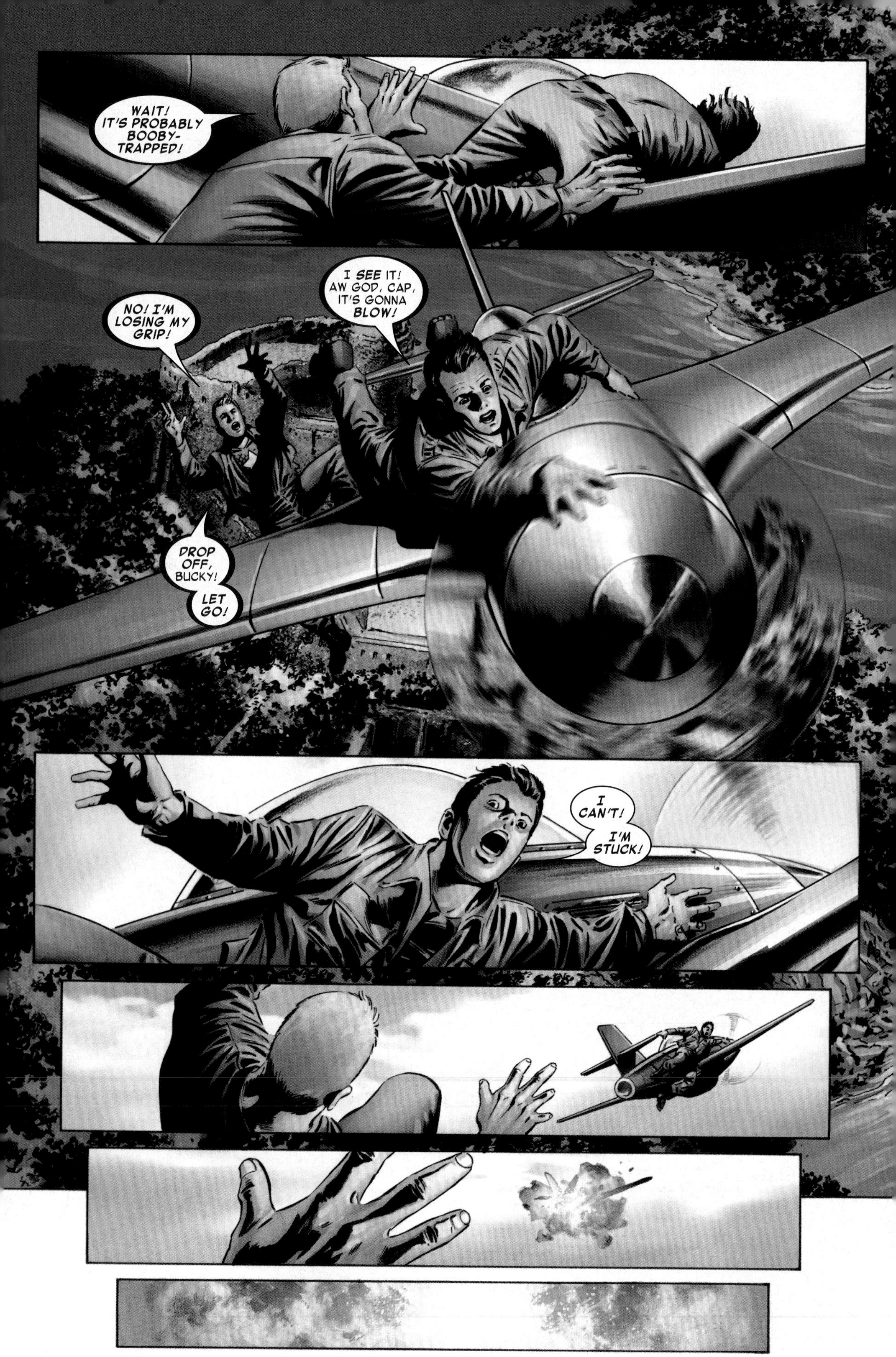
WAIT! IT'S PROBABLY BOOBY-TRAPPED!
I SEE IT! AW GOD, CAP, IT'S GONNA BLOW!
NO! I'M LOSING MY GRIP!
DROP OFF, BUCKY!
LET GO!
I CAN'T!
I'M STUCK!

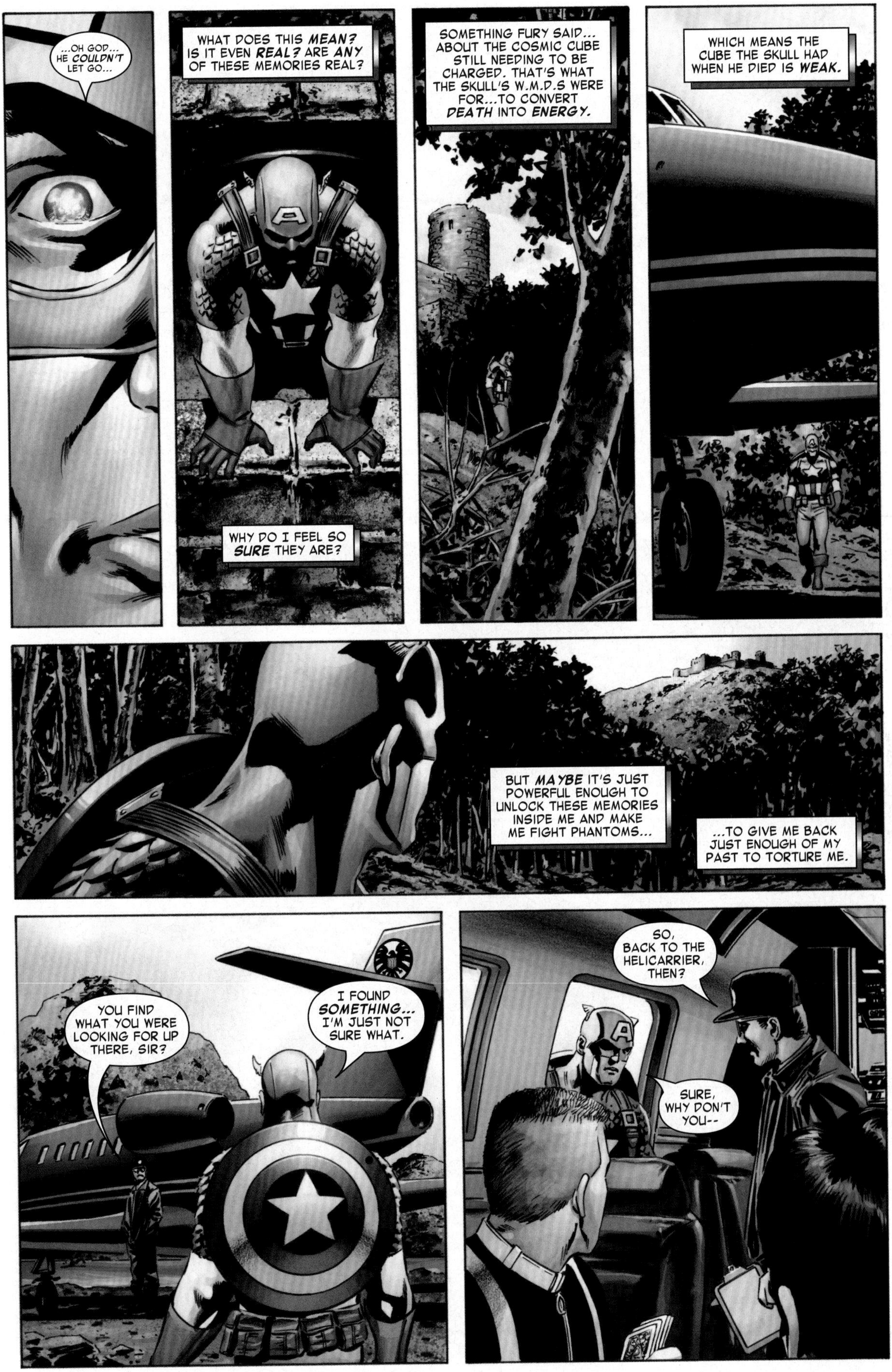
...OH GOD... HE COULDN'T LET GO...
WHAT DOES THIS MEAN? IS IT EVEN REAL? ARE ANY OF THESE MEMORIES REAL?
WHY DO I FEEL SO SURE THEY ARE?
SOMETHING FURY SAID... ABOUT THE COSMIC CUBE STILL NEEDING TO BE CHARGED. THAT'S WHAT THE SKULL'S W.M.D.S WERE FOR...TO CONVERT DEATH INTO ENERGY.
WHICH MEANS THE CUBE THE SKULL HAD WHEN HE DIED IS WEAK.
BUT MAYBE IT'S JUST POWERFUL ENOUGH TO UNLOCK THESE MEMORIES INSIDE ME AND MAKE ME FIGHT PHANTOMS...
...TO GIVE ME BACK JUST ENOUGH OF MY PAST TO TORTURE ME.
YOU FIND WHAT YOU WERE LOOKING FOR UP THERE, SIR?
I FOUND SOMETHING... I'M JUST NOT SURE WHAT.
SO, BACK TO THE HELICARRIER, THEN?
SURE, WHY DON'T YOU--

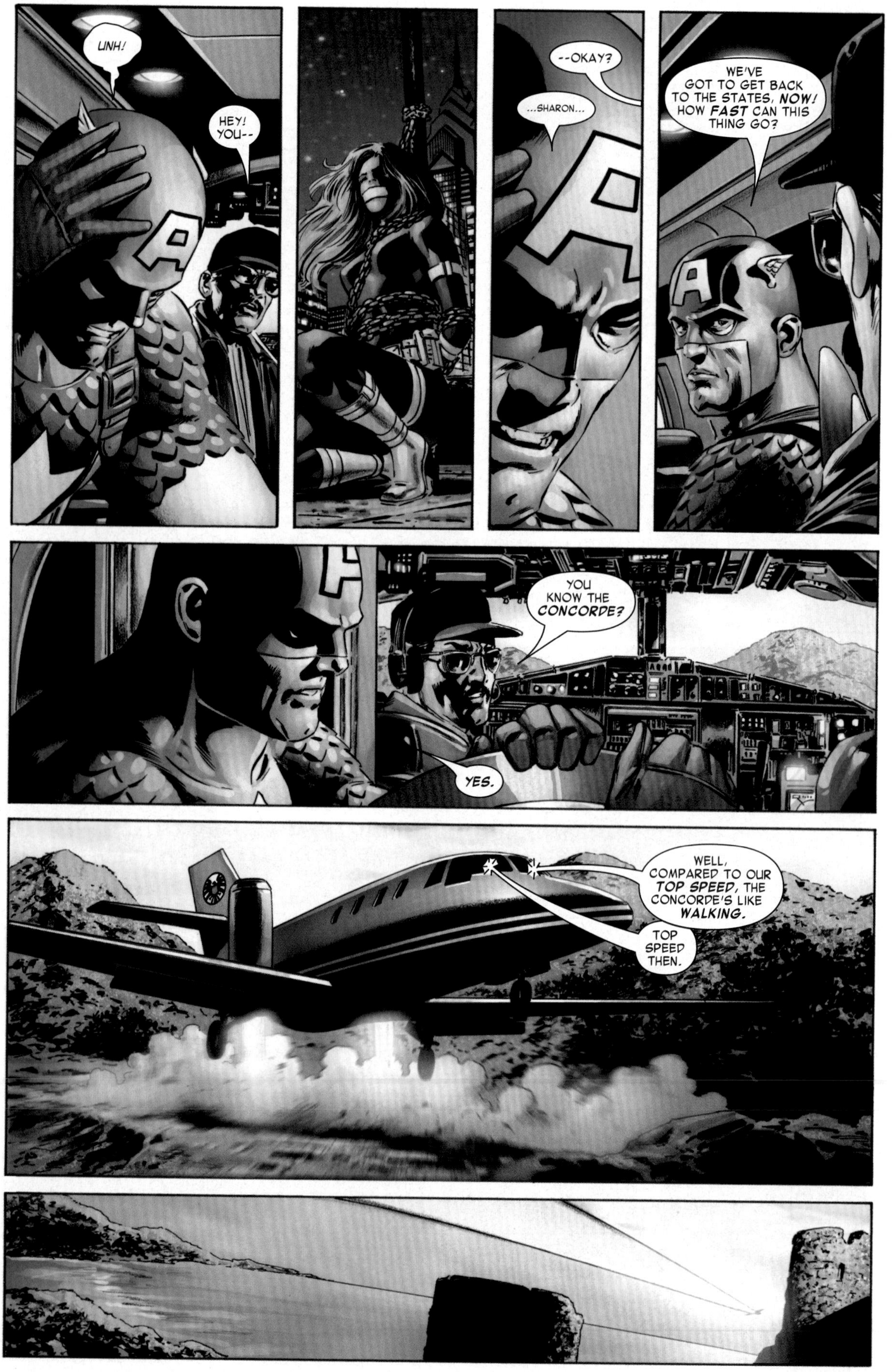
UNH!
HEY! YOU--
...SHARON...
--OKAY?
WE'VE GOT TO GET BACK TO THE STATES, NOW! HOW FAST CAN THIS THING GO?
YOU KNOW THE CONCORDE?
YES.
WELL, COMPARED TO OUR TOP SPEED, THE CONCORDE'S LIKE WALKING.
TOP SPEED THEN.

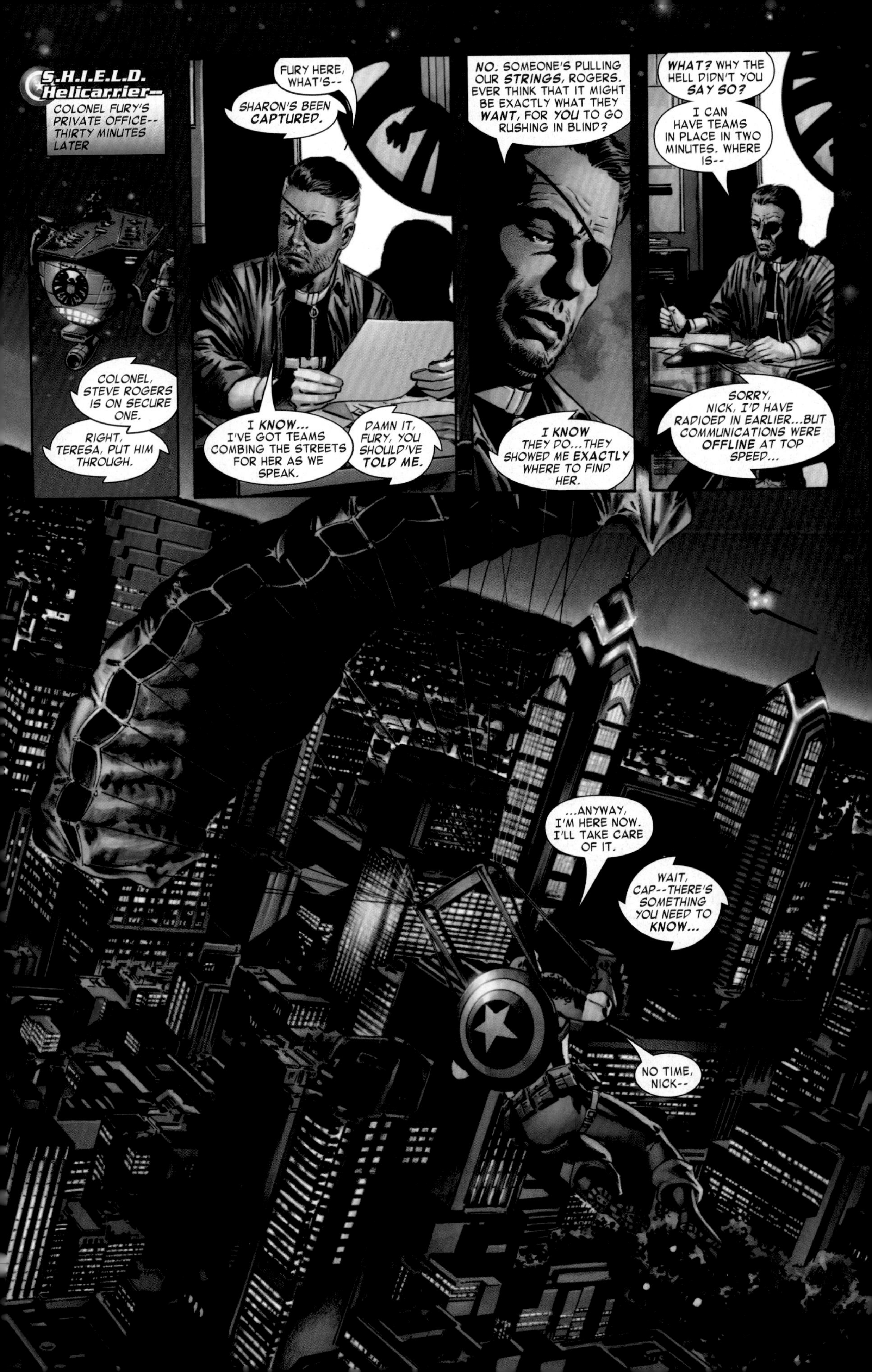
S.H.I.E.L.D. Helicarrier--
COLONEL FURY'S PRIVATE OFFICE--THIRTY MINUTES LATER
COLONEL, STEVE ROGERS IS ON SECURE ONE.
RIGHT, TERESA, PUT HIM THROUGH.
FURY HERE, WHAT'S--
SHARON'S BEEN CAPTURED.
I KNOW... I'VE GOT TEAMS COMBING THE STREETS FOR HER AS WE SPEAK.
DAMN IT, FURY, YOU SHOULD'VE TOLD ME.
NO. SOMEONE'S PULLING OUR STRINGS, ROGERS. EVER THINK THAT IT MIGHT BE EXACTLY WHAT THEY WANT, FOR YOU TO GO RUSHING IN BLIND?
I KNOW THEY DO... THEY SHOWED ME EXACTLY WHERE TO FIND HER.
WHAT? WHY THE HELL DIDN'T YOU SAY SO?
I CAN HAVE TEAMS IN PLACE IN TWO MINUTES. WHERE IS--
SORRY, NICK, I'D HAVE RADIOED IN EARLIER...BUT COMMUNICATIONS WERE OFFLINE AT TOP SPEED...
...ANYWAY, I'M HERE NOW. I'LL TAKE CARE OF IT.
WAIT, CAP--THERE'S SOMETHING YOU NEED TO KNOW...
NO TIME, NICK--

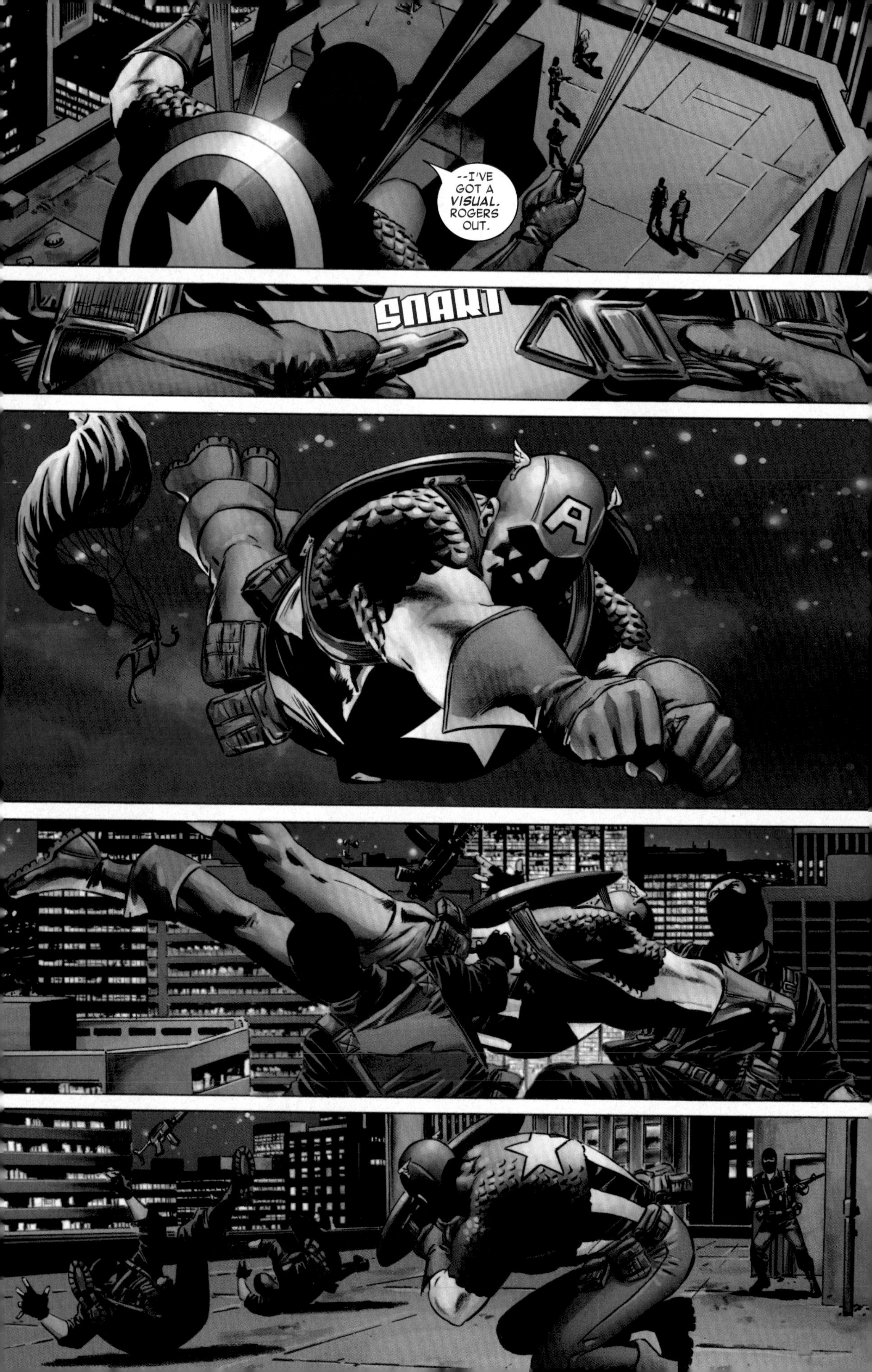
--I'VE GOT A VISUAL. ROGERS OUT.
SNAKT

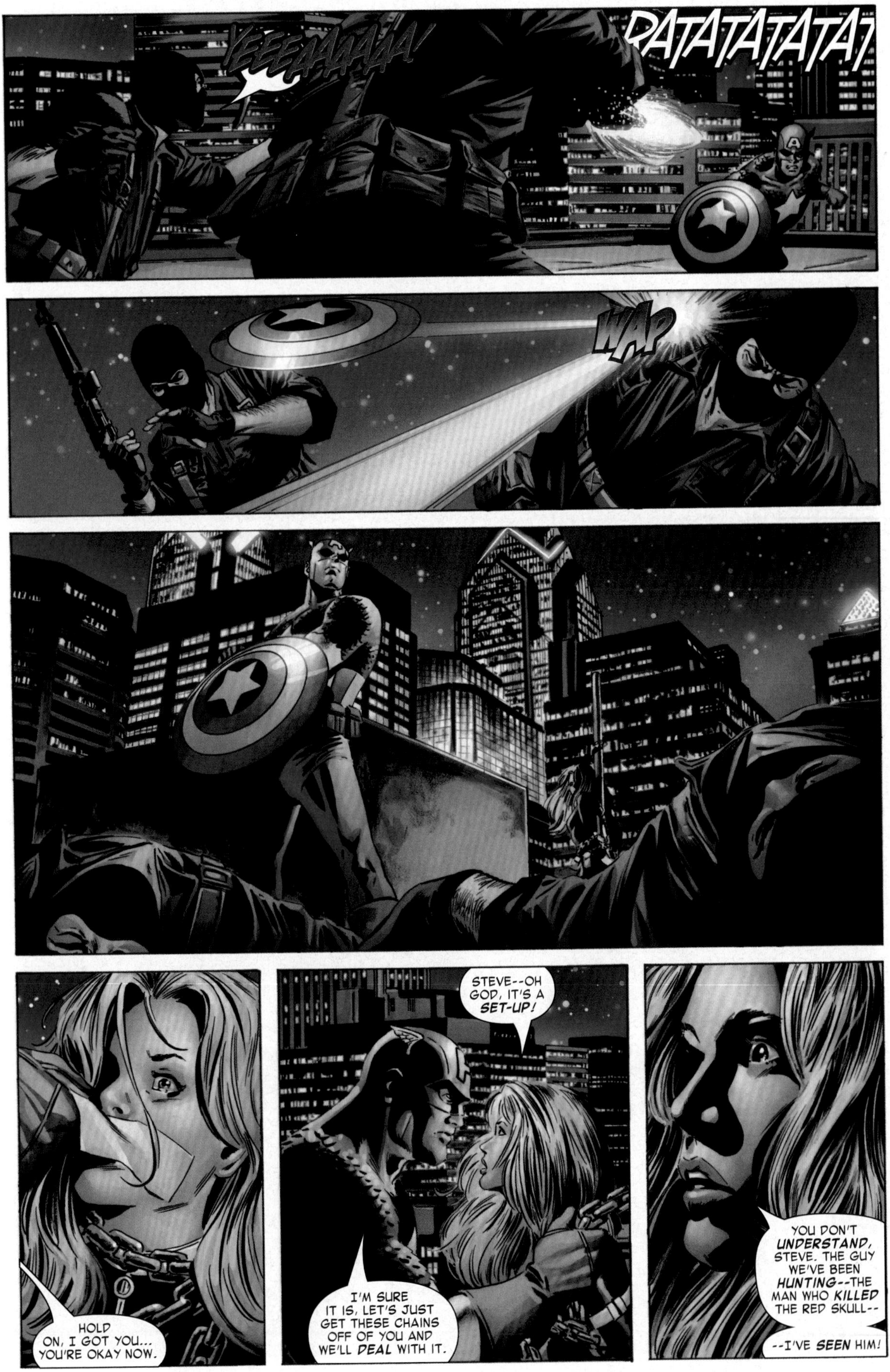
YEEEAAAAAAA!
RATATATATAT
WAP
HOLD ON, I GOT YOU... YOU'RE OKAY NOW.
STEVE--OH GOD, IT'S A SET-UP!
I'M SURE IT IS, LET'S JUST GET THESE CHAINS OFF OF YOU AND WE'LL DEAL WITH IT.
YOU DON'T UNDERSTAND, STEVE. THE GUY WE'VE BEEN HUNTING--THE MAN WHO KILLED THE RED SKULL--
--I'VE SEEN HIM!

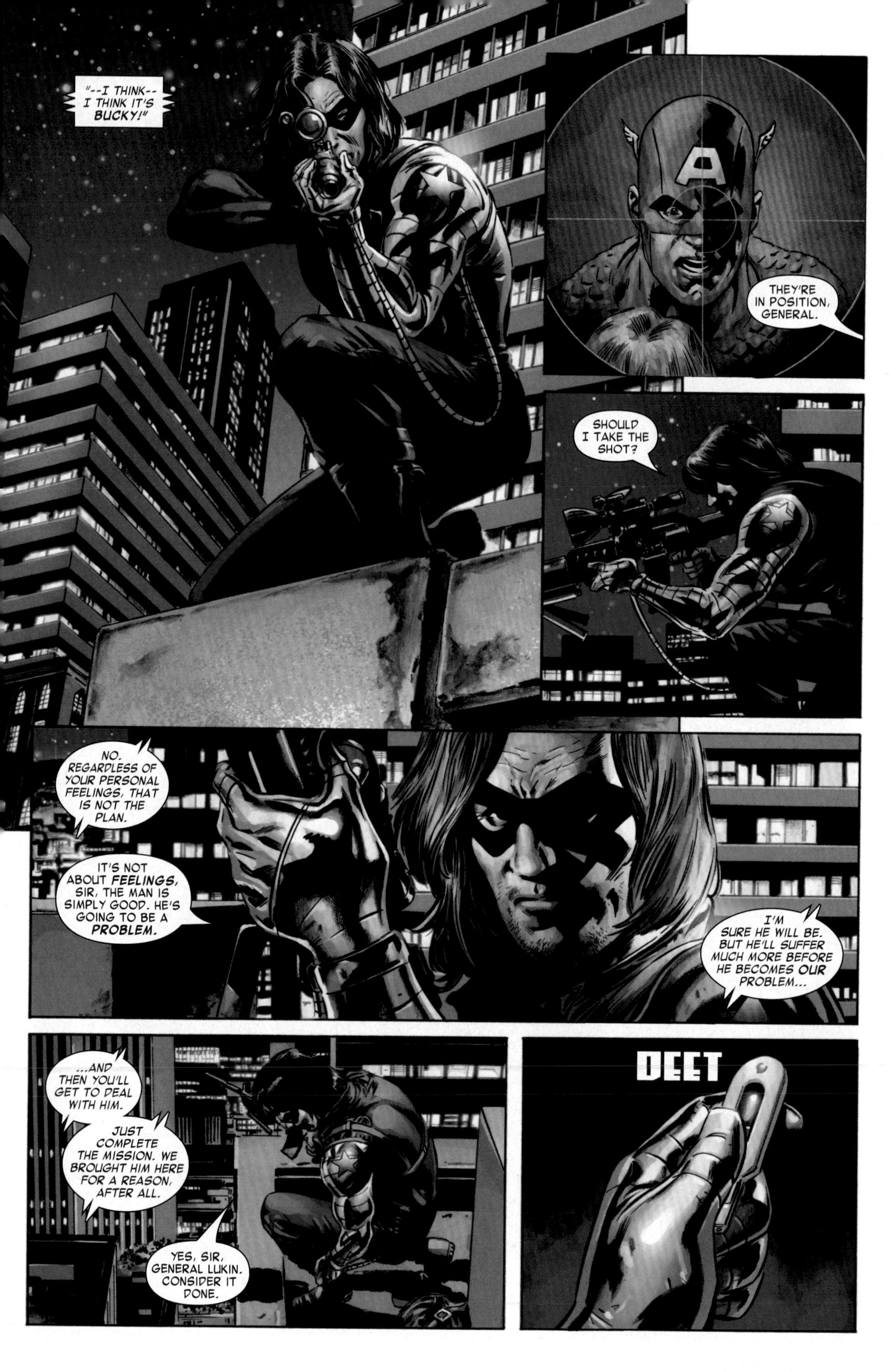
"--I THINK--
I THINK IT'S
BUCKY!"
THEY'RE IN POSITION, GENERAL.
SHOULD I TAKE THE SHOT?
NO. REGARDLESS OF YOUR PERSONAL FEELINGS, THAT IS NOT THE PLAN.
IT'S NOT ABOUT FEELINGS, SIR, THE MAN IS SIMPLY GOOD. HE'S GOING TO BE A PROBLEM.
I'M SURE HE WILL BE. BUT HE'LL SUFFER MUCH MORE BEFORE HE BECOMES OUR PROBLEM...
...AND THEN YOU'LL GET TO DEAL WITH HIM.
JUST COMPLETE THE MISSION. WE BROUGHT HIM HERE FOR A REASON, AFTER ALL.
YES, SIR, GENERAL LUKIN. CONSIDER IT DONE.
DEET

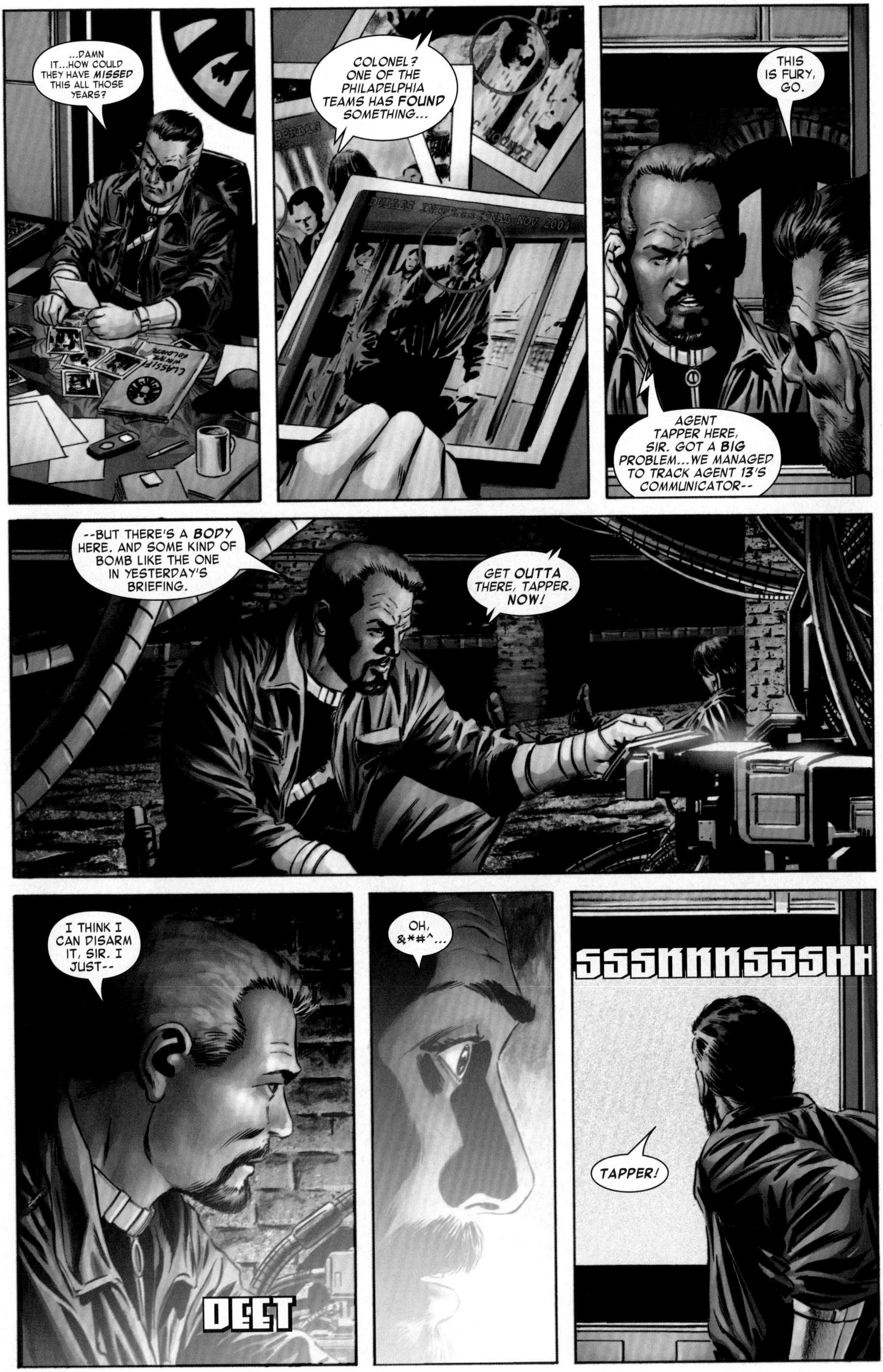
...DAMN IT...HOW COULD THEY HAVE MISSED THIS ALL THOSE YEARS?
COLONEL? ONE OF THE PHILADELPHIA TEAMS HAS FOUND SOMETHING...
THIS IS FURY, GO.
AGENT TAPPER HERE, SIR. GOT A BIG PROBLEM...WE MANAGED TO TRACK AGENT 13'S COMMUNICATOR--
--BUT THERE'S A BODY HERE. AND SOME KIND OF BOMB LIKE THE ONE IN YESTERDAY'S BRIEFING.
GET OUTTA THERE, TAPPER. NOW!
I THINK I CAN DISARM IT, SIR. I JUST--
DEET
OH, &*#^...
SSSKKKSSSHH
TAPPER!

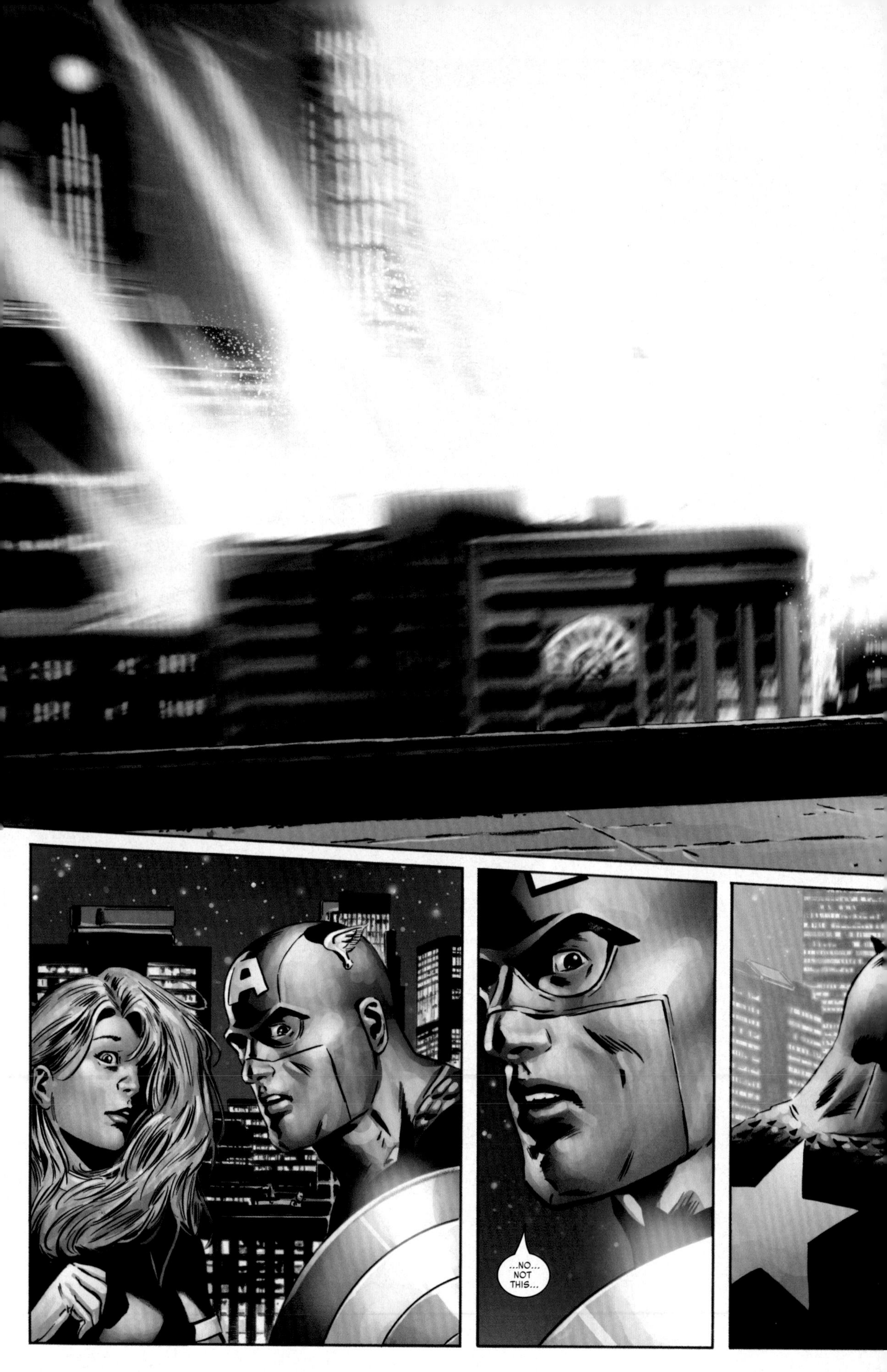
...NO... NOT THIS...

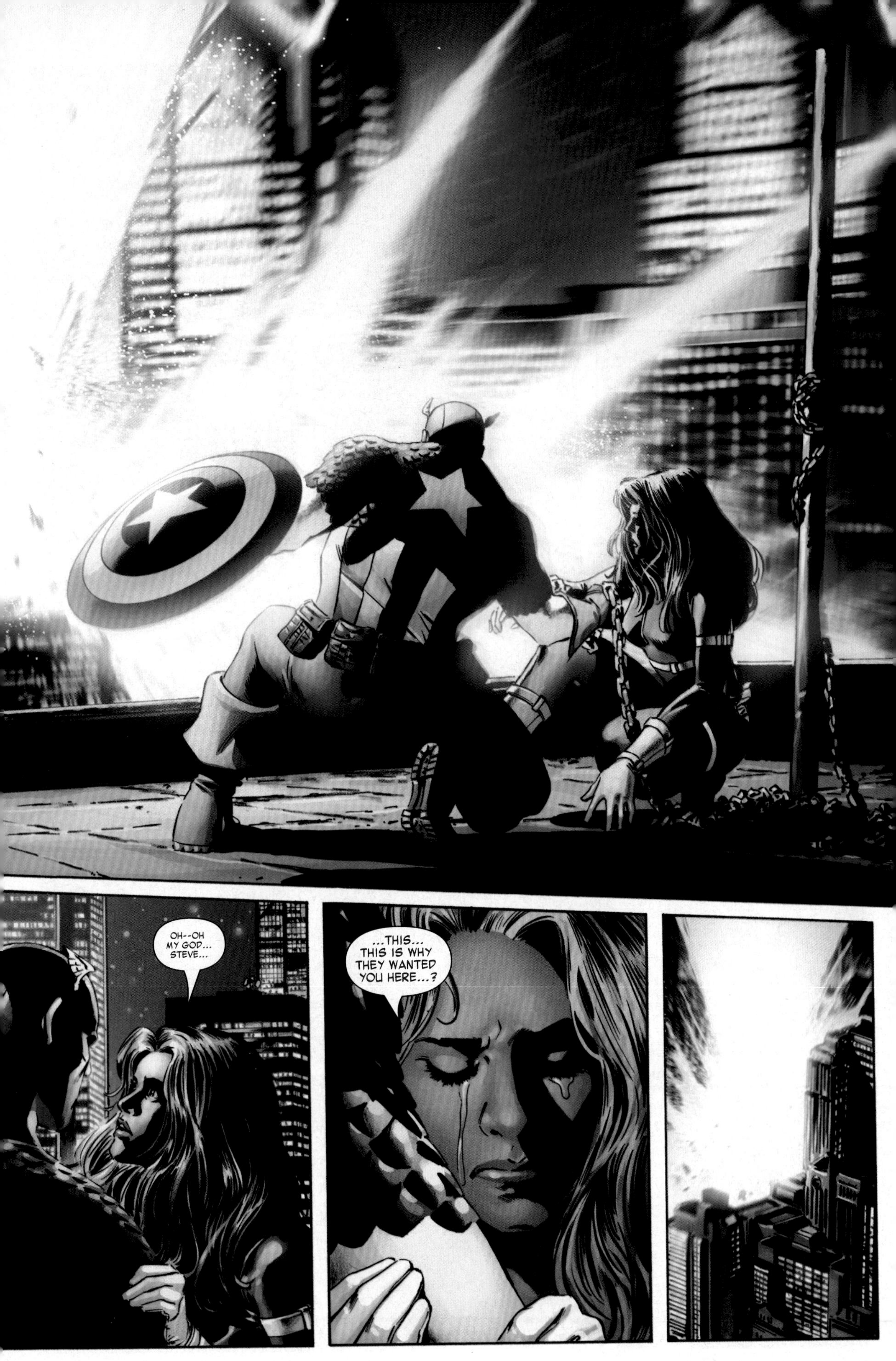
OH--OH MY GOD... STEVE...
...THIS... THIS IS WHY THEY WANTED YOU HERE...?

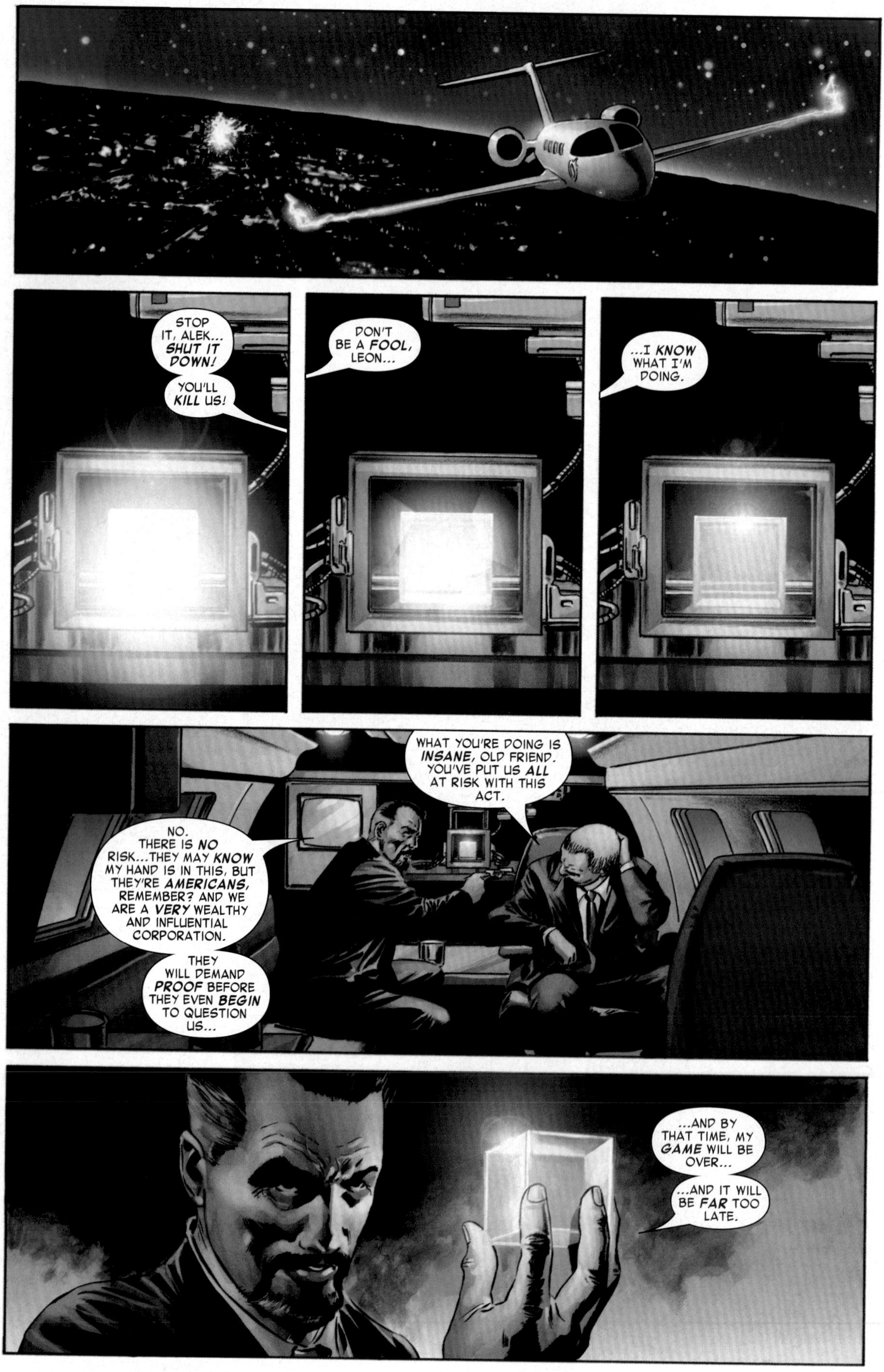
STOP IT, ALEK... SHUT IT DOWN!
YOU'LL KILL US!
DON'T BE A FOOL, LEON...
...I KNOW WHAT I'M DOING.
WHAT YOU'RE DOING IS INSANE, OLD FRIEND. YOU'VE PUT US ALL AT RISK WITH THIS ACT.
NO. THERE IS NO RISK...THEY MAY KNOW MY HAND IS IN THIS, BUT THEY'RE AMERICANS, REMEMBER? AND WE ARE A VERY WEALTHY AND INFLUENTIAL CORPORATION.
THEY WILL DEMAND PROOF BEFORE THEY EVEN BEGIN TO QUESTION US...
...AND BY THAT TIME, MY GAME WILL BE OVER...
...AND IT WILL BE FAR TOO LATE.

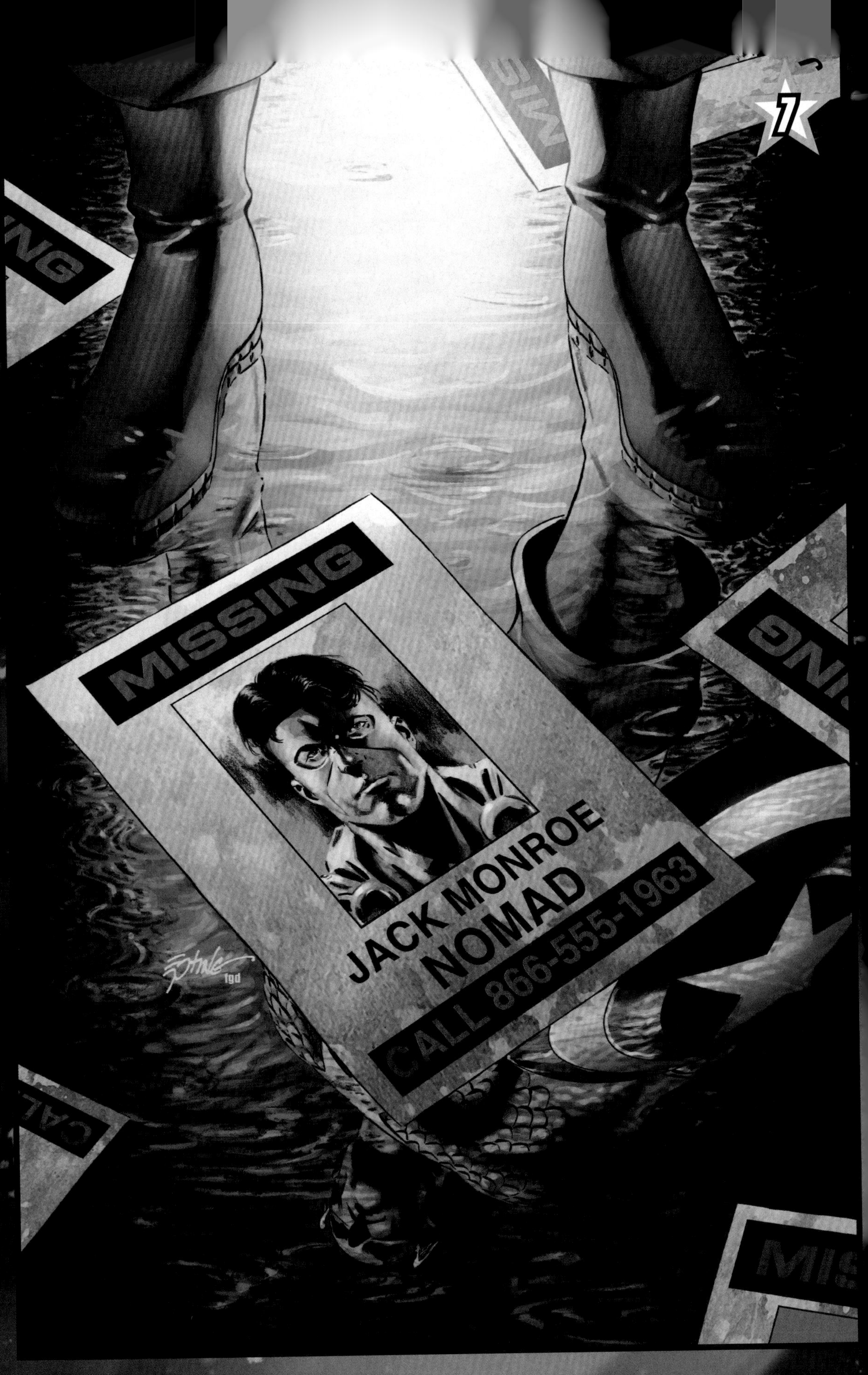
7
MISSING
JACK MONROE
NOMAD
CALL 866-555-1963

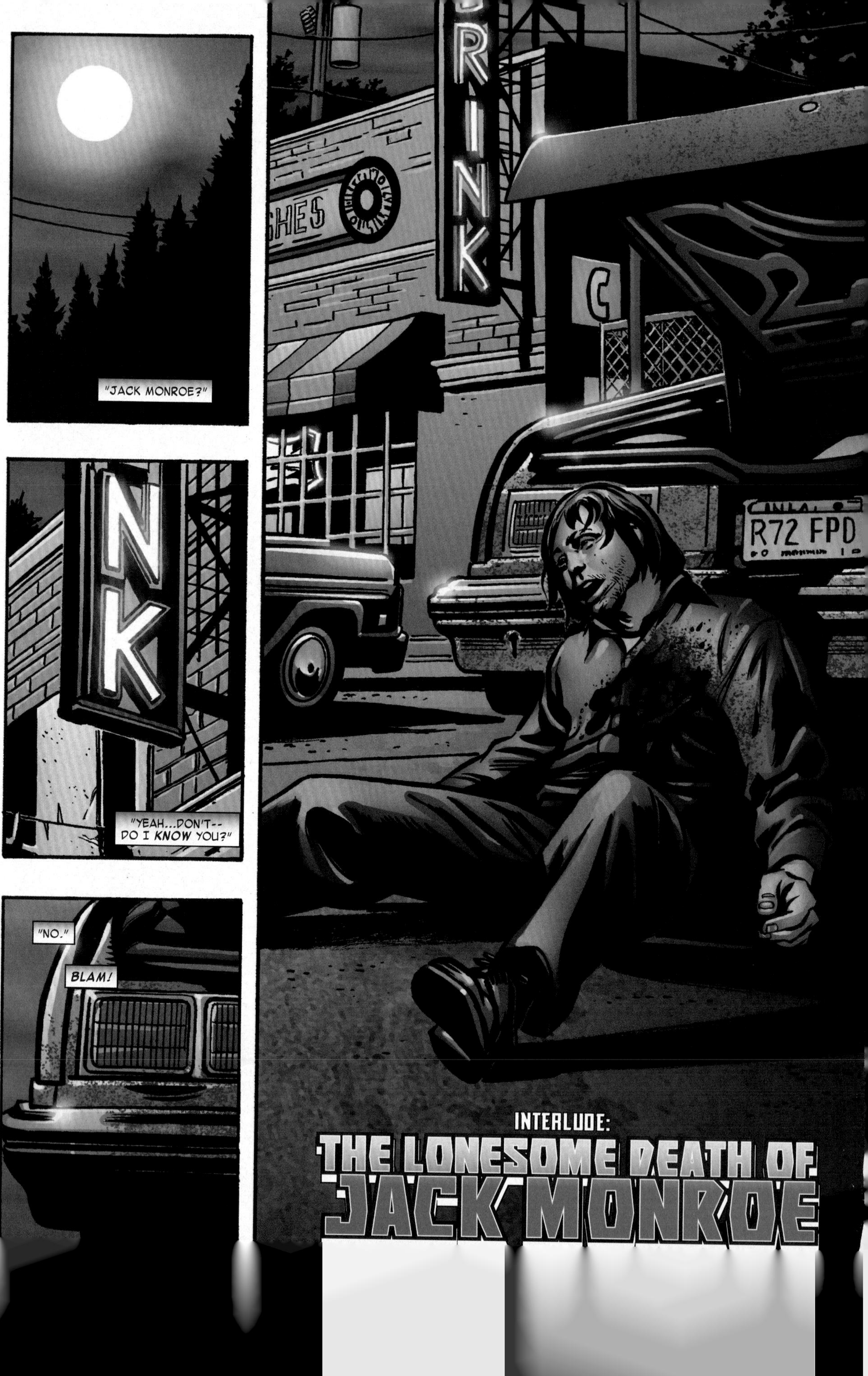
"JACK MONROE?"
NK
"YEAH...DON'T--
DO I KNOW YOU?"
"NO."
BLAM!
RINK
SHES
C
R72 FPD
INTERLUDE:
THE LONESOME DEATH OF
JACK MONROE

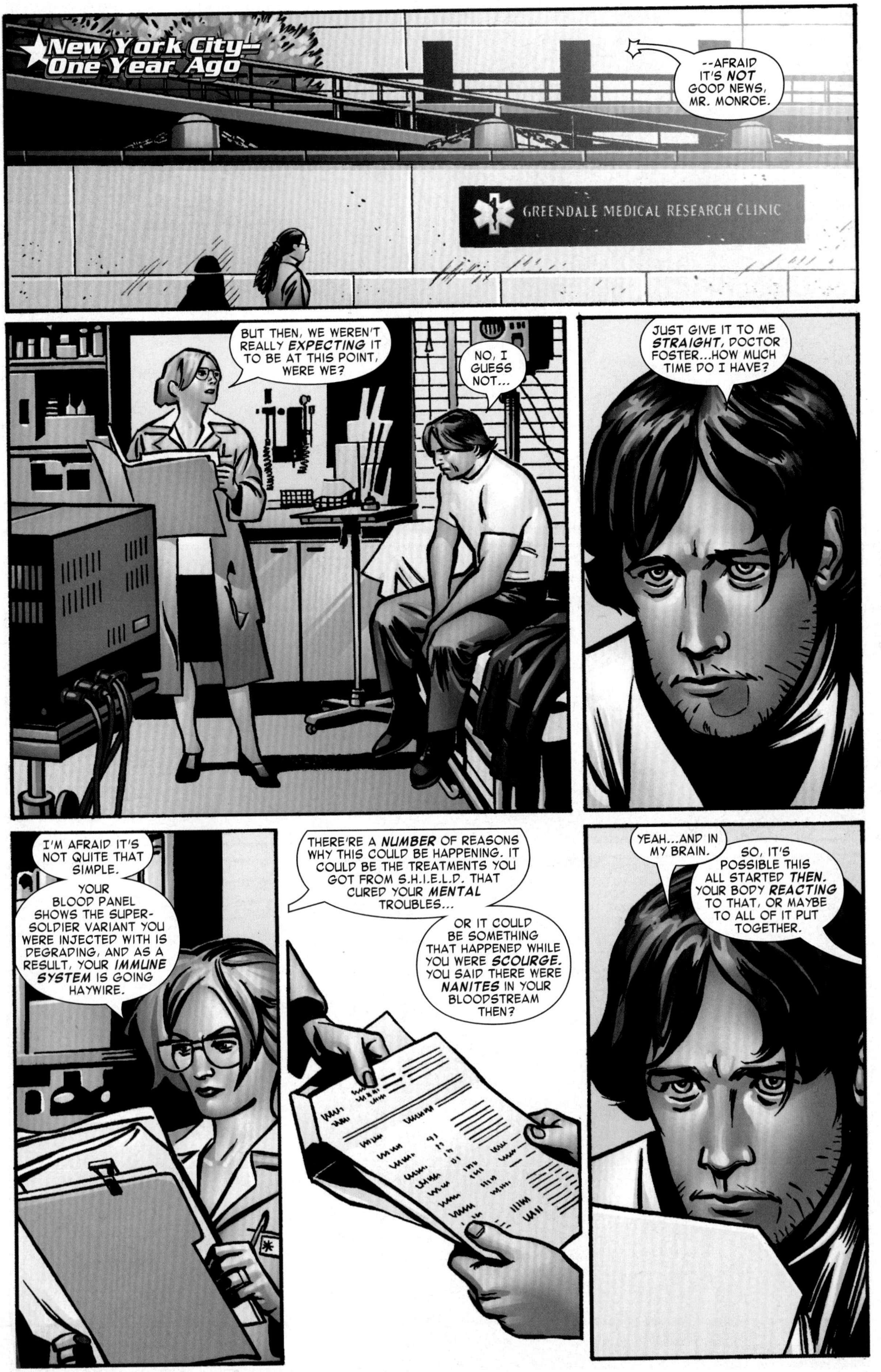
New York City-- One Year Ago
--AFRAID IT'S NOT GOOD NEWS, MR. MONROE.
GREENDALE MEDICAL RESEARCH CLINIC
BUT THEN, WE WEREN'T REALLY EXPECTING IT TO BE AT THIS POINT, WERE WE?
NO, I GUESS NOT...
JUST GIVE IT TO ME STRAIGHT, DOCTOR FOSTER...HOW MUCH TIME DO I HAVE?
I'M AFRAID IT'S NOT QUITE THAT SIMPLE.
YOUR BLOOD PANEL SHOWS THE SUPER-SOLDIER VARIANT YOU WERE INJECTED WITH IS DEGRADING, AND AS A RESULT, YOUR IMMUNE SYSTEM IS GOING HAYWIRE.
THERE'RE A NUMBER OF REASONS WHY THIS COULD BE HAPPENING. IT COULD BE THE TREATMENTS YOU GOT FROM S.H.I.E.L.D. THAT CURED YOUR MENTAL TROUBLES...
OR IT COULD BE SOMETHING THAT HAPPENED WHILE YOU WERE SCOURGE. YOU SAID THERE WERE NANITES IN YOUR BLOODSTREAM THEN?
YEAH...AND IN MY BRAIN.
SO, IT'S POSSIBLE THIS ALL STARTED THEN. YOUR BODY REACTING TO THAT, OR MAYBE TO ALL OF IT PUT TOGETHER.

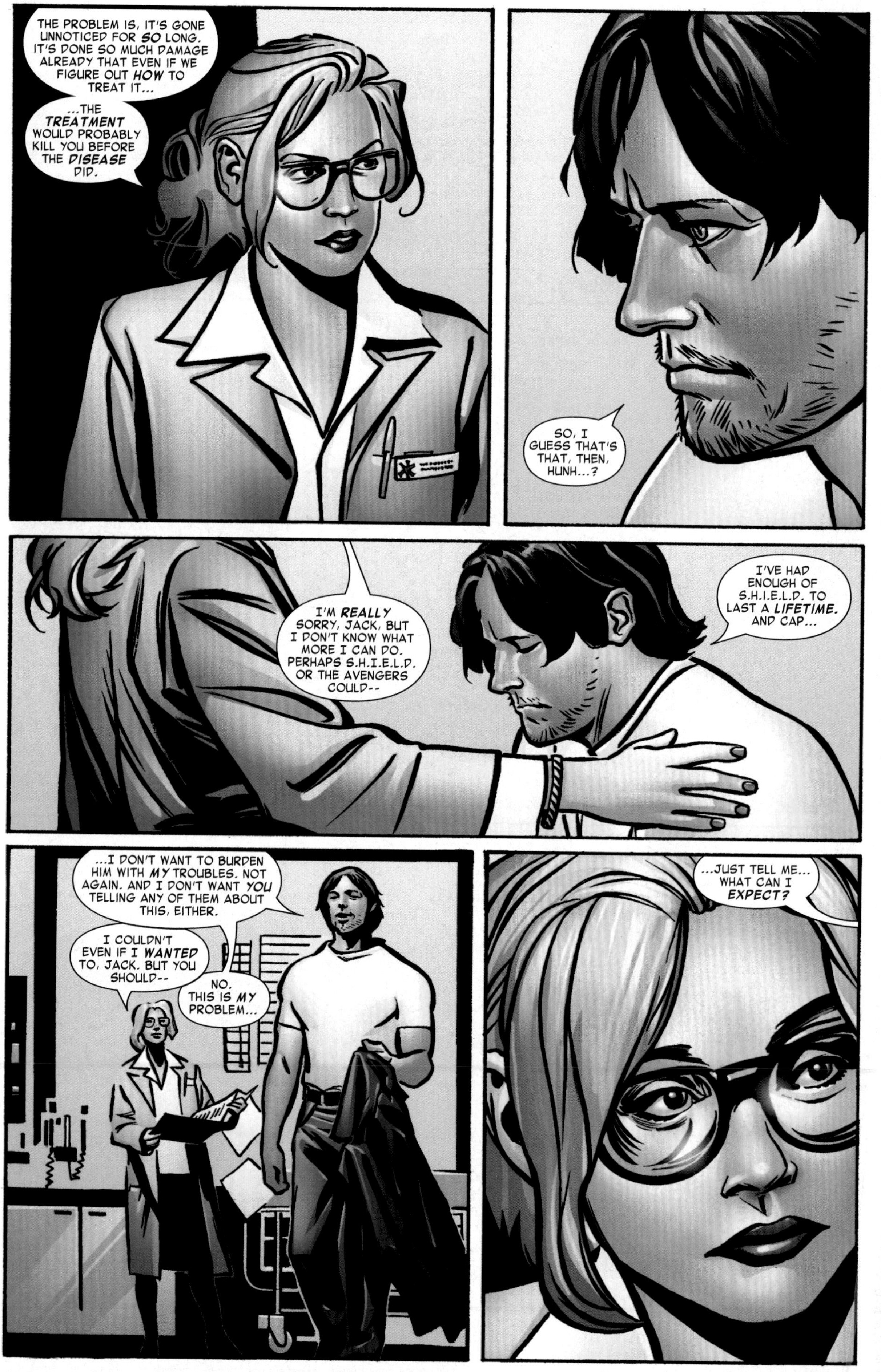
THE PROBLEM IS, IT'S GONE UNNOTICED FOR SO LONG. IT'S DONE SO MUCH DAMAGE ALREADY THAT EVEN IF WE FIGURE OUT HOW TO TREAT IT...
...THE TREATMENT WOULD PROBABLY KILL YOU BEFORE THE DISEASE DID.
SO, I GUESS THAT'S THAT, THEN, HUNH...?
I'M REALLY SORRY, JACK, BUT I DON'T KNOW WHAT MORE I CAN DO. PERHAPS S.H.I.E.L.D. OR THE AVENGERS COULD--
I'VE HAD ENOUGH OF S.H.I.E.L.D. TO LAST A LIFETIME. AND CAP...
...I DON'T WANT TO BURDEN HIM WITH MY TROUBLES. NOT AGAIN. AND I DON'T WANT YOU TELLING ANY OF THEM ABOUT THIS, EITHER.
I COULDN'T EVEN IF I WANTED TO, JACK. BUT YOU SHOULD--
NO. THIS IS MY PROBLEM...
...JUST TELL ME... WHAT CAN I EXPECT?

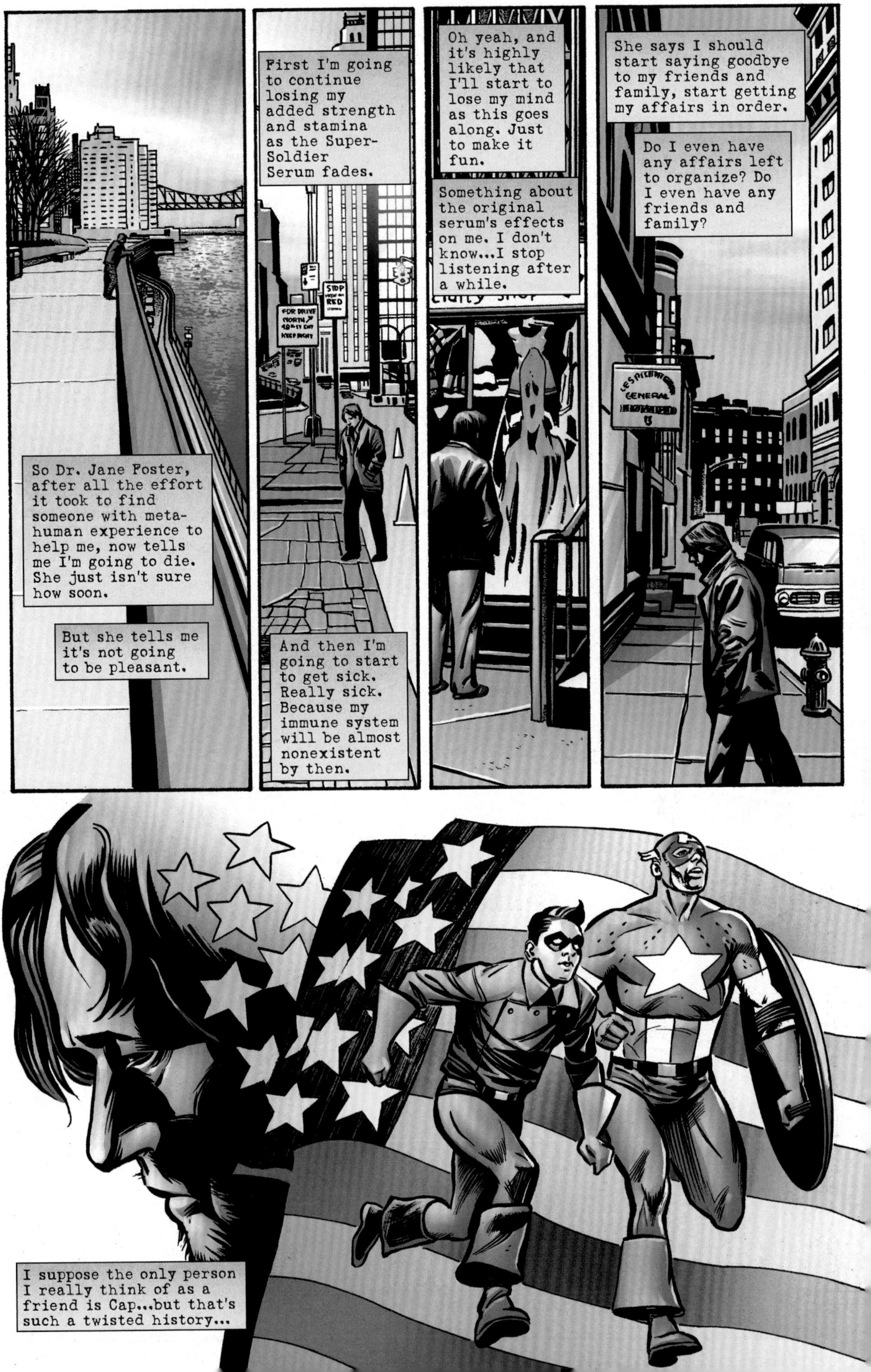
So Dr. Jane Foster, after all the effort it took to find someone with meta-human experience to help me, now tells me I'm going to die. She just isn't sure how soon.
But she tells me it's not going to be pleasant.
First I'm going to continue losing my added strength and stamina as the Super-Soldier Serum fades.
And then I'm going to start to get sick. Really sick. Because my immune system will be almost nonexistent by then.
Oh yeah, and it's highly likely that I'll start to lose my mind as this goes along. Just to make it fun.
Something about the original serum's effects on me. I don't know...I stop listening after a while.
She says I should start saying goodbye to my friends and family, start getting my affairs in order.
Do I even have any affairs left to organize? Do I even have any friends and family?
I suppose the only person I really think of as a friend is Cap...but that's such a twisted history...

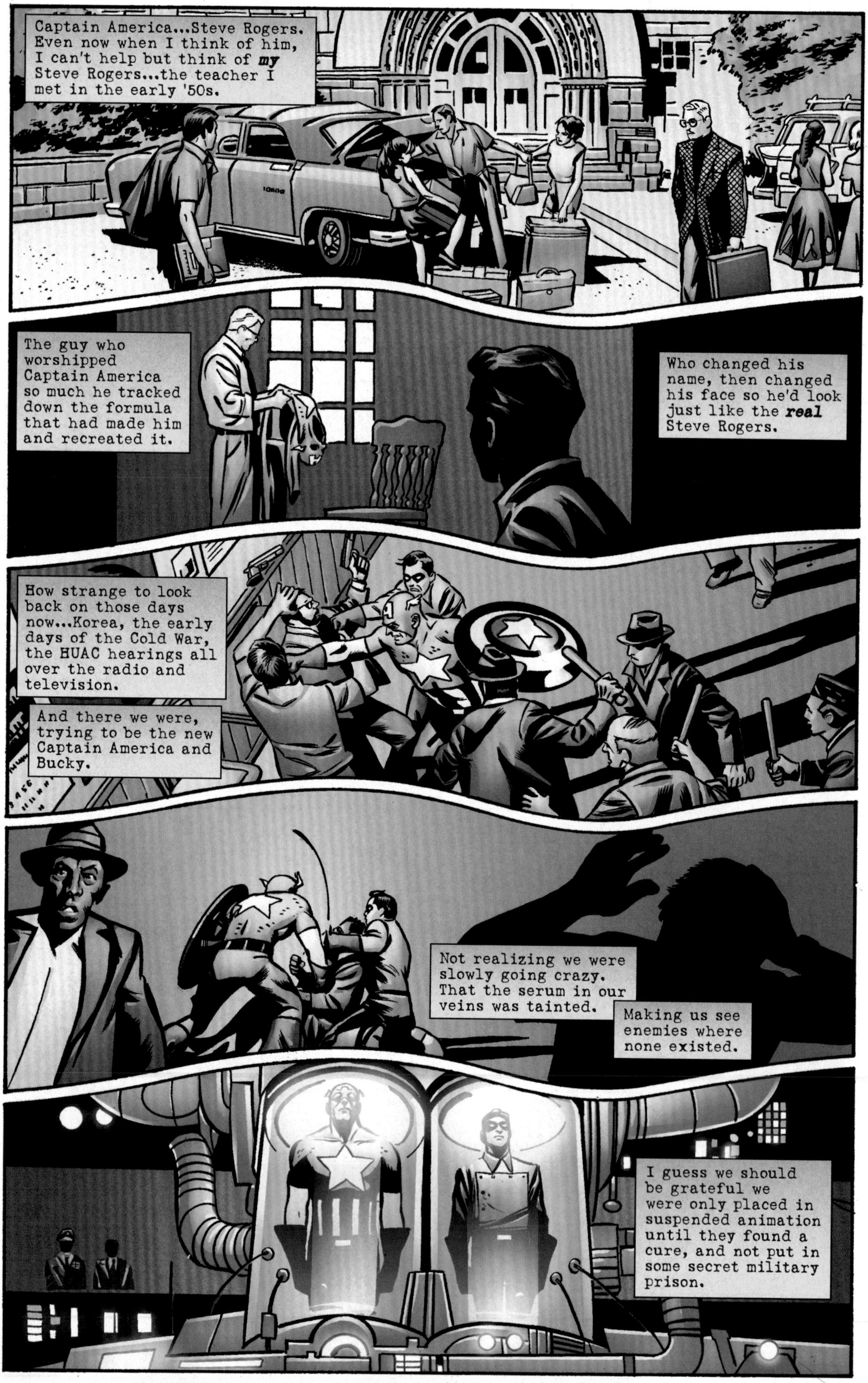
Captain America...Steve Rogers. Even now when I think of him, I can't help but think of *my* Steve Rogers...the teacher I met in the early '50s.
The guy who worshipped Captain America so much he tracked down the formula that had made him and recreated it.
Who changed his name, then changed his face so he'd look just like the *real* Steve Rogers.
How strange to look back on those days now...Korea, the early days of the Cold War, the HUAC hearings all over the radio and television.
And there we were, trying to be the new Captain America and Bucky.
Not realizing we were slowly going crazy. That the serum in our veins was tainted.
Making us see enemies where none existed.
I guess we should be grateful we were only placed in suspended animation until they found a cure, and not put in some secret military prison.

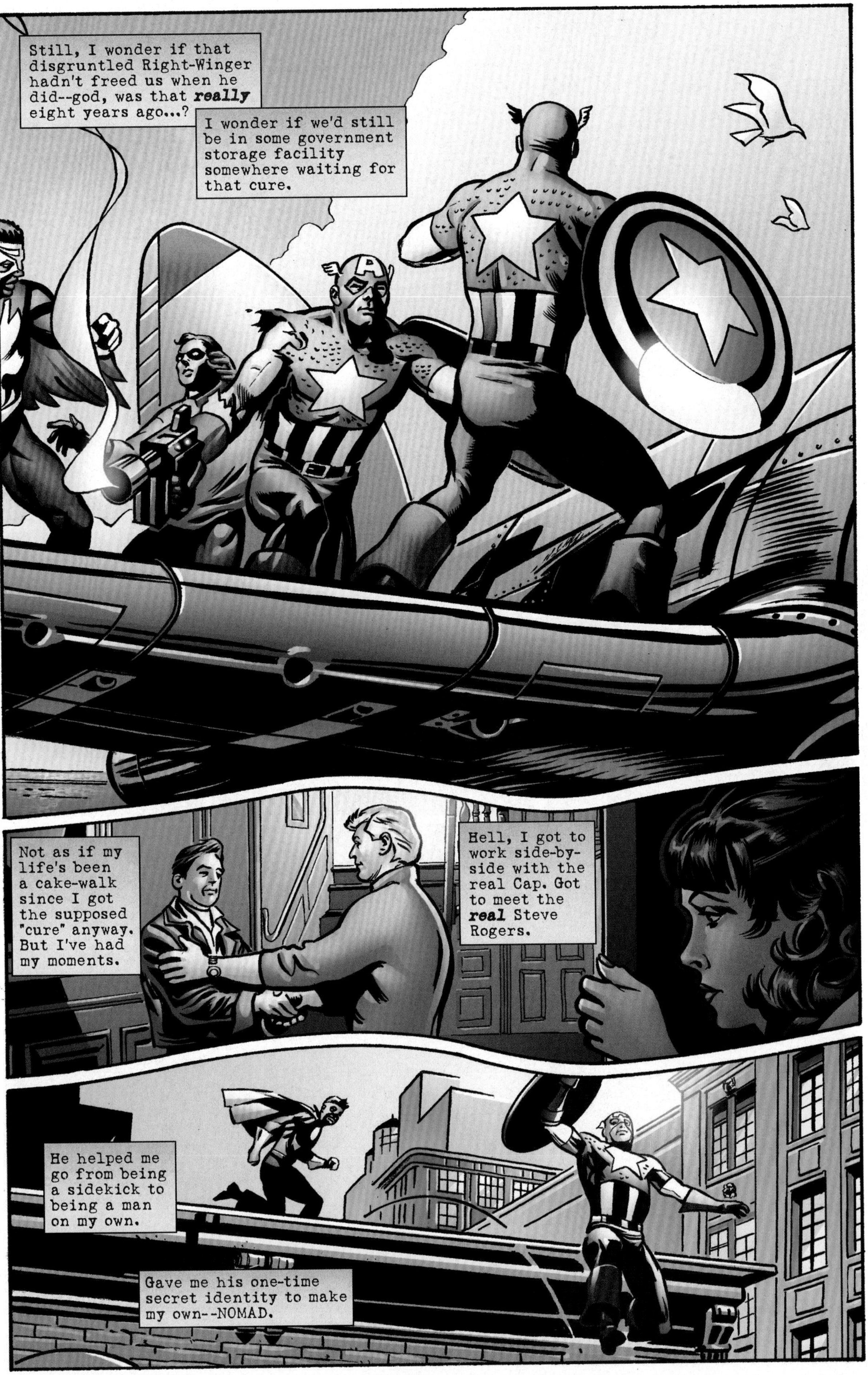
Still, I wonder if that disgruntled Right-Winger hadn't freed us when he did--god, was that **really** eight years ago...?
I wonder if we'd still be in some government storage facility somewhere waiting for that cure.
Not as if my life's been a cake-walk since I got the supposed "cure" anyway. But I've had my moments.
Hell, I got to work side-by-side with the real Cap. Got to meet the **real** Steve Rogers.
He helped me go from being a sidekick to being a man on my own.
Gave me his one-time secret identity to make my own--NOMAD.

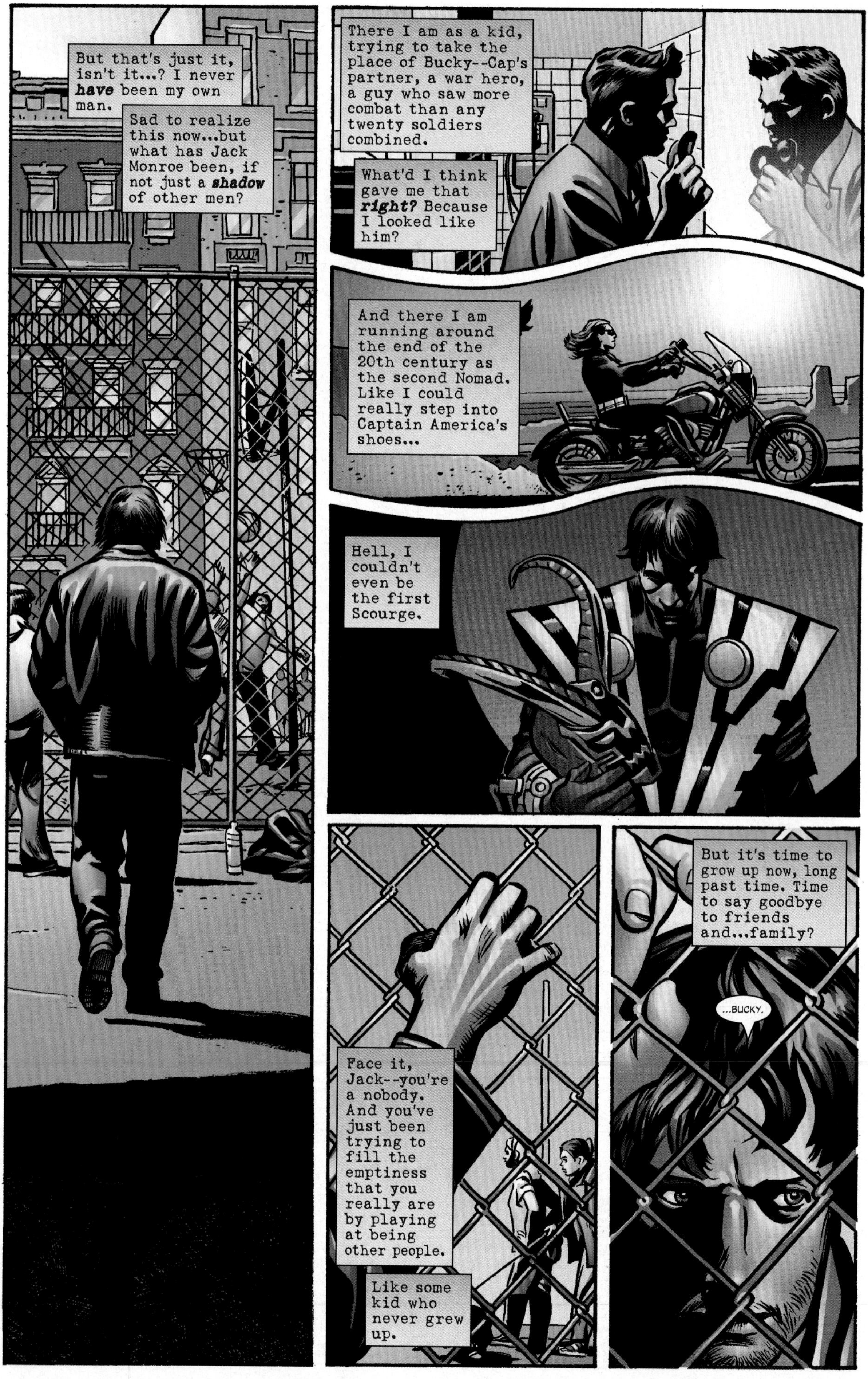

But that's just it, isn't it...? I never **have** been my own man.
Sad to realize this now...but what has Jack Monroe been, if not just a **shadow** of other men?
There I am as a kid, trying to take the place of Bucky--Cap's partner, a war hero, a guy who saw more combat than any twenty soldiers combined.
What'd I think gave me that **right?** Because I looked like him?
And there I am running around the end of the 20th century as the second Nomad. Like I could really step into Captain America's shoes...
Hell, I couldn't even be the first Scourge.
Face it, Jack--you're a nobody. And you've just been trying to fill the emptiness that you really are by playing at being other people.
Like some kid who never grew up.
But it's time to grow up now, long past time. Time to say goodbye to friends and...family?
...BUCKY.

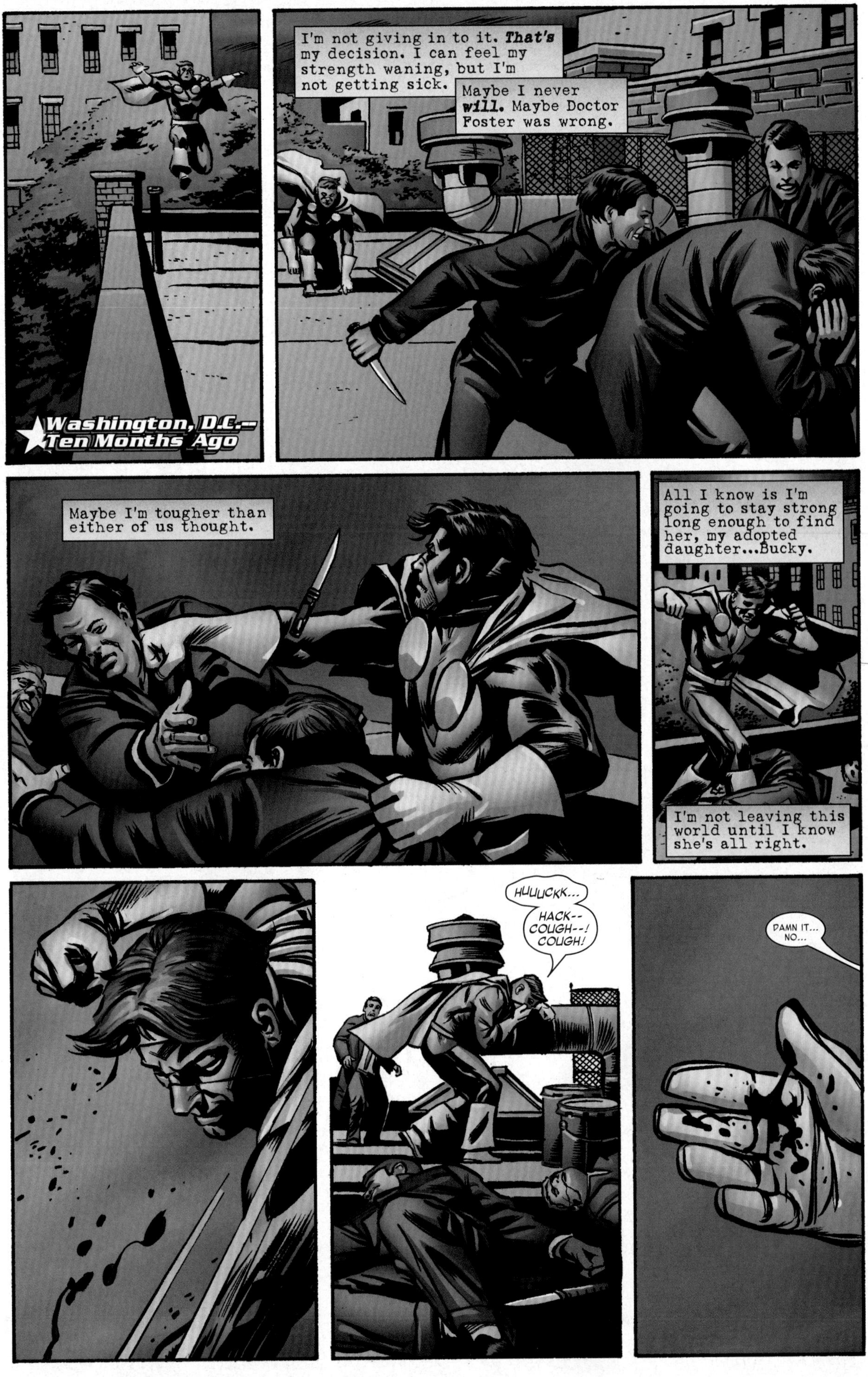
Washington, D.C.--
Ten Months Ago
I'm not giving in to it. That's my decision. I can feel my strength waning, but I'm not getting sick.
Maybe I never will. Maybe Doctor Foster was wrong.
Maybe I'm tougher than either of us thought.
All I know is I'm going to stay strong long enough to find her, my adopted daughter...Bucky.
I'm not leaving this world until I know she's all right.
HUUUCKK...
HACK--
COUGH--!
COUGH!
DAMN IT...
NO...

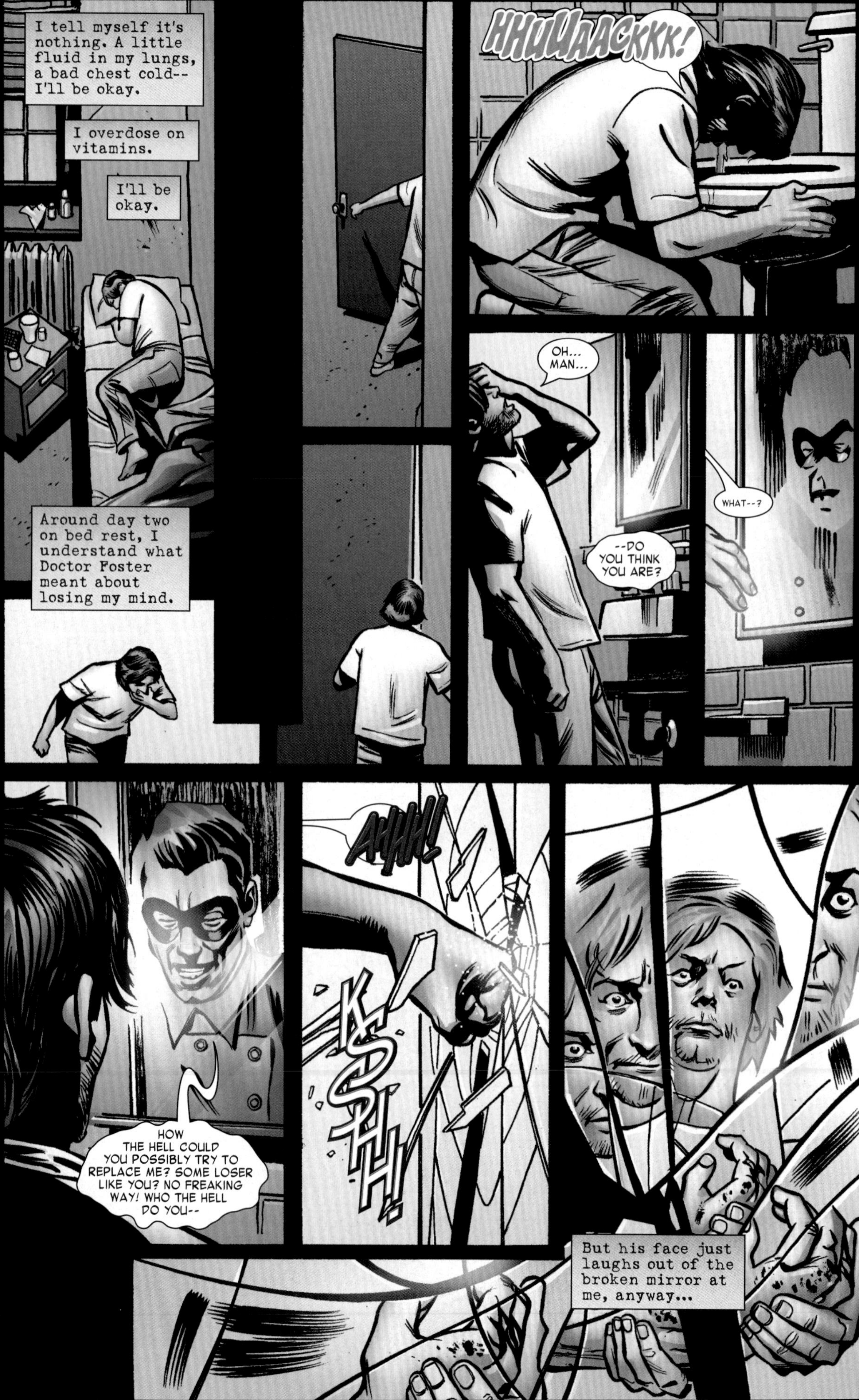

I tell myself it's nothing. A little fluid in my lungs, a bad chest cold-- I'll be okay.
I overdose on vitamins.
I'll be okay.
HHUUAACKKK!
Around day two on bed rest, I understand what Doctor Foster meant about losing my mind.
OH... MAN...
WHAT--?
--DO YOU THINK YOU ARE?
HOW THE HELL COULD YOU POSSIBLY TRY TO REPLACE ME? SOME LOSER LIKE YOU? NO FREAKING WAY! WHO THE HELL DO YOU--
AHHH!
KSSHH!
But his face just laughs out of the broken mirror at me, anyway...

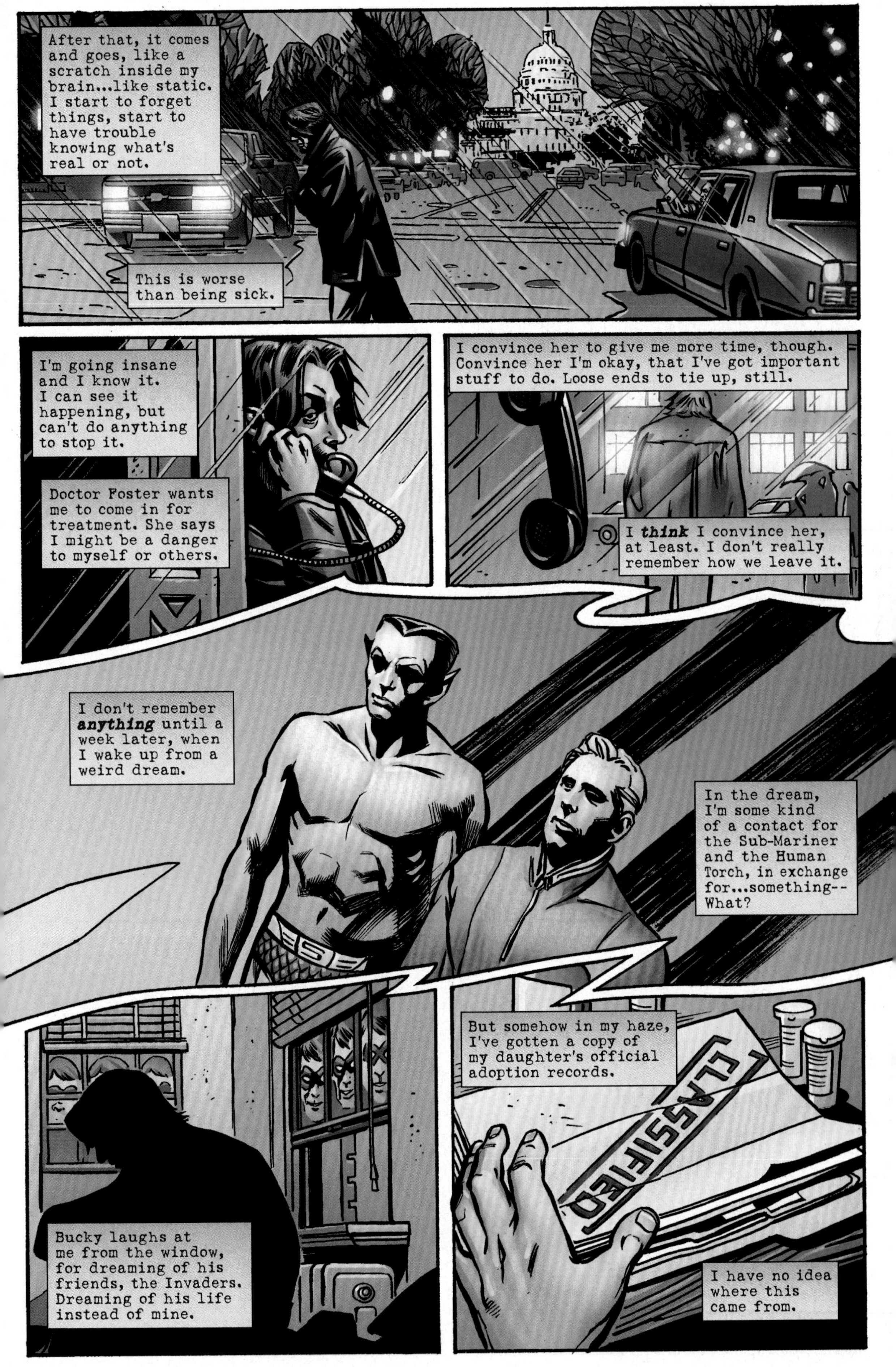
After that, it comes and goes, like a scratch inside my brain...like static. I start to forget things, start to have trouble knowing what's real or not.
This is worse than being sick.
I'm going insane and I know it. I can see it happening, but can't do anything to stop it.
Doctor Foster wants me to come in for treatment. She says I might be a danger to myself or others.
I convince her to give me more time, though. Convince her I'm okay, that I've got important stuff to do. Loose ends to tie up, still.
I *think* I convince her, at least. I don't really remember how we leave it.
I don't remember *anything* until a week later, when I wake up from a weird dream.
In the dream, I'm some kind of a contact for the Sub-Mariner and the Human Torch, in exchange for...something-- What?
Bucky laughs at me from the window, for dreaming of his friends, the Invaders. Dreaming of his life instead of mine.
But somehow in my haze, I've gotten a copy of my daughter's official adoption records.
CLASSIFIED
I have no idea where this came from.

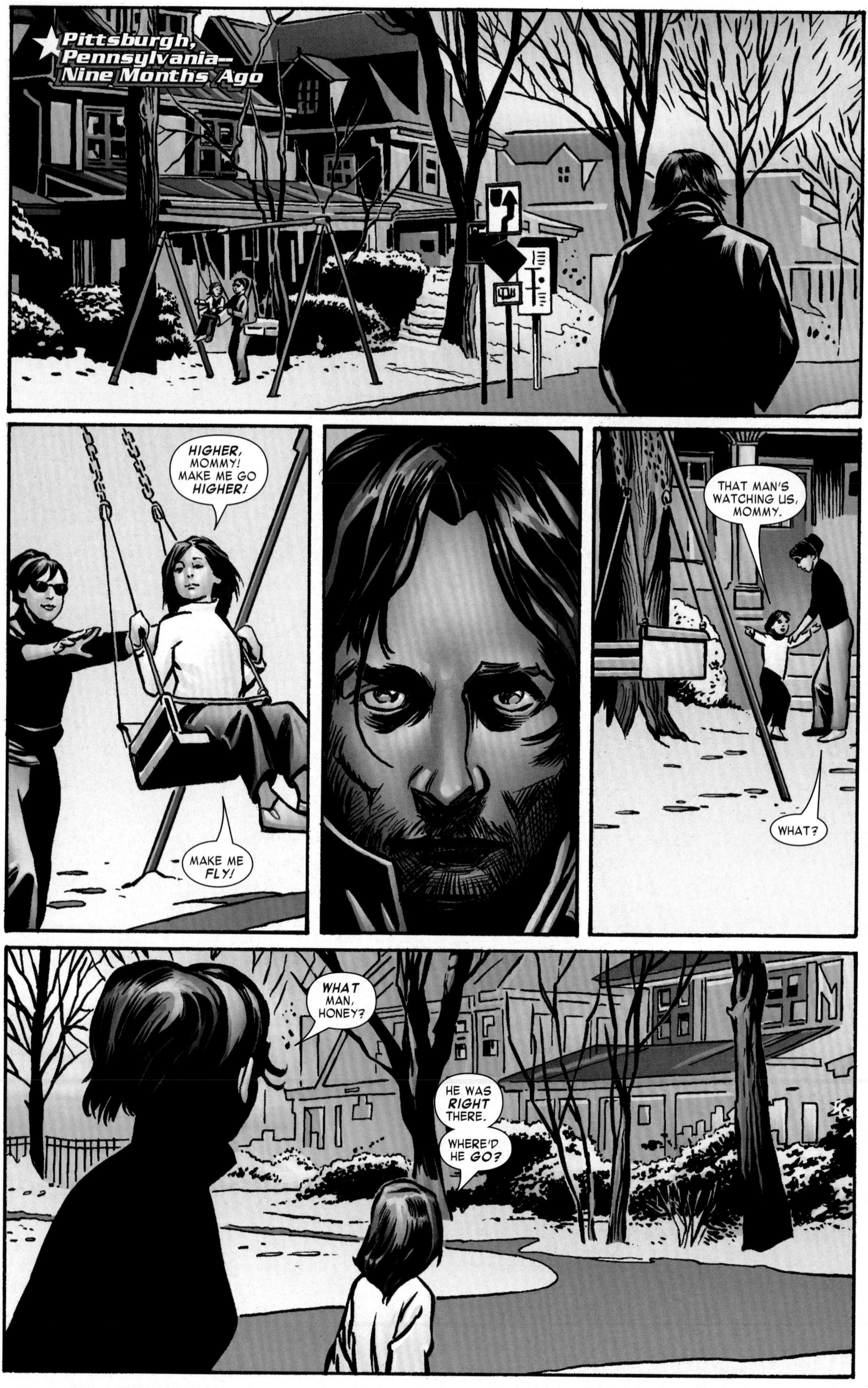
Pittsburgh, Pennsylvania-- Nine Months Ago
HIGHER, MOMMY! MAKE ME GO HIGHER!
MAKE ME FLY!
THAT MAN'S WATCHING US, MOMMY.
WHAT?
WHAT MAN, HONEY?
HE WAS RIGHT THERE.
WHERE'D HE GO?

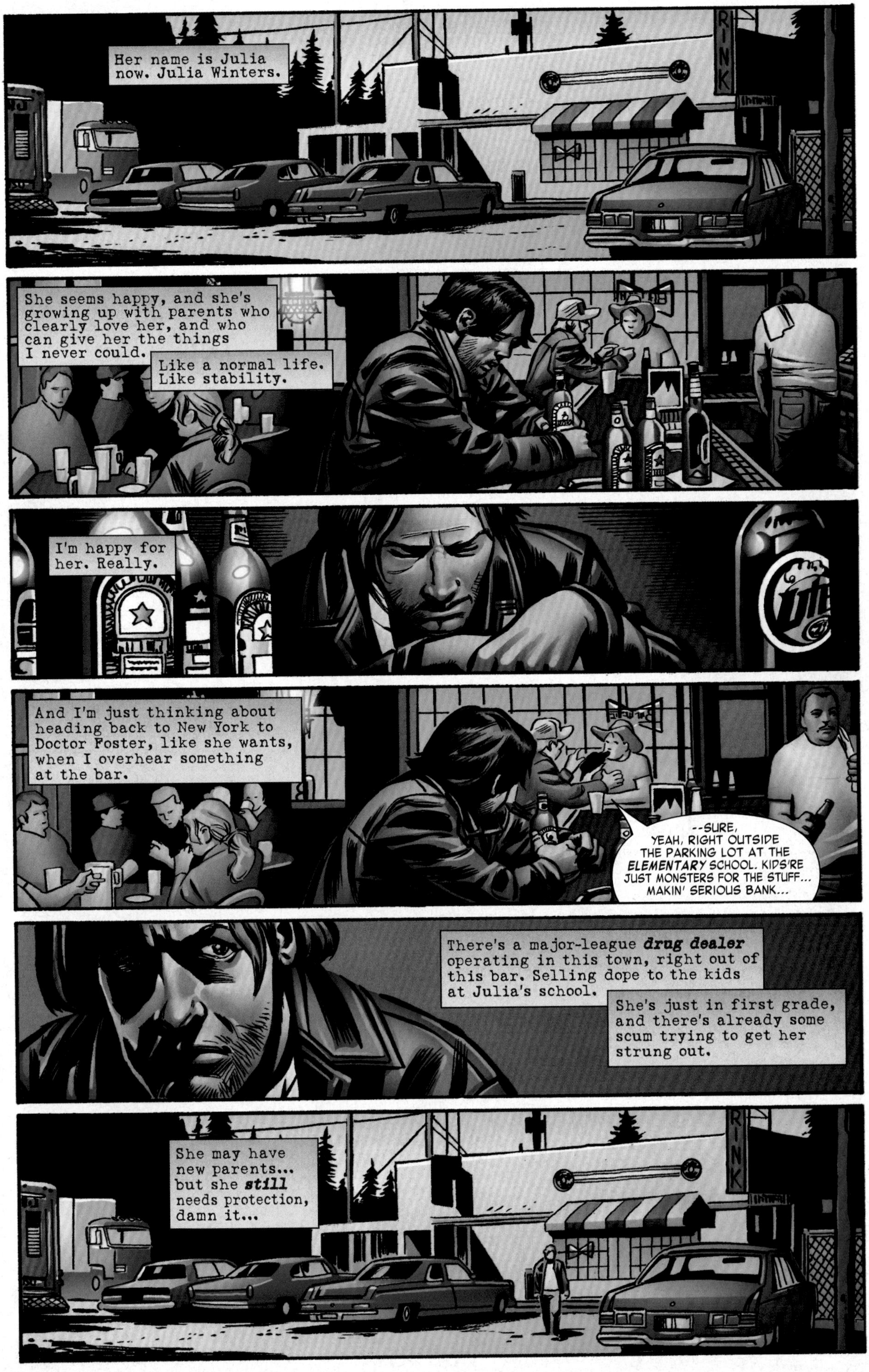
Her name is Julia now. Julia Winters.
RINK
She seems happy, and she's growing up with parents who clearly love her, and who can give her the things I never could.
Like a normal life. Like stability.
I'm happy for her. Really.
And I'm just thinking about heading back to New York to Doctor Foster, like she wants, when I overhear something at the bar.
--SURE, YEAH, RIGHT OUTSIDE THE PARKING LOT AT THE ELEMENTARY SCHOOL. KIDS'RE JUST MONSTERS FOR THE STUFF... MAKIN' SERIOUS BANK...
There's a major-league drug dealer operating in this town, right out of this bar. Selling dope to the kids at Julia's school.
She's just in first grade, and there's already some scum trying to get her strung out.
She may have new parents... but she still needs protection, damn it...
RINK

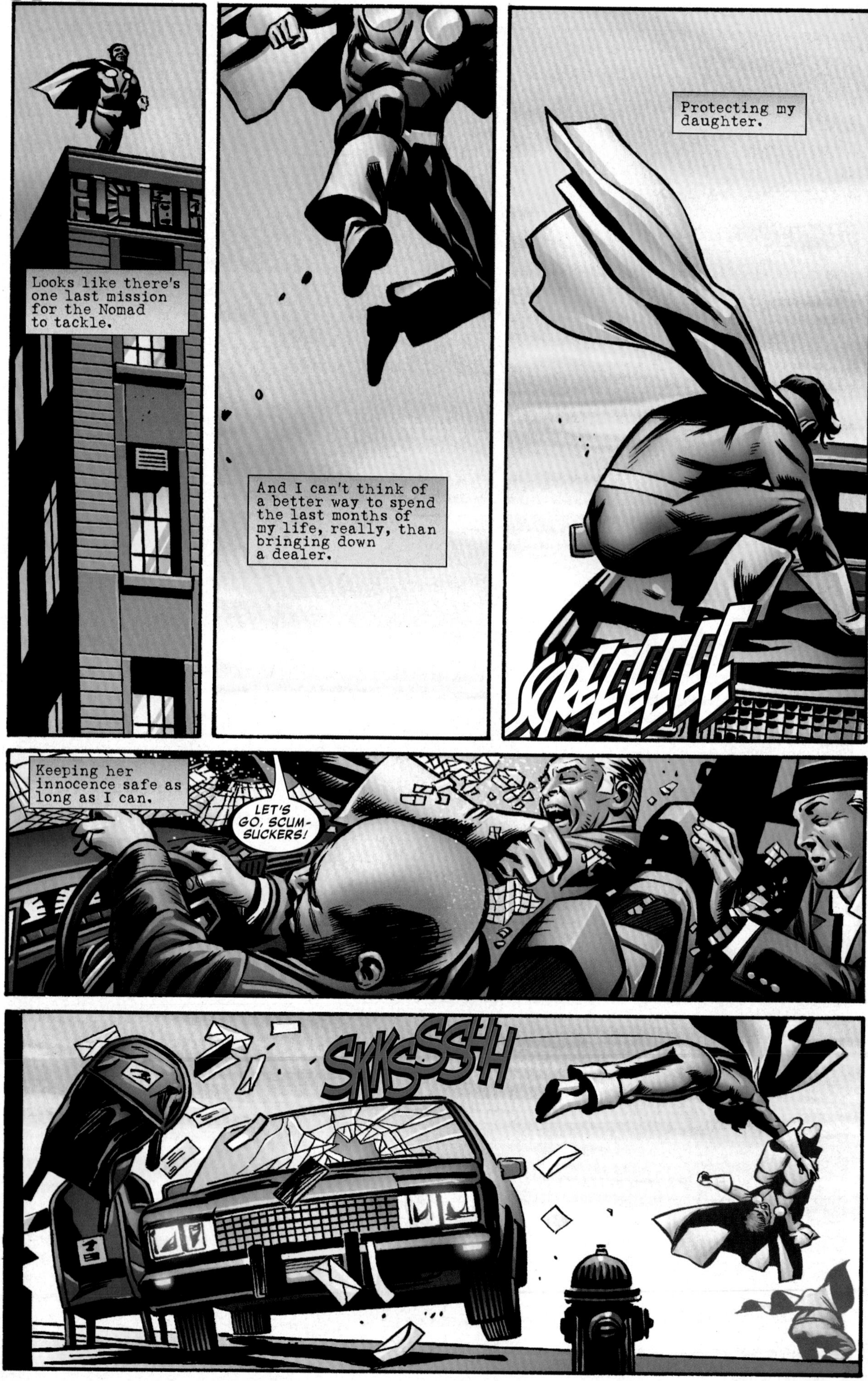
Looks like there's one last mission for the Nomad to tackle.
And I can't think of a better way to spend the last months of my life, really, than bringing down a dealer.
Protecting my daughter.
SCREEEEEE
Keeping her innocence safe as long as I can.
LET'S GO, SCUM-SUCKERS!
SKKSSSHH

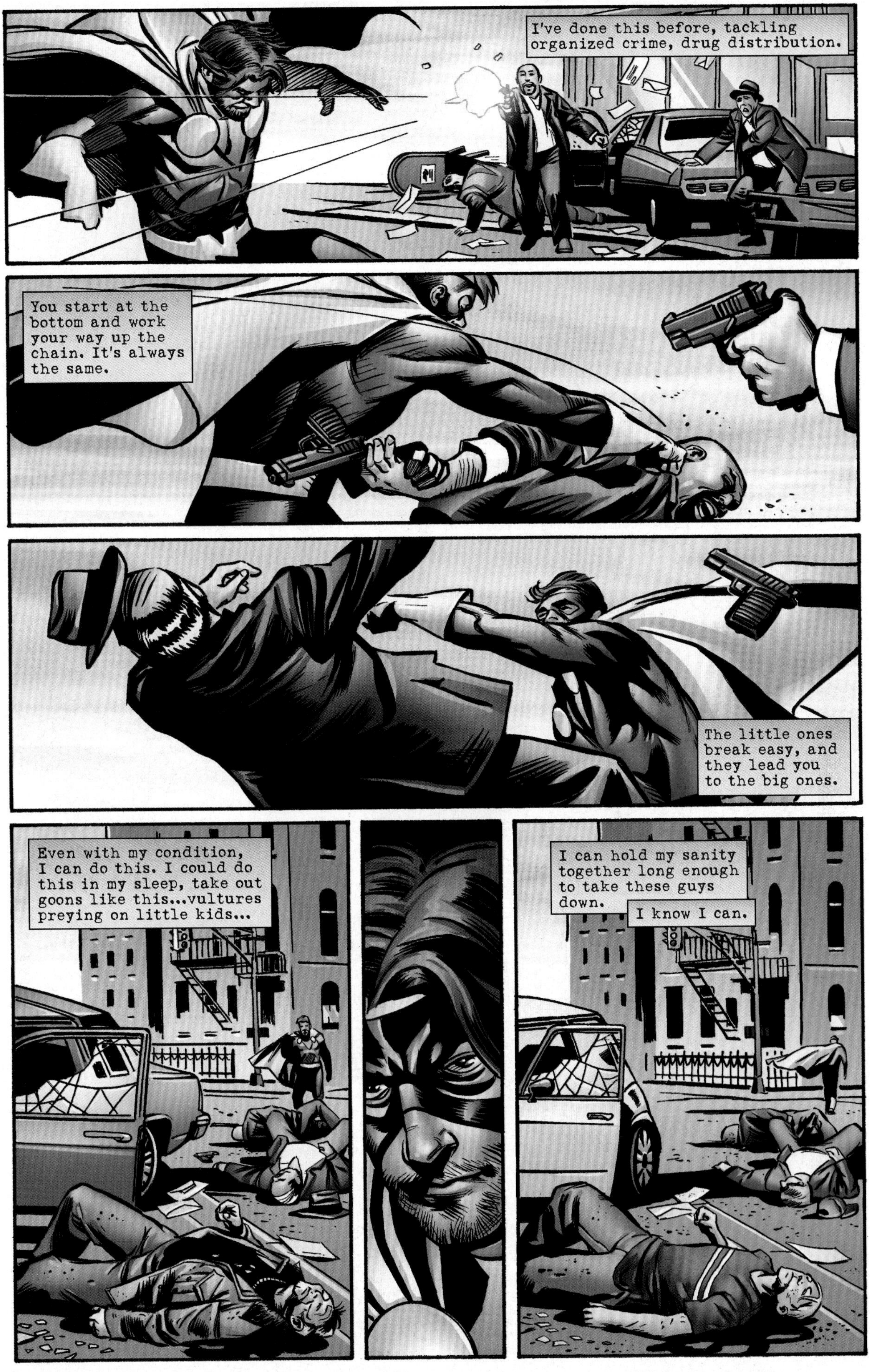

I've done this before, tackling organized crime, drug distribution.
You start at the bottom and work your way up the chain. It's always the same.
The little ones break easy, and they lead you to the big ones.
Even with my condition, I can do this. I could do this in my sleep, take out goons like this...vultures preying on little kids...
I can hold my sanity together long enough to take these guys down.
I know I can.

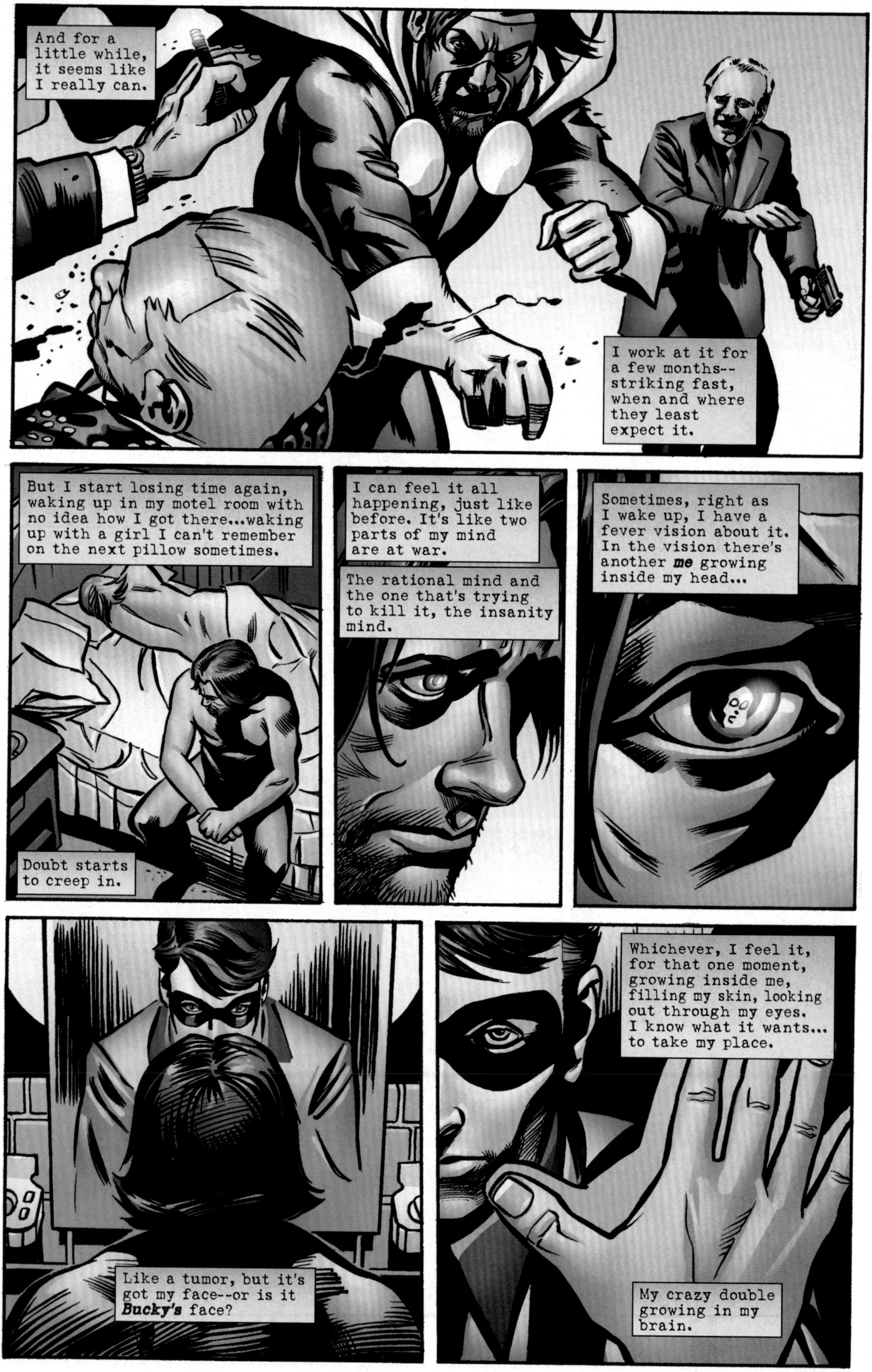
And for a little while, it seems like I really can.
I work at it for a few months--striking fast, when and where they least expect it.
But I start losing time again, waking up in my motel room with no idea how I got there...waking up with a girl I can't remember on the next pillow sometimes.
Doubt starts to creep in.
I can feel it all happening, just like before. It's like two parts of my mind are at war.
The rational mind and the one that's trying to kill it, the insanity mind.
Sometimes, right as I wake up, I have a fever vision about it. In the vision there's another *me* growing inside my head...
Like a tumor, but it's got my face--or is it ***Bucky's*** face?
Whichever, I feel it, for that one moment, growing inside me, filling my skin, looking out through my eyes. I know what it wants... to take my place.
My crazy double growing in my brain.

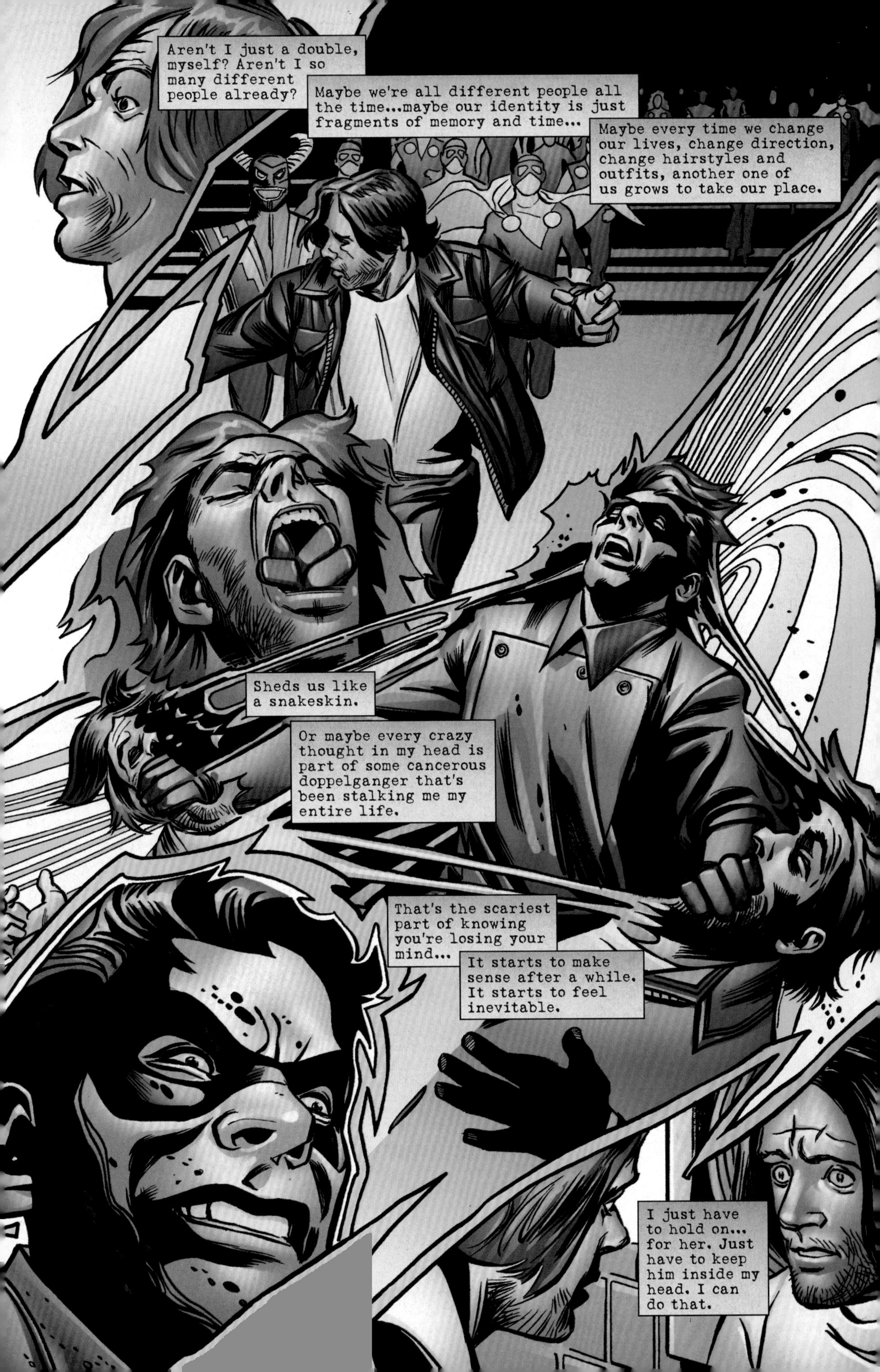
Aren't I just a double, myself? Aren't I so many different people already?
Maybe we're all different people all the time...maybe our identity is just fragments of memory and time...
Maybe every time we change our lives, change direction, change hairstyles and outfits, another one of us grows to take our place.
Sheds us like a snakeskin.
Or maybe every crazy thought in my head is part of some cancerous doppelganger that's been stalking me my entire life.
That's the scariest part of knowing you're losing your mind...
It starts to make sense after a while. It starts to feel inevitable.
I just have to hold on... for her. Just have to keep him inside my head. I can do that.

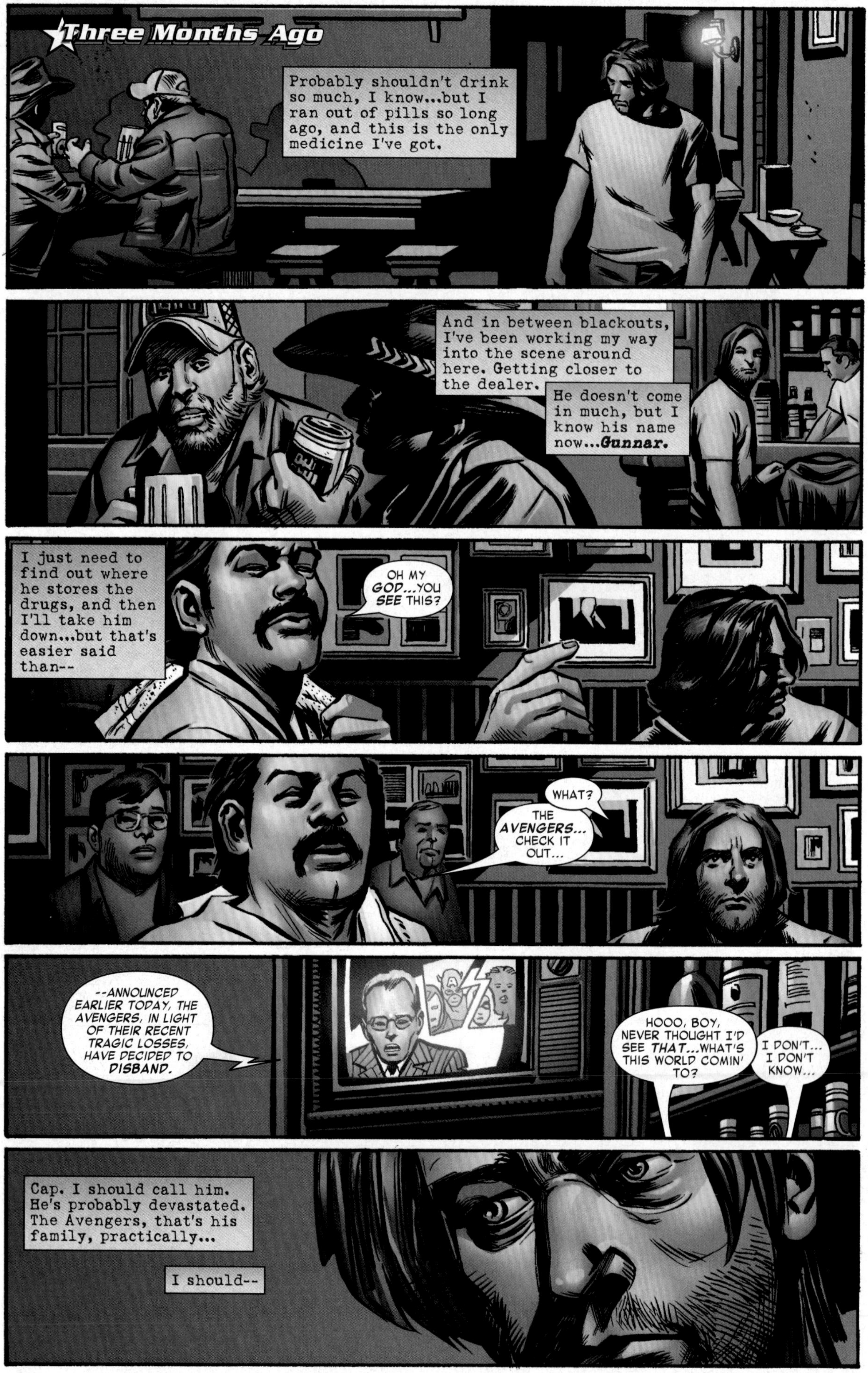
Three Months Ago
Probably shouldn't drink so much, I know...but I ran out of pills so long ago, and this is the only medicine I've got.
And in between blackouts, I've been working my way into the scene around here. Getting closer to the dealer.
He doesn't come in much, but I know his name now...Gunnar.
I just need to find out where he stores the drugs, and then I'll take him down...but that's easier said than--
OH MY GOD...YOU SEE THIS?
WHAT?
THE AVENGERS... CHECK IT OUT...
--ANNOUNCED EARLIER TODAY, THE AVENGERS, IN LIGHT OF THEIR RECENT TRAGIC LOSSES, HAVE DECIDED TO DISBAND.
HOOO, BOY, NEVER THOUGHT I'D SEE THAT...WHAT'S THIS WORLD COMIN' TO?
I DON'T... I DON'T KNOW...
Cap. I should call him. He's probably devastated. The Avengers, that's his family, practically...
I should--

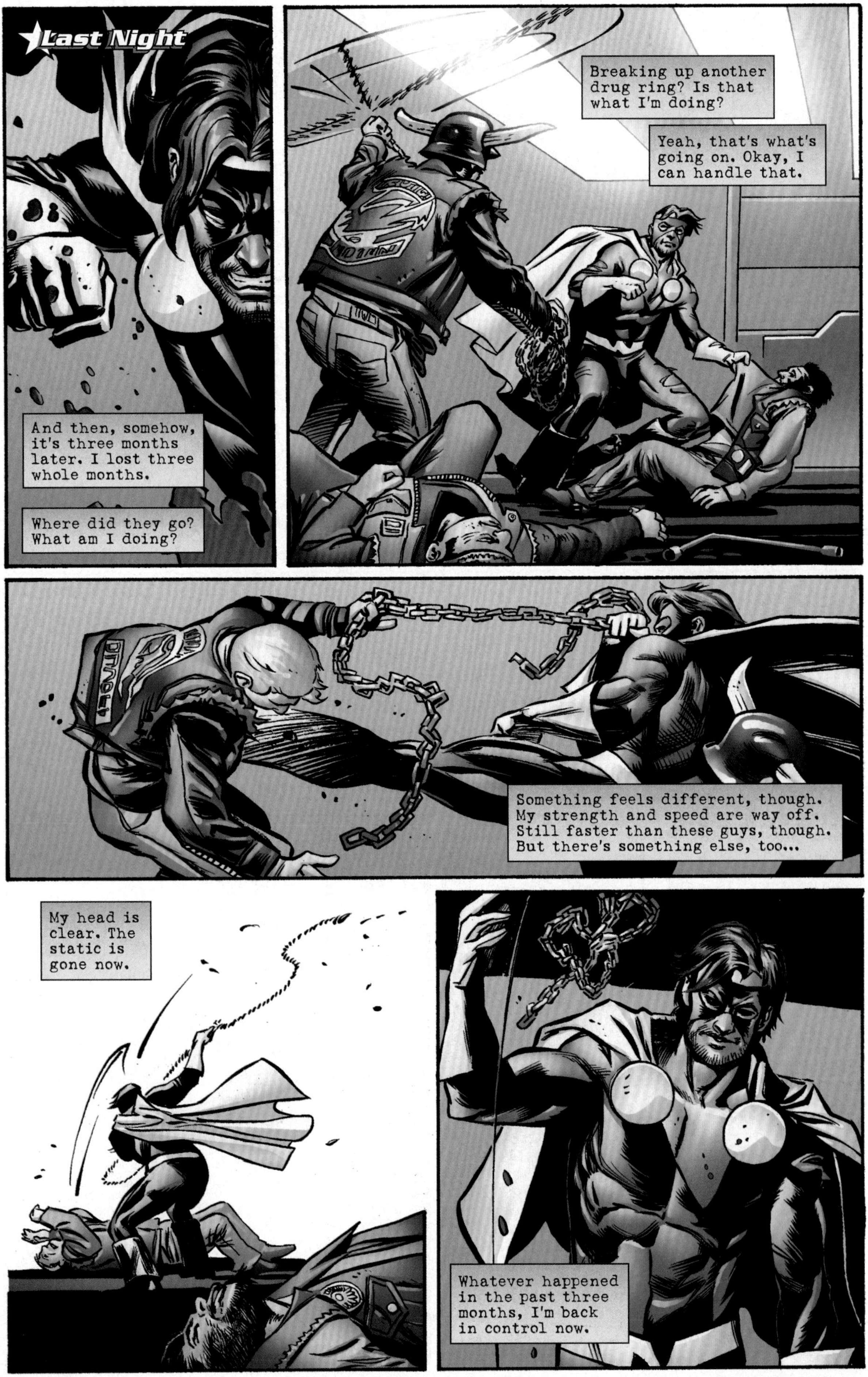
Last Night
And then, somehow, it's three months later. I lost three whole months.
Where did they go? What am I doing?
Breaking up another drug ring? Is that what I'm doing?
Yeah, that's what's going on. Okay, I can handle that.
Something feels different, though. My strength and speed are way off. Still faster than these guys, though. But there's something else, too...
My head is clear. The static is gone now.
Whatever happened in the past three months, I'm back in control now.

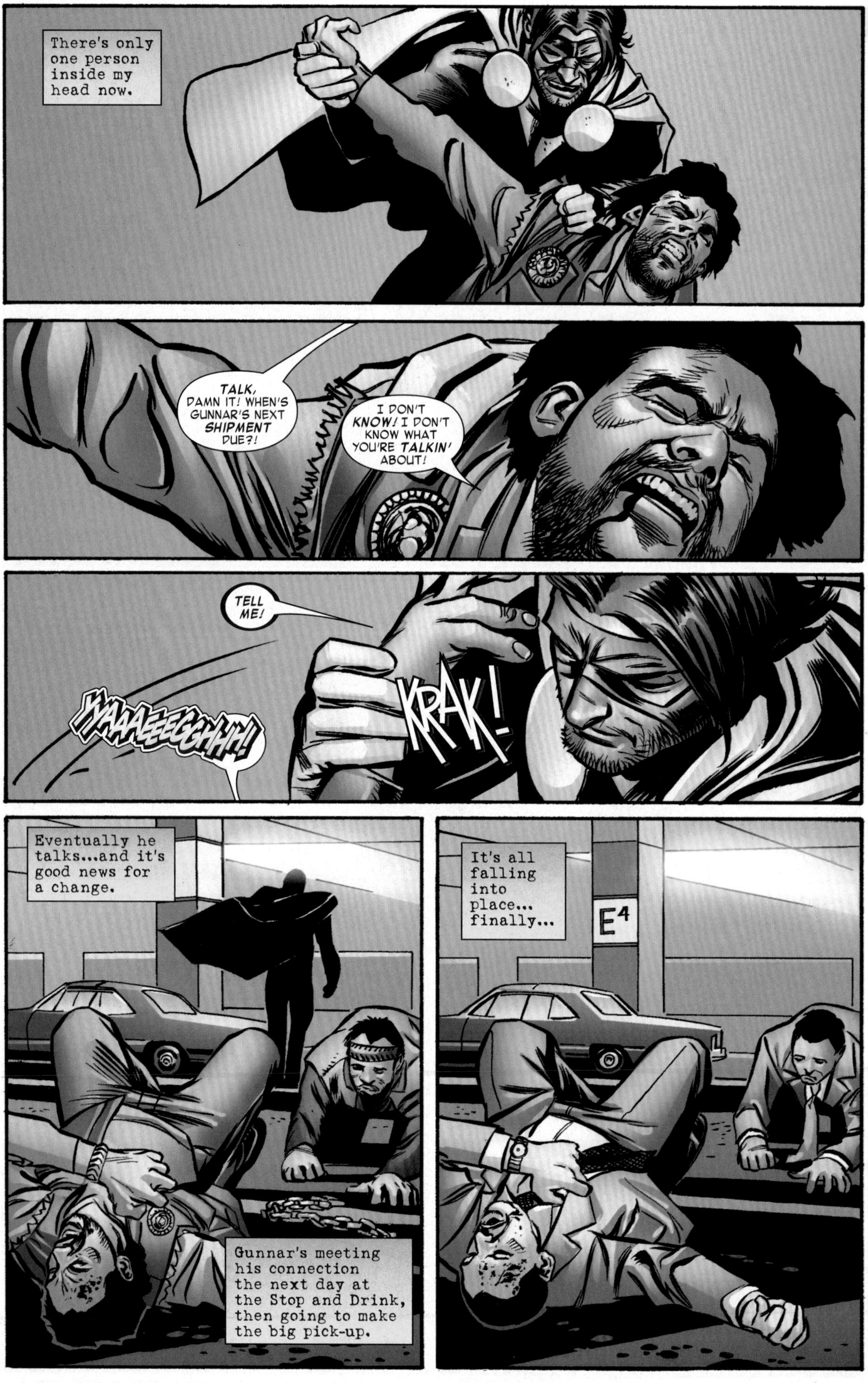

There's only one person inside my head now.
TALK, DAMN IT! WHEN'S GUNNAR'S NEXT SHIPMENT DUE?!
I DON'T KNOW! I DON'T KNOW WHAT YOU'RE TALKIN' ABOUT!
TELL ME!
YYAAAEEEGGHHH!
KRAK!
Eventually he talks...and it's good news for a change.
Gunnar's meeting his connection the next day at the Stop and Drink, then going to make the big pick-up.
It's all falling into place... finally...
E4

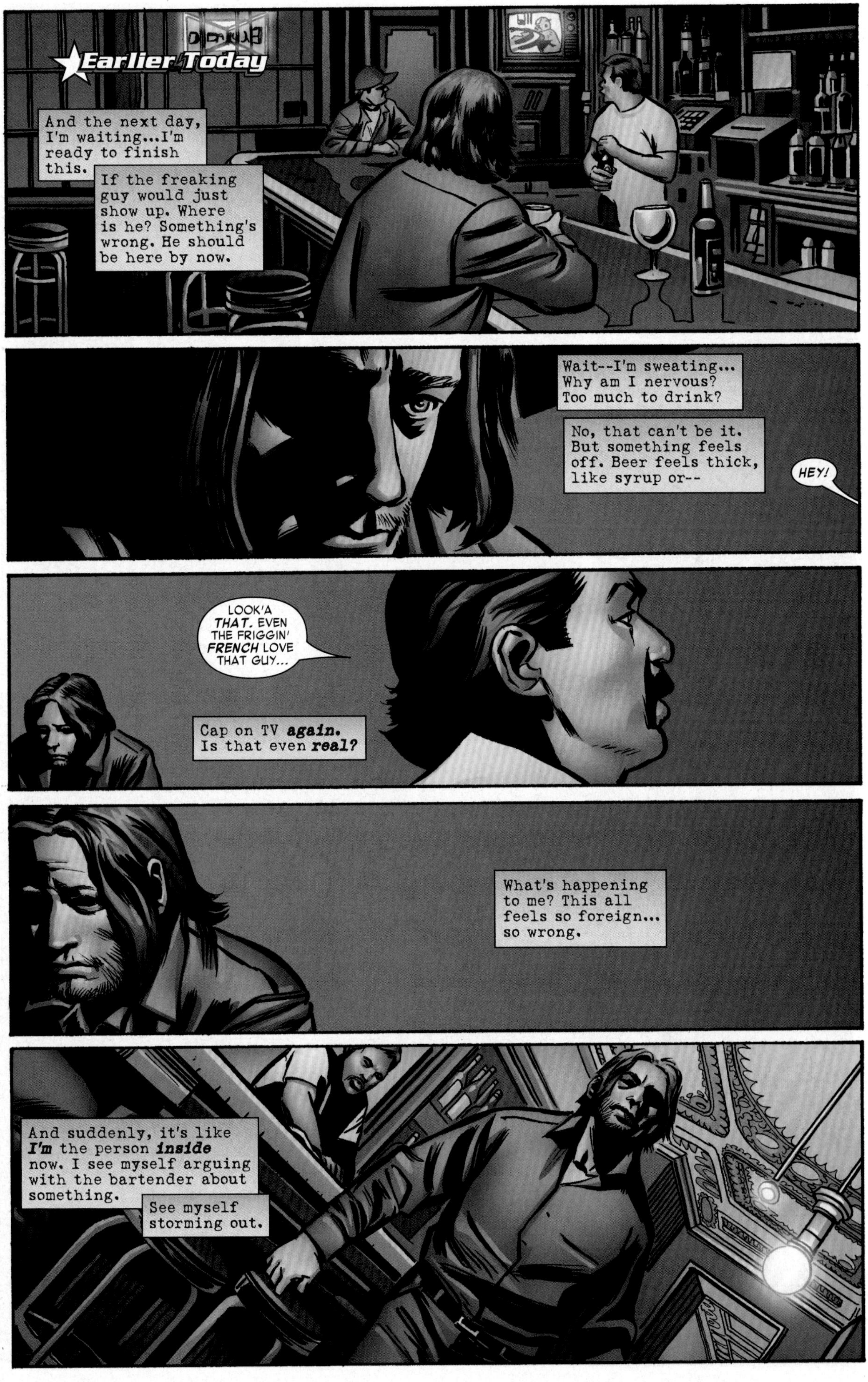
Earlier Today
And the next day, I'm waiting...I'm ready to finish this.
If the freaking guy would just show up. Where is he? Something's wrong. He should be here by now.
Wait--I'm sweating... Why am I nervous? Too much to drink?
No, that can't be it. But something feels off. Beer feels thick, like syrup or--
HEY!
LOOK'A THAT. EVEN THE FRIGGIN' FRENCH LOVE THAT GUY...
Cap on TV again. Is that even real?
What's happening to me? This all feels so foreign... so wrong.
And suddenly, it's like I'm the person inside now. I see myself arguing with the bartender about something.
See myself storming out.

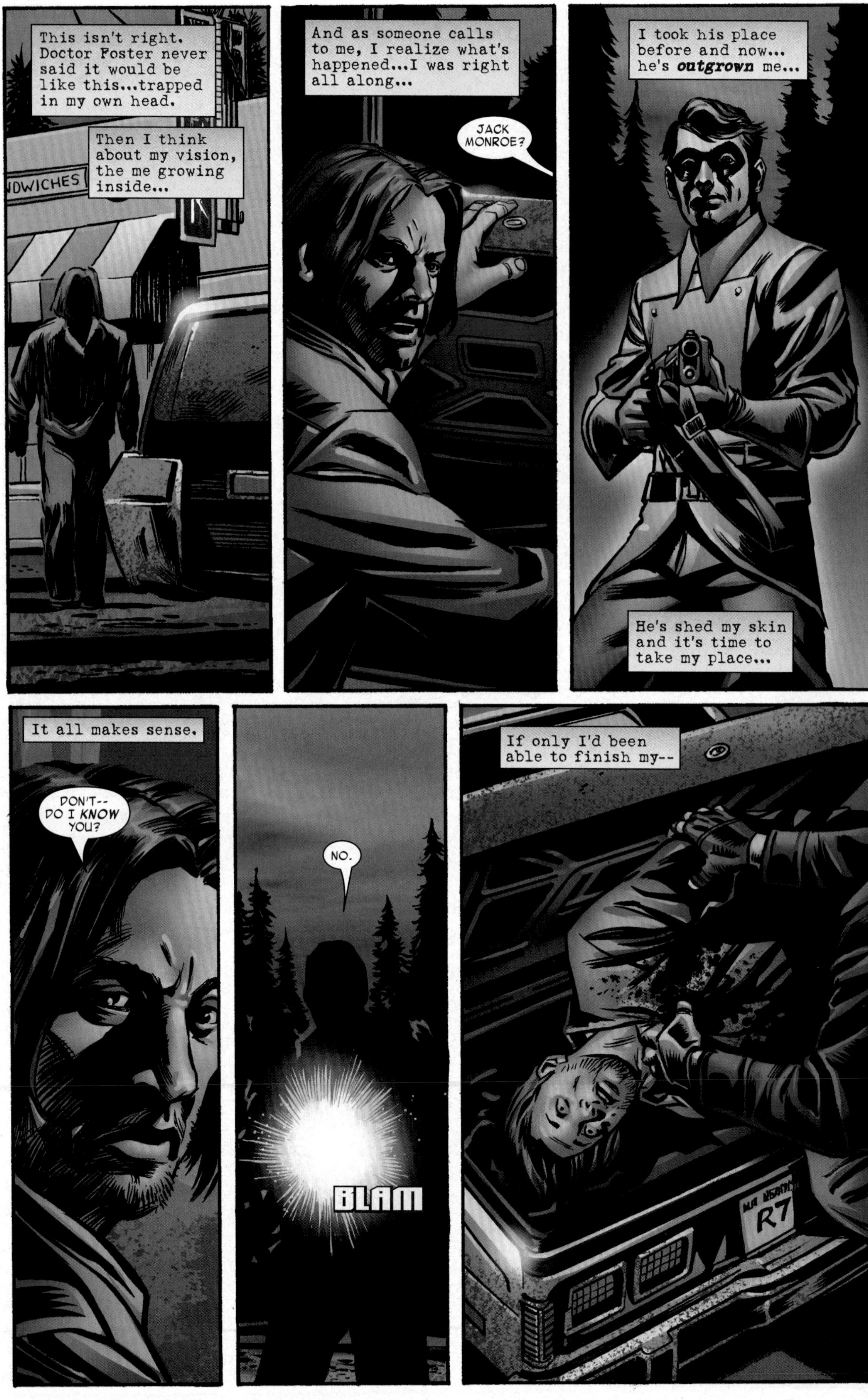
This isn't right. Doctor Foster never said it would be like this...trapped in my own head.
Then I think about my vision, the me growing inside...
NDWICHES
And as someone calls to me, I realize what's happened...I was right all along...
JACK MONROE?
I took his place before and now... he's *outgrown* me...
He's shed my skin and it's time to take my place...
It all makes sense.
DON'T-- DO I *KNOW* YOU?
NO.
BLAM
If only I'd been able to finish my--
R7

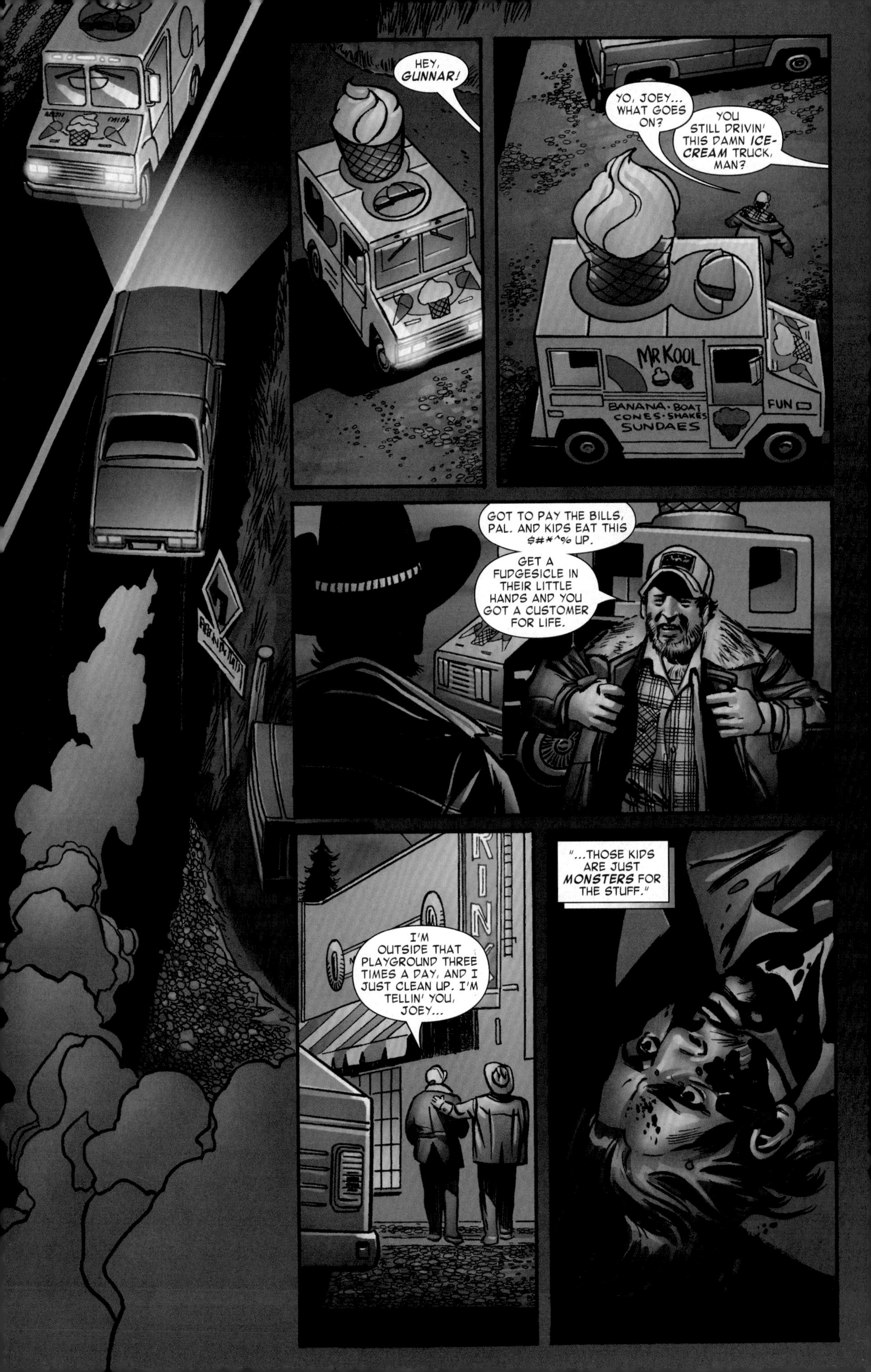

HEY, GUNNAR!
YO, JOEY... WHAT GOES ON?
YOU STILL DRIVIN' THIS DAMN ICE-CREAM TRUCK, MAN?
MR KOOL
BANANA·BOAT CONES·SHAKES SUNDAES
FUN
GOT TO PAY THE BILLS, PAL. AND KIDS EAT THIS $#*^% UP.
GET A FUDGESICLE IN THEIR LITTLE HANDS AND YOU GOT A CUSTOMER FOR LIFE.
I'M OUTSIDE THAT PLAYGROUND THREE TIMES A DAY, AND I JUST CLEAN UP. I'M TELLIN' YOU, JOEY...
"...THOSE KIDS ARE JUST MONSTERS FOR THE STUFF."

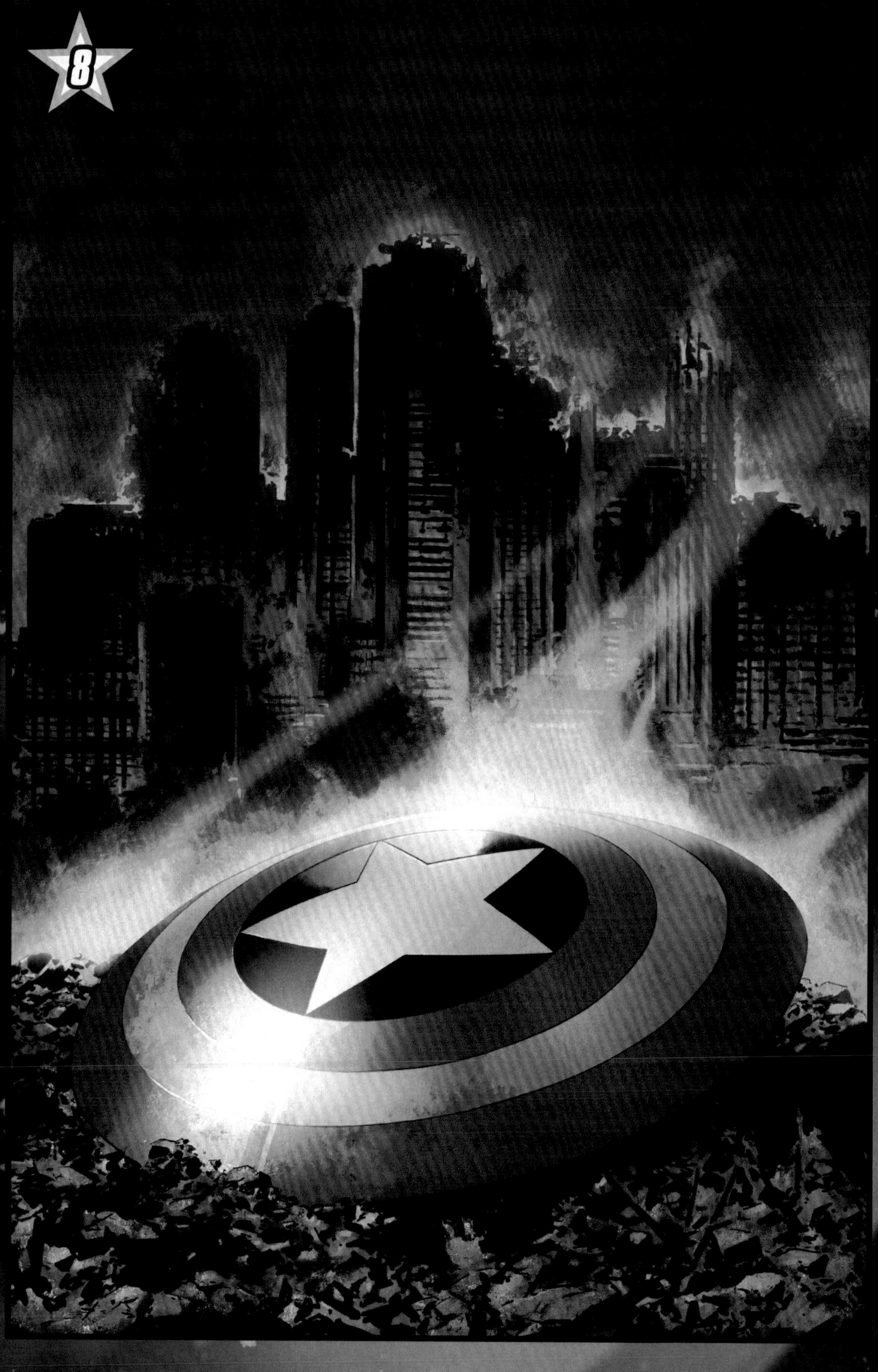
8

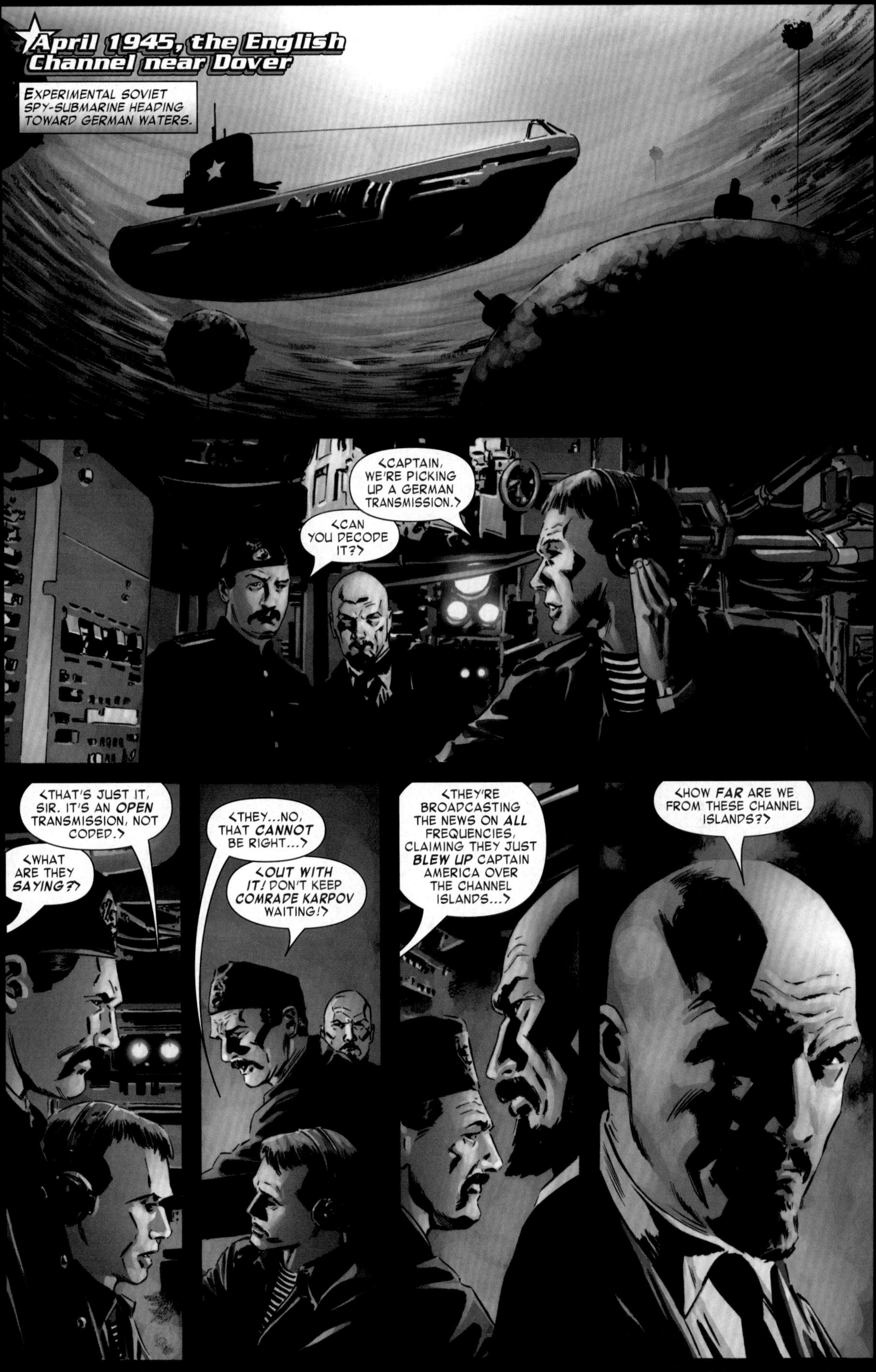
April 1945, the English Channel near Dover
EXPERIMENTAL SOVIET SPY-SUBMARINE HEADING TOWARD GERMAN WATERS.
<CAPTAIN, WE'RE PICKING UP A GERMAN TRANSMISSION.>
<CAN YOU DECODE IT?>
<THAT'S JUST IT, SIR. IT'S AN OPEN TRANSMISSION, NOT CODED.>
<WHAT ARE THEY SAYING?>
<THEY...NO, THAT CANNOT BE RIGHT...>
<OUT WITH IT! DON'T KEEP COMRADE KARPOV WAITING!>
<THEY'RE BROADCASTING THE NEWS ON ALL FREQUENCIES, CLAIMING THEY JUST BLEW UP CAPTAIN AMERICA OVER THE CHANNEL ISLANDS...>
<HOW FAR ARE WE FROM THESE CHANNEL ISLANDS?>

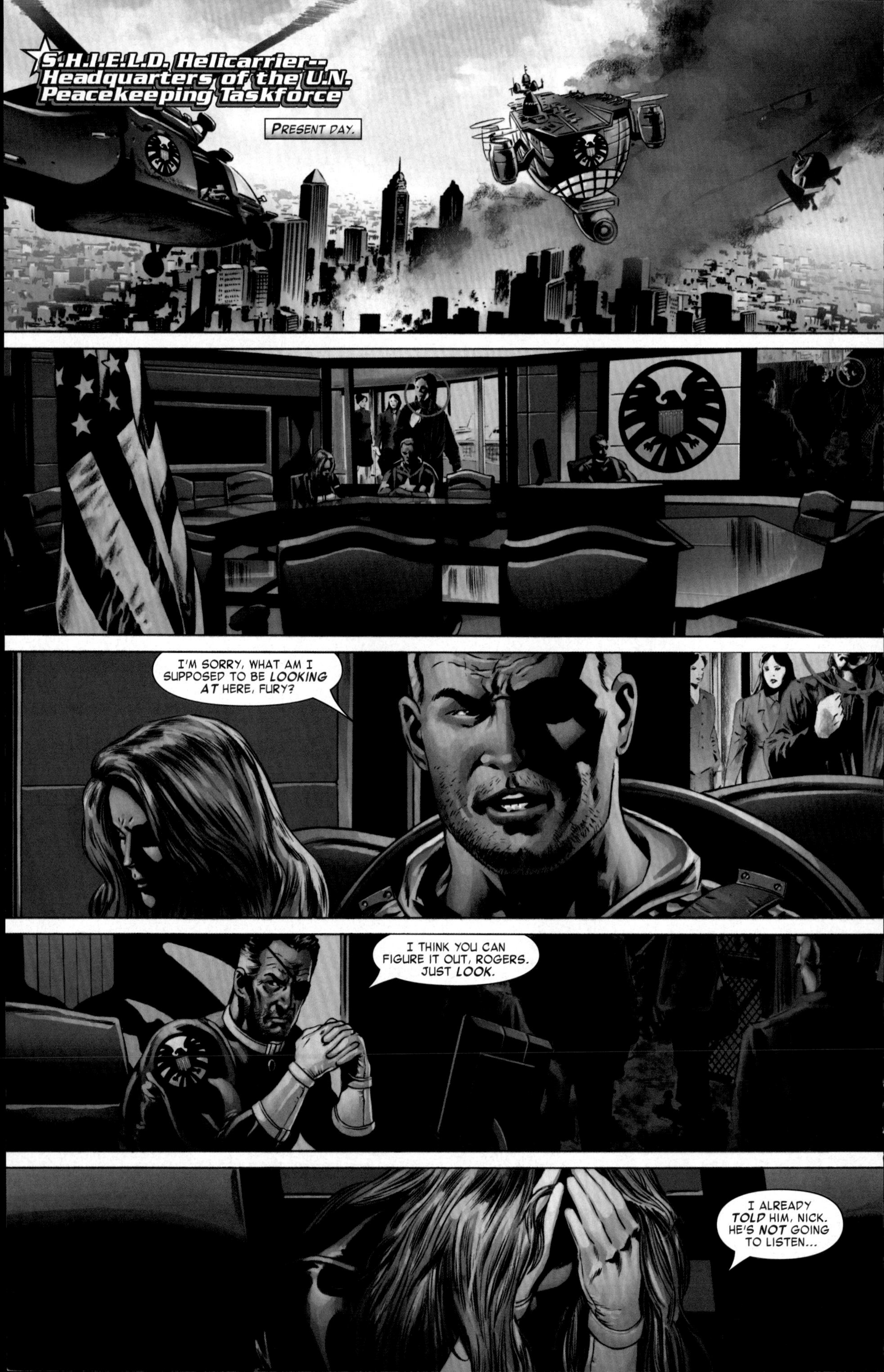
S.H.I.E.L.D. Helicarrier--
Headquarters of the U.N.
Peacekeeping Taskforce
PRESENT DAY.
I'M SORRY, WHAT AM I SUPPOSED TO BE LOOKING AT HERE, FURY?
I THINK YOU CAN FIGURE IT OUT, ROGERS. JUST LOOK.
I ALREADY TOLD HIM, NICK. HE'S NOT GOING TO LISTEN...

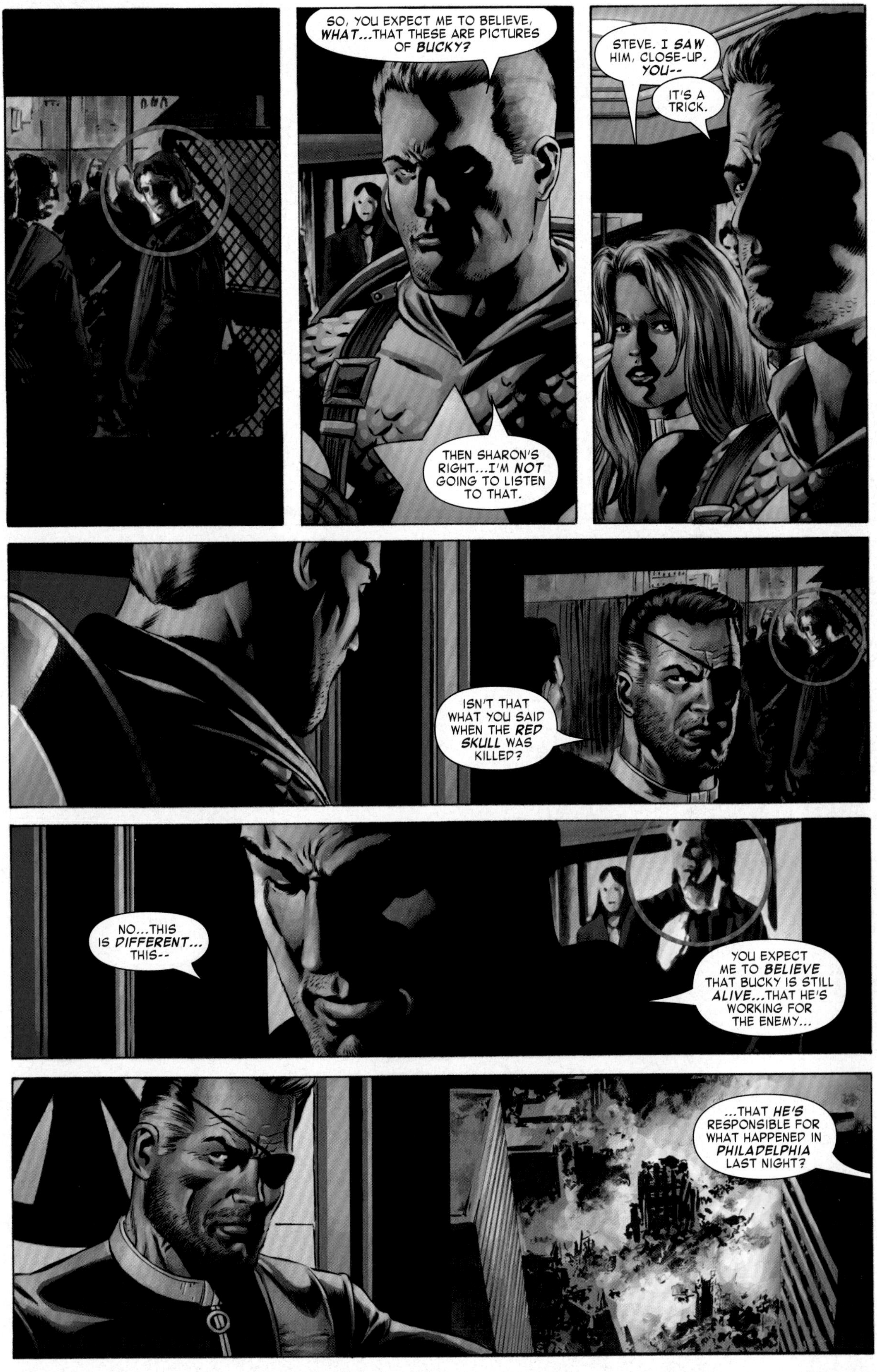
SO, YOU EXPECT ME TO BELIEVE, WHAT...THAT THESE ARE PICTURES OF BUCKY?
THEN SHARON'S RIGHT...I'M NOT GOING TO LISTEN TO THAT.
STEVE. I SAW HIM, CLOSE-UP. YOU--
IT'S A TRICK.
ISN'T THAT WHAT YOU SAID WHEN THE RED SKULL WAS KILLED?
NO...THIS IS DIFFERENT... THIS--
YOU EXPECT ME TO BELIEVE THAT BUCKY IS STILL ALIVE...THAT HE'S WORKING FOR THE ENEMY...
...THAT HE'S RESPONSIBLE FOR WHAT HAPPENED IN PHILADELPHIA LAST NIGHT?

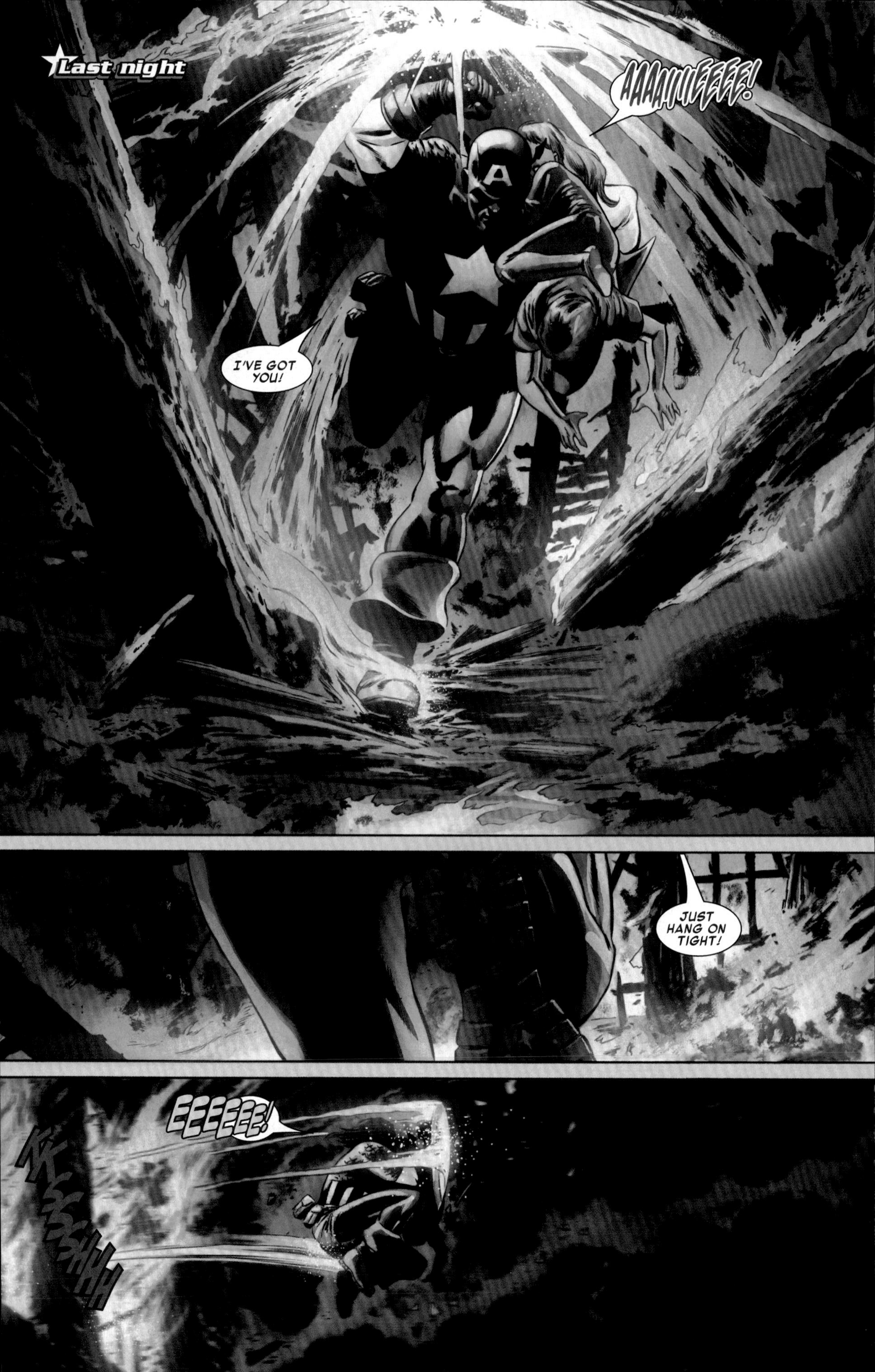
Last night
AAAAIIIIEEEE!
I'VE GOT YOU!
JUST HANG ON TIGHT!
EEEEEE!
KKSSHHH

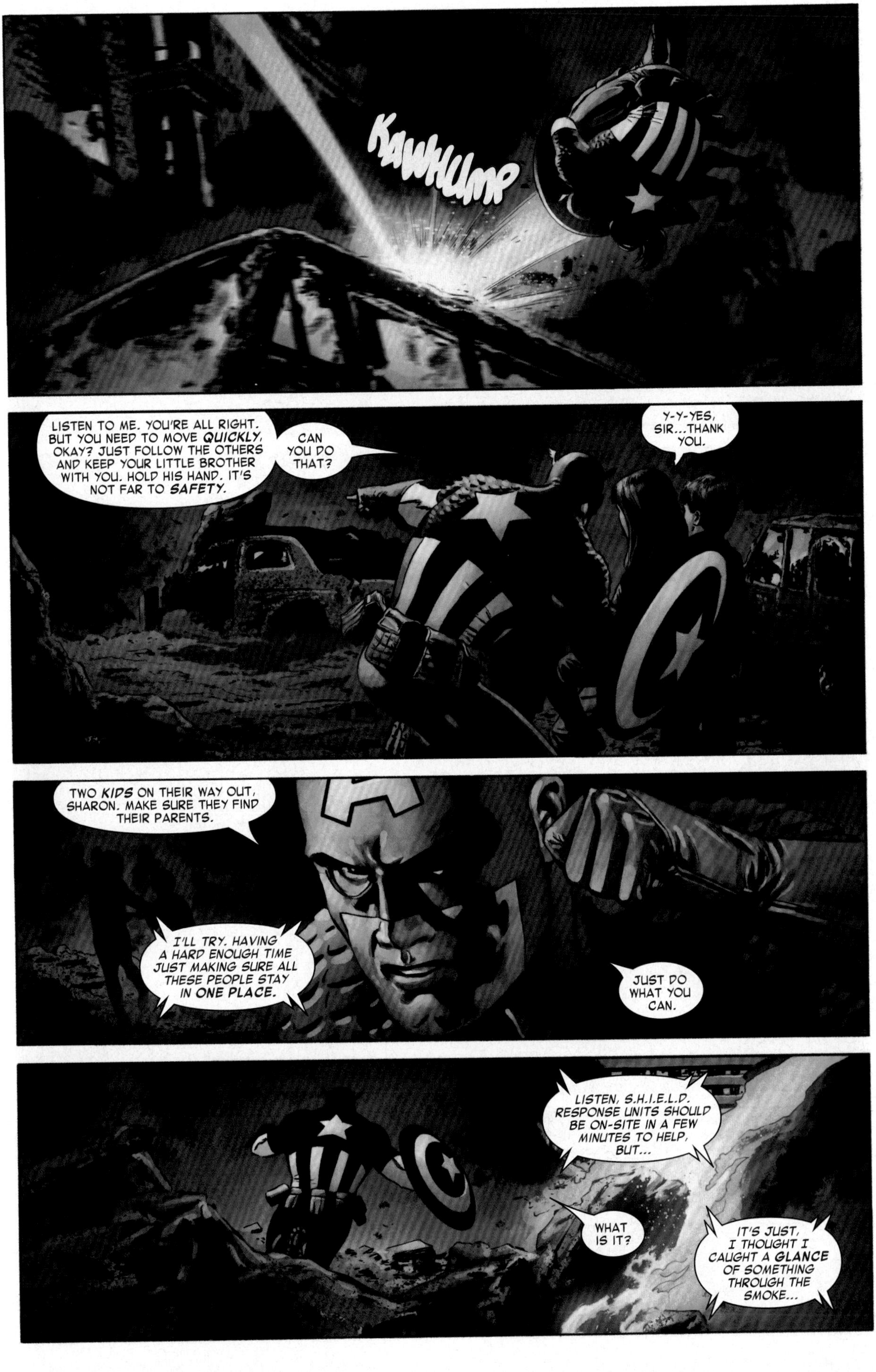
KAWHUMP
LISTEN TO ME. YOU'RE ALL RIGHT. BUT YOU NEED TO MOVE QUICKLY, OKAY? JUST FOLLOW THE OTHERS AND KEEP YOUR LITTLE BROTHER WITH YOU. HOLD HIS HAND. IT'S NOT FAR TO SAFETY.
CAN YOU DO THAT?
Y-Y-YES, SIR...THANK YOU.
TWO KIDS ON THEIR WAY OUT, SHARON. MAKE SURE THEY FIND THEIR PARENTS.
I'LL TRY. HAVING A HARD ENOUGH TIME JUST MAKING SURE ALL THESE PEOPLE STAY IN ONE PLACE.
JUST DO WHAT YOU CAN.
LISTEN, S.H.I.E.L.D. RESPONSE UNITS SHOULD BE ON-SITE IN A FEW MINUTES TO HELP, BUT...
WHAT IS IT?
IT'S JUST, I THOUGHT I CAUGHT A GLANCE OF SOMETHING THROUGH THE SMOKE...

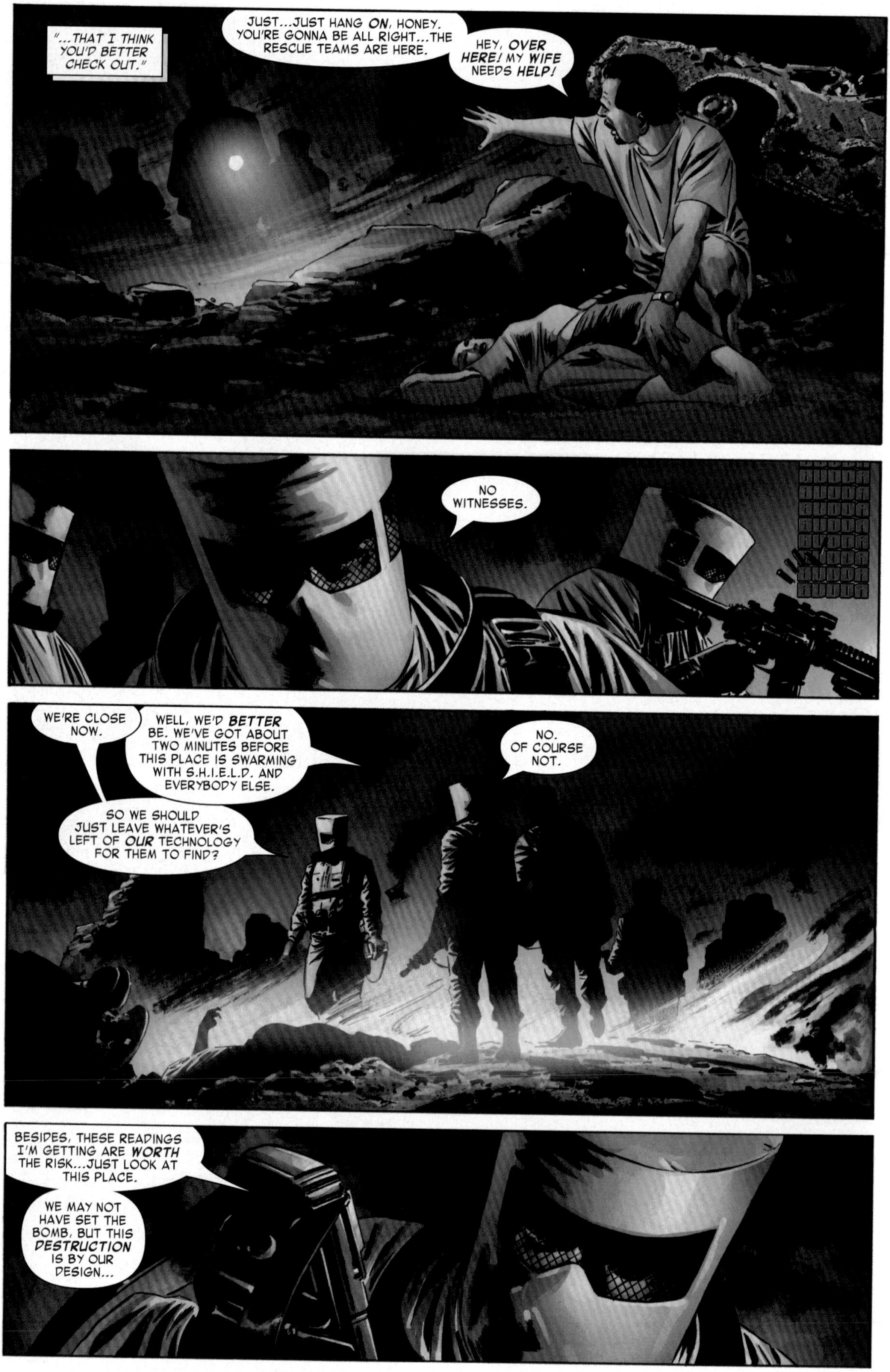
"...THAT I THINK YOU'D BETTER CHECK OUT."
JUST...JUST HANG ON, HONEY. YOU'RE GONNA BE ALL RIGHT...THE RESCUE TEAMS ARE HERE.
HEY, OVER HERE! MY WIFE NEEDS HELP!
NO WITNESSES.
BUDDA BUDDA BUDDA BUDDA BUDDA BUDDA BUDDA BUDDA
WE'RE CLOSE NOW.
WELL, WE'D BETTER BE. WE'VE GOT ABOUT TWO MINUTES BEFORE THIS PLACE IS SWARMING WITH S.H.I.E.L.D. AND EVERYBODY ELSE.
SO WE SHOULD JUST LEAVE WHATEVER'S LEFT OF OUR TECHNOLOGY FOR THEM TO FIND?
NO. OF COURSE NOT.
BESIDES, THESE READINGS I'M GETTING ARE WORTH THE RISK...JUST LOOK AT THIS PLACE.
WE MAY NOT HAVE SET THE BOMB, BUT THIS DESTRUCTION IS BY OUR DESIGN...

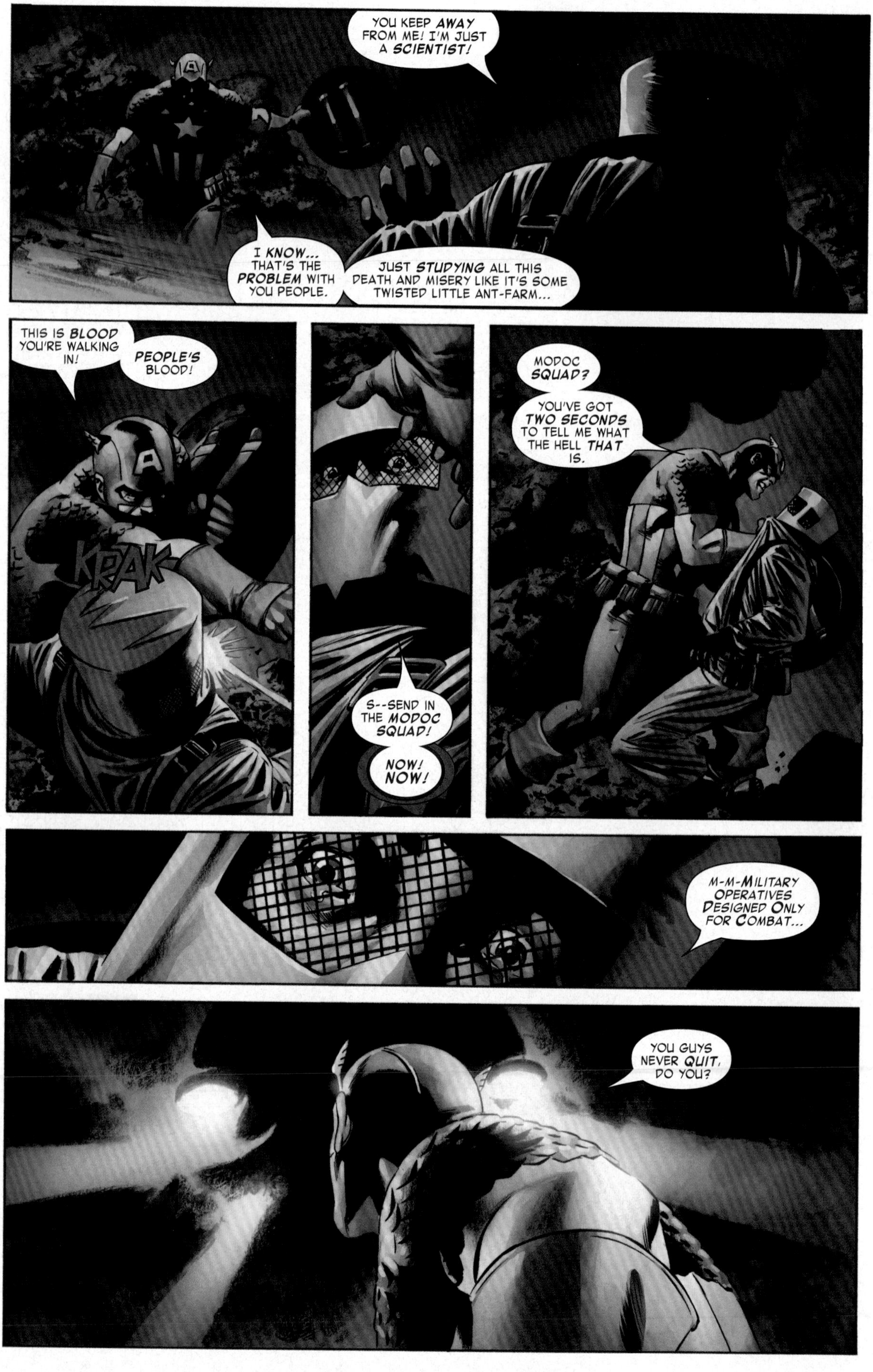

YOU KEEP AWAY FROM ME! I'M JUST A SCIENTIST!
I KNOW... THAT'S THE PROBLEM WITH YOU PEOPLE.
JUST STUDYING ALL THIS DEATH AND MISERY LIKE IT'S SOME TWISTED LITTLE ANT-FARM...
THIS IS BLOOD YOU'RE WALKING IN!
PEOPLE'S BLOOD!
KRAK
S--SEND IN THE MODOC SQUAD!
NOW! NOW!
MODOC SQUAD?
YOU'VE GOT TWO SECONDS TO TELL ME WHAT THE HELL THAT IS.
M-M-MILITARY OPERATIVES DESIGNED ONLY FOR COMBAT...
YOU GUYS NEVER QUIT, DO YOU?

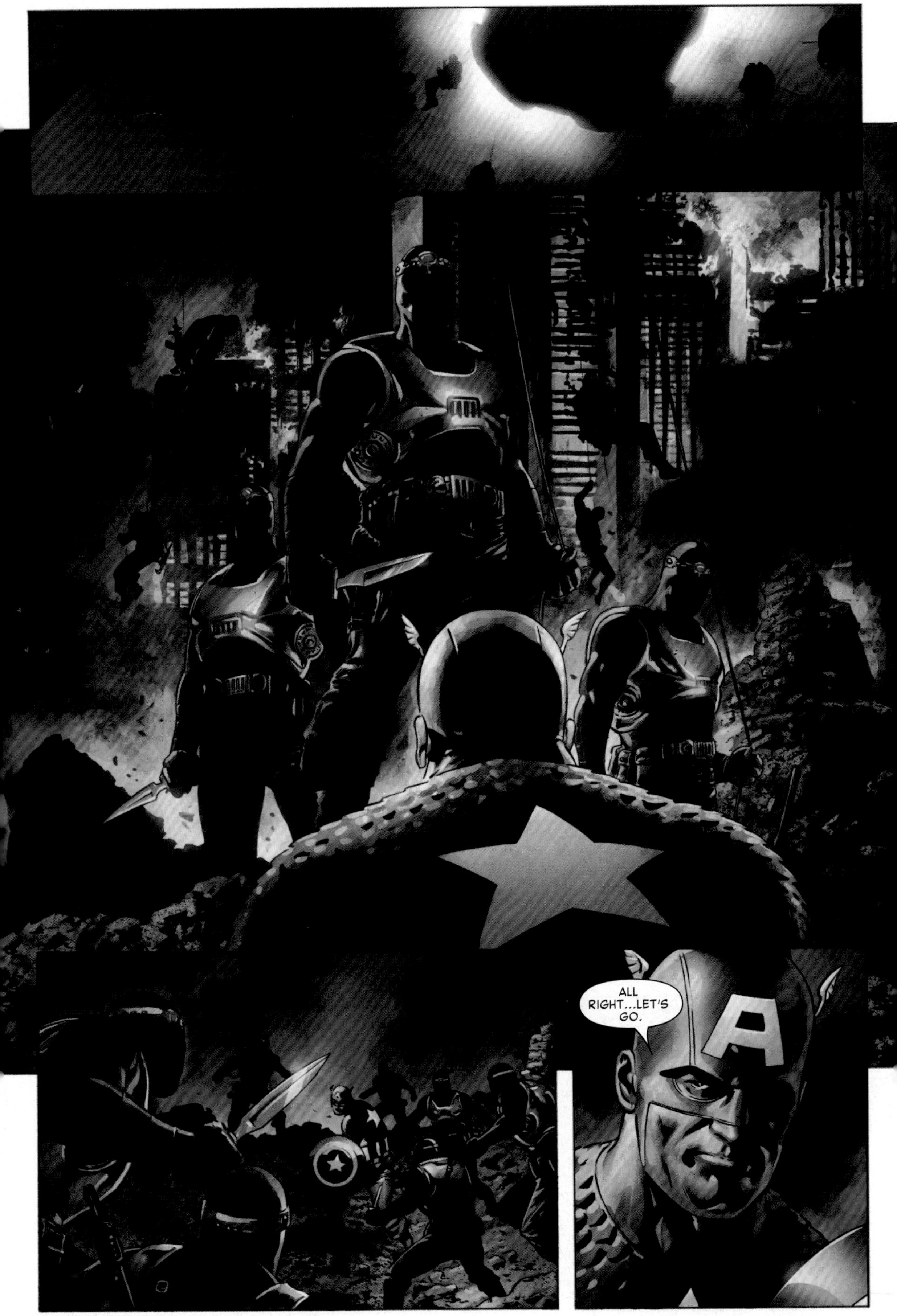
ALL RIGHT...LET'S GO.

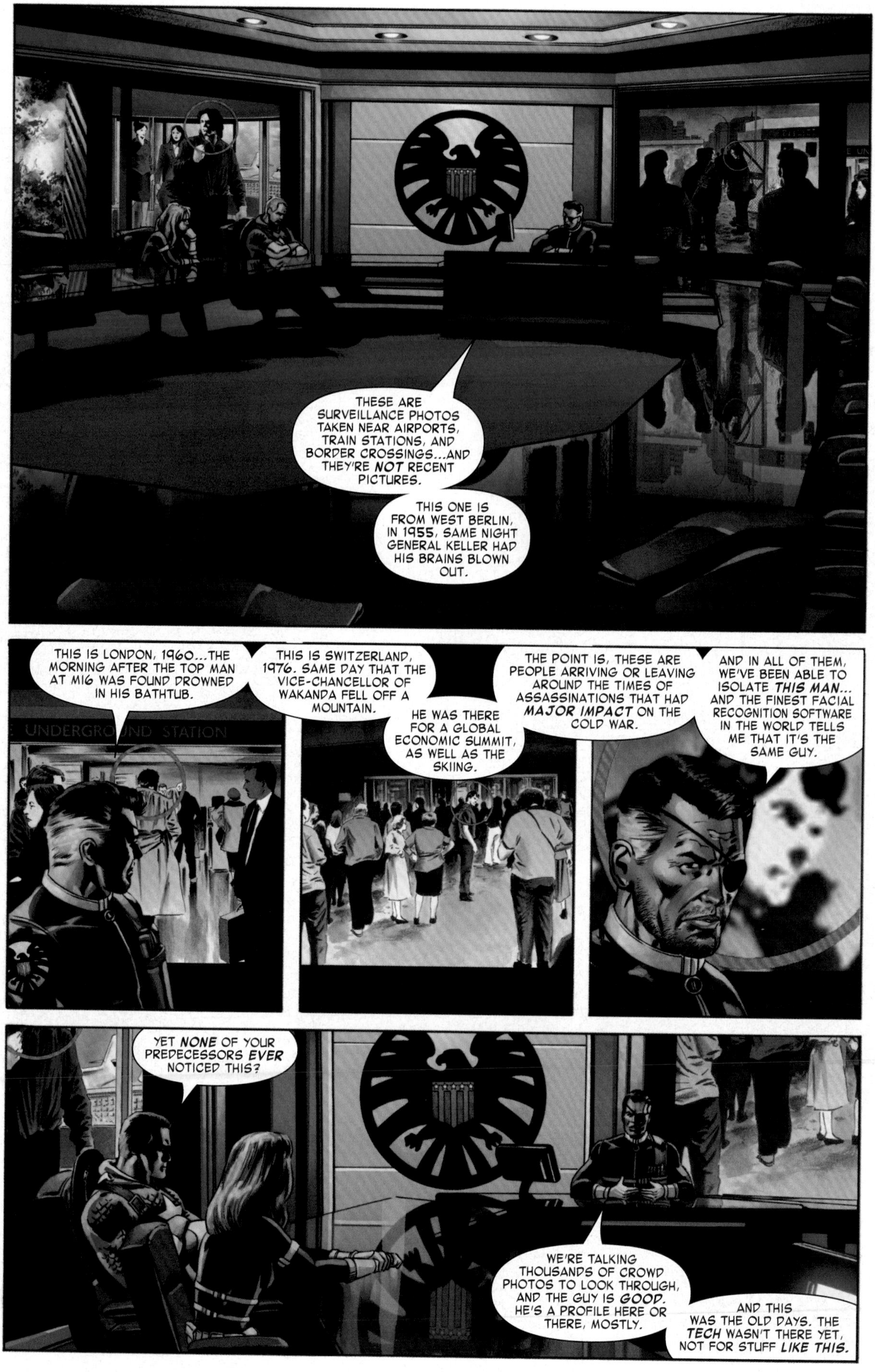

THESE ARE SURVEILLANCE PHOTOS TAKEN NEAR AIRPORTS, TRAIN STATIONS, AND BORDER CROSSINGS...AND THEY'RE NOT RECENT PICTURES.
THIS ONE IS FROM WEST BERLIN, IN 1955, SAME NIGHT GENERAL KELLER HAD HIS BRAINS BLOWN OUT.
THIS IS LONDON, 1960...THE MORNING AFTER THE TOP MAN AT MI6 WAS FOUND DROWNED IN HIS BATHTUB.
UNDERGROUND STATION
THIS IS SWITZERLAND, 1976. SAME DAY THAT THE VICE-CHANCELLOR OF WAKANDA FELL OFF A MOUNTAIN.
HE WAS THERE FOR A GLOBAL ECONOMIC SUMMIT, AS WELL AS THE SKIING.
THE POINT IS, THESE ARE PEOPLE ARRIVING OR LEAVING AROUND THE TIMES OF ASSASSINATIONS THAT HAD MAJOR IMPACT ON THE COLD WAR.
AND IN ALL OF THEM, WE'VE BEEN ABLE TO ISOLATE THIS MAN... AND THE FINEST FACIAL RECOGNITION SOFTWARE IN THE WORLD TELLS ME THAT IT'S THE SAME GUY.
YET NONE OF YOUR PREDECESSORS EVER NOTICED THIS?
WE'RE TALKING THOUSANDS OF CROWD PHOTOS TO LOOK THROUGH, AND THE GUY IS GOOD. HE'S A PROFILE HERE OR THERE, MOSTLY.
AND THIS WAS THE OLD DAYS. THE TECH WASN'T THERE YET, NOT FOR STUFF LIKE THIS.

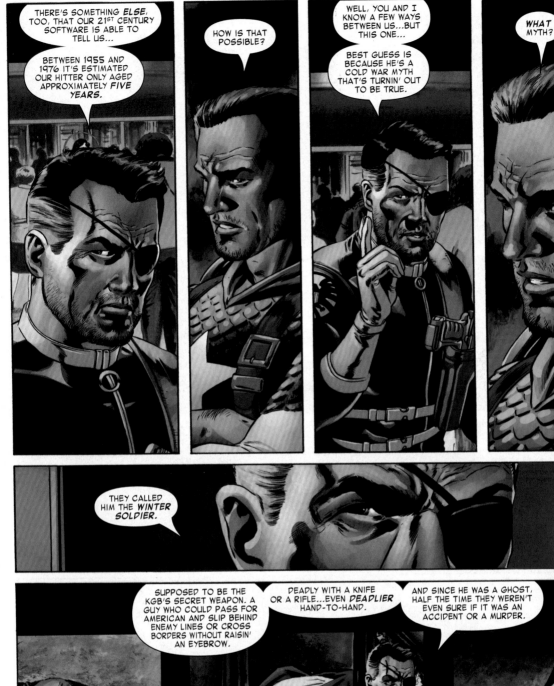

THERE'S SOMETHING *ELSE*, TOO, THAT OUR 21ST CENTURY SOFTWARE IS ABLE TO TELL US...

BETWEEN 1955 AND 1976 IT'S ESTIMATED OUR HITTER ONLY AGED APPROXIMATELY *FIVE YEARS.*

HOW IS THAT POSSIBLE?

WELL, YOU AND I KNOW A FEW WAYS BETWEEN US...BUT THIS ONE...

BEST GUESS IS BECAUSE HE'S A COLD WAR MYTH THAT'S TURNIN' OUT TO BE TRUE.

WHAT MYTH?

THEY CALLED HIM THE *WINTER SOLDIER.*

SUPPOSED TO BE THE KGB'S SECRET WEAPON. A GUY WHO COULD PASS FOR AMERICAN AND SLIP BEHIND ENEMY LINES OR CROSS BORDERS WITHOUT RAISIN' AN EYEBROW.

DEADLY WITH A KNIFE OR A RIFLE...EVEN *DEADLIER* HAND-TO-HAND.

AND SINCE HE WAS A GHOST, HALF THE TIME THEY WEREN'T EVEN SURE IF IT WAS AN ACCIDENT OR A MURDER.

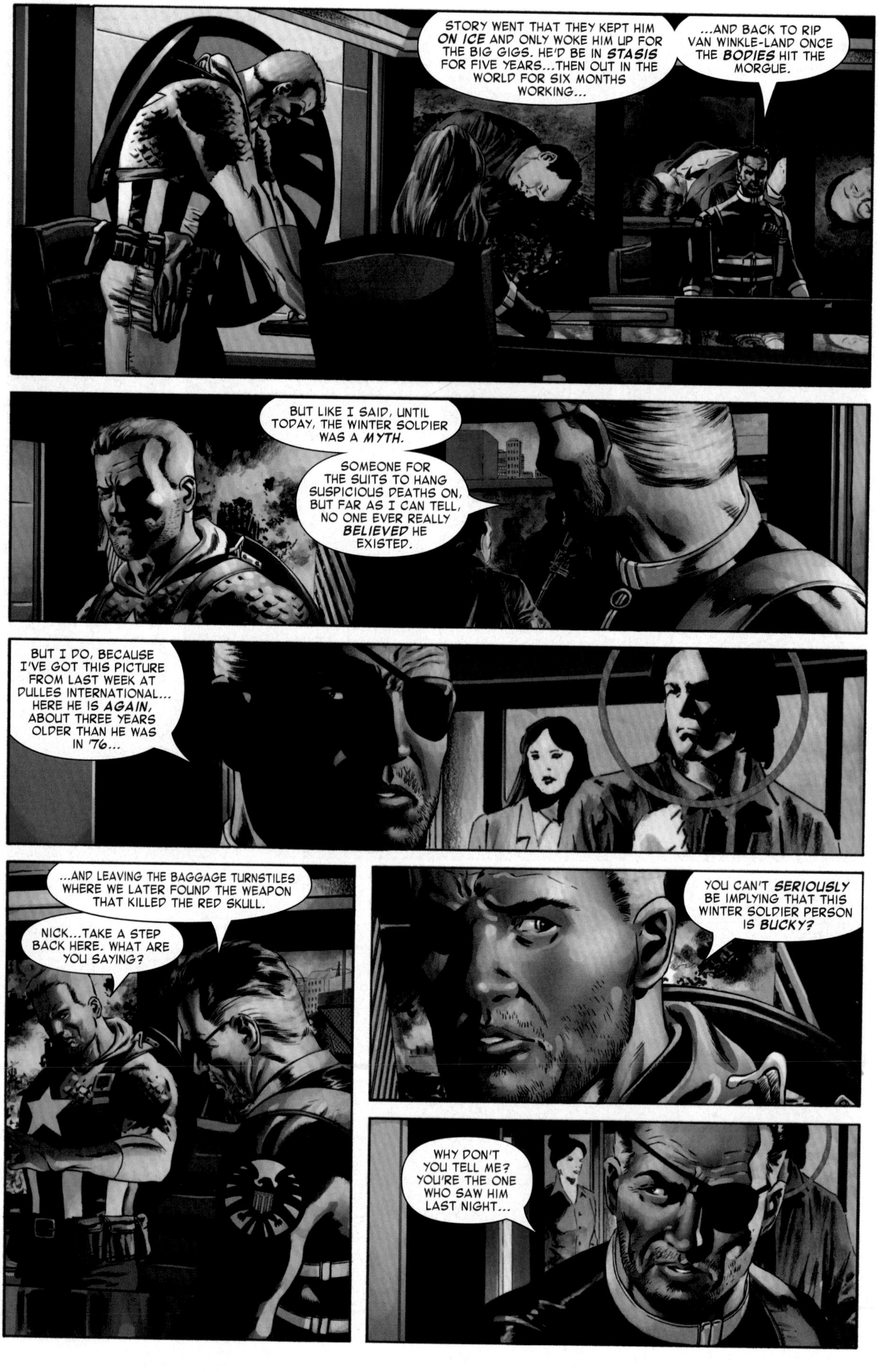
STORY WENT THAT THEY KEPT HIM ON ICE AND ONLY WOKE HIM UP FOR THE BIG GIGS. HE'D BE IN STASIS FOR FIVE YEARS...THEN OUT IN THE WORLD FOR SIX MONTHS WORKING...
...AND BACK TO RIP VAN WINKLE-LAND ONCE THE BODIES HIT THE MORGUE.
BUT LIKE I SAID, UNTIL TODAY, THE WINTER SOLDIER WAS A MYTH.
SOMEONE FOR THE SUITS TO HANG SUSPICIOUS DEATHS ON, BUT FAR AS I CAN TELL, NO ONE EVER REALLY BELIEVED HE EXISTED.
BUT I DO, BECAUSE I'VE GOT THIS PICTURE FROM LAST WEEK AT DULLES INTERNATIONAL... HERE HE IS AGAIN, ABOUT THREE YEARS OLDER THAN HE WAS IN '76...
...AND LEAVING THE BAGGAGE TURNSTILES WHERE WE LATER FOUND THE WEAPON THAT KILLED THE RED SKULL.
NICK...TAKE A STEP BACK HERE. WHAT ARE YOU SAYING?
YOU CAN'T SERIOUSLY BE IMPLYING THAT THIS WINTER SOLDIER PERSON IS BUCKY?
WHY DON'T YOU TELL ME? YOU'RE THE ONE WHO SAW HIM LAST NIGHT...

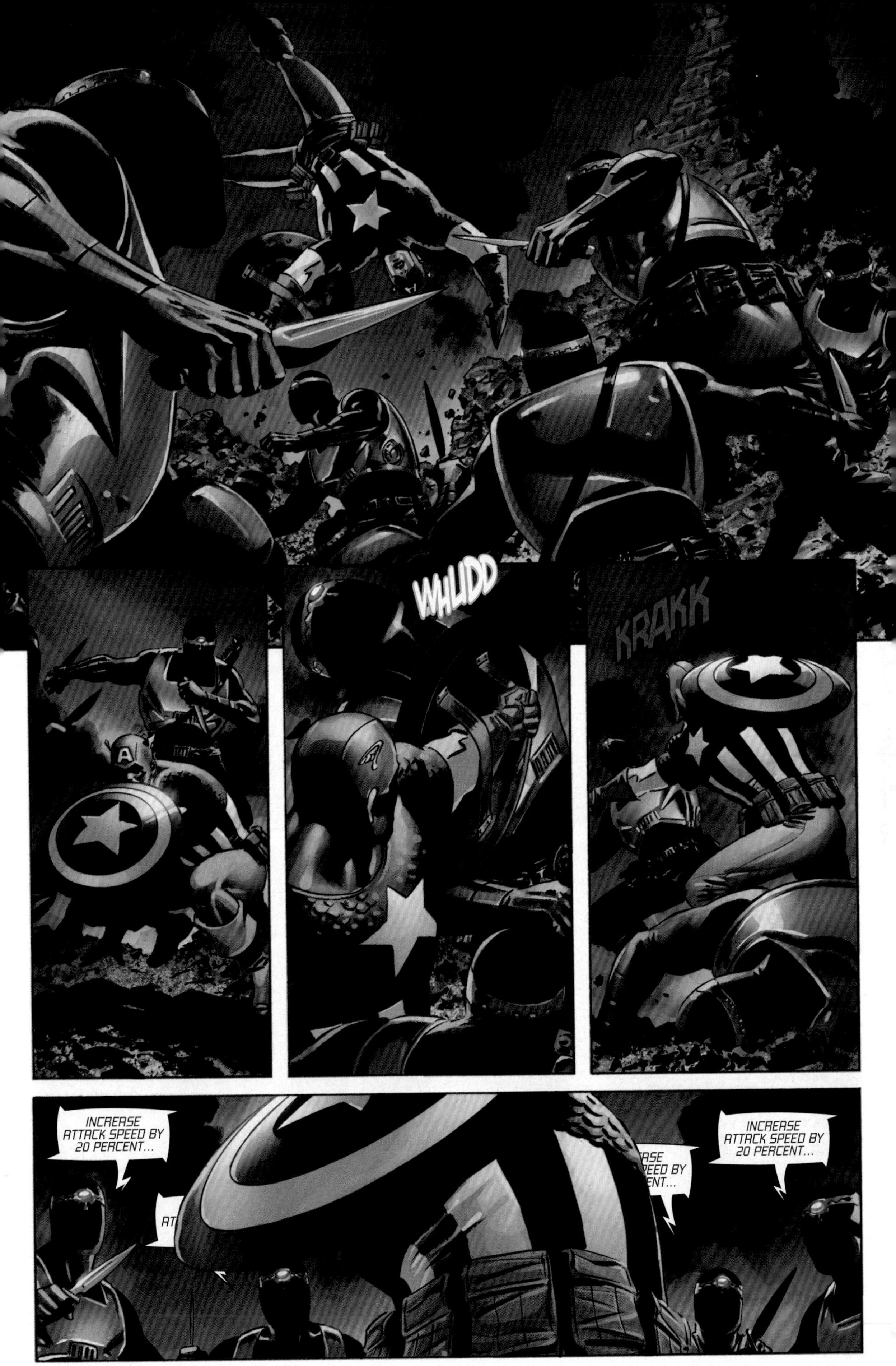

WHUDD
KRAKK
INCREASE ATTACK SPEED BY 20 PERCENT...
AT
ASE PEED BY ENT...
INCREASE ATTACK SPEED BY 20 PERCENT...

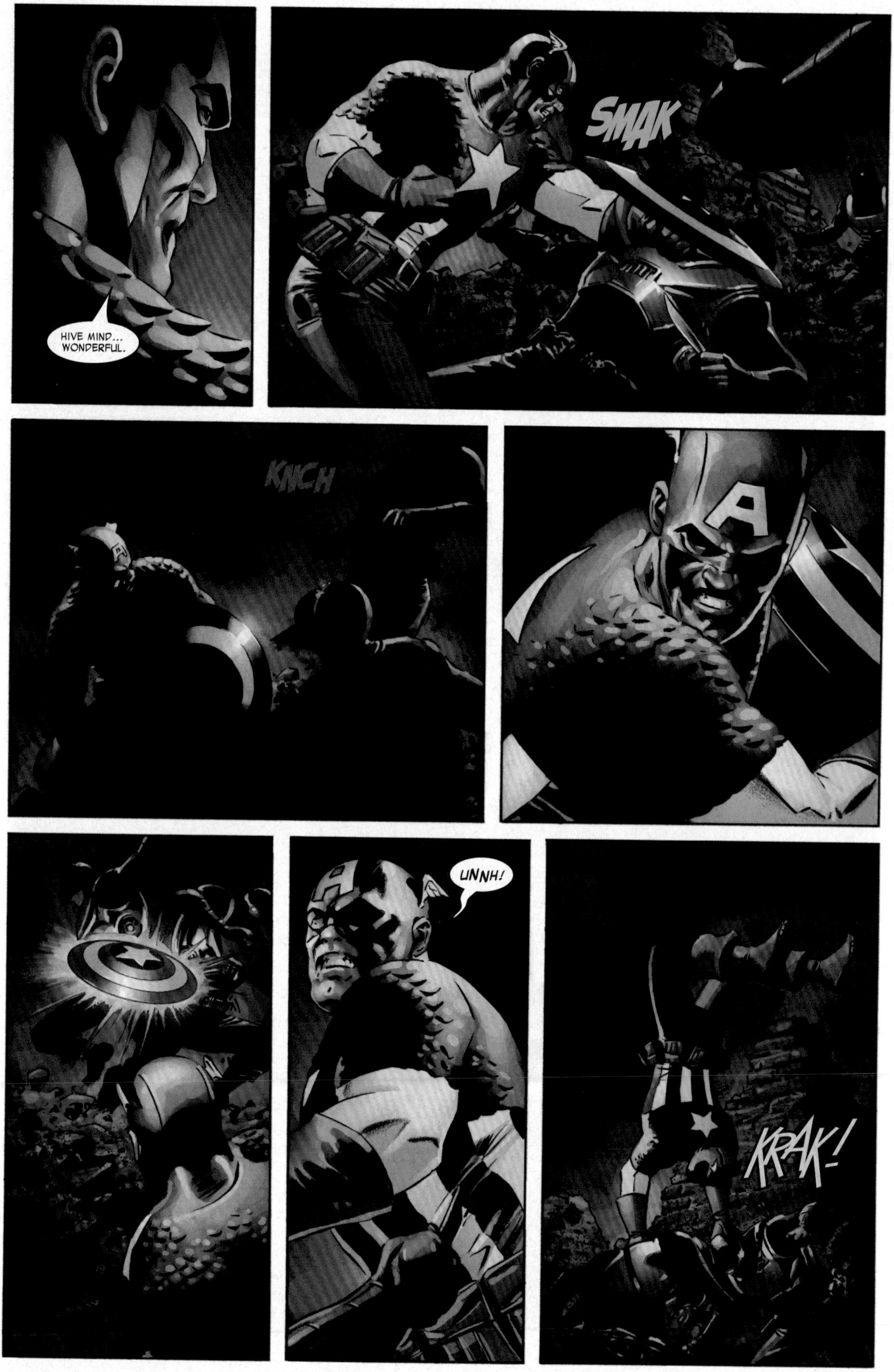
HIVE MIND... WONDERFUL.
SMAK
KNCH
UNNH!
KRAK!

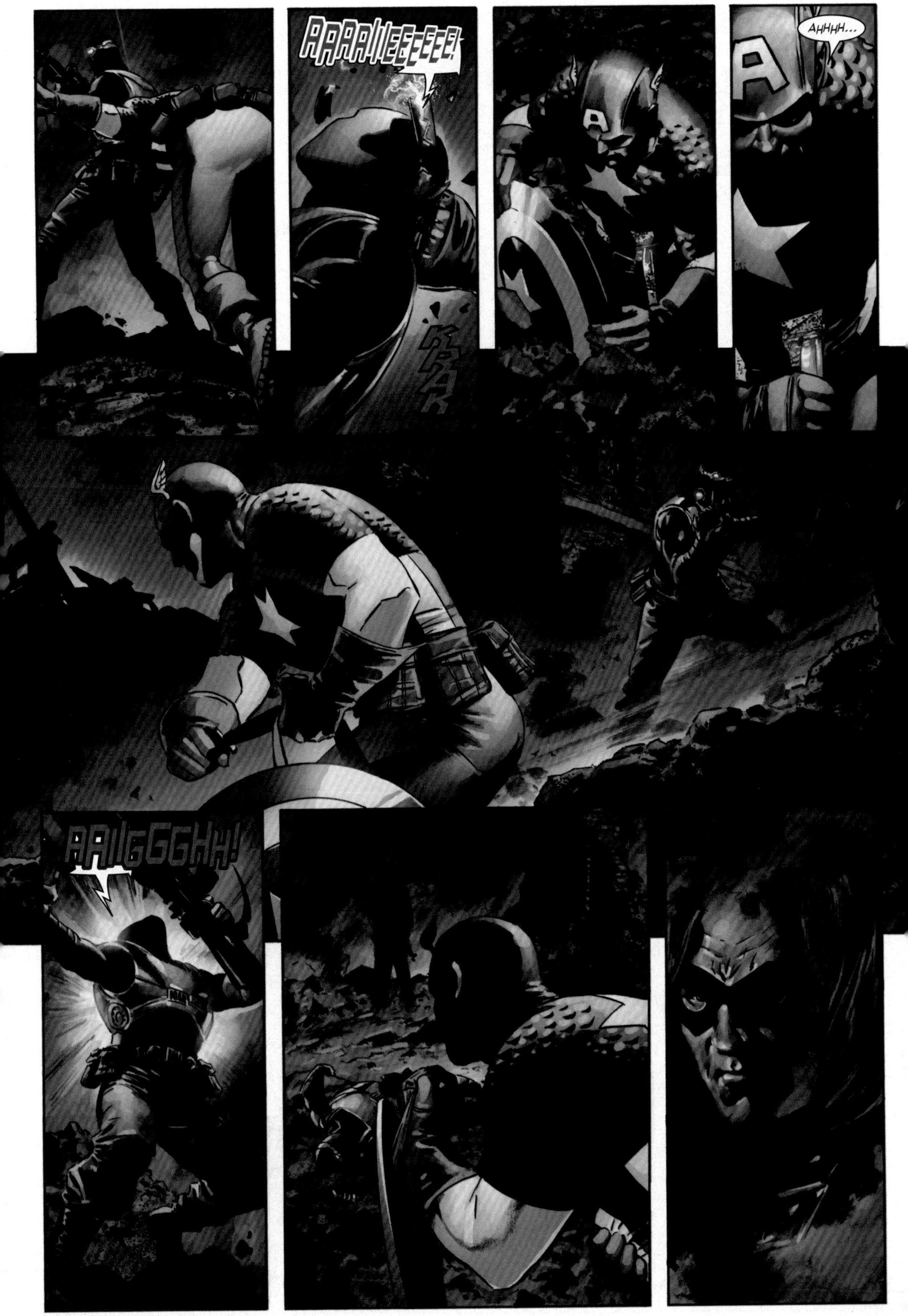
AAARRIIEEEEEE!
KRAK
AHHHH...
ARRGGGHH!

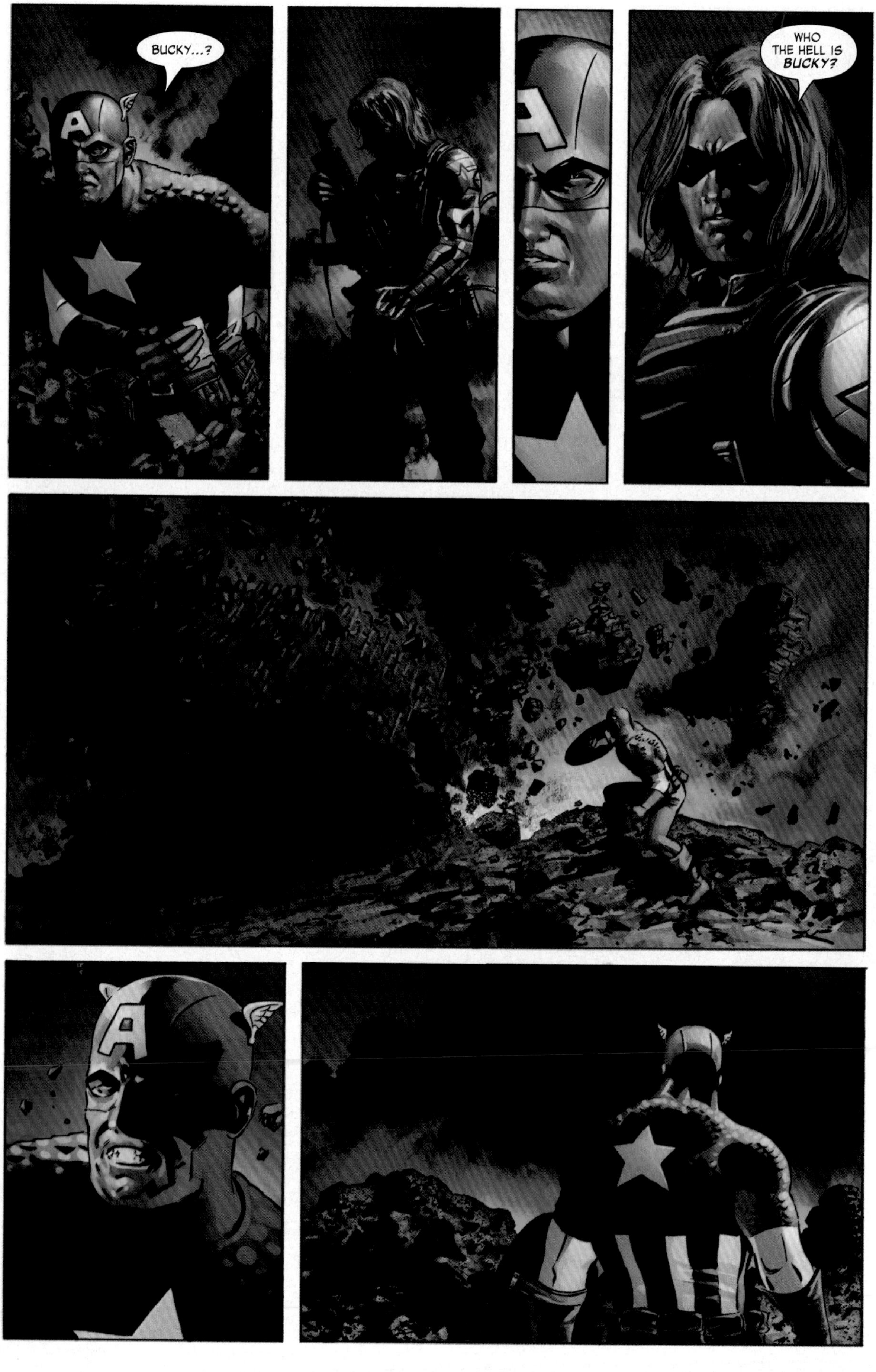
BUCKY...?
WHO THE HELL IS BUCKY?

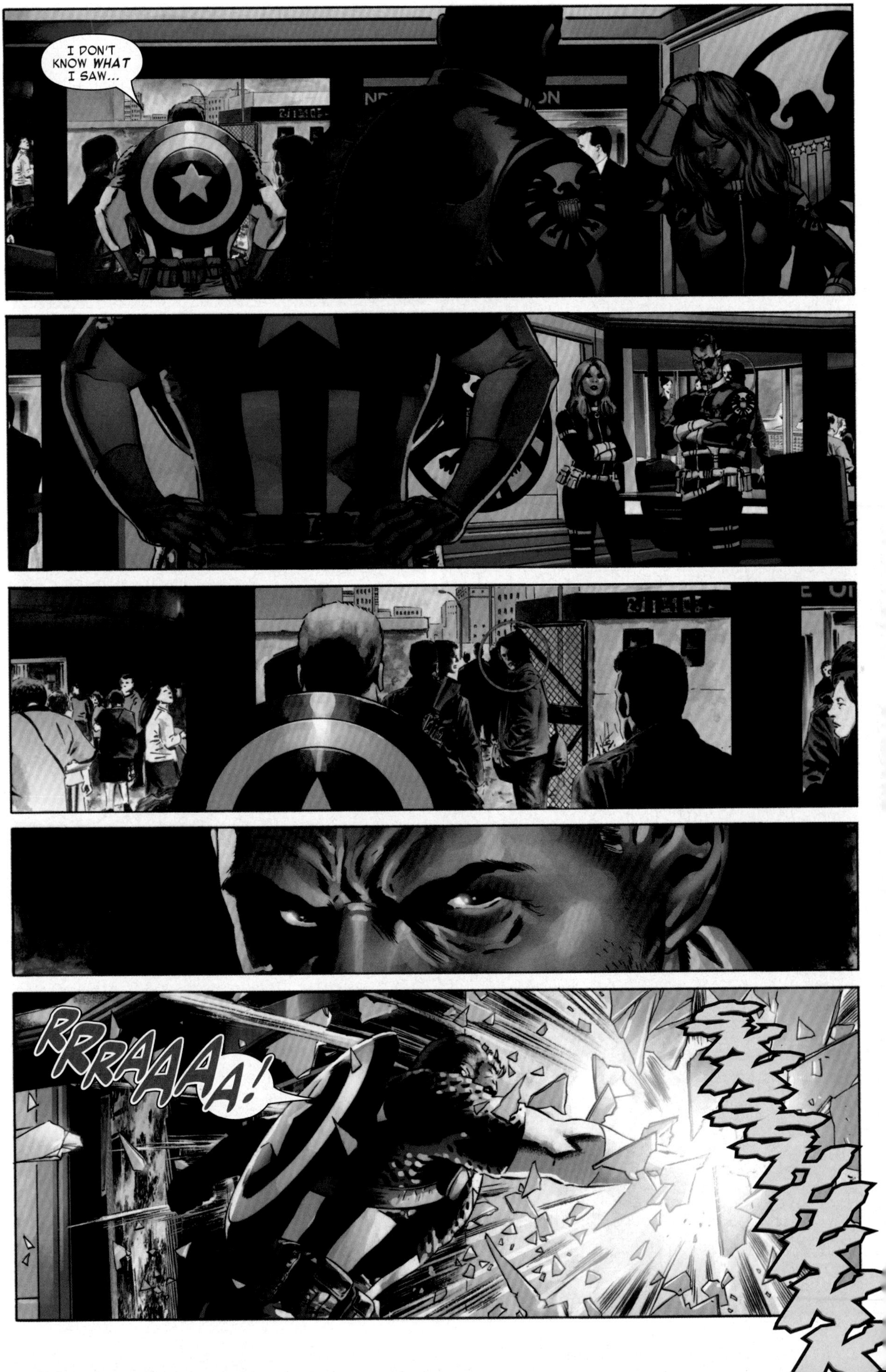
I DON'T KNOW WHAT I SAW...
RRRAAAAA!

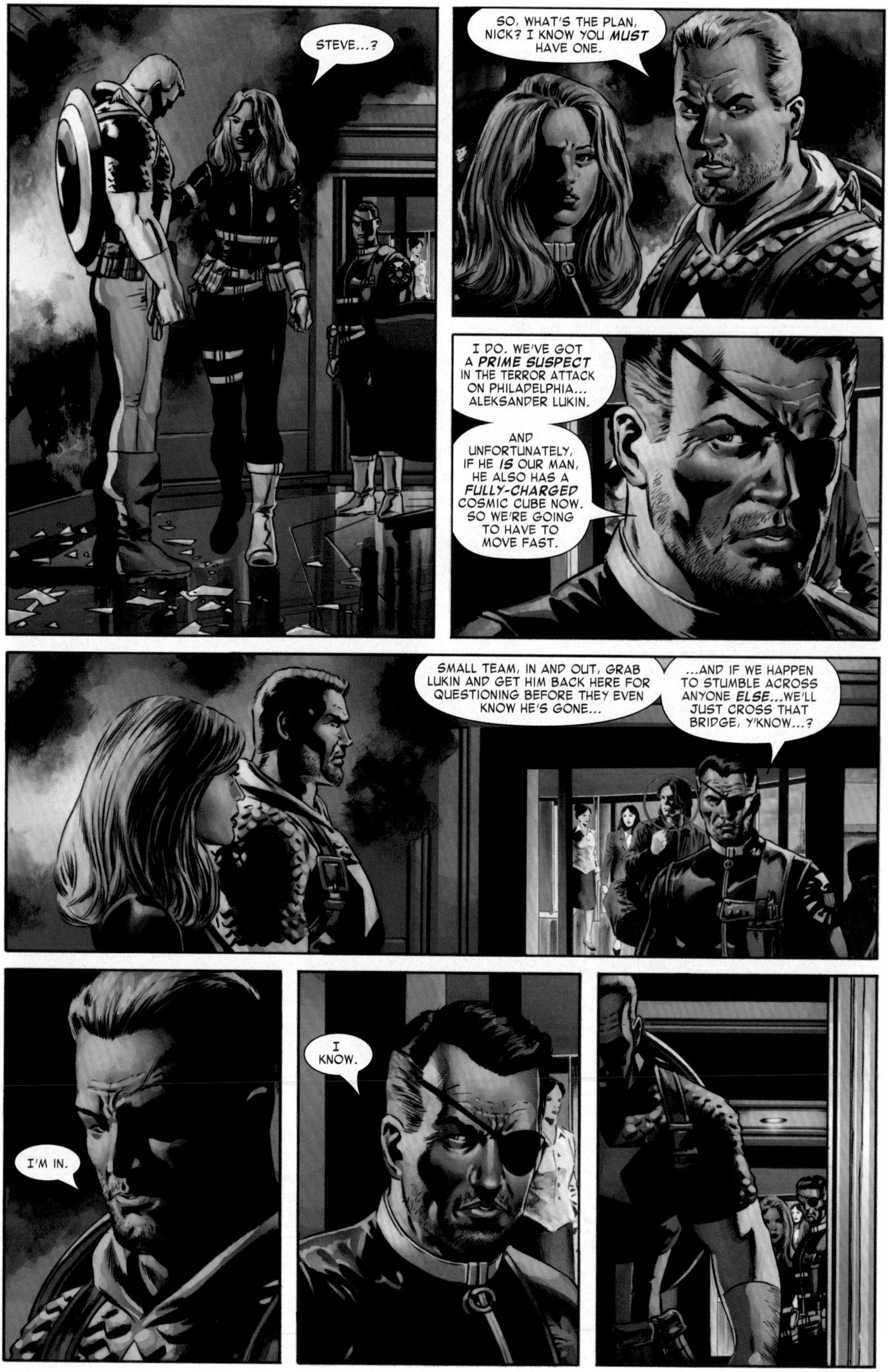
STEVE...?
SO, WHAT'S THE PLAN, NICK? I KNOW YOU MUST HAVE ONE.
I DO. WE'VE GOT A PRIME SUSPECT IN THE TERROR ATTACK ON PHILADELPHIA... ALEKSANDER LUKIN.
AND UNFORTUNATELY, IF HE IS OUR MAN, HE ALSO HAS A FULLY-CHARGED COSMIC CUBE NOW. SO WE'RE GOING TO HAVE TO MOVE FAST.
SMALL TEAM, IN AND OUT, GRAB LUKIN AND GET HIM BACK HERE FOR QUESTIONING BEFORE THEY EVEN KNOW HE'S GONE...
...AND IF WE HAPPEN TO STUMBLE ACROSS ANYONE ELSE...WE'LL JUST CROSS THAT BRIDGE, Y'KNOW...?
I'M IN.
I KNOW.

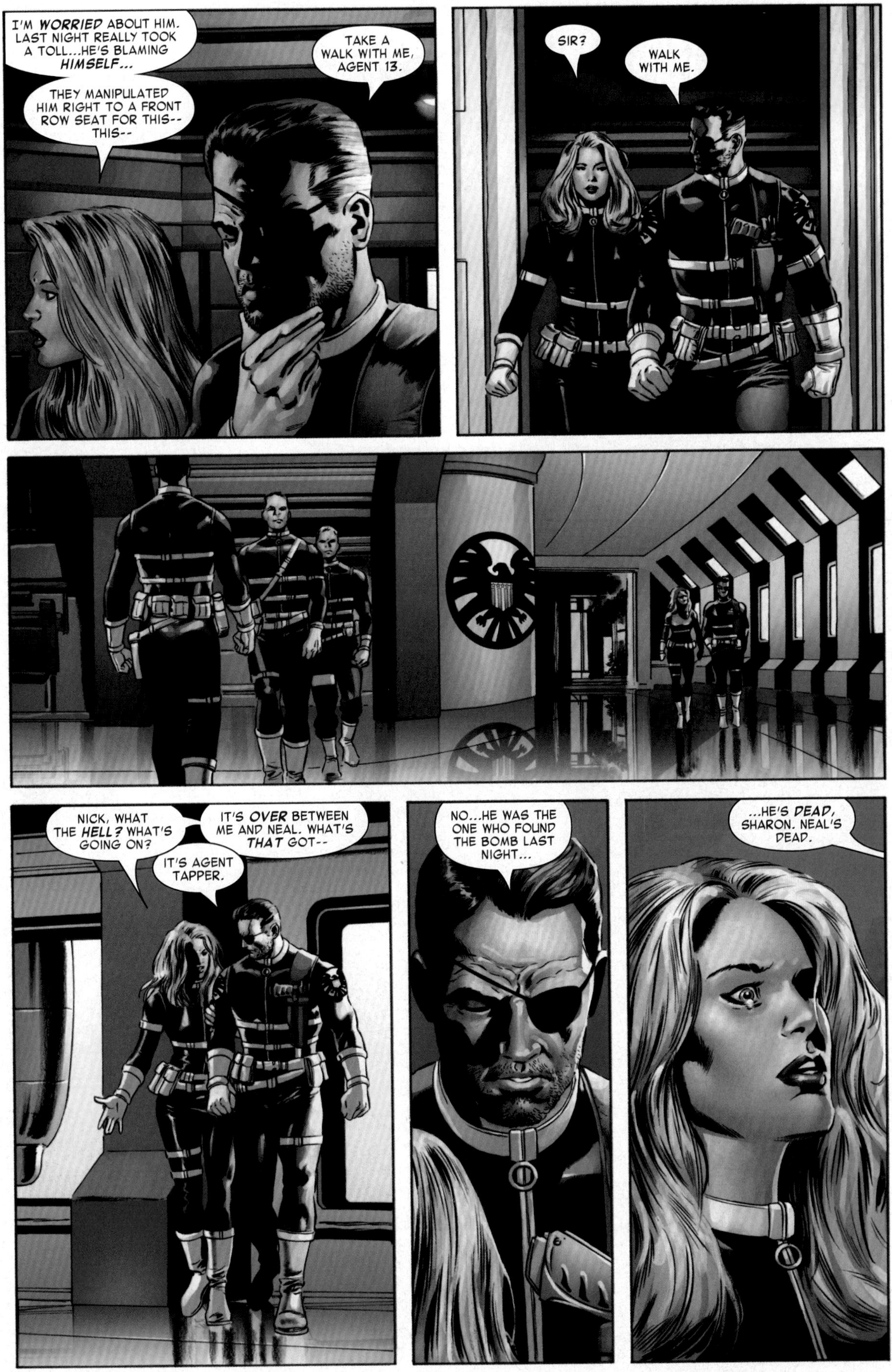
I'M WORRIED ABOUT HIM. LAST NIGHT REALLY TOOK A TOLL...HE'S BLAMING HIMSELF...
THEY MANIPULATED HIM RIGHT TO A FRONT ROW SEAT FOR THIS-- THIS--
TAKE A WALK WITH ME, AGENT 13.
SIR?
WALK WITH ME.
NICK, WHAT THE HELL? WHAT'S GOING ON?
IT'S OVER BETWEEN ME AND NEAL. WHAT'S THAT GOT--
IT'S AGENT TAPPER.
NO...HE WAS THE ONE WHO FOUND THE BOMB LAST NIGHT...
...HE'S DEAD, SHARON. NEAL'S DEAD.

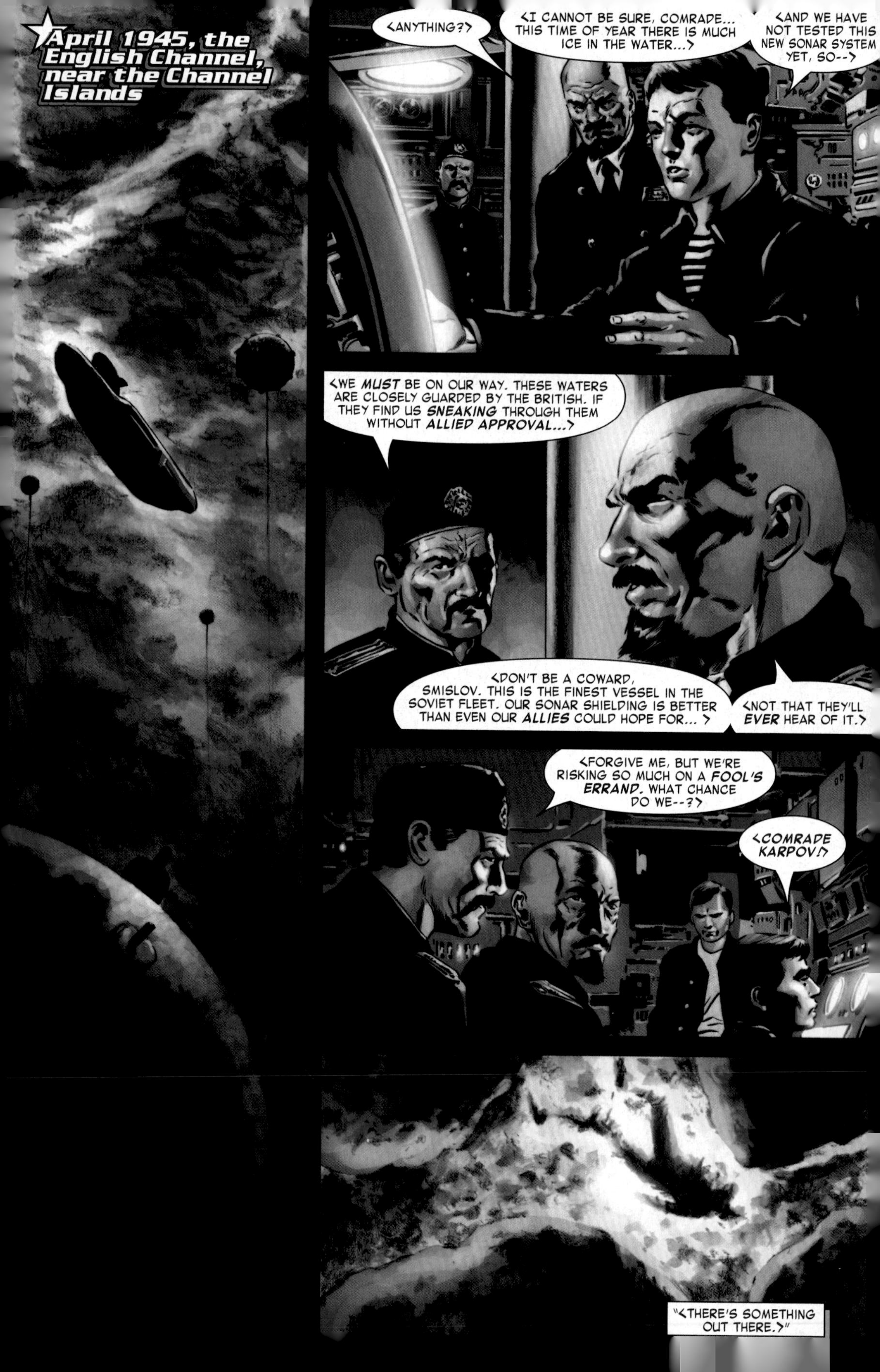
April 1945, the English Channel, near the Channel Islands
<ANYTHING?>
<I CANNOT BE SURE, COMRADE... THIS TIME OF YEAR THERE IS MUCH ICE IN THE WATER...>
<AND WE HAVE NOT TESTED THIS NEW SONAR SYSTEM YET, SO-->
<WE MUST BE ON OUR WAY. THESE WATERS ARE CLOSELY GUARDED BY THE BRITISH. IF THEY FIND US SNEAKING THROUGH THEM WITHOUT ALLIED APPROVAL...>
<DON'T BE A COWARD, SMISLOV. THIS IS THE FINEST VESSEL IN THE SOVIET FLEET. OUR SONAR SHIELDING IS BETTER THAN EVEN OUR ALLIES COULD HOPE FOR...>
<NOT THAT THEY'LL EVER HEAR OF IT.>
<FORGIVE ME, BUT WE'RE RISKING SO MUCH ON A FOOL'S ERRAND. WHAT CHANCE DO WE--?>
<COMRADE KARPOV!>
"<THERE'S SOMETHING OUT THERE.>"

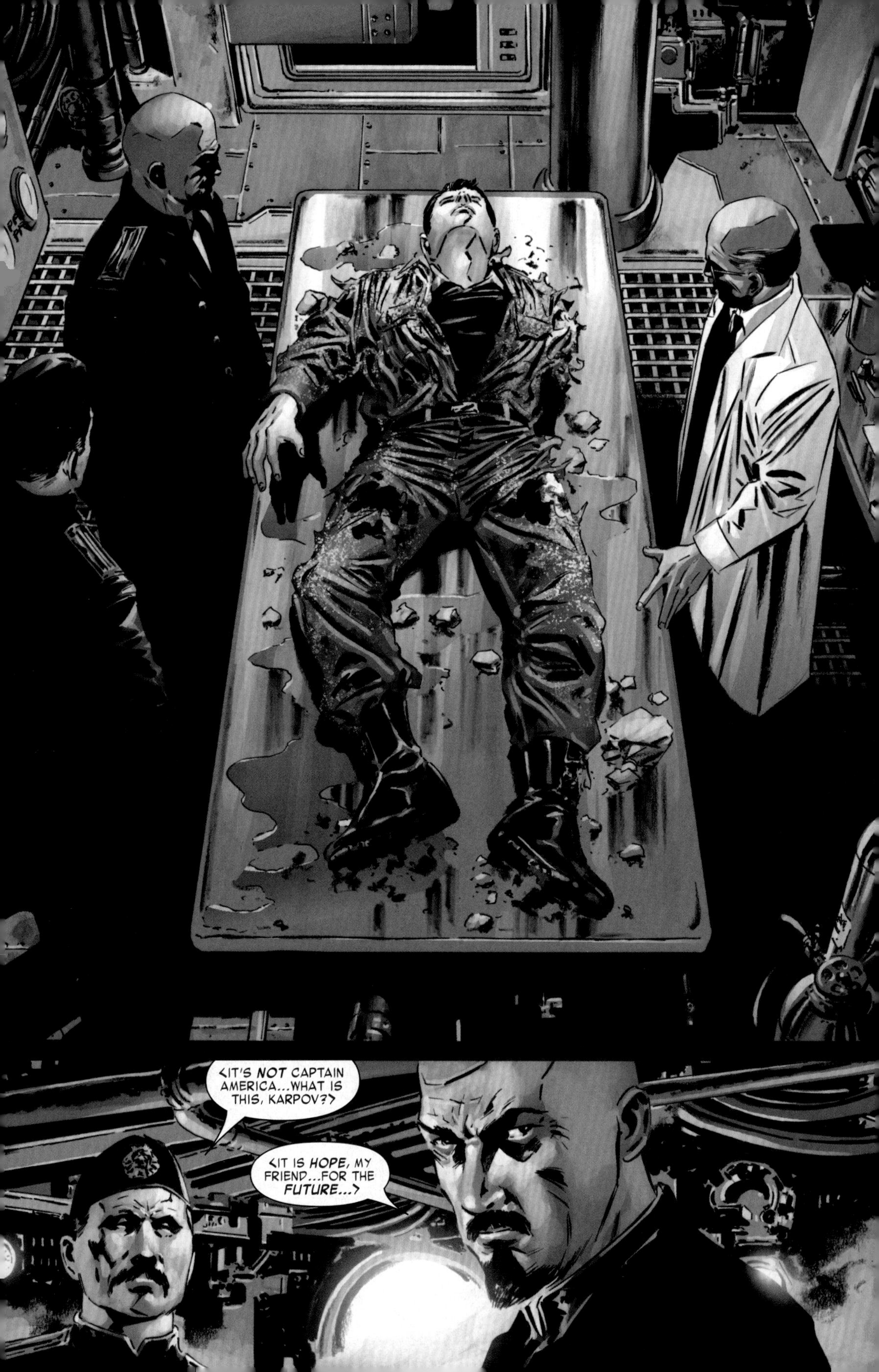
<IT'S NOT CAPTAIN AMERICA...WHAT IS THIS, KARPOV?>
<IT IS HOPE, MY FRIEND...FOR THE FUTURE...>

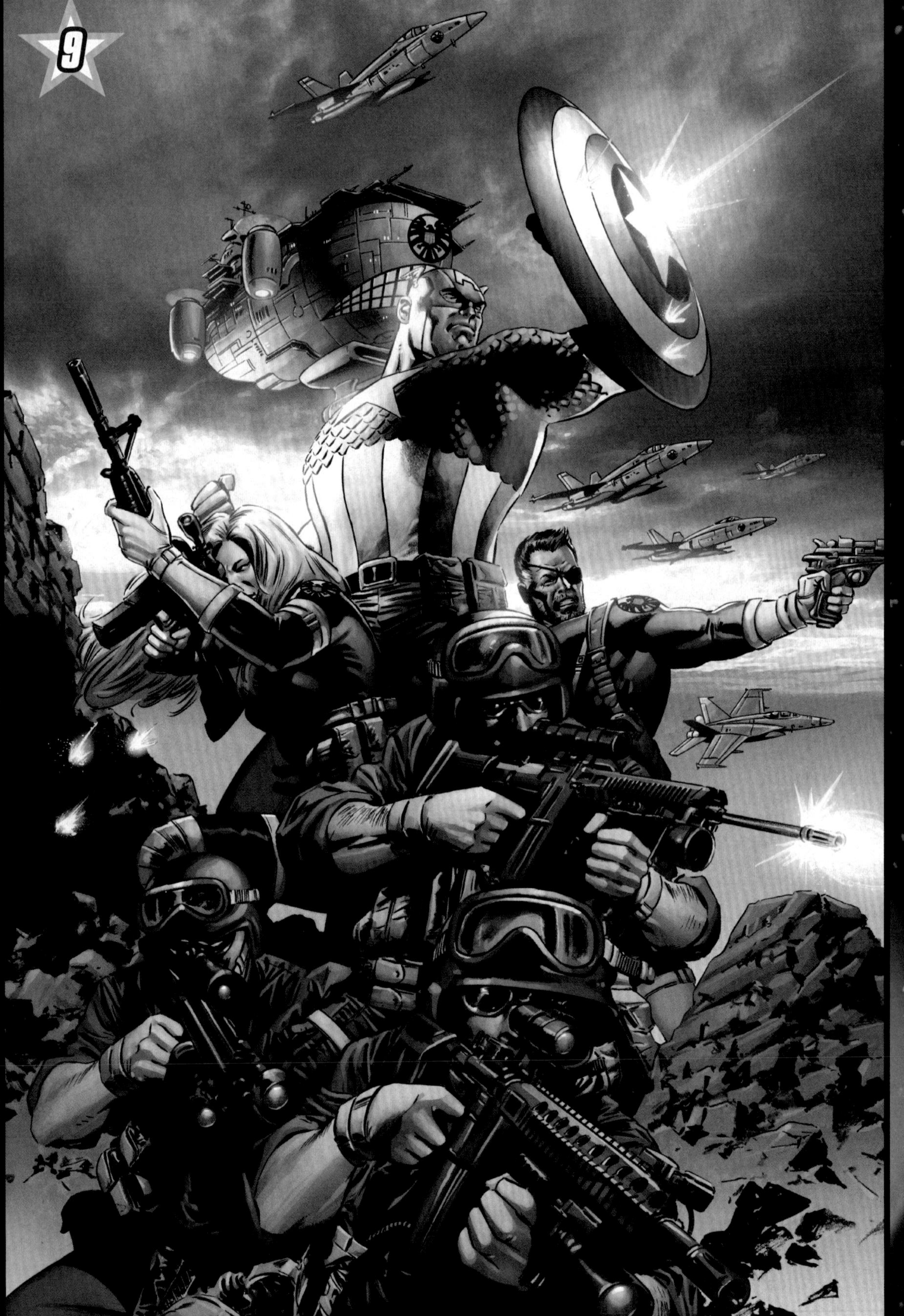
9

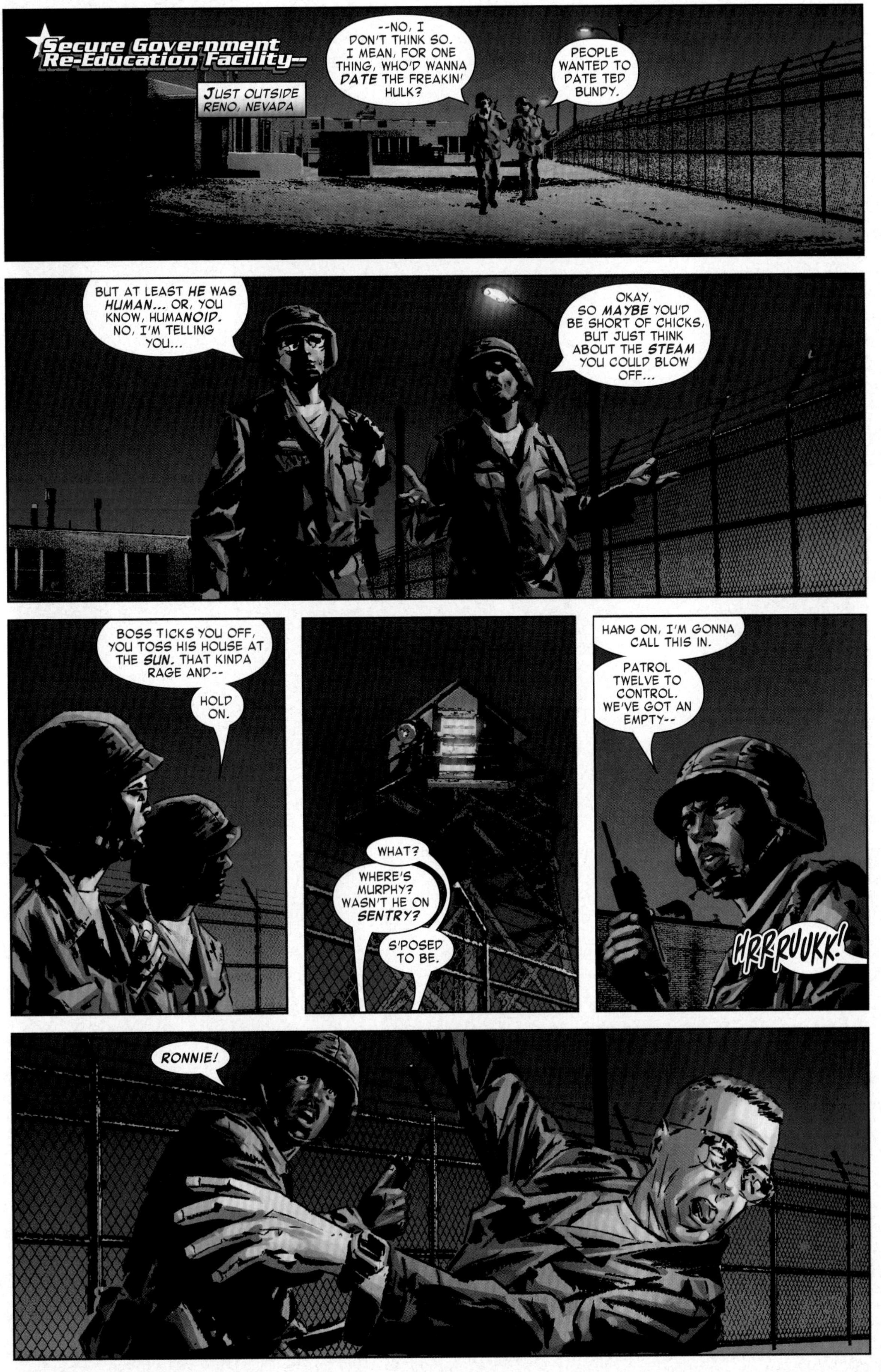
Secure Government Re-Education Facility--
JUST OUTSIDE RENO, NEVADA
--NO, I DON'T THINK SO. I MEAN, FOR ONE THING, WHO'D WANNA DATE THE FREAKIN' HULK?
PEOPLE WANTED TO DATE TED BUNDY.
BUT AT LEAST HE WAS HUMAN... OR, YOU KNOW, HUMANOID. NO, I'M TELLING YOU...
OKAY, SO MAYBE YOU'D BE SHORT OF CHICKS, BUT JUST THINK ABOUT THE STEAM YOU COULD BLOW OFF...
BOSS TICKS YOU OFF, YOU TOSS HIS HOUSE AT THE SUN. THAT KINDA RAGE AND--
HOLD ON.
WHAT?
WHERE'S MURPHY? WASN'T HE ON SENTRY?
S'POSED TO BE.
HANG ON, I'M GONNA CALL THIS IN.
PATROL TWELVE TO CONTROL. WE'VE GOT AN EMPTY--
HRRRUUKK!
RONNIE!

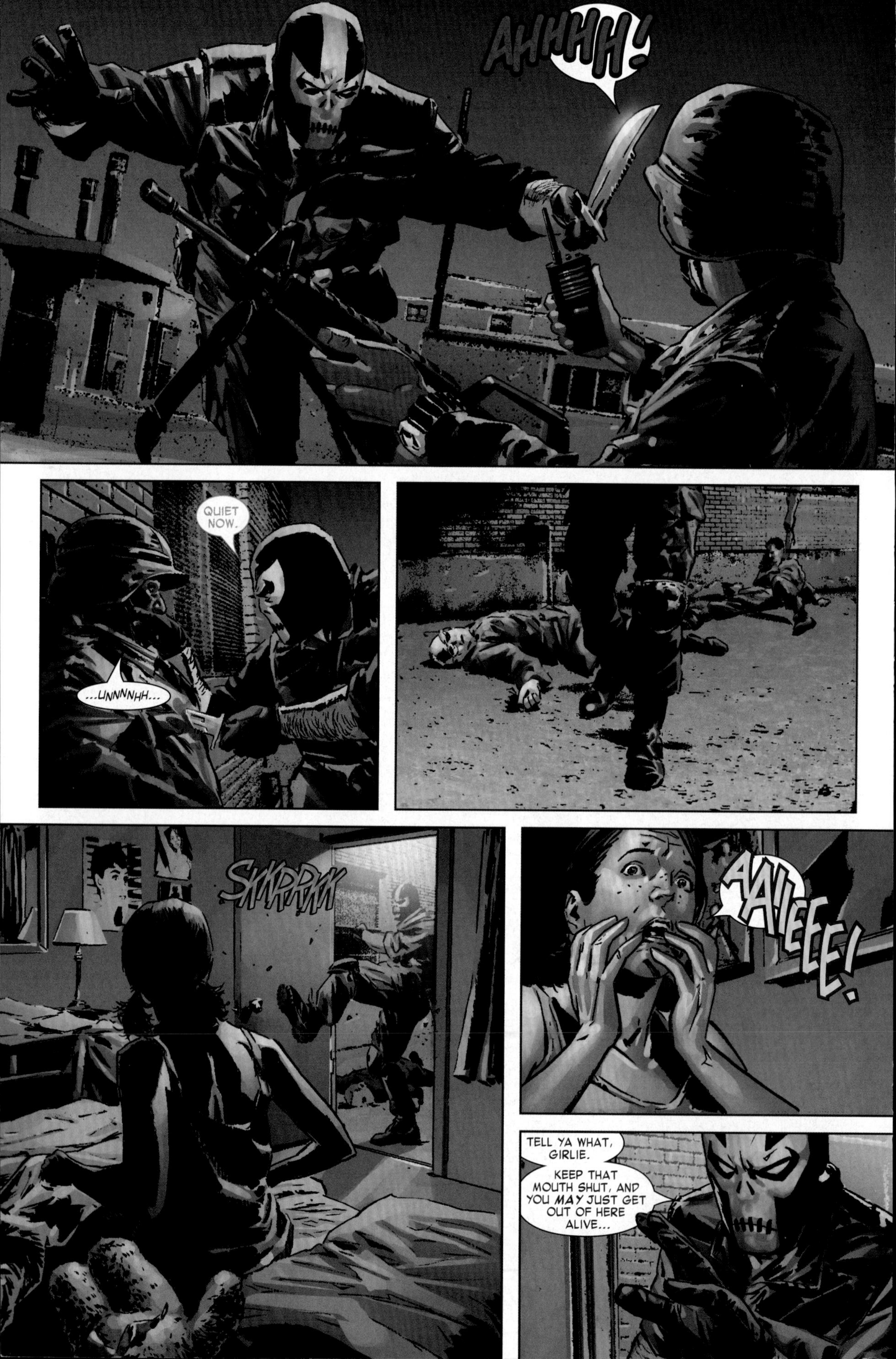
AHHHH!
QUIET NOW.
...UNNNNHH...
SKKRRKK
AAIIEEEE!
TELL YA WHAT, GIRLIE.
KEEP THAT MOUTH SHUT, AND YOU *MAY* JUST GET OUT OF HERE ALIVE...

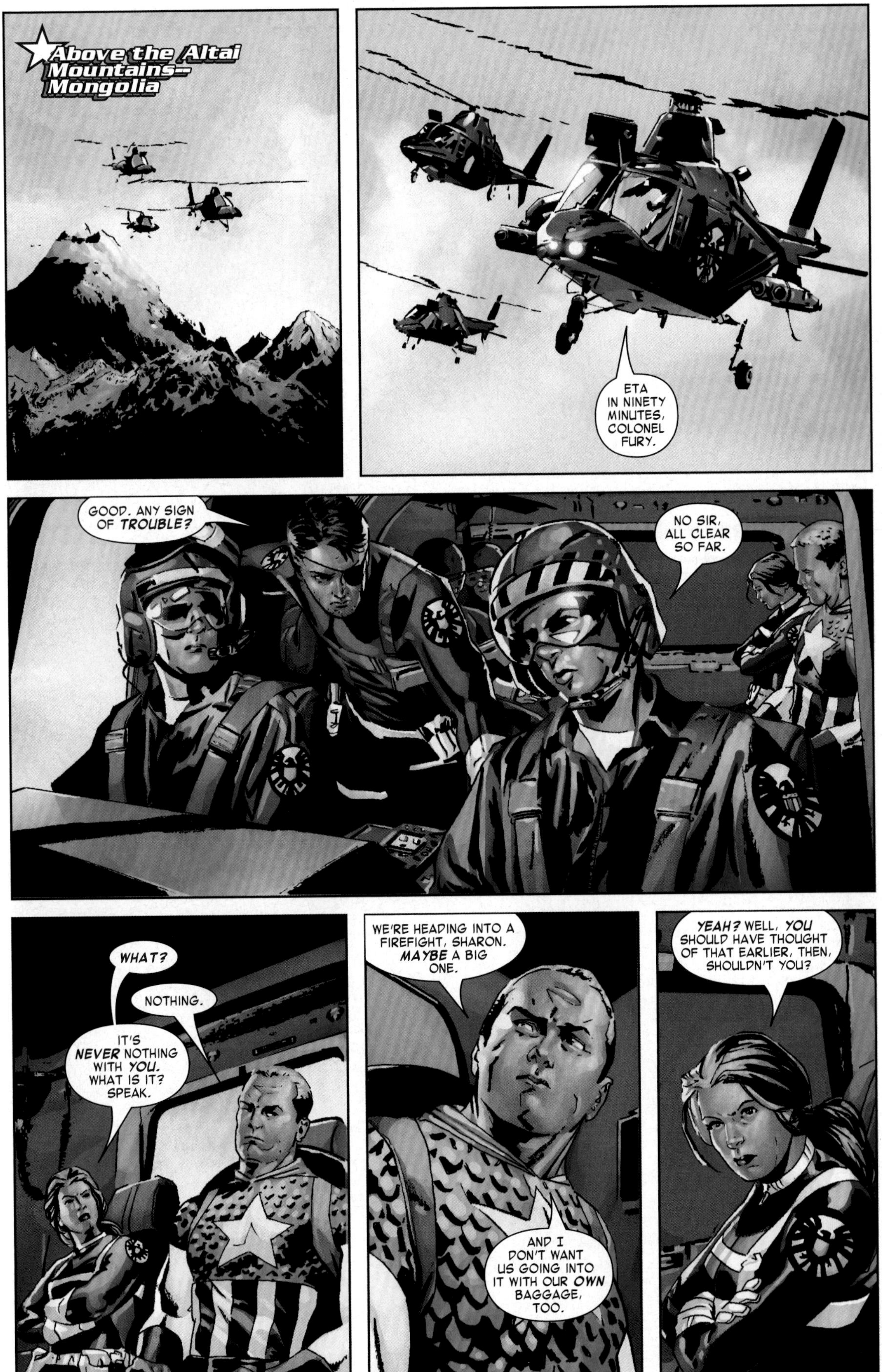
Above the Altai Mountains-- Mongolia
ETA IN NINETY MINUTES, COLONEL FURY.
GOOD. ANY SIGN OF TROUBLE?
NO SIR, ALL CLEAR SO FAR.
WHAT?
NOTHING.
IT'S NEVER NOTHING WITH YOU. WHAT IS IT? SPEAK.
WE'RE HEADING INTO A FIREFIGHT, SHARON. MAYBE A BIG ONE.
AND I DON'T WANT US GOING INTO IT WITH OUR OWN BAGGAGE, TOO.
YEAH? WELL, YOU SHOULD HAVE THOUGHT OF THAT EARLIER, THEN, SHOULDN'T YOU?

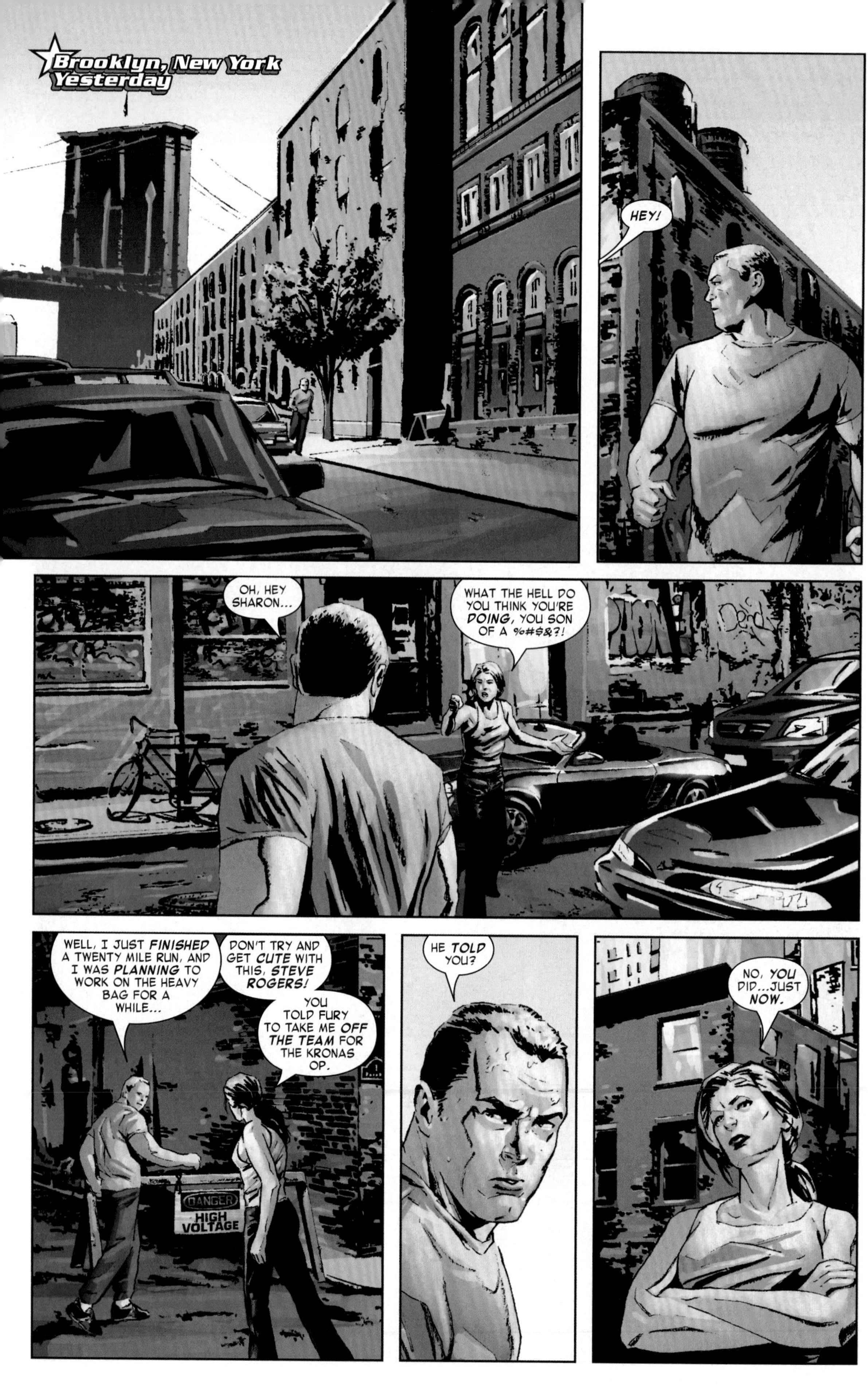
Brooklyn, New York
Yesterday
HEY!
OH, HEY SHARON...
WHAT THE HELL DO YOU THINK YOU'RE DOING, YOU SON OF A %#$&?!
WELL, I JUST FINISHED A TWENTY MILE RUN, AND I WAS PLANNING TO WORK ON THE HEAVY BAG FOR A WHILE...
DON'T TRY AND GET CUTE WITH THIS, STEVE ROGERS!
YOU TOLD FURY TO TAKE ME OFF THE TEAM FOR THE KRONAS OP.
DANGER
HIGH VOLTAGE
HE TOLD YOU?
NO, YOU DID...JUST NOW.

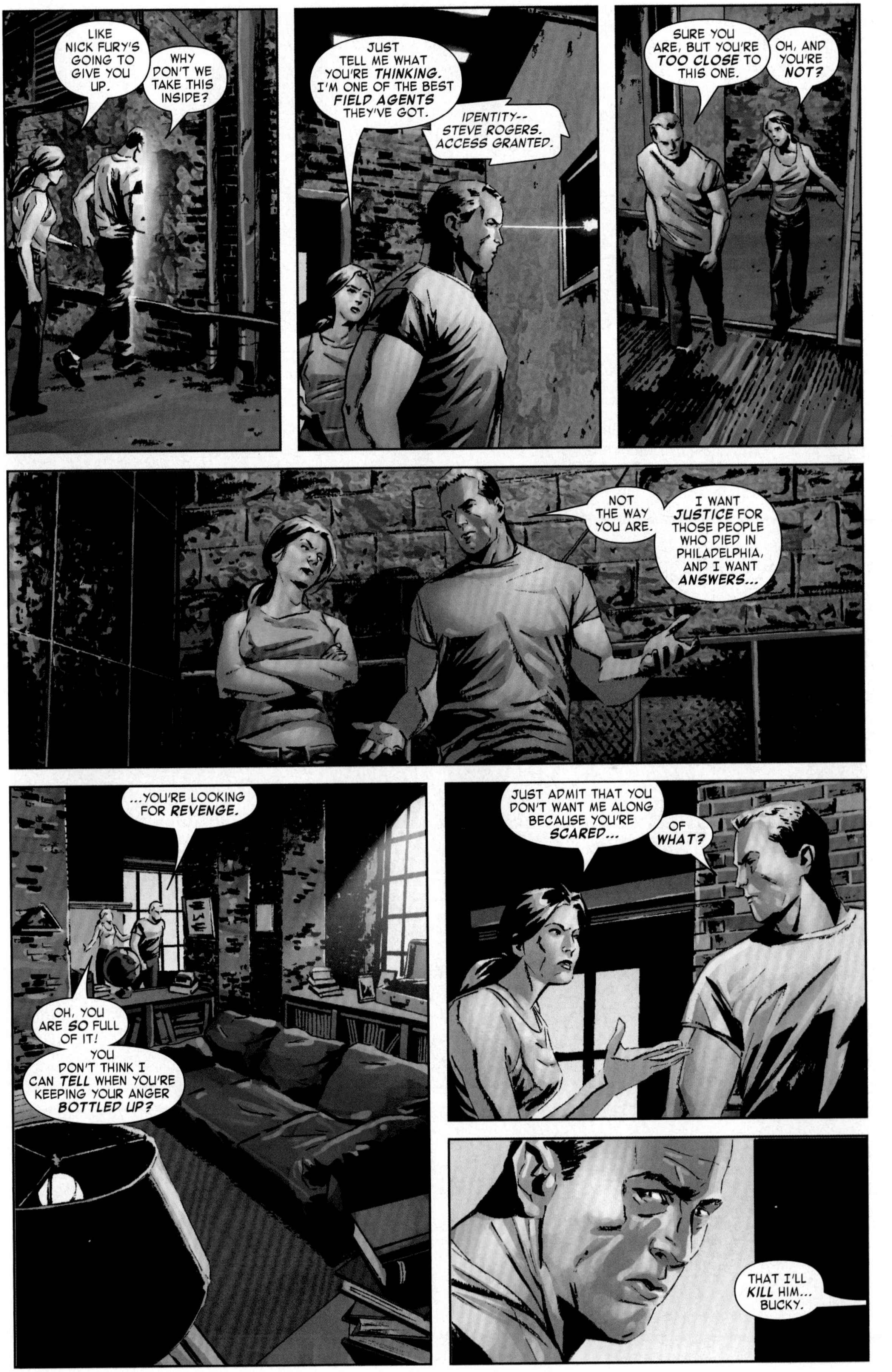
LIKE NICK FURY'S GOING TO GIVE YOU UP.
WHY DON'T WE TAKE THIS INSIDE?
JUST TELL ME WHAT YOU'RE THINKING. I'M ONE OF THE BEST FIELD AGENTS THEY'VE GOT.
IDENTITY-- STEVE ROGERS. ACCESS GRANTED.
SURE YOU ARE, BUT YOU'RE TOO CLOSE TO THIS ONE.
OH, AND YOU'RE NOT?
NOT THE WAY YOU ARE.
I WANT JUSTICE FOR THOSE PEOPLE WHO DIED IN PHILADELPHIA, AND I WANT ANSWERS...
...YOU'RE LOOKING FOR REVENGE.
OH, YOU ARE SO FULL OF IT!
YOU DON'T THINK I CAN TELL WHEN YOU'RE KEEPING YOUR ANGER BOTTLED UP?
JUST ADMIT THAT YOU DON'T WANT ME ALONG BECAUSE YOU'RE SCARED...
OF WHAT?
THAT I'LL KILL HIM... BUCKY.

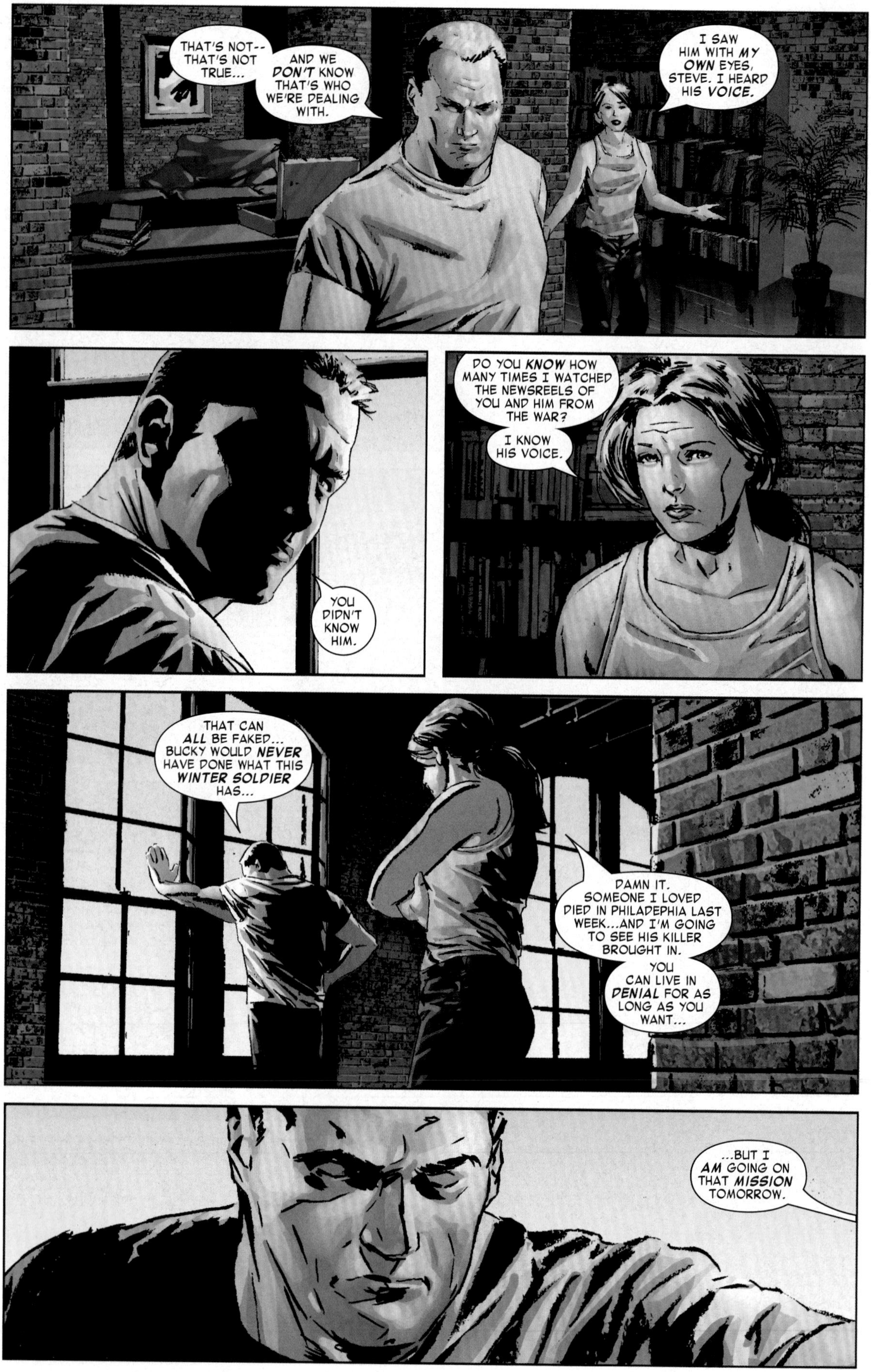

THAT'S NOT-- THAT'S NOT TRUE...
AND WE DON'T KNOW THAT'S WHO WE'RE DEALING WITH.
I SAW HIM WITH MY OWN EYES, STEVE. I HEARD HIS VOICE.
YOU DIDN'T KNOW HIM.
DO YOU KNOW HOW MANY TIMES I WATCHED THE NEWSREELS OF YOU AND HIM FROM THE WAR?
I KNOW HIS VOICE.
THAT CAN ALL BE FAKED... BUCKY WOULD NEVER HAVE DONE WHAT THIS WINTER SOLDIER HAS...
DAMN IT. SOMEONE I LOVED DIED IN PHILADEPHIA LAST WEEK...AND I'M GOING TO SEE HIS KILLER BROUGHT IN.
YOU CAN LIVE IN DENIAL FOR AS LONG AS YOU WANT...
...BUT I AM GOING ON THAT MISSION TOMORROW.

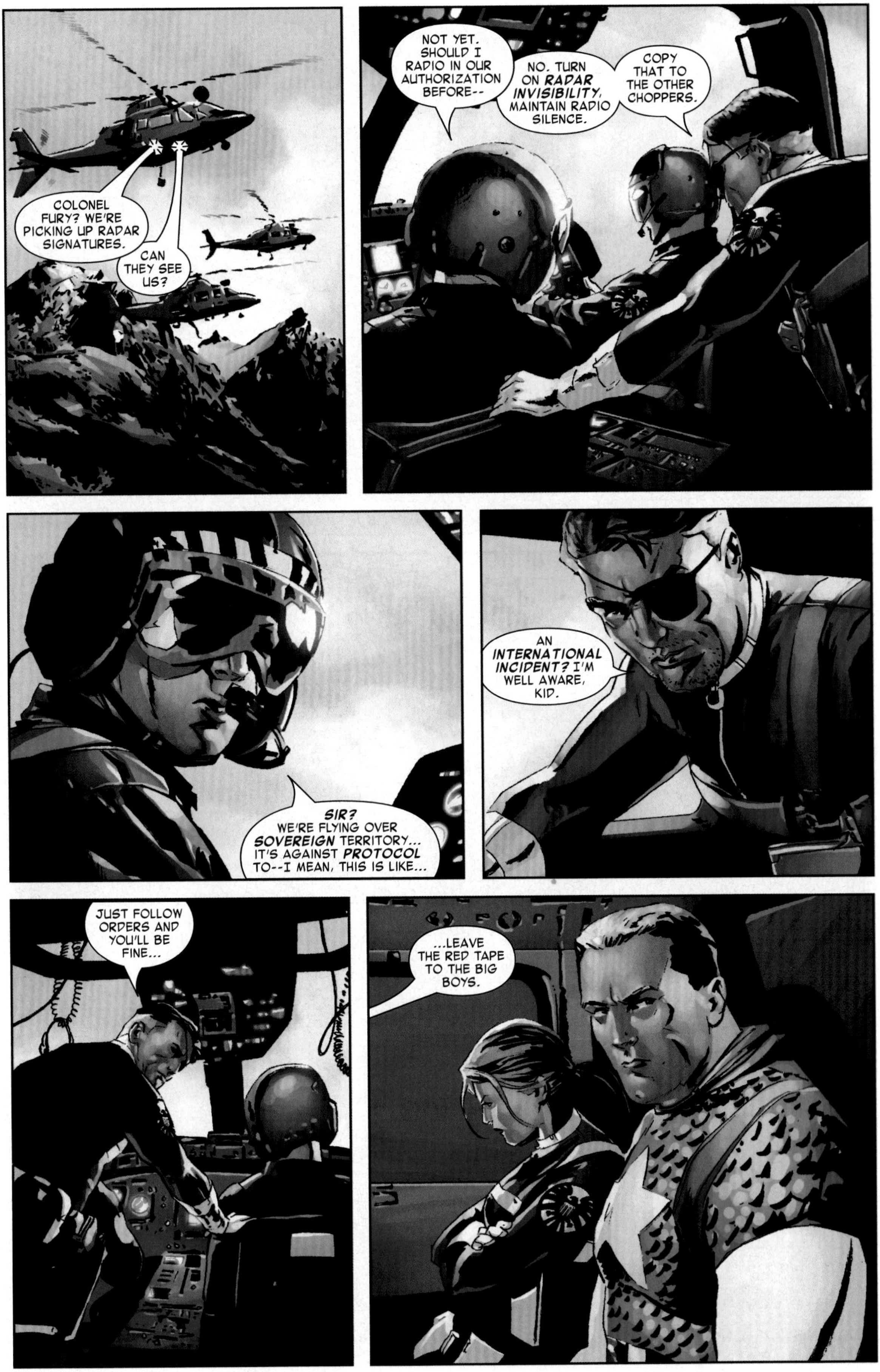
COLONEL FURY? WE'RE PICKING UP RADAR SIGNATURES.
CAN THEY SEE US?
NOT YET. SHOULD I RADIO IN OUR AUTHORIZATION BEFORE--
NO. TURN ON RADAR INVISIBILITY, MAINTAIN RADIO SILENCE.
COPY THAT TO THE OTHER CHOPPERS.
SIR? WE'RE FLYING OVER SOVEREIGN TERRITORY... IT'S AGAINST PROTOCOL TO--I MEAN, THIS IS LIKE...
AN INTERNATIONAL INCIDENT? I'M WELL AWARE, KID.
JUST FOLLOW ORDERS AND YOU'LL BE FINE...
...LEAVE THE RED TAPE TO THE BIG BOYS.

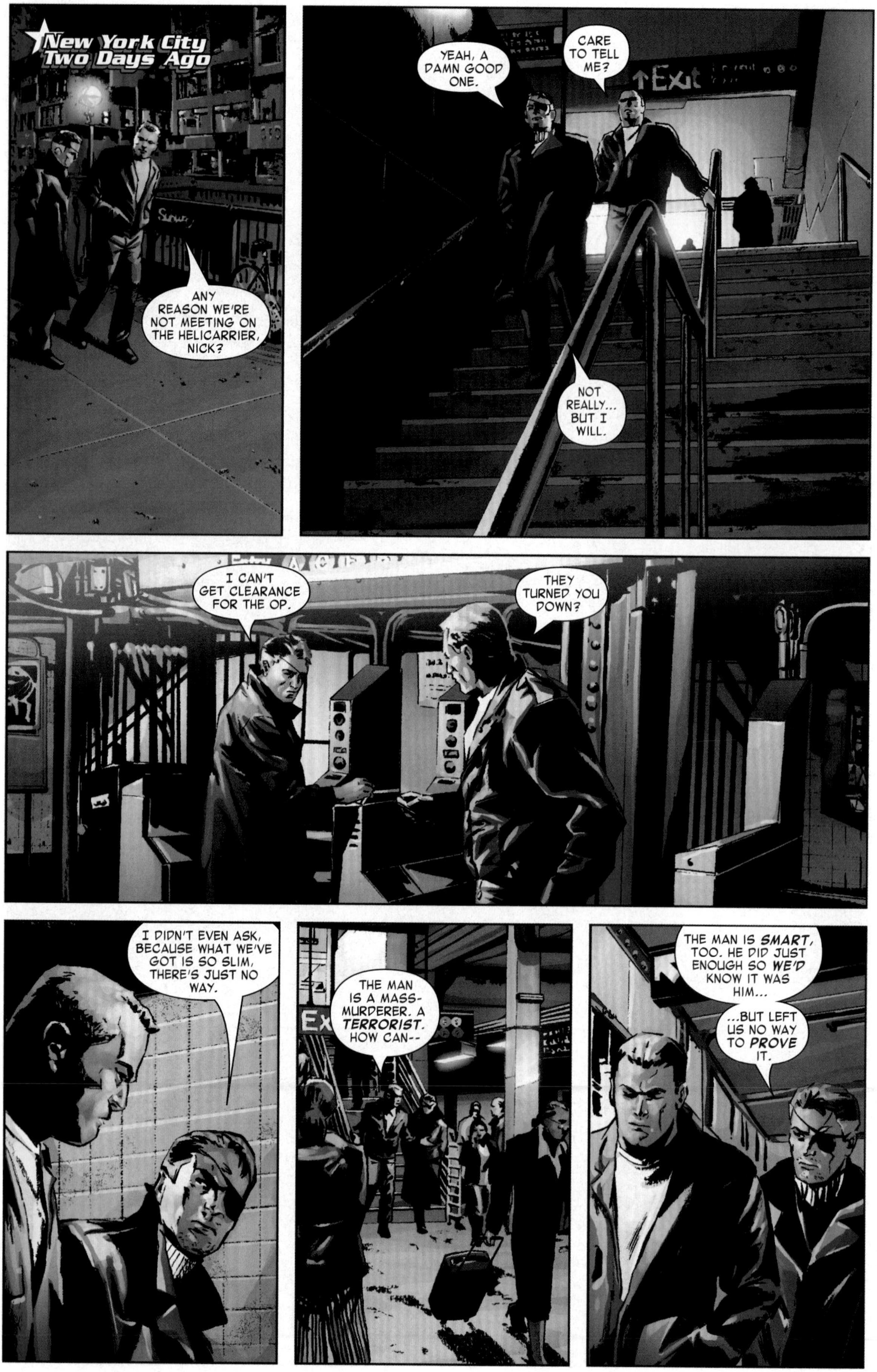
New York City Two Days Ago
ANY REASON WE'RE NOT MEETING ON THE HELICARRIER, NICK?
YEAH, A DAMN GOOD ONE.
CARE TO TELL ME?
NOT REALLY... BUT I WILL.
Exit
I CAN'T GET CLEARANCE FOR THE OP.
THEY TURNED YOU DOWN?
I DIDN'T EVEN ASK, BECAUSE WHAT WE'VE GOT IS SO SLIM, THERE'S JUST NO WAY.
THE MAN IS A MASS-MURDERER. A TERRORIST. HOW CAN--
THE MAN IS SMART, TOO. HE DID JUST ENOUGH SO WE'D KNOW IT WAS HIM...
...BUT LEFT US NO WAY TO PROVE IT.

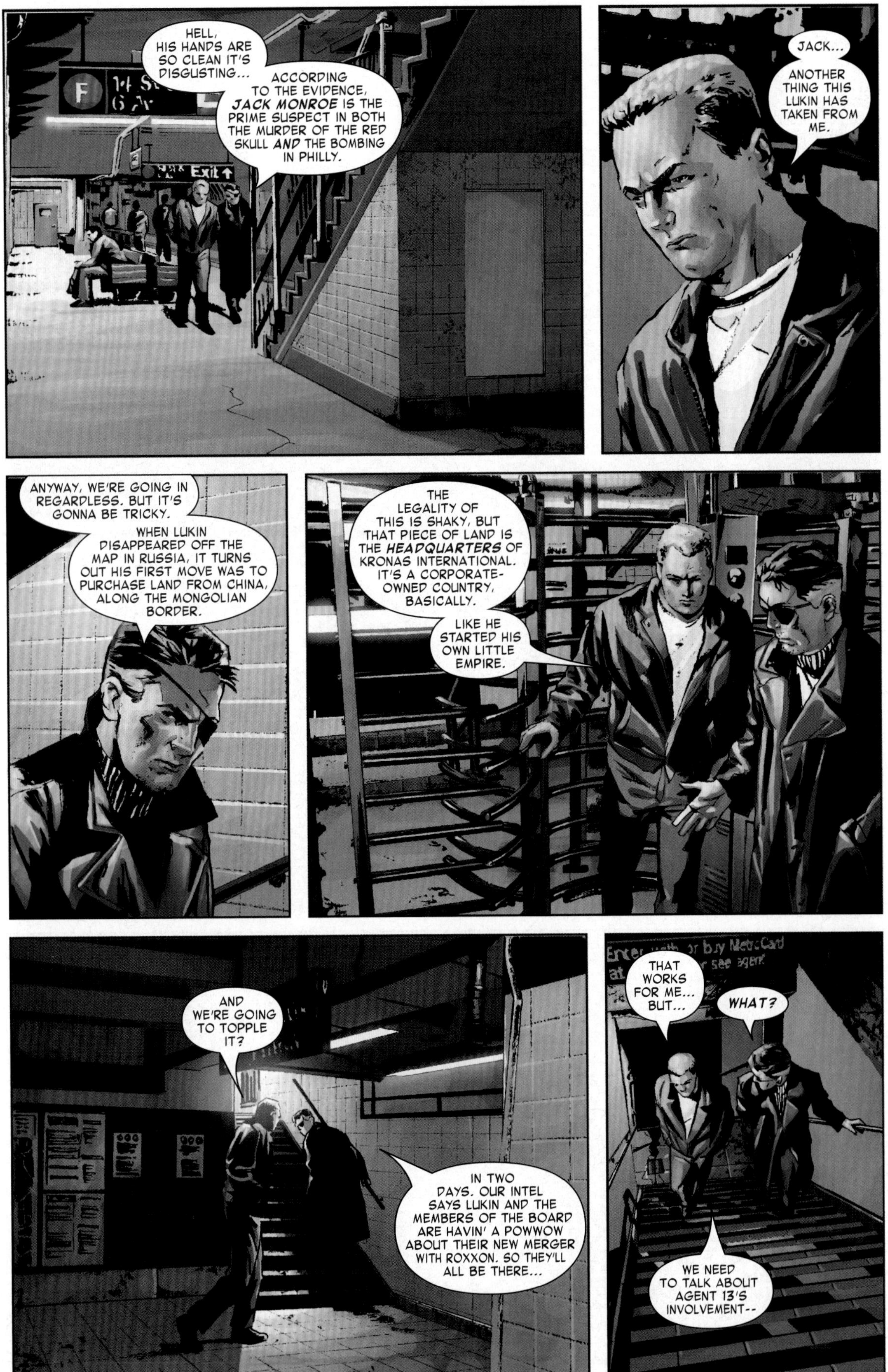
HELL, HIS HANDS ARE SO CLEAN IT'S DISGUSTING...
ACCORDING TO THE EVIDENCE, JACK MONROE IS THE PRIME SUSPECT IN BOTH THE MURDER OF THE RED SKULL AND THE BOMBING IN PHILLY.
JACK...
ANOTHER THING THIS LUKIN HAS TAKEN FROM ME.
ANYWAY, WE'RE GOING IN REGARDLESS. BUT IT'S GONNA BE TRICKY.
WHEN LUKIN DISAPPEARED OFF THE MAP IN RUSSIA, IT TURNS OUT HIS FIRST MOVE WAS TO PURCHASE LAND FROM CHINA, ALONG THE MONGOLIAN BORDER.
THE LEGALITY OF THIS IS SHAKY, BUT THAT PIECE OF LAND IS THE HEADQUARTERS OF KRONAS INTERNATIONAL. IT'S A CORPORATE-OWNED COUNTRY, BASICALLY.
LIKE HE STARTED HIS OWN LITTLE EMPIRE.
AND WE'RE GOING TO TOPPLE IT?
IN TWO DAYS. OUR INTEL SAYS LUKIN AND THE MEMBERS OF THE BOARD ARE HAVIN' A POWWOW ABOUT THEIR NEW MERGER WITH ROXXON. SO THEY'LL ALL BE THERE...
THAT WORKS FOR ME... BUT...
WHAT?
WE NEED TO TALK ABOUT AGENT 13'S INVOLVEMENT--

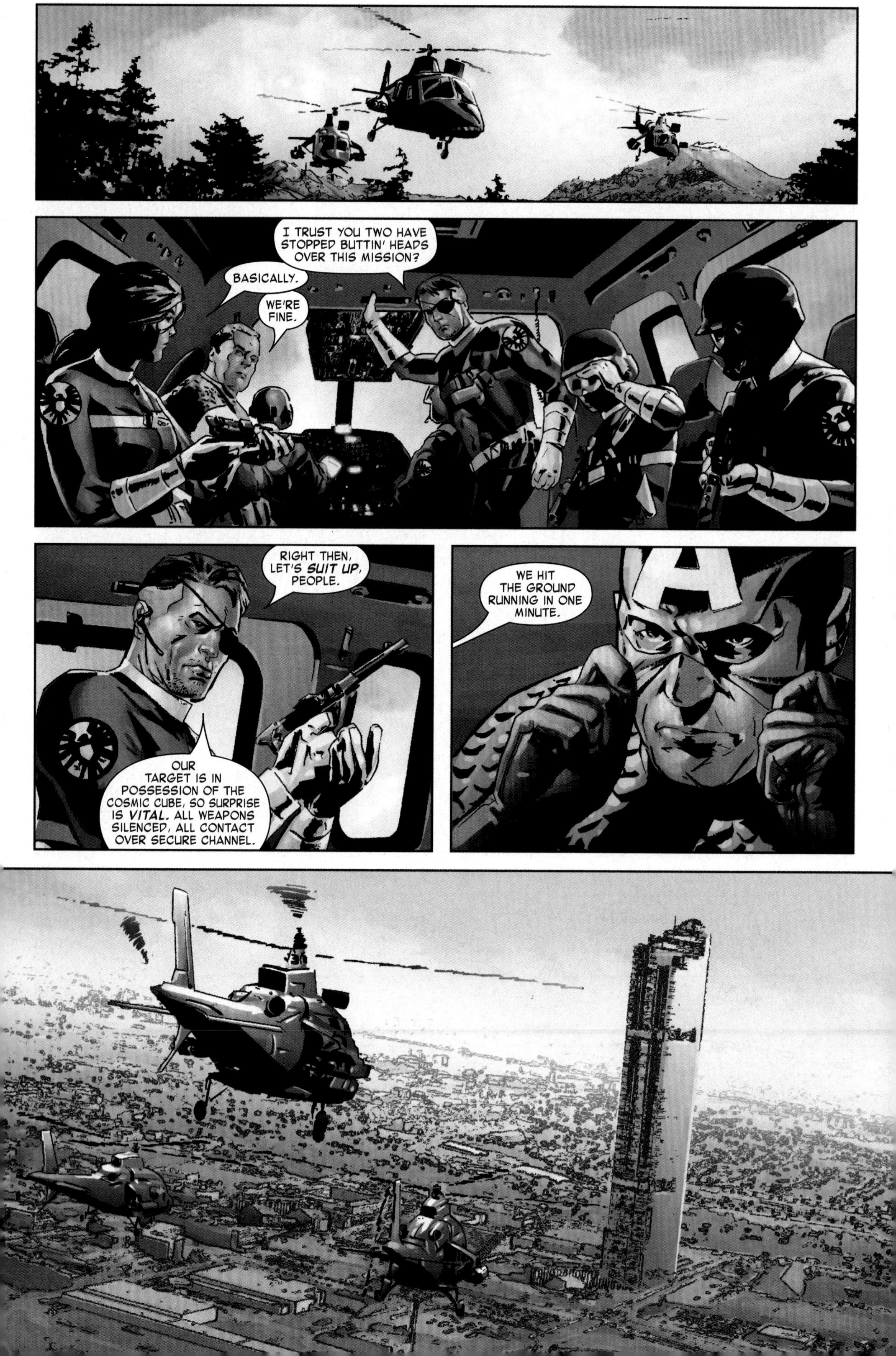
I TRUST YOU TWO HAVE STOPPED BUTTIN' HEADS OVER THIS MISSION?
BASICALLY.
WE'RE FINE.
RIGHT THEN, LET'S SUIT UP, PEOPLE.
OUR TARGET IS IN POSSESSION OF THE COSMIC CUBE, SO SURPRISE IS VITAL. ALL WEAPONS SILENCED, ALL CONTACT OVER SECURE CHANNEL.
WE HIT THE GROUND RUNNING IN ONE MINUTE.

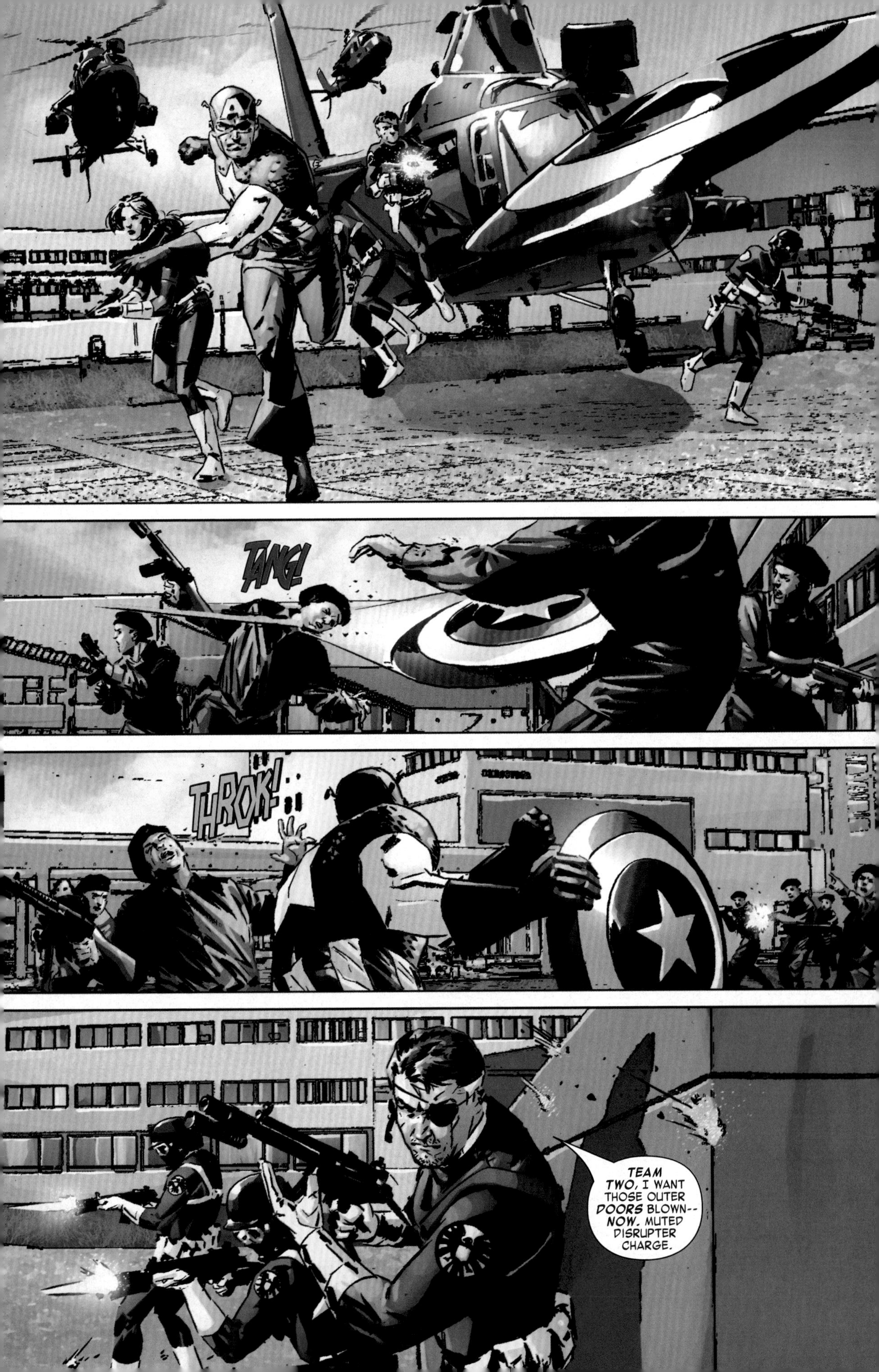

TANG!
THROK!
TEAM TWO, I WANT THOSE OUTER DOORS BLOWN--NOW. MUTED DISRUPTER CHARGE.

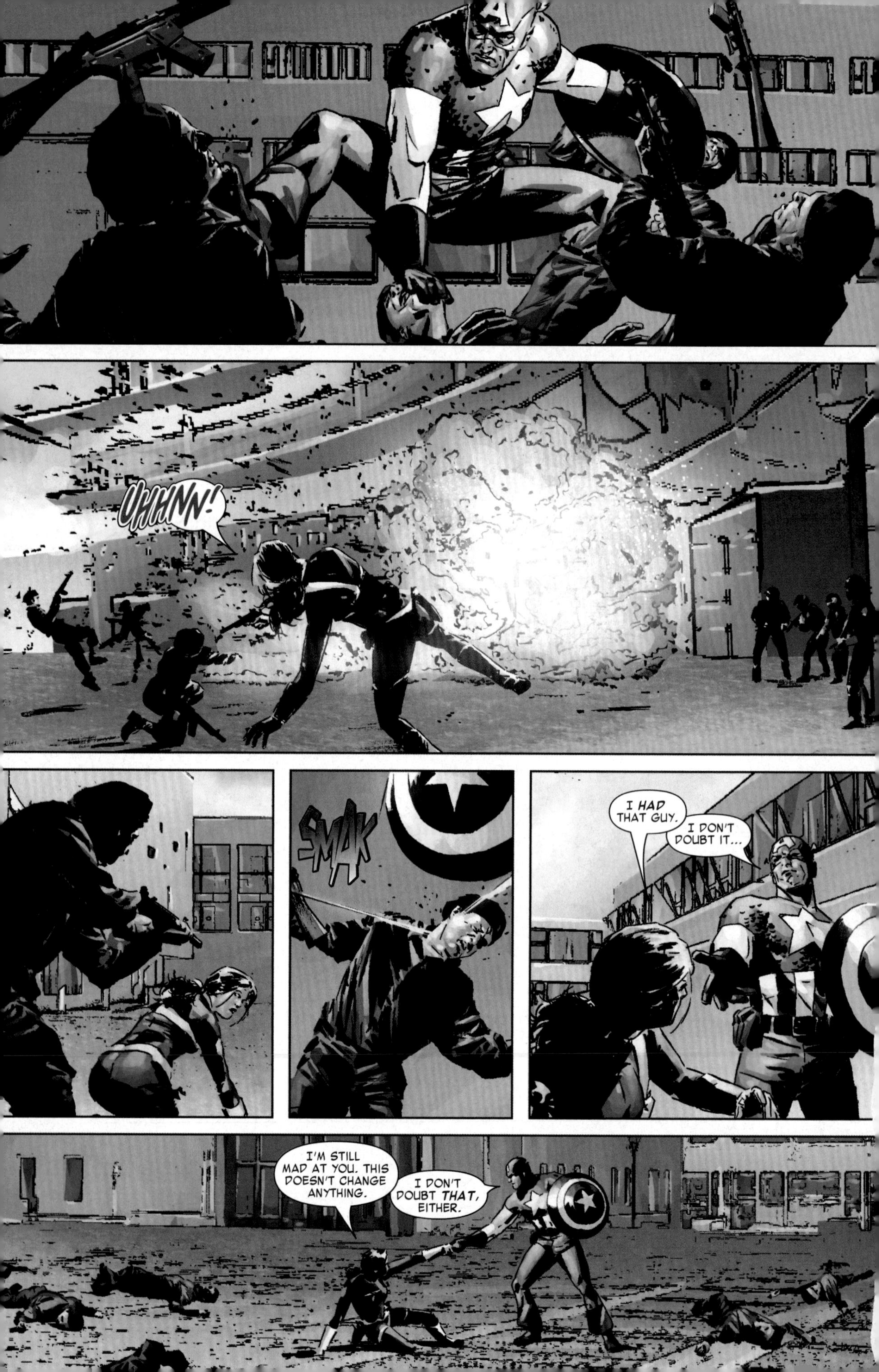
UHHNN!
SMAK
I HAD THAT GUY.
I DON'T DOUBT IT...
I'M STILL MAD AT YOU. THIS DOESN'T CHANGE ANYTHING.
I DON'T DOUBT THAT, EITHER.

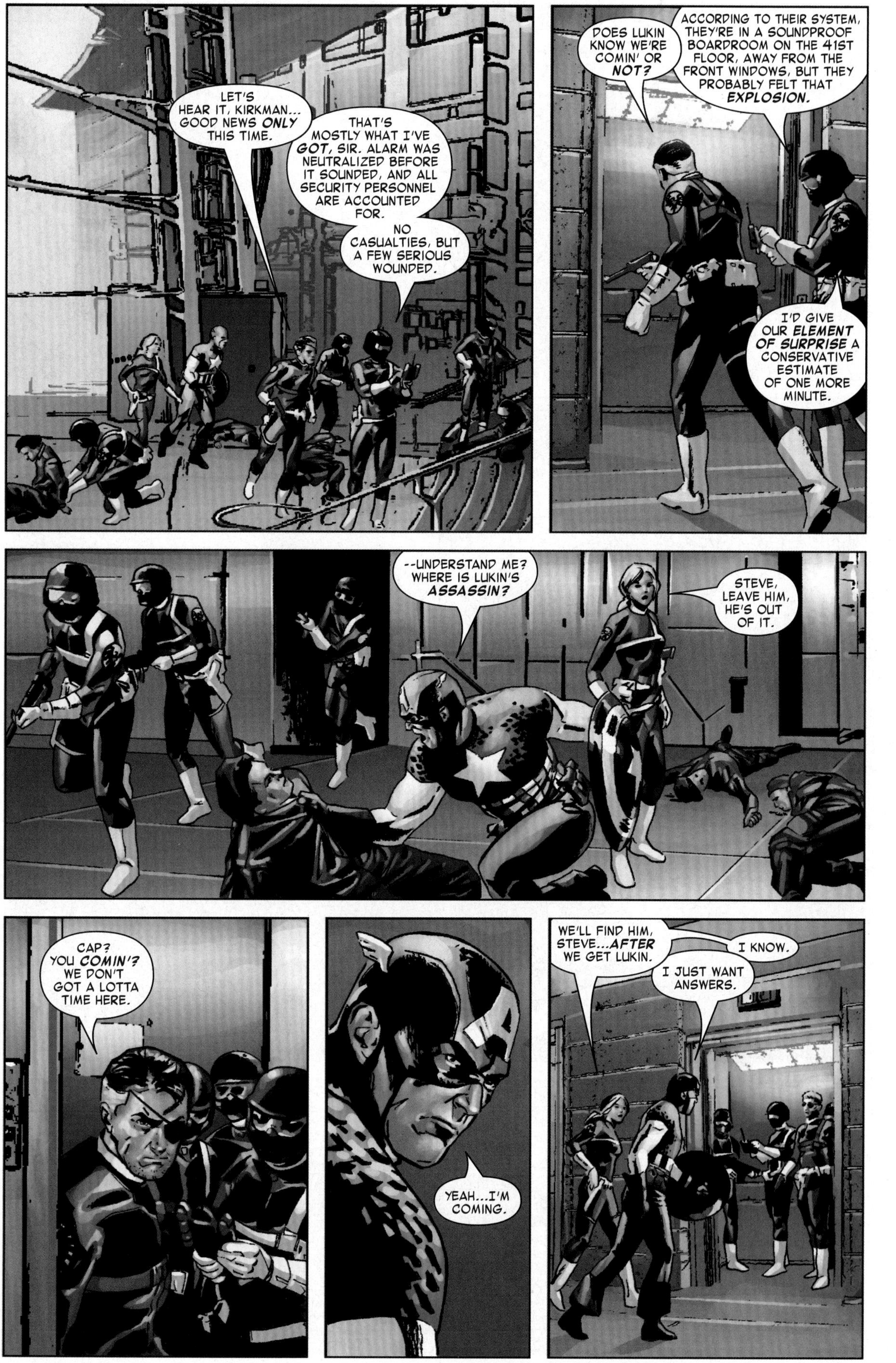
LET'S HEAR IT, KIRKMAN... GOOD NEWS ONLY THIS TIME.
THAT'S MOSTLY WHAT I'VE GOT, SIR. ALARM WAS NEUTRALIZED BEFORE IT SOUNDED, AND ALL SECURITY PERSONNEL ARE ACCOUNTED FOR.
NO CASUALTIES, BUT A FEW SERIOUS WOUNDED.
DOES LUKIN KNOW WE'RE COMIN' OR NOT?
ACCORDING TO THEIR SYSTEM, THEY'RE IN A SOUNDPROOF BOARDROOM ON THE 41ST FLOOR, AWAY FROM THE FRONT WINDOWS, BUT THEY PROBABLY FELT THAT EXPLOSION.
I'D GIVE OUR ELEMENT OF SURPRISE A CONSERVATIVE ESTIMATE OF ONE MORE MINUTE.
--UNDERSTAND ME? WHERE IS LUKIN'S ASSASSIN?
STEVE, LEAVE HIM, HE'S OUT OF IT.
CAP? YOU COMIN'? WE DON'T GOT A LOTTA TIME HERE.
YEAH...I'M COMING.
WE'LL FIND HIM, STEVE...AFTER WE GET LUKIN.
I KNOW.
I JUST WANT ANSWERS.

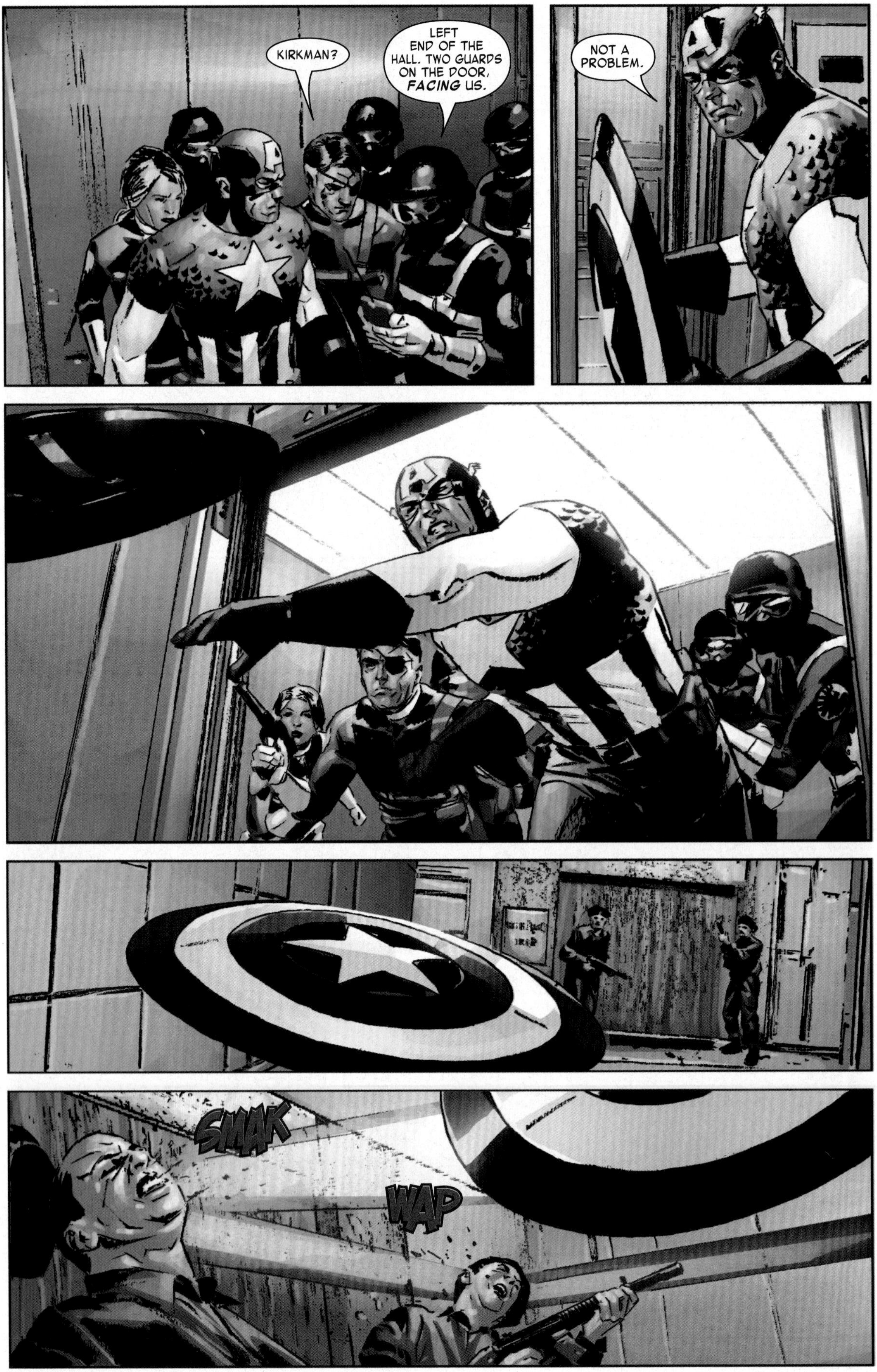
KIRKMAN?
LEFT END OF THE HALL. TWO GUARDS ON THE DOOR, *FACING* US.
NOT A PROBLEM.
SMAK
WAP

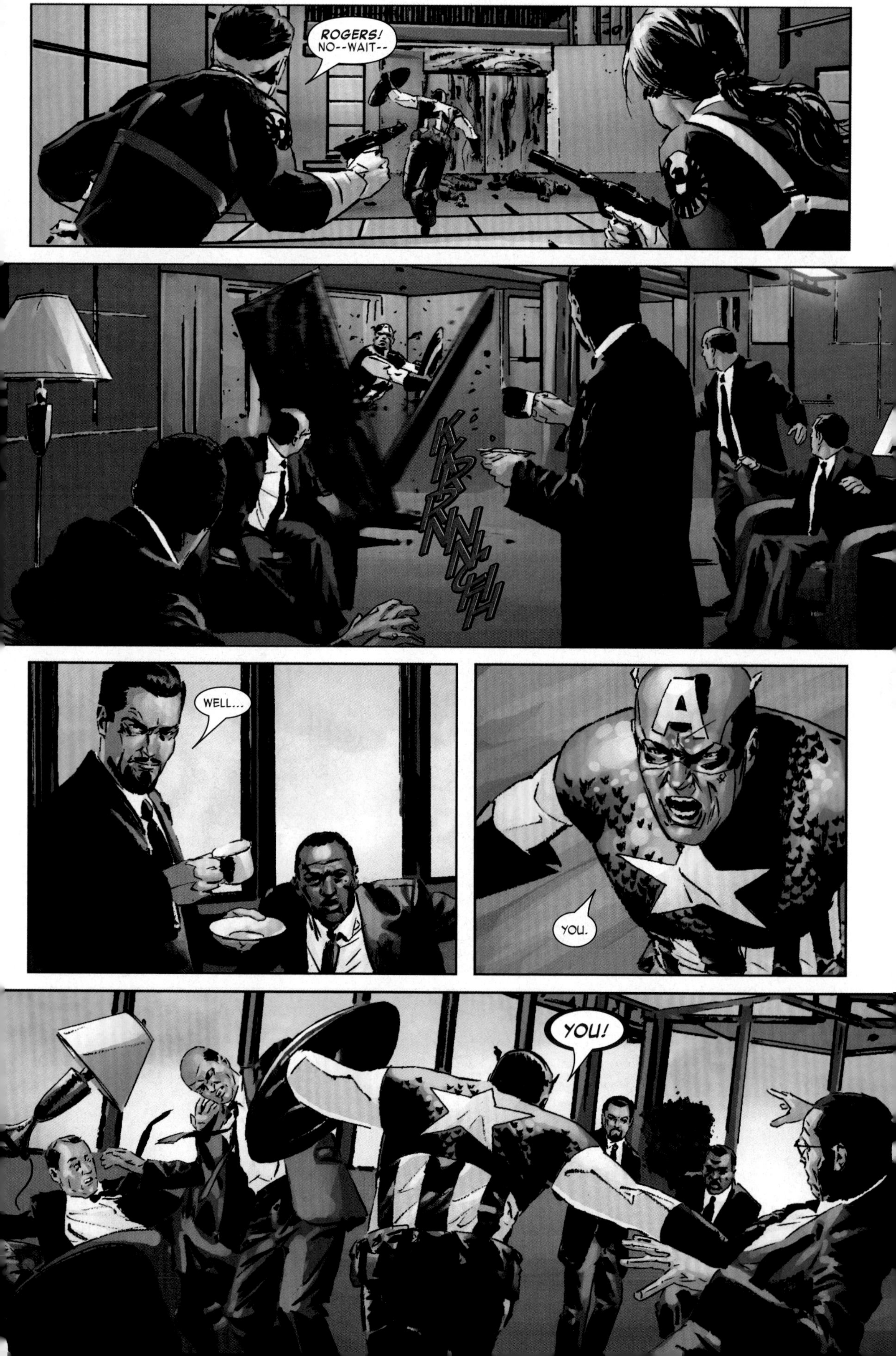
ROGERS! NO--WAIT--
KKRRNNCHH
WELL...
YOU.
YOU!

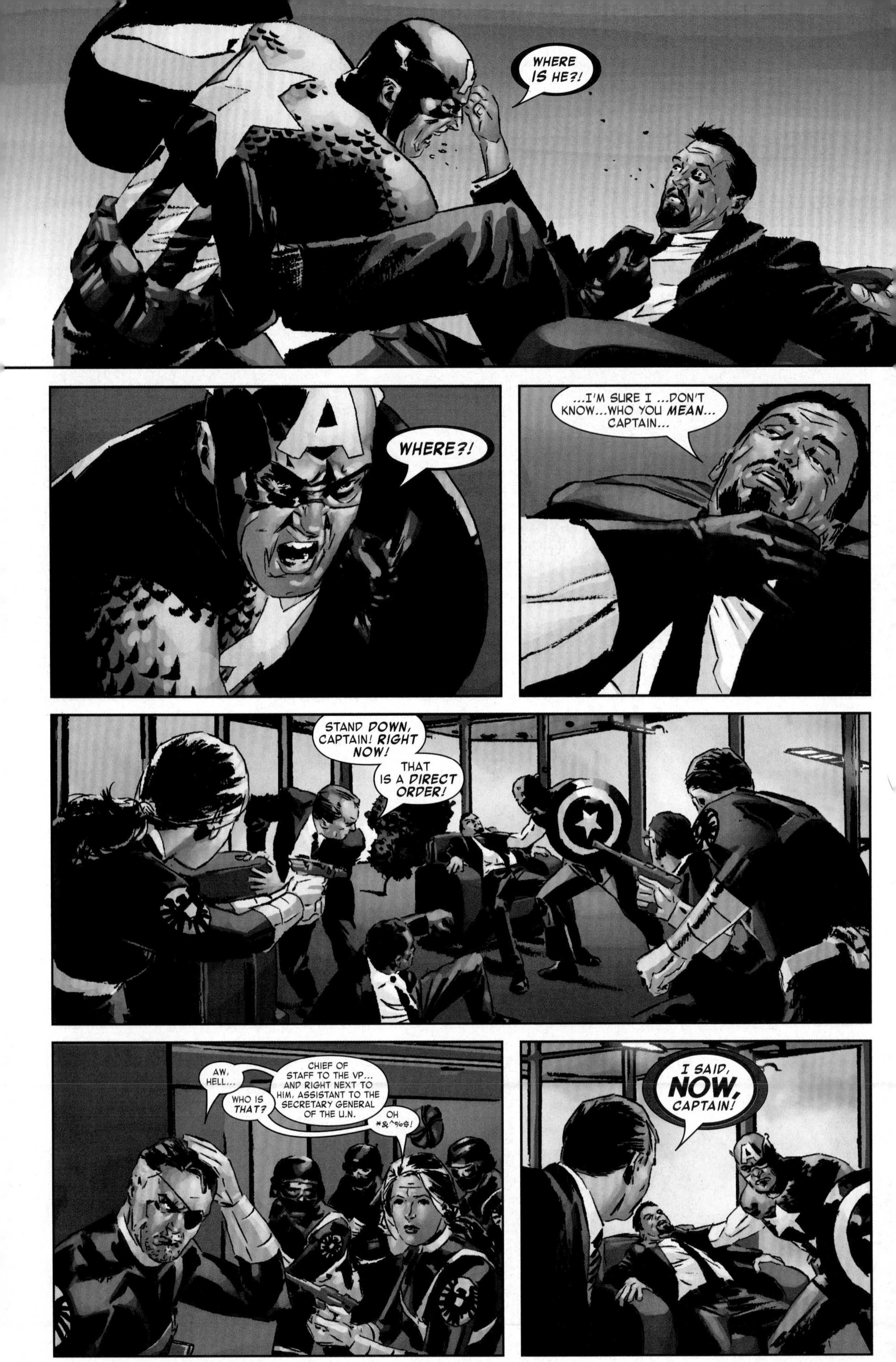
WHERE IS HE?!
WHERE?!
...I'M SURE I ...DON'T KNOW...WHO YOU MEAN... CAPTAIN...
STAND DOWN, CAPTAIN! RIGHT NOW!
THAT IS A DIRECT ORDER!
AW, HELL...
WHO IS THAT?
CHIEF OF STAFF TO THE VP... AND RIGHT NEXT TO HIM, ASSISTANT TO THE SECRETARY GENERAL OF THE U.N.
OH *&^%$!
I SAID, NOW, CAPTAIN!

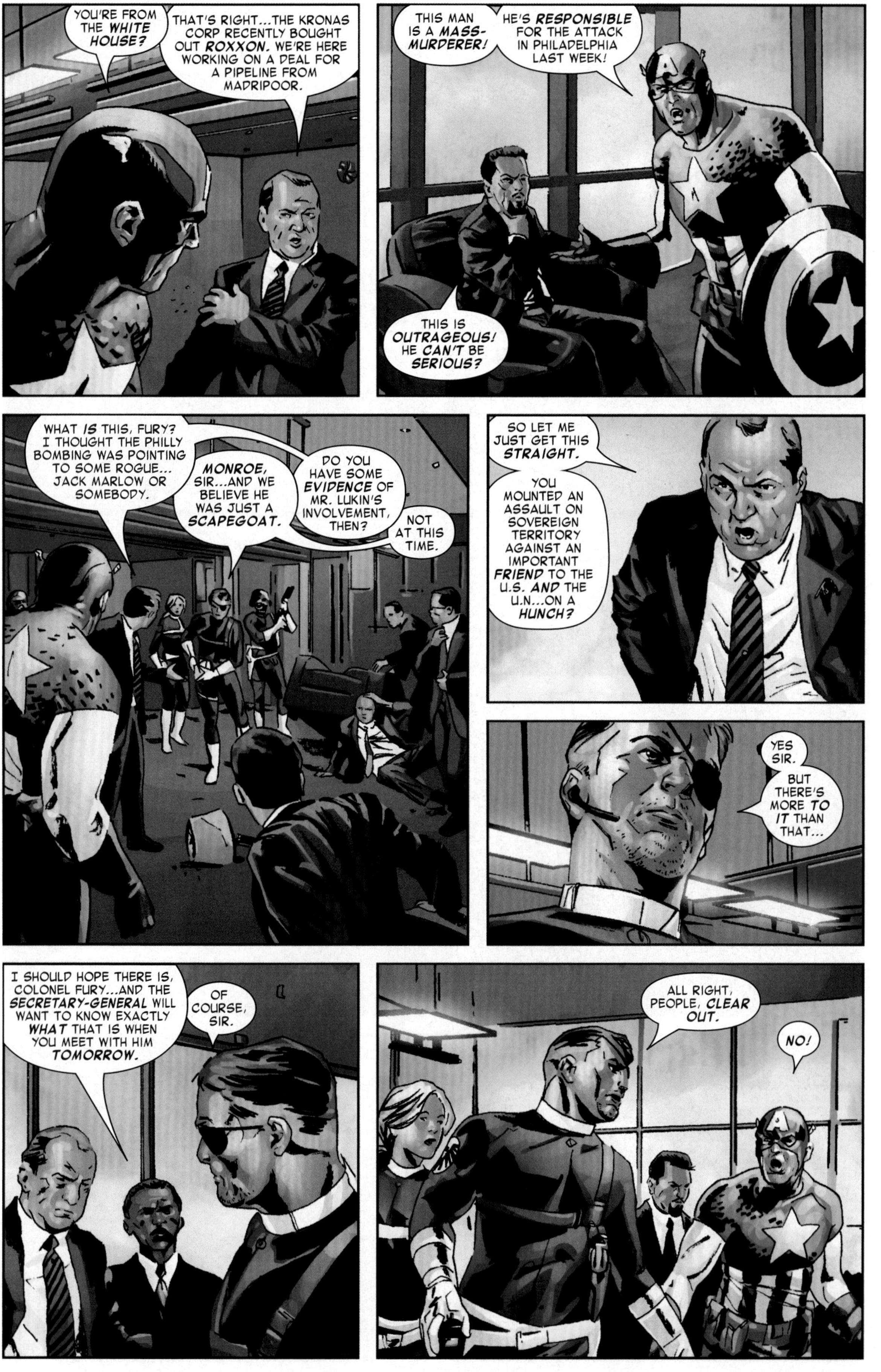
YOU'RE FROM THE WHITE HOUSE?
THAT'S RIGHT...THE KRONAS CORP RECENTLY BOUGHT OUT ROXXON. WE'RE HERE WORKING ON A DEAL FOR A PIPELINE FROM MADRIPOOR.
THIS MAN IS A MASS-MURDERER!
HE'S RESPONSIBLE FOR THE ATTACK IN PHILADELPHIA LAST WEEK!
THIS IS OUTRAGEOUS! HE CAN'T BE SERIOUS?
WHAT IS THIS, FURY? I THOUGHT THE PHILLY BOMBING WAS POINTING TO SOME ROGUE... JACK MARLOW OR SOMEBODY.
MONROE, SIR...AND WE BELIEVE HE WAS JUST A SCAPEGOAT.
DO YOU HAVE SOME EVIDENCE OF MR. LUKIN'S INVOLVEMENT, THEN?
NOT AT THIS TIME.
SO LET ME JUST GET THIS STRAIGHT.
YOU MOUNTED AN ASSAULT ON SOVEREIGN TERRITORY AGAINST AN IMPORTANT FRIEND TO THE U.S. AND THE U.N...ON A HUNCH?
YES SIR.
BUT THERE'S MORE TO IT THAN THAT...
I SHOULD HOPE THERE IS, COLONEL FURY...AND THE SECRETARY-GENERAL WILL WANT TO KNOW EXACTLY WHAT THAT IS WHEN YOU MEET WITH HIM TOMORROW.
OF COURSE, SIR.
ALL RIGHT, PEOPLE, CLEAR OUT.
NO!

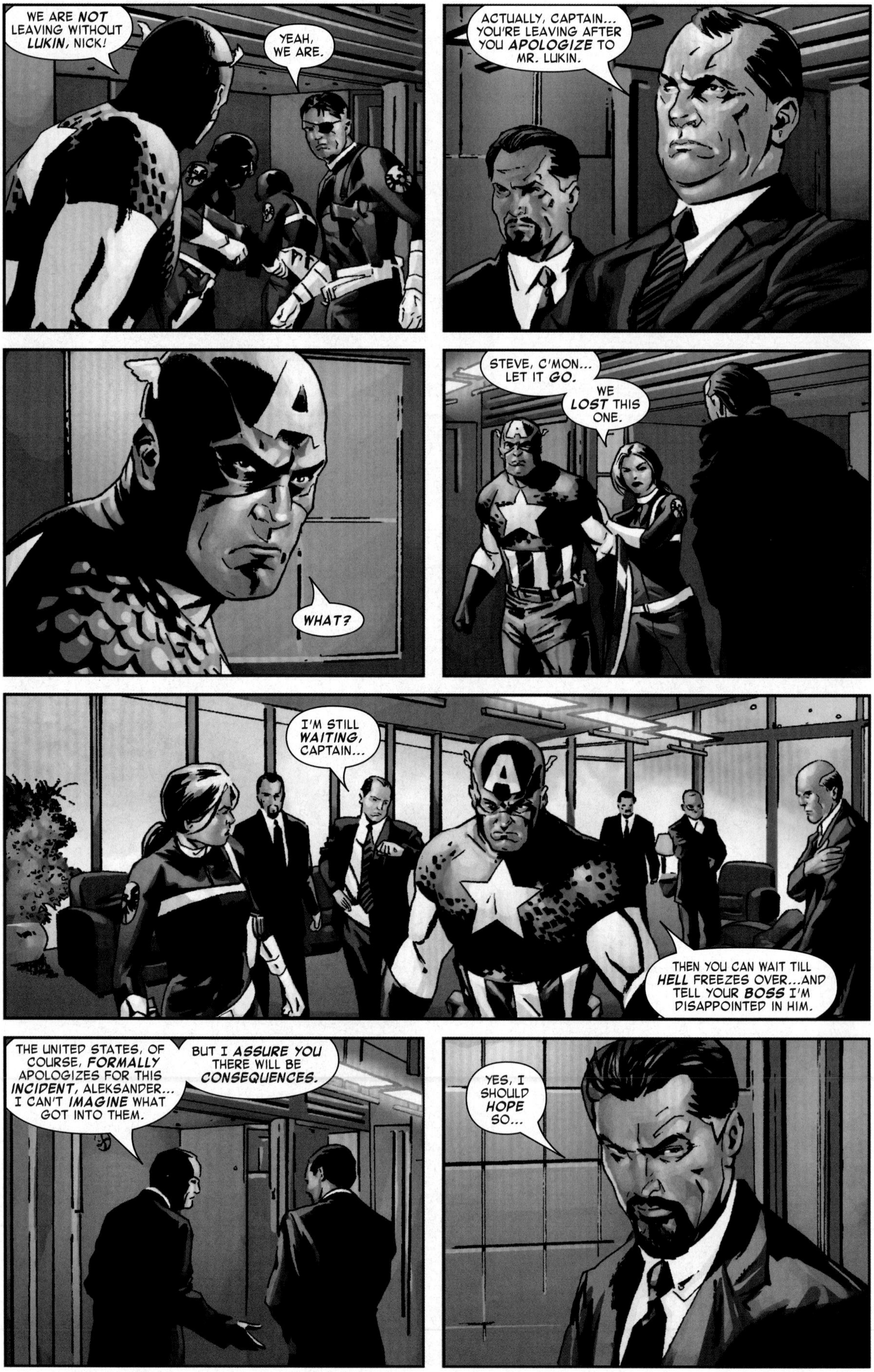
WE ARE NOT LEAVING WITHOUT LUKIN, NICK!
YEAH, WE ARE.
ACTUALLY, CAPTAIN... YOU'RE LEAVING AFTER YOU APOLOGIZE TO MR. LUKIN.
WHAT?
STEVE, C'MON... LET IT GO.
WE LOST THIS ONE.
I'M STILL WAITING, CAPTAIN...
THEN YOU CAN WAIT TILL HELL FREEZES OVER...AND TELL YOUR BOSS I'M DISAPPOINTED IN HIM.
THE UNITED STATES, OF COURSE, FORMALLY APOLOGIZES FOR THIS INCIDENT, ALEKSANDER... I CAN'T IMAGINE WHAT GOT INTO THEM.
BUT I ASSURE YOU THERE WILL BE CONSEQUENCES.
YES, I SHOULD HOPE SO...

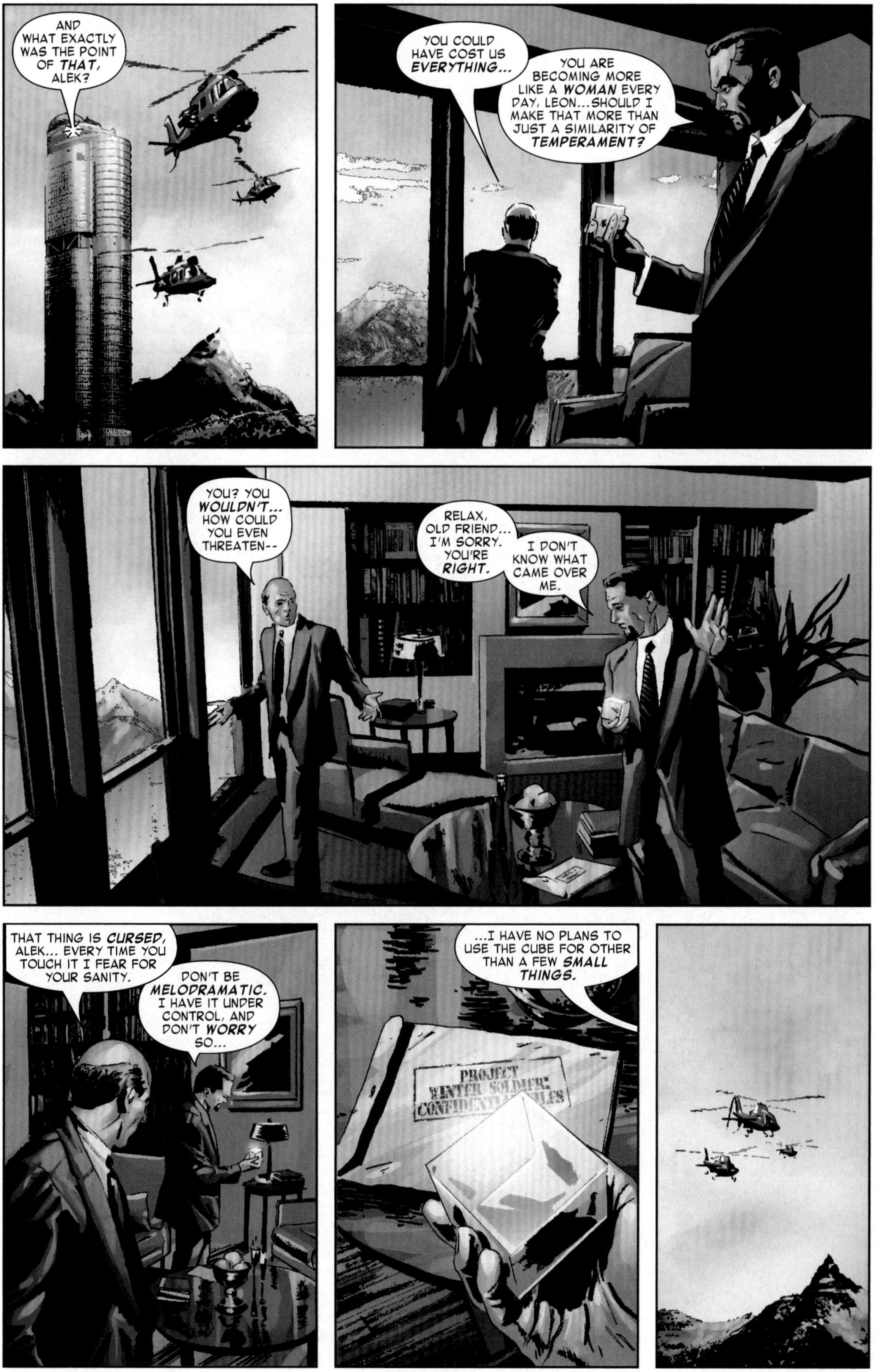

AND WHAT EXACTLY WAS THE POINT OF *THAT*, ALEK?
YOU COULD HAVE COST US *EVERYTHING...*
YOU ARE BECOMING MORE LIKE A *WOMAN* EVERY DAY, LEON...SHOULD I MAKE THAT MORE THAN JUST A SIMILARITY OF *TEMPERAMENT?*
YOU? YOU *WOULDN'T...* HOW COULD YOU EVEN THREATEN--
RELAX, OLD FRIEND... I'M SORRY. YOU'RE *RIGHT.*
I DON'T KNOW WHAT CAME OVER ME.
THAT THING IS *CURSED*, ALEK... EVERY TIME YOU TOUCH IT I FEAR FOR YOUR SANITY.
DON'T BE *MELODRAMATIC.* I HAVE IT UNDER CONTROL, AND DON'T *WORRY* SO...
PROJECT WINTER SOLDIER: CONFIDENTIAL FILES
...I HAVE NO PLANS TO USE THE CUBE FOR OTHER THAN A FEW *SMALL THINGS.*

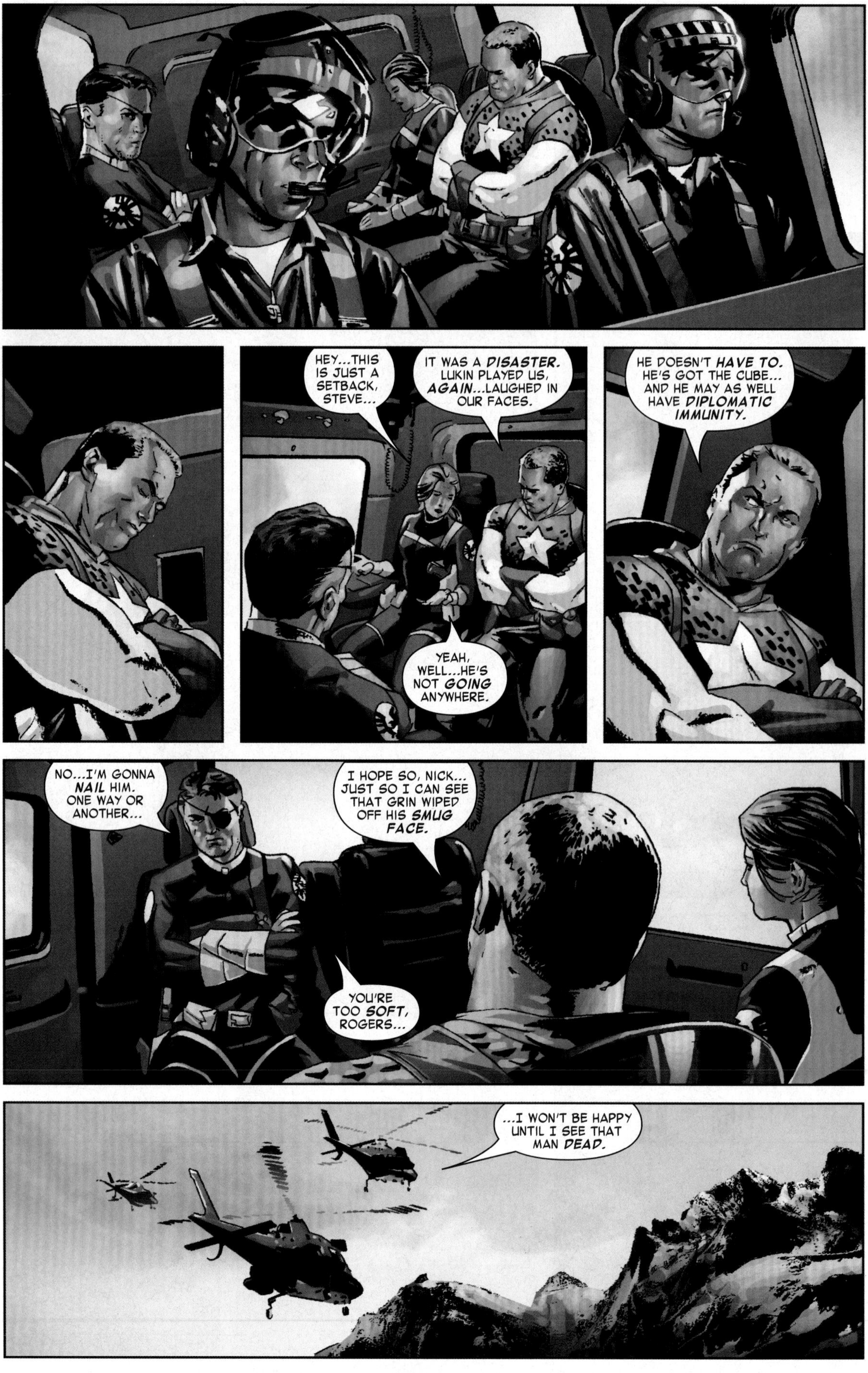
HEY...THIS IS JUST A SETBACK, STEVE...
IT WAS A DISASTER. LUKIN PLAYED US, AGAIN...LAUGHED IN OUR FACES.
YEAH, WELL...HE'S NOT GOING ANYWHERE.
HE DOESN'T HAVE TO. HE'S GOT THE CUBE... AND HE MAY AS WELL HAVE DIPLOMATIC IMMUNITY.
NO...I'M GONNA NAIL HIM. ONE WAY OR ANOTHER...
I HOPE SO, NICK... JUST SO I CAN SEE THAT GRIN WIPED OFF HIS SMUG FACE.
YOU'RE TOO SOFT, ROGERS...
...I WON'T BE HAPPY UNTIL I SEE THAT MAN DEAD.

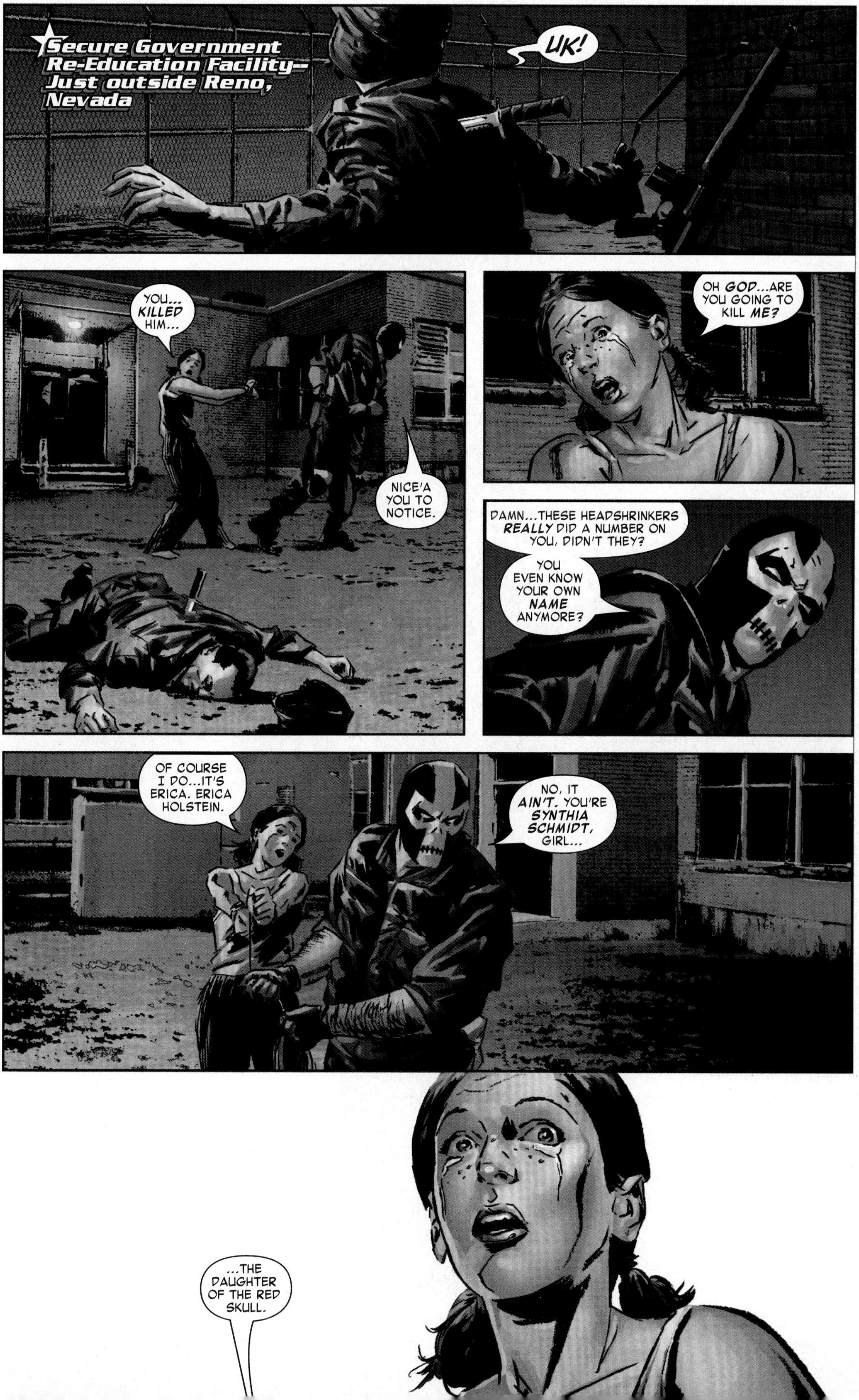
Secure Government Re-Education Facility-- Just outside Reno, Nevada
UK!
YOU... KILLED HIM...
NICE'A YOU TO NOTICE.
OH GOD...ARE YOU GOING TO KILL ME?
DAMN...THESE HEADSHRINKERS REALLY DID A NUMBER ON YOU, DIDN'T THEY?
YOU EVEN KNOW YOUR OWN NAME ANYMORE?
OF COURSE I DO...IT'S ERICA. ERICA HOLSTEIN.
NO, IT AIN'T. YOU'RE SYNTHIA SCHMIDT, GIRL...
...THE DAUGHTER OF THE RED SKULL.

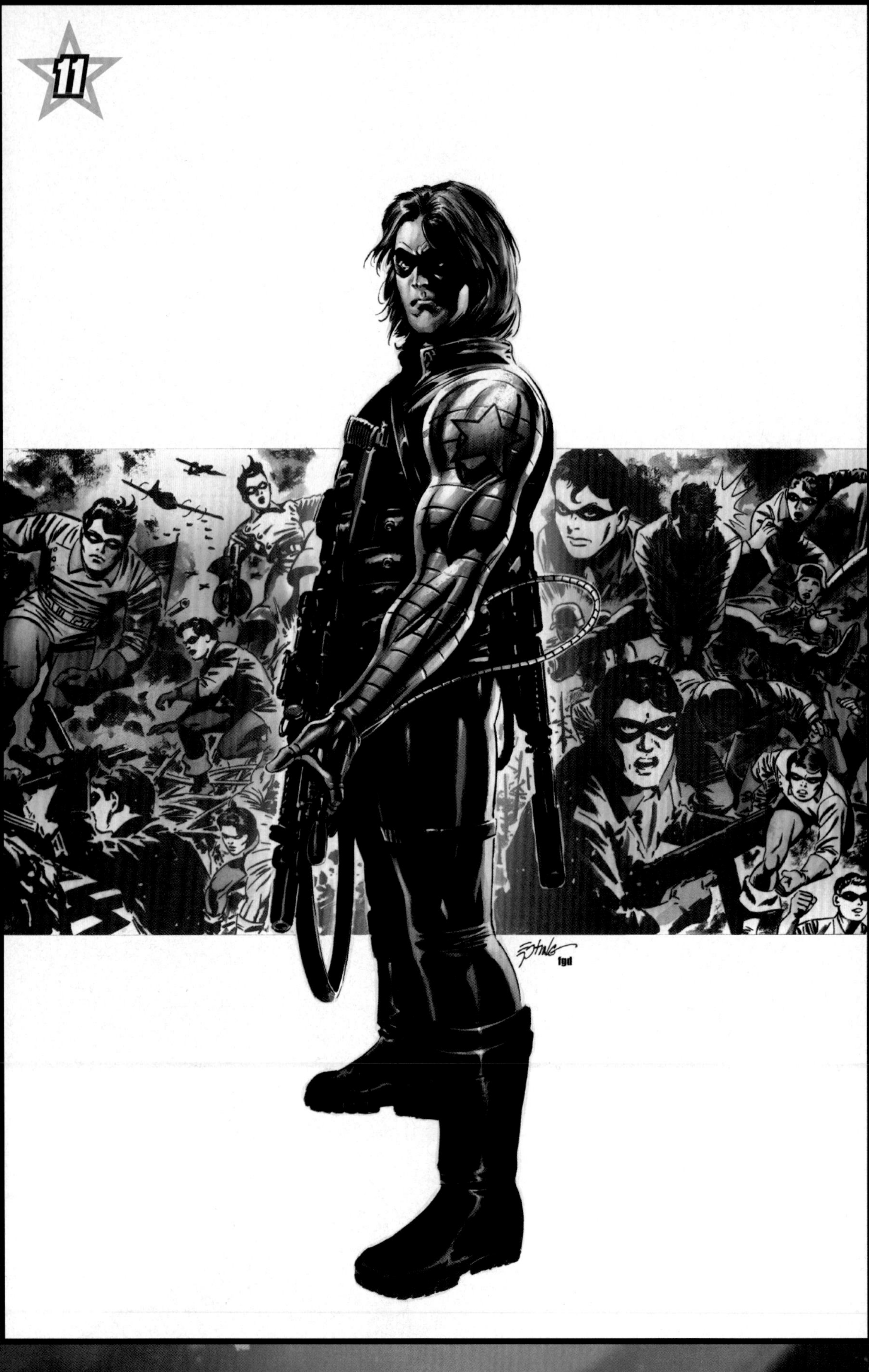
11

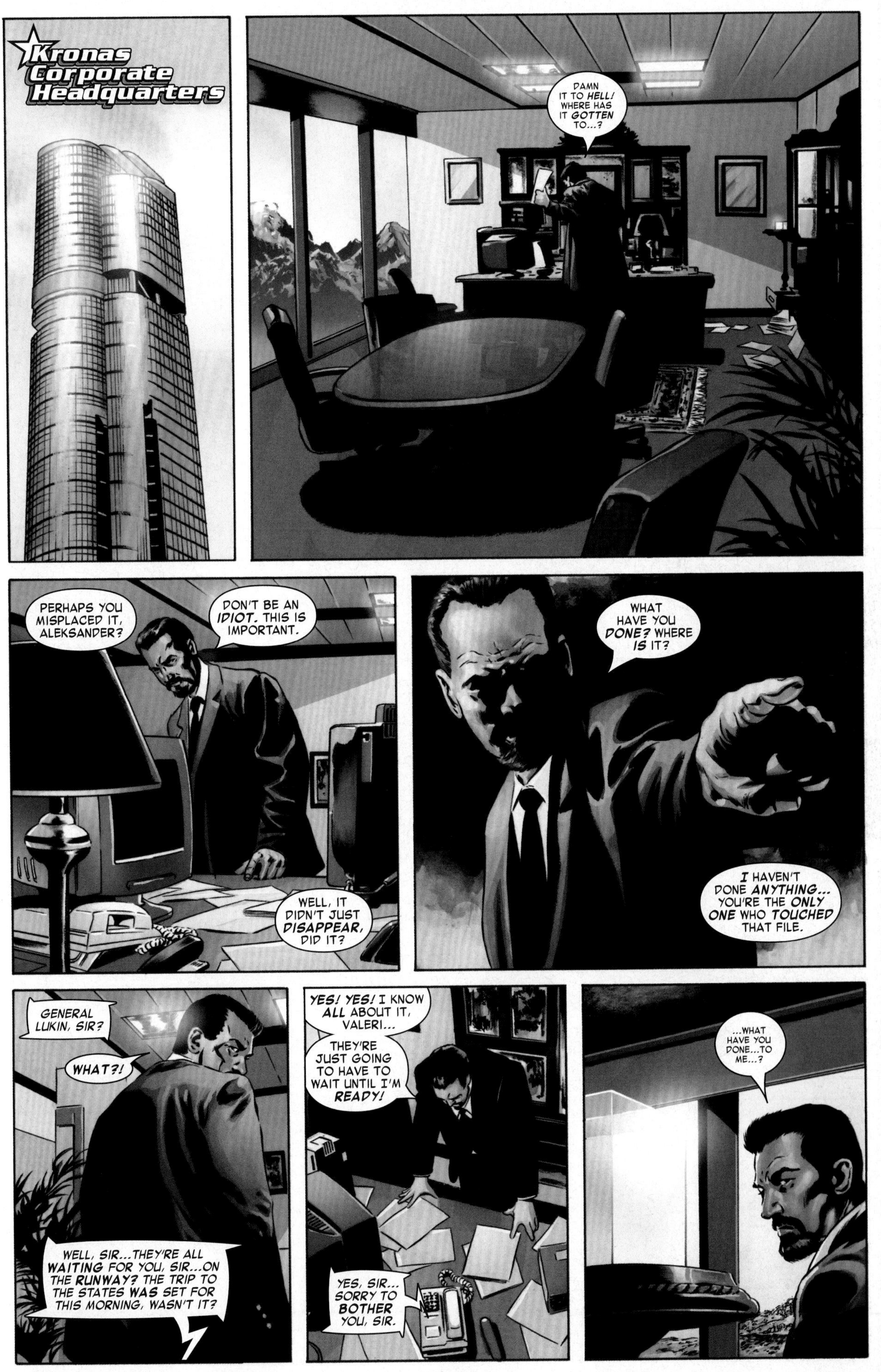
Kronas Corporate Headquarters
DAMN IT TO HELL! WHERE HAS IT GOTTEN TO...?
PERHAPS YOU MISPLACED IT, ALEKSANDER?
DON'T BE AN IDIOT. THIS IS IMPORTANT.
WELL, IT DIDN'T JUST DISAPPEAR, DID IT?
WHAT HAVE YOU DONE? WHERE IS IT?
I HAVEN'T DONE ANYTHING... YOU'RE THE ONLY ONE WHO TOUCHED THAT FILE.
GENERAL LUKIN, SIR?
WHAT?!
WELL, SIR...THEY'RE ALL WAITING FOR YOU, SIR...ON THE RUNWAY? THE TRIP TO THE STATES WAS SET FOR THIS MORNING, WASN'T IT?
YES! YES! I KNOW ALL ABOUT IT, VALERI...
THEY'RE JUST GOING TO HAVE TO WAIT UNTIL I'M READY!
YES, SIR... SORRY TO BOTHER YOU, SIR.
...WHAT HAVE YOU DONE...TO ME...?

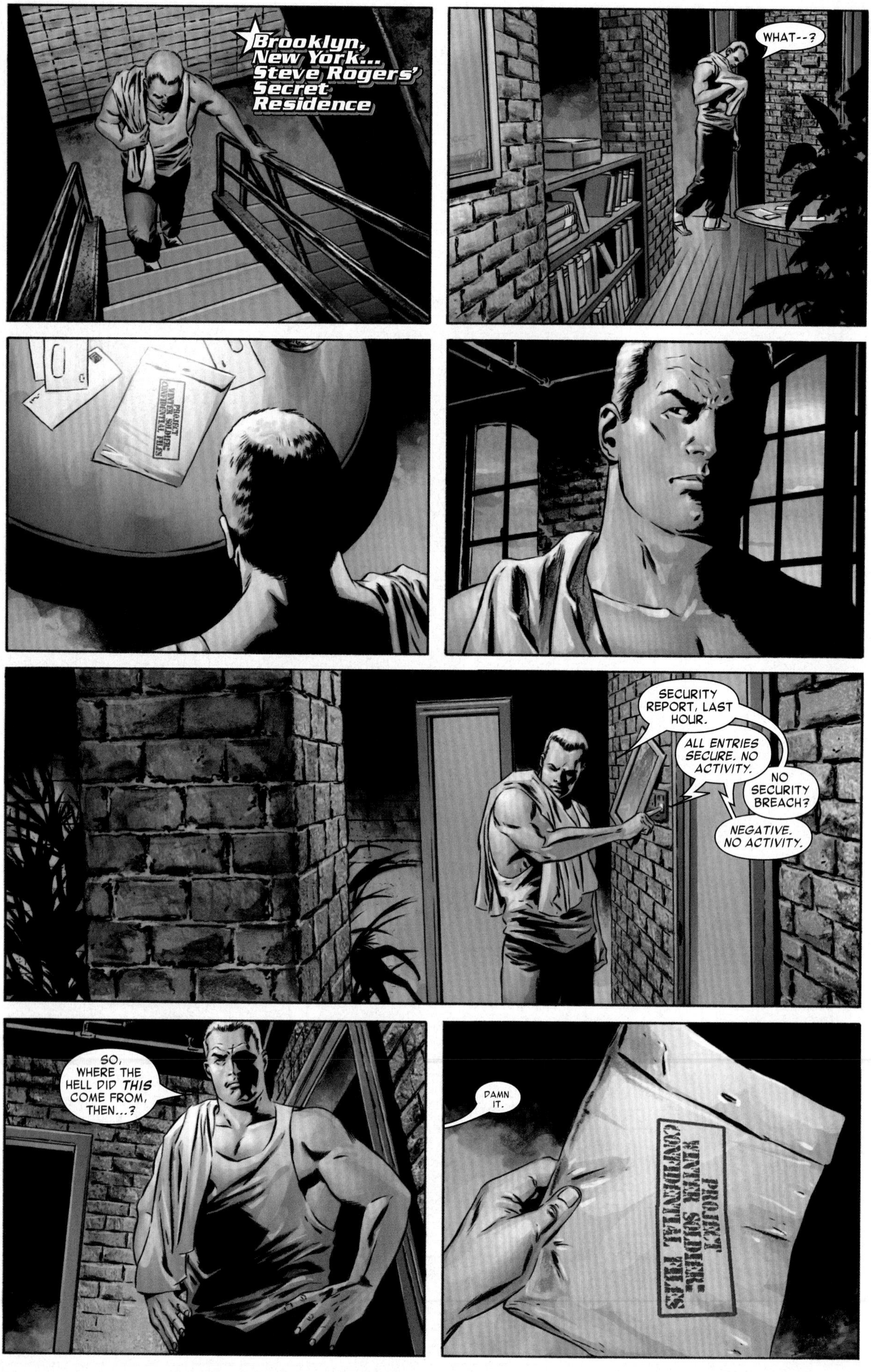
Brooklyn, New York... Steve Rogers' Secret Residence
WHAT--?
PROJECT WINTER SOLDIER CONFIDENTIAL FILES
SECURITY REPORT, LAST HOUR.
ALL ENTRIES SECURE. NO ACTIVITY.
NO SECURITY BREACH?
NEGATIVE. NO ACTIVITY.
SO, WHERE THE HELL DID THIS COME FROM, THEN...?
DAMN IT.
PROJECT WINTER SOLDIER CONFIDENTIAL FILES

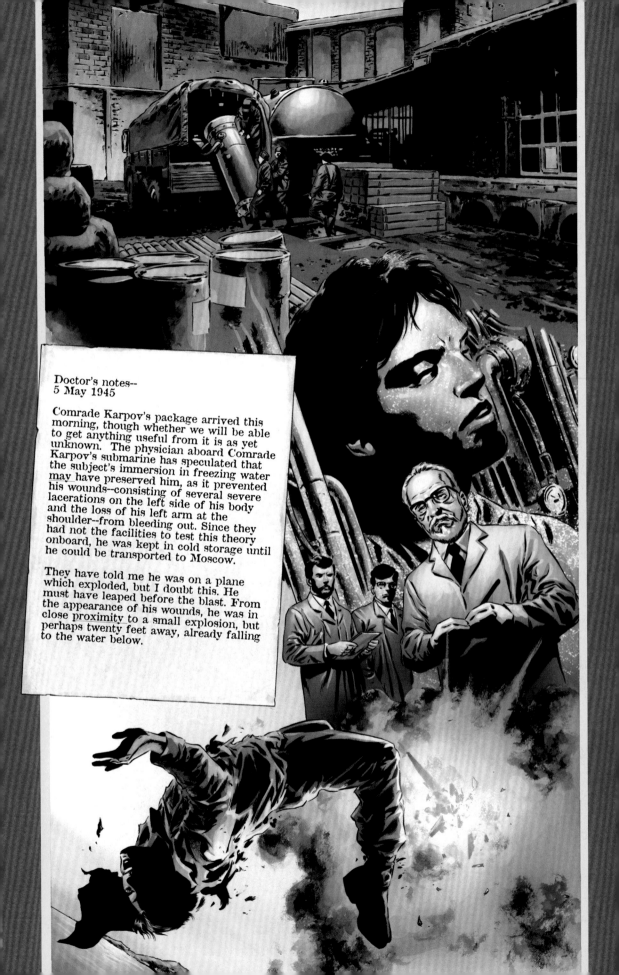

Doctor's notes--
5 May 1945

Comrade Karpov's package arrived this morning, though whether we will be able to get anything useful from it is as yet unknown. The physician aboard Comrade Karpov's submarine has speculated that the subject's immersion in freezing water may have preserved him, as it prevented his wounds--consisting of several severe lacerations on the left side of his body and the loss of his left arm at the shoulder--from bleeding out. Since they had not the facilities to test this theory onboard, he was kept in cold storage until he could be transported to Moscow.

They have told me he was on a plane which exploded, but I doubt this. He must have leaped before the blast. From the appearance of his wounds, he was in close proximity to a small explosion, but perhaps twenty feet away, already falling to the water below.

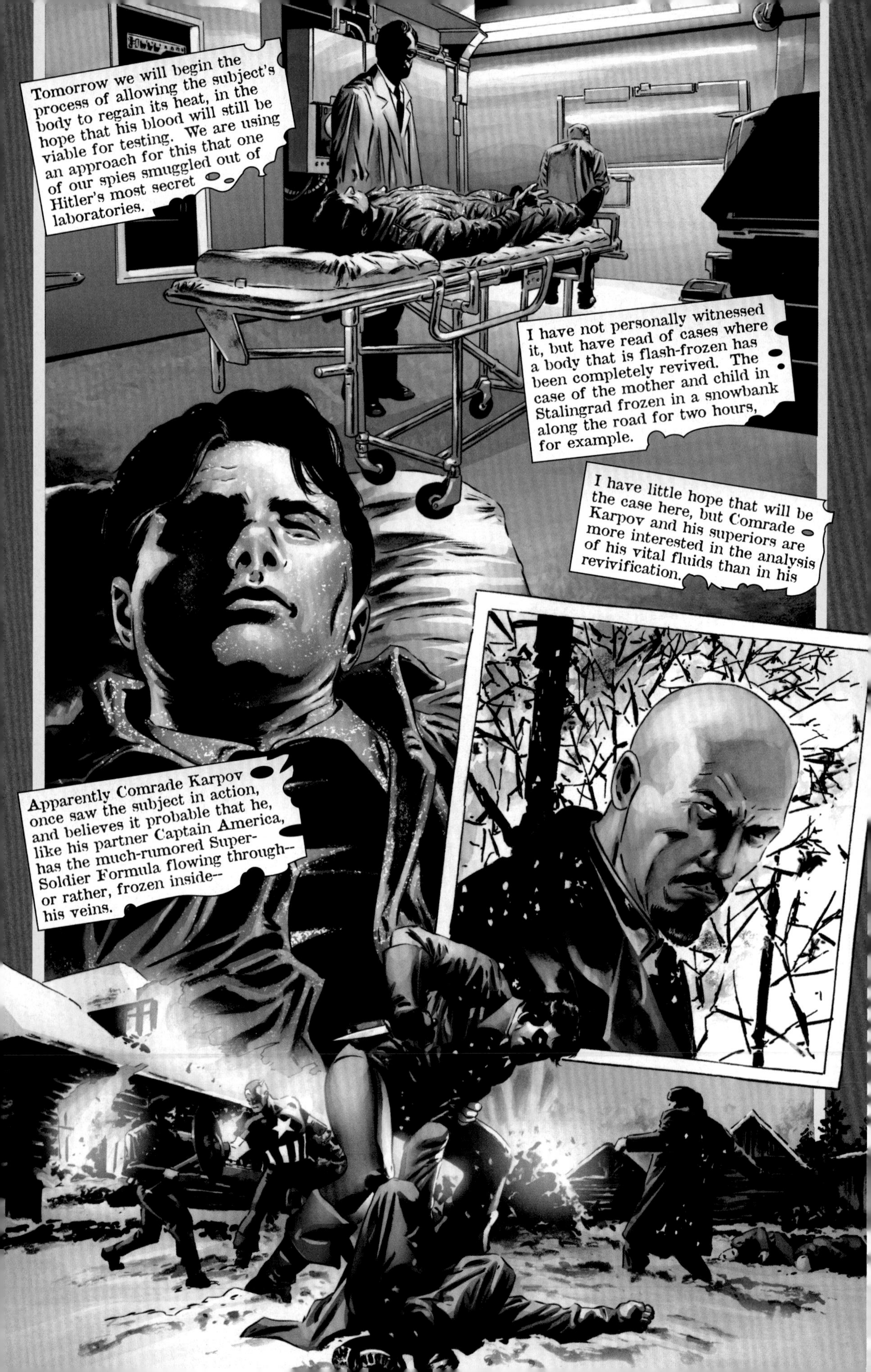
Tomorrow we will begin the process of allowing the subject's body to regain its heat, in the hope that his blood will still be viable for testing. We are using an approach for this that one of our spies smuggled out of Hitler's most secret laboratories.
I have not personally witnessed it, but have read of cases where a body that is flash-frozen has been completely revived. The case of the mother and child in Stalingrad frozen in a snowbank along the road for two hours, for example.
I have little hope that will be the case here, but Comrade Karpov and his superiors are more interested in the analysis of his vital fluids than in his revivification.
Apparently Comrade Karpov once saw the subject in action, and believes it probable that he, like his partner Captain America, has the much-rumored Super-Soldier Formula flowing through-- or rather, frozen inside-- his veins.

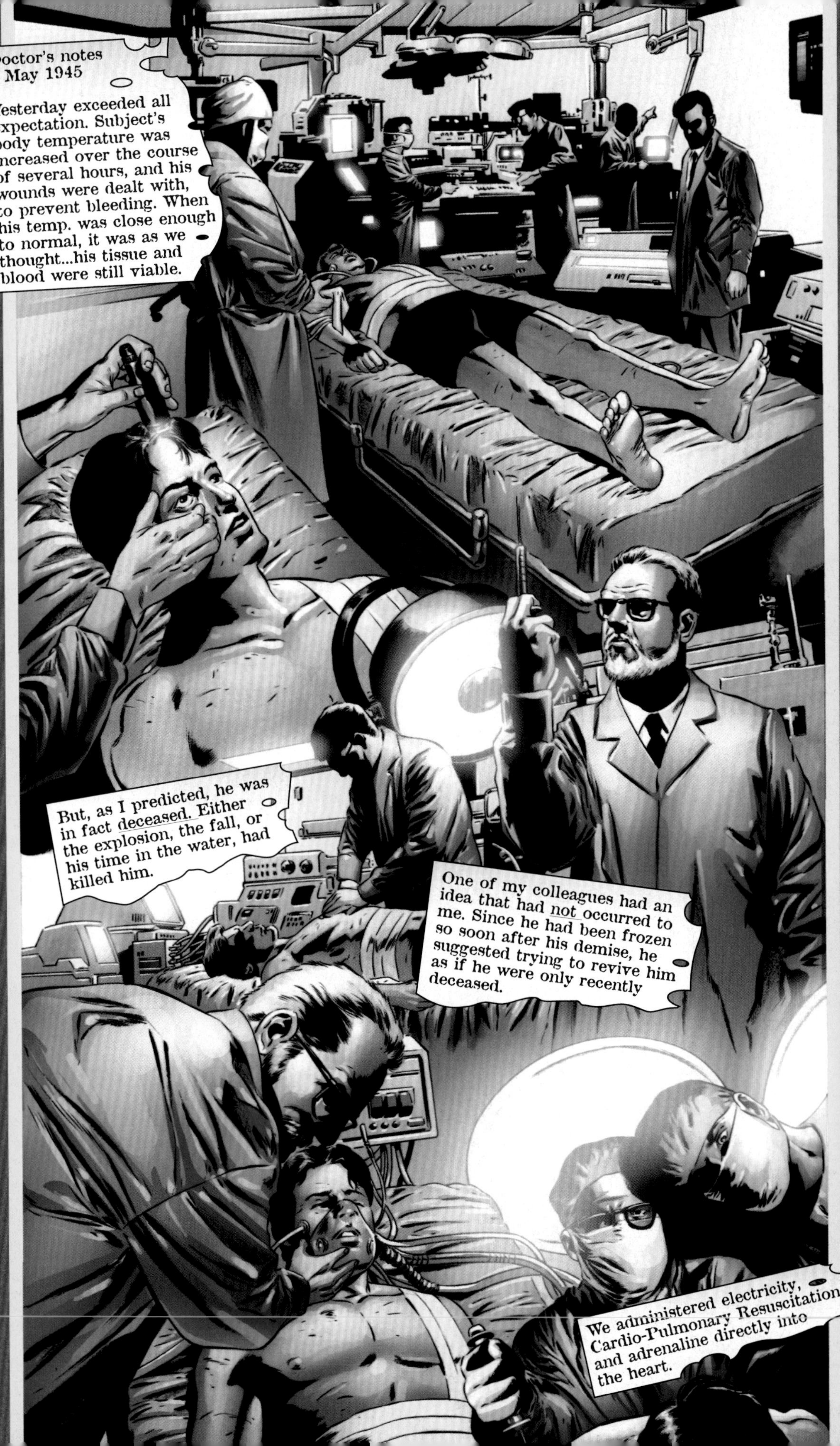
Doctor's notes
7 May 1945
Yesterday exceeded all expectation. Subject's body temperature was increased over the course of several hours, and his wounds were dealt with, to prevent bleeding. When his temp. was close enough to normal, it was as we thought...his tissue and blood were still viable.
But, as I predicted, he was in fact deceased. Either the explosion, the fall, or his time in the water, had killed him.
One of my colleagues had an idea that had not occurred to me. Since he had been frozen so soon after his demise, he suggested trying to revive him as if he were only recently deceased.
We administered electricity, Cardio-Pulmonary Resuscitation, and adrenaline directly into the heart.

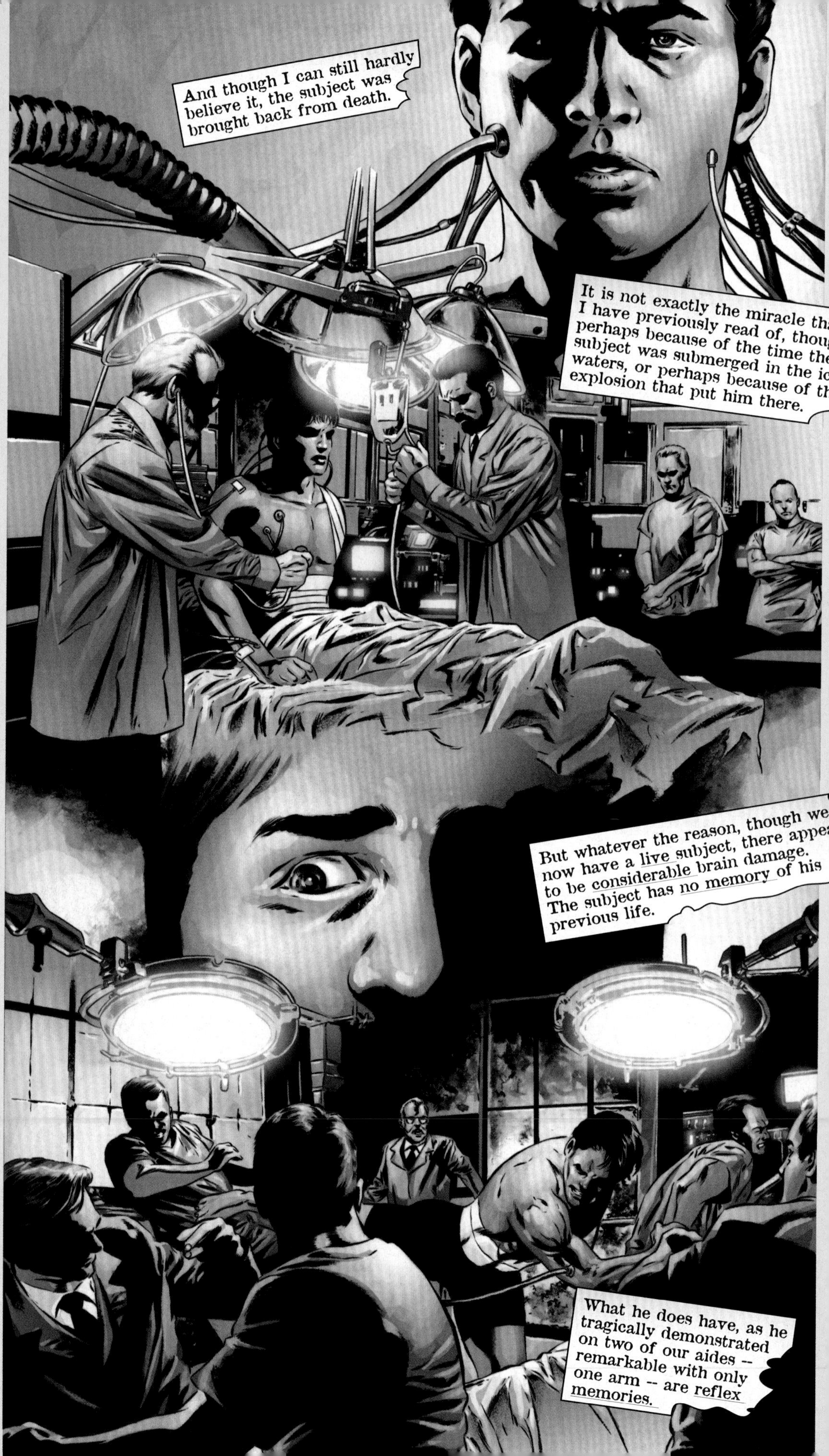

And though I can still hardly believe it, the subject was brought back from death.
It is not exactly the miracle tha I have previously read of, thoug perhaps because of the time the subject was submerged in the ic waters, or perhaps because of th explosion that put him there.
But whatever the reason, though we now have a live subject, there appea to be considerable brain damage. The subject has no memory of his previous life.
What he does have, as he tragically demonstrated on two of our aides -- remarkable with only one arm -- are reflex memories.

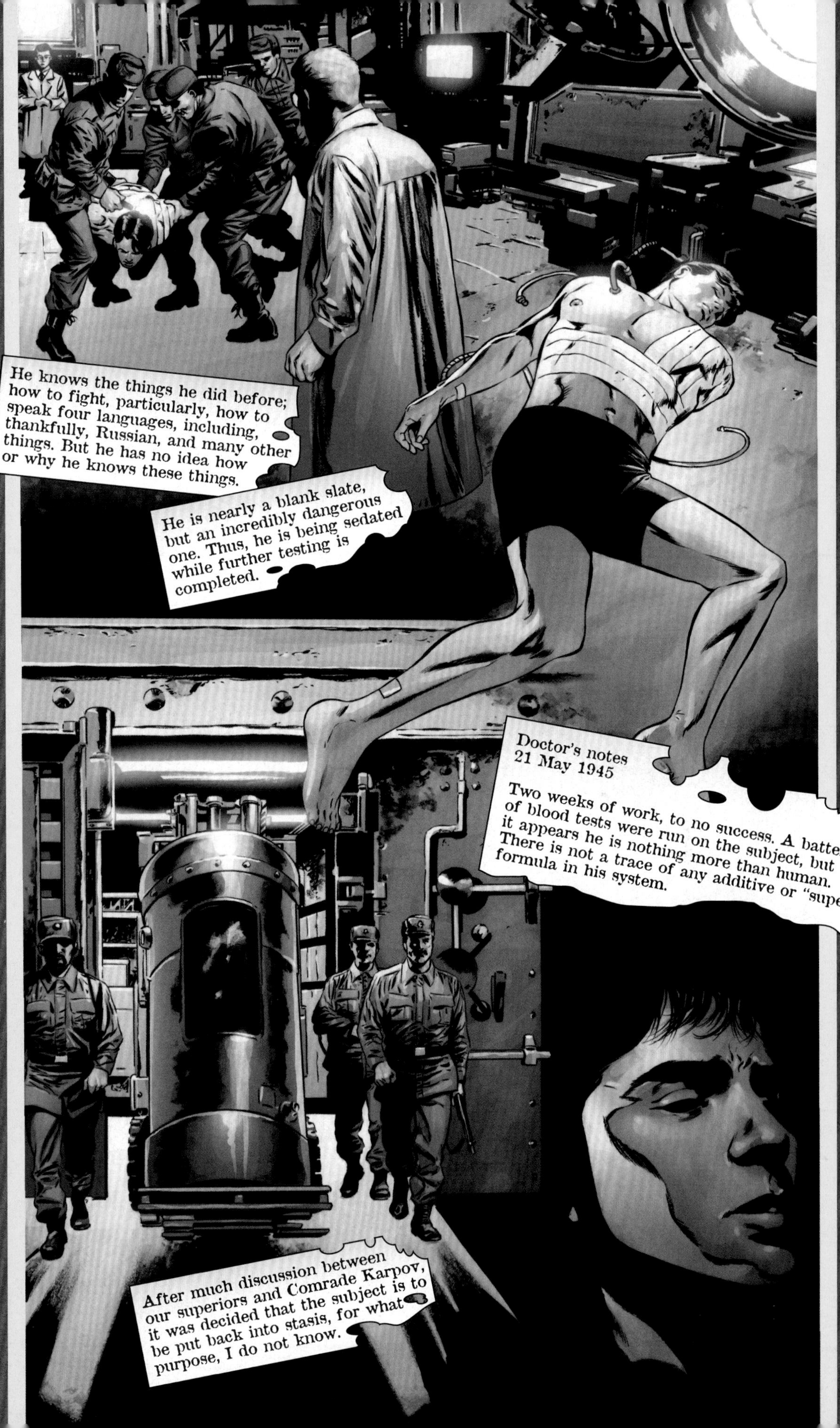
He knows the things he did before; how to fight, particularly, how to speak four languages, including, thankfully, Russian, and many other things. But he has no idea how or why he knows these things.
He is nearly a blank slate, but an incredibly dangerous one. Thus, he is being sedated while further testing is completed.
Doctor's notes 21 May 1945
Two weeks of work, to no success. A battery of blood tests were run on the subject, but it appears he is nothing more than human. There is not a trace of any additive or "super" formula in his system.
After much discussion between our superiors and Comrade Karpov, it was decided that the subject is to be put back into stasis, for what purpose, I do not know.

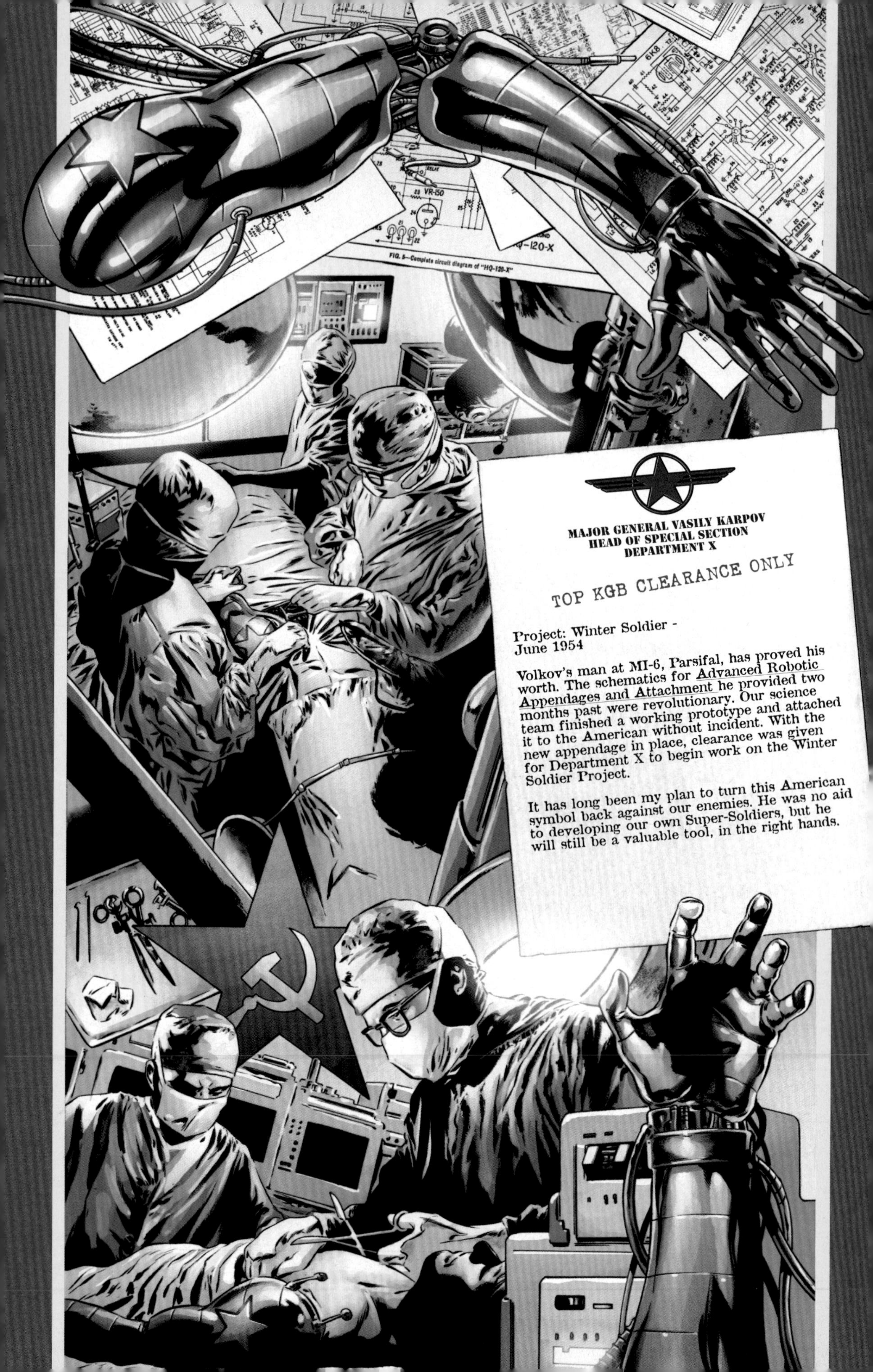
MAJOR GENERAL VASILY KARPOV
HEAD OF SPECIAL SECTION
DEPARTMENT X
TOP KGB CLEARANCE ONLY
Project: Winter Soldier -
June 1954
Volkov's man at MI-6, Parsifal, has proved his worth. The schematics for Advanced Robotic Appendages and Attachment he provided two months past were revolutionary. Our science team finished a working prototype and attached it to the American without incident. With the new appendage in place, clearance was given for Department X to begin work on the Winter Soldier Project.
It has long been my plan to turn this American symbol back against our enemies. He was no aid to developing our own Super-Soldiers, but he will still be a valuable tool, in the right hands.

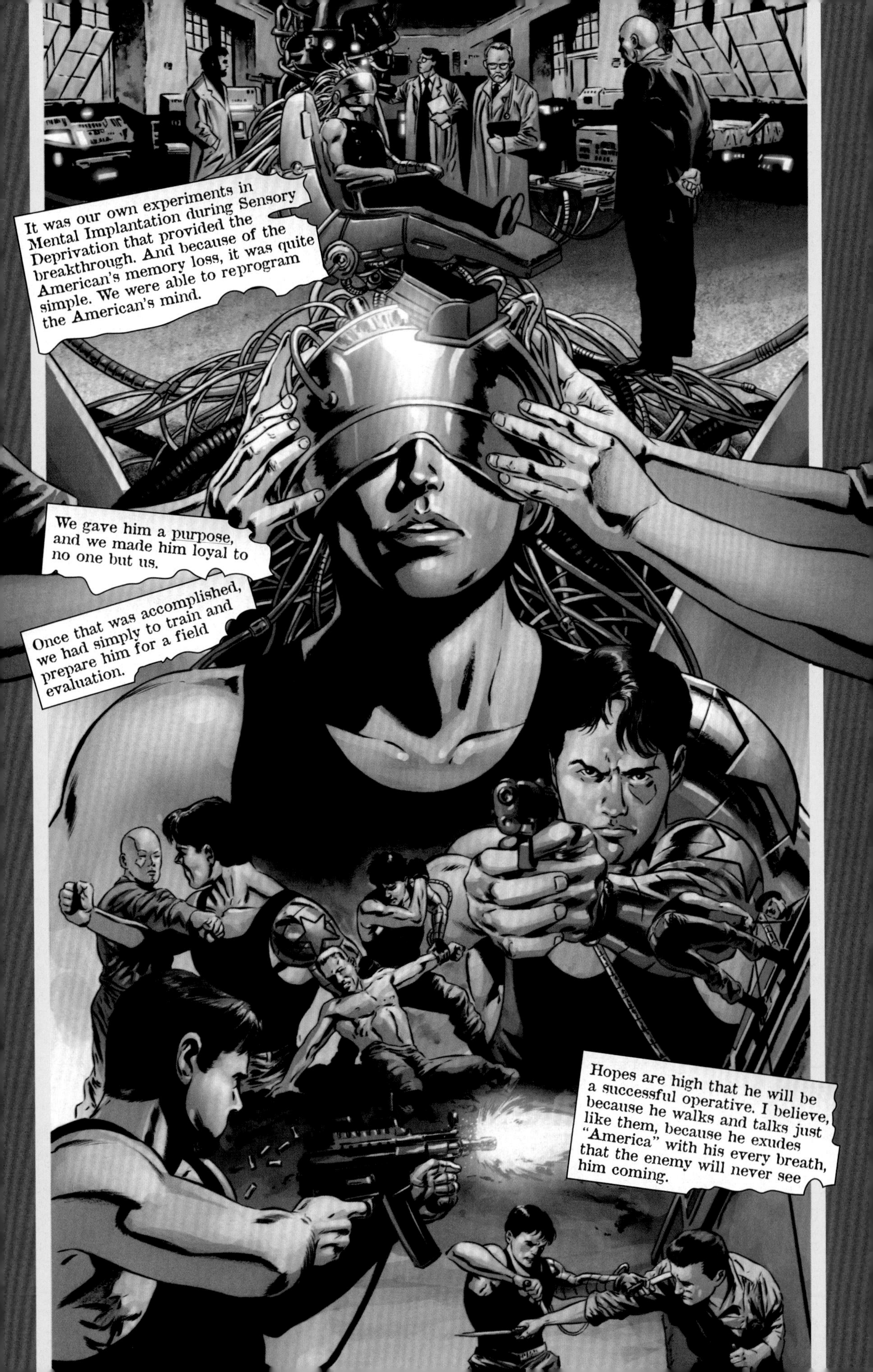
It was our own experiments in Mental Implantation during Sensory Deprivation that provided the breakthrough. And because of the American's memory loss, it was quite simple. We were able to reprogram the American's mind.
We gave him a purpose, and we made him loyal to no one but us.
Once that was accomplished, we had simply to train and prepare him for a field evaluation.
Hopes are high that he will be a successful operative. I believe, because he walks and talks just like them, because he exudes "America" with his every breath, that the enemy will never see him coming.

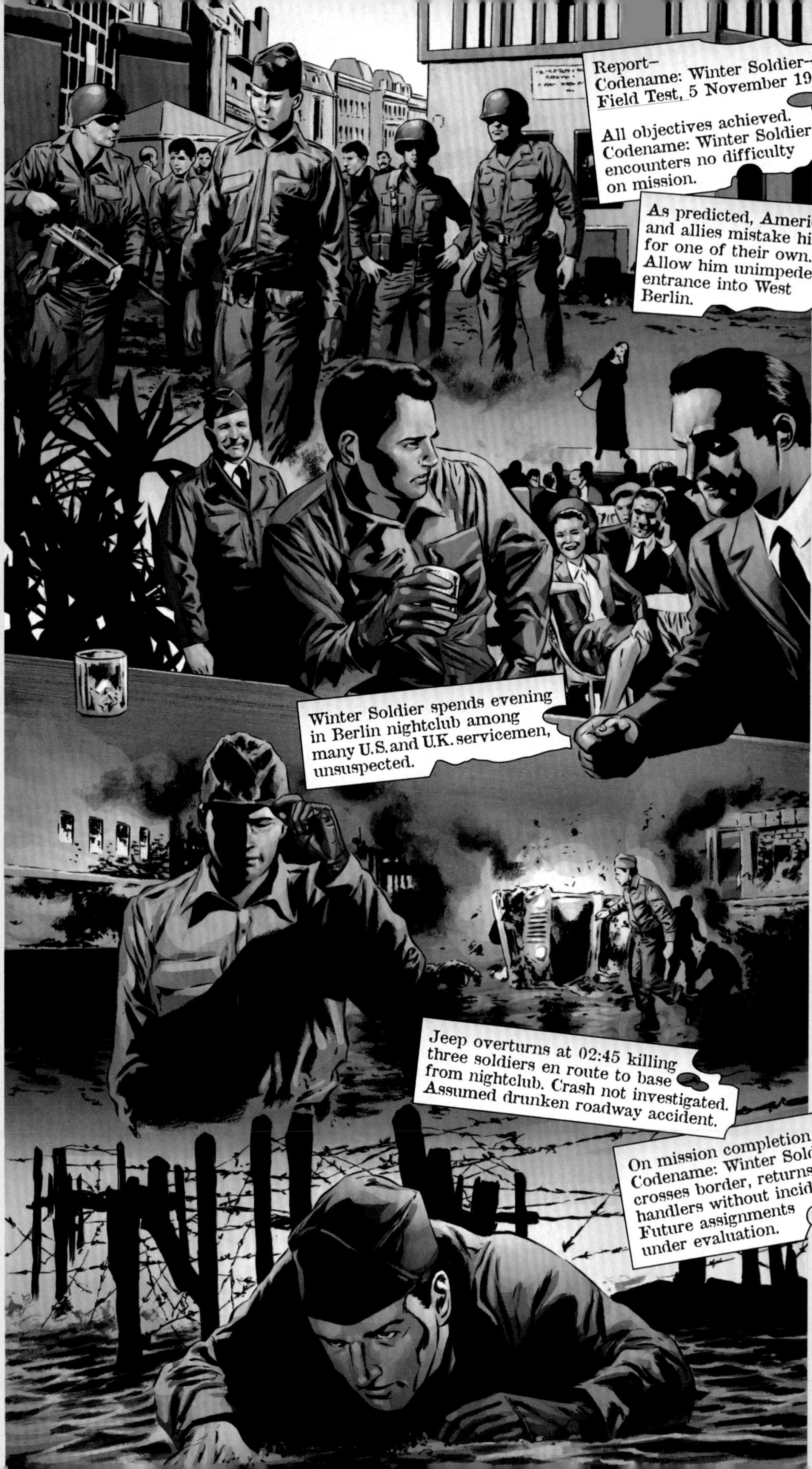
Report–
Codename: Winter Soldier--
Field Test, 5 November 1954
All objectives achieved. Codename: Winter Soldier encounters no difficulty on mission.
As predicted, Americans and allies mistake him for one of their own. Allow him unimpeded entrance into West Berlin.
Winter Soldier spends evening in Berlin nightclub among many U.S. and U.K. servicemen, unsuspected.
Jeep overturns at 02:45 killing three soldiers en route to base from nightclub. Crash not investigated. Assumed drunken roadway accident.
On mission completion, Codename: Winter Soldier crosses border, returns to handlers without incident. Future assignments under evaluation.

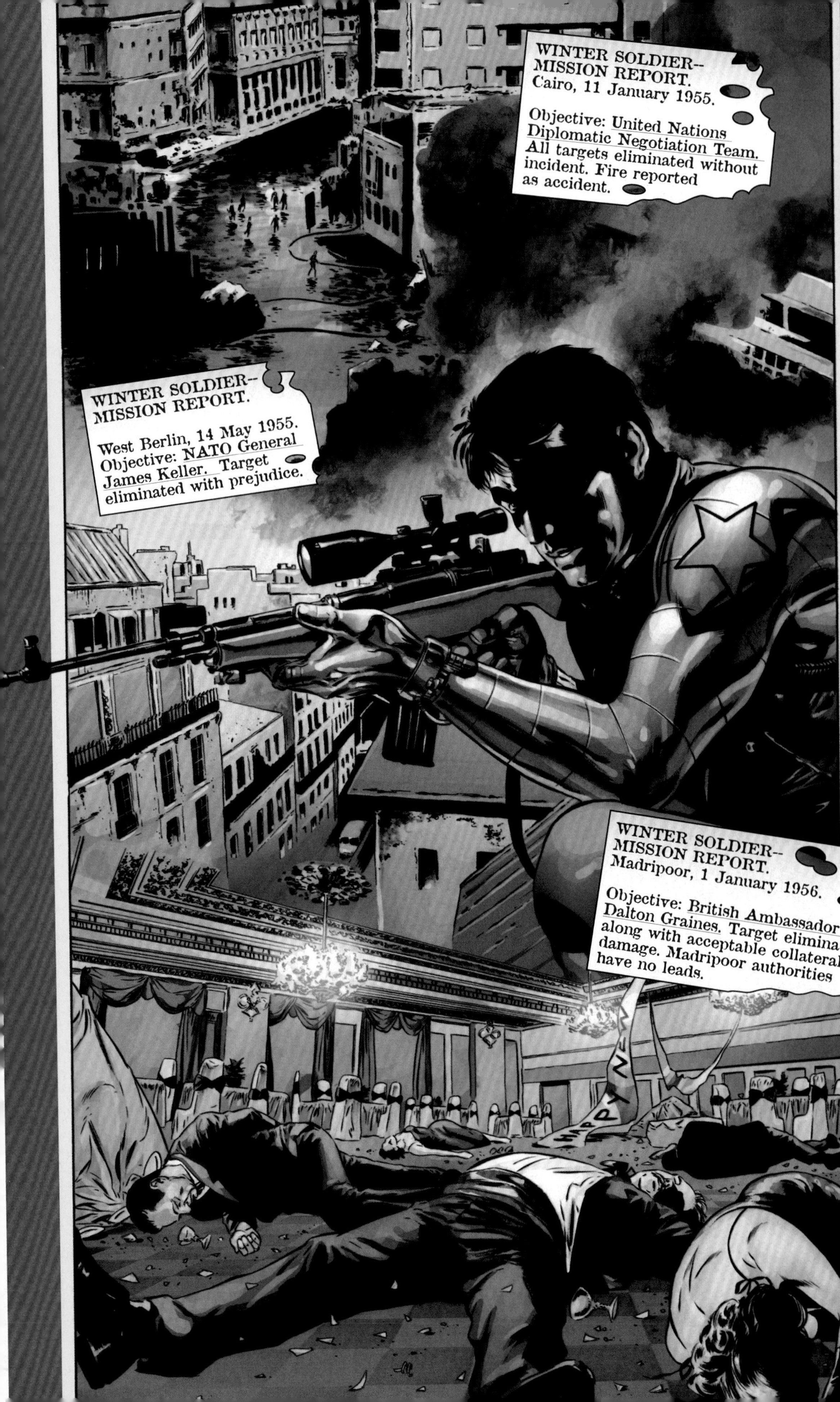
WINTER SOLDIER--
MISSION REPORT.
Cairo, 11 January 1955.
Objective: United Nations Diplomatic Negotiation Team. All targets eliminated without incident. Fire reported as accident.
WINTER SOLDIER--
MISSION REPORT.
West Berlin, 14 May 1955. Objective: NATO General James Keller. Target eliminated with prejudice.
WINTER SOLDIER--
MISSION REPORT.
Madripoor, 1 January 1956.
Objective: British Ambassador Dalton Graines. Target eliminated, along with acceptable collateral damage. Madripoor authorities have no leads.
HAPPY NEW

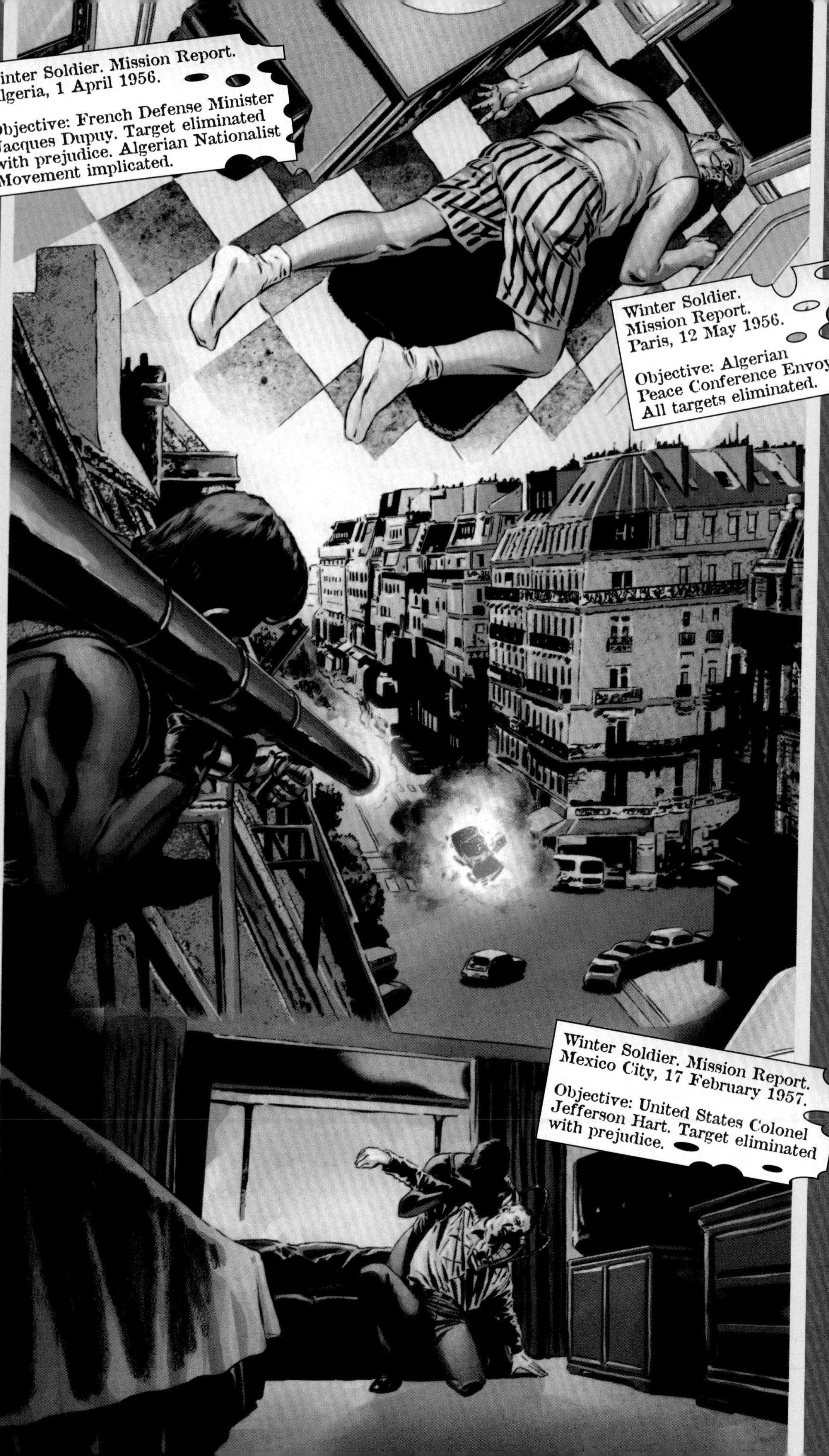
Winter Soldier. Mission Report. Algeria, 1 April 1956.
Objective: French Defense Minister Jacques Dupuy. Target eliminated with prejudice. Algerian Nationalist Movement implicated.
Winter Soldier. Mission Report. Paris, 12 May 1956.
Objective: Algerian Peace Conference Envoy. All targets eliminated.
Winter Soldier. Mission Report. Mexico City, 17 February 1957.
Objective: United States Colonel Jefferson Hart. Target eliminated with prejudice.

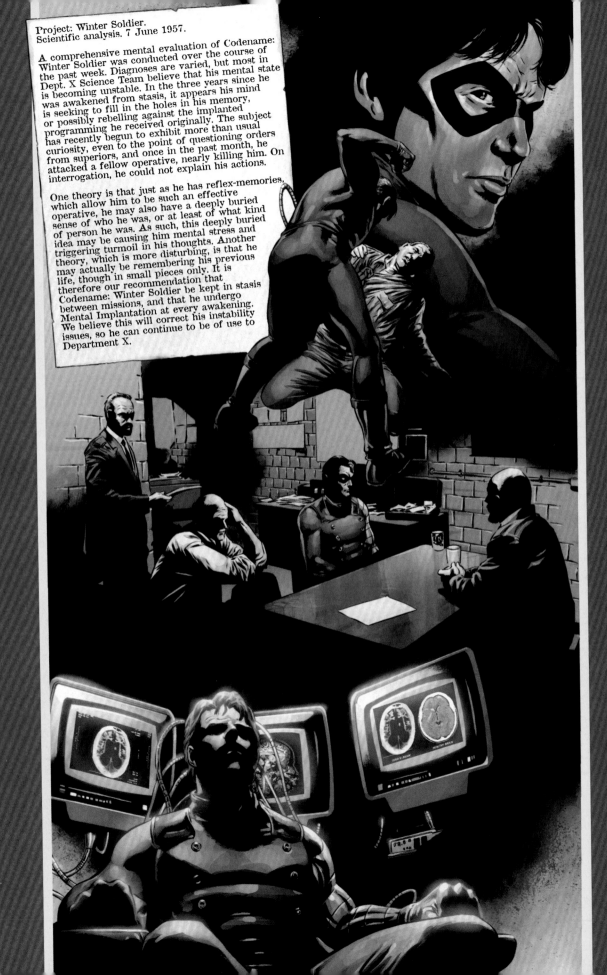

Project: Winter Soldier.
Scientific analysis. 7 June 1957.

A comprehensive mental evaluation of Codename: Winter Soldier was conducted over the course of the past week. Diagnoses are varied, but most in Dept. X Science Team believe that his mental state is becoming unstable. In the three years since he was awakened from stasis, it appears his mind is seeking to fill in the holes in his memory, or possibly rebelling against the implanted programming he received originally. The subject has recently begun to exhibit more than usual curiosity, even to the point of questioning orders from superiors, and once in the past month, he attacked a fellow operative, nearly killing him. On interrogation, he could not explain his actions.

One theory is that just as he has reflex-memories, which allow him to be such an effective operative, he may also have a deeply buried sense of who he was, or at least of what kind of person he was. As such, this deeply buried idea may be causing him mental stress and triggering turmoil in his thoughts. Another theory, which is more disturbing, is that he may actually be remembering his previous life, though in small pieces only. It is therefore our recommendation that Codename: Winter Soldier be kept in stasis between missions, and that he undergo Mental Implantation at every awakening. We believe this will correct his instability issues, so he can continue to be of use to Department X.

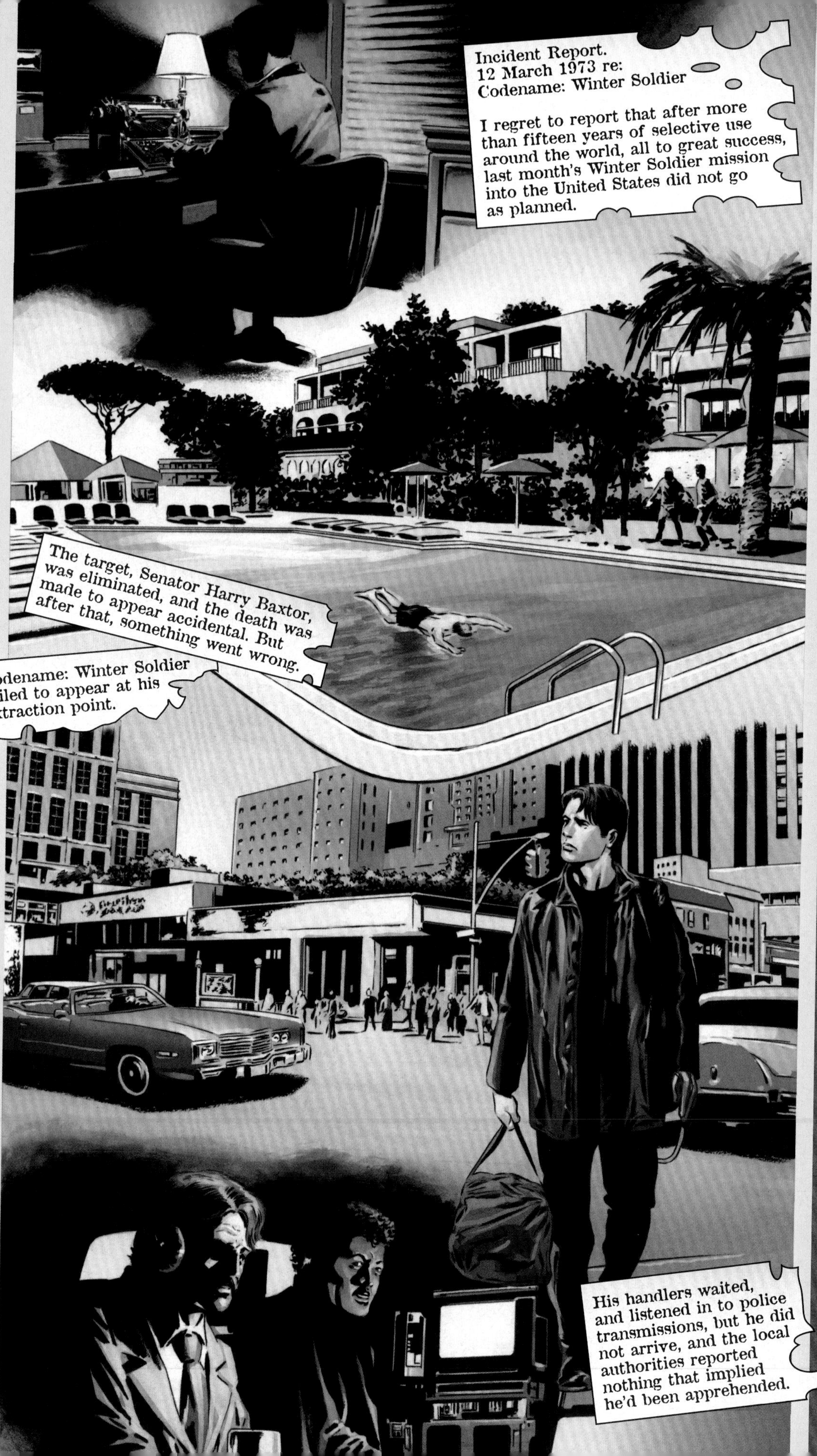
Incident Report.
12 March 1973 re:
Codename: Winter Soldier
I regret to report that after more than fifteen years of selective use around the world, all to great success, last month's Winter Soldier mission into the United States did not go as planned.
The target, Senator Harry Baxtor, was eliminated, and the death was made to appear accidental. But after that, something went wrong.
Codename: Winter Soldier failed to appear at his extraction point.
His handlers waited, and listened in to police transmissions, but he did not arrive, and the local authorities reported nothing that implied he'd been apprehended.

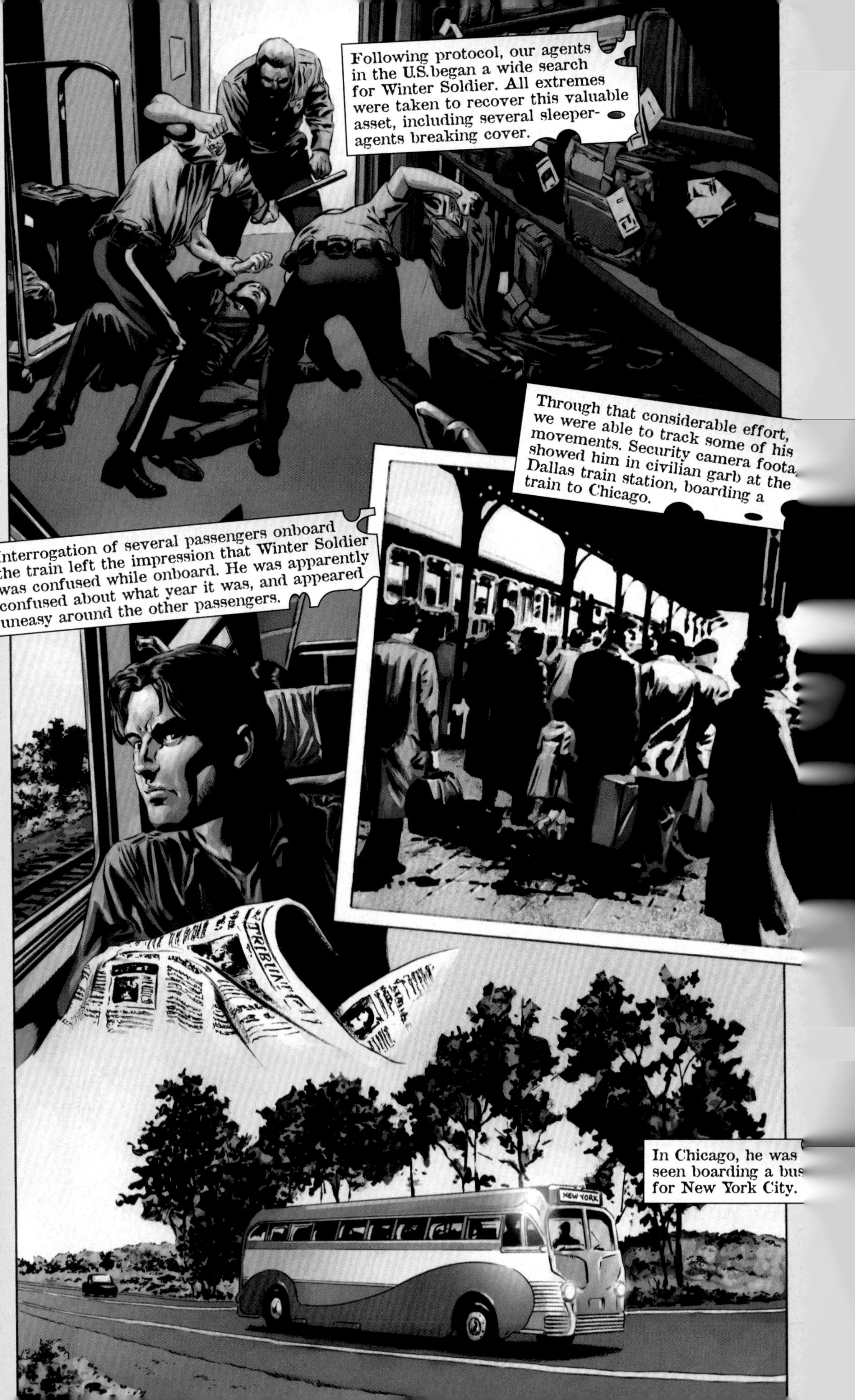
Following protocol, our agents in the U.S. began a wide search for Winter Soldier. All extremes were taken to recover this valuable asset, including several sleeper-agents breaking cover.
Through that considerable effort, we were able to track some of his movements. Security camera foota showed him in civilian garb at the Dallas train station, boarding a train to Chicago.
Interrogation of several passengers onboard the train left the impression that Winter Soldier was confused while onboard. He was apparently confused about what year it was, and appeared uneasy around the other passengers.
TRIBUNE
In Chicago, he was seen boarding a bus for New York City.
NEW YORK

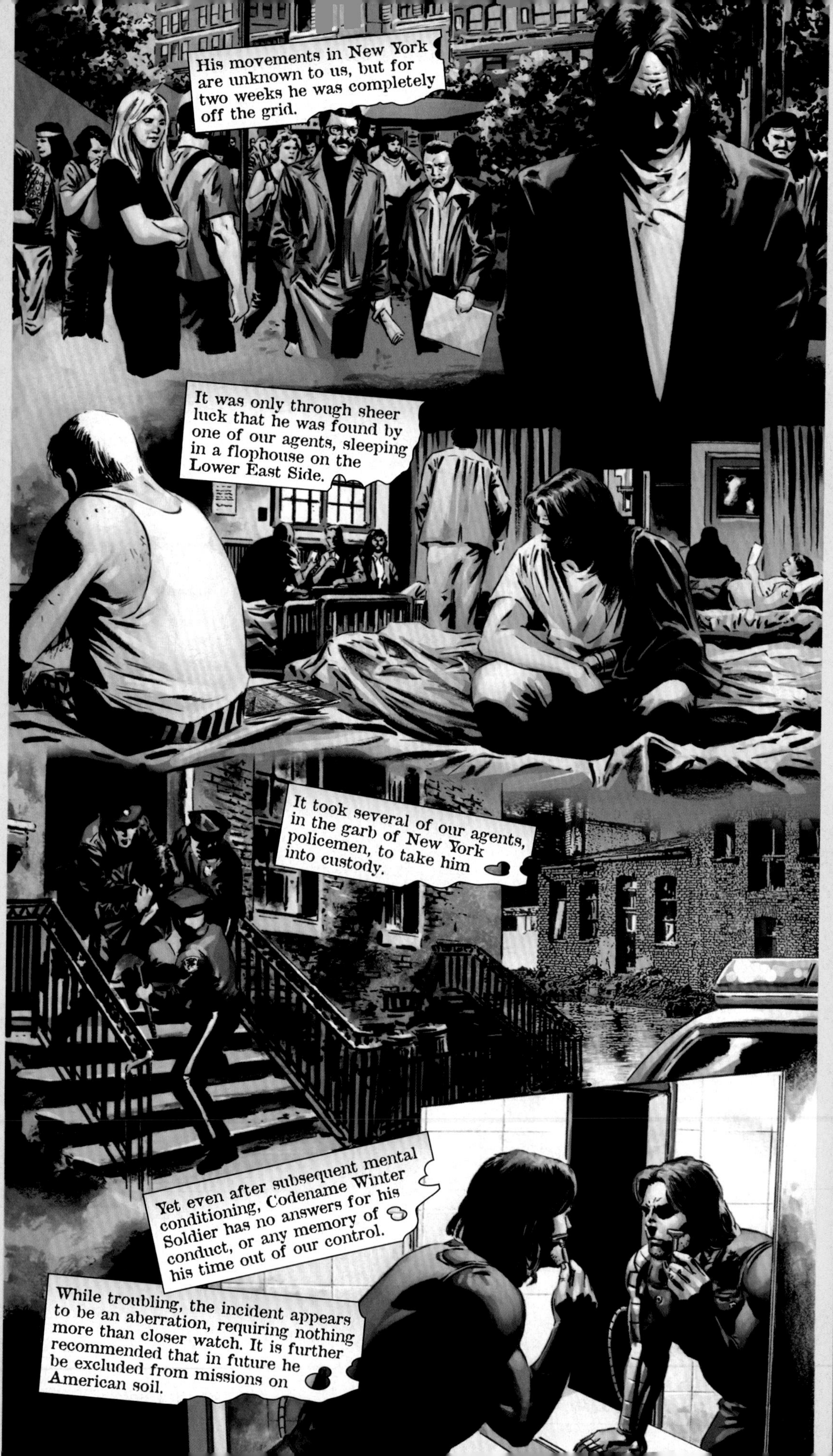
His movements in New York are unknown to us, but for two weeks he was completely off the grid.
It was only through sheer luck that he was found by one of our agents, sleeping in a flophouse on the Lower East Side.
It took several of our agents, in the garb of New York policemen, to take him into custody.
Yet even after subsequent mental conditioning, Codename Winter Soldier has no answers for his conduct, or any memory of his time out of our control.
While troubling, the incident appears to be an aberration, requiring nothing more than closer watch. It is further recommended that in future he be excluded from missions on American soil.

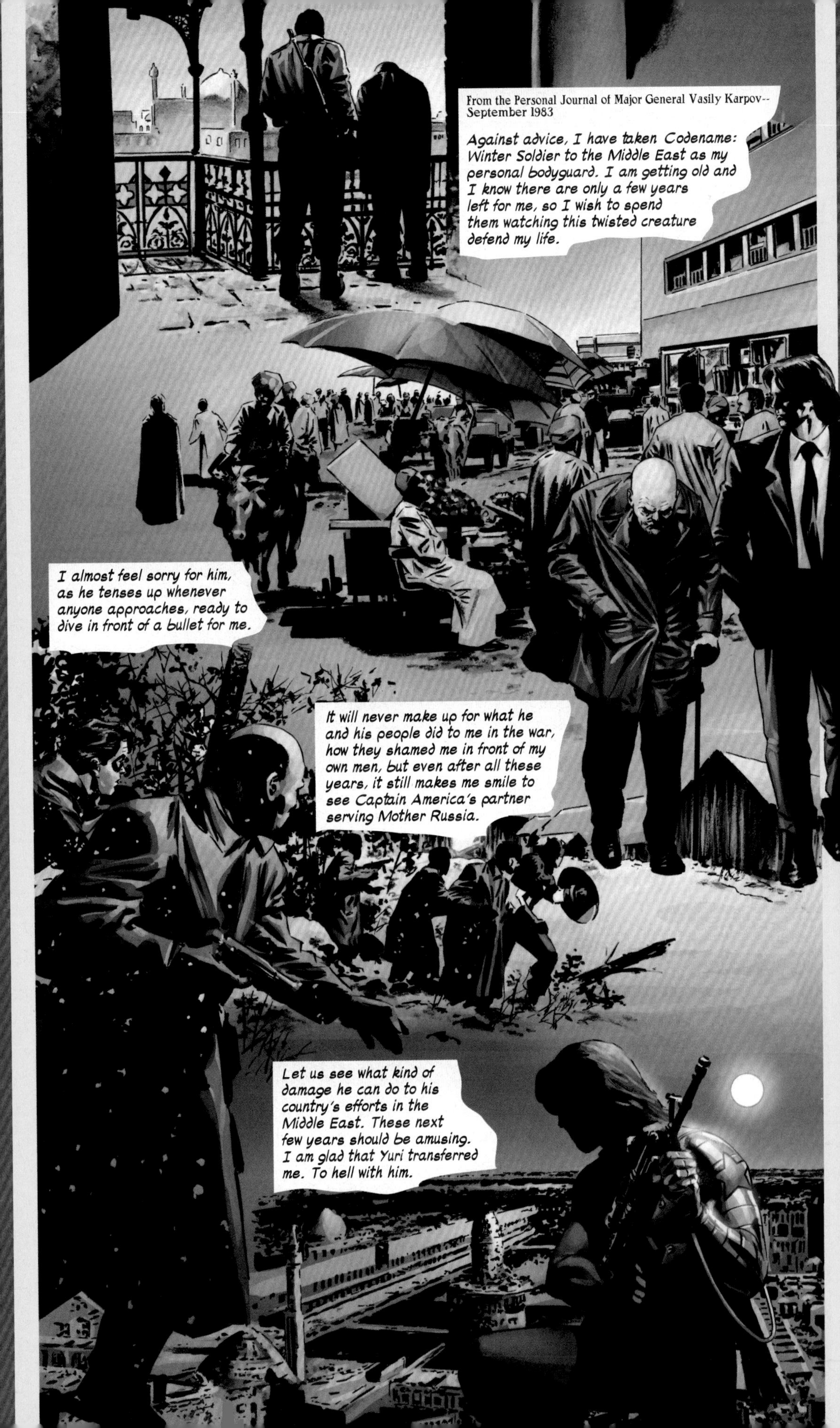
From the Personal Journal of Major General Vasily Karpov-- September 1983
Against advice, I have taken Codename: Winter Soldier to the Middle East as my personal bodyguard. I am getting old and I know there are only a few years left for me, so I wish to spend them watching this twisted creature defend my life.
I almost feel sorry for him, as he tenses up whenever anyone approaches, ready to dive in front of a bullet for me.
It will never make up for what he and his people did to me in the war, how they shamed me in front of my own men, but even after all these years, it still makes me smile to see Captain America's partner serving Mother Russia.
Let us see what kind of damage he can do to his country's efforts in the Middle East. These next few years should be amusing. I am glad that Yuri transferred me. To hell with him.

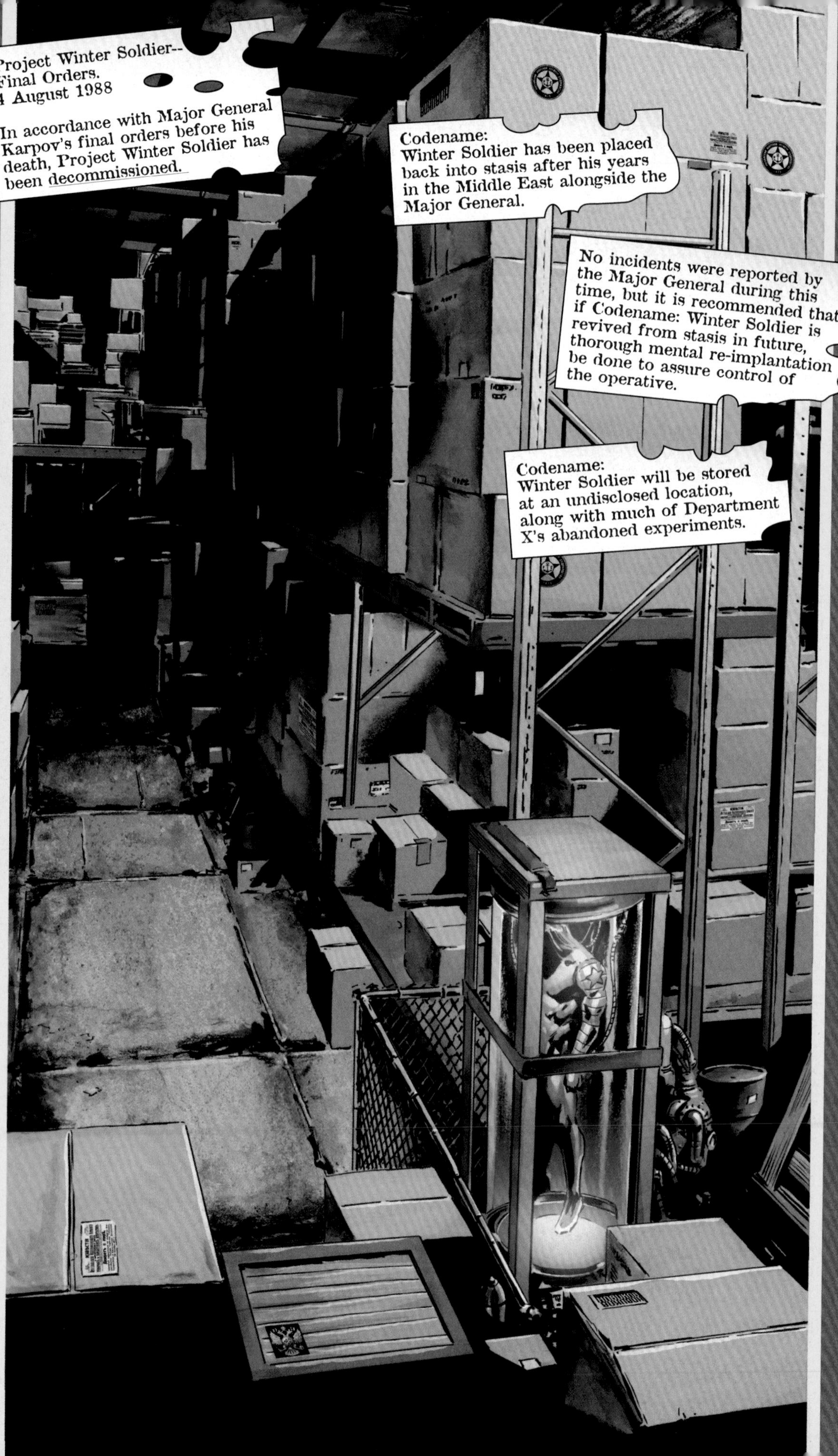
Project Winter Soldier--
Final Orders.
4 August 1988
In accordance with Major General Karpov's final orders before his death, Project Winter Soldier has been decommissioned.
Codename:
Winter Soldier has been placed back into stasis after his years in the Middle East alongside the Major General.
No incidents were reported by the Major General during this time, but it is recommended that if Codename: Winter Soldier is revived from stasis in future, thorough mental re-implantation be done to assure control of the operative.
Codename:
Winter Soldier will be stored at an undisclosed location, along with much of Department X's abandoned experiments.

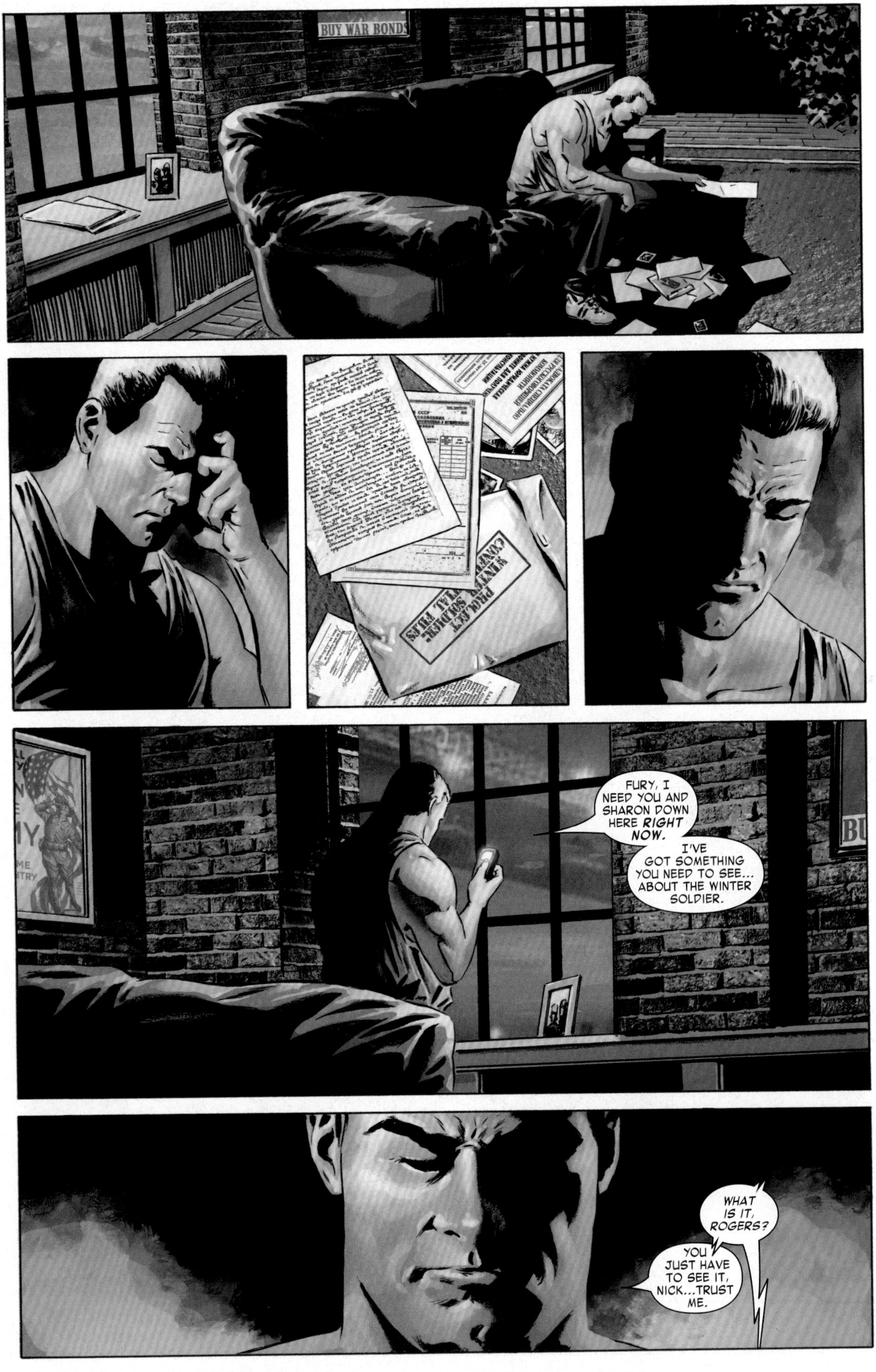
BUY WAR BONDS
FURY, I NEED YOU AND SHARON DOWN HERE RIGHT NOW.
I'VE GOT SOMETHING YOU NEED TO SEE... ABOUT THE WINTER SOLDIER.
WHAT IS IT, ROGERS?
YOU JUST HAVE TO SEE IT, NICK...TRUST ME.

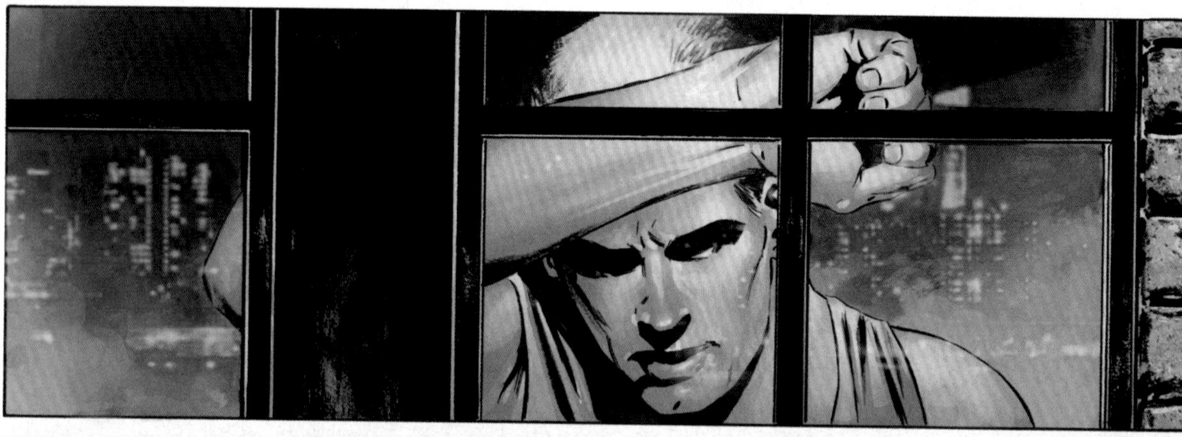

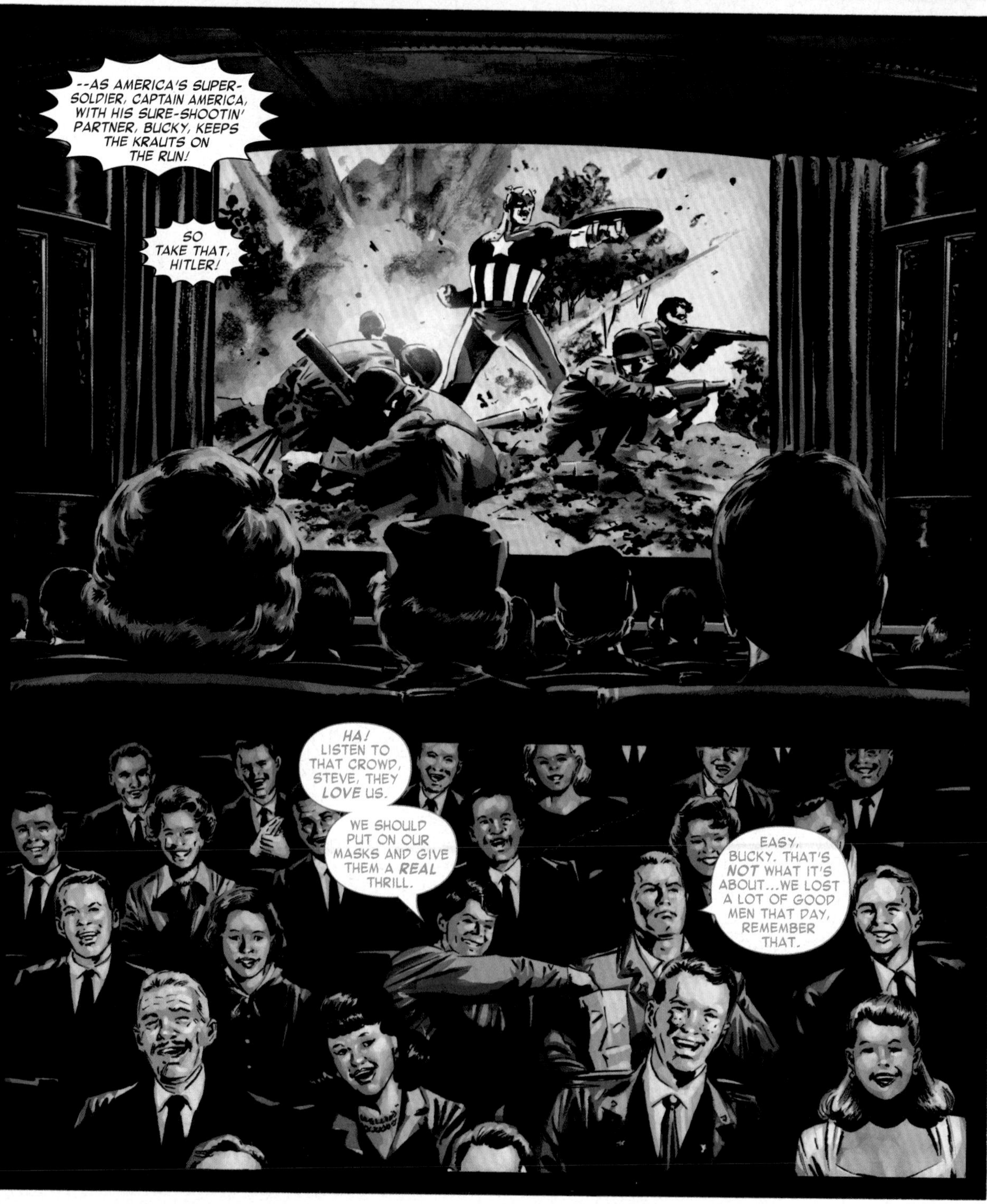
--AS AMERICA'S SUPER-SOLDIER, CAPTAIN AMERICA, WITH HIS SURE-SHOOTIN' PARTNER, BUCKY, KEEPS THE KRAUTS ON THE RUN!
SO TAKE THAT, HITLER!
HA! LISTEN TO THAT CROWD, STEVE, THEY LOVE US.
WE SHOULD PUT ON OUR MASKS AND GIVE THEM A REAL THRILL.
EASY, BUCKY. THAT'S NOT WHAT IT'S ABOUT...WE LOST A LOT OF GOOD MEN THAT DAY, REMEMBER THAT.

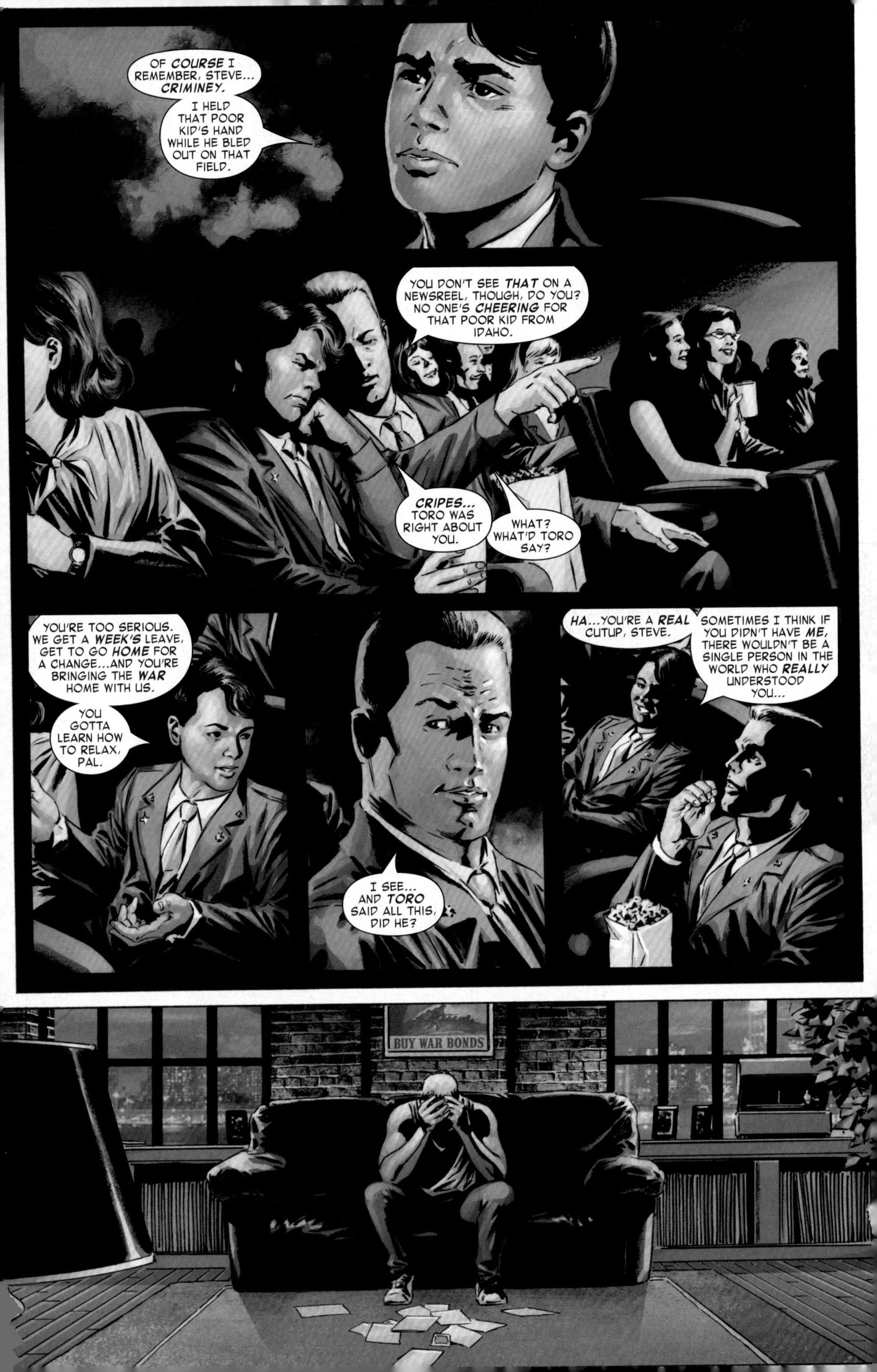
OF COURSE I REMEMBER, STEVE... CRIMINEY.
I HELD THAT POOR KID'S HAND WHILE HE BLED OUT ON THAT FIELD.
YOU DON'T SEE THAT ON A NEWSREEL, THOUGH, DO YOU? NO ONE'S CHEERING FOR THAT POOR KID FROM IDAHO.
CRIPES... TORO WAS RIGHT ABOUT YOU.
WHAT? WHAT'D TORO SAY?
YOU'RE TOO SERIOUS. WE GET A WEEK'S LEAVE, GET TO GO HOME FOR A CHANGE...AND YOU'RE BRINGING THE WAR HOME WITH US.
YOU GOTTA LEARN HOW TO RELAX, PAL.
I SEE... AND TORO SAID ALL THIS, DID HE?
HA...YOU'RE A REAL CUTUP, STEVE.
SOMETIMES I THINK IF YOU DIDN'T HAVE ME, THERE WOULDN'T BE A SINGLE PERSON IN THE WORLD WHO REALLY UNDERSTOOD YOU...
BUY WAR BONDS

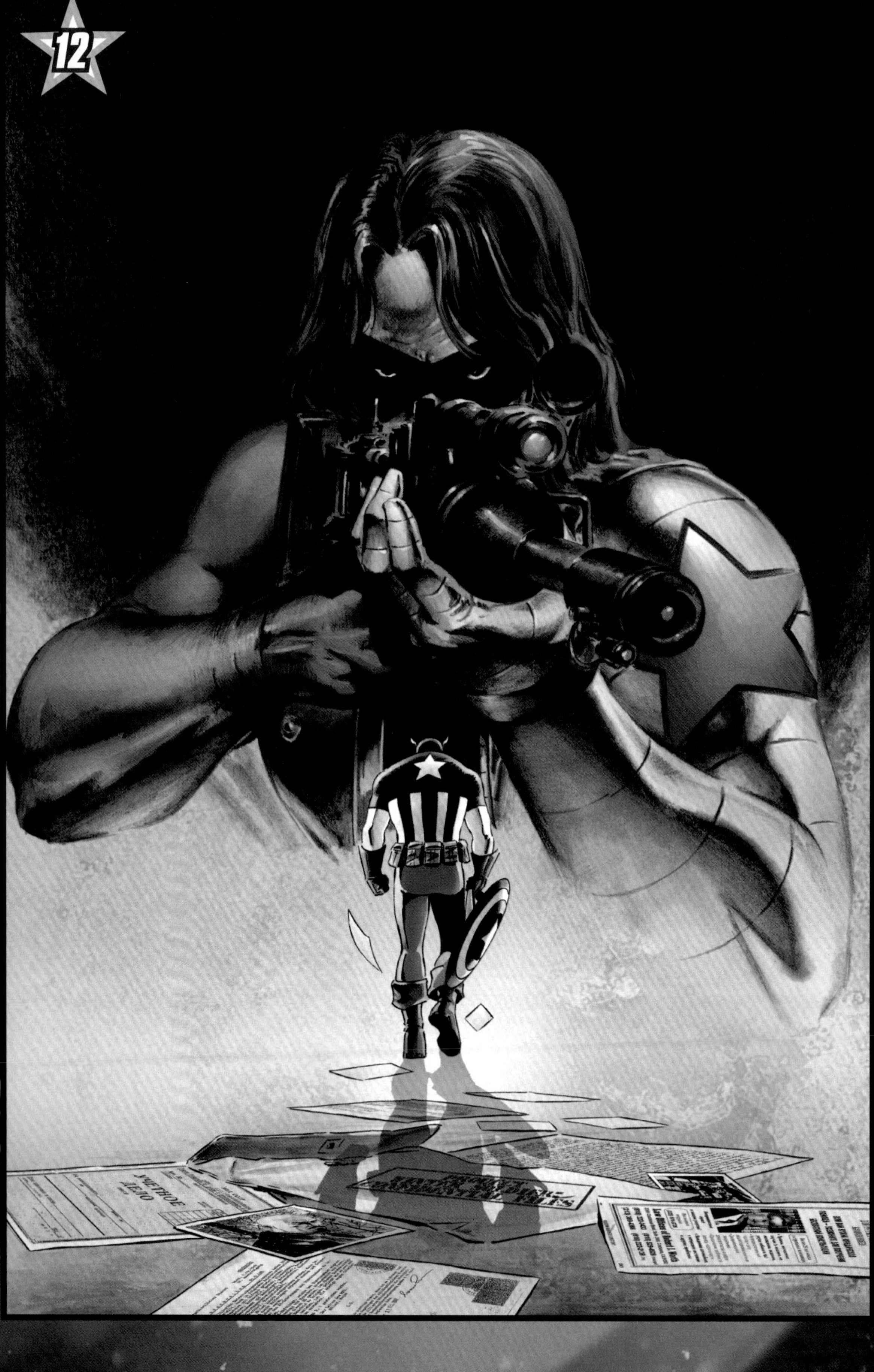
12

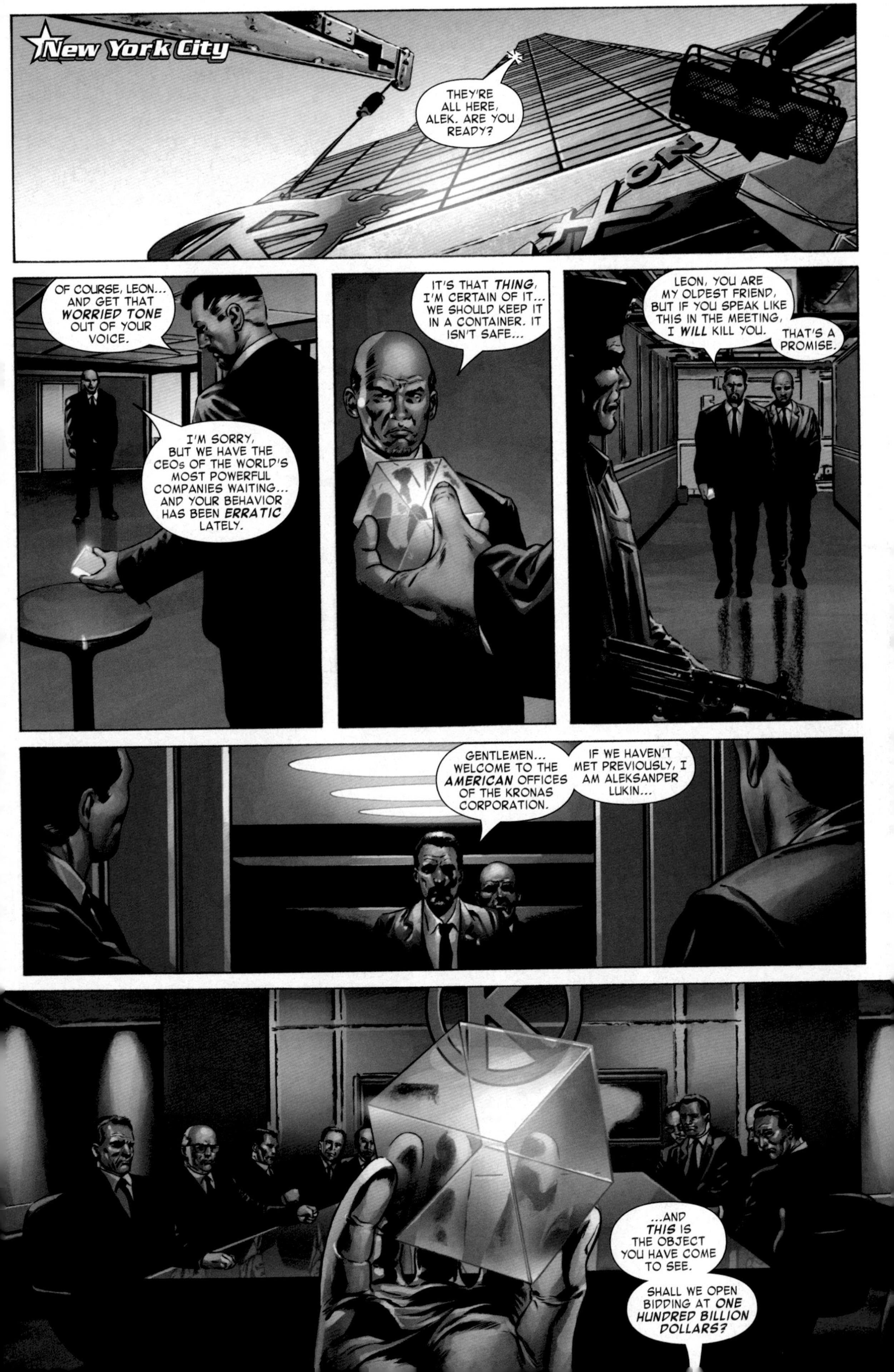
New York City
THEY'RE ALL HERE, ALEK. ARE YOU READY?
OF COURSE, LEON... AND GET THAT WORRIED TONE OUT OF YOUR VOICE.
I'M SORRY, BUT WE HAVE THE CEOs OF THE WORLD'S MOST POWERFUL COMPANIES WAITING... AND YOUR BEHAVIOR HAS BEEN ERRATIC LATELY.
IT'S THAT THING, I'M CERTAIN OF IT... WE SHOULD KEEP IT IN A CONTAINER. IT ISN'T SAFE...
LEON, YOU ARE MY OLDEST FRIEND, BUT IF YOU SPEAK LIKE THIS IN THE MEETING, I WILL KILL YOU.
THAT'S A PROMISE.
GENTLEMEN... WELCOME TO THE AMERICAN OFFICES OF THE KRONAS CORPORATION.
IF WE HAVEN'T MET PREVIOUSLY, I AM ALEKSANDER LUKIN...
...AND THIS IS THE OBJECT YOU HAVE COME TO SEE.
SHALL WE OPEN BIDDING AT ONE HUNDRED BILLION DOLLARS?

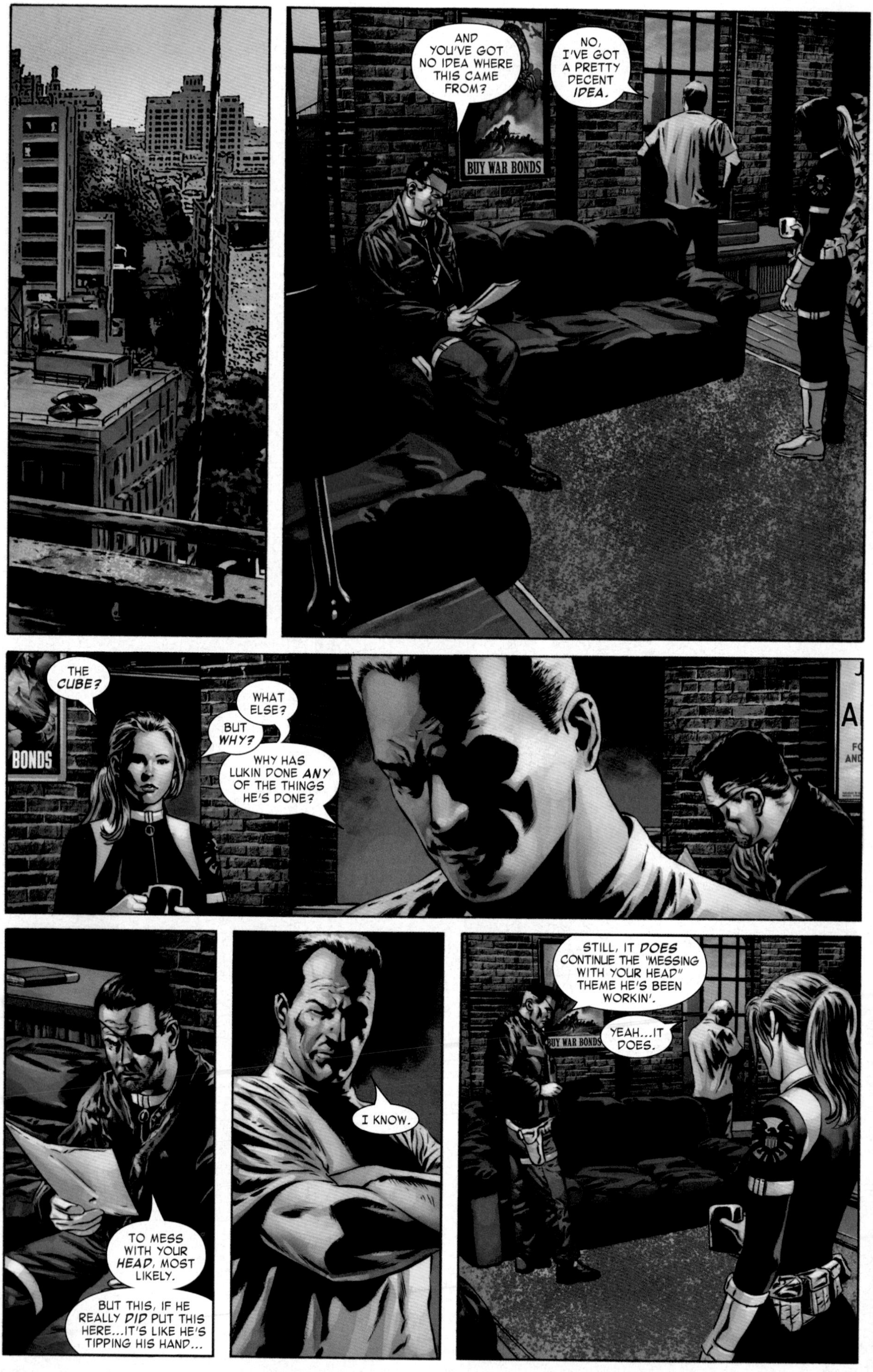

AND YOU'VE GOT NO IDEA WHERE THIS CAME FROM?
NO, I'VE GOT A PRETTY DECENT IDEA.
BUY WAR BONDS
THE CUBE?
WHAT ELSE?
BUT WHY?
WHY HAS LUKIN DONE ANY OF THE THINGS HE'S DONE?
BONDS
TO MESS WITH YOUR HEAD, MOST LIKELY.
BUT THIS, IF HE REALLY DID PUT THIS HERE...IT'S LIKE HE'S TIPPING HIS HAND...
I KNOW.
STILL, IT DOES CONTINUE THE "MESSING WITH YOUR HEAD" THEME HE'S BEEN WORKIN'.
YEAH...IT DOES.
BUY WAR BONDS

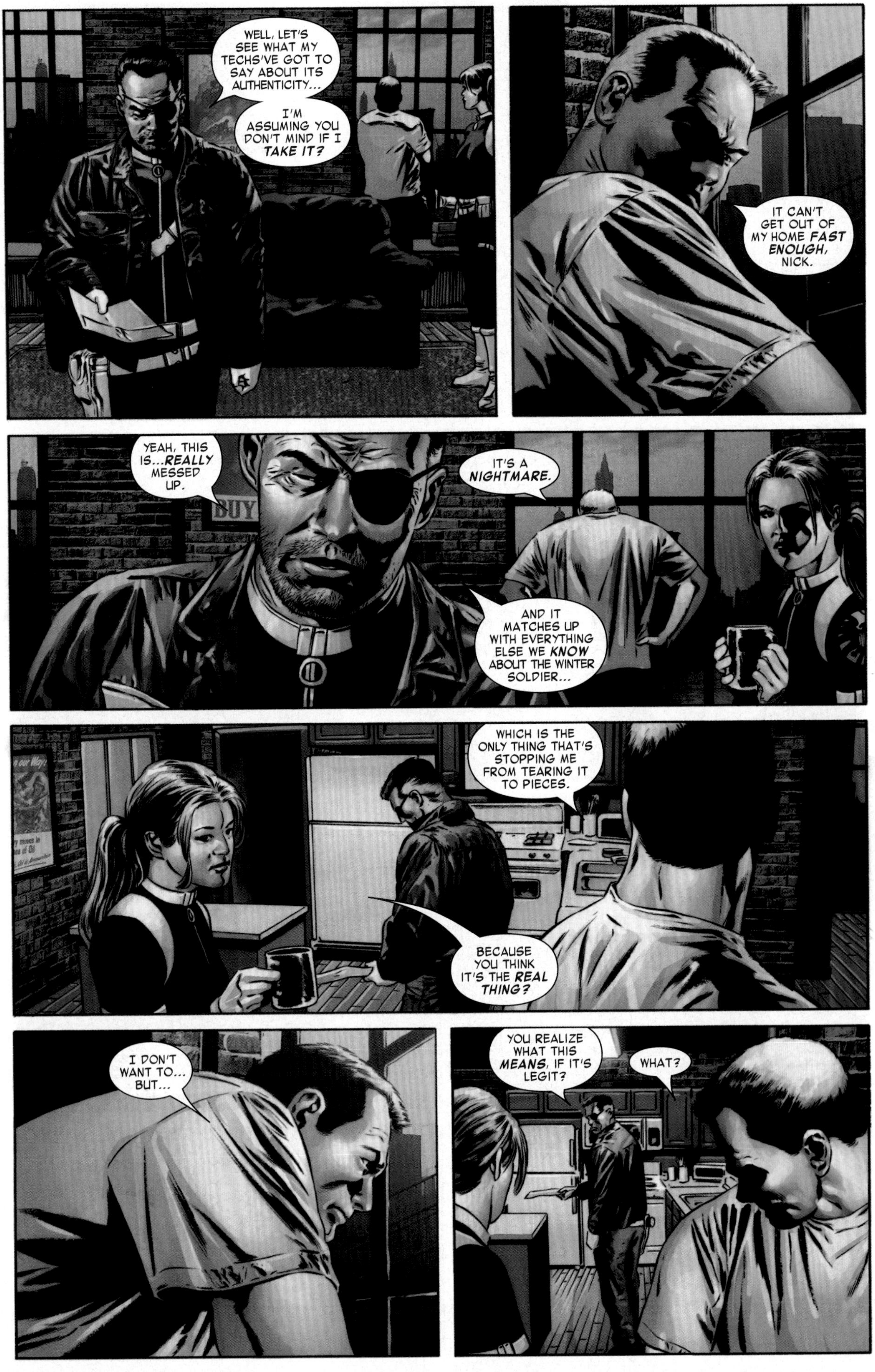
WELL, LET'S SEE WHAT MY TECHS'VE GOT TO SAY ABOUT ITS AUTHENTICITY...
I'M ASSUMING YOU DON'T MIND IF I TAKE IT?
IT CAN'T GET OUT OF MY HOME FAST ENOUGH, NICK.
YEAH, THIS IS...REALLY MESSED UP.
BUY
IT'S A NIGHTMARE.
AND IT MATCHES UP WITH EVERYTHING ELSE WE KNOW ABOUT THE WINTER SOLDIER...
WHICH IS THE ONLY THING THAT'S STOPPING ME FROM TEARING IT TO PIECES.
BECAUSE YOU THINK IT'S THE REAL THING?
I DON'T WANT TO... BUT...
YOU REALIZE WHAT THIS MEANS, IF IT'S LEGIT?
WHAT?

THAT IT'S NOT *REALLY* BUCKY... IT'S JUST WHATEVER WAS LEFT OF HIM THAT THEY COULD *MANIPULATE* FOR THEIR OWN ENDS.

IS THAT SUPPOSED TO MAKE ME FEEL BETTER?

WELL, IT *DOESN'T*... AND YOU SHOULD READ THAT FILE *CLOSER,* SHARON.

YEAH.

HE KEPT TURNING *AGAINST* THEM, AND HE *DISAPPEARED* WHEN THEY SENT HIM TO AMERICA.

THERE'S SOME PART OF HIM, OF WHO HE IS, STILL *TRAPPED* INSIDE... SOMEWHERE INSIDE THAT *THING* THEY TURNED HIM INTO, IS WHATEVER'S *LEFT* OF BUCKY BARNES' *HUMANITY.*

WE DON'T KNOW THAT, ROGERS...

HE WAS MY *PARTNER,* DAMN IT...

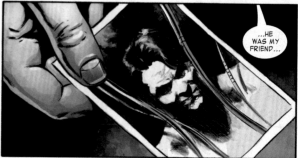

...HE WAS MY *FRIEND...*

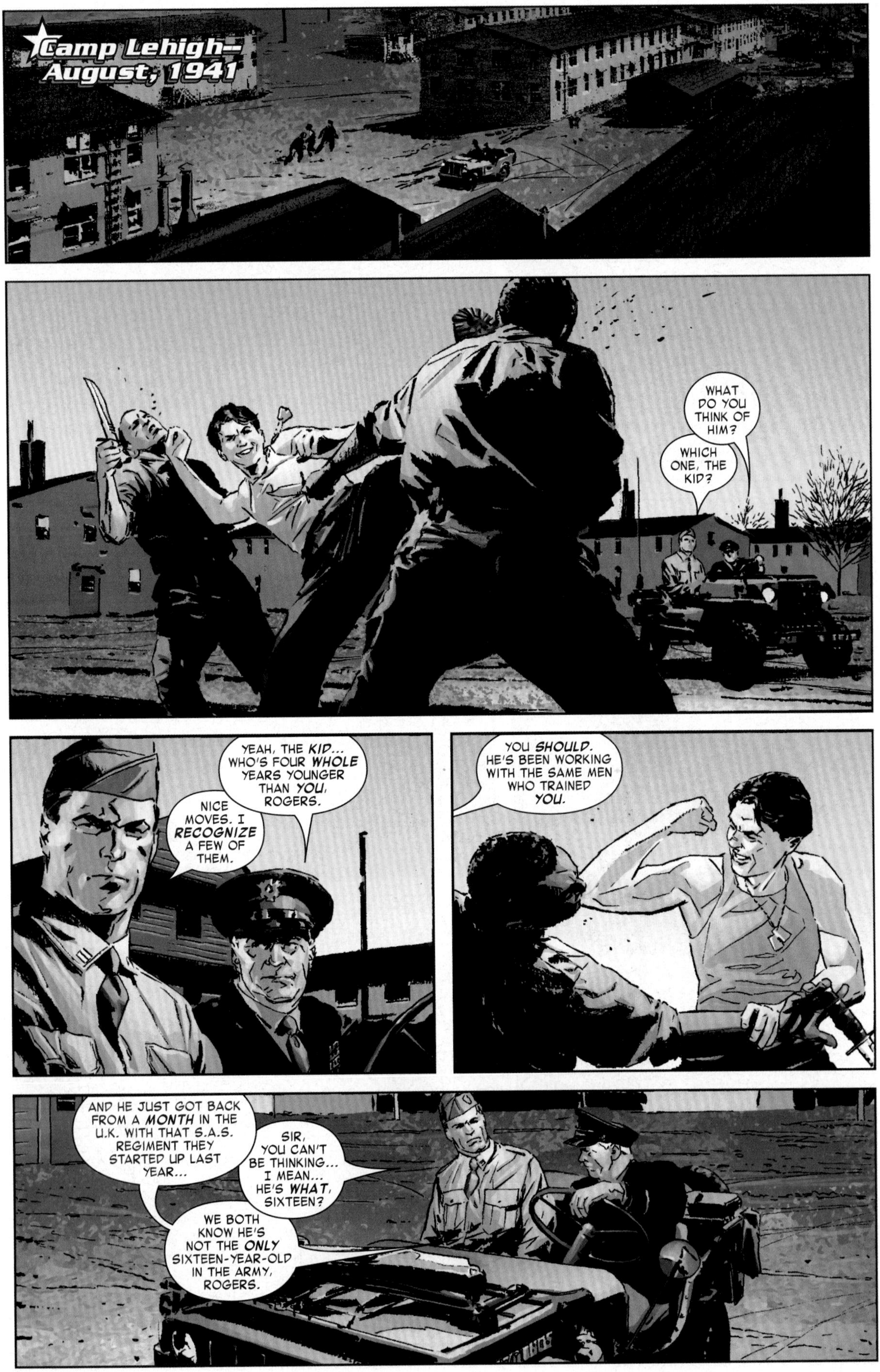
Camp Lehigh—August, 1941
WHAT DO YOU THINK OF HIM?
WHICH ONE, THE KID?
NICE MOVES. I RECOGNIZE A FEW OF THEM.
YEAH, THE KID... WHO'S FOUR WHOLE YEARS YOUNGER THAN YOU, ROGERS.
YOU SHOULD. HE'S BEEN WORKING WITH THE SAME MEN WHO TRAINED YOU.
AND HE JUST GOT BACK FROM A MONTH IN THE U.K. WITH THAT S.A.S. REGIMENT THEY STARTED UP LAST YEAR...
SIR, YOU CAN'T BE THINKING... I MEAN... HE'S WHAT, SIXTEEN?
WE BOTH KNOW HE'S NOT THE ONLY SIXTEEN-YEAR-OLD IN THE ARMY, ROGERS.

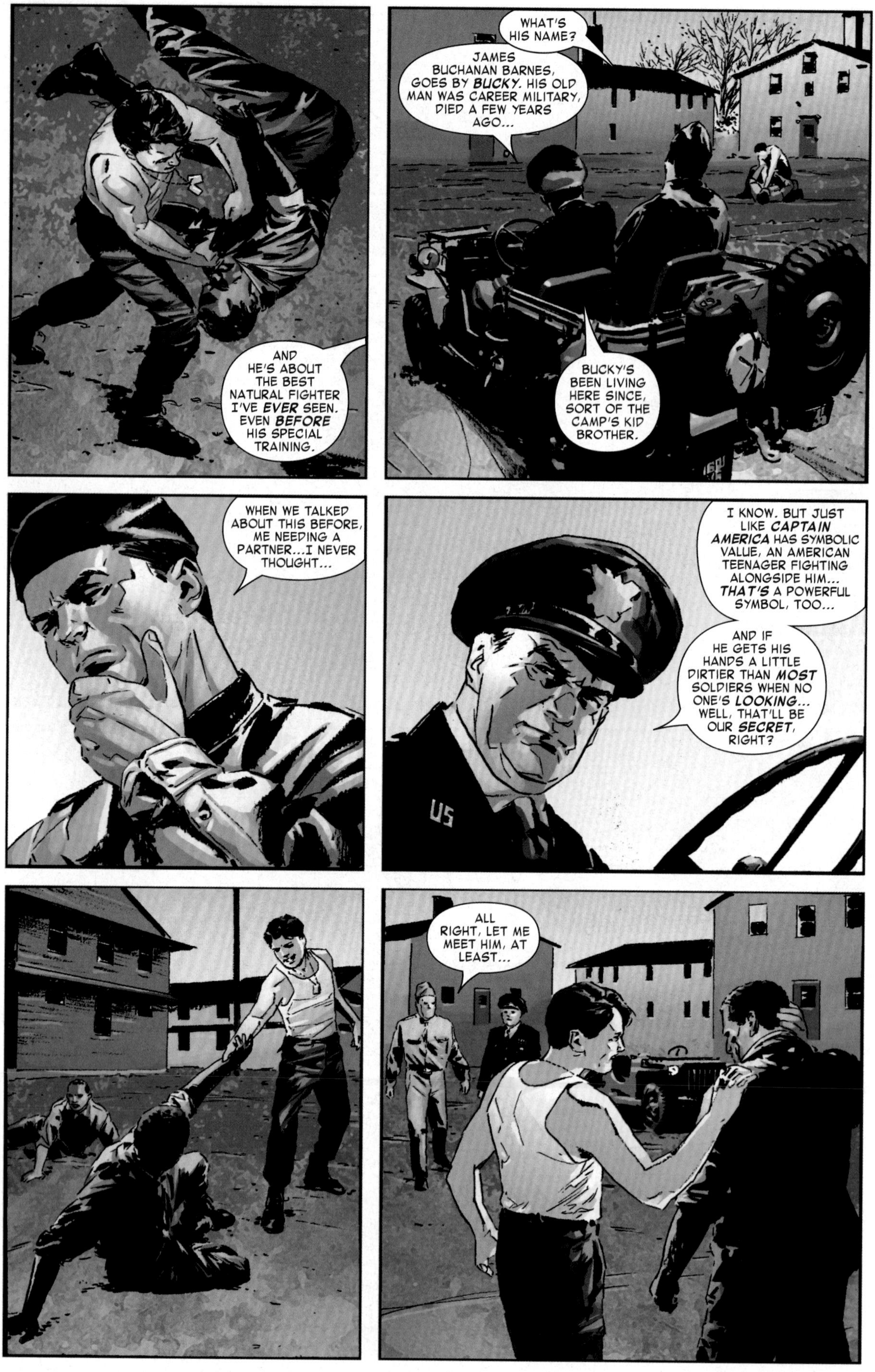
AND HE'S ABOUT THE BEST NATURAL FIGHTER I'VE EVER SEEN. EVEN BEFORE HIS SPECIAL TRAINING.
WHAT'S HIS NAME?
JAMES BUCHANAN BARNES, GOES BY BUCKY. HIS OLD MAN WAS CAREER MILITARY, DIED A FEW YEARS AGO...
BUCKY'S BEEN LIVING HERE SINCE, SORT OF THE CAMP'S KID BROTHER.
WHEN WE TALKED ABOUT THIS BEFORE, ME NEEDING A PARTNER...I NEVER THOUGHT...
I KNOW. BUT JUST LIKE CAPTAIN AMERICA HAS SYMBOLIC VALUE, AN AMERICAN TEENAGER FIGHTING ALONGSIDE HIM... THAT'S A POWERFUL SYMBOL, TOO...
AND IF HE GETS HIS HANDS A LITTLE DIRTIER THAN MOST SOLDIERS WHEN NO ONE'S LOOKING... WELL, THAT'LL BE OUR SECRET, RIGHT?
ALL RIGHT, LET ME MEET HIM, AT LEAST...

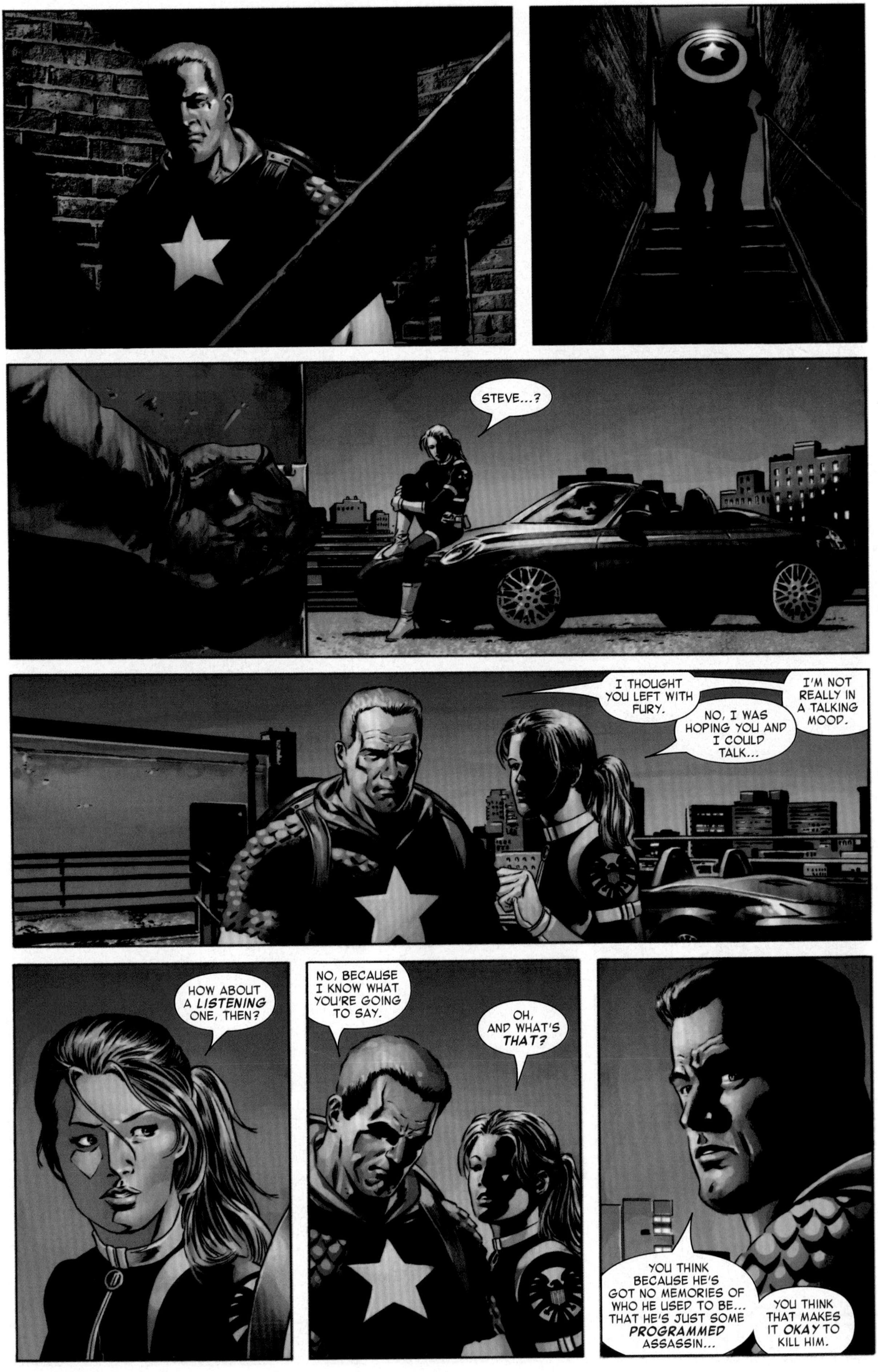
STEVE...?
I THOUGHT YOU LEFT WITH FURY.
NO, I WAS HOPING YOU AND I COULD TALK...
I'M NOT REALLY IN A TALKING MOOD.
HOW ABOUT A *LISTENING* ONE, THEN?
NO, BECAUSE I KNOW WHAT YOU'RE GOING TO SAY.
OH, AND WHAT'S *THAT?*
YOU THINK BECAUSE HE'S GOT NO MEMORIES OF WHO HE USED TO BE... THAT HE'S JUST SOME *PROGRAMMED* ASSASSIN...
YOU THINK THAT MAKES IT *OKAY* TO KILL HIM.

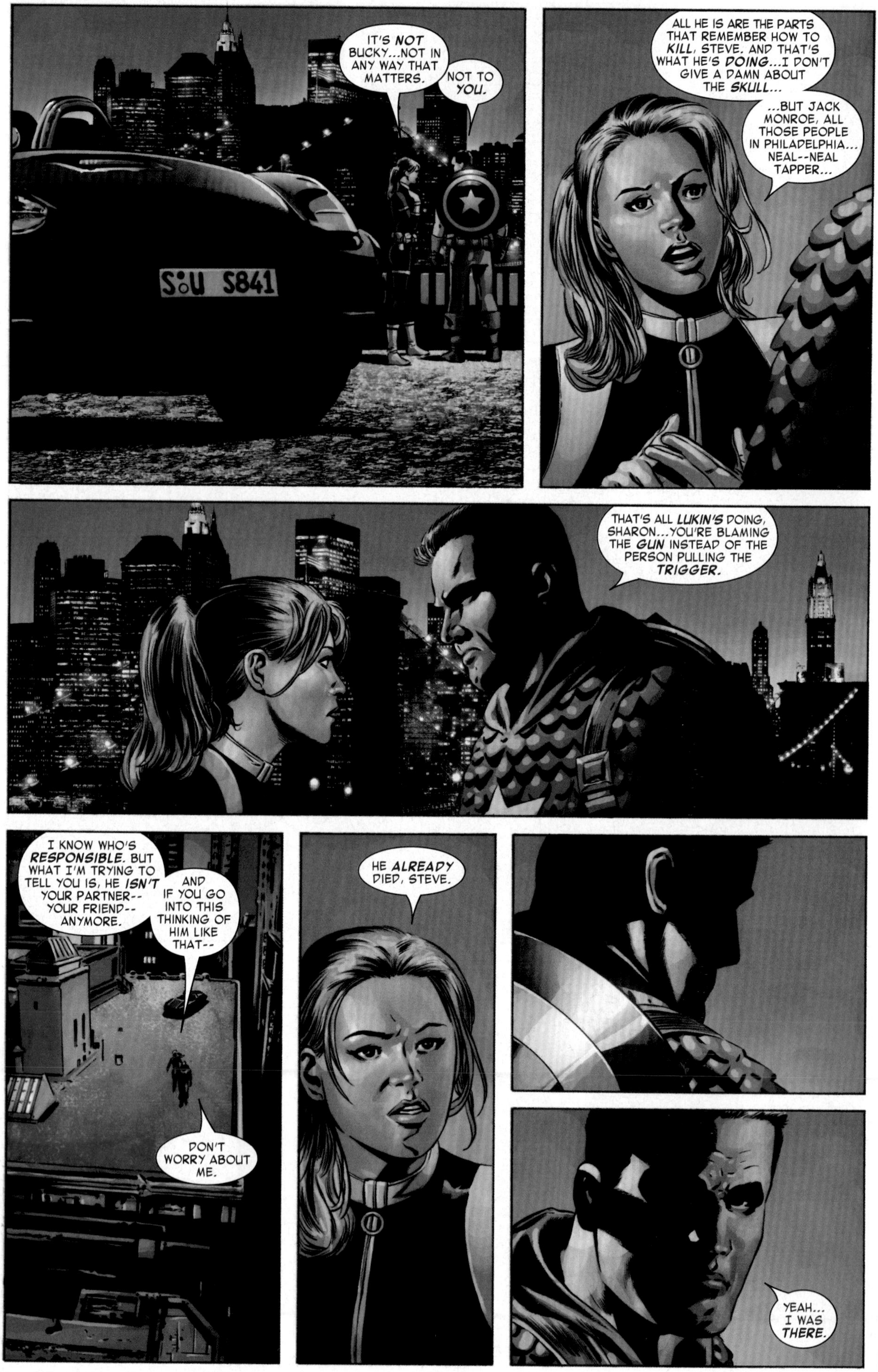
IT'S NOT BUCKY...NOT IN ANY WAY THAT MATTERS.
NOT TO YOU.
S◦U S841
ALL HE IS ARE THE PARTS THAT REMEMBER HOW TO KILL, STEVE. AND THAT'S WHAT HE'S DOING...I DON'T GIVE A DAMN ABOUT THE SKULL...
...BUT JACK MONROE, ALL THOSE PEOPLE IN PHILADELPHIA... NEAL--NEAL TAPPER...
THAT'S ALL LUKIN'S DOING, SHARON...YOU'RE BLAMING THE GUN INSTEAD OF THE PERSON PULLING THE TRIGGER.
I KNOW WHO'S RESPONSIBLE. BUT WHAT I'M TRYING TO TELL YOU IS, HE ISN'T YOUR PARTNER-- YOUR FRIEND-- ANYMORE.
AND IF YOU GO INTO THIS THINKING OF HIM LIKE THAT--
DON'T WORRY ABOUT ME.
HE ALREADY DIED, STEVE.
YEAH... I WAS THERE.

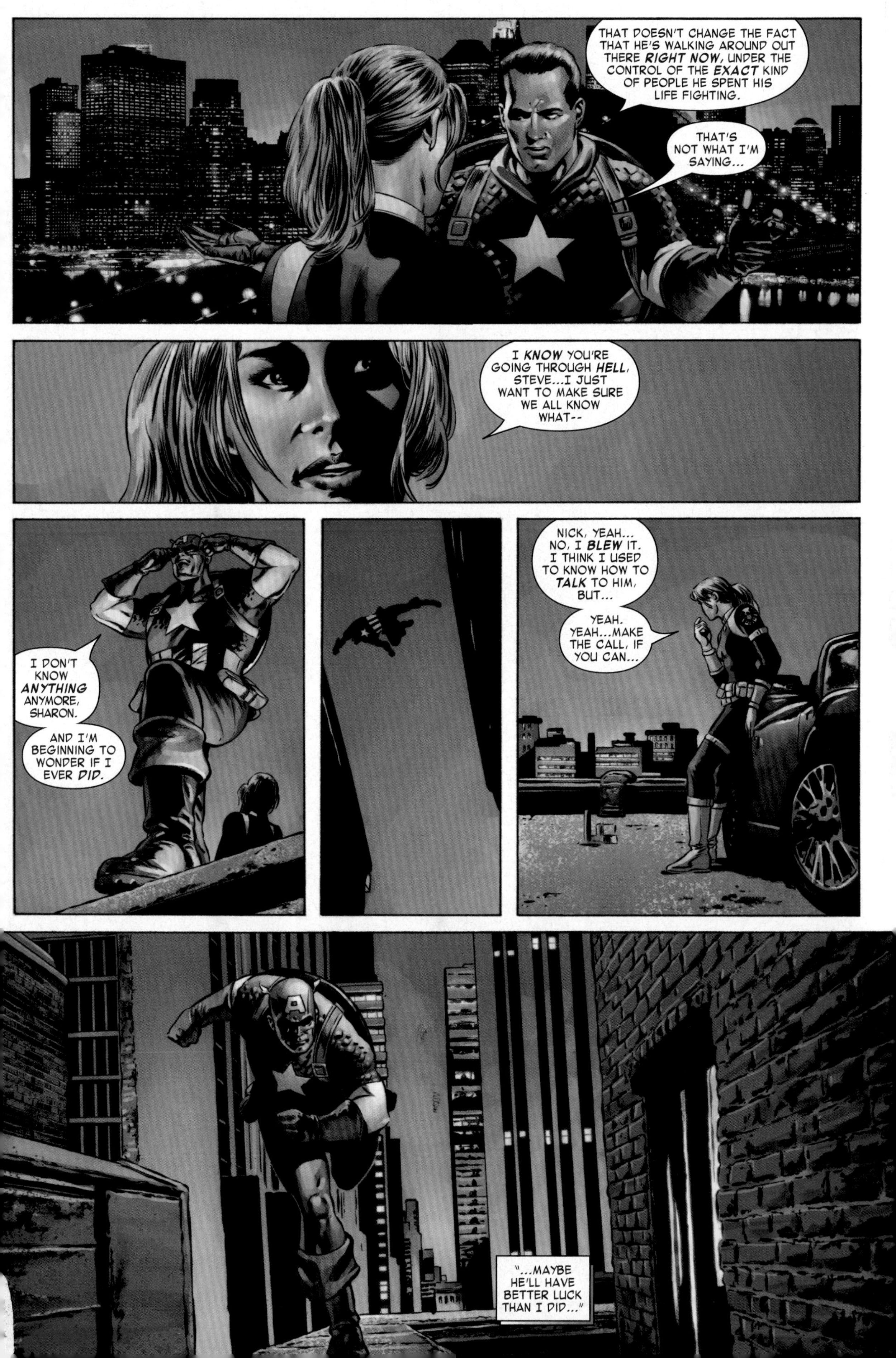
THAT DOESN'T CHANGE THE FACT THAT HE'S WALKING AROUND OUT THERE RIGHT NOW, UNDER THE CONTROL OF THE EXACT KIND OF PEOPLE HE SPENT HIS LIFE FIGHTING.
THAT'S NOT WHAT I'M SAYING...
I KNOW YOU'RE GOING THROUGH HELL, STEVE...I JUST WANT TO MAKE SURE WE ALL KNOW WHAT--
I DON'T KNOW ANYTHING ANYMORE, SHARON.
AND I'M BEGINNING TO WONDER IF I EVER DID.
NICK, YEAH... NO, I BLEW IT. I THINK I USED TO KNOW HOW TO TALK TO HIM, BUT...
YEAH. YEAH...MAKE THE CALL, IF YOU CAN...
"...MAYBE HE'LL HAVE BETTER LUCK THAN I DID..."

ONE HUNDRED AND TWENTY BILLION!

MATCHED! AND A THIRTY PERCENT SHARE IN STOCK OPTIONS!

ONE HUNDRED FIFTY!

WAIT! WAIT A DAMN SECOND!

JUST *HOLD ON*, LUKIN...YOU'RE *ENJOYING* THIS, SEEING US FALL ALL OVER OURSELVES...

BUT HOW DO WE EVEN KNOW THAT REALLY *IS* THE COSMIC CUBE?

YOU'RE PHILIP HOCKNEY, RIGHT? FROM CHEMAXONE?

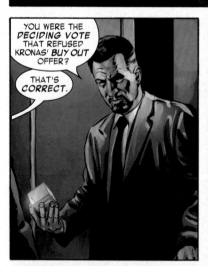

YOU WERE THE *DECIDING VOTE* THAT REFUSED KRONAS' *BUY OUT* OFFER?

THAT'S *CORRECT*.

AND NOW YOU'D LIKE SOME KIND OF DEMONSTRATION THAT THIS REALLY IS WHAT I SAY IT IS?

I THINK WE'RE ALL OWED AT LEAST THAT, DON'T YOU?

WELL, YOU'D THINK THE FACT THAT YOU ARE ALL *HERE*, AT A SECRET MEETING TOGETHER, WOULD BE PROOF ENOUGH...

SINCE THERE'S *NEVER* BEEN A TIME WHEN YOU TRAVELED WITHOUT YOUR *SECURITY*...

AND I CAN ASSURE YOU IT WAS THE CUBE THAT MADE THAT SEEM LIKE A *WISE* IDEA...WHICH IT *WASN'T*.

BUT STILL, PERHAPS A MORE *CONCRETE* DEMONSTRATION *IS* IN ORDER...

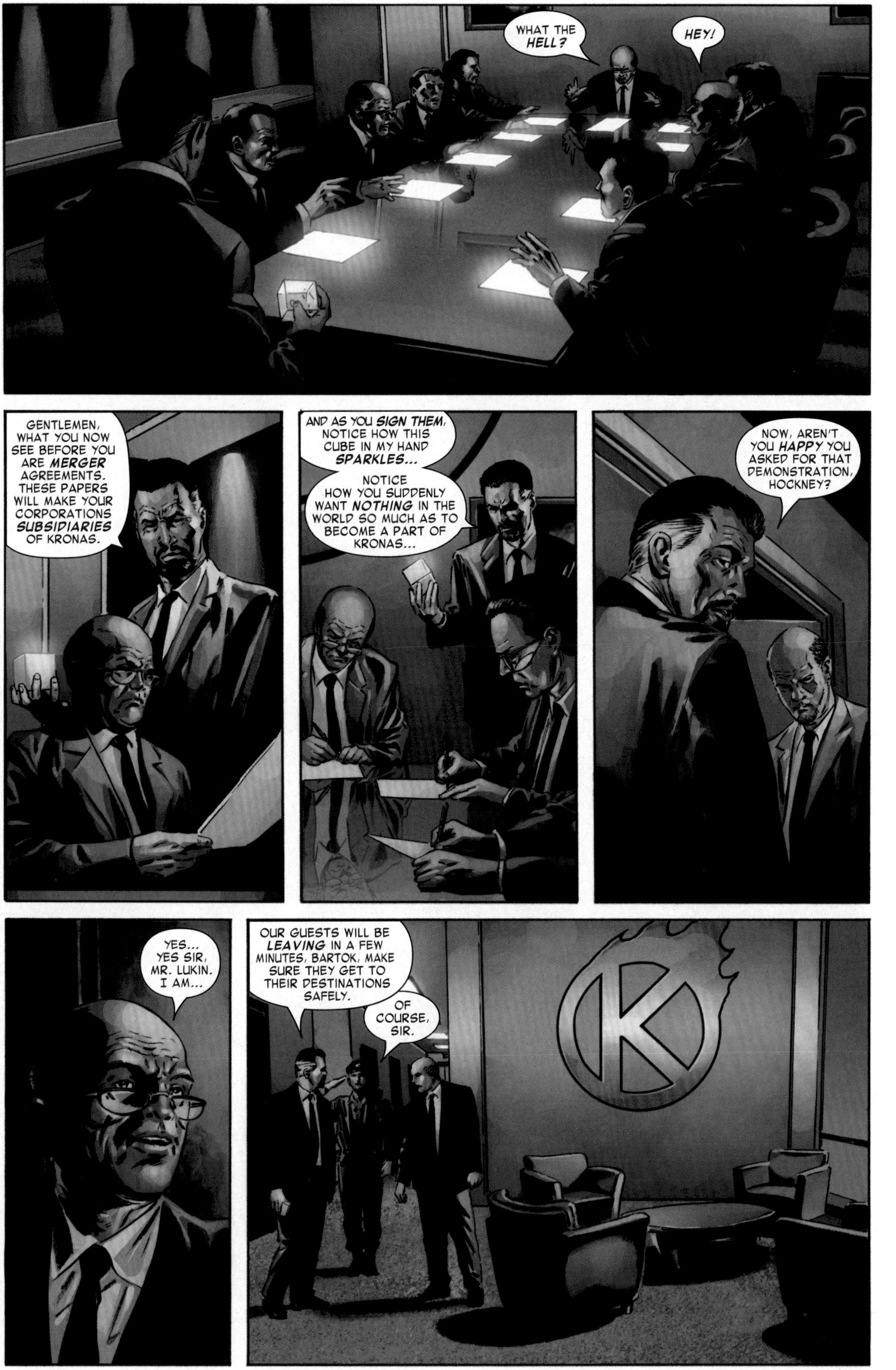
WHAT THE HELL?
HEY!
GENTLEMEN, WHAT YOU NOW SEE BEFORE YOU ARE MERGER AGREEMENTS. THESE PAPERS WILL MAKE YOUR CORPORATIONS SUBSIDIARIES OF KRONAS.
AND AS YOU SIGN THEM, NOTICE HOW THIS CUBE IN MY HAND SPARKLES...
NOTICE HOW YOU SUDDENLY WANT NOTHING IN THE WORLD SO MUCH AS TO BECOME A PART OF KRONAS...
NOW, AREN'T YOU HAPPY YOU ASKED FOR THAT DEMONSTRATION, HOCKNEY?
YES... YES SIR, MR. LUKIN. I AM...
OUR GUESTS WILL BE LEAVING IN A FEW MINUTES, BARTOK, MAKE SURE THEY GET TO THEIR DESTINATIONS SAFELY.
OF COURSE, SIR.

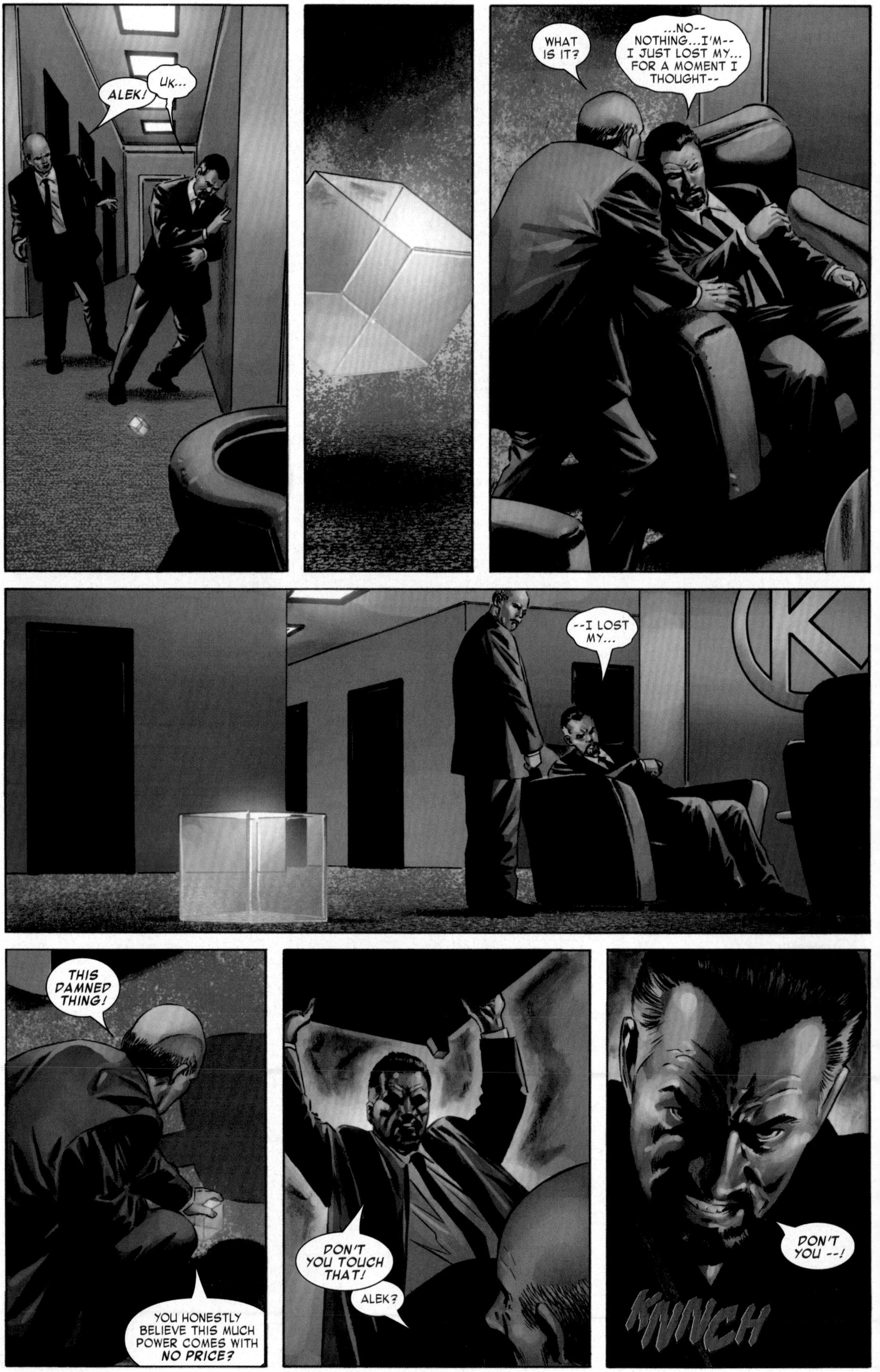
ALEK!
UK...
WHAT IS IT?
...NO-- NOTHING...I'M-- I JUST LOST MY... FOR A MOMENT I THOUGHT--
--I LOST MY...
THIS DAMNED THING!
YOU HONESTLY BELIEVE THIS MUCH POWER COMES WITH NO PRICE?
DON'T YOU TOUCH THAT!
ALEK?
DON'T YOU --!
KNNCH

DAMN IT.

THIS IS NO WAY TO FUNCTION... WORK THROUGH IT, STEVE.

ANGER WILL NOT HELP YOU DEAL WITH THIS.

IT'LL JUST MAKE SURE THAT *WHATEVER* YOU DO NEXT IS THE WRONG MOVE.

AND YOU CAN'T AFFORD THAT.

YOU'VE LET LUKIN PUSH ALL YOUR BUTTONS TOO EASILY SO FAR... YOU CAN'T AFFORD ANYTHING BUT A CLEAR HEAD FROM THIS POINT ON...

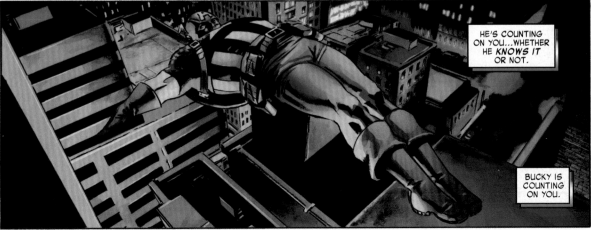

HE'S COUNTING ON YOU...WHETHER HE *KNOWS IT* OR NOT.

BUCKY IS COUNTING ON YOU.

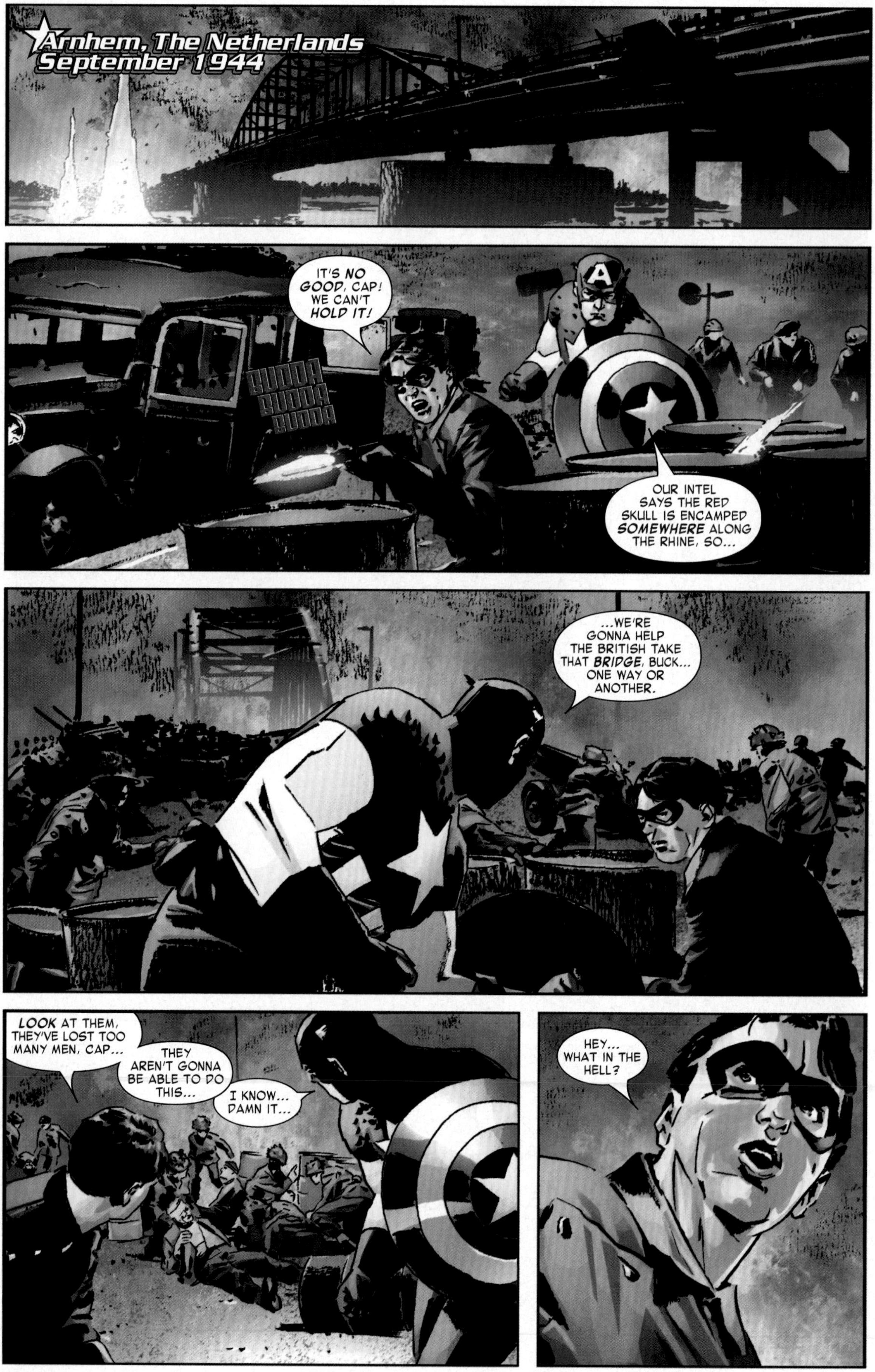
Arnhem, The Netherlands
September 1944
IT'S NO GOOD, CAP! WE CAN'T HOLD IT!
BUDDA BUDDA BUDDA
OUR INTEL SAYS THE RED SKULL IS ENCAMPED SOMEWHERE ALONG THE RHINE, SO...
...WE'RE GONNA HELP THE BRITISH TAKE THAT BRIDGE, BUCK... ONE WAY OR ANOTHER.
LOOK AT THEM, THEY'VE LOST TOO MANY MEN, CAP...
THEY AREN'T GONNA BE ABLE TO DO THIS...
I KNOW... DAMN IT...
HEY... WHAT IN THE HELL?

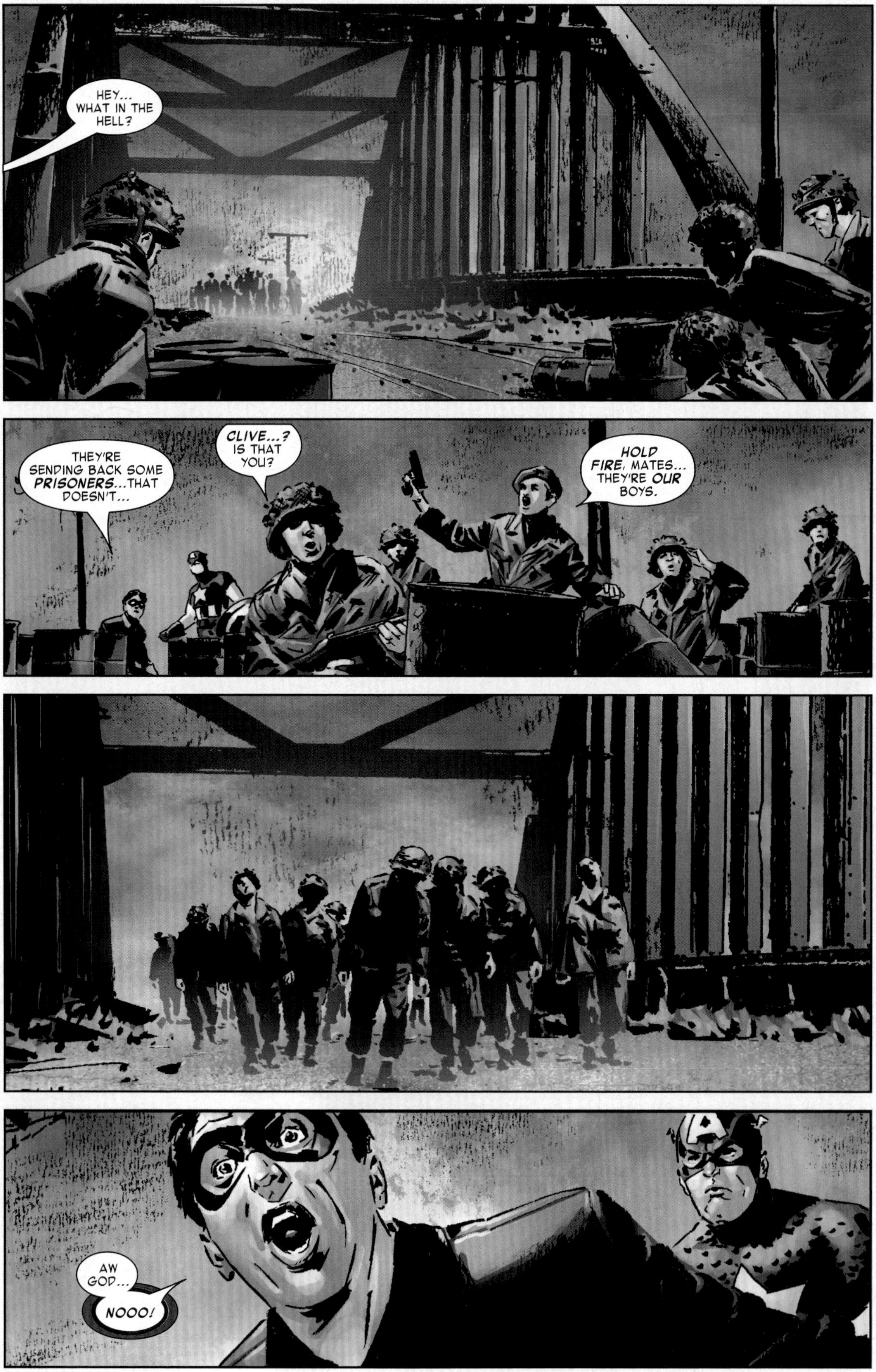
HEY... WHAT IN THE HELL?
THEY'RE SENDING BACK SOME PRISONERS...THAT DOESN'T...
CLIVE...? IS THAT YOU?
HOLD FIRE, MATES... THEY'RE OUR BOYS.
AW GOD...
NOOO!

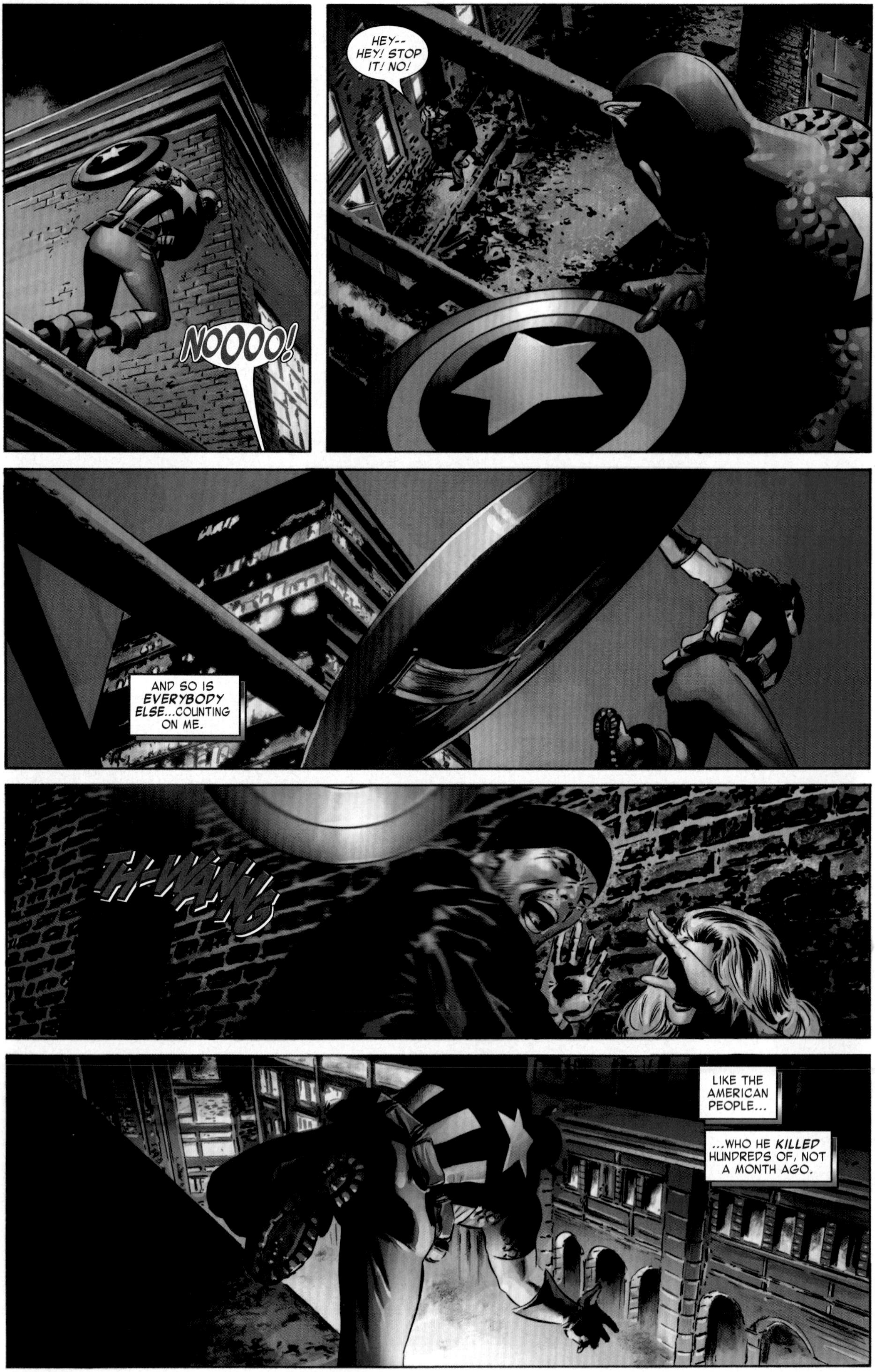
NOOOO!
HEY-- HEY! STOP IT! NO!
AND SO IS EVERYBODY ELSE...COUNTING ON ME.
TH-WANG
LIKE THE AMERICAN PEOPLE...
...WHO HE KILLED HUNDREDS OF, NOT A MONTH AGO.

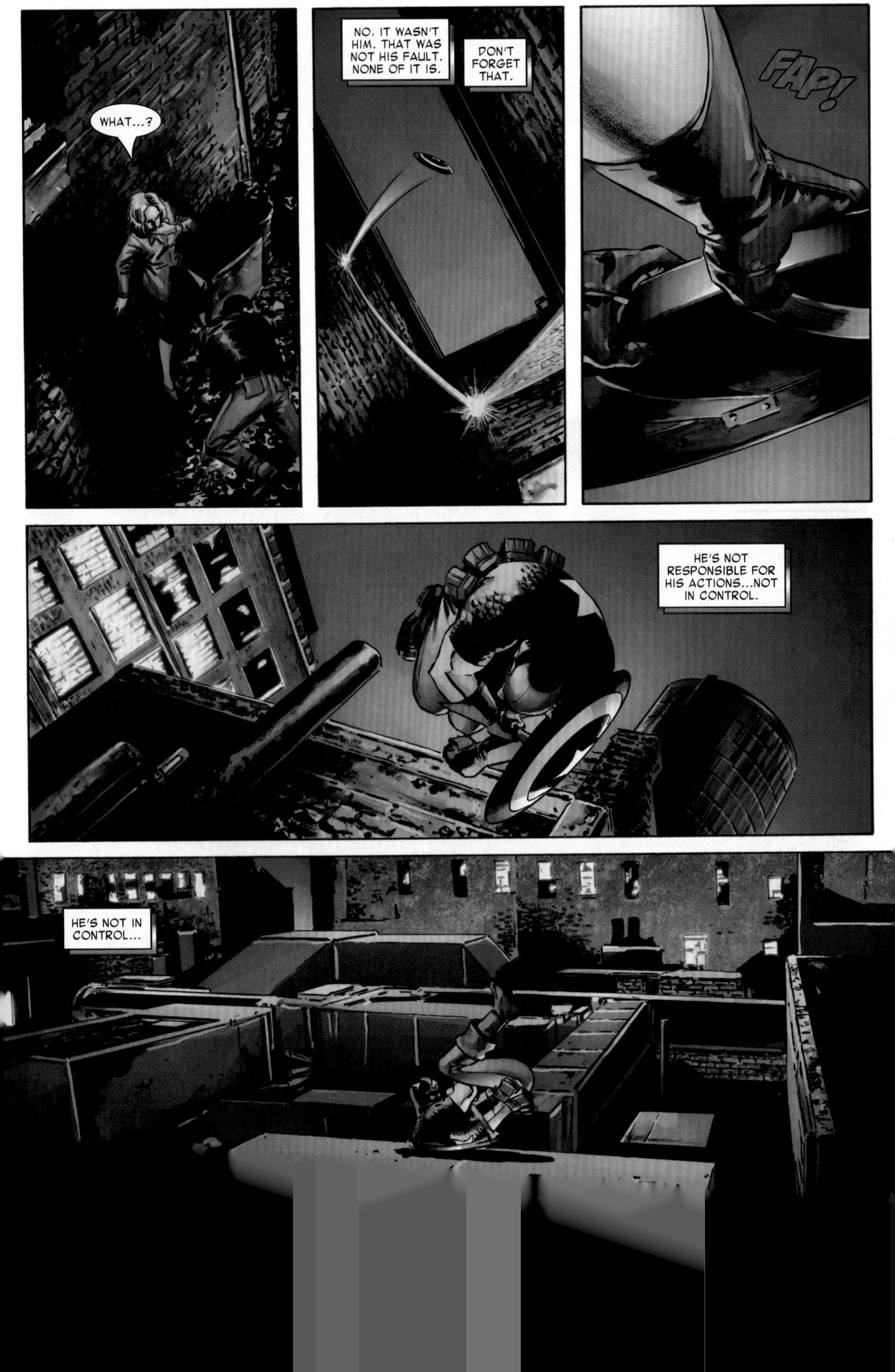
WHAT...?
NO, IT WASN'T HIM. THAT WAS NOT HIS FAULT. NONE OF IT IS.
DON'T FORGET THAT.
FAP!
HE'S NOT RESPONSIBLE FOR HIS ACTIONS...NOT IN CONTROL.
HE'S NOT IN CONTROL...

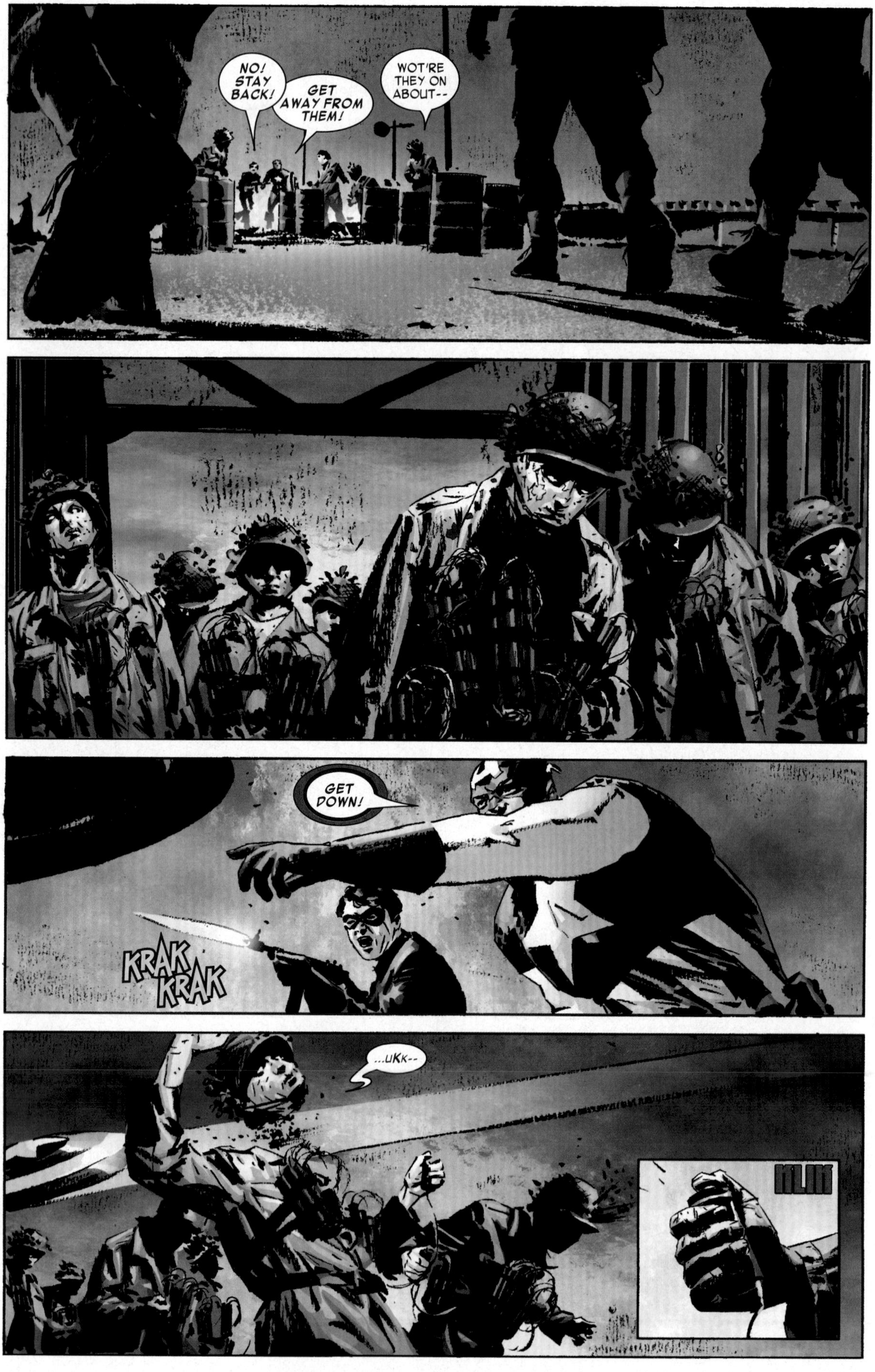
NO! STAY BACK!
GET AWAY FROM THEM!
WOT'RE THEY ON ABOUT--
GET DOWN!
KRAK KRAK
...UKK--
KLIK

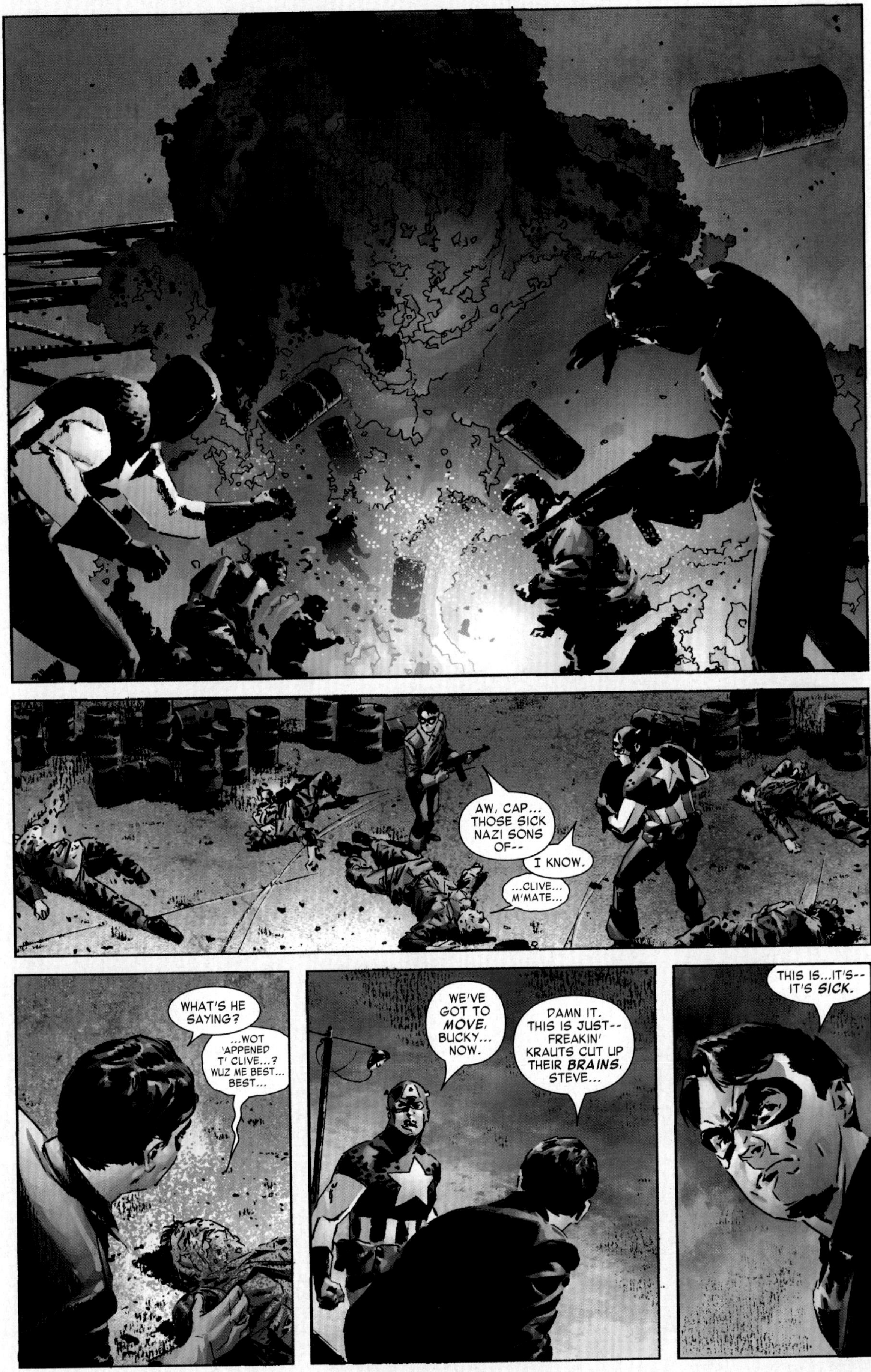
AW, CAP... THOSE SICK NAZI SONS OF--
I KNOW.
...CLIVE... M'MATE...
WHAT'S HE SAYING?
...WOT 'APPENED T' CLIVE...? WUZ ME BEST... BEST...
WE'VE GOT TO MOVE, BUCKY... NOW.
DAMN IT. THIS IS JUST-- FREAKIN' KRAUTS CUT UP THEIR BRAINS, STEVE...
THIS IS...IT'S-- IT'S SICK.

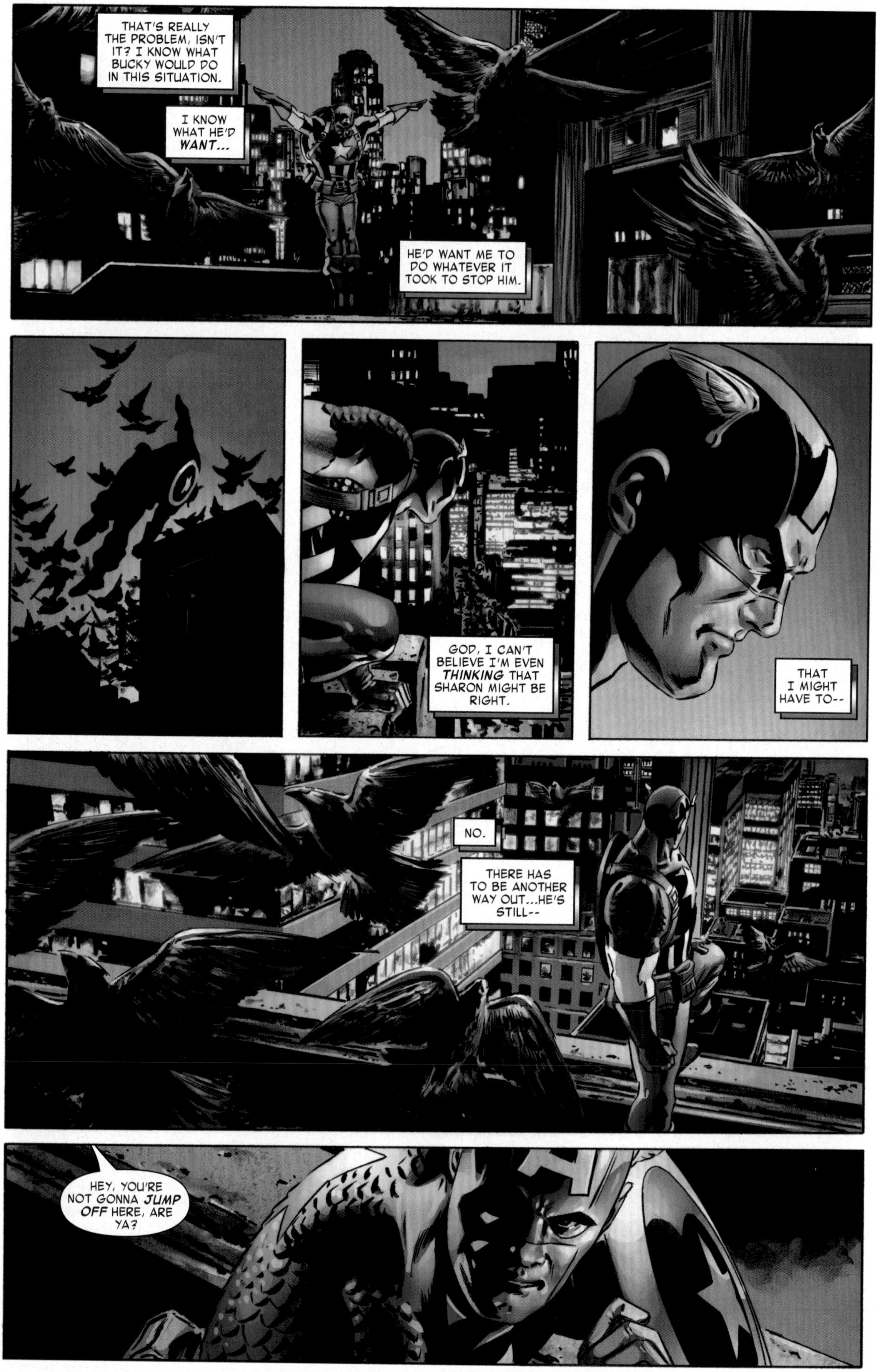
THAT'S REALLY THE PROBLEM, ISN'T IT? I KNOW WHAT BUCKY WOULD DO IN THIS SITUATION.
I KNOW WHAT HE'D *WANT...*
HE'D WANT ME TO DO WHATEVER IT TOOK TO STOP HIM.
GOD, I CAN'T BELIEVE I'M EVEN *THINKING* THAT SHARON MIGHT BE RIGHT.
THAT I MIGHT HAVE TO--
NO.
THERE HAS TO BE ANOTHER WAY OUT...HE'S STILL--
HEY, YOU'RE NOT GONNA *JUMP OFF* HERE, ARE YA?

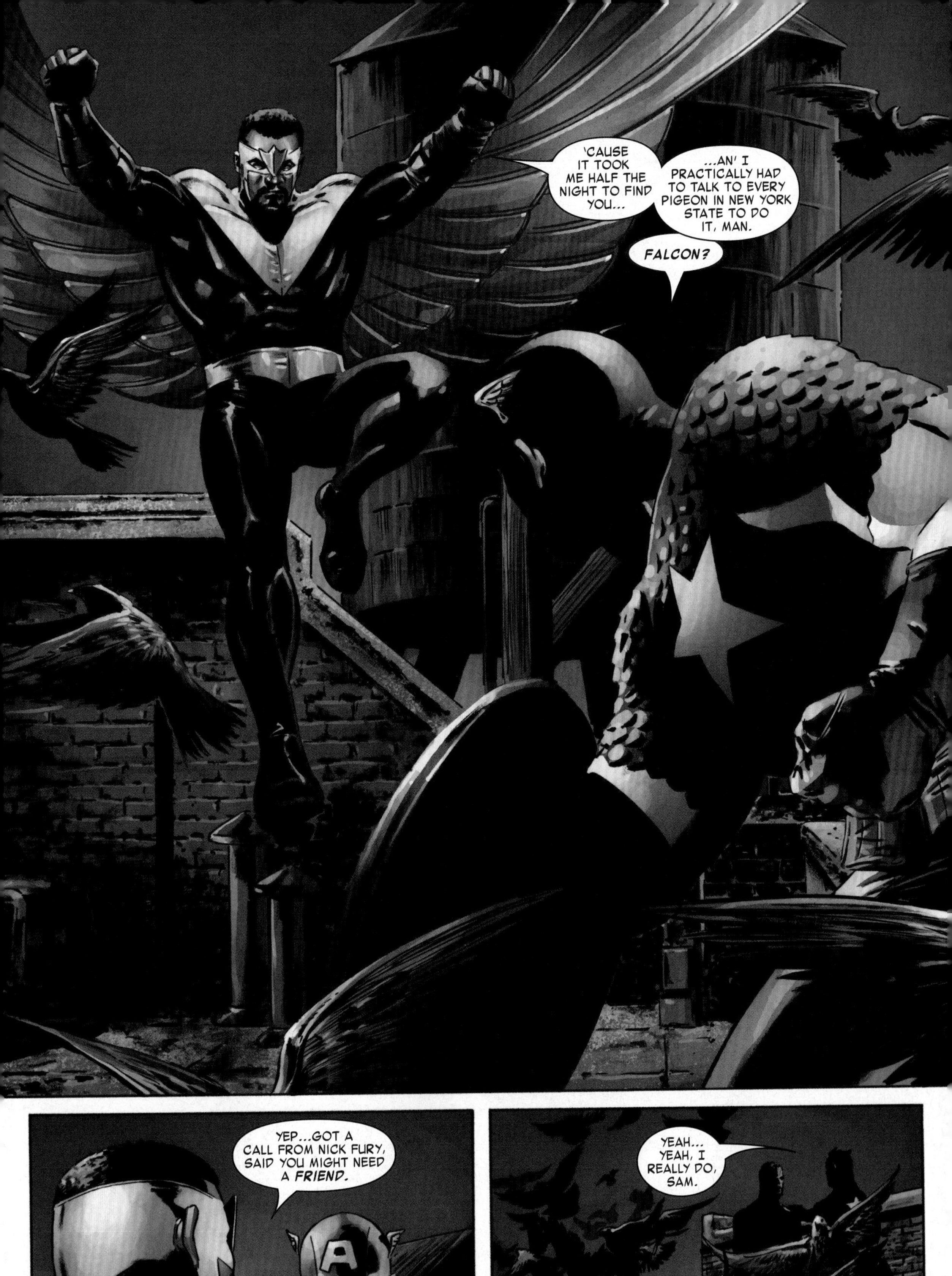
'CAUSE IT TOOK ME HALF THE NIGHT TO FIND YOU...
...AN' I PRACTICALLY HAD TO TALK TO EVERY PIGEON IN NEW YORK STATE TO DO IT, MAN.
FALCON?

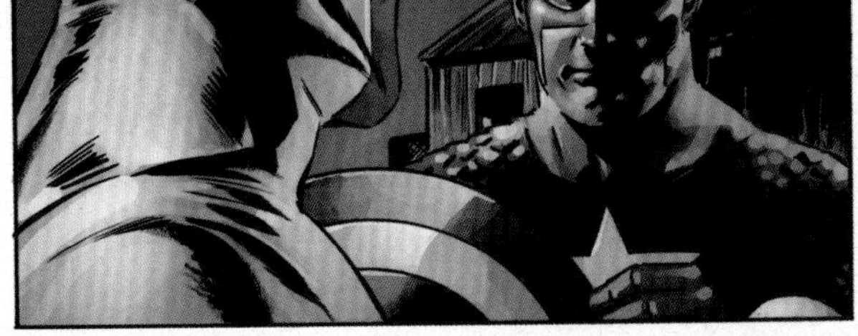
YEP...GOT A CALL FROM NICK FURY, SAID YOU MIGHT NEED A FRIEND.

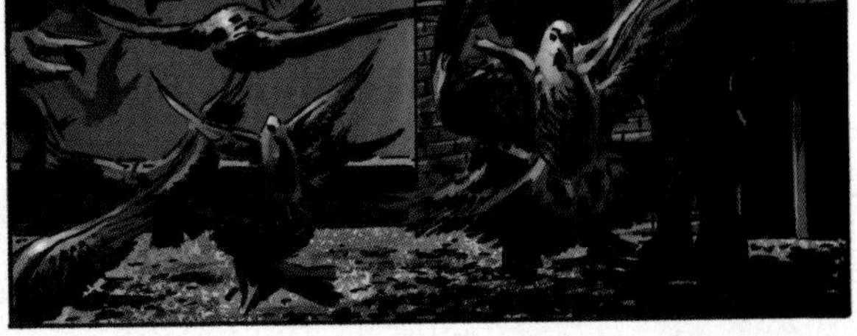
YEAH... YEAH, I REALLY DO, SAM.

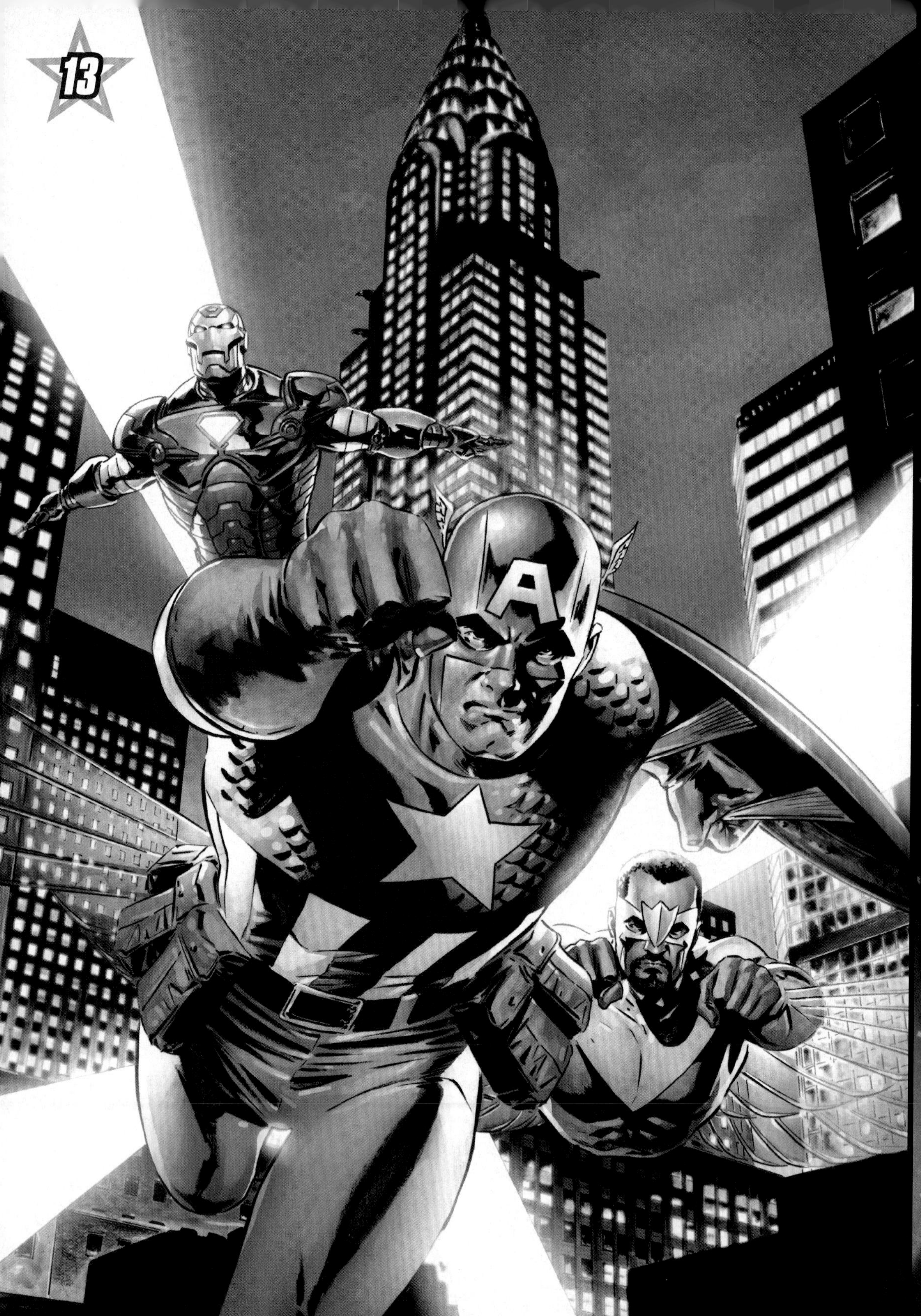
13

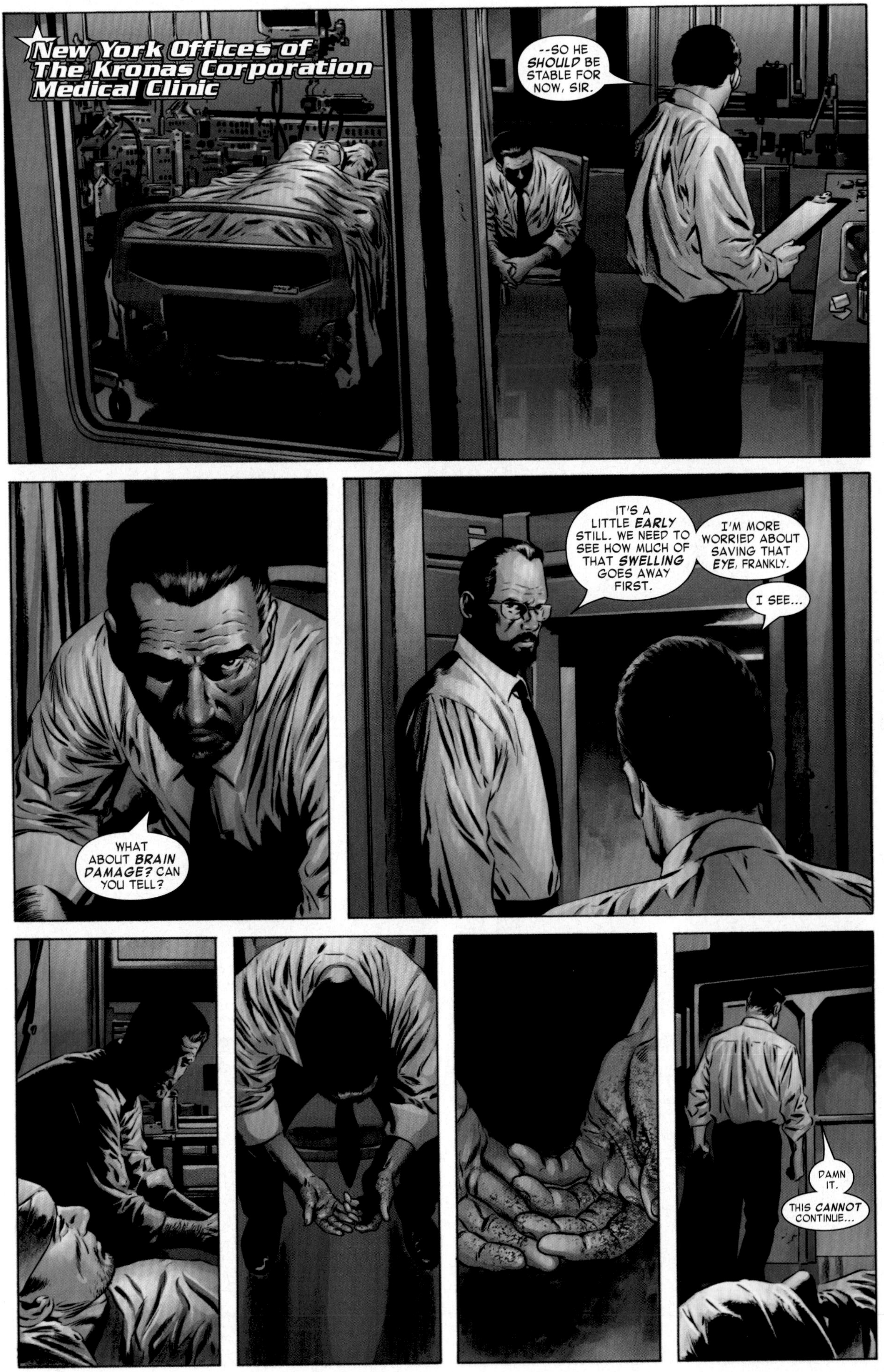
New York Offices of The Kronas Corporation Medical Clinic
--SO HE SHOULD BE STABLE FOR NOW, SIR.
WHAT ABOUT BRAIN DAMAGE? CAN YOU TELL?
IT'S A LITTLE EARLY STILL. WE NEED TO SEE HOW MUCH OF THAT SWELLING GOES AWAY FIRST.
I'M MORE WORRIED ABOUT SAVING THAT EYE, FRANKLY.
I SEE...
DAMN IT.
THIS CANNOT CONTINUE...

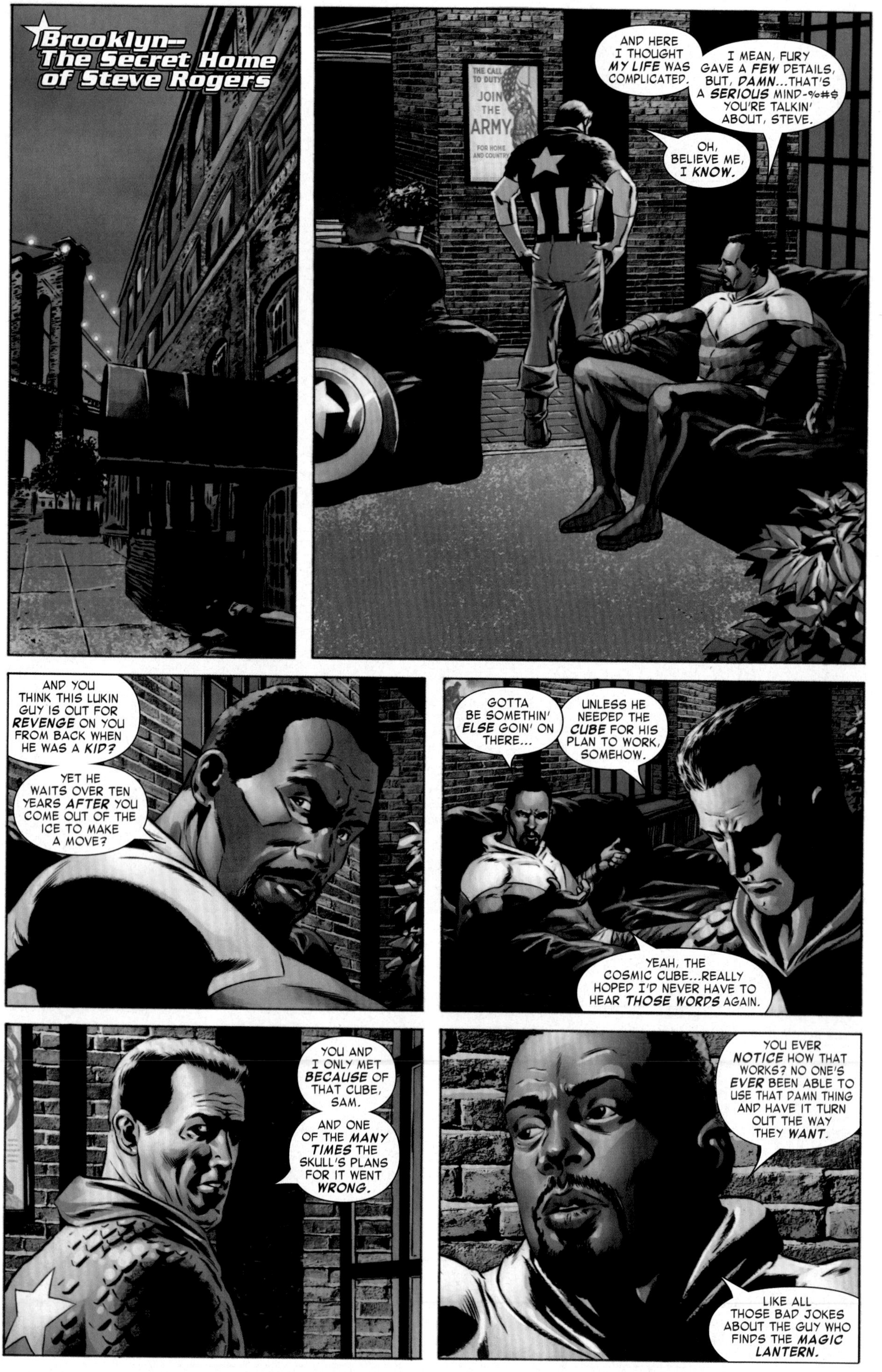
Brooklyn--The Secret Home of Steve Rogers
THE CALL TO DUTY! JOIN THE ARMY FOR HOME AND COUNTRY
AND HERE I THOUGHT MY LIFE WAS COMPLICATED.
I MEAN, FURY GAVE A FEW DETAILS, BUT, DAMN...THAT'S A SERIOUS MIND-%#$ YOU'RE TALKIN' ABOUT, STEVE.
OH, BELIEVE ME, I KNOW.
AND YOU THINK THIS LUKIN GUY IS OUT FOR REVENGE ON YOU FROM BACK WHEN HE WAS A KID?
YET HE WAITS OVER TEN YEARS AFTER YOU COME OUT OF THE ICE TO MAKE A MOVE?
GOTTA BE SOMETHIN' ELSE GOIN' ON THERE...
UNLESS HE NEEDED THE CUBE FOR HIS PLAN TO WORK, SOMEHOW.
YEAH, THE COSMIC CUBE...REALLY HOPED I'D NEVER HAVE TO HEAR THOSE WORDS AGAIN.
YOU AND I ONLY MET BECAUSE OF THAT CUBE, SAM.
AND ONE OF THE MANY TIMES THE SKULL'S PLANS FOR IT WENT WRONG.
YOU EVER NOTICE HOW THAT WORKS? NO ONE'S EVER BEEN ABLE TO USE THAT DAMN THING AND HAVE IT TURN OUT THE WAY THEY WANT.
LIKE ALL THOSE BAD JOKES ABOUT THE GUY WHO FINDS THE MAGIC LANTERN.

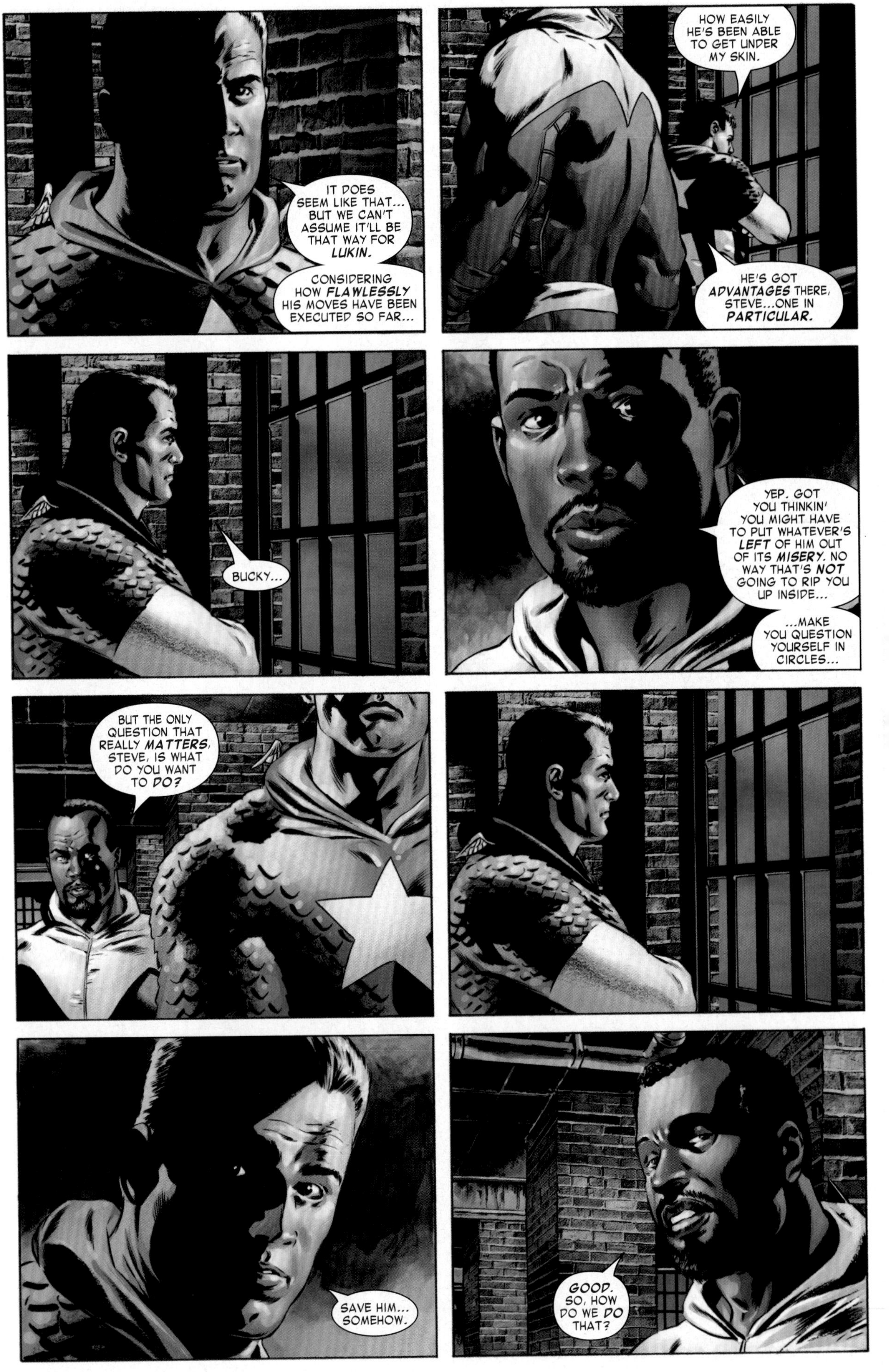
IT DOES SEEM LIKE THAT... BUT WE CAN'T ASSUME IT'LL BE THAT WAY FOR LUKIN.
CONSIDERING HOW FLAWLESSLY HIS MOVES HAVE BEEN EXECUTED SO FAR...
HOW EASILY HE'S BEEN ABLE TO GET UNDER MY SKIN.
HE'S GOT ADVANTAGES THERE, STEVE...ONE IN PARTICULAR.
BUCKY...
YEP. GOT YOU THINKIN' YOU MIGHT HAVE TO PUT WHATEVER'S LEFT OF HIM OUT OF ITS MISERY. NO WAY THAT'S NOT GOING TO RIP YOU UP INSIDE...
...MAKE YOU QUESTION YOURSELF IN CIRCLES...
BUT THE ONLY QUESTION THAT REALLY MATTERS, STEVE, IS WHAT DO YOU WANT TO DO?
SAVE HIM... SOMEHOW.
GOOD. SO, HOW DO WE DO THAT?

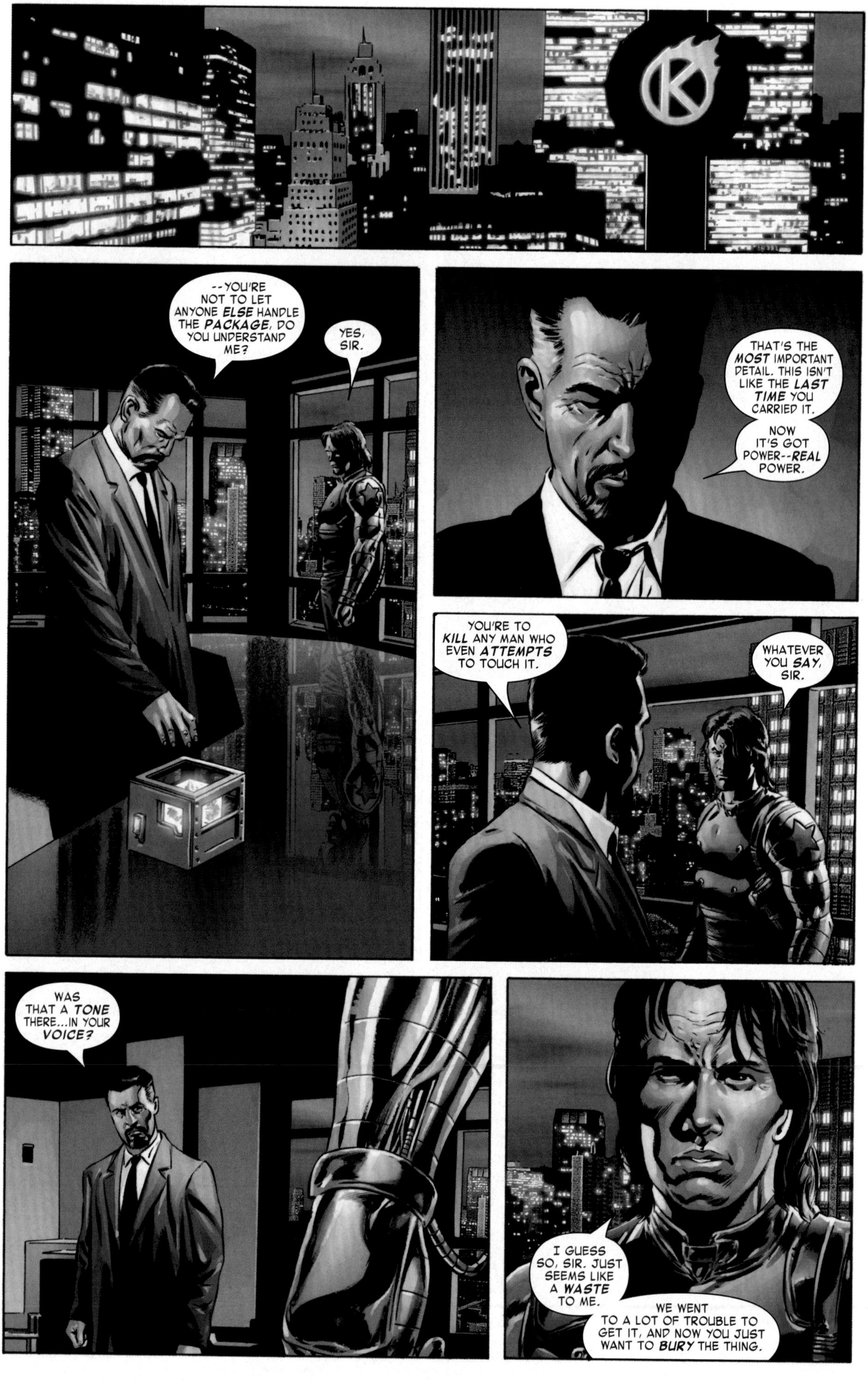
--YOU'RE NOT TO LET ANYONE ELSE HANDLE THE PACKAGE, DO YOU UNDERSTAND ME?
YES, SIR.
THAT'S THE MOST IMPORTANT DETAIL. THIS ISN'T LIKE THE LAST TIME YOU CARRIED IT.
NOW IT'S GOT POWER--REAL POWER.
YOU'RE TO KILL ANY MAN WHO EVEN ATTEMPTS TO TOUCH IT.
WHATEVER YOU SAY, SIR.
WAS THAT A TONE THERE...IN YOUR VOICE?
I GUESS SO, SIR. JUST SEEMS LIKE A WASTE TO ME.
WE WENT TO A LOT OF TROUBLE TO GET IT, AND NOW YOU JUST WANT TO BURY THE THING.

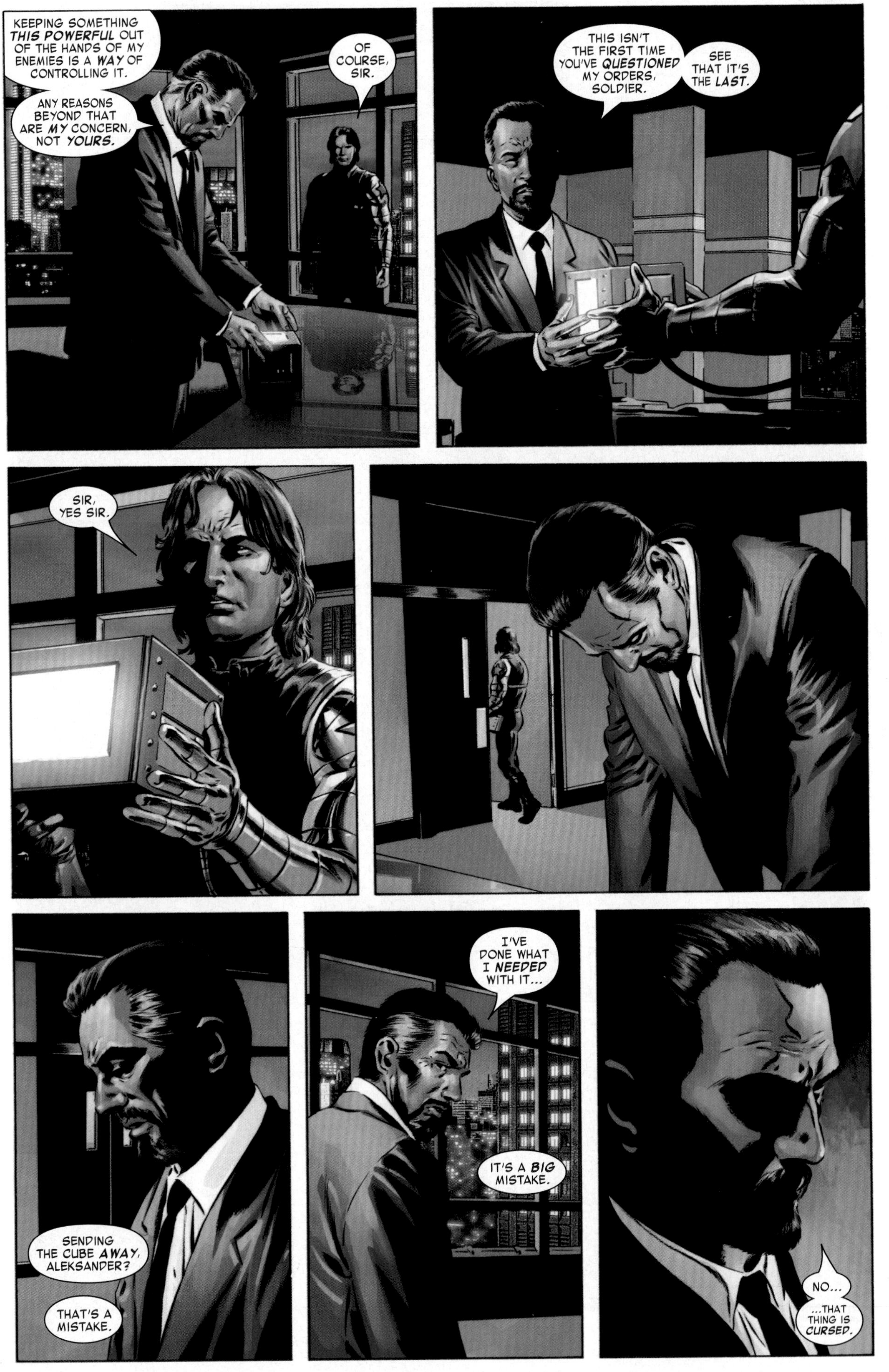

KEEPING SOMETHING THIS POWERFUL OUT OF THE HANDS OF MY ENEMIES IS A WAY OF CONTROLLING IT.
ANY REASONS BEYOND THAT ARE MY CONCERN, NOT YOURS.
OF COURSE, SIR.
THIS ISN'T THE FIRST TIME YOU'VE QUESTIONED MY ORDERS, SOLDIER.
SEE THAT IT'S THE LAST.
SIR, YES SIR.
SENDING THE CUBE AWAY, ALEKSANDER?
THAT'S A MISTAKE.
I'VE DONE WHAT I NEEDED WITH IT...
IT'S A BIG MISTAKE.
NO...
...THAT THING IS CURSED.

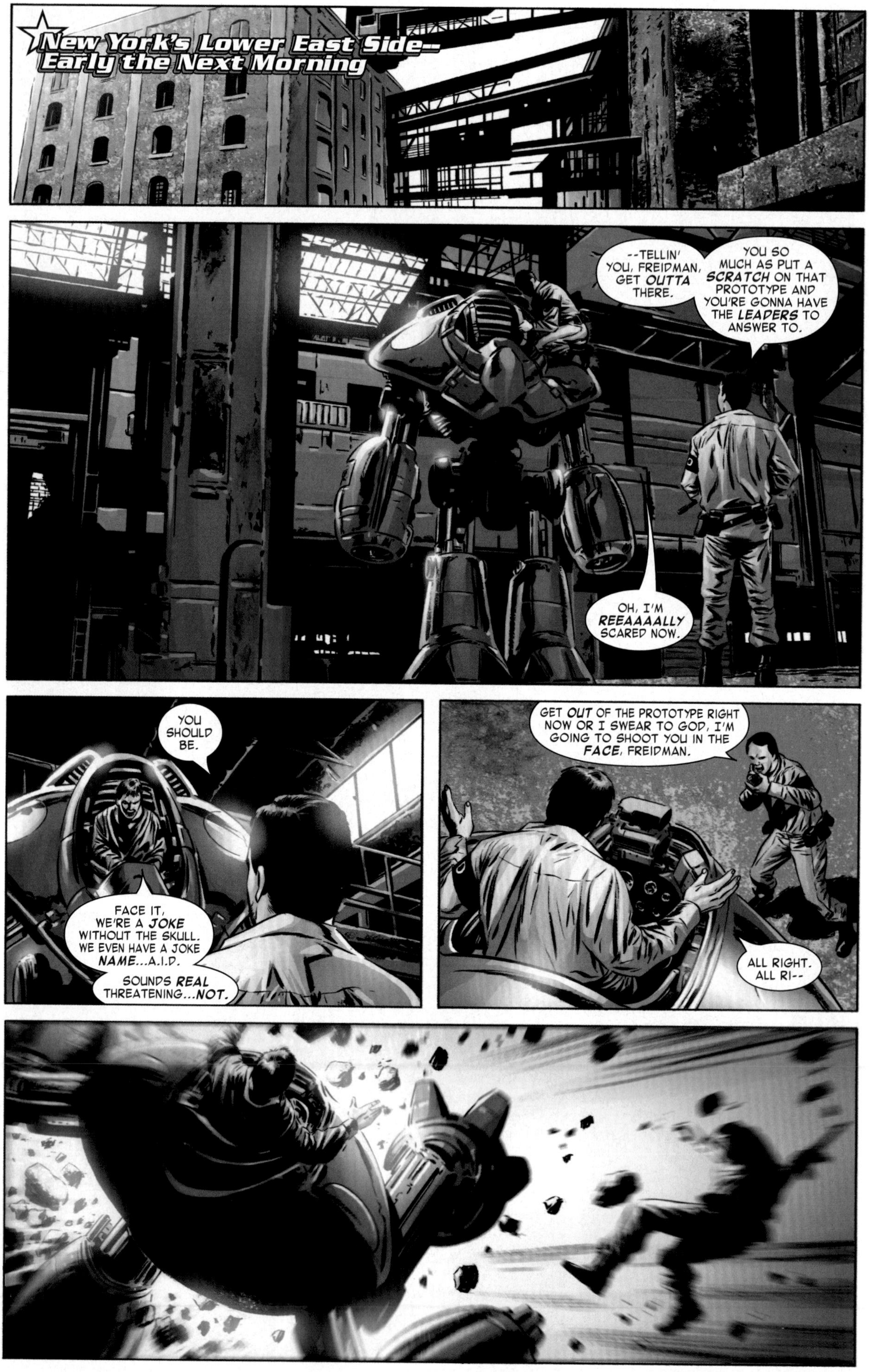
New York's Lower East Side--
Early the Next Morning
--TELLIN' YOU, FREIDMAN, GET OUTTA THERE.
YOU SO MUCH AS PUT A SCRATCH ON THAT PROTOTYPE AND YOU'RE GONNA HAVE THE LEADERS TO ANSWER TO.
OH, I'M REEAAAALLY SCARED NOW.
YOU SHOULD BE.
FACE IT, WE'RE A JOKE WITHOUT THE SKULL. WE EVEN HAVE A JOKE NAME...A.I.D.
SOUNDS REAL THREATENING...NOT.
GET OUT OF THE PROTOTYPE RIGHT NOW OR I SWEAR TO GOD, I'M GOING TO SHOOT YOU IN THE FACE, FREIDMAN.
ALL RIGHT. ALL RI--

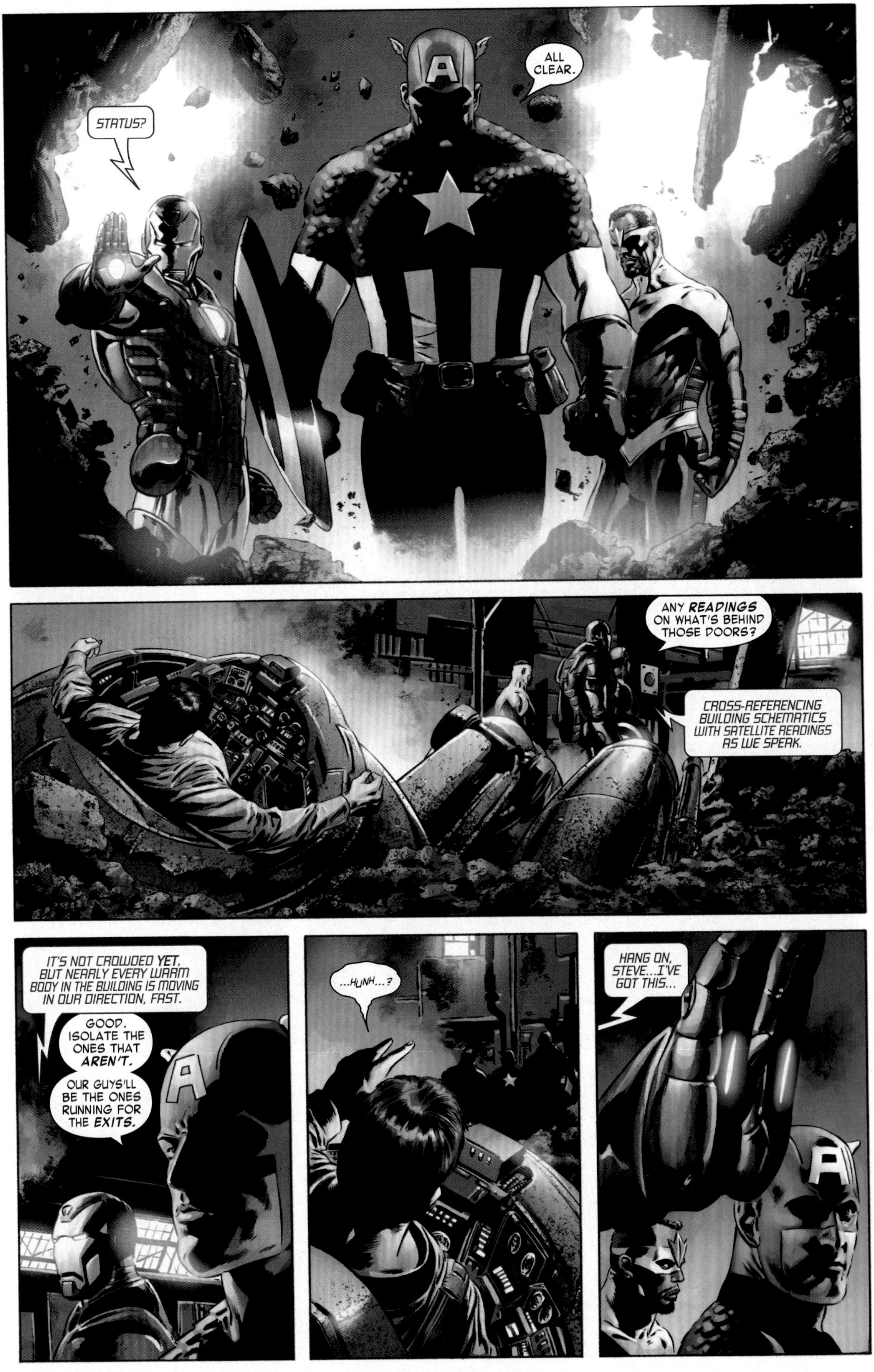
STATUS?
ALL CLEAR.
ANY READINGS ON WHAT'S BEHIND THOSE DOORS?
CROSS-REFERENCING BUILDING SCHEMATICS WITH SATELLITE READINGS AS WE SPEAK.
IT'S NOT CROWDED YET, BUT NEARLY EVERY WARM BODY IN THE BUILDING IS MOVING IN OUR DIRECTION, FAST.
GOOD. ISOLATE THE ONES THAT AREN'T.
OUR GUYS'LL BE THE ONES RUNNING FOR THE EXITS.
...HUNH...?
HANG ON, STEVE...I'VE GOT THIS...

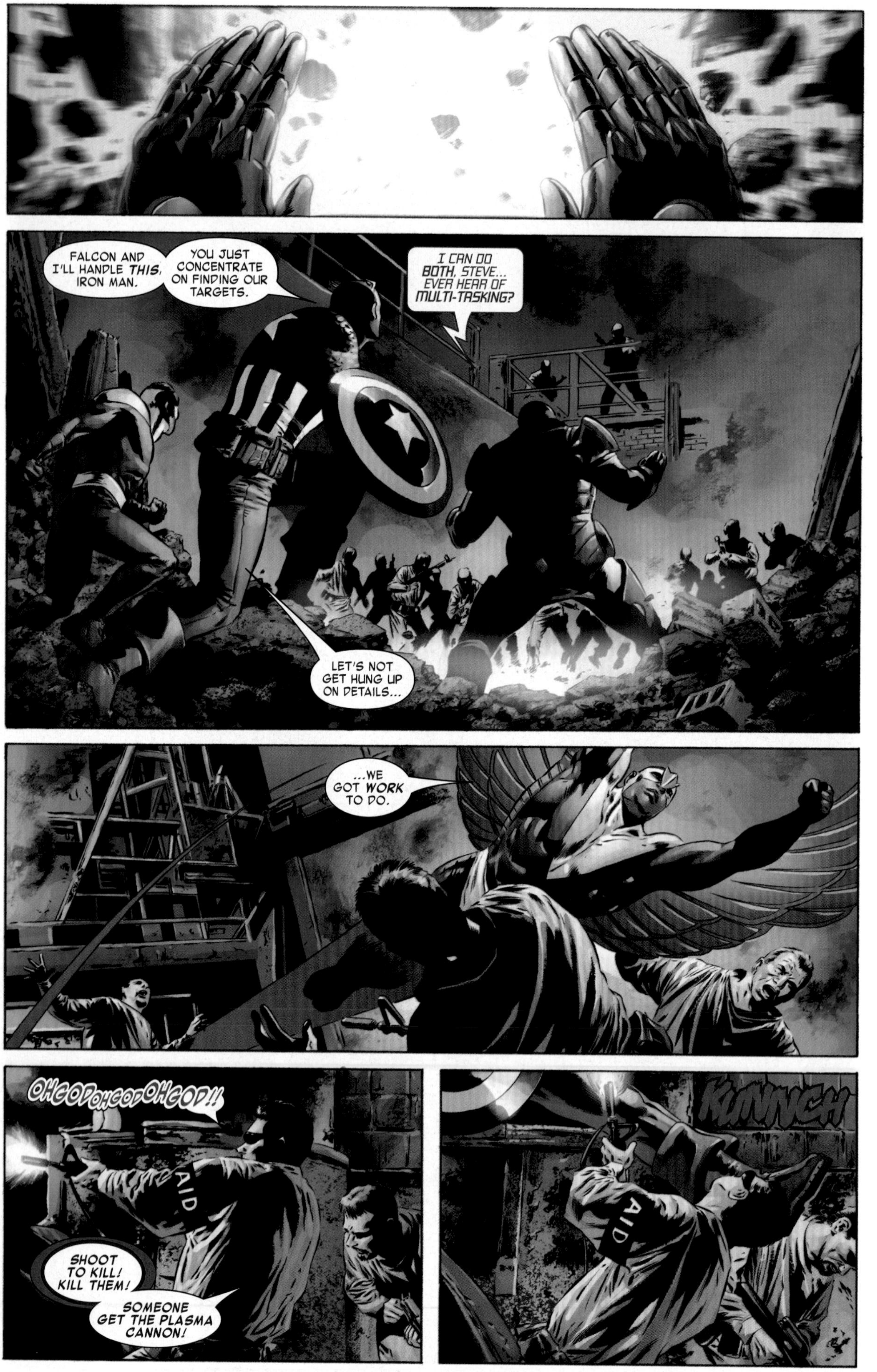

FALCON AND I'LL HANDLE THIS, IRON MAN.
YOU JUST CONCENTRATE ON FINDING OUR TARGETS.
I CAN DO BOTH, STEVE... EVER HEAR OF MULTI-TASKING?
LET'S NOT GET HUNG UP ON DETAILS...
...WE GOT WORK TO DO.
OHGODOHGODOHGOD!!
AID
SHOOT TO KILL! KILL THEM!
SOMEONE GET THE PLASMA CANNON!
KUNNCH
AID

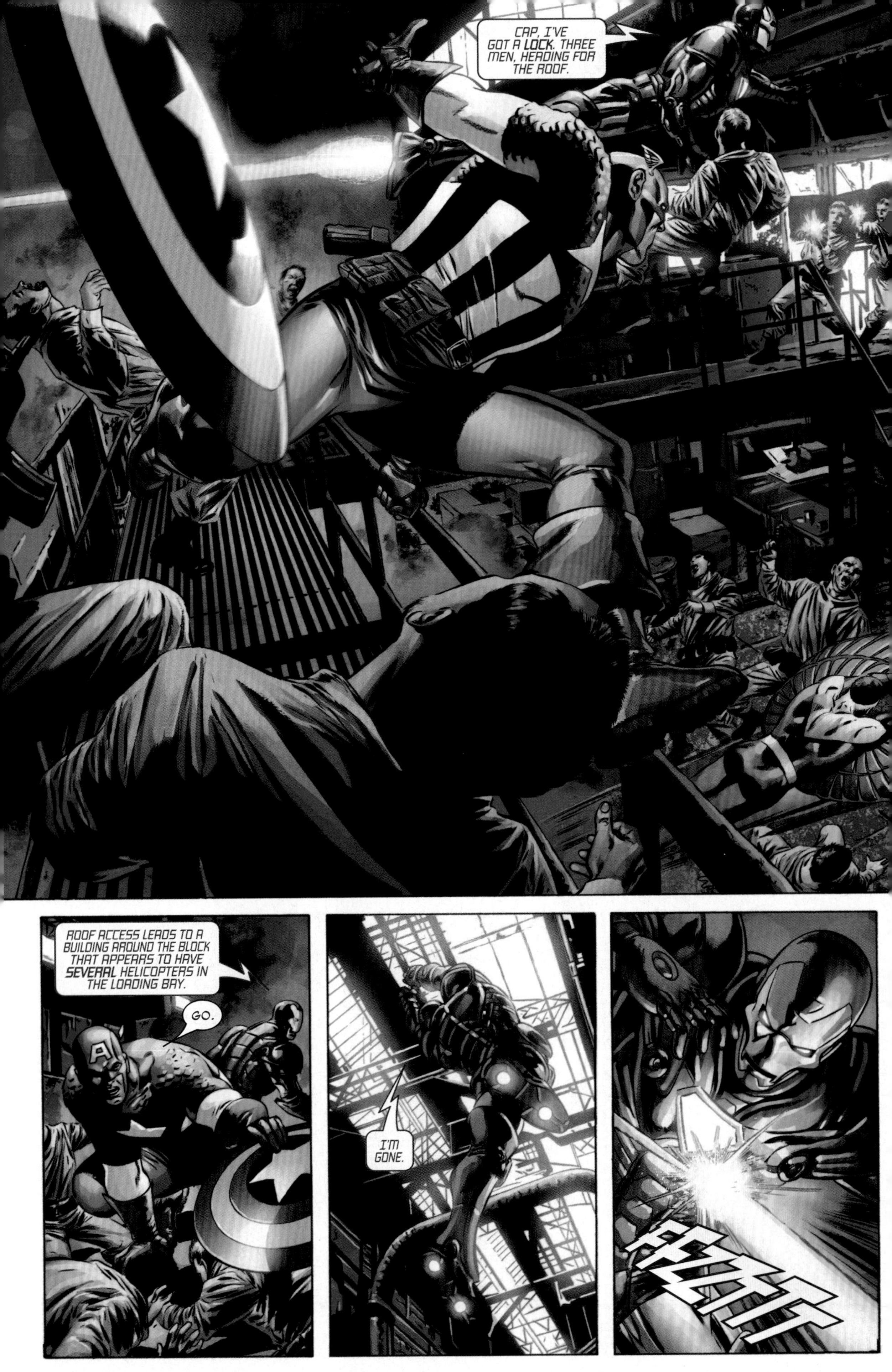
CAP, I'VE GOT A LOCK. THREE MEN, HEADING FOR THE ROOF.
ROOF ACCESS LEADS TO A BUILDING AROUND THE BLOCK THAT APPEARS TO HAVE SEVERAL HELICOPTERS IN THE LOADING BAY.
GO.
I'M GONE.
FZZTT

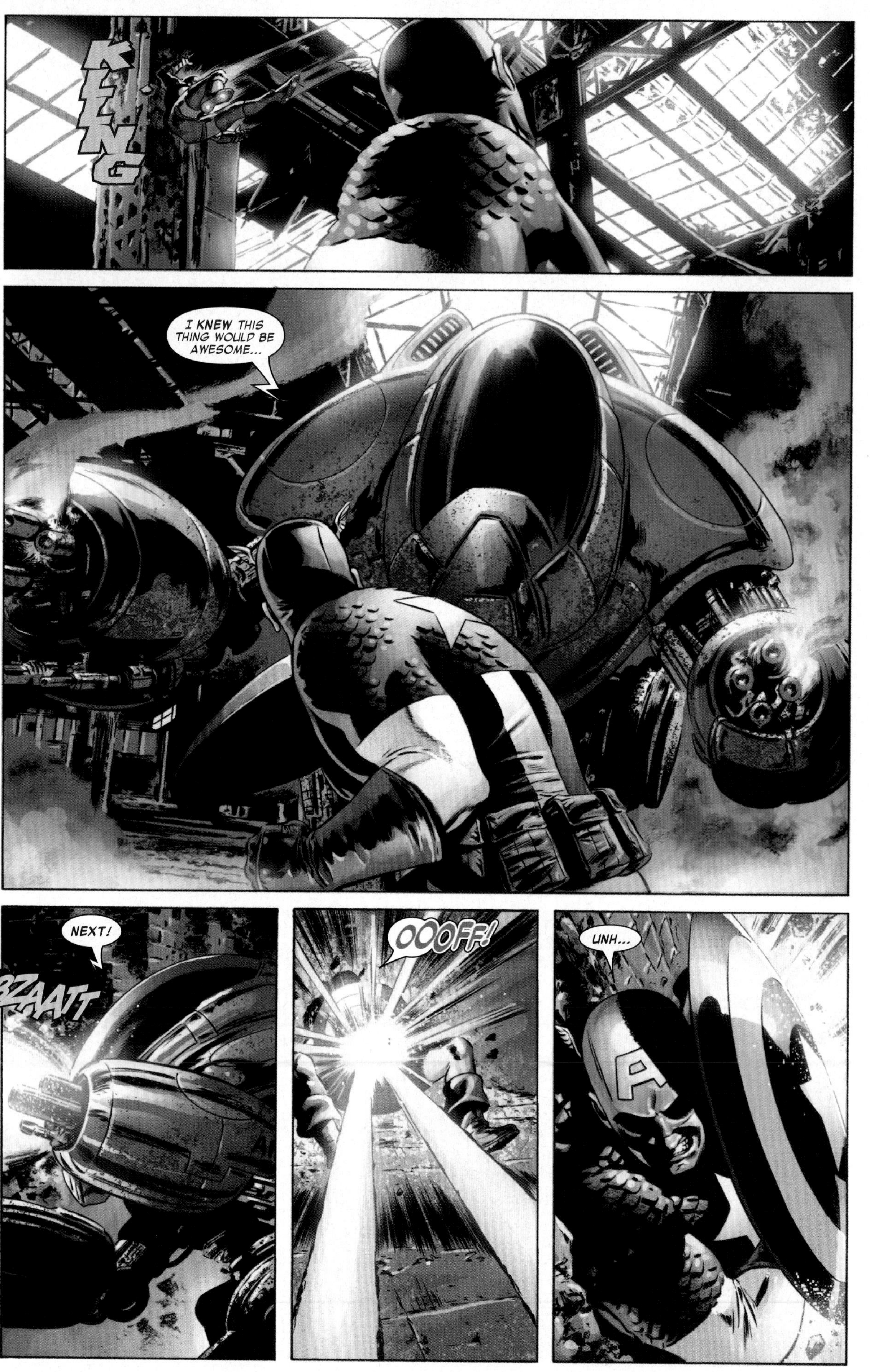
KLING
I KNEW THIS THING WOULD BE AWESOME...
NEXT!
BZAATT
OOOFF!
UNH...

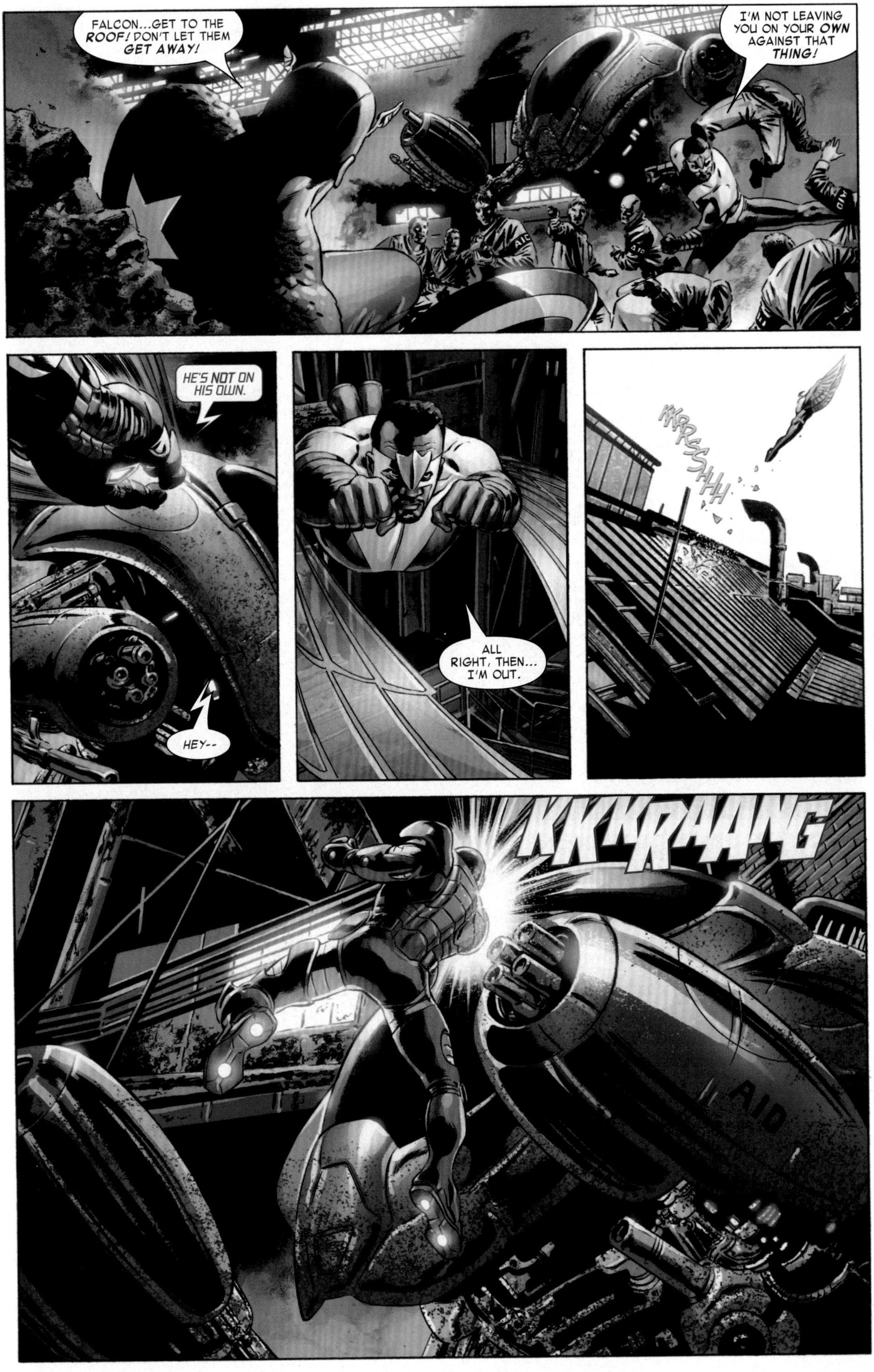

FALCON...GET TO THE ROOF! DON'T LET THEM GET AWAY!
I'M NOT LEAVING YOU ON YOUR OWN AGAINST THAT THING!
HE'S NOT ON HIS OWN.
HEY--
ALL RIGHT, THEN... I'M OUT.
KKRRSSHHH
KKKRAANG

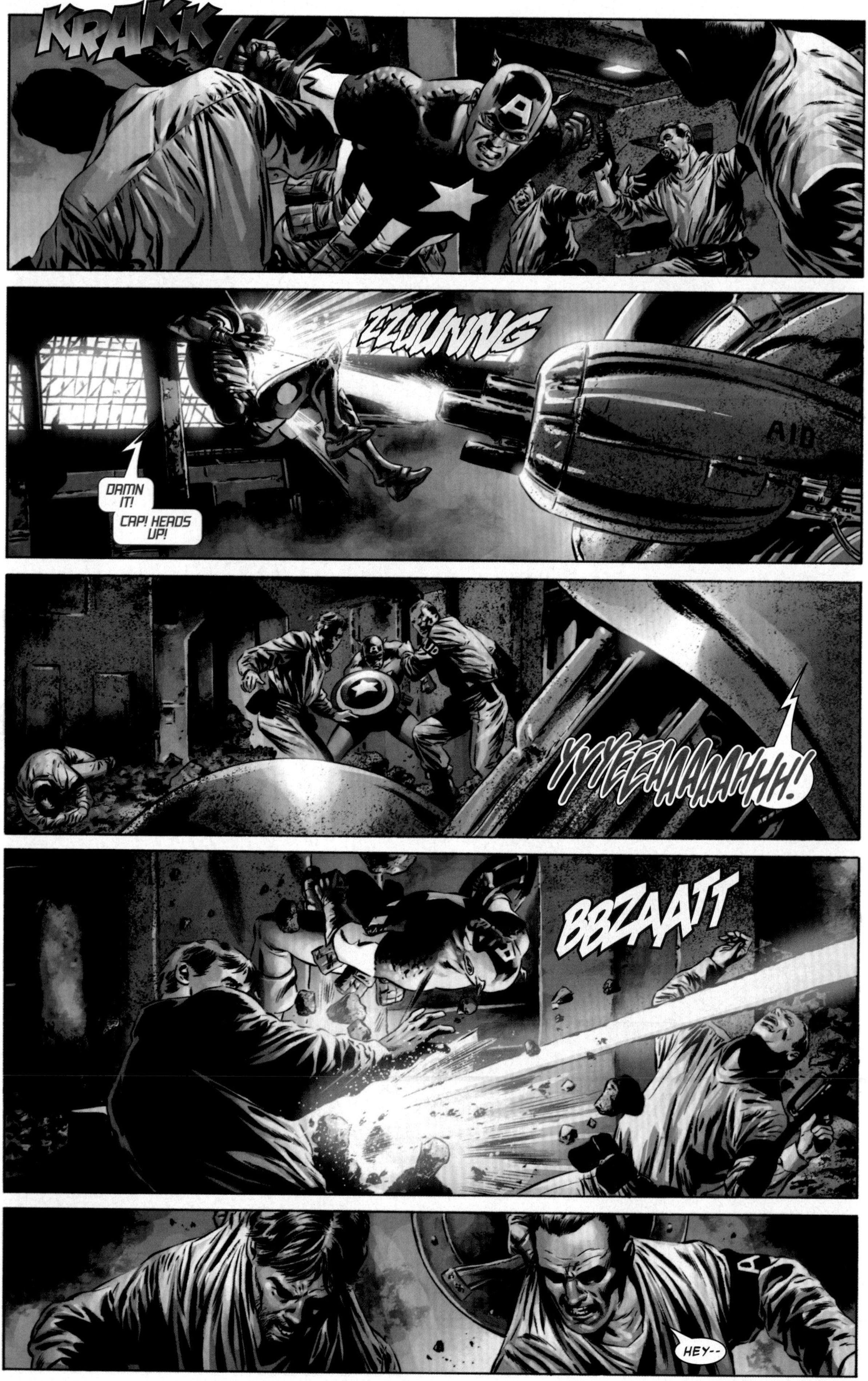
KRAKK
ZZUUNNG
DAMN IT!
CAP! HEADS UP!
YYYEEAAAAAHHH!
BBZAATT
HEY--

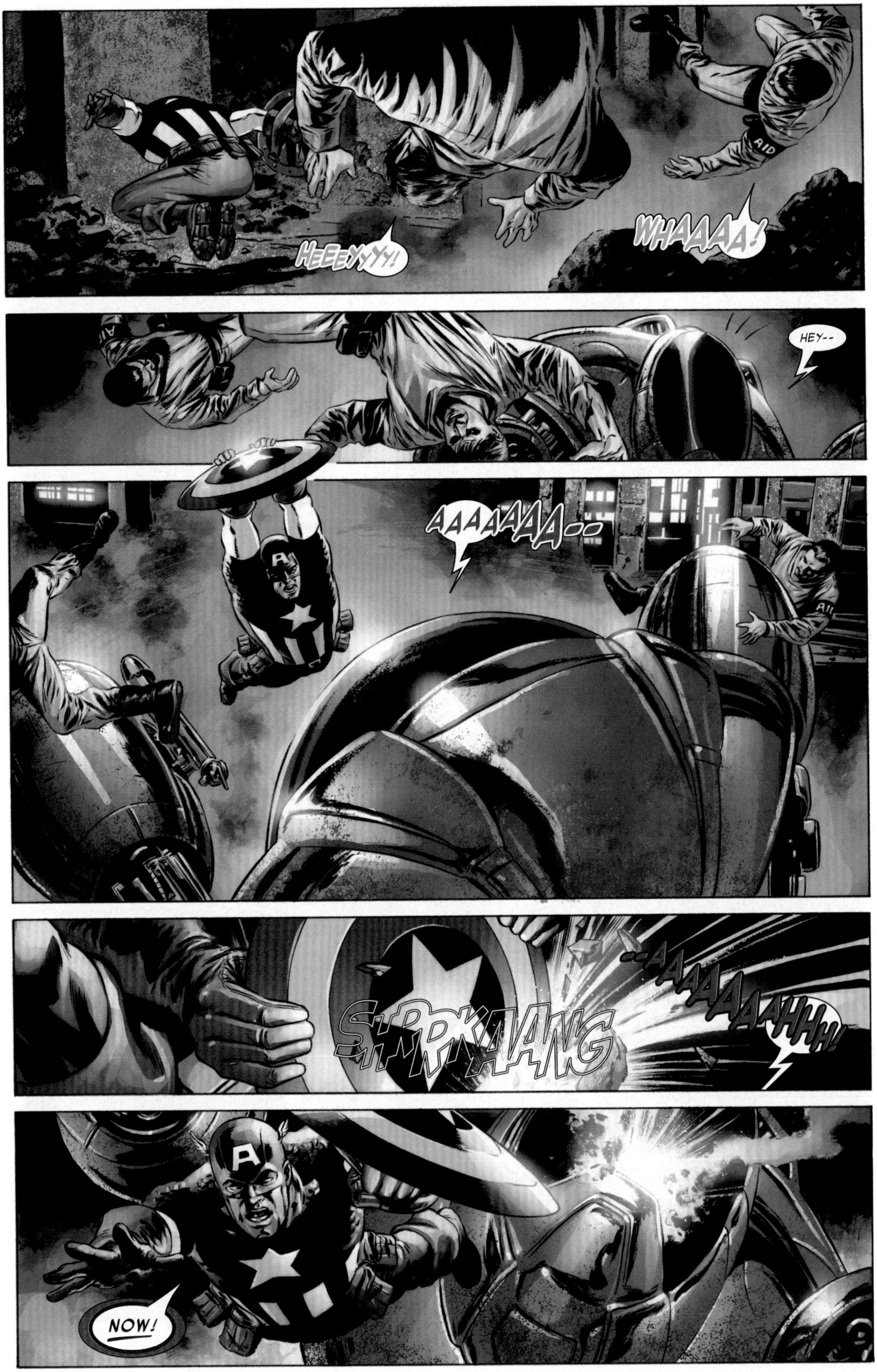
HEEEYYYY!
WHAAAAA!
HEY--
AAAAAAA--
SHRRKAANG
--AAAAAAAHHH!
NOW!

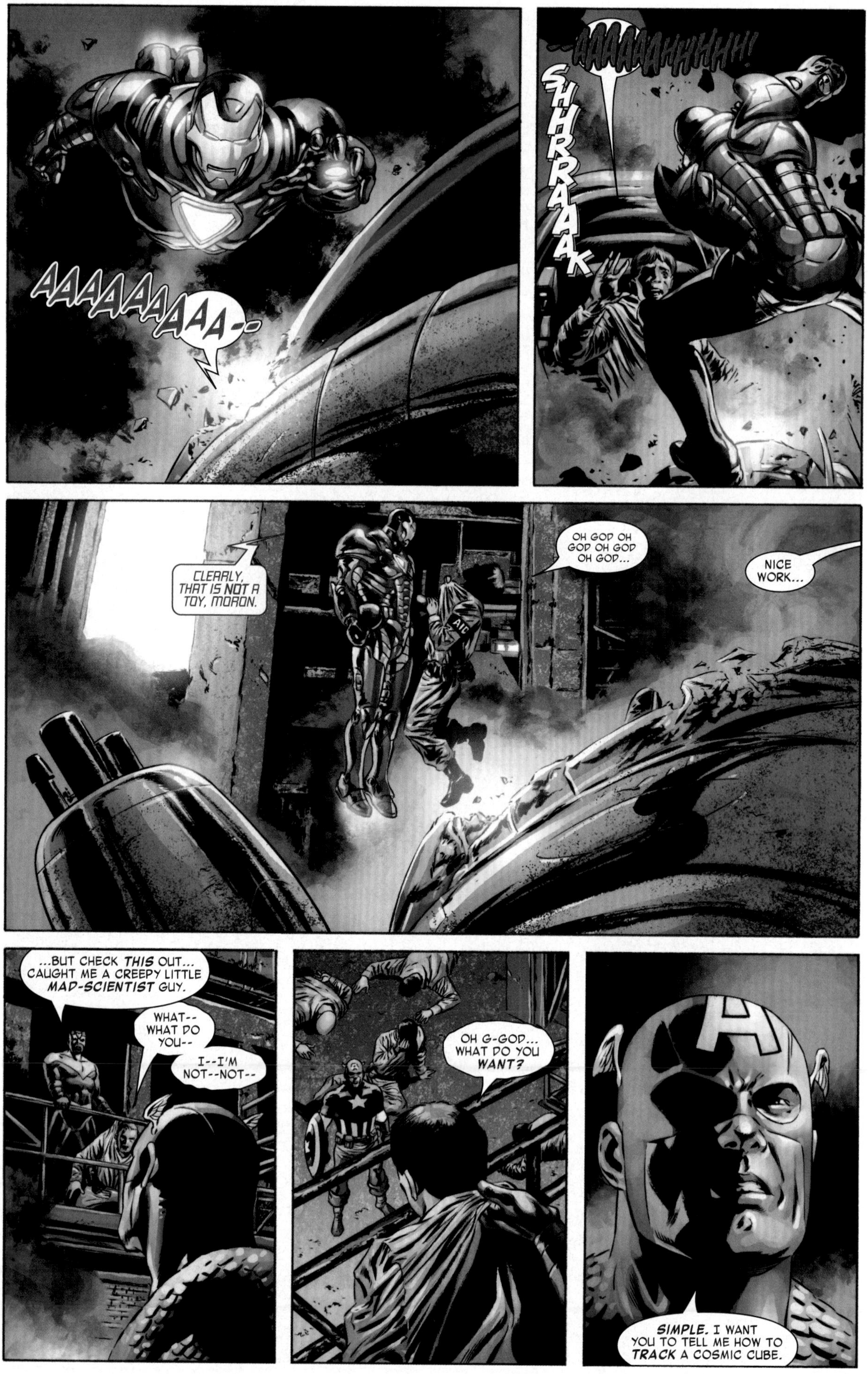
AAAAAAAAAA--
--AAAAAAAHHHHH!
SHHRAAAK
CLEARLY, THAT IS NOT A TOY, MORON.
OH GOD OH GOD OH GOD OH GOD...
NICE WORK...
...BUT CHECK THIS OUT... CAUGHT ME A CREEPY LITTLE MAD-SCIENTIST GUY.
WHAT-- WHAT DO YOU--
I--I'M NOT--NOT--
OH G-GOD... WHAT DO YOU WANT?
SIMPLE. I WANT YOU TO TELL ME HOW TO TRACK A COSMIC CUBE.

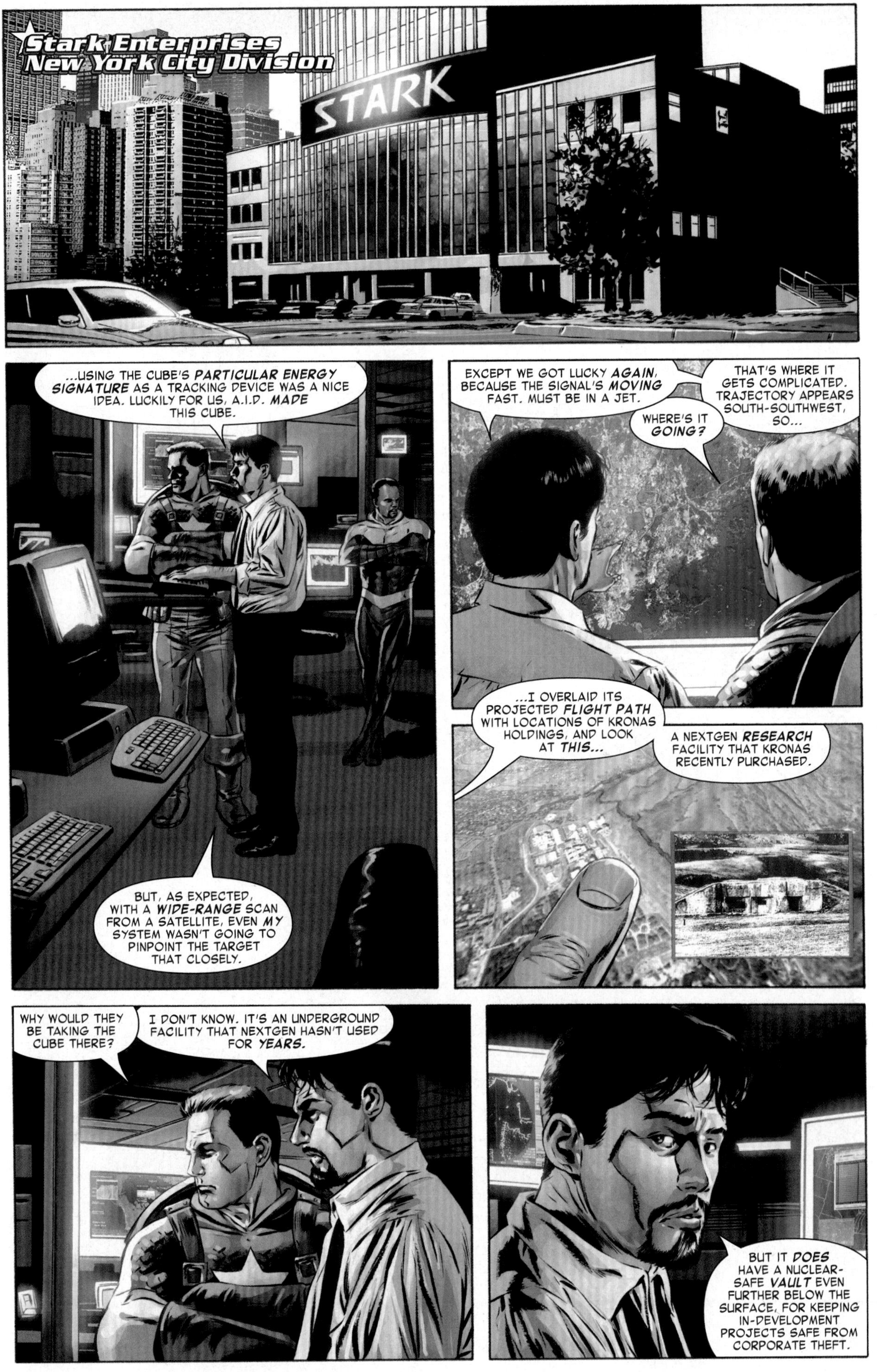
Stark Enterprises New York City Division
STARK
...USING THE CUBE'S PARTICULAR ENERGY SIGNATURE AS A TRACKING DEVICE WAS A NICE IDEA. LUCKILY FOR US, A.I.D. MADE THIS CUBE.
BUT, AS EXPECTED, WITH A WIDE-RANGE SCAN FROM A SATELLITE, EVEN MY SYSTEM WASN'T GOING TO PINPOINT THE TARGET THAT CLOSELY.
EXCEPT WE GOT LUCKY AGAIN, BECAUSE THE SIGNAL'S MOVING FAST. MUST BE IN A JET.
WHERE'S IT GOING?
THAT'S WHERE IT GETS COMPLICATED. TRAJECTORY APPEARS SOUTH-SOUTHWEST, SO...
...I OVERLAID ITS PROJECTED FLIGHT PATH WITH LOCATIONS OF KRONAS HOLDINGS, AND LOOK AT THIS...
A NEXTGEN RESEARCH FACILITY THAT KRONAS RECENTLY PURCHASED.
WHY WOULD THEY BE TAKING THE CUBE THERE?
I DON'T KNOW. IT'S AN UNDERGROUND FACILITY THAT NEXTGEN HASN'T USED FOR YEARS.
BUT IT DOES HAVE A NUCLEAR-SAFE VAULT EVEN FURTHER BELOW THE SURFACE, FOR KEEPING IN-DEVELOPMENT PROJECTS SAFE FROM CORPORATE THEFT.

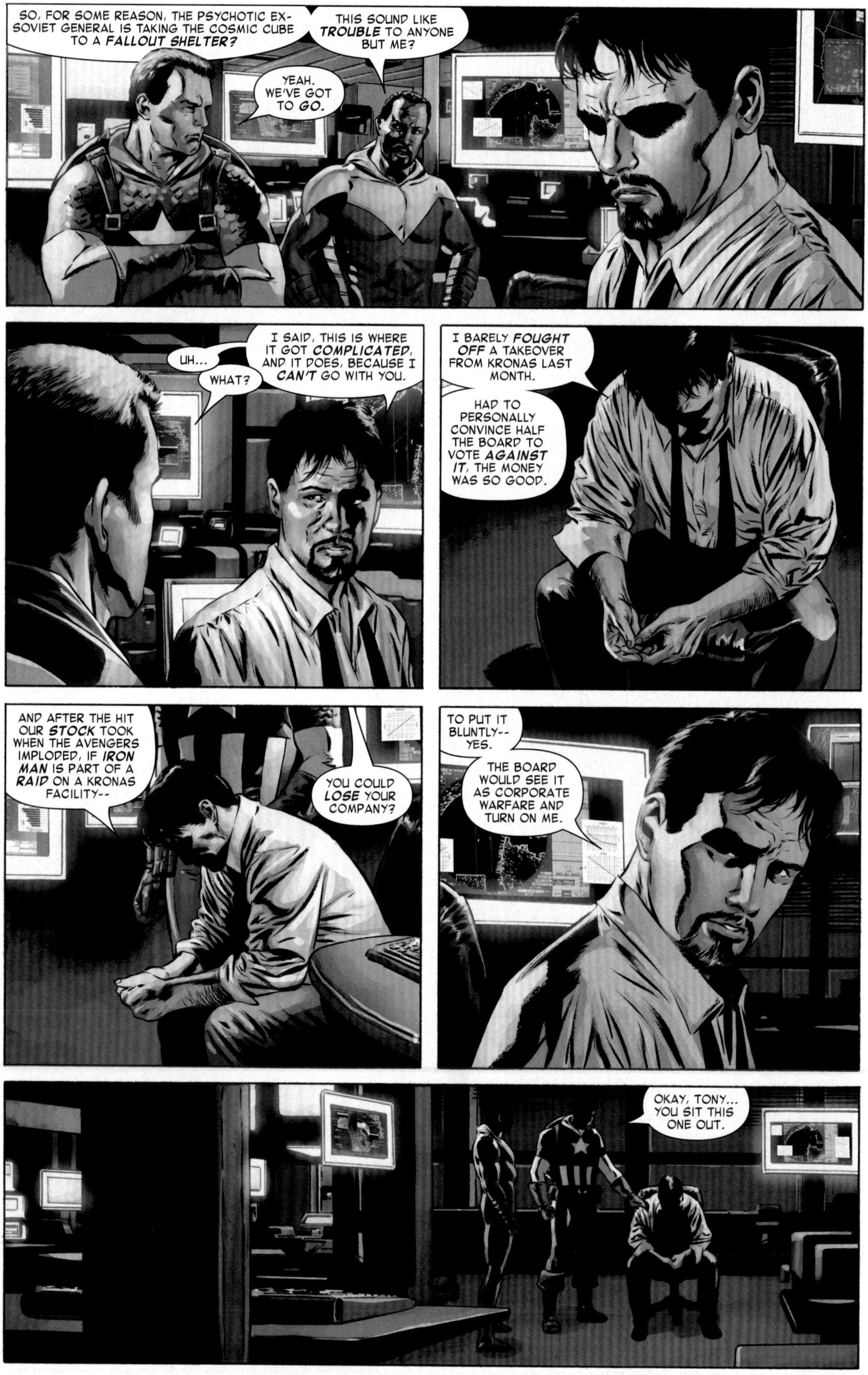
SO, FOR SOME REASON, THE PSYCHOTIC EX-SOVIET GENERAL IS TAKING THE COSMIC CUBE TO A FALLOUT SHELTER?
THIS SOUND LIKE TROUBLE TO ANYONE BUT ME?
YEAH. WE'VE GOT TO GO.
I SAID, THIS IS WHERE IT GOT COMPLICATED, AND IT DOES, BECAUSE I CAN'T GO WITH YOU.
UH...
WHAT?
I BARELY FOUGHT OFF A TAKEOVER FROM KRONAS LAST MONTH.
HAD TO PERSONALLY CONVINCE HALF THE BOARD TO VOTE AGAINST IT, THE MONEY WAS SO GOOD.
AND AFTER THE HIT OUR STOCK TOOK WHEN THE AVENGERS IMPLODED, IF IRON MAN IS PART OF A RAID ON A KRONAS FACILITY--
YOU COULD LOSE YOUR COMPANY?
TO PUT IT BLUNTLY--YES.
THE BOARD WOULD SEE IT AS CORPORATE WARFARE AND TURN ON ME.
OKAY, TONY... YOU SIT THIS ONE OUT.

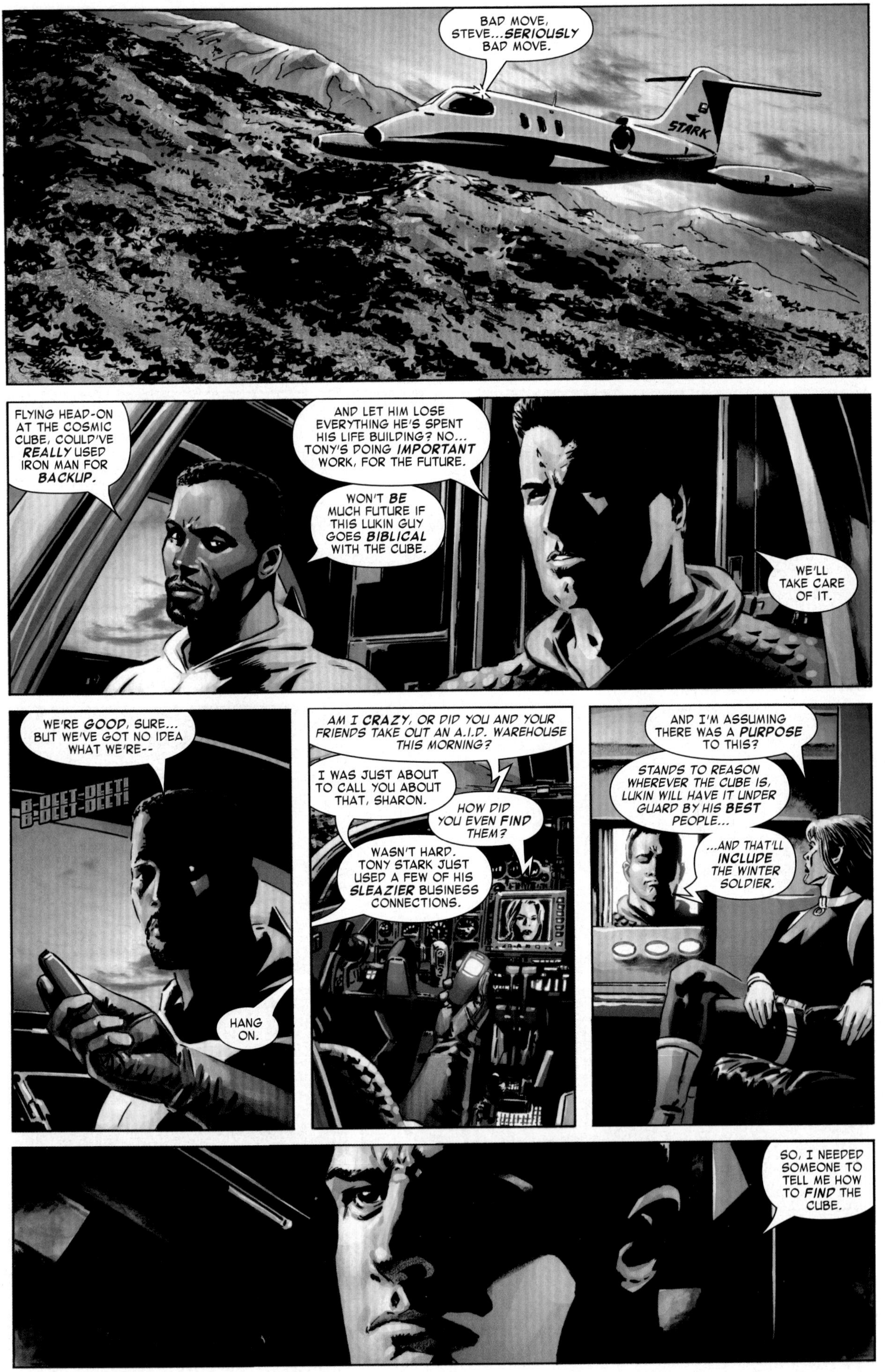
BAD MOVE, STEVE...SERIOUSLY BAD MOVE.
STARK
FLYING HEAD-ON AT THE COSMIC CUBE, COULD'VE REALLY USED IRON MAN FOR BACKUP.
AND LET HIM LOSE EVERYTHING HE'S SPENT HIS LIFE BUILDING? NO... TONY'S DOING IMPORTANT WORK, FOR THE FUTURE.
WON'T BE MUCH FUTURE IF THIS LUKIN GUY GOES BIBLICAL WITH THE CUBE.
WE'LL TAKE CARE OF IT.
WE'RE GOOD, SURE... BUT WE'VE GOT NO IDEA WHAT WE'RE--
B-DEET-DEET! B-DEET-DEET!
HANG ON.
AM I CRAZY, OR DID YOU AND YOUR FRIENDS TAKE OUT AN A.I.D. WAREHOUSE THIS MORNING?
I WAS JUST ABOUT TO CALL YOU ABOUT THAT, SHARON.
HOW DID YOU EVEN FIND THEM?
WASN'T HARD. TONY STARK JUST USED A FEW OF HIS SLEAZIER BUSINESS CONNECTIONS.
AND I'M ASSUMING THERE WAS A PURPOSE TO THIS?
STANDS TO REASON WHEREVER THE CUBE IS, LUKIN WILL HAVE IT UNDER GUARD BY HIS BEST PEOPLE...
...AND THAT'LL INCLUDE THE WINTER SOLDIER.
SO, I NEEDED SOMEONE TO TELL ME HOW TO FIND THE CUBE.

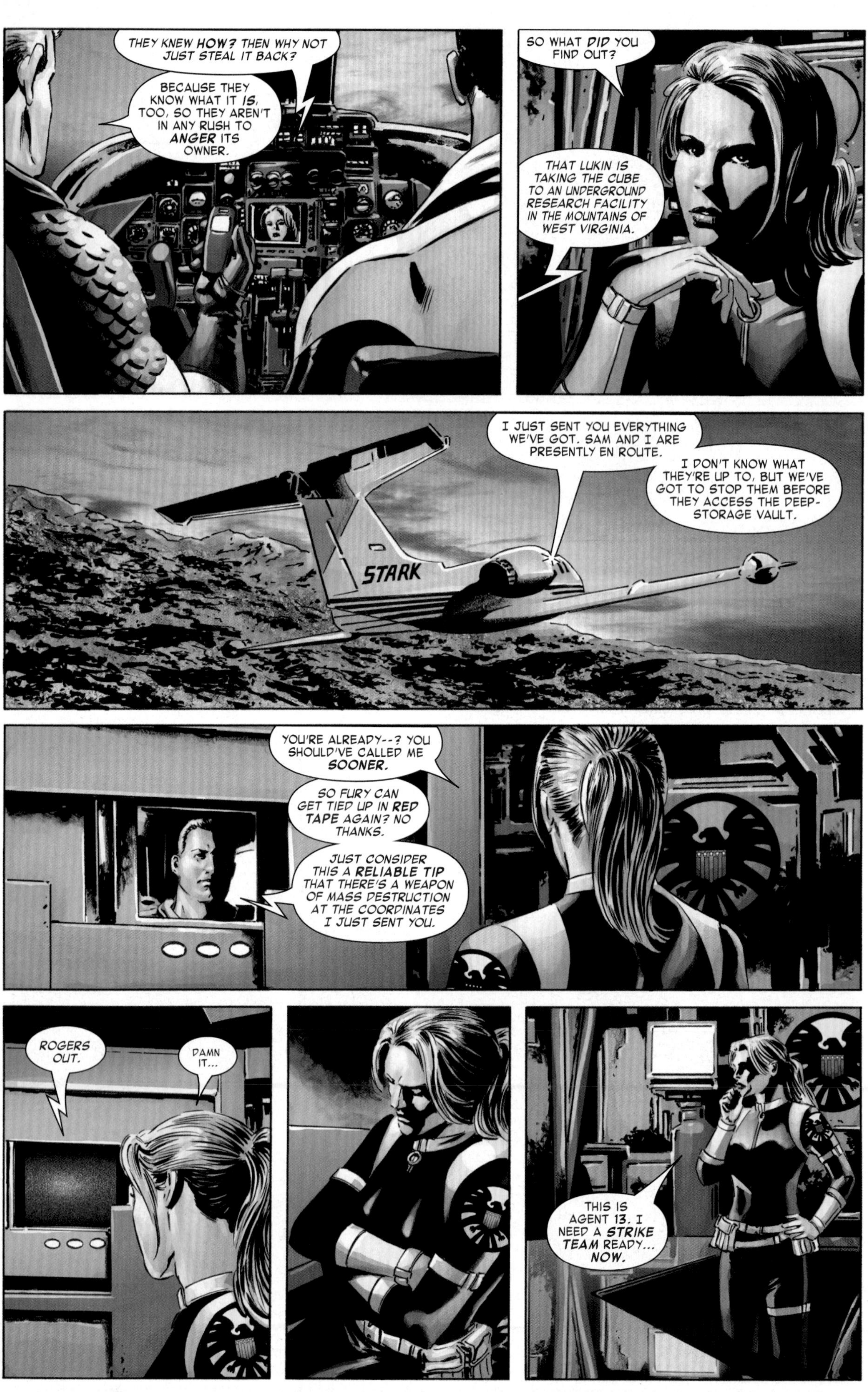
THEY KNEW **HOW?** THEN WHY NOT JUST STEAL IT BACK?
BECAUSE THEY KNOW WHAT IT *IS*, TOO, SO THEY AREN'T IN ANY RUSH TO **ANGER** ITS OWNER.
SO WHAT *DID* YOU FIND OUT?
THAT LUKIN IS TAKING THE CUBE TO AN UNDERGROUND RESEARCH FACILITY IN THE MOUNTAINS OF WEST VIRGINIA.
I JUST SENT YOU EVERYTHING WE'VE GOT. SAM AND I ARE PRESENTLY EN ROUTE.
I DON'T KNOW WHAT THEY'RE UP TO, BUT WE'VE GOT TO STOP THEM BEFORE THEY ACCESS THE DEEP-STORAGE VAULT.
STARK
YOU'RE ALREADY--? YOU SHOULD'VE CALLED ME **SOONER.**
SO FURY CAN GET TIED UP IN **RED TAPE** AGAIN? NO THANKS.
JUST CONSIDER THIS A **RELIABLE TIP** THAT THERE'S A WEAPON OF MASS DESTRUCTION AT THE COORDINATES I JUST SENT YOU.
ROGERS OUT.
DAMN IT...
THIS IS AGENT 13. I NEED A **STRIKE TEAM** READY... **NOW.**

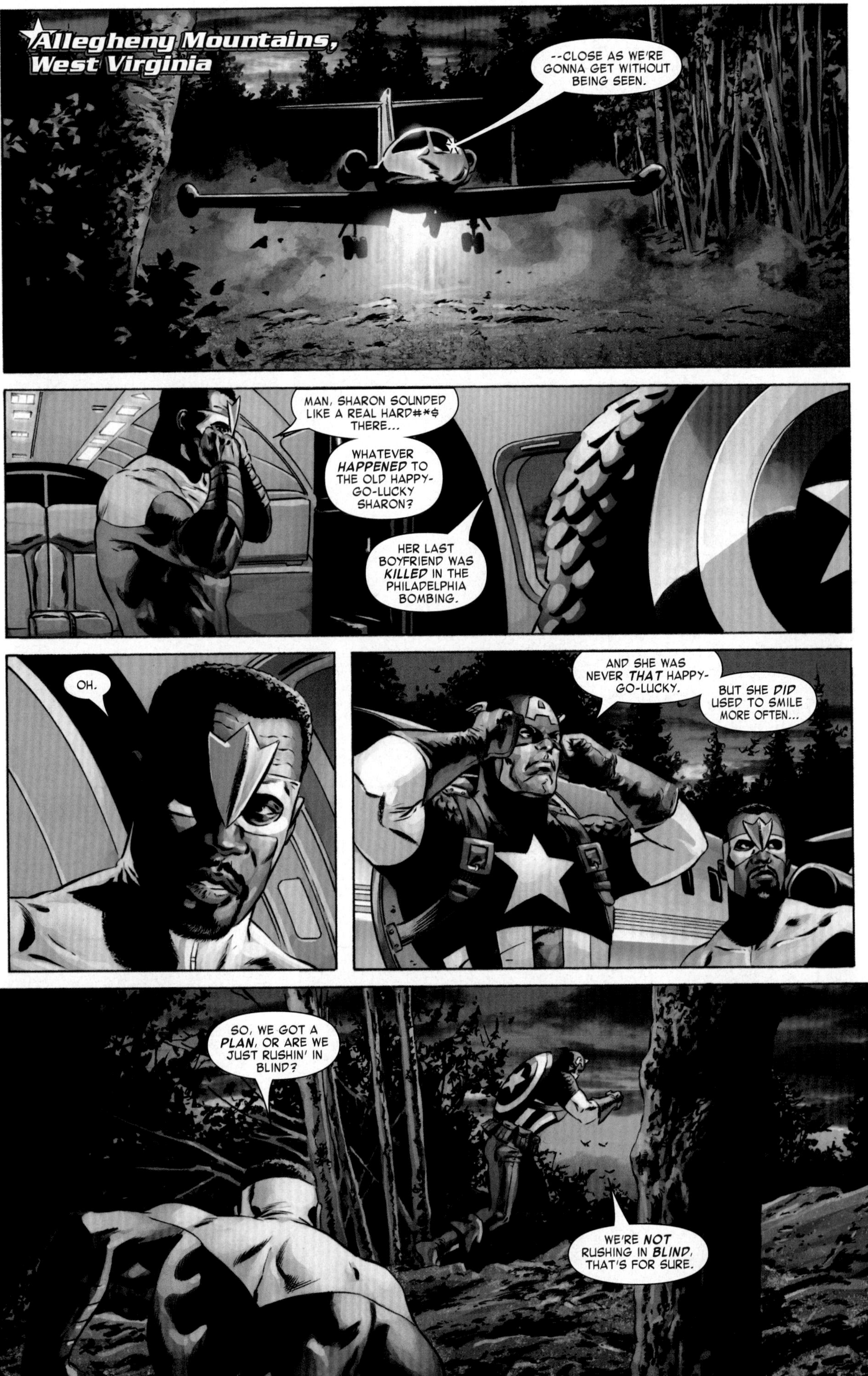
Allegheny Mountains, West Virginia
--CLOSE AS WE'RE GONNA GET WITHOUT BEING SEEN.
MAN, SHARON SOUNDED LIKE A REAL HARD#*$ THERE...
WHATEVER HAPPENED TO THE OLD HAPPY-GO-LUCKY SHARON?
HER LAST BOYFRIEND WAS KILLED IN THE PHILADELPHIA BOMBING.
OH.
AND SHE WAS NEVER THAT HAPPY-GO-LUCKY.
BUT SHE DID USED TO SMILE MORE OFTEN...
SO, WE GOT A PLAN, OR ARE WE JUST RUSHIN' IN BLIND?
WE'RE NOT RUSHING IN BLIND, THAT'S FOR SURE.

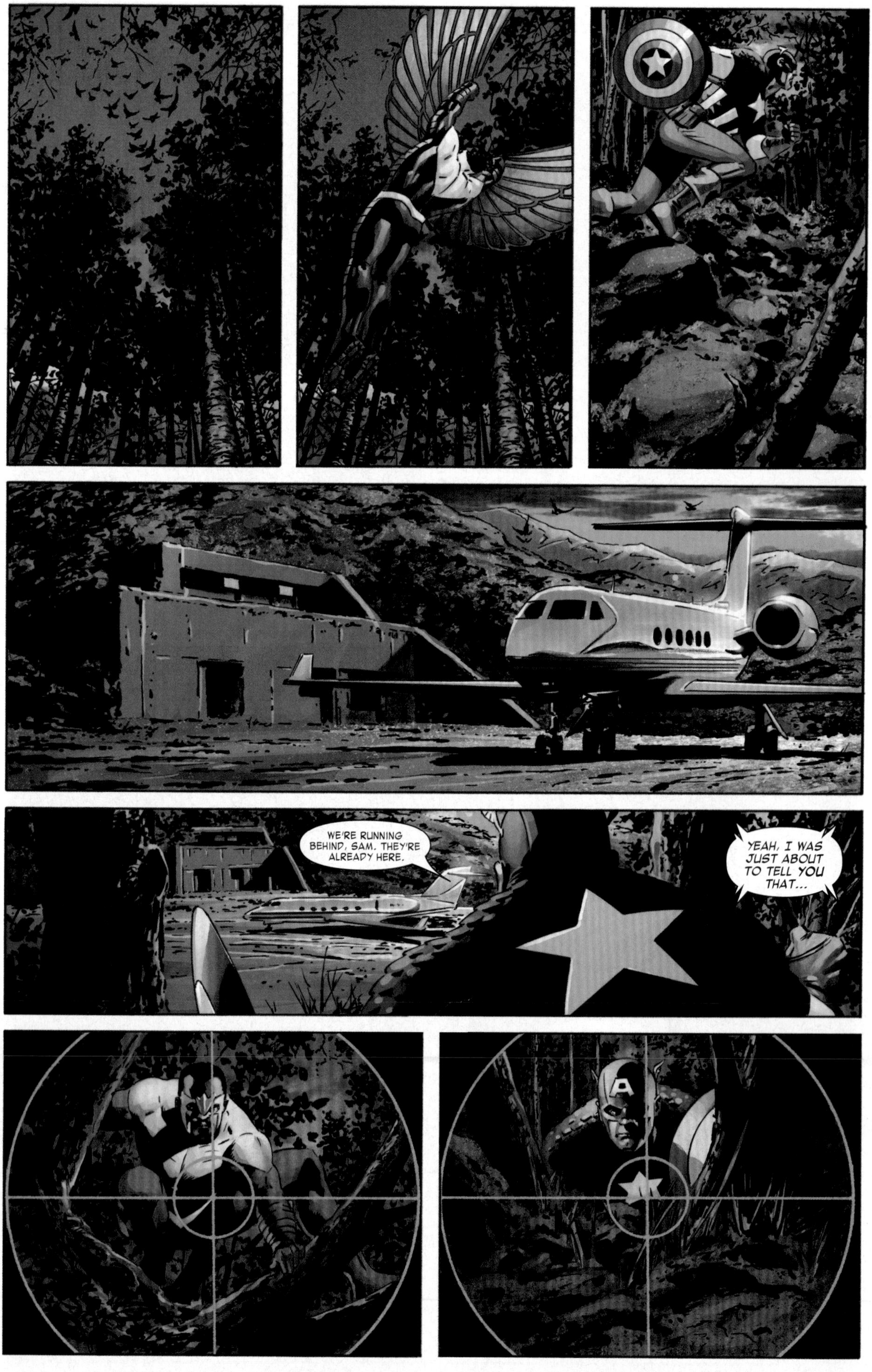
WE'RE RUNNING BEHIND, SAM. THEY'RE ALREADY HERE.
YEAH, I WAS JUST ABOUT TO TELL YOU THAT...

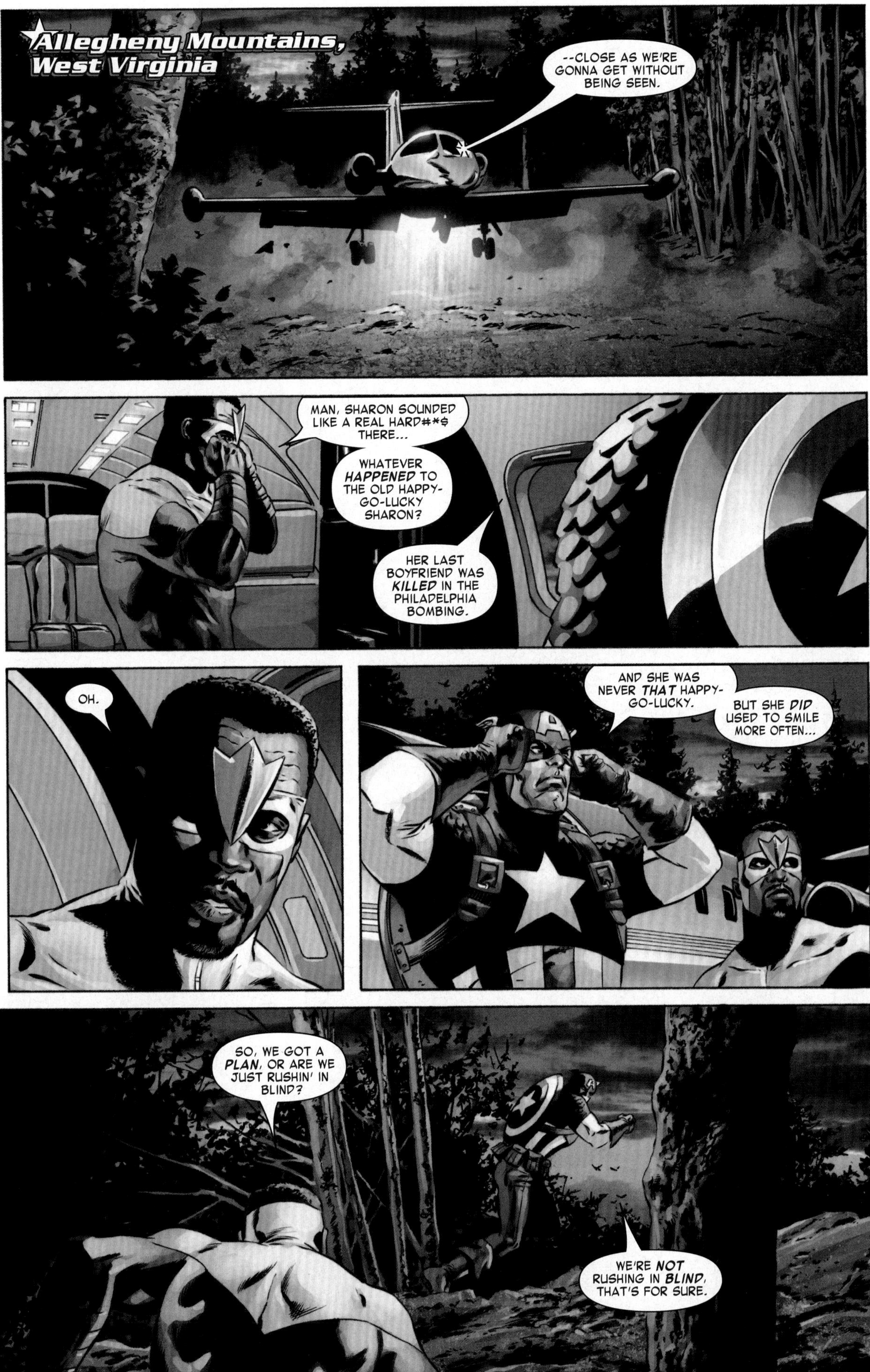
Allegheny Mountains, West Virginia
--CLOSE AS WE'RE GONNA GET WITHOUT BEING SEEN.
MAN, SHARON SOUNDED LIKE A REAL HARD#*$ THERE...
WHATEVER HAPPENED TO THE OLD HAPPY-GO-LUCKY SHARON?
HER LAST BOYFRIEND WAS KILLED IN THE PHILADELPHIA BOMBING.
OH.
AND SHE WAS NEVER THAT HAPPY-GO-LUCKY.
BUT SHE DID USED TO SMILE MORE OFTEN...
SO, WE GOT A PLAN, OR ARE WE JUST RUSHIN' IN BLIND?
WE'RE NOT RUSHING IN BLIND, THAT'S FOR SURE.

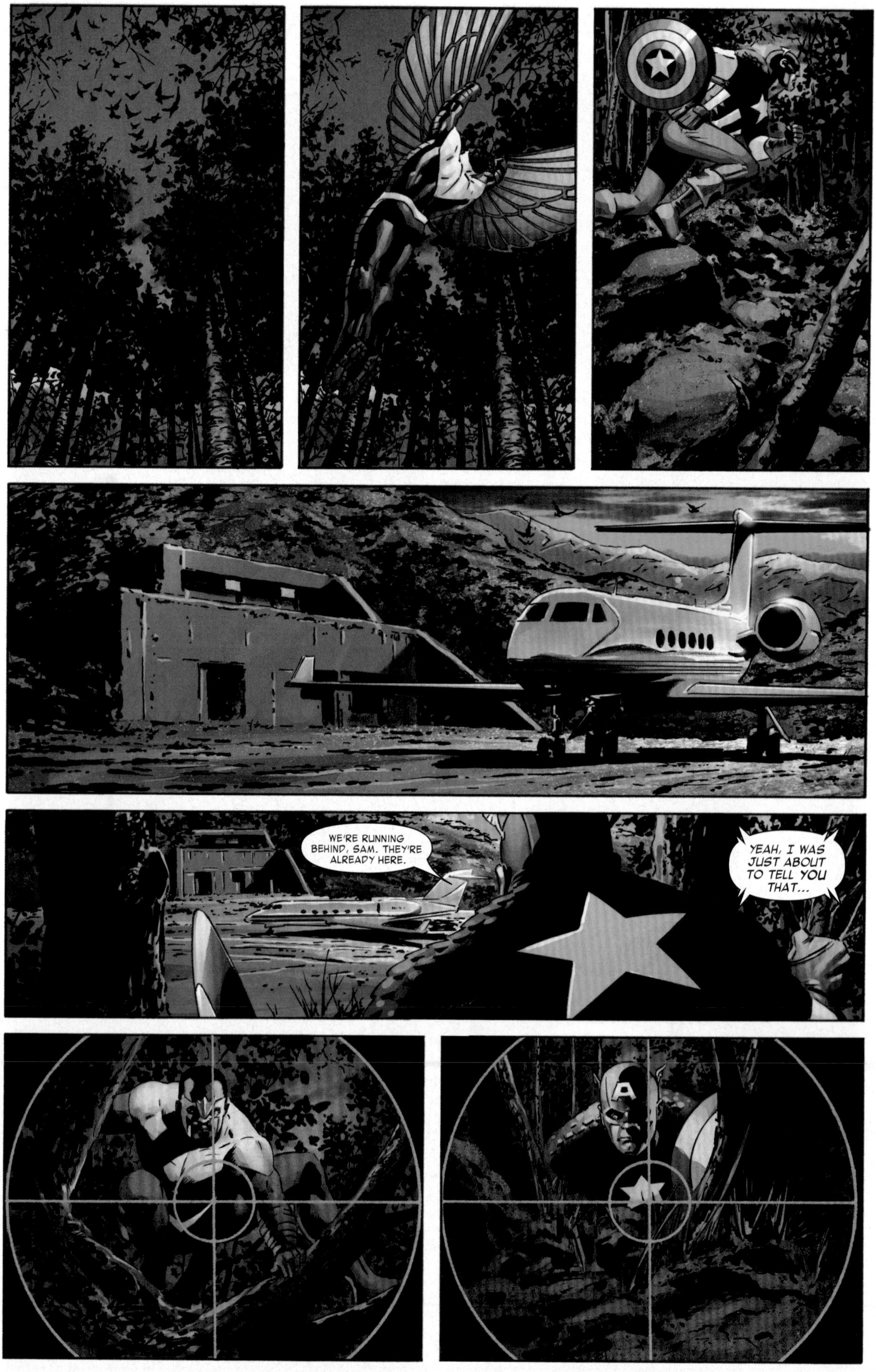
WE'RE RUNNING BEHIND, SAM. THEY'RE ALREADY HERE.
YEAH, I WAS JUST ABOUT TO TELL YOU THAT...

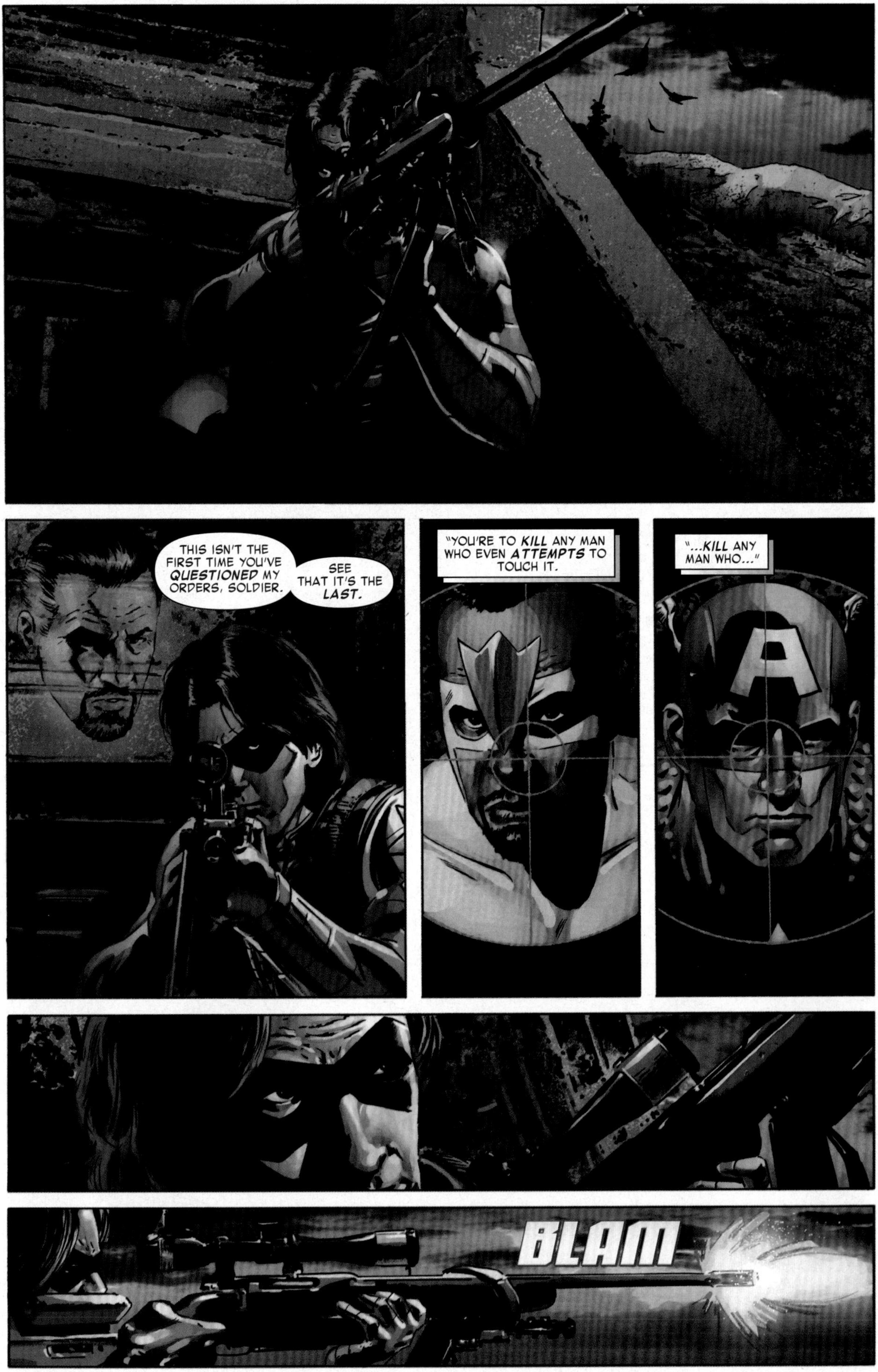

THIS ISN'T THE FIRST TIME YOU'VE QUESTIONED MY ORDERS, SOLDIER.
SEE THAT IT'S THE LAST.
"YOU'RE TO KILL ANY MAN WHO EVEN ATTEMPTS TO TOUCH IT.
"...KILL ANY MAN WHO..."
BLAM

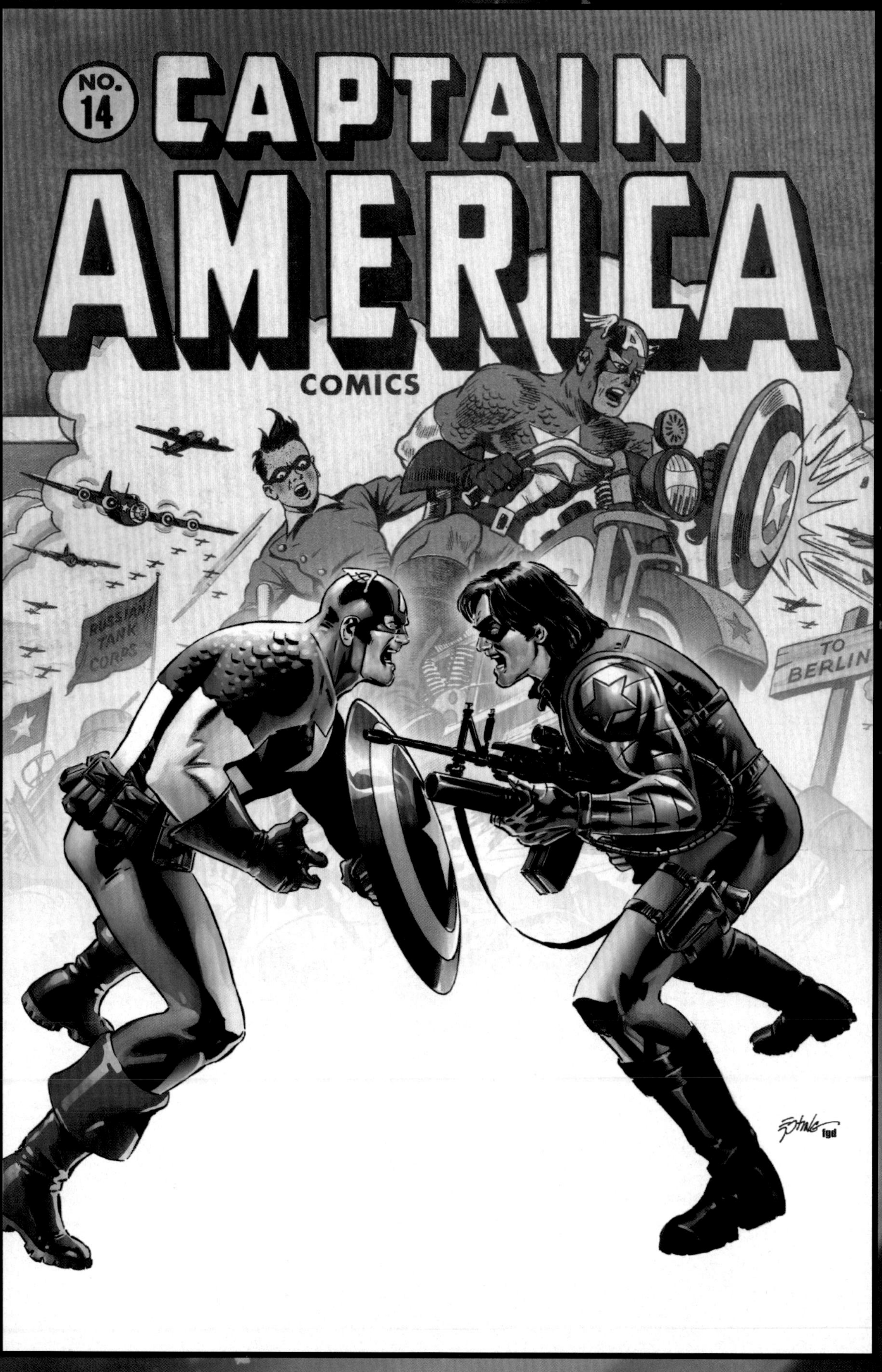
NO. 14
CAPTAIN
AMERICA
COMICS
RUSSIAN TANK CORPS
TO BERLIN

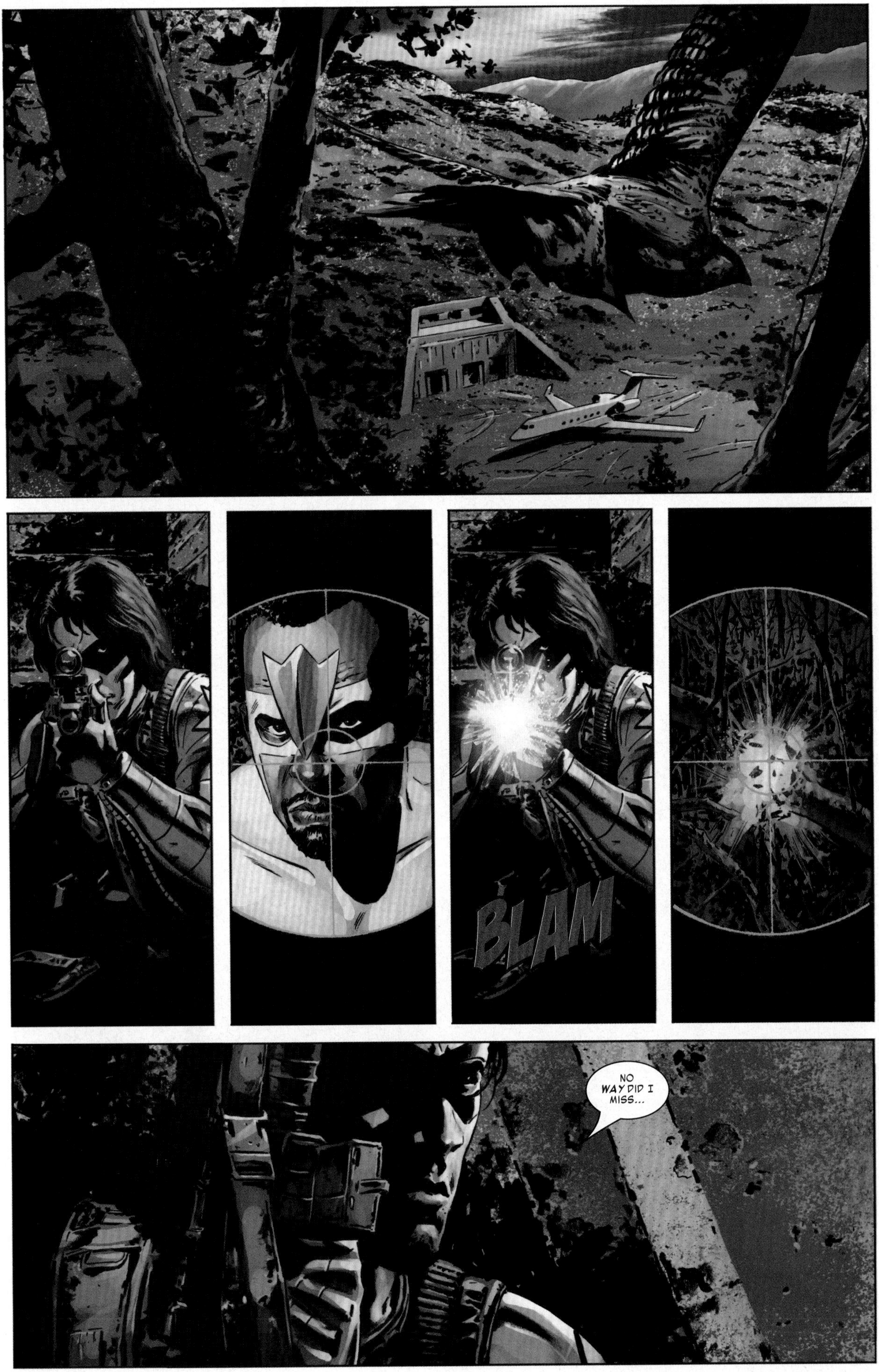
BLAM
NO WAY DID I MISS...

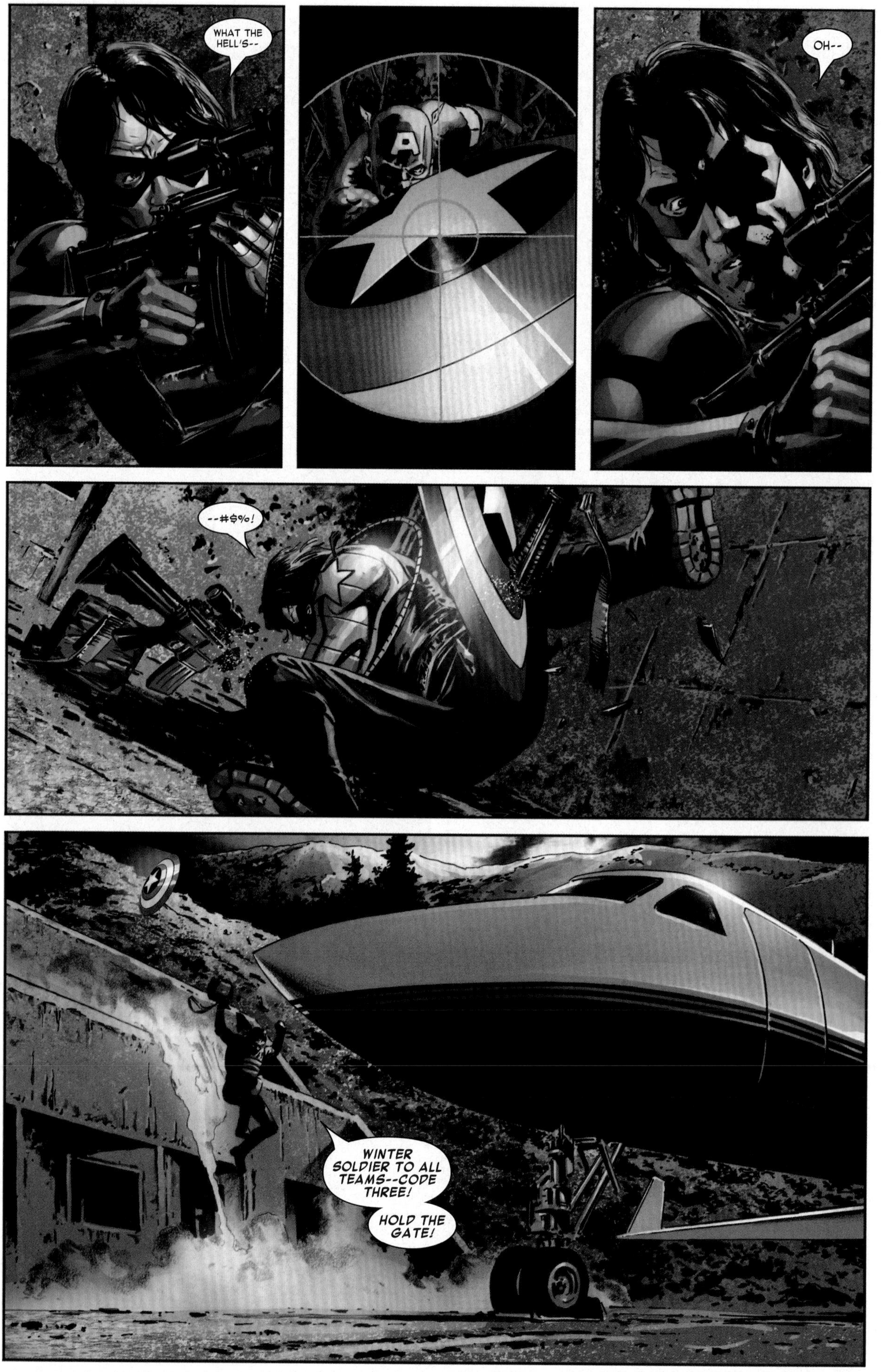
WHAT THE HELL'S--
OH--
--#$%!
WINTER SOLDIER TO ALL TEAMS--CODE THREE!
HOLD THE GATE!

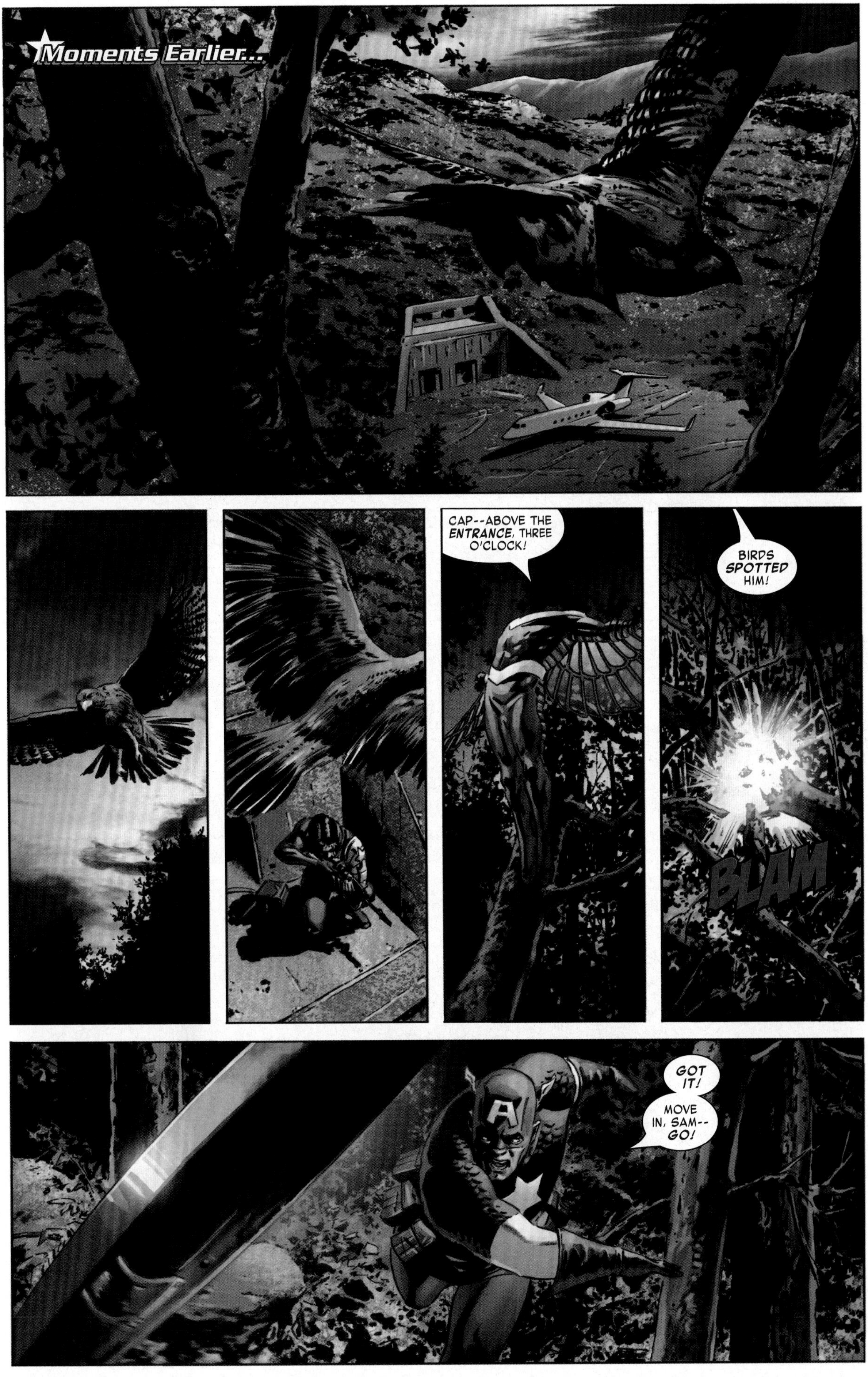
Moments Earlier...
CAP--ABOVE THE ENTRANCE, THREE O'CLOCK!
BIRDS SPOTTED HIM!
BLAM
GOT IT!
MOVE IN, SAM-- GO!

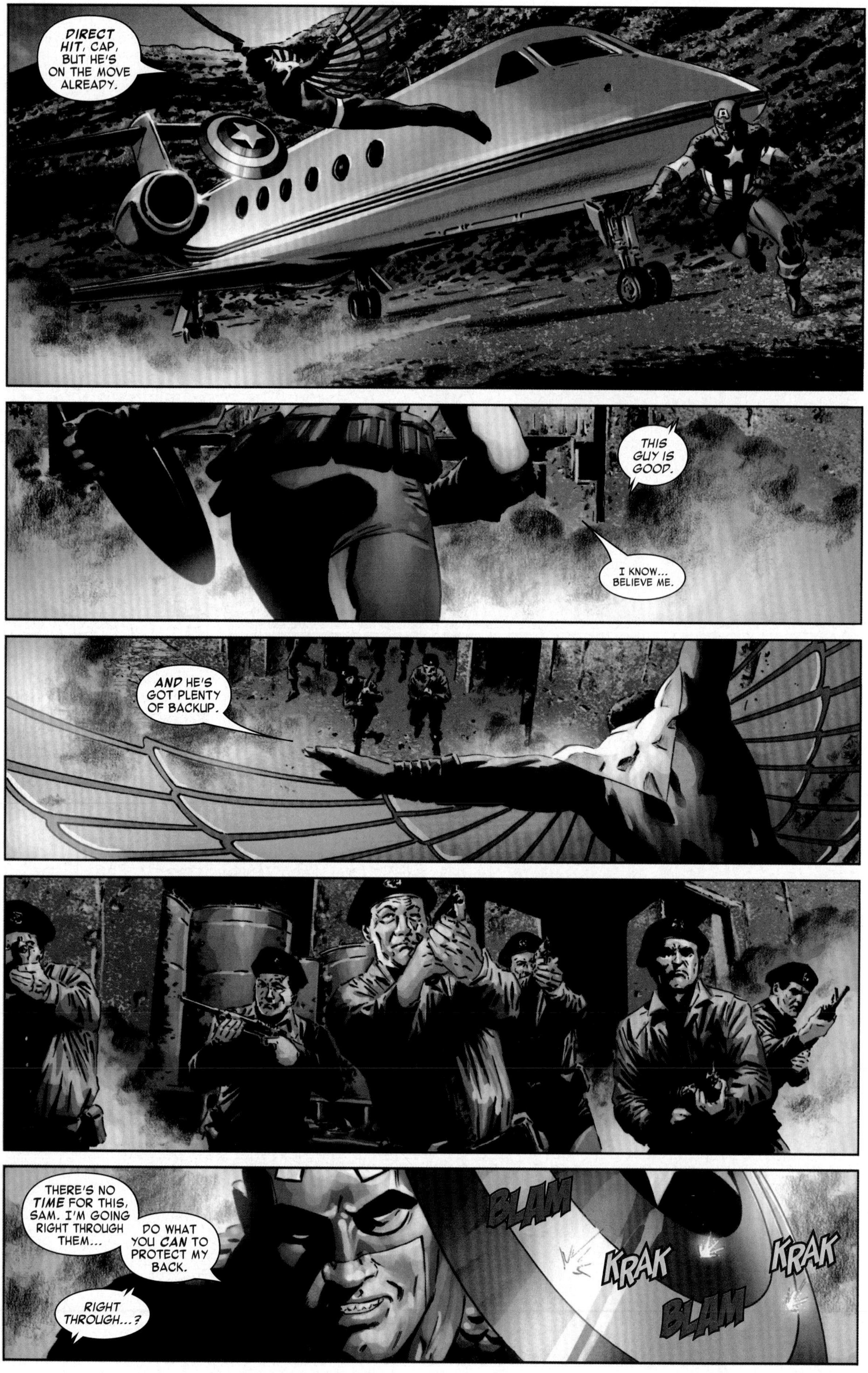

DIRECT HIT, CAP, BUT HE'S ON THE MOVE ALREADY.
THIS GUY IS GOOD.
I KNOW... BELIEVE ME.
AND HE'S GOT PLENTY OF BACKUP.
THERE'S NO *TIME* FOR THIS, SAM. I'M GOING RIGHT THROUGH THEM...
DO WHAT YOU *CAN* TO PROTECT MY BACK.
RIGHT THROUGH...?
BLAM
KRAK
KRAK
BLAM

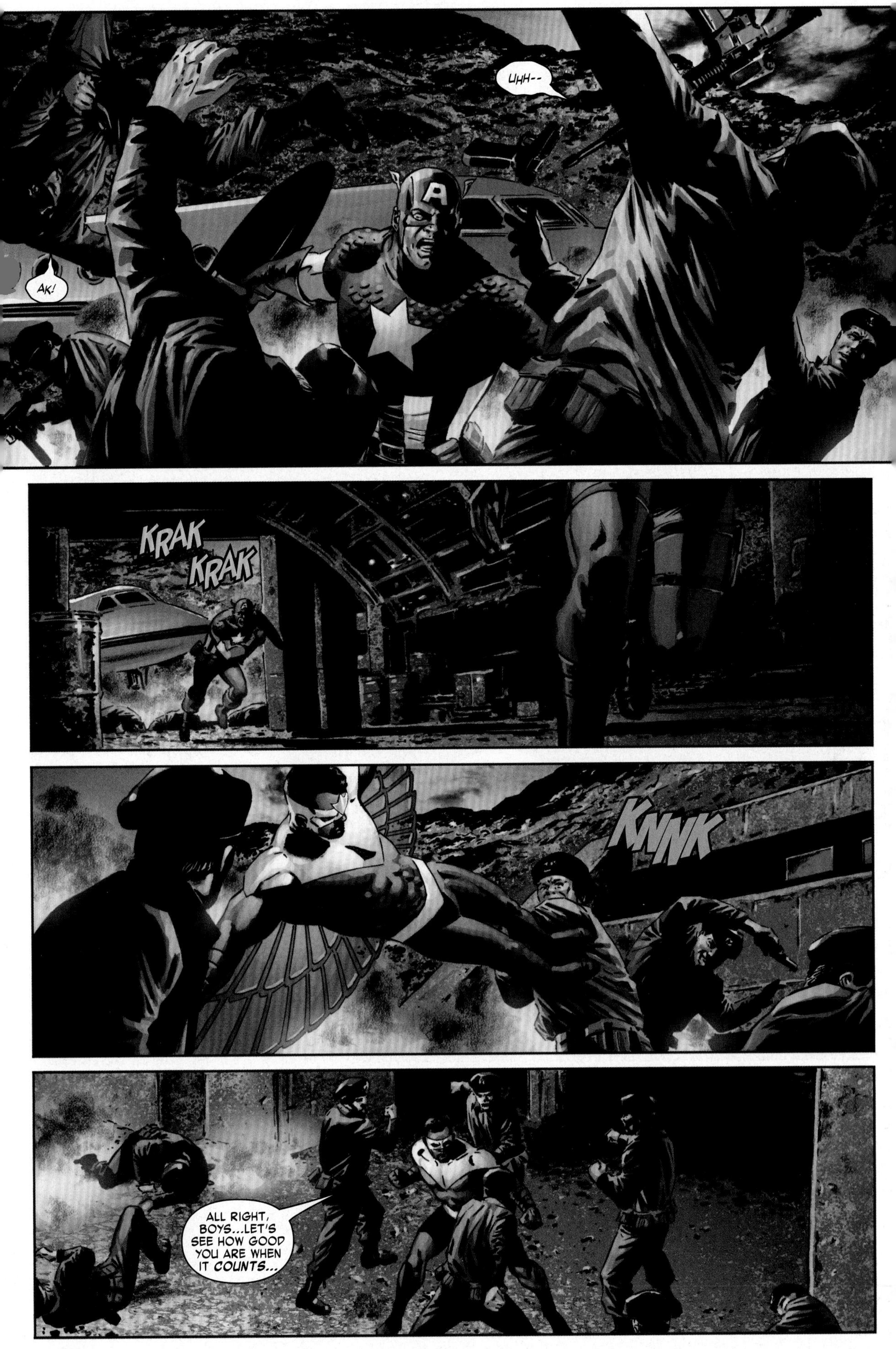
UHH--
AK!
KRAK
KRAK
KNNK
ALL RIGHT, BOYS...LET'S SEE HOW GOOD YOU ARE WHEN IT COUNTS...

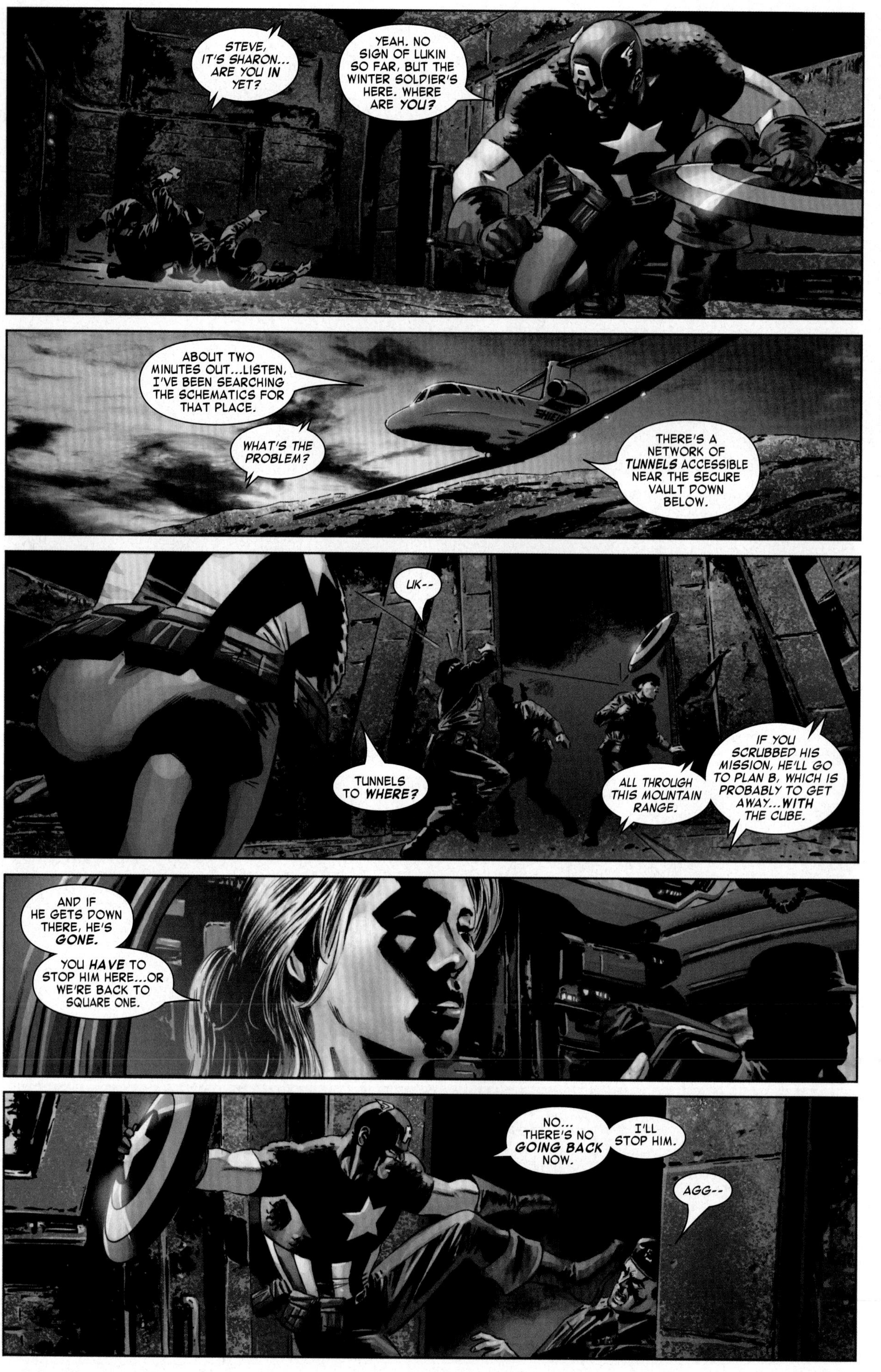
STEVE, IT'S SHARON... ARE YOU IN YET?
YEAH. NO SIGN OF LUKIN SO FAR, BUT THE WINTER SOLDIER'S HERE. WHERE ARE YOU?
ABOUT TWO MINUTES OUT...LISTEN, I'VE BEEN SEARCHING THE SCHEMATICS FOR THAT PLACE.
WHAT'S THE PROBLEM?
THERE'S A NETWORK OF TUNNELS ACCESSIBLE NEAR THE SECURE VAULT DOWN BELOW.
UK--
TUNNELS TO WHERE?
ALL THROUGH THIS MOUNTAIN RANGE.
IF YOU SCRUBBED HIS MISSION, HE'LL GO TO PLAN B, WHICH IS PROBABLY TO GET AWAY...WITH THE CUBE.
AND IF HE GETS DOWN THERE, HE'S GONE.
YOU HAVE TO STOP HIM HERE...OR WE'RE BACK TO SQUARE ONE.
NO... THERE'S NO GOING BACK NOW.
I'LL STOP HIM.
AGG--

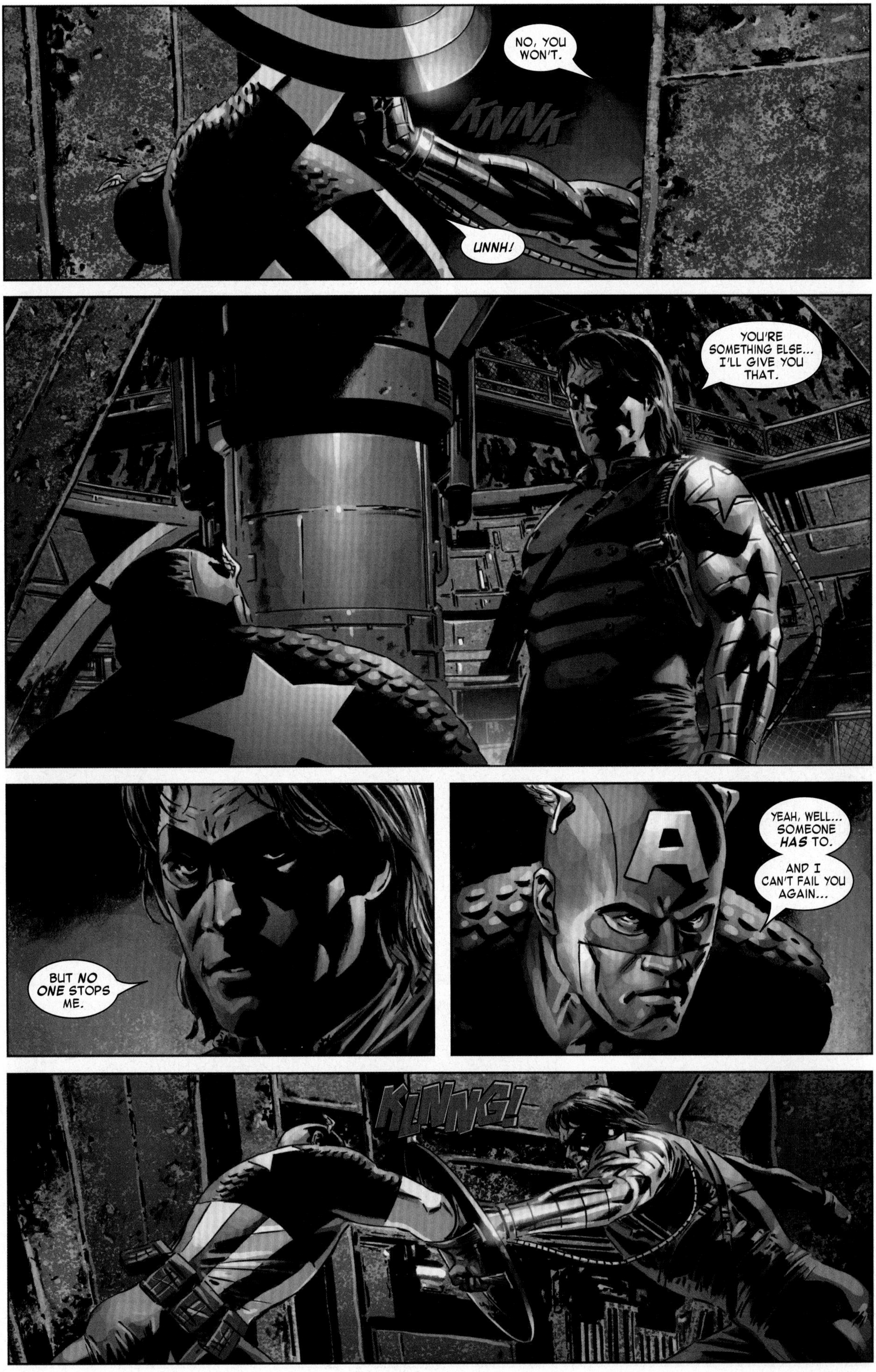
NO, YOU WON'T.
KNNK
UNNH!
YOU'RE SOMETHING ELSE... I'LL GIVE YOU THAT.
BUT NO ONE STOPS ME.
YEAH, WELL... SOMEONE HAS TO.
AND I CAN'T FAIL YOU AGAIN...
KLNNNG!

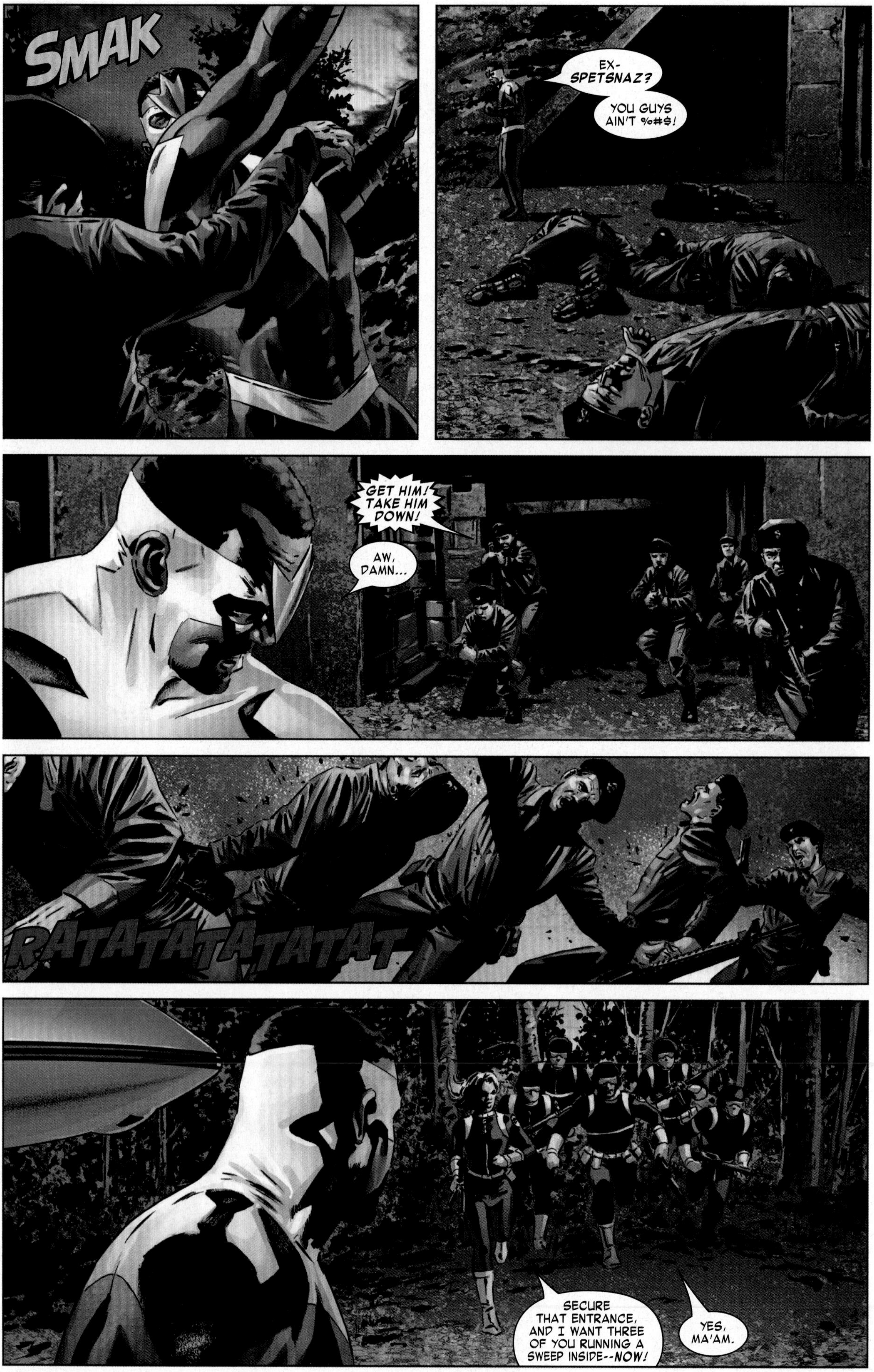
SMAK
EX-SPETSNAZ?
YOU GUYS AIN'T %#$!
GET HIM! TAKE HIM DOWN!
AW, DAMN...
RATATATATATATAT
SECURE THAT ENTRANCE, AND I WANT THREE OF YOU RUNNING A SWEEP INSIDE--NOW!
YES, MA'AM.

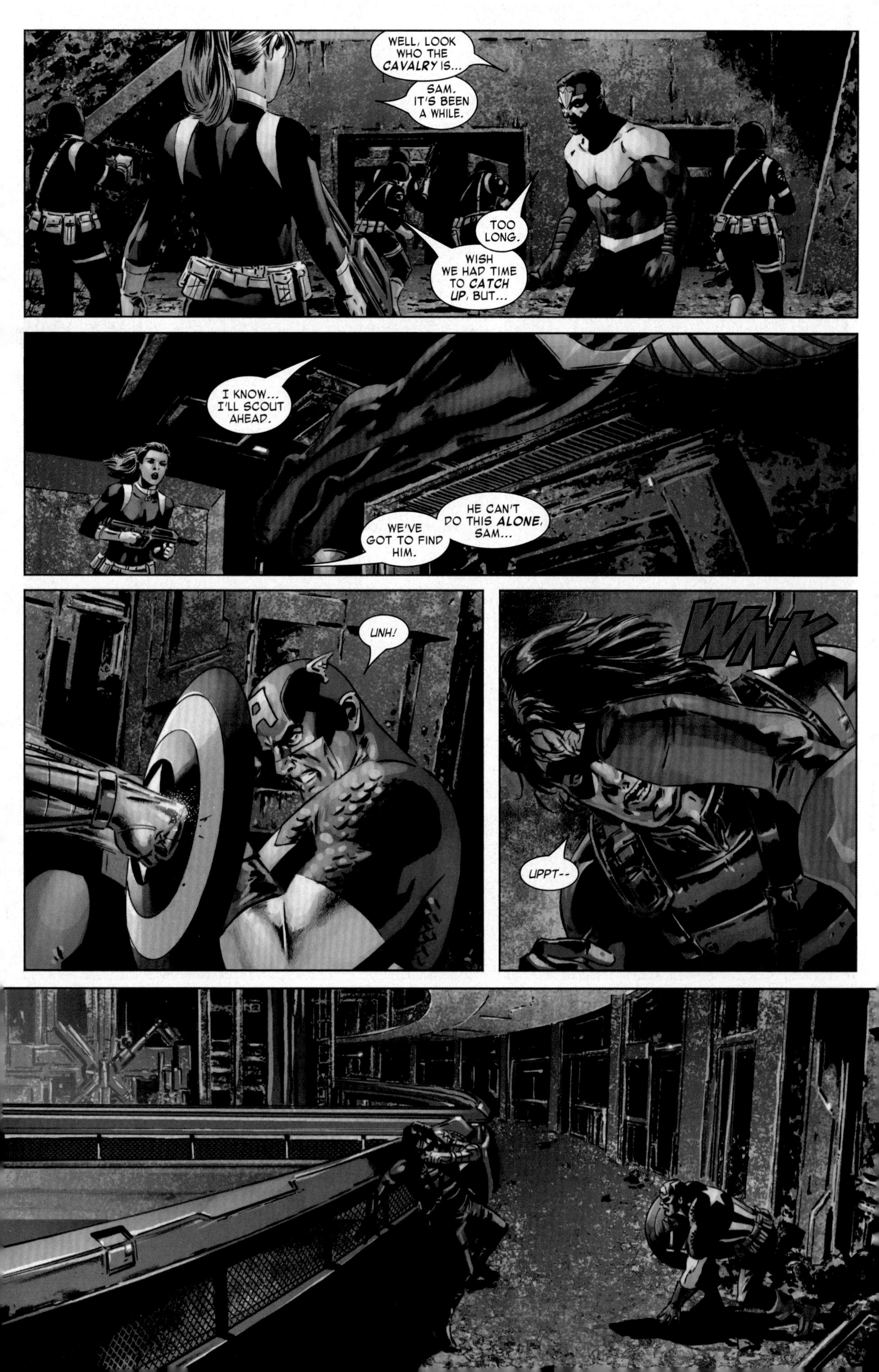
WELL, LOOK WHO THE CAVALRY IS...
SAM. IT'S BEEN A WHILE.
TOO LONG.
WISH WE HAD TIME TO CATCH UP, BUT...
I KNOW... I'LL SCOUT AHEAD.
HE CAN'T DO THIS ALONE, SAM...
WE'VE GOT TO FIND HIM.
UNH!
WNK
UPPT--

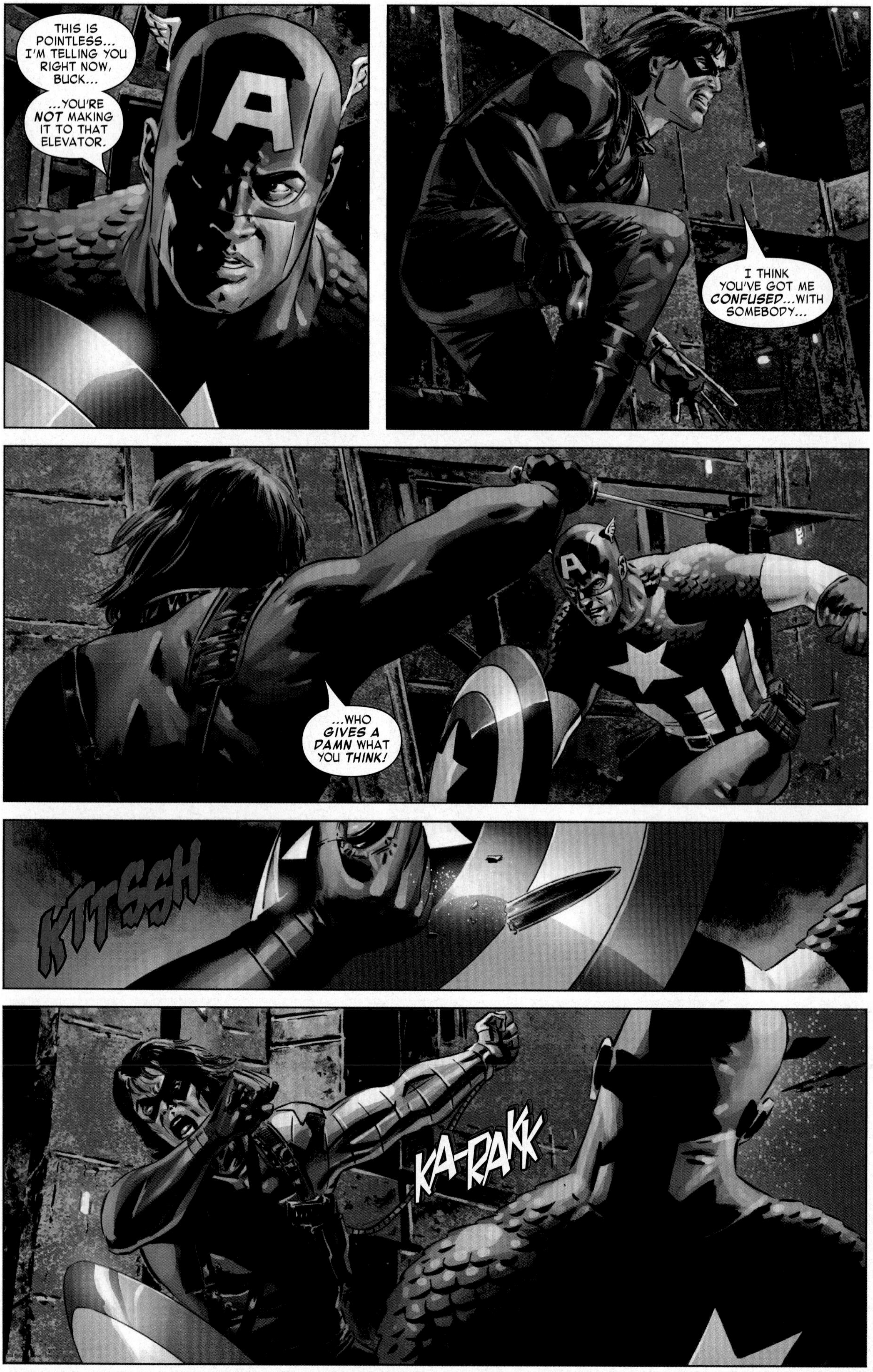

THIS IS POINTLESS... I'M TELLING YOU RIGHT NOW, BUCK...
...YOU'RE NOT MAKING IT TO THAT ELEVATOR.
I THINK YOU'VE GOT ME CONFUSED...WITH SOMEBODY...
...WHO GIVES A DAMN WHAT YOU THINK!
KTTSSH
KA-RAKK

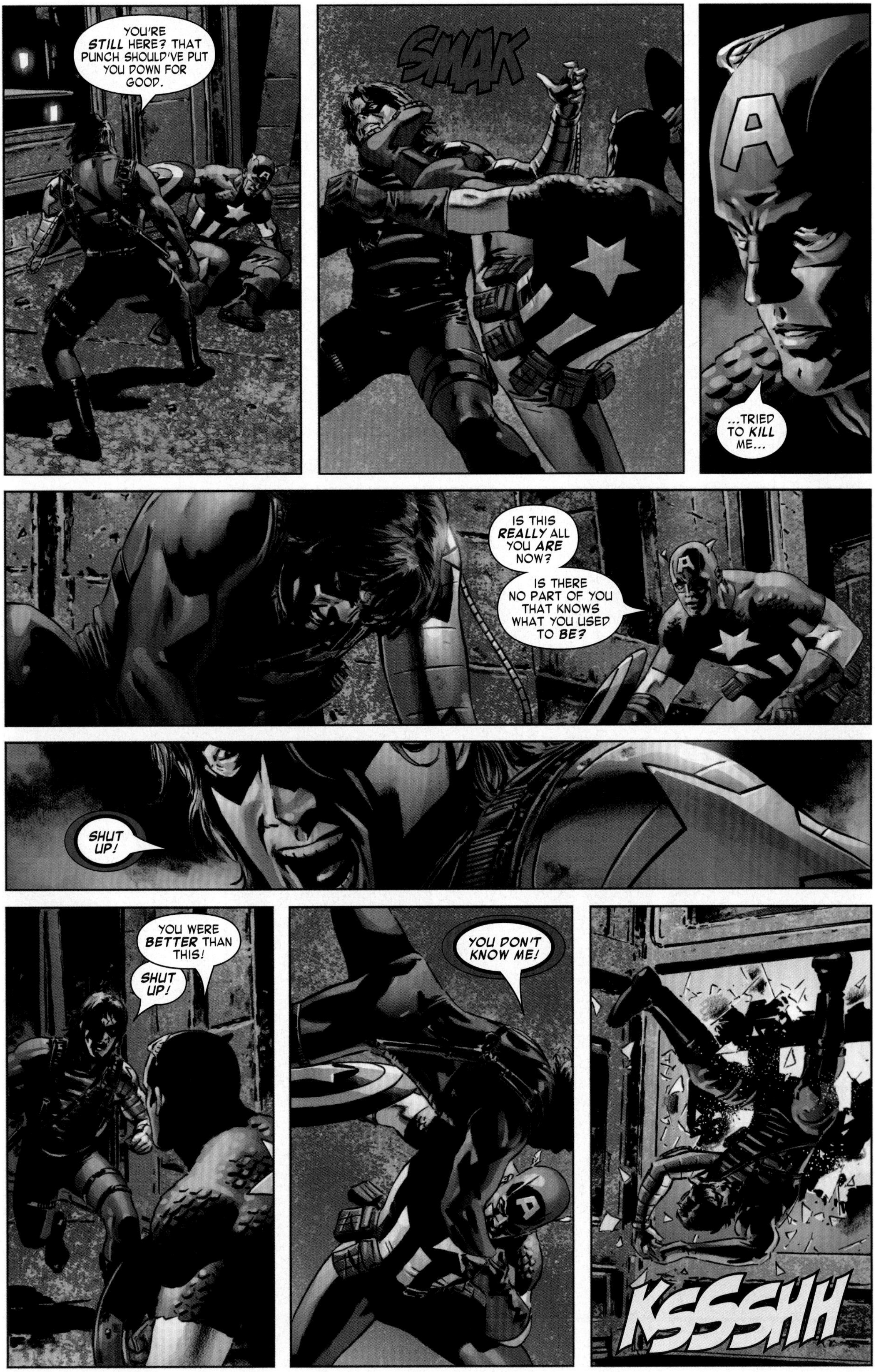

YOU'RE STILL HERE? THAT PUNCH SHOULD'VE PUT YOU DOWN FOR GOOD.
SMAK
...TRIED TO KILL ME...
IS THIS REALLY ALL YOU ARE NOW?
IS THERE NO PART OF YOU THAT KNOWS WHAT YOU USED TO BE?
SHUT UP!
YOU WERE BETTER THAN THIS!
SHUT UP!
YOU DON'T KNOW ME!
KSSSHH

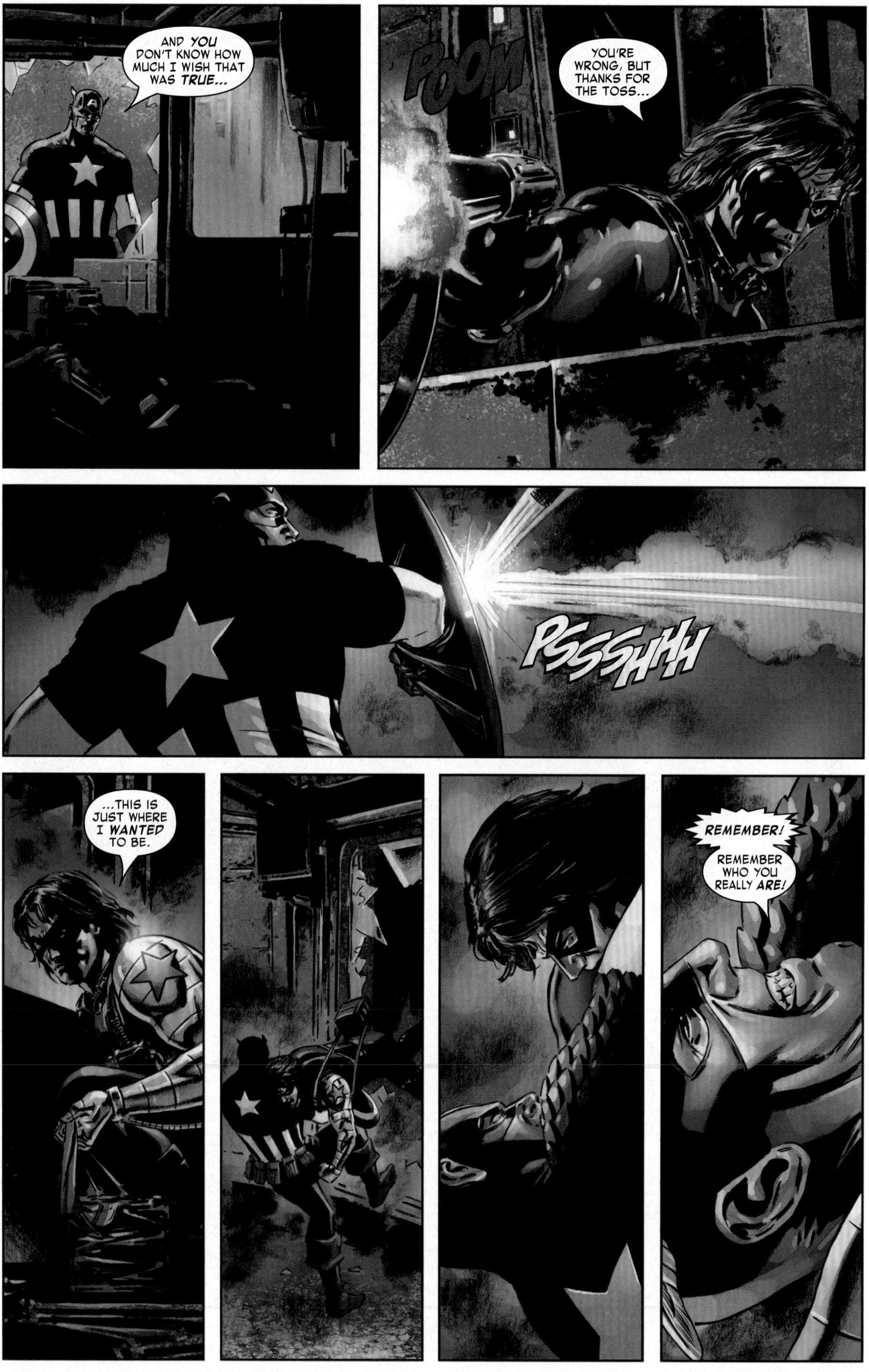
AND YOU DON'T KNOW HOW MUCH I WISH THAT WAS TRUE...
POOM
YOU'RE WRONG, BUT THANKS FOR THE TOSS...
PSSSHHH
...THIS IS JUST WHERE I WANTED TO BE.
REMEMBER!
REMEMBER WHO YOU REALLY ARE!

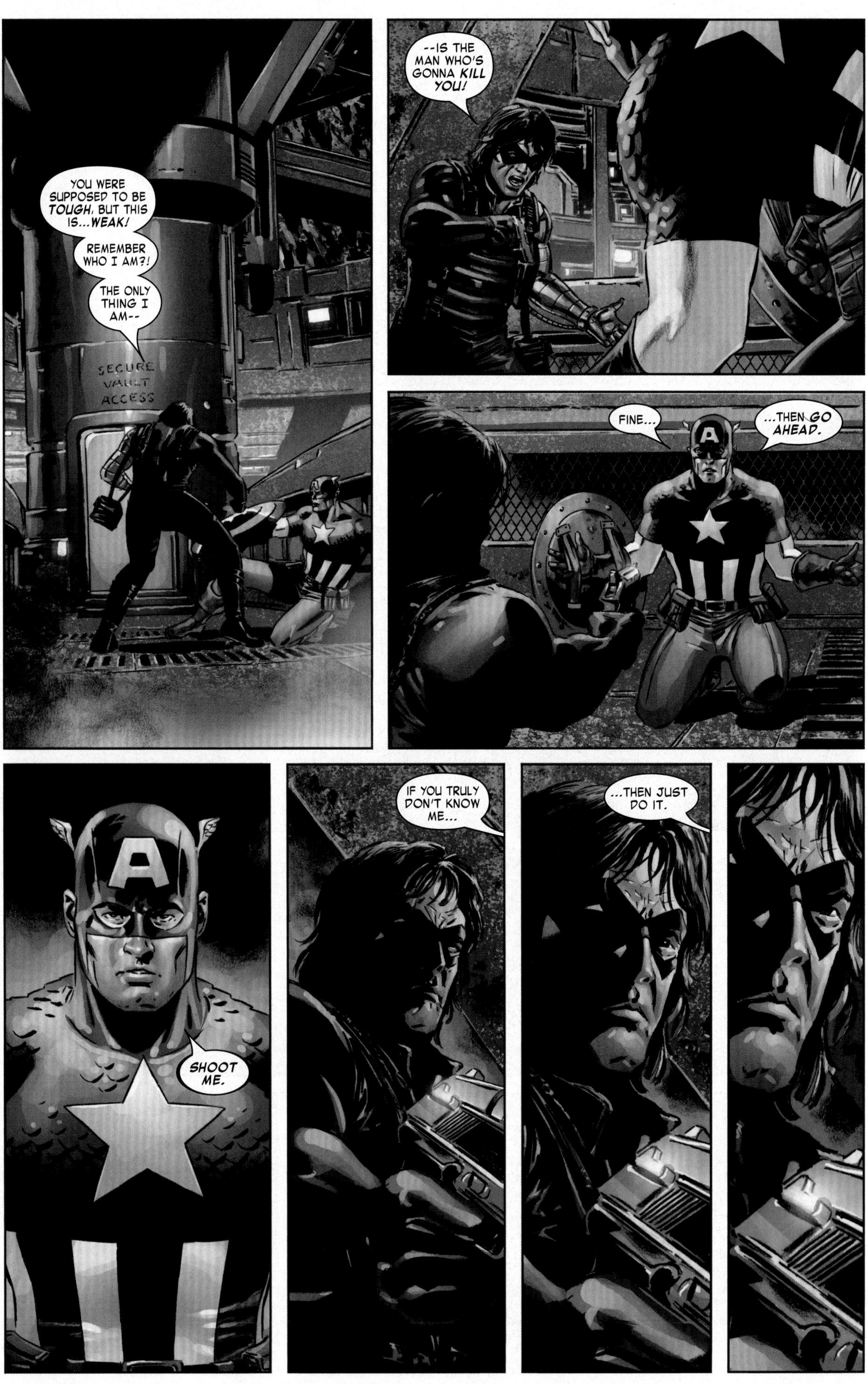
YOU WERE SUPPOSED TO BE TOUGH, BUT THIS IS...WEAK!
REMEMBER WHO I AM?!
THE ONLY THING I AM--
SECURE VAULT ACCESS
--IS THE MAN WHO'S GONNA KILL YOU!
FINE...
...THEN GO AHEAD.
SHOOT ME.
IF YOU TRULY DON'T KNOW ME...
...THEN JUST DO IT.

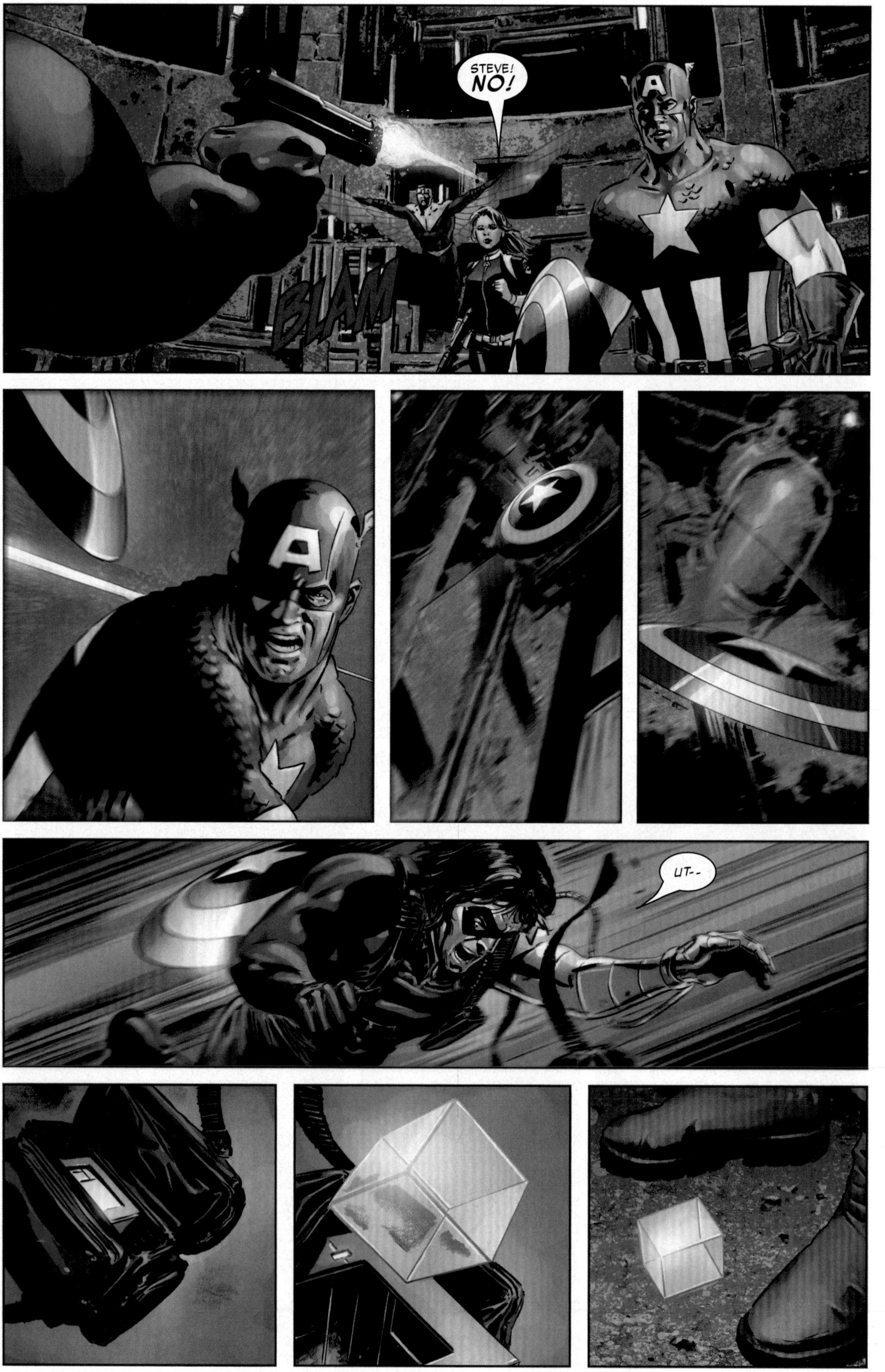
STEVE! NO!
BLAM
UT--

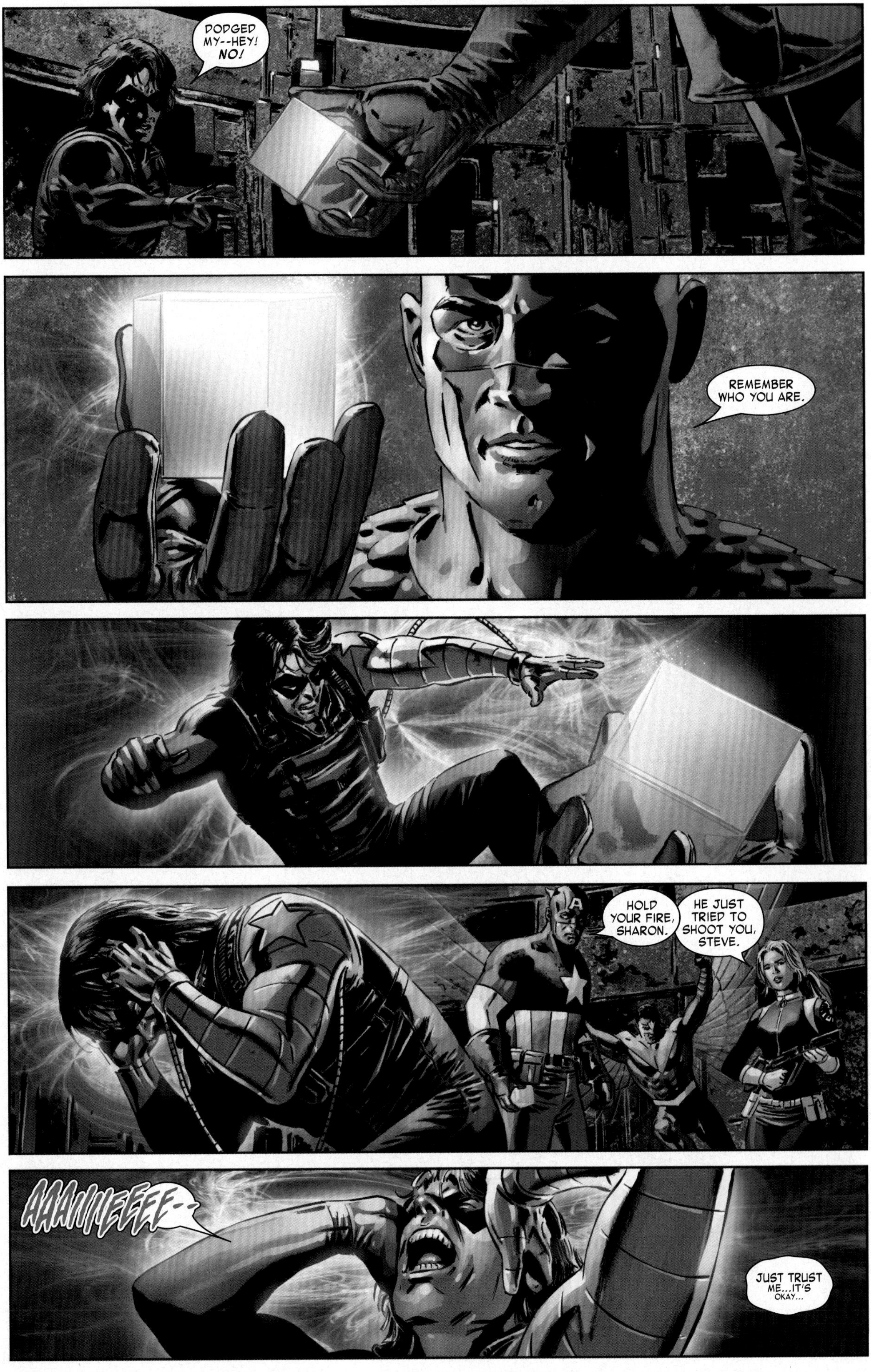
DODGED MY--HEY! NO!
REMEMBER WHO YOU ARE.
HOLD YOUR FIRE, SHARON.
HE JUST TRIED TO SHOOT YOU, STEVE.
AAAIIIEEEE--
JUST TRUST ME...IT'S OKAY...

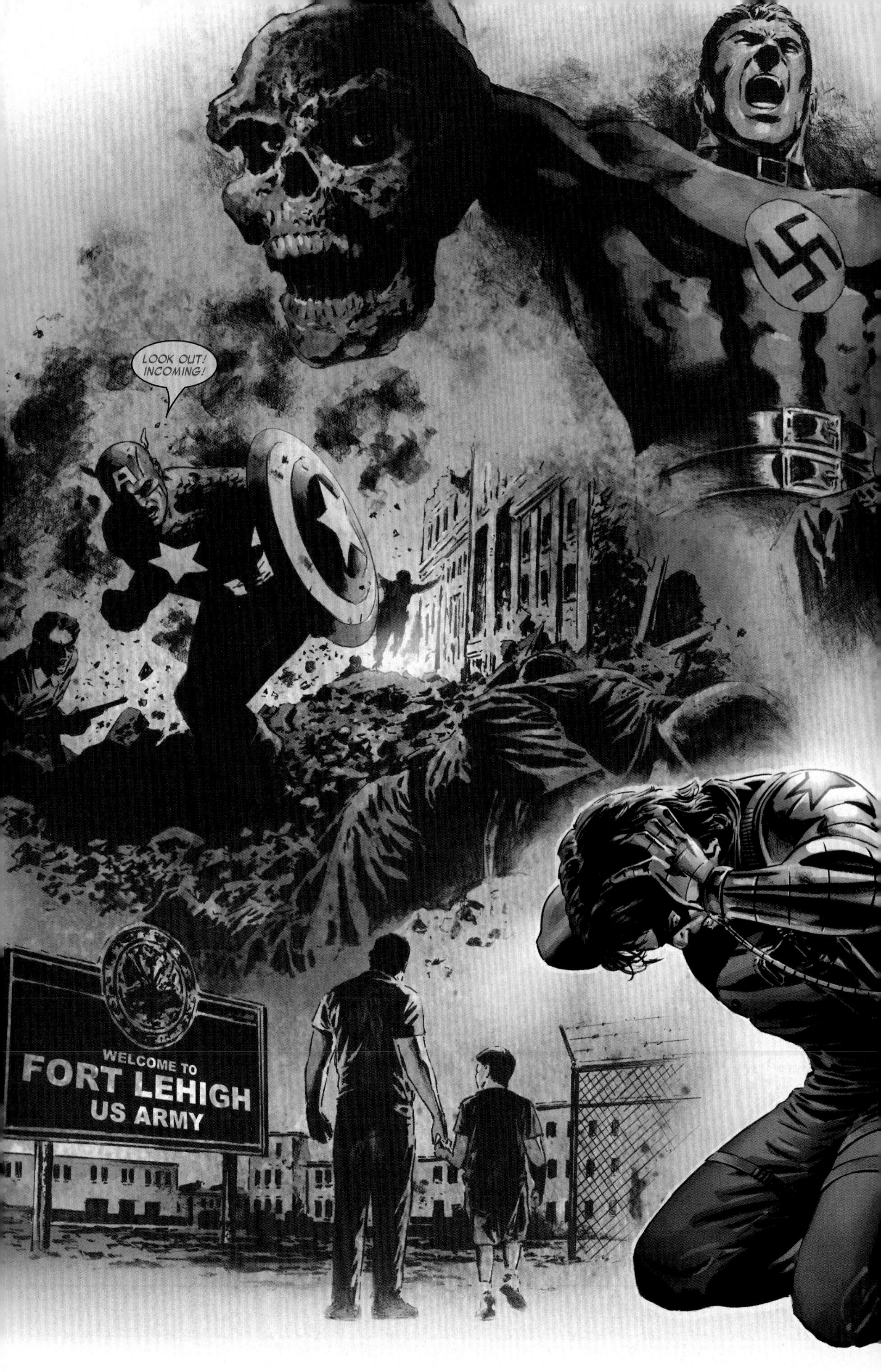
LOOK OUT! INCOMING!
WELCOME TO FORT LEHIGH US ARMY

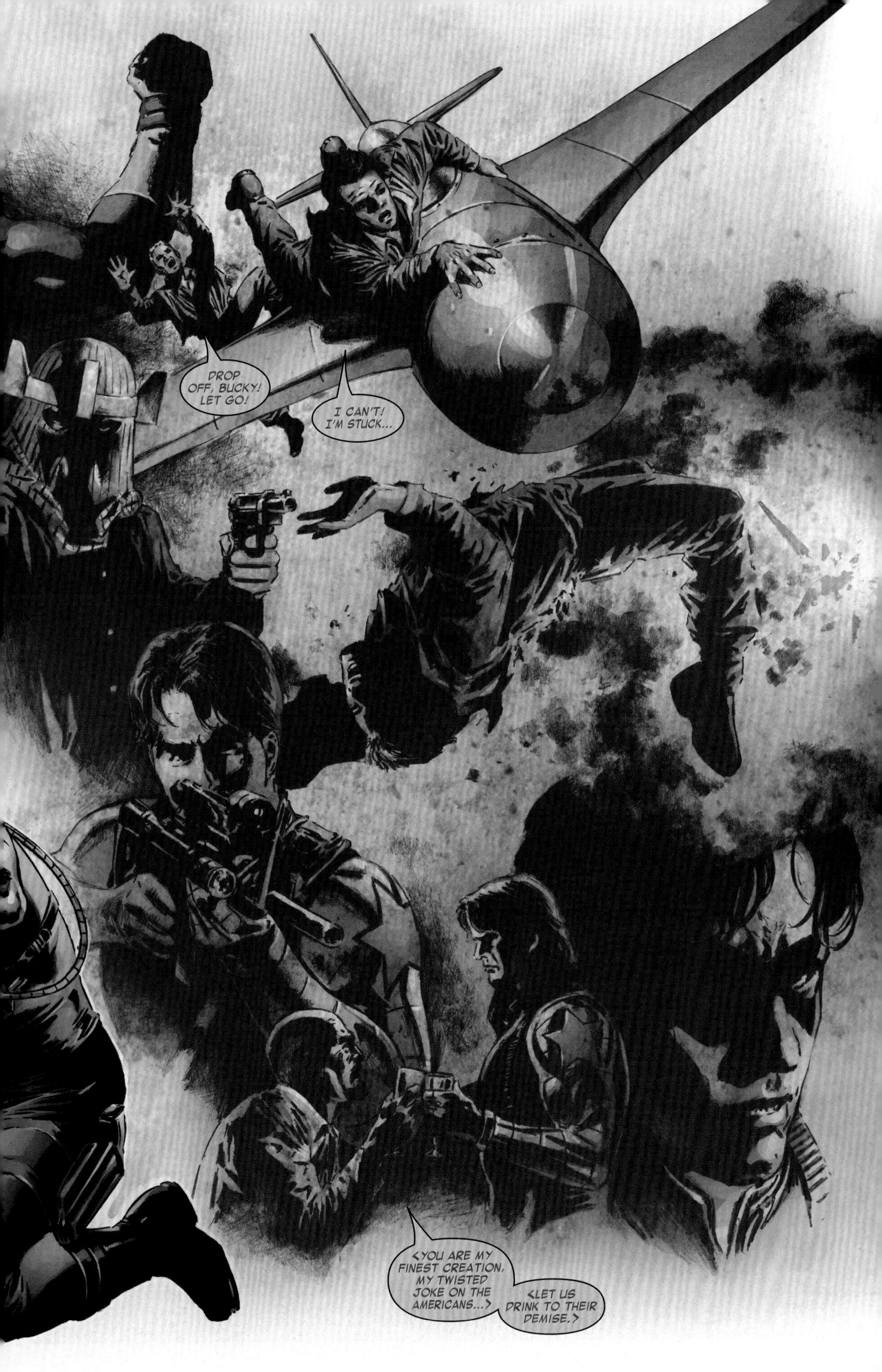
DROP OFF, BUCKY! LET GO!
I CAN'T! I'M STUCK...
<YOU ARE MY FINEST CREATION, MY TWISTED JOKE ON THE AMERICANS...>
<LET US DRINK TO THEIR DEMISE.>

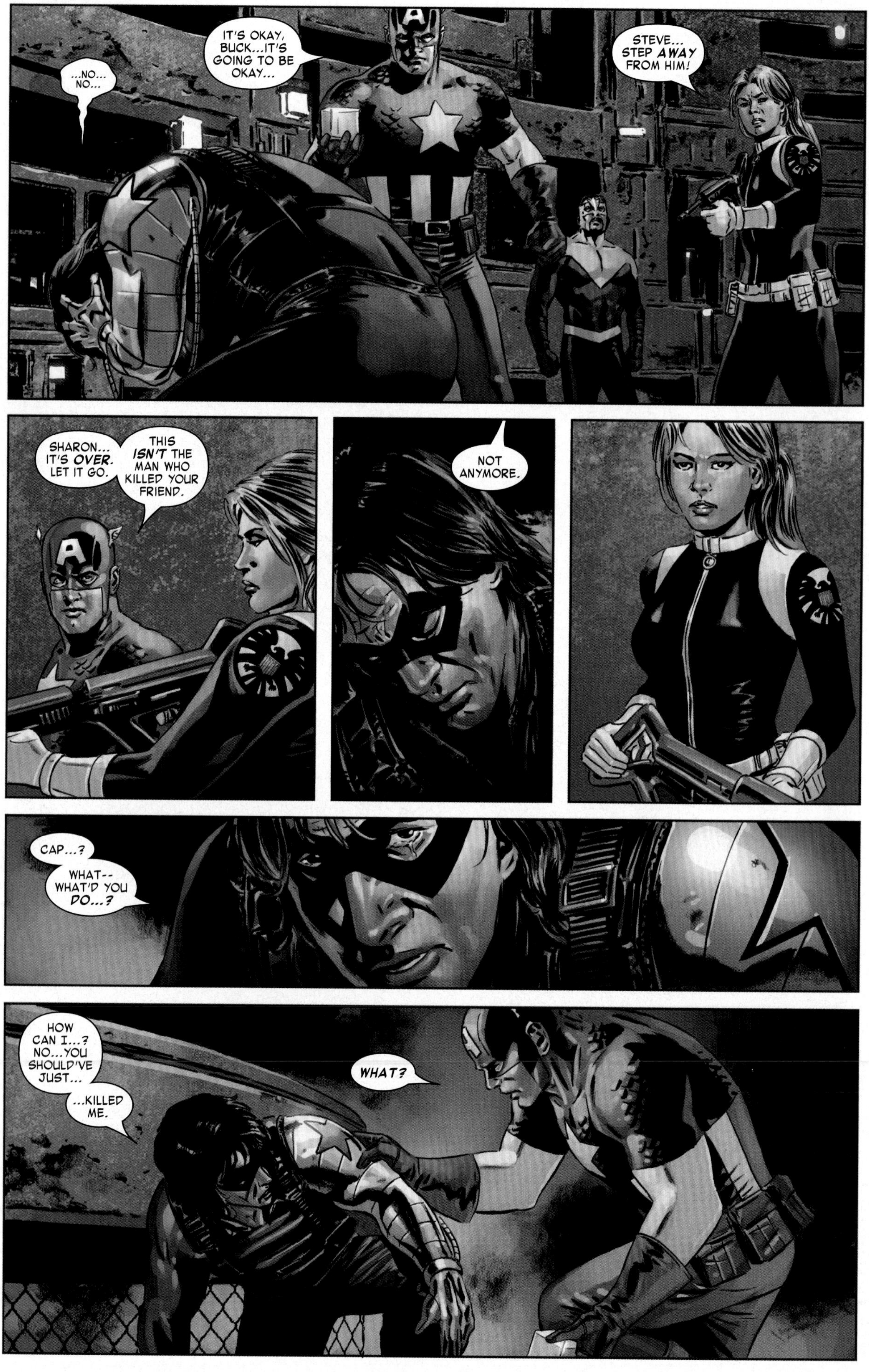
...NO... NO...
IT'S OKAY, BUCK...IT'S GOING TO BE OKAY...
STEVE... STEP AWAY FROM HIM!
SHARON... IT'S OVER. LET IT GO.
THIS ISN'T THE MAN WHO KILLED YOUR FRIEND.
NOT ANYMORE.
CAP...?
WHAT-- WHAT'D YOU DO...?
HOW CAN I...? NO...YOU SHOULD'VE JUST...
...KILLED ME.
WHAT?

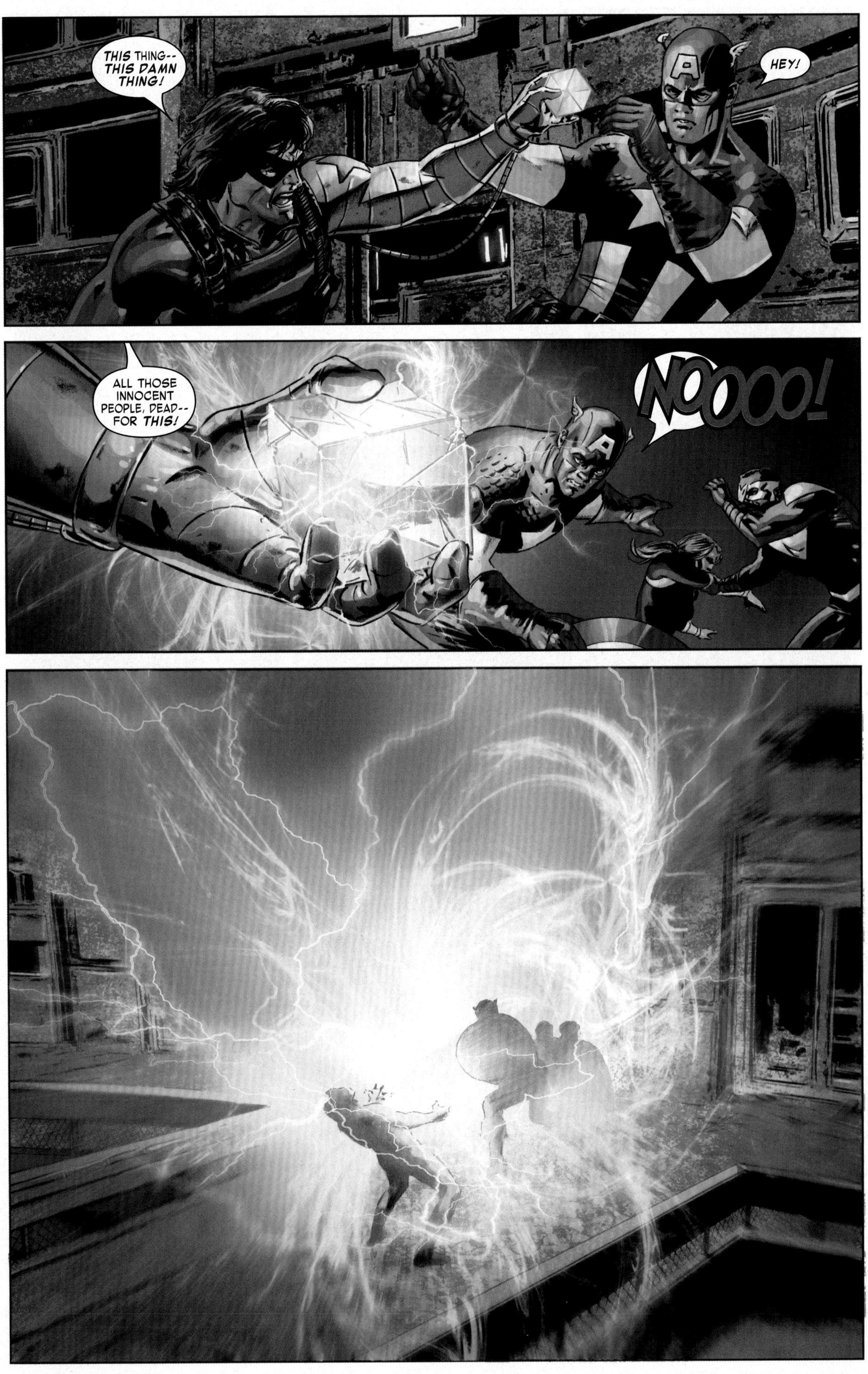
THIS THING--
THIS DAMN THING!
HEY!
ALL THOSE INNOCENT PEOPLE, DEAD--
FOR THIS!
NOOOO!

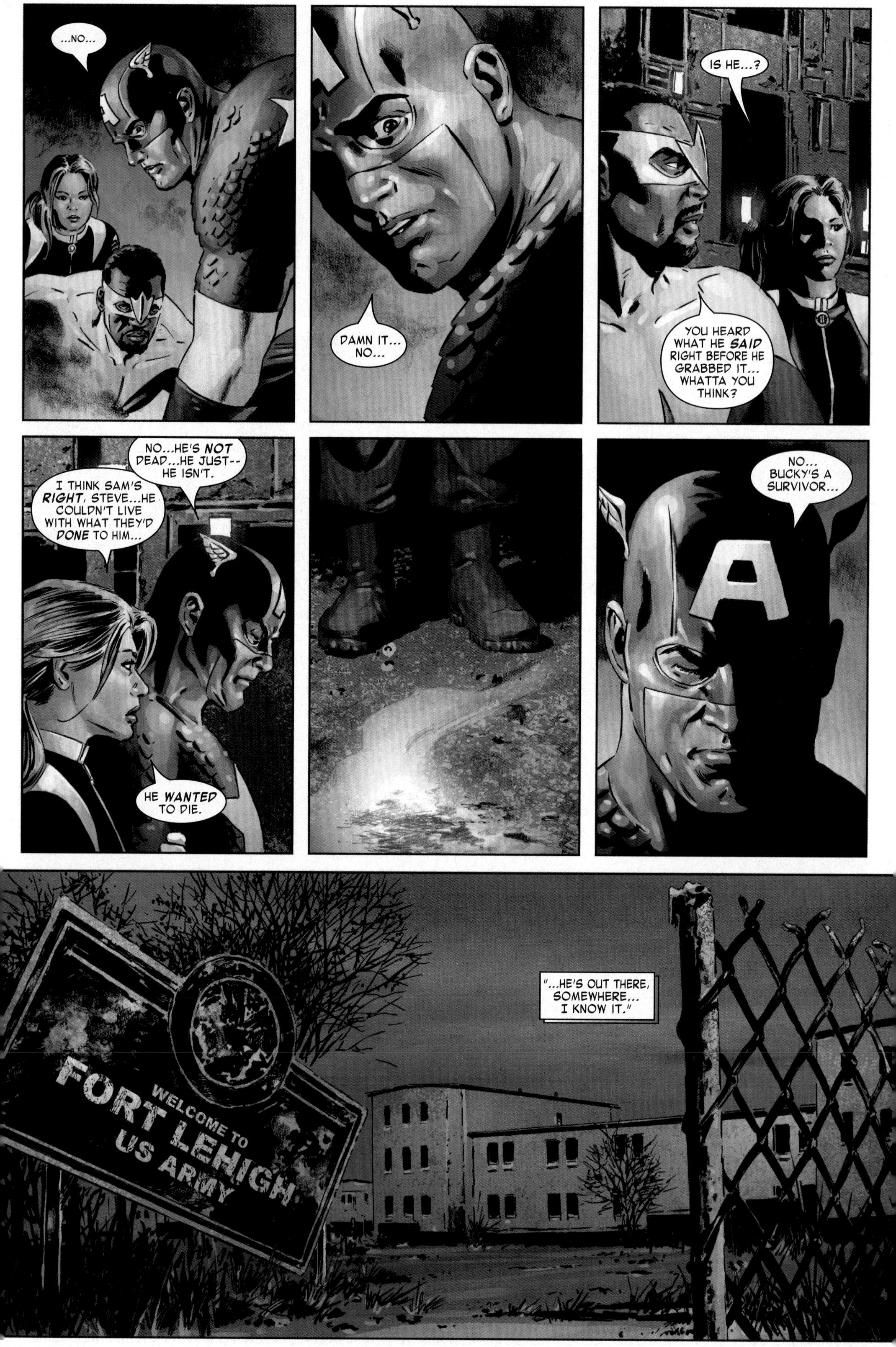
...NO...
DAMN IT... NO...
IS HE...?
YOU HEARD WHAT HE SAID RIGHT BEFORE HE GRABBED IT... WHATTA YOU THINK?
I THINK SAM'S RIGHT, STEVE...HE COULDN'T LIVE WITH WHAT THEY'D DONE TO HIM...
HE WANTED TO DIE.
NO...HE'S NOT DEAD...HE JUST--HE ISN'T.
NO... BUCKY'S A SURVIVOR...
WELCOME TO
FORT LEHIGH
US ARMY
"...HE'S OUT THERE, SOMEWHERE... I KNOW IT."

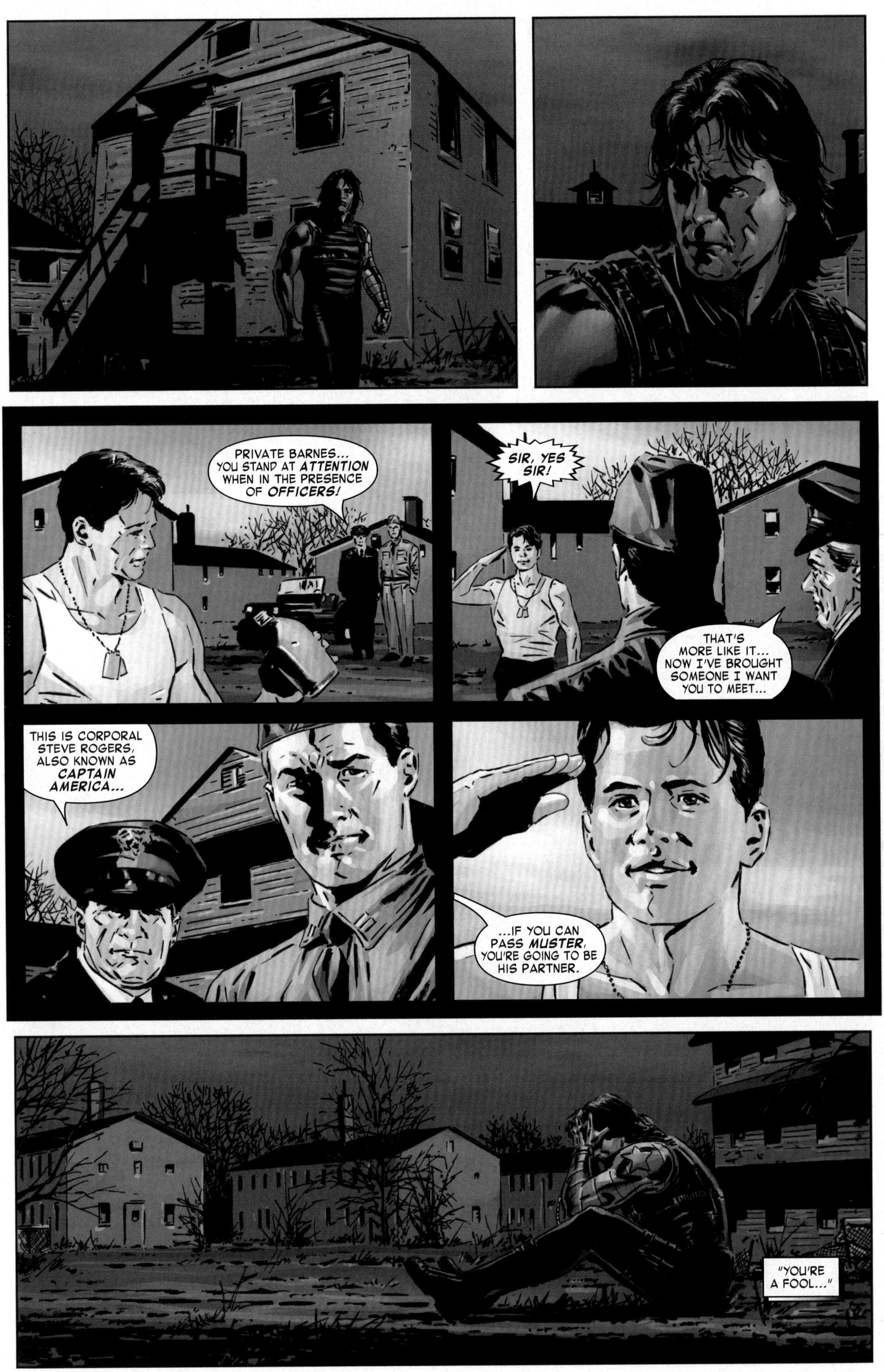
PRIVATE BARNES... YOU STAND AT ATTENTION WHEN IN THE PRESENCE OF OFFICERS!
SIR, YES SIR!
THAT'S MORE LIKE IT... NOW I'VE BROUGHT SOMEONE I WANT YOU TO MEET...
THIS IS CORPORAL STEVE ROGERS, ALSO KNOWN AS CAPTAIN AMERICA...
...IF YOU CAN PASS MUSTER, YOU'RE GOING TO BE HIS PARTNER.
"YOU'RE A FOOL..."

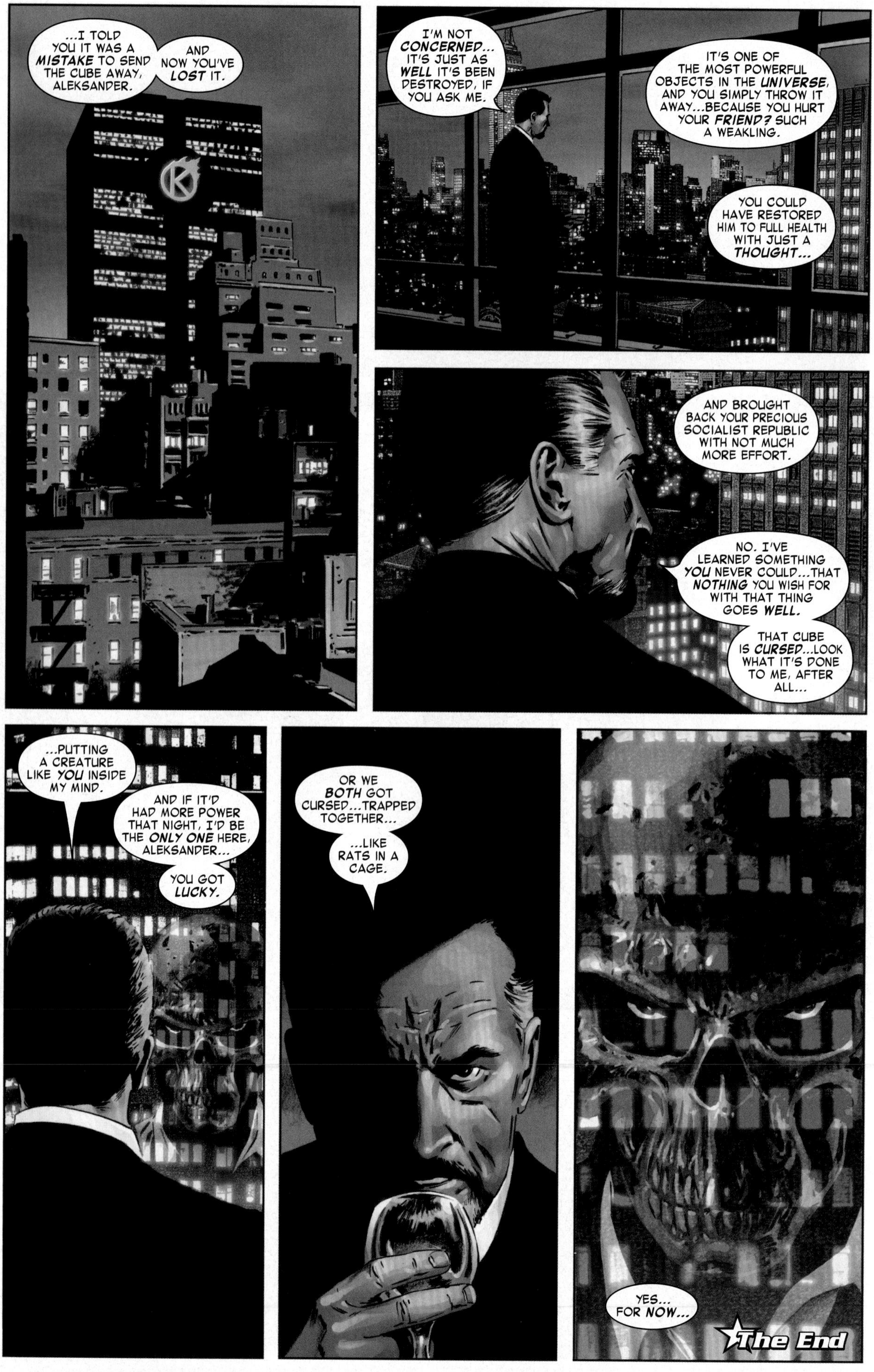
...I TOLD YOU IT WAS A MISTAKE TO SEND THE CUBE AWAY, ALEKSANDER.
AND NOW YOU'VE LOST IT.
I'M NOT CONCERNED... IT'S JUST AS WELL IT'S BEEN DESTROYED, IF YOU ASK ME.
IT'S ONE OF THE MOST POWERFUL OBJECTS IN THE UNIVERSE, AND YOU SIMPLY THROW IT AWAY...BECAUSE YOU HURT YOUR FRIEND? SUCH A WEAKLING.
YOU COULD HAVE RESTORED HIM TO FULL HEALTH WITH JUST A THOUGHT...
AND BROUGHT BACK YOUR PRECIOUS SOCIALIST REPUBLIC WITH NOT MUCH MORE EFFORT.
NO. I'VE LEARNED SOMETHING YOU NEVER COULD...THAT NOTHING YOU WISH FOR WITH THAT THING GOES WELL.
THAT CUBE IS CURSED...LOOK WHAT IT'S DONE TO ME, AFTER ALL...
...PUTTING A CREATURE LIKE YOU INSIDE MY MIND.
AND IF IT'D HAD MORE POWER THAT NIGHT, I'D BE THE ONLY ONE HERE, ALEKSANDER...
YOU GOT LUCKY.
OR WE BOTH GOT CURSED...TRAPPED TOGETHER...
...LIKE RATS IN A CAGE.
YES... FOR NOW...
The End

PROMOTIONAL ART FOR *CAPTAIN AMERICA #1* BY STEVE EPTING & LAURA MARTI

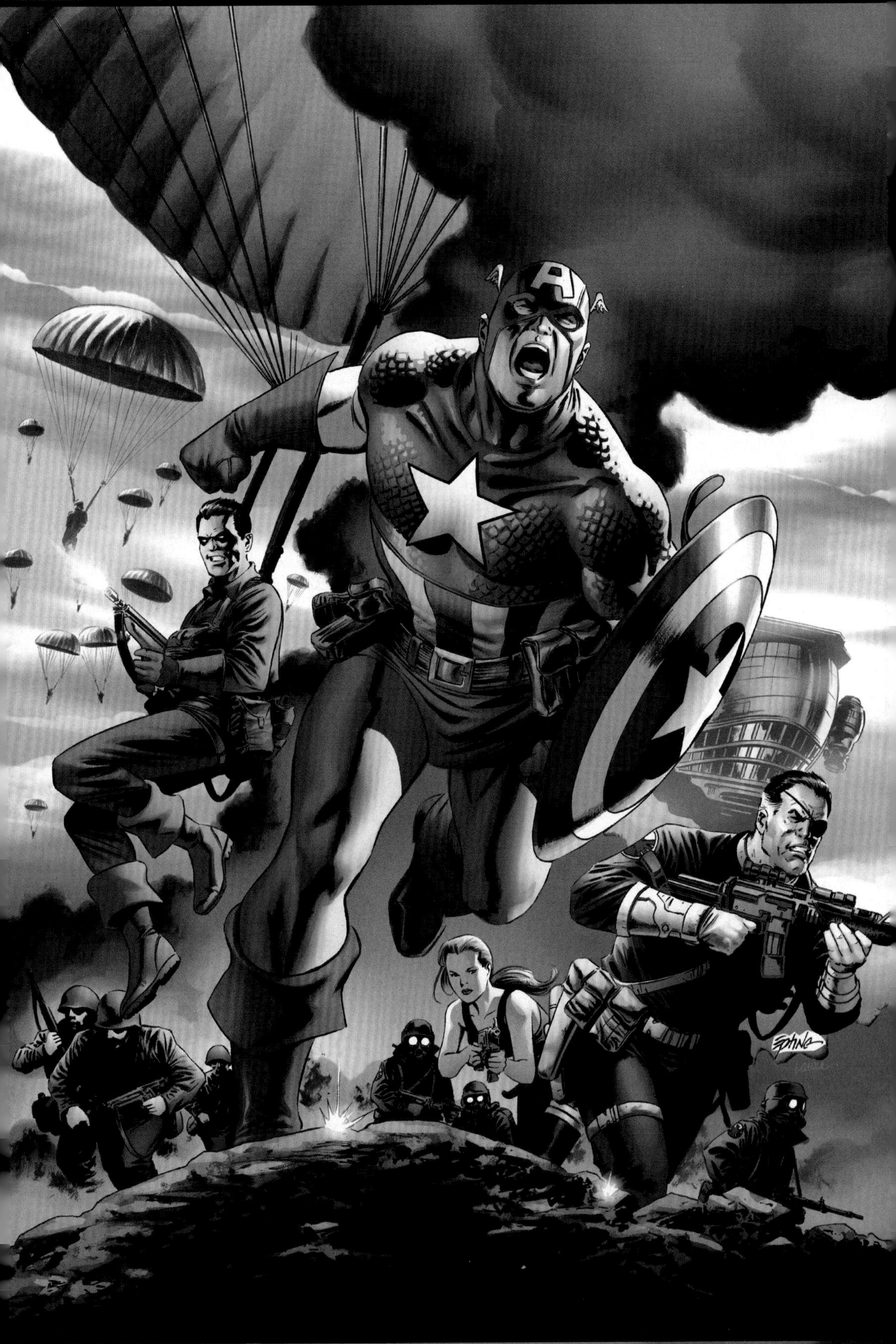

APTAIN AMERICA #6 VARIANT COVER BY STEVE EPTING & FRANK D'ARMATA

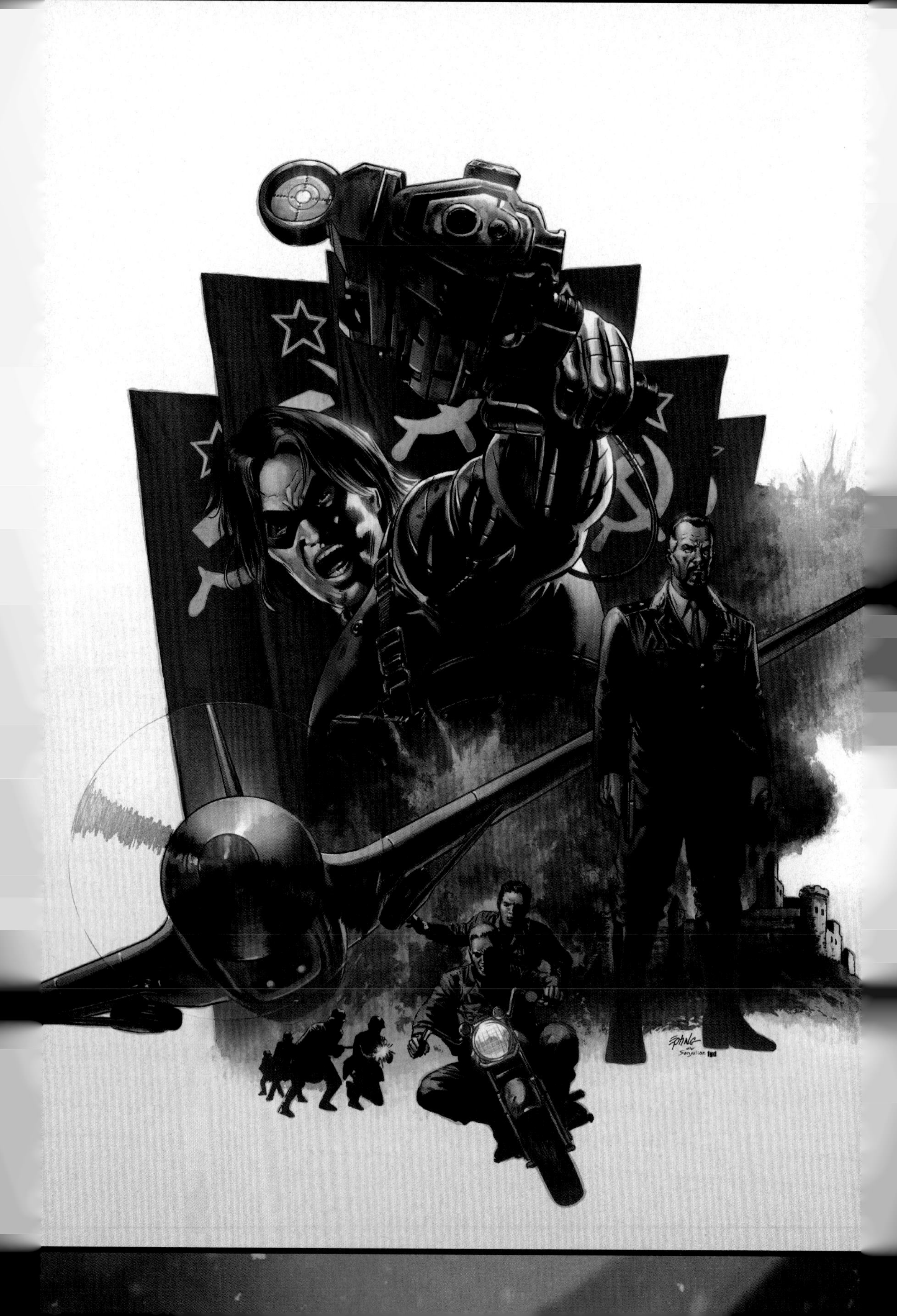

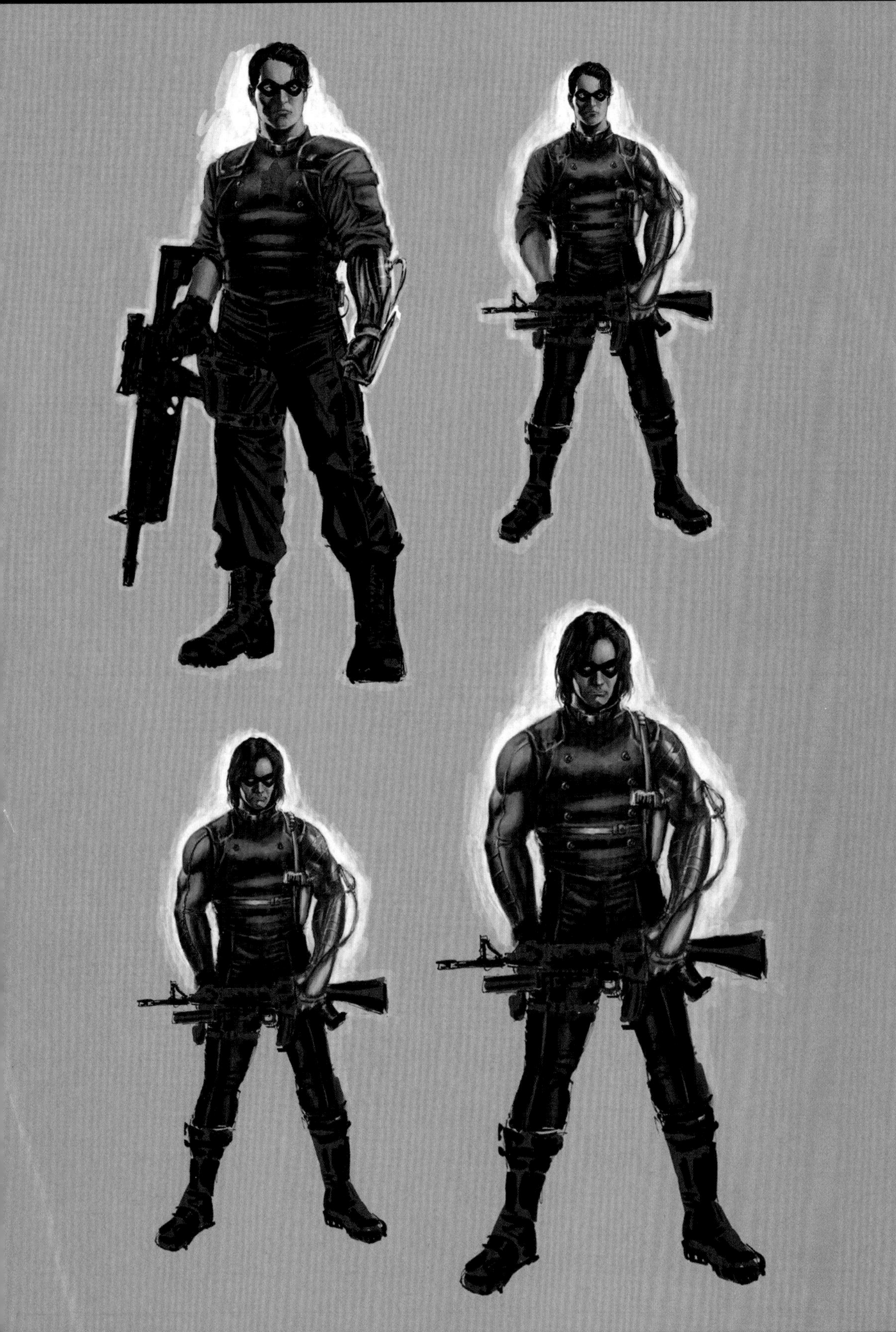

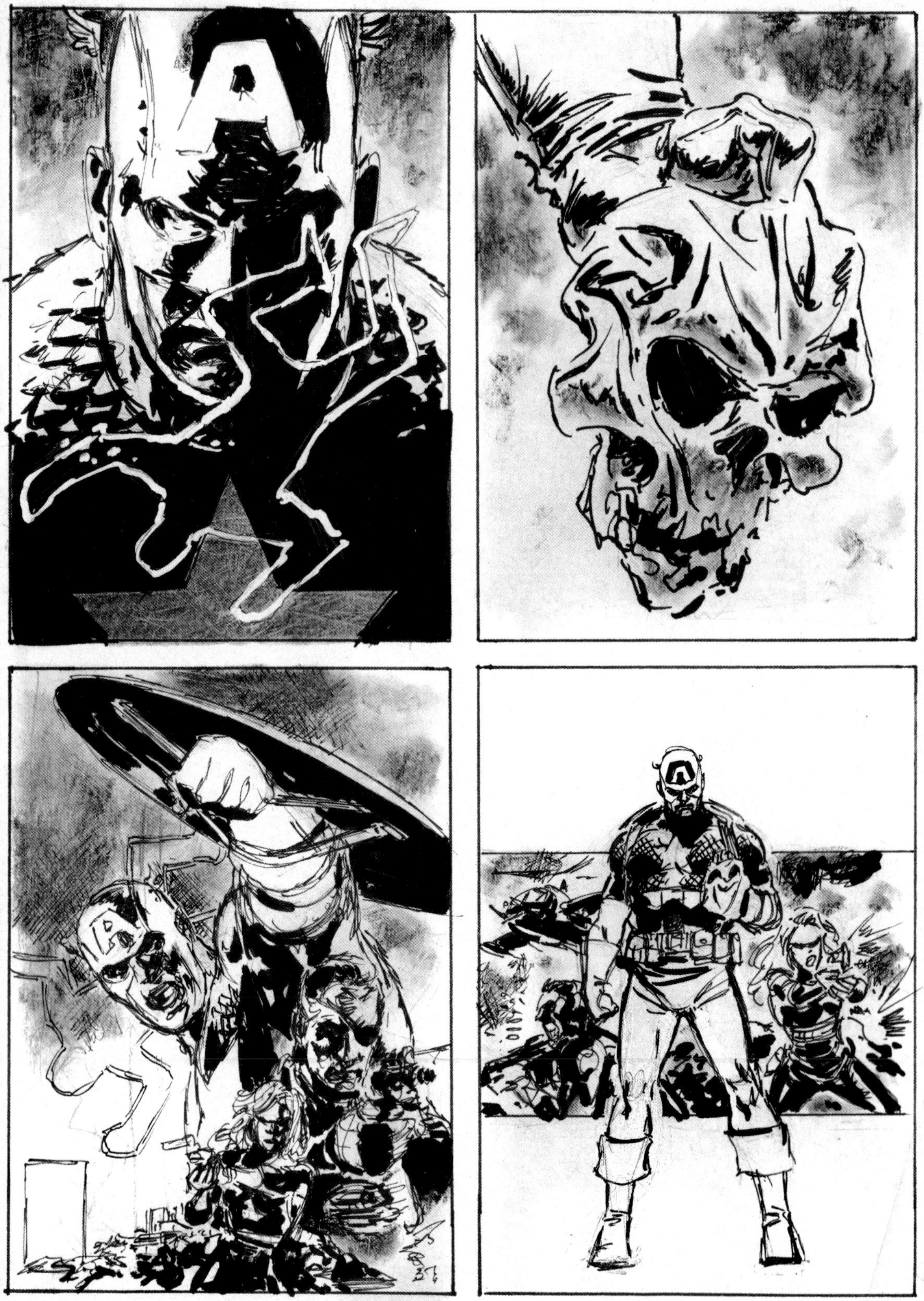

CAPTAIN AMERICA #4, #7, #12 & #13 COVER ROUGHS BY STEVE EPTING

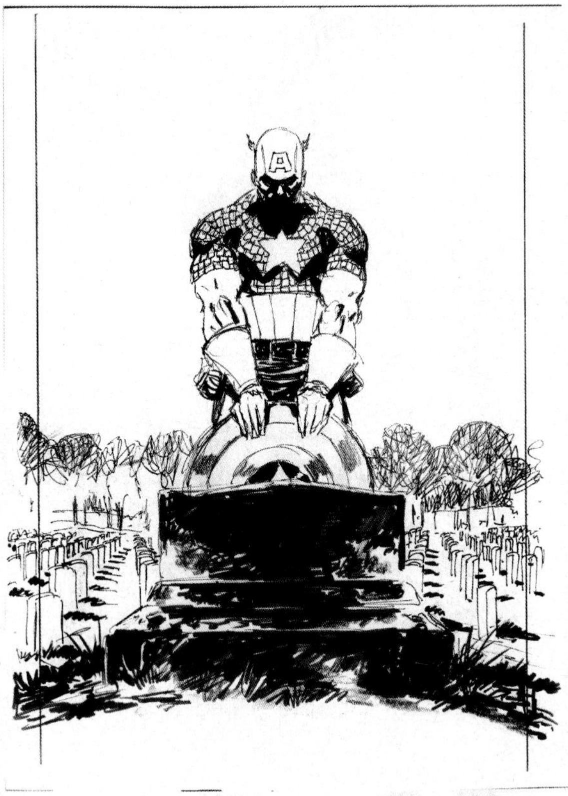

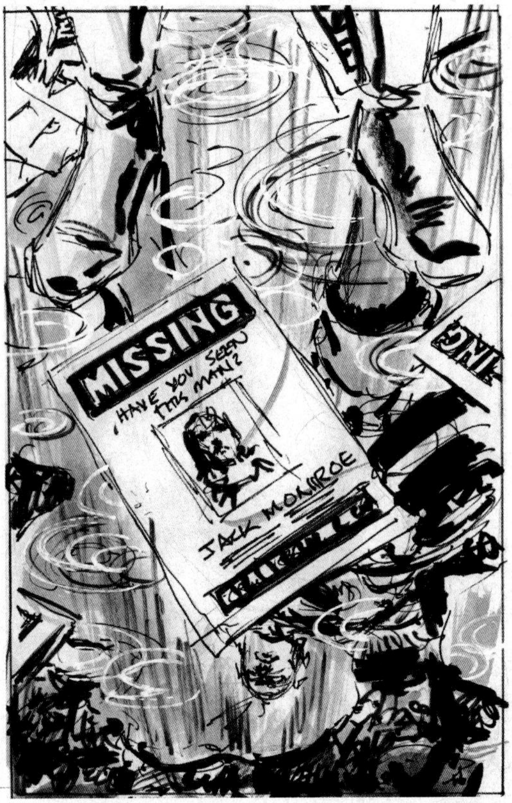
MISSING
HAVE YOU SEEN THIS MAN?
JACK MONROE

CAP COVER ROUGH 13

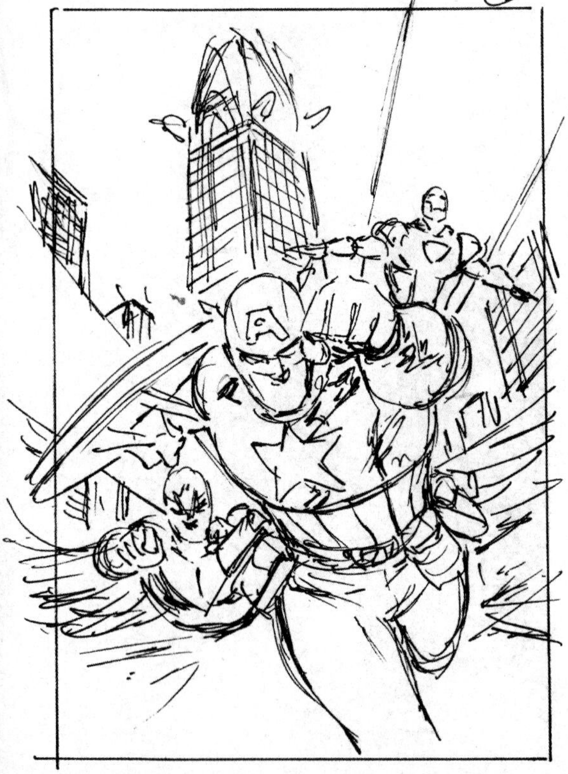

CAP COVER ROUGH 12

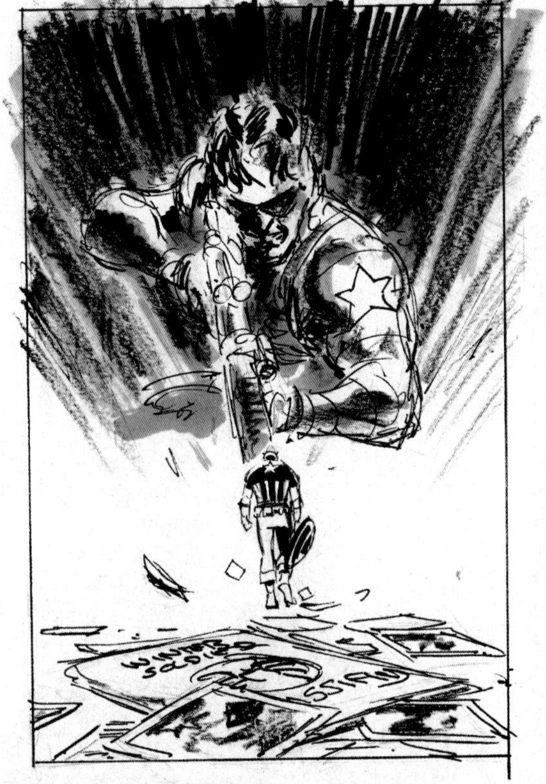

CAPTAIN AMERICA #8 VARIANT COVER BY JOE JUSKO

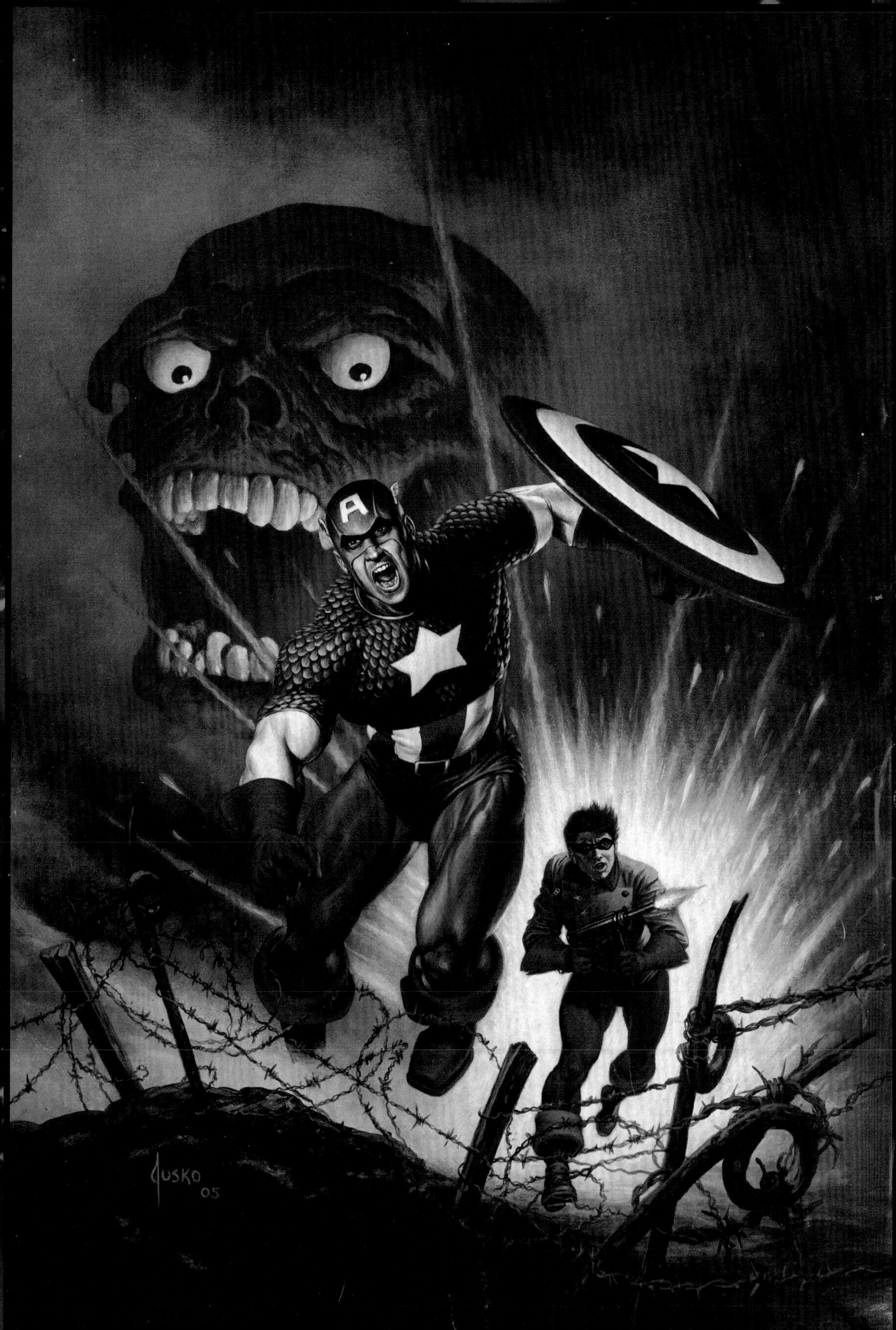
JUSKO
05